Lecture Notes in Computer Science 14479

The series Lecture Notes in Computer Science (LNCS), including its subseries Lecture Notes in Artificial Intelligence (LNAI) and Lecture Notes in Bioinformatics (LNBI), has established itself as a medium for the publication of new developments in computer science and information technology research, teaching, and education.

LNCS enjoys close cooperation with the computer science R & D community, the series counts many renowned academics among its volume editors and paper authors, and collaborates with prestigious societies. Its mission is to serve this international community by providing an invaluable service, mainly focused on the publication of conference and workshop proceedings and postproceedings. LNCS commenced publication in 1973.

Minh Hoàng Hà · Xingquan Zhu · My T. Thai
Editors

Computational Data and Social Networks

12th International Conference, CSoNet 2023
Hanoi, Vietnam, December 11–13, 2023
Proceedings

Editors
Minh Hoàng Hà
National Economics University
Hanoi, Vietnam

Xingquan Zhu
Florida Atlantic University
Boca Raton, FL, USA

My T. Thai 🆔
University of Florida
Gainesville, FL, USA

ISSN 0302-9743   ISSN 1611-3349 (electronic)
Lecture Notes in Computer Science
ISBN 978-981-97-0668-6   ISBN 978-981-97-0669-3 (eBook)
https://doi.org/10.1007/978-981-97-0669-3

This Springer imprint is published by the registered company Springer Nature Singapore Pte Ltd.
The registered company address is: 152 Beach Road, #21-01/04 Gateway East, Singapore 189721, Singapore

Paper in this product is recyclable.

Preface

This book constitutes the refereed proceedings of the 12th International Conference on Computational Data and Social Networks (CSoNet 2023), held at the National Economics University (NEU) in Hanoi, Vietnam, December 11–13, 2023. This conference provided a premier interdisciplinary forum to bring together researchers and practitioners from all fields of big data networks, such as billion-scale network computing, data network analysis, mining, security and privacy, optimization, and learning. CSoNet 2023 welcomed not only the presentation of original research results, but also the exchange and dissemination of innovative, practical development experiences. The topics of CSoNet 2023 covered the fundamental background, theoretical technology development, and real-world applications associated with the aforementioned fields.

The target audience of this book mainly consists of researchers, students, and practitioners in complex networks, machine and deep learning, combinatorial optimization, security, and blockchain. The book is also of interest to researchers and industrial practitioners in emerging areas such as Internet of Things, blockchain modeling, cloud computing, fraud detection, rumor blocking, crime detection, intelligent transportation systems, and many more.

CSoNet 2023 has received papers from 20 countries in four major areas of research including machine learning & forecasting, optimization, network analysis, and security & blockchain. The Program Committee has followed a formal standard reviewing process; bidding, single-blind reviewing, and deliberating resulted in acceptance of 23 regular papers, 14 short papers, and 4 extended-abstract papers for presentation and publication in the proceedings. Each paper was reviewed by at least two experts in the field. It was our great honor to receive a keynote talk on "Learning with graphs" given by a world-class invited speaker, Roger Wattenhofer (ETH Zurich, Switzerland). We also organized a panel discussion about "Large Language Models: Theory, Applications, and Challenges" with the participation of My T. Tra (University of Florida, USA), Xingquan Zhu (Florida Atlantic University, USA), Tu-Bao Ho (Viasm, Vietnam), David Mohaisen (University of Central Florida, USA), and Tien Mai (Singapore Management University, Singapore).

We would like to express our appreciation to all contributors and the conference committee members. A special thank you goes to the National Economics University for its support of this conference. We sincerely thank all authors for submitting their high-quality work to the conference. Our thanks also go to all Technical Program Committee members and sub-reviewers for their willingness to provide timely and detailed reviews of all submissions. Their hard work made the success of the conference possible. Furthermore, without the tremendous efforts from general co-chair Hong Chuong Pham (President of NEU), local chair Thanh Hieu Nguyen (Vice-president of NEU) and team members, publication co-chairs Duc Minh Vu and Hung Tran, publicity co-chairs Phi Le Nguyen and Min Shi, financial chair Thang Dinh, and website chair Canh V. Pham, our conference would not have been so successful in its 12th year. Lastly, we acknowledge the support and patience of Springer staff members throughout the process.

December 2023   Minh Hoàng Hà
                                                                    Xingquan Zhu
                                                                     My T. Thai

Organization

General Co-chairs

Pham Hong Chuong   National Economics University, Vietnam
Sergiy Butenko   Texas A&M University, USA

TPC Co-chairs

Minh Hoàng Hà   National Economics University, Vietnam
Xingquan Zhu   Florida Atlantic University, USA

TPC Members

Thien Luong	Phenikaa University, Vietnam
Akrati Saxena	Eindhoven University of Technology, The Netherlands
Cảnh V. Pham	Phenikaa University, Vietnam
Hocine Cherifi	University of Burgundy, France
Son Ha Xuan	RMIT, Vietnam
Min Shi	Harvard University, USA
Viet Anh Nguyen	Chinese University of Hong Kong, China
Duc Minh Vu	National Economics University, Vietnam
Thu-Huong Dang	Lancaster University, UK
Ralucca Gera	Naval Postgraduate School, USA
Anurag Singh	National Institute of Technology Delhi, India
Vincenzo Moscato	University of Naples, Italy
Lu-An Tang	NEC Labs America, USA
Mohammed Abuhamad	Loyola University Chicago, USA
Gang Li	Deakin University, Australia
Hasan Davulcu	Arizona State University, USA
Xin Huang	Hong Kong Baptist University, China
Jinyoung Han	Sungkyunkwan University, South Korea
Gianni D'Angelo	University of Salerno, Italy
Weizhi Meng	Technical University of Denmark, Denmark
Hoang Long Nguyen	Meharry Medical College, USA
Rhongho Jang	Wayne State University, USA

Yongge Wang	UNC Charlotte, USA
Lara Quijano-Sanchez	Universidad Autónoma de Madrid, Spain
Marek Ogiela	AGH University of Science and Technology, Poland
Trung Thanh Nguyen	Phenikaa University, Vietnam
Tien Mai	Singapore Management University, Singapore
Thanh Binh Nguyen	VNUHCM University of Science, Vietnam
Xuan-Hieu Phan	VNU University of Engineering and Technology, Vietnam
Ngoc Le	Hanoi University of Science and Technology, Vietnam
Thanh Nguyen	University of Oregon, USA
Raul Monroy	Tecnológico de Monterrey, Campus Estado de México, Mexico
Hoang Quynh Le	VNU University of Engineering and Technology, Vietnam
Thuy Nguyen	RMIT, Vietnam
Huy Hieu Pham	VinUniversity, Vietnam
Duy Dung Le	VinUniversity, Vietnam
Cong-Thanh Le	University of Melbourne, Australia
Duc Tan Tran	Phenikaa University, Vietnam
Thi Diep Hoang	VNU University of Engineering and Technology, Vietnam
Tin Nguyen	Auburn University, USA
Hop Nguyen	VNUHCM International University, Vietnam
Viet Hung Nguyen	LIMOS, France
Cam Van Nguyen Thi	VNU University of Engineering and Technology, Vietnam
Tuan Anh Hoang	RMIT, Vietnam
Viet Lai	University of Oregon, USA
Quoc Trung Bui	Hanoi University of Science and Technology, Vietnam
Viet Sang Dinh	Hanoi University of Science and Technology, Vietnam
An Dang	Phenikaa University, Vietnam

Publicity Co-chairs

Nguyen Phi Le	Hanoi University of Science and Technology, Vietnam
Min Shi	Harvard University, USA

Web Chair

Canh V. Pham   Phenikaa University, Vietnam

Publication Co-chairs

Duc Minh Vu   National Economics University, Vietnam
Hung Tran   Phenikaa University, Vietnam

Local Committee

Thanh Hieu Nguyen (Chair)   National Economics University, Vietnam
Trung Thanh To   National Economics University, Vietnam
Thanh Tung Dao   National Economics University, Vietnam
Trung Tuan Nguyen   National Economics University, Vietnam

Steering Committee

My T. Thai (Chair)   University of Florida, USA
Kim-Kwang Raymond Choo   University of Texas at San Antonio, USA
Zhi-Li Zhang   University of Minnesota, USA
Weili Wu   University of Texas, USA

Contents

Machine Learning and Prediction

Security and Blockchain

Network Analysis

Machine Learning and Prediction

An Approach Using Threshold-Based Noise Reduction and Fine-Tuned ShuffleNetV2 for Plant Leaf Disease Detection

Hai Thanh Nguyen, Phat Minh Nguyen, Quang Duy Tran,
and Phuong Ha Dang Bui[✉]

Can Tho University, Can Tho, Vietnam
{nthai.cit,tdquang,bdhphuong}@ctu.edu.vn

Abstract. Diagnosing plant leaf diseases is essential for agricultural development. Leaves are an important part of the plant and are often where signs of disease appear. With the support of image processing algorithms, researchers have widely used them to support disease detection tasks on plant leaves. Transfer learning approaches have revealed encouraging results in many domains but require fine-tuning hyperparameter values. Additionally, a combination with noise reduction can lead to positive potential effects in improving performance. This study proposes an approach leveraging a noise reduction technique based on Soft-Thresholding with Lasso regression and then performing the disease classification with a fine-tuned ShuffleNetV2. The experimental results on 14,400 images of 24 plant leaf disease classes of 10 various plant species show that the Threshold-based noise reduction combined with a fine-tuned ShuffleNetV2 can obtain better performance in disease classification on plant leaves than the original model and several considered transfer learning methods.

Keywords: plant leaf diseases · threshold · noise reduction · ShuffleNetV2

1 Introduction

The development of agriculture, particularly in crops, is one of the critical areas to promote economic growth [1]. In recent years, Vietnam has transformed the cultivation of crops, i.e., the production of one crop per year has increased to two crops per year, which helps Vietnam become one of the largest exporters of agricultural products in Southeast Asia [2]. Applying high technology and modern machinery has effectively supported farmers in growing agricultural products. However, the difficulties in growing plants, such as the appearance of diseases, e.g., brown leaf spots, bacterial leaf blight, leaf fungus, powdery mildew, etc., have reduced both the yield and the quality of plant cultivation. Therefore, detecting common diseases on crops is an urgent matter for supporting farmers to improve productivity [3].

© The Author(s), under exclusive license to Springer Nature Singapore Pte Ltd. 2024
M. H. Hà et al. (Eds.): CSoNet 2023, LNCS 14479, pp. 3–14, 2024.
https://doi.org/10.1007/978-981-97-0669-3_1

Most plant diseases have evident symptoms and can be diagnosed through infected plant leaf observation by an experienced plant pathologist. However, the excessive diversity of plants, the diversity, and the faster spread of plant leaf diseases make them challenging to diagnose. Therefore, applying deep learning in plant leaf disease diagnosis is crucial. In addition, the noise reduction techniques give a promising performance for removing Gaussian noise in CT medical images [4], in color digital images [5].

This research proposes a novel deep learning-based diagnosis model, which uses the PlantVillage dataset, based on a Threshold-based noise reduction technique and fine-tuned ShuffleNetV2 architecture, to classify common diseases on plant leaves for supporting farmers in growing agricultural products in practical ways. The performance of the proposed model is compared to the original model and several considered transfer learning methods for classifying plant leaf diseases.

2   Related Work

Deep learning frameworks have been applied recently in numerous plant leaf disease detection studies, especially convolutional neural network (CNN) based approaches. In addition, an exciting work in [6] deployed deep learning architectures, which include VGG16, InceptionV4, ResNet50, ResNet101, Resnet152, and DenseNet121, using PlantVillage dataset for plant disease identification. In a study [7], the authors presented a deep learning-based approach applying CNN-based pre-trained models, encompassing DenseNet121, ResNet50, VGG16, and InceptionV4, which trained on the PlantVillage dataset for leaf disease detection. Binnar and Sharma [8] proposed detection models that deployed four deep learning models, e.g., AlexNet, simple sequential model, MobileNet, and Inception-v3, for detecting plant leaf diseases. An improved MobileNet was used in [9] to perform disease detection tasks on tomato leaves. Exciting work in [10] presented a model using improved ShuffleNetV2, which deeply integrated the Squeeze-and-Excitation module with the ShuffleNetV2 network to recognize edible fungi fruit body diseases.

Although studies based on CNN algorithms have been proposed in plant leaf disease detection, usually only on a specific plant, examining the effects of noise reduction techniques for improving the performance of CNN-based architectures needs to be thoroughly investigated on numerous types of plants. Therefore, our study has attempted a threshold-based noise reduction technique and evaluated its effects on accuracy in plant leaf disease detection tasks.

3   Methods

Figure 1 exhibits an approach for disease detection in plant leaves with ShuffleNetV2 [11], LeNet [12], and ResNet50 [13], including the main stages. In the first phase, we collect the data for the experiment and divide the dataset into two main subsets, including the training set and the testing set. Then, we per-form data processing by applying Soft-Thresholding with Lasso regression to reduce the noise. Next, the data are fetched into learning architectures such as ShuffleNetV2, LeNet, and ResNet50 for disease classification tasks.

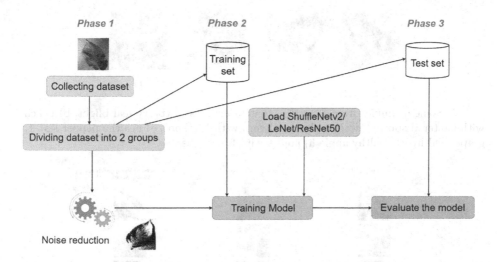

Fig. 1. The proposed workflow for Disease Detection on Plant Leaves.

3.1 Dataset

PlantVillage dataset [14] was collected with 24 plant leaf disease classes, including 14,400 images of 10 different plant species. Figure 2 shows some examples from PlantVillage dataset. The original images had different resolutions, and because the crop data were of a substandard size, this dataset was preprocessed to resize images to 224×224 pixels for fetching into models. We use 80% for the training set (11,520 images) and 20% for testing (2,880 images).

3.2 Soft-Thresholding with Lasso Regression for Noise Reduction

We leverage Soft-Thresholding by using Lasso regression. Soft-thresholding is an essential technique in data and feature processing in the case of statistical prediction and analysis. This technique eliminates features that are not essential or that contribute little to the model; thereby, it helps to improve the overall ability of the Lasso model. In this study, the Soft-Thresholding was estimated with a value of 0.5. Figure 3 compares the threshold applied to the image and the original ones.

Lasso regression is ordinary least squares plus an L1 norm, with $Cost(\beta)$ computed as Eq. 1 [15], where $Cost(\beta)$ is the loss function (cost function) calculated based on a set of training data and a set of coefficients β. At the same

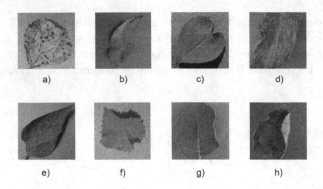

Fig. 2. Some examples from PlantVillage dataset: a) strawberry leaf blight, b) peach with bacterial spot, c) healthy cherry, d) corn with leaf spot, e) healthy pepper leaf, f) grape healthy g) healthy apple h) apples with fungal disease.

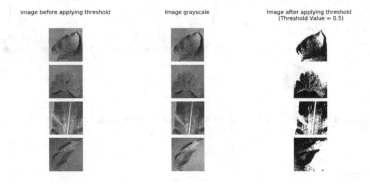

Fig. 3. Before and after applying threshold images and grayscale images.

time, the Residual Sum of Squares (RSS) denotes the sum of the squared errors between the values actual y_i and predicted value $\sum_{j=0}^{M} \beta_j x_{ij}$ for each data point. λ reveals a regularization parameter used to control the level of regularization applied to the model.

$$Cost(\beta) = RSS + \lambda \, (\text{sum of absolute value of weights})$$
$$= \sum_{i=0}^{N} \left(y_i - \sum_{j=0}^{M} \beta_j x_{ij} \right)^2 + \lambda \sum_{j=0}^{M} |\beta_j| \tag{1}$$

We use soft-thresholding function $S(a, \lambda)$. This allows us to solve the subdifferential of the Lasso cost function [16] as follows Eq. 2, In this case, we use the L1 regularization function with the regularization coefficient λ. $S(\lambda, \beta)$: This is approximately the derivative of the normalization component for β, and it is called the subdifferential of the function $|\beta|$. It depends on the values of λ and

β as Eq. 2.

$$\therefore \frac{\partial}{\partial \beta}(\text{Cost}) = \sum_{i=1}^{n} 2(y_i - x_i\beta)(-x_i) + \frac{\partial}{\partial \beta}[\lambda|\beta|]$$

$$= \sum_{i=1}^{n} 2(y_i - x_i\beta)(-x_i) + S(\lambda, \beta)$$

(2)

We can use this function during slope reduction to estimate λ with α. However, in the context of using Gaussian [17] and Lasso regression [15], it is common to use the Lasso model to estimate the regression coefficients of a predictive model, and Soft-Thresholding is applied to perform variable selection through setting the coefficients of non-critical variables based on defined thresholds. Gaussian and Soft-Thresholding in Lasso Regression appear when assuming that the coefficients of the Lasso model have a Gaussian distribution. This could allow you to estimate the regression coefficients through Lasso's goal optimization process and apply Soft-Thresholding to the model by setting the coefficients to be less than a threshold.

3.3 Deep Learning Architectures for Disease Detection on Leaf Images

Deep learning architectures used in this study include ShuffleNetV2, LeNet, and ResNet50. Table 1 shows the main features of each considered CNN model used to prepare for the training phase. Many CNN models are provided, but the model was chosen because of its high results in the training process.

Table 1. Some considered deep learning architectures

Architecture	Main Features	#Params (millions)
ShuffleNetV2	Solves tasks such as recognition images	10.81
ResNet50	Helps significantly improve performance in disease classification and image classification tasks	376.99
LeNet	Developing machine learning applications related to image processing	29.62

4 Experimental Results

4.1 Experimental Setup

The tests are conducted on the command line parameter with 12 GB RAM and 1.8 GHz Core i5 Intel CPU-assisted GPU with 8 GB. The proposed model is trained using ten epochs and a batch size of 32.

4.2   Scenario 1: Disease Performance with ShuffleNetV2

The original ShuffleNetV2 includes default hyper-parameters: epoch value of 5, step size of 3, gamma value of 0.01, and batch size of 8. In the experiment of using fine-tuned ShuffleNetV2 for disease detection on leaves, we fine-tune the hyper-parameters, including the epoch value of 10, a learning speed value of 0.001, a batch size of 32, a step size of 5, and leaving the same gamma value of 0.01. The loss and accuracy during epochs are shown in the Fig. 4a

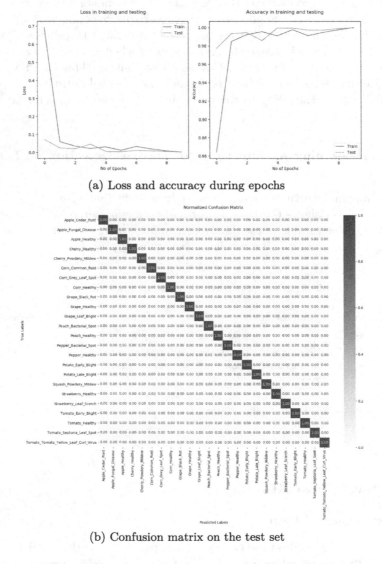

(a) Loss and accuracy during epochs

(b) Confusion matrix on the test set

Fig. 4. Classification performance with ShuffleNetV2

Fig. 4b shows the confusion matrix on the testing set in scenario 1. The results of fining-tune the hyper-parameters show that the fine-tuned ShuffleNetV2 model achieves an accuracy of 99.61% compared to the results of original ShuffleNetV2 model with an accuracy of 99.41%.

4.3   Scenario 2: Disease Performance with ResNet50

The original ResNet50 has hyper-parameters with default values: epoch value of 5, step size of 3, gamma value of 0.01, and batch size of 8. In the experiment using fine-tuned ResNet50, we fine-tuned the hyper-parameters, including the epoch value of 10, a learning speed value of 0.001, a batch size of 32, a step size of 5, and leaving the same gamma value of 0.01. Figure 5a shows the loss and accuracy during epochs.

Figure 5b shows the confusion matrix on the testing set in scenario 2. The results of fine-tuning the hyper-parameters show that the fine-tuned ResNet50 model achieves an accuracy of 99.21% compared to the results of the original ResNet50 model with an accuracy of 98.63%.

4.4   Scenario 3: Disease Performance with LeNet

The original LeNet has hyper-parameters with default values: epoch value of 5, step size of 3, gamma value of 0.01, and batch size of 8. In the experiment of using fine-tuned LeNet, we fine-tuned the hyper-parameters, including the epoch value of 10, a learning speed value of 0.001, a batch size of 32, a step size of 5, and leaving the same gamma value of 0.01. Figure 6a shows the loss and accuracy during epochs.

From the illustration of Fig. 6b shows the confusion matrix on the testing set in scenario 3. The results of fining-tune the hyper-parameters show that the fine-tuned LeNet model achieves an accuracy of 94.45% compared to the results of the original LeNet model with an accuracy of 92.20%.

4.5   Scenario 4: Soft-Thresholding with Lasso Regression

Figure 7 illustrates the Soft-Thresholding with Lasso Regression analysis. Figure 7a shows that when increasing the threshold value, the recall value will increase to help to choose a better model, and Fig. 7b shows that when the value of Soft-Thresholding increases, the beta value will decrease, which helps reduce unnecessary features. In addition, results achieved after applying the Soft-Thresholding with Lasso regression to the fine-tuned ShuffleNetV2 model show promising results in Table 2 and can be applied in practice to implement diagnostic software for plant diseases.

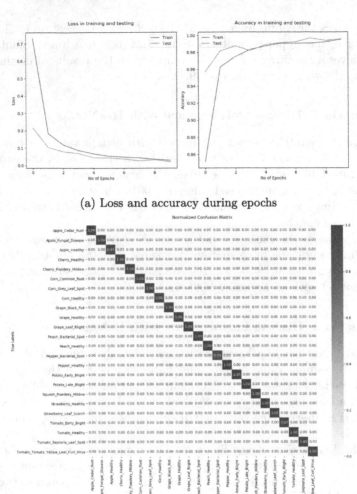

(a) Loss and accuracy during epochs

(b) Confusion matrix on the test set

Fig. 5. Classification performance with ResNet50

4.6   Discussion

The four scenarios show that the four prediction cases are more than 0.9 accurate. In scenario 3, LeNet with the unexpected result is 0.94453; In scenario 1, the discriminating rate between disease and healthy disease is close to 100%. There is almost no confusion in the learning process. Based on the above experimental results, the statistics are presented in Table 2. The results show that the model applying the Soft-Thresholding with Lasso regression to the fine-tuned

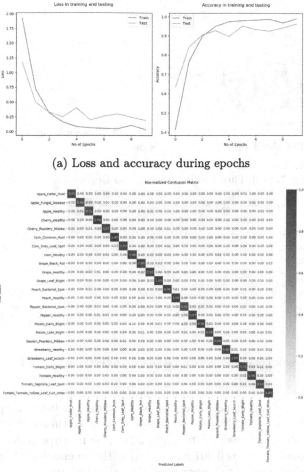

(a) Loss and accuracy during epochs

(b) Confusion matrix on the test set

Fig. 6. Classification performance with LeNet

Table 2. The result of applying the Soft-Thresholding with Lasso regression to the fine-tuned model

	Fine-tuned + Thresholding
ShuffleNetV2	0.99610
ResNet50	0.99211
LeNet	0.94453

ShuffleNetV2 outperforms the most recently published efforts in identifying disease signals. Similarly, based on the experimental results, the machine learning process on the ShuffleNetV2 model for positive and promising results. In this

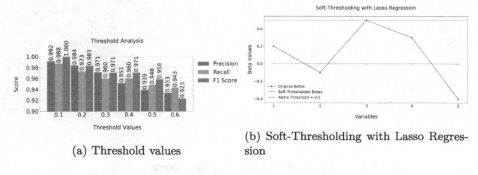

(a) Threshold values

(b) Soft-Thresholding with Lasso Regression

Fig. 7. Soft-Thresholding with Lasso Regression Analysis

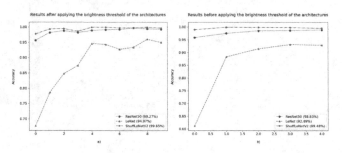

Fig. 8. Result comparison with various architectures on the testing set.

experiment, the default hyperparameter values used include an epoch value of 10 and a batch size of 32. The model uses a gamma optimization function. The initial image will be normalized to 224×224. The hyperparameters have been refined: The learning rate is 0.001 and tested with ten epochs. These parameters can be determined using a hyperparameter search. The accuracy and loss during the training phase show that the accuracy increases after iterations, and the error gradually decreases and stabilizes after ten epochs.

Table 3. Results comparison between fine-tuned architectures and original values of hyper-parameters

	Fine-tuned + Thresholding	Original Values of Hyper-parameters
ShuffleNetV2	0.99610	0.99411
ResNet50	0.99211	0.98630
LeNet	0.94453	0.92202

This study selected three architectures, including ShffleNetV2, ResNet50, and LeNet, to compare making more prominent benefits, improving accuracy, and choosing parameters. As shown in (a) and (b) in Fig. 8, there is a comparison of brightness accuracy on experimental recognition by ShuffleNet V2, ResNet50, and LeNet in modern architectures. With training comparison, it works and corresponds to a corresponding authentication. By observing Fig. 8, the exact form identified by different models increases with the increase of the primitives. It should be noted that the accuracy of our model is currently higher than that of other models. Figure 8 determines that the preliminary calibration results of the method are exported. Priority of the output model, Table 3 illustrates a comparison between the results of applying the Soft-Thresholding with Lasso regression to the fine-tuned architectures and those of original values of hyper-parameters.

5   Conclusion

Deep learning methods have recently become famous for image processing and pattern recognition. This study proposes a learning architecture using a Threshold-based noise reduction technique and a fine-tuned ShuffleNetV2 app-roach for classifying plant leaf images of 24 plant leaf disease classes in the PlantVillage dataset. The success of the proposed architecture is compared with the most advanced deep learning architectures used to detect leaf diseases in the literature. Research experiments were conducted in the original and denoised versions of the PlantVillage Dataset. Regarding average accuracy, the proposed ShuffleNetV2 outperforms other CNN architectures on both the original and denoised datasets with accuracies of 0.99411 and 0.99610, respectively. Future work is expected to expand the foliage disease dataset by increasing plant diversity and several classes. This will help develop models that can make more accurate predictions under challenging environments. Plant pathologists and farmers can quickly diagnose plant diseases and take necessary preventive measures by deploying these innovative models on environmental mobile devices.

References

1. Nayik, G.A., Gull, A.: Antioxidants in Vegetables and Nuts - Properties and Health Benefits. Springer, Singapore (2020). https://doi.org/10.1007/978-981-15-7470-2
2. Alsaeedi, A., El-Ramady, H., Alshaal, T., El-Garawany, M., Elhawat, N., Al-Otaibi, A.: Silica nanoparticles boost growth and productivity of cucumber under water deficit and salinity stresses by balancing nutrients uptake. Plant Physiol. Biochem. **139**, 1–10 (2019). https://doi.org/10.1016/j.plaphy.2019.03.008
3. Omari, R., Frempong, G.K., Arthur, W.: Public perceptions and worry about food safety hazards and risks in Ghana. Food Control **93**, 76–82 (2018). https://doi.org/10.1016/j.foodcont.2018.05.026
4. Arnal, J., Súcar, L.: Fast method based on fuzzy logic for gaussian-impulsive noise reduction in CT medical images. Mathematics **10**(19), 3652 (2022). https://doi.org/10.3390/math10193652
5. Arnal, J., Súcar, L.: Hybrid filter based on fuzzy techniques for mixed noise reduction in color images. Appl. Sci. **10**(1), 243 (2019). https://doi.org/10.3390/app10010243

6. Too, E.C., Yujian, L., Njuki, S., Yingchun, L.: A comparative study of fine-tuning deep learning models for plant disease identification. Comput. Electron. Agric. **161**, 272–279 (2019). https://doi.org/10.1016/j.compag.2018.03.032

7. Eunice, J., Popescu, D.E., Chowdary, M.K., Hemanth, J.: Deep learning-based leaf disease detection in crops using images for agricultural applications. Agronomy **12**(10), 2395 (2022). https://doi.org/10.3390/agronomy12102395

8. Binnar, V., Sharma, S.: Plant leaf diseases detection using deep learning algorithms. In: Doriya, R., Soni, B., Shukla, A., Gao, X.Z. (eds.) Machine Learning, Image Processing, Network Security and Data Sciences. Lecture Notes in Electrical Engineering, vol. 946, pp. 217–228. Springer, Singapore (2023). https://doi.org/10.1007/978-981-19-5868-7_17

9. Nguyen, H.T., Luong, H.H., Huynh, L.B., Le, B.Q.H., Doan, N.H., Le, D.T.D.: An improved MobileNet for disease detection on tomato leaves. Adv. Technol. Innov. **8**(3), 192–209 (2023). https://doi.org/10.46604/aiti.2023.11568

10. Xu, X., Zhang, Y., Cao, H., Yang, D., Zhou, L., Yu, H.: Recognition of edible fungi fruit body diseases based on improved ShuffleNetV2. Agronomy **13**(6), 1530 (2023). https://doi.org/10.3390/agronomy13061530

11. Zhang, X., Zhou, X., Lin, M., Sun, J.: ShuffleNet: an extremely efficient convolutional neural network for mobile devices (2017). https://arxiv.org/abs/1707.01083

12. Zhang, Z.H., Yang, Z., Sun, Y., Wu, Y.F., Xing, Y.D.: Lenet-5 convolution neural network with mish activation function and fixed memory step gradient descent method. In: 2019 16th International Computer Conference on Wavelet Active Media Technology and Information Processing, pp. 196–199 (2019)

13. LeCun, Y., et al.: Backpropagation applied to handwritten zip code recognition. Neural Comput. **1**(4), 541–551 (1989). https://doi.org/10.1162/neco.1989.1.4.541

14. Zhou, L.: Plant disease dataset (2022). https://data.mendeley.com/datasets/tsfxgsp3z6/2

15. Tibshirani, R., Saunders, M., Rosset, S., Zhu, J., Knight, K.: Sparsity and smoothness via the fused lasso. J. R. Stat. Soc. Ser. B Stat Methodol. **67**(1), 91–108 (2004). https://doi.org/10.1111/j.1467-9868.2005.00490.x

16. Mazlan, A.U., Sahabudin, N.A., Remli, M.A., Ismail, N.S.N., Adenuga, K.I.: An enhanced feature selection and cancer classification for microarray data using relaxed lasso and support vector machine. In: Translational Bioinformatics in Healthcare and Medicine, pp. 193–200. Elsevier (2021). https://doi.org/10.1016/b978-0-323-89824-9.00016-1

17. Miriyagalla, R., et al.: On the effectiveness of using machine learning and gaussian plume model for plant disease dispersion prediction and simulation. In: 2019 International Conference on Advancements in Computing (ICAC). IEEE (2019). https://doi.org/10.1109/icac49085.2019.9103383

Enhancing Visual Question Answering with Generated Image Caption

Kieu-Anh Thi Truong[(✉)], Truong-Thuy Tran, Cam- Van Thi Nguyen, and Duc-Trong Le

VNU University of Engineering and Technology, Ha Noi, Viet Nam
{kieuanhtt,truongthuyuet,vanntc,trongld}@vnu.edu.vn

Abstract. Visual Question Answering (VQA) poses a formidable challenge, necessitating computer systems to proficiently execute essential computer vision tasks, grasp the intricate contextual relationship between a posed question and a coexisting image, and produce precise responses. Nonetheless, a recurrent issue in numerous VQA models pertains to their inclination to prioritize language-based information over the rich contextual cues embedded within images, which are pivotal for answering questions comprehensively. To mitigate this limitation, this paper investigates the utility of image captioning-a technique that generates one or more descriptive sentences pertaining to the content of an image-as a means to augment answer quality within the framework of VQA, leveraging a language-centric approach. Towards this goal, we propose two model variants, namely **BLIP-C** and **BLIP-CL**, to aggregate the caption-grounded and vision-grounded representations to enrich the contextual question representation to improve the quality of answer generation. Experimental results on a public dataset demonstrate that utilizing captions significantly improves the accuracy and detail of answers compared to the baseline model.

Keywords: vqa · blip · blip-c · vision-language fusion

1 Introduction

Visual Question Answering (VQA) is a complex and interdisciplinary task that bridges the domains of computer vision (CV) and natural language processing (NLP). To accomplish this task, a VQA system relies on different algorithms to integrate input in the form of a natural language question with an image and generate an answer as output. The role of NLP is to address challenges such as question understanding and answer generation based on visual understanding using CV. VQA task has various practical applications in our life such as recommendation systems, education, advertising [3].

However, VQA models exhibit a bias towards learning from question features rather than giving equal importance to image features [12]. Previous studies [1, 20, 26] mainly focus on image features such as object recognition, attributes,

M. H. Hà et al. (Eds.): CSoNet 2023, LNCS 14479, pp. 15–26, 2024.
https://doi.org/10.1007/978-981-97-0669-3_2

Question 1: "where is the *lady sitting*",
Ground truth answer: "on a tree branch in a forest"

Question 2: "how do the *woman* wear clothes",
Ground truth answer: " a blue south vietnamese pajama shirt, south vietnamese pajama pants"

Generated caption by BLIP: a young woman in blue jacket and pink pants hanging on an old tree with her

Question 3: "where is the woman?",
Ground truth answer: " *sitting* in a forest"

Fig. 1. Example of our caption informative the model to answer question. Words relevant to the question and answer are marked by the same color, synonyms are italic

and relationships between object pairs. As another direction, several works [13,30] leverage textual features from images that can provide relevant information for answering questions. Nevertheless, these approaches heavily rely on descriptive, lengthy sentences to extract visual information and make decisions for answer generation, which can introduce bias towards additional information. In this paper, we hypothesize that image captions can be useful in facilitating answer construction. For VQA, if image captions are not readily available, they could be generated using pre-trained image captioning models, e.g., BLIP Image Captioning [15]. Figure 1 shows examples of generated captions, which have the potential to provide informative content for answer construction by reflecting various aspects and relationships among multiple objects or entities in the input question.

To incorporate the semantic information in captions, for each image input, we run a pre-processing step to generate a descriptive caption using a pre-trained image captioning module. *As the main contribution*, the generated caption is utilized to enrich the question representation, i.e., *caption-grounded representation*, besides the visual input, referred to as *image-grounded representation*. To combine these representations, we propose two variants namely **BLIP-C** and **BLIP-CL** built upon the VQA module of **BLIP** [15]. The former utilizes a hyperparameter to control the aggregation while the latter seeks to learn the trade-off ratio automatically. The joint representation is subsequently fed into the answer decoder to generate the appropriate answer. *As the second contribution*, we conduct extensive experiments on the VLSP-EJVQA datasets for English. Experimental results show that our proposed models demonstrate the ability to generate better answers with statistically significant improvements in terms of BLEU scores. For BLEU-1, **BLIP-C**, and **BLIP-CL** increase 3.35% and 0.93% respectively from the baseline **BLIP**.

The paper is organized as follows: Sect. 2 presents our literature review on related work for the VQA task while we thoroughly describe our approach in Sect. 3. In Sect. 4, various experiments on the VLSP-EJVQA datasets for English are performed to validate the effectiveness of the proposed approach. Section 5 summarizes the main content of the paper.

2   Related Work

2.1   Visual Question Answering

VQA was first introduced in [2] which is a combination of LSTM question encoder and VGG image encoder. Image embedding and question embedding after joint using point-wise multiplication goes through a fully-connected neural network to output the answer. Ren et al. [21], Malinowski et al. [19], Gao et al. [10] propose extracting image features from CNNs and text features from LSTM cells. Image features are fed into each LSTM cell of question encoder or answers decoder. Learning the important local features of image and question instead of using global features alone, some attentive models are proposed. Models designed in a top-down manner cannot effectively represent clear boundaries between regions, making it challenging to filter out noise from different parts of an image [23]. Likewise, Anderson et al. [1] ensures clear boundaries in object detection; however, it cannot guarantee the appropriate incorporation of semantic parts without explicitly classifying the objects and supervising the semantic connections between them. Multimodal Bottom-Up and Top-Down Cues [9], MBC for short, employs attention mechanisms for image and text features. However, to combine these two types of information, MBC proposes a deeper analysis of the combination between images and natural language by estimating the outer product of image features and text features. This mechanism has been shown to perform better than element-wise multiplication or concatenation of feature vectors. MBC achieves the best VQA results on the COCO VQA dataset. Additionally, another drawback of this method is its complexity and computational cost. Yang et al. [35], generate answers from fixed space and employ the VQA as a classification problem. Stack Attention Network (SAN) [35], is proposed to stack multiple question-guided attention layers, and representation of each layer is used as a query to attend to image grids. Following the EJVQA-VLSP dataset, we require a model with the ability to generate open-ended answers instead of a region of answers.

Recently, along with the advancement of pre-trained models, vision and language (VL) fusion models have gotten a lot of attention. These models exhibit improved capabilities in representing both images and text, enhancing generalization and the ability to generate descriptive captions for images. VilBERT [18] and LXMERT [25] utilize dual stream models with two separated Transformers to encode image and text input, and then the output features are inserted into a cross-modal Transformer for multimodal embeddings. VL-BERT [24], Pixel-BERT [11] use a only single stream of Transformer to fuse input from two modalities simultaneously. SemVLP [14] proposed a model architecture that applies both single stream encoder and dual stream by training them iteratively. In the effort of building a generic pre-trained BERT, BLIP [15] employs BERT for text encoder and Vision Transformer (ViT) for visual encoder, and feeds image embedding to the text encoder to generate output.

The top-5 methods in the VLSP competition for the EVJQA dataset mostly focus on addressing the multilingual VQA problem. Thai et al. [27] integrates a pre-trained vision language model to extract hints for the answers. Seq2Seq architecture is proposed to generate the corresponding answers in free-form natural language. Dong et al. [6] using an encoder-decoder architecture with object prefixes for inputs and proposing an additional object detection component for capturing the image's semantics. Multimodal sequence-to-sequence transformer model derived from the T5 encoder-decoder architecture is proposed in [5]. The input question includes text-based prompts to indicate language, image augmentation is added to generate more various input for different types of questions. Truong et al. [29] combine two modules of question-answer embedding and visual embedding as custom encode for transformer-based architecture. Our approach concentrates on using image captioning to enrich visual features for specific English VQA task.

2.2   VQA with Image Captioning

There are efforts to improve the VQA performance with the support of the image captioning task. Wu et al. [33] utilize a word prediction pre-trained on ImageNet to generate attributes and a separated image captioning model to generate captions. Likewise, Li et al. [16] leverages attributes to generate related knowledge and image captions. Both attributes, captions, and knowledge embeddings are fed into LSTM before fusing with modalities vectors. Changpinyo et al. [4] using captions to generate question-answer pair for training dataset of vqa model. Captions, generated question-answer pairs, and answers are inputs for the model. Li et al. [17] also use captions to construct the dataset with explanation for answers. Wu et al. [31] and Sharma et al. [22] employ question and image features to generate captions. Next, caption-based image feature, question representation, and the attended image feature are fed into LSTM unit to generate answers. Instead of using images as input, Tiong et al. [28] takes captions. Wu et al. [32] choose the question-relevant image descriptions to reduce question learning bias. Du et al. [8] apply a pre-trained language model to propose answers. As a direction using large language models, Yang et al. [34] propose the utilization of GPT-3 for answering knowledge-based visual questions. Different from mentioned works, our model uses a separate caption module to extract captions from the images and captions as input of VQA model. We demonstrate that utilizing image captions independently in the VQA task yields significant results, even when having no prior information about the questions.

3   Methodology

In this section, we present our methodology for improving the visual question answering task via exploiting generated captions of input images. Figure 2 illustrates the overall architecture of our approach.

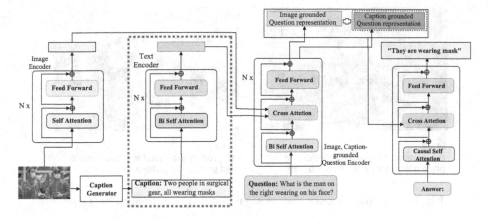

Fig. 2. Our framework architecture for VQA . Red dash-line boxes highlight novel components compared to BLIP [15] (Color figure online).

3.1   Caption Generation

As a preprocessing step, we adopt the pre-trained image caption module of BLIP to produce the caption for every image input. First, it takes image embedding injected from the ViT [7] module as input for the cross-attention layer of Transformer block. Next, a nucleus sample is utilized to generate more diverse and surprising captions, which may contain more useful information for the VQA task compared to beam search. Figure 3 shows some generated caption examples using BLIP Image Captioning.

3.2   Feature Representation

Inspired by BLIP [15], we employ a vision transformer (ViT) image encoder and a BERT-based text encoder to represent visual and text modalities respectively. Given an input tuple of (question, image, generated caption), the images are transformed into latent representations using ViT. In the case of the caption and question, we have implemented an image-grounded text encoder comprising three components namely bi-directional self-attention, cross-attention, and feedforward. The bi-directional self-attention module is to extract the contextual information in the sentences while the cross-attention module is to fuse the contextual representation with the visual representation to extract the image-text multimodal representation. Suppose that L is the length of the sentences, V is latent dimension of image embeddings from ViT, $\mathbf{C} \in \mathbb{R}^{L_c \times V}$ and $\mathbf{B}^{iq} \in \mathbb{R}^{L_q \times V}$ are denoted as enriched representation of image caption embedding and image question embedding respectively. Furthermore, we introduce a caption-grounded question encoder, which shares a similar architecture with the image-grounded question encoder but differs in the cross-attention layer where we replace the

id = 92
the crowds at an event with the first
place number 1 on the poster in red

id = 6340
An grocery attendant with face mask
and protective, picking vegetables.

Fig. 3. Examples of generated captions by BLIP [15] Image Captioning

image embedding with caption feature representation $\mathbf{C}$ to extract caption-grounded question representation $\mathbf{B}^{cq} \in \mathbb{R}^{L_q \times V}$. The aggregation of question-caption $\mathbf{B}^{cq}$ and question-image representation $\mathbf{B}^{iq}$ is the input of cross attention layer for Answer decoder block. The combination of these representations will described in the next section.

3.3 Multimodal Representation Aggregation

We propose two approaches to aggregate image- and caption-grounded question representation as the following: **BLIP-C**: The main idea is to combine these representations using a trade-off hyperparameter $\alpha \in [0, 1]$.

$$\mathbf{B}_{ques-out} = \alpha \times \mathbf{B}^{iq} + (1 - \alpha) \times \mathbf{B}^{cq} \tag{1}$$

BLIP-CL: Instead of using a trade-off hyperparameter, this variant leverages the importance of these representations by an additional parameter $\mathbf{D} \in \mathbb{R}^V$ as:

$$\mathbf{W}_{iq} = \mathbf{B}^{iq} \times \mathbf{D} \tag{2}$$

$$\mathbf{W}_{cq} = \mathbf{B}^{cq} \times \mathbf{D} \tag{3}$$

$$\mathbf{W}_l = Softmax([\mathbf{W}_{iq}, \mathbf{W}_{cq}]) \tag{4}$$

$$\mathbf{B}_{ques-out} = \mathbf{W}_l[:, 0] \times \mathbf{B}^{iq} + \mathbf{W}_l[:, 1] \times \mathbf{B}^{cq} \tag{5}$$

3.4 Answers Decoder

The aggregated representation $\mathbf{B}_{ques-out}$ of the image-grounded and caption-grounded question vector is fed into cross-attention layer of the Transformer block. In this decoder block, the bi-directional self-attention layer in the image-grounded encoder is replaced by a casual self-attention layer. A [Decode] token is used to signal the beginning of a sequence, and an end-of-sequence (EOF) token is to signify its end. With the objective of generating textual descriptions

Table 1. Statistics of EJVQA-VSLP dataset for English

	Training set	Test set
Images	3,285	478
English question-answer pairs	5,763	1,441

given an image, the answer decoder optimizes a cross-entropy loss which trains the model to maximize the likelihood of the text in an autoregressive manner

$$L_{CE} = -\sum_{n} H(y^{(n)} \hat{y}^{(n)}) \tag{6}$$

where y is ground-truth value and $\hat{y}$ is predicted probability.

4 Experiments

4.1 Dataset

We use the English dataset the VLSP Multilingual Visual Question Answering Competition (EVJVQA) 2022[1]. This dataset contains 7,928 English question-answer pairs from 3,763 images of various types such as landscapes, specific objects, markets, and human activities. Additionally, there are images capturing signs, information on posters, and some images are paintings. A single question may apply to multiple images. Unlike previous VQA datasets, which often aimed to transform VQA into a classification problem, the answers in the EJVQA-VLSP dataset are typically detailed. Some answers even include complete sentences with both subject and predicate. This raises a challenge in solving the task as the original BLIP model tends to create short answers.

Following the BLIP architecture and considering the constraints imposed by a limited dataset, we split the dataset into training and test sets of 5,763/1,441 question-answer pairs. Each training image has an image caption of length from 12 to 20 words. Table 1 illustrates the statistics of the dataset.

4.2 Metrics

BLEU score is used to evaluate the generation answers. In particular, we use BLEU-1, and BLEU-2 as the evaluation metric for visual question answering. The BLEU score is calculated using the following formula.

$$\text{BLEU} = BP \cdot \exp\left(\frac{1}{n}\sum_{i=1}^{n}\log P_i\right) \tag{7}$$

---

[1] https://vlsp.org.vn/vlsp2022/eval/evjvqa.

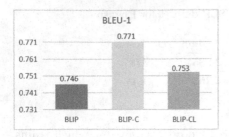
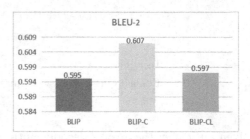

Fig. 4. Experiment results compare with the baseline method **BLIP**

where BP stands for *Brevity Penalty* computed as follows:

$$BP = min(1, \exp(1 - r/c)) \tag{8}$$

with r is the number of words or characters in the generated sentence, and c is the number of words or characters in the reference sentence; P_i is the ratio of the number of matching n-grams between the generated and the reference sentence; n is size of the n-gram used.

4.3   Implementation Details

The model is implemented using PyTorch with GPU. The Transformer block for images is initialized with parameters similar to the ViT model trained on the ImageNet dataset, while the Transformer block for text is initialized from the pre-trained $BERT_{base}$ model. The model is trained for 5 epochs with a batch size of 3 due to the large amount of data and GPU limitations. To optimize the training, the model uses AdamW optimizer with a weight decay of 0.05. The learning rate is set to 2e-5, and the decay linearly with the rate of 0.85. Images are trained at a resolution of 384×384 pixels. To mitigate the risk of overfitting, we terminate training when the loss stabilizes without further reduction. During the inference process for VQA, we employ the decoder to generate answers. In our approach, the output words from the previous step are used as input for the current step instead of ranking a predefined number of answers. Notably, captions are not employed in generating answers during inference. Both baseline model **BLIP** and proposed models, i.e., **BLIP-C**, **BLIP-CL**, are finetuned using the EJVQA-VLSP dataset. Each model is run ten times with different seeds and reports the average performance. Remarkably, without incorporating captions during inference, two models demonstrate their proficiency in generating high-quality answers by effectively leveraging both visual and textual features.

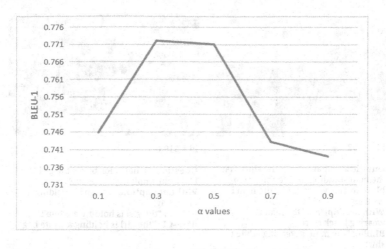

Fig. 5. The effect of α on the BLIP-C's performance

4.4 Results and Discussions

Quantitative Results. We further analyze our model quantitatively in the context of two research questions below.

Is the generated caption is useful for the VQA task? As shown in Fig. 4, our proposed models, i.e., BLIP-C and BLIP-CL, improve BLEU scores compared to the baseline BLIP model. In BLEU-1, the **BLIP-C**, and **BLIP-CL** increase 3.35% and 0.93% respectively from the baseline BLIP. **BLIP-C** is the best performing variant because it is simpler than **BLIP-CL**. Likewise, we observe similar phenomena. All improvements are validated by the statistical student *t-test* with *p-value* 0.05. These observations imply that the integration of captions helps improve VQA model performance.

What is the effect of α in BLIP-C? We vary α and observe the BLEU-1 metric as Fig. 5. The results showed that with $\alpha = 0.3$, indicating a larger role of the caption-question features over the image, the best result was achieved with a BLEU-1 score of 0.772. $\alpha = 0.5$, where both features are considered equally important, shows a similar result of 0.771. Results with α values lower (0.1) or higher (0.7, 0.9) did not yield significant values. This demonstrates that when the image-question or caption-question features are given too much weight, the model lacks the information provided by the other feature. The fact that a value of $\alpha = 0.7$ and image feature alone ($\alpha = 1$, baseline model not using caption) resulted in a lower score than $\alpha = 0.3$ also confirms that the image feature alone is insufficient in forming accurate answers.

Qualitative Results. We conduct several qualitative experiments to show the effectiveness of the proposed methods, namely **BLIP-C, BLIP-CL** in improving the quality of generated answers for the VQA task as Fig. 6. For example, considering the image with *id = 6092* and the question "What color is the shirt that the man standing next to the girl in a black shirt is wearing? " Both proposed models correctly color answer "white", with the BLIP-C model providing

id = 6092

id = 5193

Question: "what color is the shirt that the man standing next to the girl in black shirt is wearing? "- "the man is wearing white shirt"
Without Caption: "the man is wearing black shirt"
BLIP-C: "the man is wearing white t - shirt"
BLIP-CL: "it is white."

Question: "what color bag is the girl in black shirt holding?" - "white"
Without Caption: "the girl is holding a black bag"
BLIP-C: "the girl is holding a white bag"
BLIP-CL: "the girl is holding a white bag"

Fig. 6. Comparison answers generated from proposed method and baseline model

an answer closer to the reference answer. In contrast, the baseline model predicts the incorrect answer "black". As another example, in the image with $id = 5193$, both **BLIP-C** and **BLIP-CL** models predict "the girl is holding a white bag" with the correct color being "white", while the baseline model provides an incorrect answer with the color "black".

5   Conclusion

In this paper, we present a novel approach for the VQA task, which exploits generated captions from input images to enhance the quality of answers. The main idea is to jointly enhance the contextual question representation with image- and caption-grounded representations. The representations are aggregated in two ways respecting to our two model variants including **BLIP-C** and **BLIP-CL**. Experimental results on the VLSP-2022 EJVQA dataset for English demonstrate the efficacy of our approach compared to the baseline **BLIP**. In the future, we aim to improve the accuracy of the model by constructing an end-to-end architecture, whereby the caption is built concurrently with the answer generation in a unified framework.

References

1. Anderson, P., et al.: Bottom-up and top-down attention for image captioning and visual question answering. In: Proceedings of the IEEE Conference on Computer Vision and Pattern Recognition, pp. 6077–6086 (2018)
2. Antol, S., et al.: VQA: visual question answering. In: Proceedings of the IEEE International Conference on Computer Vision, pp. 2425–2433 (2015)

3. Barra, S., Bisogni, C., De Marsico, M., Ricciardi, S.: Visual question answering: which investigated applications? Pattern Recogn. Lett. **151**, 325–331 (2021)
4. Changpinyo, S., Kukliansky, D., Szpektor, I., Chen, X., Ding, N., Soricut, R.: All you may need for VQA are image captions. arXiv preprint: arXiv:2205.01883 (2022)
5. Dinh, H.L., Phan, L.: A jointly language-image model for multilingual visual question answering. In: The 9th International Workshop on Vietnamese Language and Speech Processing (2022)
6. Dong, N.V.N., Loi: A multi-modal transformer-based method with object prefixes for multilingual visual question answering. In: The 9th International Workshop on Vietnamese Language and Speech Processing (2022)
7. Dosovitskiy, A., et al.: An image is worth 16x16 words: transformers for image recognition at scale. arXiv preprint: arXiv:2010.11929 (2020)
8. Du, Y., Li, J., Tang, T., Zhao, W.X., Wen, J.R.: Zero-shot visual question answering with language model feedback. arXiv preprint: arXiv:2305.17006 (2023)
9. Fukui, A., Park, D.H., Yang, D., Rohrbach, A., Darrell, T., Rohrbach, M.: Multimodal compact bilinear pooling for visual question answering and visual grounding. arXiv preprint: arXiv:1606.01847 (2016)
10. Gao, H., Mao, J., Zhou, J., Huang, Z., Wang, L., Xu, W.: Are you talking to a machine? Dataset and methods for multilingual image question. In: Advances in Neural Information Processing Systems, vol. 28 (2015)
11. Huang, Z., Zeng, Z., Liu, B., Fu, D., Fu, J.: Pixel-BERT: aligning image pixels with text by deep multi-modal transformers. arXiv preprint: arXiv:2004.00849 (2020)
12. Kafle, K., Kanan, C.: Visual question answering: datasets, algorithms, and future challenges. Comput. Vis. Image Underst. **163**, 3–20 (2017)
13. Kim, H., Bansal, M.: Improving visual question answering by referring to generated paragraph captions. arXiv preprint: arXiv:1906.06216 (2019)
14. Li, C., et al.: SemVLP: vision-language pre-training by aligning semantics at multiple levels. arXiv preprint: arXiv:2103.07829 (2021)
15. Li, J., Li, D., Xiong, C., Hoi, S.: BLIP: bootstrapping language-image pre-training for unified vision-language understanding and generation. In: International Conference on Machine Learning, pp. 12888–12900. PMLR (2022)
16. Li, Q., Fu, J., Yu, D., Mei, T., Luo, J.: Tell-and-answer: towards explainable visual question answering using attributes and captions. arXiv preprint: arXiv:1801.09041 (2018)
17. Li, Q., Tao, Q., Joty, S., Cai, J., Luo, J.: VQA-E: explaining, elaborating, and enhancing your answers for visual questions. In: Ferrari, V., Hebert, M., Sminchisescu, C., Weiss, Y. (eds.) Computer Vision – ECCV 2018. Lecture Notes in Computer Science(), vol. 11211, pp. 552–567. Springer, Cham (2018). https://doi.org/10.1007/978-3-030-01234-2_34
18. Lu, J., Batra, D., Parikh, D., Lee, S.: VilBERT: pretraining task-agnostic visiolinguistic representations for vision-and-language tasks. In: Advances in Neural Information Processing Systems, vol. 32 (2019)
19. Malinowski, M., Rohrbach, M., Fritz, M.: Ask your neurons: a neural-based approach to answering questions about images. In: Proceedings of the IEEE International Conference on Computer Vision, pp. 1–9 (2015)
20. Pedersoli, M., Lucas, T., Schmid, C., Verbeek, J.: Areas of attention for image captioning. In: Proceedings of the IEEE International Conference on Computer Vision, pp. 1242–1250 (2017)
21. Ren, M., Kiros, R., Zemel, R.: Exploring models and data for image question answering. In: Advances in Neural Information Processing Systems, vol. 28 (2015)

22. Sharma, H., Jalal, A.S.: Image captioning improved visual question answering. Multimedia Tools Appl. **81**, 1–22 (2021)
23. Singh, J., Ying, V., Nutkiewicz, A.: Attention on attention: architectures for visual question answering (VQA). arXiv preprint: arXiv:1803.07724 (2018)
24. Su, W., et al.: VL-BERT: pre-training of generic visual-linguistic representations. arXiv preprint: arXiv:1908.08530 (2019)
25. Tan, H., Bansal, M.: LXMERT: learning cross-modality encoder representations from transformers. arXiv preprint: arXiv:1908.07490 (2019)
26. Teney, D., Anderson, P., He, X., Van Den Hengel, A.: Tips and tricks for visual question answering: learnings from the 2017 challenge. In: Proceedings of the IEEE Conference on Computer Vision and Pattern Recognition, pp. 4223–4232 (2018)
27. Thai, T.M., Luu, S.T.: Integrating image features with convolutional sequence-to-sequence network for multilingual visual question answering. arXiv preprint: arXiv:2303.12671 (2023)
28. Tiong, A.M.H., Li, J., Li, B., Savarese, S., Hoi, S.C.: Plug-and-play VQA: Zero-shot VQA by conjoining large pretrained models with zero training. arXiv preprint: arXiv:2210.08773 (2022)
29. Truong, L.X., Pham, V.Q.: Multi-modal feature extraction for multilingual visual question answering. In: The 9th International Workshop on Vietnamese Language and Speech Processing (2022)
30. Wu, J., Chen, L., Mooney, R.J.: Improving VQA and its explanations\\by comparing competing explanations. arXiv preprint: arXiv:2006.15631 (2020)
31. Wu, J., Hu, Z., Mooney, R.J.: Joint image captioning and question answering. arXiv preprint: arXiv:1805.08389 (2018)
32. Wu, J., Hu, Z., Mooney, R.J.: Generating question relevant captions to aid visual question answering. arXiv preprint: arXiv:1906.00513 (2019)
33. Wu, Q., Shen, C., Wang, P., Dick, A., Van Den Hengel, A.: Image captioning and visual question answering based on attributes and external knowledge. IEEE Trans. Pattern Anal. Mach. Intell. **40**(6), 1367–1381 (2017)
34. Yang, Z., et al.: An empirical study of GPT-3 for few-shot knowledge-based VQA. In: Proceedings of the AAAI Conference on Artificial Intelligence, vol. 36, pp. 3081–3089 (2022)
35. Yang, Z., He, X., Gao, J., Deng, L., Smola, A.: Stacked attention networks for image question answering. In: Proceedings of the IEEE Conference on Computer Vision and Pattern Recognition, pp. 21–29 (2016)

A Gaussian Distribution Labeling Method for Speech Quality Assessment

Minh Tu Le[1,2]([✉]), Bao Thang Ta[1,2], Nhat Minh Le[1], Phi Le Nguyen[2], and Van Hai Do[1,3]

[1] Viettel Cyberspace Center, Viettel Group, Hanoi, Vietnam
minhtutx@gmail.com
[2] Hanoi University of Science and Technology, Hanoi, Vietnam
[3] Thuyloi University, Hanoi, Vietnam

Abstract. Speech Quality Assessment (SQA) plays a critical role in speech processing systems by predicting the quality of input speech signals. Traditionally, quality is represented as mean of scores provided by many listeners' opinions and is a floating-point value, so the straightforward approach is treating SQA as a regression task. However, speech quality score is labeled by crowdsourcing, resulting in a lack of uniformity among listeners. This discrepancy makes it challenging to accurately represent speech quality. Some recent works have proposed transforming SQA into a classification task by converting continuous scores into discrete classes. These approaches simplify the training of SQA models but not consider valuable variance information, which capture the differences among listeners and the difficulties to evaluate.

To address this limitation, in addition to directly learning score values through the regression task, we propose using a classification task in a multitask setting. We assume that quality labels for each class follow a Gaussian distribution, considering not only the mean ratings but also the variance among them. To ensure that the improvements can be confidently attributed to our approach, we adopt a Conformer-based architecture, a state-of-the-art architectural framework for representing speech information, as the core for our model and baseline models. Through a comprehensive series of experiments conducted on the NISQA speech quality assessment dataset, we provide conclusive evidence that our proposed method consistently enhances results across all dimensions of speech quality.

Keywords: Speech Quality Assessment · MOS · distribution labeling

1 Introduction

With the development of information and communication technology, people can easily communicate with others through the Internet and telecommunication systems. The most popular forms are voice calls and online meetings, where people can talk to others. However, speech transmitted over networks can be degraded

M. H. Hà et al. (Eds.): CSoNet 2023, LNCS 14479, pp. 27–38, 2024.
https://doi.org/10.1007/978-981-97-0669-3_3

and may not ensure the original quality, leading to annoyance and potential misunderstandings among end-users. Consequently, speech quality assessment is a crucial task in evaluating the performance of communication systems, garnering attention from telephone companies and Internet service providers.

The primary approach for assessing speech quality is the subjective method, where a group of human listens to and evaluates the speech. Normally, each listener rates the speech quality on a scale from 1 to 5, and the Mean Opinion Score (MOS), calculated as the average score, represents the overall quality [6]. While this method provides authentic insights into users' experiences, it is expensive, time-consuming, and impractical for real-time and large-scale systems.

To address these limitations, alternative objective methods have been developed [14]. The International Telecommunication Union - Telecommunication (ITU-T) has recommended standard objective methods, including PESQ [7] and POLQA [8]. These methods are double-ended, requiring a clean or reference speech signal for comparison with the degraded signal. By analyzing the differences between them, these algorithms provide a measure of the quality of the degraded speech. However, the double-ended method faces limitations due to the unavailability of reference speech signals in many practical scenarios. As a result, single-ended methods have garnered considerable attention and emerged as an active research area in speech quality assessment. Not relying on reference speech signals, single-ended methods overcome the limitations of double-ended methods and are more applicable in real-world settings.

Recently, deep learning-based approaches have achieved remarkable results in single-ended speech quality assessment by predicting MOS. Researchers have explored various neural network architectures and different methods of extracting speech features. For instance, [24] propose a model using Long Short-Term Memory (LSTM) module. Additionally, certain models comprise bidirectional LSTM and densely connected convolutional (DCC) layers [4], while others incorporate convolutional neural networks (CNNs) [13]. In a different approach, authors in [20] introduced transformer-based learning to the domain of audio quality assessment, using three essential audio features: Mel-frequency cepstral coefficients, chroma, and Mel-scaled spectrogram. Furthermore, [23] proposed a model called Subband Adaptive Attention Temporal Convolutional Neural Network (SAA-TCN), which takes subband magnitude spectrograms as input. These research efforts have yielded promising results in predicting speech quality and have provided valuable insights for the development of effective models for this critical task.

All of these research efforts aim to predict MOS, a real-value label determined by individual opinions. However, the scoring range of 1 to 5 can often confuse listeners when selecting a suitable level. Therefore, predicting MOS can be challenging, particularly when listeners assign different scores to the same speech sample. To overcome this limitation, several studies have explored alternative labeling schemes and objective functions. For instance, [11] provides a posterior distribution of MOS by predicting both the mean and standard deviation. In [9], researchers compared the Mean Squared Error (MSE) loss with Kullback-Leibler divergence (KLD) in regression approach and cross-entropy (CE) in classification approach. The KLD loss was used to train models to predict a normal distribution with mean and variance similar to human-labeled scores, while the cross-entropy loss was employed with converting the MOS scale, ranging from 1 to 5, into a 5-class setting. Additionally, [29] and [15] employed the Earth Mover's Distance (EMD) as a loss function with blended label distributions. Similarly, in [16], the speech quality quantification task was formulated as a classification problem, and Gaussian-smoothed labels were introduced as part of the solution. These alternative approaches aim to enhance the robustness and accuracy of speech quality prediction models by considering various methods for interpreting and handling the subjective nature of MOS labels.

To transform the problem to classification task, existing labeling methods are inflexibility, only labeling a few classes around the MOS value and not utilizing the variance information present in individual listener opinions. While [9] and [11] try to predict it but still regard it as a regression task and treat all badly and well labeled samples equally. In our work, we proposes a Gaussian distribution labeling approach for speech quality assessment, which captures the varying degrees of speech quality opinions expressed by different listeners and helps training model phase focus on the samples labeled well. This distribution-based labeling is then utilized within a classification framework to predict speech quality. Moreover, we implement Conformer blocks, which include convolution sub-sampling layers and Transformer blocks [5], to represent speech information. Not only Automatic Speech Recognition (ASR), Conformer has been applied for other tasks, such as Speech Emotion Recognition [27], Accent Recognition [25]. A recent work [26] showed that Conformer gave state-of-the-art performance in speech quality assessment. With the same neural architecture, we compare the proposed labeling method with the traditional method of predicting MOS and Gaussian-smoothed-labels, a labeling method used in [15,16,29]. The experiments evaluate not only on overall quality but also other criteria: noisiness, discontinuity, coloration and loudness [28]. In predicting overall quality, the experiments show that our propose outperforms Gaussian-smoothed-labels and traditional regression approach in all test cases. In other criteria of speech quality, our labeling method also gives the improvement. Moreover, the combination of classification approach using Gaussian distribution labeling and regression approach achieves best performance.

The paper is organized as follows: Sect. 2 details the proposed distribution labeling method along with speech quality assessment model. The effectiveness of the proposed approach is then confirmed through experimental results, presented in Sect. 3. Finally, Sect. 4 provides a summary of the research findings and outlines potential future directions for this work.

2   Proposed Method

2.1   Gaussian Distribution Labeling

Usually, conventional methods aim to predict MOS directly, but MOS values are labeled by a group and can be different among listeners. To simplify the prediction process, some researchers [15,16,29] convert speech quality prediction into a classification task by dividing the MOS range into discrete classes.

For instance, [16] introduced a label distribution learning method, named by Gaussian-smooth-labeled. Within this, MOS range of 1–5 is divided into C distinct classes and v represents the class index containing the MOS value, smooth labels at k^{th} class (x^k) is formulated as follows:

$$x^k = \begin{cases} 0.6 & \text{if } k = v \\ 0.2 & \text{if } k = v \pm 1 \\ 0 & \text{otherwise} \end{cases} \tag{1}$$

However, this conventional approach only assigns labels to the two classes adjacent to the one containing the MOS value. [15,29] share the similar idea with four adjacent class. Furthermore, they did not leverage the variance information, which indicates the different of listeners' opinions are rating speech samples.

Hence, we propose a novel approach of smoothing the labels using a Gaussian distribution. We assume that the scores provided by listeners follow a Gaussian distribution, and the model's task is to reconstruct this distribution, ensuring representation for each class relative ratio of ratings at each score, as illustrated in Fig. 1.

For a sample with a mean score of μ and a standard deviation of σ, given a variable $s \sim \mathcal{N}(\mu, \sigma)$. C is the number of discrete classes. We define the range of each class 2δ:

$$2\delta = \frac{MOS_{max} - MOS_{min}}{C - 1} = \frac{4}{C - 1} \tag{2}$$

The centroid of the kth class (c^k):

$$c^k = MOS_{min} + \frac{(k - 1) * (MOS_{max} - MOS_{min})}{C - 1} = 1 + \frac{(k - 1) * 4}{C - 1} \tag{3}$$

The smoothed label for the sample corresponds to the probability of s falling within the range of each class.

$$x^k = \begin{cases} p(s < 1 + \delta) & \text{if } k = 1 \\ p(c^k - \delta < s < c^k + \delta) & \text{if } 1 < k < C \\ p(5 - \delta < s) & \text{if } k = C \end{cases} \tag{4}$$

Note that first and last class respectively have centroids of 1 and 5 and class range are $[-\infty, 1 + \delta]$ and $[5 - \delta, +\infty]$ while others have range $[c^k - \delta, c^k + \delta]$. This difference aims to handle the samples has MOS at border value.

By using this labeling method, the training process become a classification problem. In inference phase, the predicted MOS is obtained by a weighted sum of all centroids:

$$\hat{y} = \sum_{i=1}^{C} c^k * p^k$$

where p^k is the predicted probability of class k^{th}.

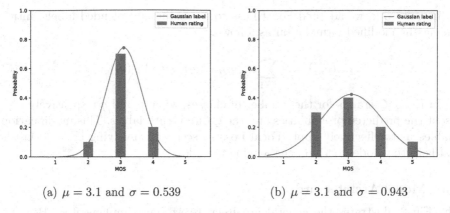

(a) $\mu = 3.1$ and $\sigma = 0.539$ (b) $\mu = 3.1$ and $\sigma = 0.943$

Fig. 1. Two speech samples have the same MOS but different standard deviation with 10 ratings. The distribution of listeners' scores are simulated by Gaussian distribution labeling method.

Consider two examples with the same mean score value but different variances as shown in Fig. 1. The previous approaches typically assign them similar labels [15,16,29] or, at the least, treats them equally [9,11]. However, with our Gaussian distribution labeling method, the sample with a lower variance gets more sharply label which concentrates higher probability in the class containing the mean value, and is more difficult for model to fit. In contrast, the label for the other is flatter, making it easier for the model to predict. This means that badly-labeled samples, that confuse listeners during evaluation, give a smaller loss during training in this approach while the well-labeled samples, which are consistent among by many listeners, contributes more to training loss.

2.2 Focal Loss

In our research, we extended the utility of the Focal Loss (FL) [12] beyond its typical application in one-hot encoding scenarios. FL was originally designed to address classification tasks and is known for its ability to prioritize challenging samples in training process, thus enhancing model's performance.

Regularly, classification task using one-hot encoding, label in true class is 1 while the others are zero. In this scenario, the standard Focal Loss is defined as:

$$\text{FL}(p) = -\alpha_t \cdot (1 - p_t)^\gamma \cdot \log(p_t) \tag{5}$$

Here, p_t represents the predicted probability of the true class t, α_t serves as the balancing factor to account for class imbalance, and γ is the focusing parameter that controls the rate at which the loss decreases when p_t approaches 1, the label of true class. In case of $\gamma = 0$, FL is equivalent to cross entropy loss.

In our work, we adapted Focal Loss to accommodate blended labels, introducing the modified formulation as follows:

$$\mathrm{FL}(p,q) = -\sum_{i=1}^{C} \alpha_i \cdot (q_i - p_i)^{\gamma} \cdot q_i \cdot \log(p_i) \qquad (6)$$

In Eq. 6, C stands for the number of classes, while p and q respectively represent the predicted probabilities and the ground truth labels. This modification enables us to effectively apply Focal Loss in scenarios involving blended labels and help the model focus on challenging samples.

2.3 Model Architecture

The Fig. 2 illustrates the general architecture we have implemented. Because our research primarily focuses on labeling method, we have adopted the architecture model proposed by [26]. Their work also proved its efficient performance of evaluating speech in overall quality and related criteria, including noisiness, discontinuity, coloration and loudness. In our experiments, we also implement these criteria but the Fig. 2 just shows one setting for simple in visualization.

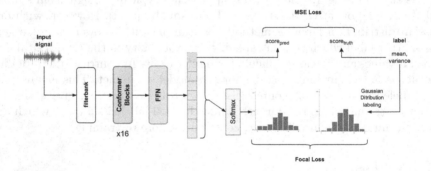

Fig. 2. General of model architecture.

An speech sample has input is waveform and label is mean and variance. The speech signal is initially extracted into to filterbanks feature, which serves as the input for the model. The core component of model consists of Conformer blocks. [5] has developed Conformer as an state-of-the-art model for ASR task and verified the efficiency of its encoder block of representing speech information. Output of the model is a $C + 1$ dimension vertex.

In regression task, the first value is considered as predicted score. We use Mean Square Error (MSE) with mean as truth value to train this task.

In classification task, C other values of output are put into softmax layer to get predicted probability of each class. True probability is provided by Guassian distribution labeling method. We train this classification task with Focal loss.

With the combination approach, the training loss is summary of regression loss and classification loss.

3 Experiments

3.1 Setup

The architecture model is configured with specific details: it consists of 16 Conformer layers with an embedding size of 320, 4 attention heads, convolution kernel size of 15, and follows other settings consistent with the medium Conformer architecture proposed by [5]. In total, the architecture encompasses approximately 43.5 million parameters.

The input features fed into the model are 120-channel filterbanks, derived from a window size of 25 ms and a frame shift of 10 ms. These Mel-spectrograms are further normalized using cepstral mean subtraction, as described by [3].

In the training phase, the models are trained for 200 epochs with a learning rate set at 0.001 and a batch size of 16. Additionally, Focal Loss is employed with a gamma value of 2.

In the context of Gaussian distribution labeling, we configure the number of classes as 9, which results in a class range of 0.5 for each class and centroid set is $\{1, 1.5, 2, ..., 4.5, 5\}$. In contrast, Gaussian-smoothed labels uses 40 classes as provided in the public source code of [16].

3.2 Datasets

We training model with two datasets, include in NISQA_TRAIN_SIM and NISQA_TRAIN_LIVE. Two validation datasets are NISQA_VAL_LIVE and NISQA_VAL_SIM. Three datasets are used for testing are NISQA_TEST_FOR, NISQA_TEST_P501, and NISQA_TEST_LIVETALK. All these datasets are obtained from the NISQA corpus [17].

The summary of them are shown in Table 1.

Table 1. The summary of used datasets

Datasets	Lang	No. Con	No. Files	Votes/File	Hours
NISQA_TRAIN_SIM	en	10,000	10,000	5	24.7
NISQA_VAL_SIM	en	2,500	2,500	5	6.0
NISQA_TRAIN_LIVE	en	1,020	1,020	5	2.6
NISQA_VAL_LIVE	en	200	200	5	0.5
NISQA_TEST_FOR	en	60	240	30	0.6
NISQA_TEST_LIVETALK	de	58	232	24	0.6
NISQA_TEST_P501	en	60	240	28	0.5

NISQA_TRAIN_SIM and NISQA_VAL_LIVE contain a large variety of different simulated distortions. The speech samples are get from sources: The Librivox audiobook clips of the DNS-Challenge dataset [22], TSP speech database [10], Crowdsourced high-quality UK and Ireland English Dialect speech dataset [2] and AusTalk [1].

In NISQA_TRAIN_LIVE and NISQA_VAL_LIVE, live calls were conducted through telephone and Skype. The clean speech files were taken from the Librivox audiobook clips of the DNS-Challenge dataset [22] and played back via a loudspeaker.

NISQA_TEST_LIVETALK, talkers used smartphones and laptops in diverse conditions and environments, including cafes, cars, areas with poor reception, elevators, shopping centers, and more. Most used mobile phones for calls through the mobile network or VoIP services like Skype or Facebook.

NISQA_TEST_FOR contains simulated distortions with different codecs, background noises, packet-loss, clipping and live conditions with WhatsApp, and Zoom. The source speech samples are taken from the "Forensic Voice Comparison Databases - Australian English: 500+ speakers" dataset [18,19].

NISQA_TEST_P501 also includes simulated distortions similar to those in NISQA_TEST_FOR and live conditions with Skype, Zoom, WhatsApp, and mobile network recordings. The source speech samples are taken from Annex C of the "ITU-T P.501" dataset [21].

3.3   Scenario

We conducted several experimental scenarios to assess the performance of our proposed labeling method. All models shared the same architecture but differed in their labeling methods and objective functions:

- Firstly, we trained a model using Mean Square Error loss to directly predict MOS, following the traditional approach [26]. This is the second baseline and denoted by $reg(MSE)$.
- Secondly , we trained a classification model using the labeling method, called Gaussian-smoothed labels (GSL), proposed by [16] with Focal loss as the first baseline. We denote it is $clf(GSL + FL)$.
- Thirdly, we implemented two variants which integrated our Gaussian distribution labeling (GDL) method with Focal loss or Cross Entropy loss. They are respectively denoted as $clf(GDL + FL)$ and $clf(GDL + CE)$.
- Finally, we combined the traditional regression task using MSE and classification task using our labeling method (GDL) and Focal loss in the training process. It is represented by $clf(GDL + FL) + reg(MSE)$.

We employed two criteria, Pearson's Correlation Coefficient (PCC) and Root Mean Squared Error (RMSE), to assess the models' performance. Higher PCC is better while lower RMSE is better.

3.4   Results and Discussion

Firstly, in Table 2, the average PCC and RMSE of overall quality per condition, as predicted by different models in each dataset, are presented.

The results clearly demonstrate that Gaussian distribution labeling, in conjunction with Cross Entropy loss or Focal loss, consistently outperforms GSL and are competitive with regression approach across all datasets. Moreover, GDL with CE or FL exhibit high PCC values and low RMSE values, with each being the best in one dataset. Remarkably, the combination of regression and classification task produces the best results in three out of the five datasets.

Table 2. Per-condition average on validation and test datasets of the Overall quality in terms of PCC and RMSE.

Model		VAL_LIVE	VAL_SIM	TEST_FOR	TEST_LIVETALK	TEST_P501
clf(GSL+FL)	PCC ↑	0.711	0.818	0.788	0.680	0.835
	RMSE ↓	0.496	0.636	0.510	0.598	0.538
reg(MSE)	PCC ↑	0.723	0.830	0.825	0.718	0.840
	RMSE ↓	0.487	0.617	0.467	0.567	0.531
clf(GDL+CE)	PCC ↑	0.745	**0.840**	0.797	0.663	0.841
	RMSE ↓	0.470	**0.599**	0.499	0.610	0.530
clf(GDL+FL)	PCC ↑	0.722	0.832	**0.857**	0.665	**0.852**
	RMSE ↓	0.488	0.613	0.427	0.609	**0.512**
clf(GDL+FL) + reg(MSE)	PCC ↑	**0.774**	0.829	**0.857**	**0.780**	0.832
	RMSE ↓	**0.446**	0.619	**0.426**	**0.510**	0.544

In addition to these findings, we also evaluated these models on various other criteria related to speech quality, encompassing noisiness (Table 3), discontinuity (Table 4), coloration (Table 5), and loudness (Table 6).

Table 3. Per-condition average on validation and test datasets of the Noisiness in terms of PCC and RMSE.

Model		VAL_LIVE	VAL_SIM	TEST_FOR	TEST_LIVETALK	TEST_P501
clf(GSL+FL)	PCC ↑	0.616	0.826	0.805	0.786	0.845
	RMSE ↓	0.571	0.535	0.416	0.446	0.500
reg(MSE)	PCC ↑	0.620	**0.838**	0.780	0.734	0.850
	RMSE ↓	0.569	**0.518**	0.439	0.490	0.493
clf(GDL+CE)	PCC ↑	**0.631**	0.833	0.806	0.723	0.853
	RMSE ↓	**0.562**	0.526	0.415	0.498	0.489
clf(GDL+FL)	PCC ↑	0.586	0.829	0.793	0.760	**0.872**
	RMSE ↓	0.587	0.531	0.428	0.469	**0.459**
clf(GDL+FL) + reg(MSE)	PCC ↑	0.621	0.835	**0.835**	**0.805**	0.863
	RMSE ↓	0.568	0.522	**0.386**	**0.428**	0.473

The proposed method consistently outperforms both the traditional regression approach and Gaussian-smooth-labels method. Specifically, across four criteria, two baseline methods achieved the best results three times in two validation datasets and only two times in three test datasets. This discrepancy can be attributed to the fact that the validation datasets only received five votes per file, while the test datasets are more confident and labeled better with more than 20 votes. This suggests that Gaussian distribution labeling better in predicting the quality of well-labeled samples, aligning with the assumption discussed in Sect. 2.1.

Table 4. Per-condition average on validation and test datasets of the Discontinuity in terms of PCC and RMSE.

Model		VAL_LIVE	VAL_SIM	TEST_FOR	TEST_LIVETALK	TEST_P501
clf(GSL+FL)	PCC ↑	0.352	0.692	0.805	**0.625**	0.762
	RMSE ↓	0.628	0.720	0.557	**0.557**	0.577
reg(MSE)	PCC ↑	0.449	**0.732**	0.893	0.560	0.825
	RMSE ↓	0.599	**0.679**	0.422	0.592	0.504
clf(GDL+CE)	PCC ↑	**0.485**	0.726	0.865	0.499	0.803
	RMSE ↓	**0.586**	0.685	0.472	0.619	0.531
clf(GDL+FL)	PCC ↑	0.435	0.715	**0.896**	0.544	**0.829**
	RMSE ↓	0.604	0.696	**0.417**	0.599	**0.499**
clf(GDL+FL) + reg(MSE)	PCC ↑	0.460	0.712	0.894	0.614	0.748
	RMSE ↓	0.596	0.700	0.421	0.564	0.592

Table 5. Per-condition average on validation and test datasets of the Coloration in terms of PCC and RMSE.

Model		VAL_LIVE	VAL_SIM	TEST_FOR	TEST_LIVETALK	TEST_P501
clf(GSL+FL)	PCC ↑	0.466	0.752	0.847	0.655	0.761
	RMSE ↓	0.458	0.615	0.378	0.482	0.492
reg(MSE)	PCC ↑	0.397	0.772	0.886	0.666	0.741
	RMSE ↓	0.475	0.594	0.329	0.476	0.509
clf(GDL+CE)	PCC ↑	0.455	0.772	0.850	0.673	0.742
	RMSE ↓	0.461	0.594	0.374	0.472	0.508
clf(GDL+FL)	PCC ↑	0.470	0.768	0.887	0.636	**0.779**
	RMSE ↓	0.457	0.599	0.329	0.492	**0.475**
clf(GDL+FL) + reg(MSE)	PCC ↑	**0.490**	**0.779**	**0.899**	**0.684**	0.763
	RMSE ↓	**0.451**	**0.586**	**0.312**	**0.466**	0.490

Table 6. Per-condition average on validation and test datasets of the Loudness in terms of PCC and RMSE.

Model		VAL_LIVE	VAL_SIM	TEST_FOR	TEST_LIVETALK	TEST_P501
clf(GSL+FL)	PCC ↑	0.518	0.712	0.488	0.587	0.654
	RMSE ↓	0.584	0.578	0.644	0.411	0.651
reg(MSE)	PCC ↑	**0.646**	0.721	0.468	0.626	**0.679**
	RMSE ↓	**0.521**	0.570	0.652	0.396	**0.632**
clf(GDL+CE)	PCC ↑	0.644	0.716	**0.507**	0.628	0.612
	RMSE ↓	0.522	0.574	**0.636**	0.395	0.681
clf(GDL+FL)	PCC ↑	0.633	0.713	0.492	0.549	0.661
	RMSE ↓	0.529	0.577	0.642	0.424	0.646
clf(GDL+FL) + reg(MSE)	PCC ↑	0.628	**0.726**	0.477	**0.705**	0.655
	RMSE ↓	0.531	**0.566**	0.648	**0.360**	0.651

4   Conclusions

In this paper, we present a Gaussian distribution labeling for speech quality assessment tasks. By transforming the problem to classification task, GDL leverage mean and the variance of human rating process and make model focus on well-labeled samples. The experiments prove our labeling method improve the result in predicting MOS, compared with traditional approach of regression and previous labeling method. Not only overall quality, GDL achieves outperform them results on various speech quality criteria.

References

1. Burnham, D., et al.: Building an audio-visual corpus of Australian English: large corpus collection with an economical portable and replicable black box. In: Proceedings of Interspeech 2011, pp. 841–844 (2011). https://doi.org/10.21437/Interspeech.2011-309
2. Demirsahin, I., Kjartansson, O., Gutkin, A., Rivera, C.: Open-source multi-speaker corpora of the English accents in the British isles. In: Proceedings of the Twelfth Language Resources and Evaluation Conference, pp. 6532–6541 (2020)
3. Desplanques, B., Thienpondt, J., Demuynck, K.: ECAPA-TDNN: emphasized channel attention, propagation and aggregation in TDNN based speaker verification. In: Proceedings of Interspeech 2020, pp. 3830–3834 (2020). https://doi.org/10.21437/Interspeech.2020-2650
4. Gong, W., Wang, J., Liu, Y., Yang, H.: A no-reference speech quality assessment method based on neural network with densely connected convolutional architecture. In: Proceedings of INTERSPEECH 2023, pp. 536–540 (2023). https://doi.org/10.21437/Interspeech.2023-811
5. Gulati, A., et al.: Conformer: convolution-augmented transformer for speech recognition. In: Proceedings of Interspeech 2020, pp. 5036–5040 (2020). https://doi.org/10.21437/Interspeech.2020-3015
6. ITU-T Recommendation P.830: Subjective performance assessment of telephone-band and wideband digital codecs (1996)
7. ITU-T Recommendation P.862: Perceptual evaluation of speech quality (PESQ): An objective method for end-to-end speech quality assessment of narrow-band telephone networks and speech codecs (2001)
8. ITU-T Recommendation P.863: Perceptual objective listening quality assessment (2011)
9. Jayesh, M.K., Sharma, M., Vonteddu, P., Shaik, M.A.B., Ganapathy, S.: Transformer networks for non-intrusive speech quality prediction. In: Proceedings of Interspeech 2022, pp. 4078–4082 (2022). https://doi.org/10.21437/Interspeech.2022-10020
10. Kabal, P.: Tsp speech database. McGill Univ., Database Version 1, 09–02 (2002)
11. Liang, X., Cumlin, F., Schüldt, C., Chatterjee, S.: DeePMOS: deep posterior mean-opinion-score of speech. In: Proceedings of INTERSPEECH 2023, pp. 526–530 (2023). https://doi.org/10.21437/Interspeech.2023-1436
12. Lin, T.Y., Goyal, P., Girshick, R., He, K., Dollár, P.: Focal loss for dense object detection. In: Proceedings of the IEEE International Conference on Computer Vision, pp. 2980–2988 (2017)
13. Liu, M., Wang, J., Xu, L., Zhang, J., Li, S., Xiang, F.: BIT-MI deep learning-based model to non-intrusive speech quality assessment challenge in online conferencing applications. In: Proceedings of Interspeech 2022, pp. 3288–3292 (2022). https://doi.org/10.21437/Interspeech.2022-10010
14. Loizou, P.C.: Speech quality assessment. In: Lin, W., Tao, D., Kacprzyk, J., Li, Z., Izquierdo, E., Wang, H. (eds.) Multimedia Analysis, Processing and Communications. Studies in Computational Intelligence, vol. 346, pp. 623–654. Springer, Berlin (2011). https://doi.org/10.1007/978-3-642-19551-8_23

15. Manocha, P., et al.: SAQAM: spatial audio quality assessment metric. In: Proceedings of Interspeech 2022, pp. 649–653 (2022). https://doi.org/10.21437/Interspeech.2022-406
16. Manocha, P., Xu, B., Kumar, A.: NORESQA: a framework for speech quality assessment using non-matching references. In: Thirty-Fifth Conference on Neural Information Processing Systems (2021). https://proceedings.neurips.cc/paper/2021/file/bc6d753857fe3dd4275dff707dedf329-Paper.pdf
17. Mittag, G., Naderi, B., Chehadi, A., Möller, S.: NISQA: a deep CNN-self-attention model for multidimensional speech quality prediction with crowdsourced datasets. In: INTERSPEECH, pp. 2127–2131 (2021)
18. Morrison, G.S., Rose, P., Zhang, C.: Protocol for the collection of databases of recordings for forensic-voice-comparison research and practice. Aust. J. Forensic Sci. **44**(2), 155–167 (2012)
19. Morrison, G., et al.: Forensic database of voice recordings of 500+ Australian English speakers (2015)
20. Mumtaz, D., Jena, A., Jakhetiya, V., Nathwani, K., Guntuku, S.C.: Transformer-based quality assessment model for generalized user-generated multimedia audio content. In: Proceedings of Interspeech 2022, pp. 674–678 (2022). https://doi.org/10.21437/Interspeech.2022-10386
21. Rec, I.: P. 501, test signals for use in telephony and other speech-based application. Int. Telecommun. Union (2020)
22. Reddy, C.K., et al.: The INTERSPEECH 2020 deep noise suppression challenge: datasets, subjective testing framework, and challenge results. In: Proceedings of Interspeech 2020, pp. 2492–2496 (2020). https://doi.org/10.21437/Interspeech.2020-3038
23. Shu, X., et al.: Non-intrusive speech quality assessment with a multi-task learning based Subband adaptive attention temporal convolutional neural network. In: Proceedings of Interspeech 2022, pp. 3298–3302 (2022). https://doi.org/10.21437/Interspeech.2022-10315
24. Sun, L., Du, J., Dai, L.R., Lee, C.H.: Multiple-target deep learning for LSTM-RNN based speech enhancement. In: 2017 Hands-free Speech Communications and Microphone Arrays (HSCMA), pp. 136–140. IEEE (2017)
25. Ta, B.T., et al.: Improving Vietnamese accent recognition using ASR transfer learning. In: 2022 25th Conference of the Oriental COCOSDA International Committee for the Co-ordination and Standardisation of Speech Databases and Assessment Techniques (O-COCOSDA), pp. 1–6. IEEE (2022)
26. Ta, B.T., Le, M.T., Le, N.M., Do, V.H.: Probing speech quality information in ASR systems. In: Proceedings of INTERSPEECH 2023, pp. 541–545 (2023). https://doi.org/10.21437/Interspeech.2023-2507
27. Ta, B.T., et al.: Improving speech emotion recognition via fine-tuning ASR with speaker information. In: 2022 Asia-Pacific Signal and Information Processing Association Annual Summit and Conference (APSIPA ASC), pp. 1–6. IEEE (2022)
28. Wältermann, M.: Dimension-Based Quality Modeling of Transmitted Speech. Springer, Cham (2013)
29. Yu, M., Zhang, C., Xu, Y., Zhang, S.X., Yu, D.: MetricNet: towards improved modeling for non-intrusive speech quality assessment. In: Proceedings of Interspeech 2021, pp. 2142–2146 (2021). https://doi.org/10.21437/Interspeech.2021-659

TextFocus: Efficient Multi-scale Detection for Arbitrary Scene Text

Do Quang Manh, Tran Minh Khoi, Duong Minh Hieu, and Phan Duy Hung[✉]

FPT University, Hanoi, Vietnam
{manhdqhe153129,khoitmhe150069,hieudmhe153146}@fpt.edu.vn,
hungpd2@fe.edu.vn

Abstract. In the age of deep learning, the emergence of high-resolution datasets containing small text presents a growing challenge in scene text detection. Scaling down entire images to address this issue often leads to text distortion and performance degradation. In this research, we introduce **TextFocus**, an innovative algorithm that **leverages a multi-scale training strategy with a focus on efficiency**. Instead of analyzing each pixel in an image pyramid, **TextFocus** will attempt to identify context regions surrounding ground-truth instances, or "chips," and then process for finding all text regions in the image sample. All text information from every chip from the model will then be combined with careful post processing methodology to obtain the final results for text detection. As a result of **TextFocus'** ability to resample very large image samples (4000x4000 pixels) into low resolution chips (640x640 pixels), our model can train twice as quickly and handle batches as large as 50 on a single GPU when scaled normally. When the larger the training size, the better the result is basic tactic, our method demonstrates that training on high resolution scale might not be ideal. Our implementation using ResNet-18 backbone with segment-like head achieves **0.828** F1 score on the SCUT-CTW1500 [1] dataset, **0.611** F1 score on the Large CTW [2] dataset with acceptable FPS for realtime purpose.

Keywords: Computer Vision · Scene Text Detection · Multi-scale Detection · High Resolution Image

1 Introduction

Scene text detection represents a pivotal and pervasive computer vision task characterized by its significance in diverse domains. This task finds extensive utility in various spheres of everyday life, encompassing document scanning, translation services, and surveillance operations entailing the extraction of information from credit cards and vehicle license plates. Moreover, its scope extends to text retrieval and text-centric visual question-answering paradigms. However, despite its multifaceted applicability, several challenges persist, impeding seamless practical integration.

The domain of shape text detection has undergone remarkable strides, primarily attributed to integrating deep learning methodologies. These advancements have been highlighted by notable contributions that encompass the adoption of models like the Fully

M. H. Há et al. (Eds.): CSoNet 2023, LNCS 14479, pp. 39–50, 2024.
https://doi.org/10.1007/978-981-97-0669-3_4

Convolutional Network [3]. These models have exhibited substantial efficacy within the confines of this specialized domain. In recent developments, a class of Transformer-based paradigms, exemplified by models such TextBPN [6] and DeepSOLO + + [5], has ascended to prominence, showcasing exceptional performance and achieving state-of-the-art outcomes.

Recent investigates in the field have predominantly revolved around the quest for novel architectural models. Nevertheless, the incremental enhancements in performance metrics achieved through these approaches have become asymptotic. Increasing accuracy by a few percent on public text datasets is not easy.

In this study, the goal is directed toward refining learning and inference strategies simultaneous with the cultivation of expanded datasets to enhance accuracy and frames per second (FPS) metrics. We introduce TextFocus (Fig. 1), a novel text detection algorithm with a dual advantage: it can quickly and accurately find instances of text within images with multiple resolutions. By harnessing the synergies afforded by multiple resolution techniques, our algorithm aims to surmount the deficiencies that often beset current methods, particularly their aptitude to discern diminutive textual elements.

2   Related Works

Arbitrary shape text detection has emerged as a critical research area within scene text detection. The problem of arbitrary-shape text detection is challenging due to the variety of shapes and appearances text can take.

Before deep learning flourished, Connected Component (CC) and Traditional sliding window based had been widely used. **Sliding window-based methods** [6, 7] involve a multi-scale window over an image and classify the current path to detect objects or

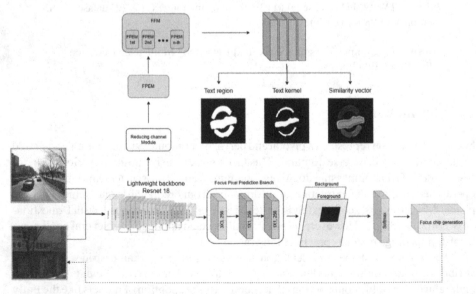

Fig. 1. The overview architecture of TextFocus

features of interest. **CC-based modes** [8, 9] get the character candidates by extracting CCs. And then, these candidates' CCs are classified as text or non-text. Recently, deep learning based methods have become popular. These methods can be divided into different groups: regression-based methods, segmentation-based methods, and contour-based methods.

Regression-based methods [10, 11] always modify box-regression-based object detection frameworks with word-level and line level for text instances. These methods comprise the text proposal generation stage, with candidate text regions generated, and the bounding box refinement stage, in which candidate text region are verified and refined to create the final detection result.

Segmentation-based methods draw inspiration from semantic segmentation to implicitly encode text instances with pixels mask. PSNET [13] employs a progress scale expansion algorithm for multi-scale segmentation map fusion. PAN [14] enhance pixel embeddings for the same text while distinguishing different texts. These methods emphasize segmentation accuracy as a key determinant of boundary detection quality. Their work on a single scale size sample still suffers from high-resolution and small item scenarios, despite their excellent studies on certain datasets. Our approach, combined with a clever multi-scale strategy, improve the model, catch small objects in high-resolution scenarios, and need minimal additional runtime or resource computation.

Contour-**based methods** directly model text boundaries to detect arbitrary shape text. ABCNet [15] and FCENet [16] employ curve modeling (Bezier-Curve and Fourier-Curve) for text instance contours, accommodation progressive approximation of closed shapes. Relative to segmentation-based methods, considerable room remains for performance and speed enhancement exploration.

3   Methodology

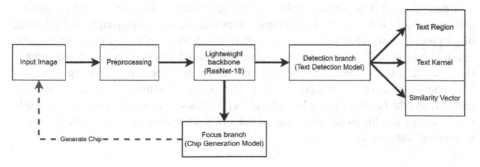

Fig. 2. TextFocus for training process

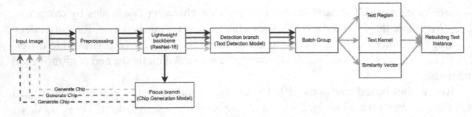

Fig. 3. TextFocus for inference process

We present distinct formulations for the training pipeline (Fig. 2) and the inference pipeline (Fig. 3) due to their slightly dissimilarity.

Illustrated in Fig. 2, the training procedure encompasses the subsequent steps: Before ingestion into the model, input images, exhibiting diverse annotator formats contingent on the dataset, undergo preprocessing to establish uniformity. Post-preprocessing, utilizing a lightweight backbone (ResNet-18 [18]), the model handles the processed inputs. It subsequently channels the outputs through dual branches, yielding outcomes instances, and focus maps intend to generate higher-level chips.

As depicted in Fig. 3, the inference procedure is outlined in some steps. The processing phase in the same as the training phase; inputs traverse a lightweight backbone with each scale iteration, yielding feature and the focus map is used to create chips that will be used in later scales. All features are combined into a batch and sent to the detection branch after chip generation has ended. This branch produces the final prediction for the text instance.

3.1 Detection Branch

Pixel Aggregation Network (PAN) is an optimized approach proposed by Wang et al. [14] for detecting text instances with arbitrary shapes, primarily due to its adept balance between speed and performance. To achieve heightened efficiency, the segmentation network's backbone must be lightweight. Nonetheless, such lightweight architectures often yield features characterized by diminutive receptive fields and limited representation capabilities. To address this challenge, the model was designed with a computationally efficient segmentation head to refine the extracted features. This segmentation head encompasses two pivotal components: The Feature Pyramid Enhancement Module (FPEM) and the Feature Fusion Module (FFM). In this study, we adopt and embrace this methodology to address the intricacies of detecting arbitrary-shaped text within images of varying resolutions.

3.2 Focus Branch

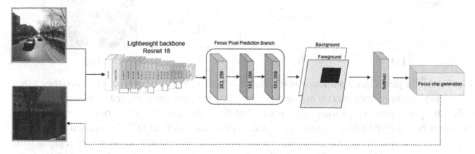

Fig. 4. The architecture of Focus branch

The process aims to predict interesting regions in the image that may contain text information and discard remaining background regions that are unlikely to have text information at the following scale (Fig. 4). The module zooms and crops from interesting regions when applying the detector at successive scales. Focus branch comprises two main parts: the first predicts Focus Pixels through learning; the second is Focus Chips Generation to produces Focus Chips. Since the first component is the only one used in the training phase, all two will be used in the inference phase.

a. *Focus Pixels Finding.*

Focus Pixels are established at the convolutional feature network's granularity from the output of the lightweight backbone. Simple modules process the feature map from the lightweight backbone and produce the focus map, which is then trained to match the interesting ground truth map accordingly. If a feature map pixel overlaps with a small sized text instance, it is referred to as a focus pixel. In the resized chip, which is input to the network, a text instance is deemed small if the root square value of the text area within the image samples falls within a range (between 3 and 50 in our implementation). If a chip contains split text covering 80% of the original text instance, all covered pixels are marked as focus pixels. In the training process, we mark Focus Pixels as positives. During training, Focus Pixels are treated as positives, while pixels with square root area values less than 5 or between 50 and 100 are ignored, and all remaining pixels are considered background, as shown in Fig. 5.

b. *Focus Chips Generation.*

Focus branching is used during inference to produce focus maps P, which are then used to predict which pixels in the foreground t and have some connected components S. With a size dxd filter, we dilate every part before merging it. Then chips were created to contains these connected components. If two chips overlap, the two chips are combined, and the overlapped chips are replaced with the boundary regions surrounding them. Be aware that sometimes, even after dilation, the number of connected components is huge, but each is very small in size. The batch inference is inefficient and takes a long time because so many small chips are produced. Therefore, we eliminate chips whose width or height is below the minimum size k.

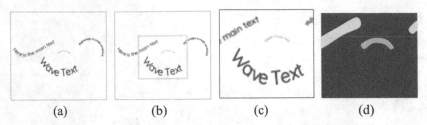

(a)   (b)   (c)   (d)

Fig. 5. All the pixels that a particular text instance covers are regarded as Focus pixels if their sizes fall within a certain range and do not deviate too much from the previous scale. When training, it is best to ignore some cases where the area is slightly higher than the upper bound or lower than the lower bound of the area range as mentioned. (a) Previous scale. (b) Chip proposed for the next scale. (c) Current scale. (d) Ground truth for focus map of the current scale, where regions with green color are positives (1), yellow color is negatives (-1), gray color is background (0)

3.3 Combination for Final Results

As depicted in Fig. 6, the outputs from the model do not inherently offer bounding box information akin to prevalent detection models. Instead, integrating region maps and kernel maps culminates in generating ultimate results. A distinctive strategy is adopted wherein all regions and kernels originating from each scale are unified to generate the final regions and kernels.

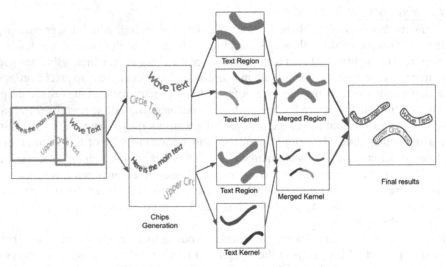

Fig. 6. Combination process for final results

4   Experiments and Results

4.1   Datasets

Table 1. The detail information of datasets.

Datasets	Range of resolution (pixel)	Real/Synthetic	Annotation level	Language in image
Large CTW [2]	320 × 240–5000 × 5000	Real	Word/line	Chinese
Total Text [20]	640 × 480–1920 × 1080	Real	Word/line	English
ICDAR2015 [19]	300 × 300–2400 × 2400	Real	Word/line	Various
SCUT-CTW1500 [1]	640 × 480–1920 × 1080	Real	Word/line	Chinese
Synth Text [22]	320 × 240–1920 × 1080	Synthetic	Word/line	Various

In this context of this study, the evaluation encompasses a comprehensive amount of datasets, where pre-existing annotations of arbitrary shapes characterize the SCUT-CTW1500 [1], ICDAR2015 [19], Total Text [20] and the Large CTW [2] dataset. Further diversifying the testing spectrum, the SynthText dataset [22] is explicitly employed to establish pre-trained models. We use the test datasets above, similar to the previous research and the baseline PAN model. The detail information of datasets as shown in Table 1.

4.2   Experiments

We tested the problem on NVIDIA GeForce GTX 1650 Ti GPU with 4Gb of VRAM. However, for training, we rely on Google Colab's and Kaggle virtual machines equipped with an Intel Xeon CPU and 40Gb of RAM, paired with NVIDIA P100 GPU boasting 40 Gb VRAM.

For evaluating system's performance, the configuration for the TextFocus is described in Table 2.

Table 2. Overall training parameters.

Parameter	Large CTW Dataset	Others Datasets
Input shape	640 × 640	320 × 320
Base lr	0.001	0.001
Batch size	32	32
Num epoch	150	150
Optimizer	Adam	Adam
Lr scheduler	Polynomial lr	Polynomial lr

In our experiments, we employ a combination of evaluation metrics, including Precision (P), Recall (R), and the F1-score, to comprehensively assess the performance of our segmentation model. These metrics are calculated based on the Intersection over Union (IoU) metric.

4.3 Result and Analysis

Table 3. Results on ICDAR2015, Total Text, SCUT-CTW1500. "P", "R", "F1" and "FPS" represent the precision, recall, F-measure and frame per second, respectively.

Method	ICDAR2015 [19]				Total Text [20]				SCUT-CTW1500 [1]			
	P	R	F1	FPS	P	R	F1	FPS	P	R	F1	**FPS**
CTPN [23]	74.2	51.6	60.9	3.55	–	–	–	–	60.4	53.8	56.9	3.57
SegLink [24]	73.1	76.8	75.0	–	30.3	23.8	26.7	–	42.3	40.0	40.8	1.35
EAST [12]	83.6	73.5	78.2	–	50.0	36.2	42.0	–	78.7	49.1	60.4	2.52
RRPN [25]	82.0	73.0	77.0	–	–	–	–	–	–	–	–	–
PSENet [13]	84.5	**86.9**	**85.7**	0.80	78.0	**84.0**	80.9	1.95	79.7	84.8	82.2	0.9
TextSnake [26]	84.9	80.4	82.6	0.55	82.7	74.5	78.4	–	67.9	**85.3**	75.6	–
PAN [14]	84.0	81.9	82.9	12.29	**83.6**	78.5	80.1	10.11	**86.4**	81.2	83.7	13.11
Ours (320)	**86.1**	74.5	79.9	8.51	82.7	74.1	78.1	**11.13**	84.8	80.9	82.8	**14.21**
Ours (640)	84.3	85.1	84.7	1.92	82.6	81.5	**82.1**	2.12	84.4	83.8	**84.9**	2.45

Table 4. Results on Large CTW. "P", "R", "F1" and "FPS" represent the precision, recall, F-measure and frame per second, respectively.

Method	Large CTW			
	P	R	F1	FPS
Ours (320)	54.6	52.3	53.4	5.12
Ours (640)	**62.1**	**60.1**	**61.1**	**1.71**

We evaluate TextFocus on the ICDAR2015, Total-Text, SCUT-CTW1500 and Large CTW. Our proposed model, with an input size of (320,320), obtained competitive results of 84.7 F1 Score on the ICDAR2015, 82.1 on the Total-Text and 84.9 on the SCUT-CTW1500 (Table. 3). Large CTW is a substantial Chinese text dataset in the wild with a very high-resolution image sample, text instances in the dataset are often tiny according to the overall image. With an input size (640,640), TextFocus obtained a 61.1 F1 Score with acceptable real-time FPS in Table 4. Figures 7 and 8 visualize some examples of the results.

Beyond just achieving efficient and balanced metrics results, TextFocus also aids in efficient training. Chips are generated sequentially for each scale to help input image size to the model always be the same to avoid performance impacted by small size input, which helps conserve resources and expedite training.

Fig. 7. Inference pipeline in TextFocus. All results are processed on the Large CTW dataset [2]. Focus Pixels masked as pink, interesting region chips are shown in yellow in the second and fourth rows. Text instances detected in each chip are shown in purple in the first and third rows, final detection results are shown in red in last row. As can be seen, high resolution image samples contain small text instances and some of them can be detected in the higher scale.

5 Conclusion

The study proposed a framework for an effective model pipeline that can streamline the inference process in real-time and reduce training's resource, time, and computing requirements. The model uses a lightweight backbone and a cascaded module strategy to increase processing speed and feature output. The model maintains input at a specific image size and uses a focus branch to identify interesting regions for the next scale. The outputs from each scale are then combined to produce the final text instance detection results. These two modules make TextFocus become an efficient, adaptive and accurate detector. In comparison to earlier state-of-the-art text detectors, experiments on the

SCUT-CTW1500, TotalText, ICDAR2015, and Large CTW show superior advantages in balancing speed, adaptability, and accuracy. The work is also a good reference for image pattern recognition problems [27–30].

Fig. 8. Visualize results on three standard benchmarks. Left: Results on SCUT-CTW1500. Middle: Results on ICDAR2015. Right: Results on TotalText.

References

1. Yuliang, L., Lianwen, J., Shuaitao, Z., Sheng, Z.: Detecting curve text in the wild: new dataset and new solution (2017). arXiv:1712.02170
2. Yuan, T.-L., Zhu, Z., Xu, K., Li, C.-J., Mu, T.-J., Hu, S.-M.: A large Chinese text dataset in the wild. J. Comput. Sci. Technol. **34**, 509–521 (2019)
3. Mukhiddinov, M.: Scene text detection and localization using fully convolutional network. In: Proceedings of the International Conference on Information Science and Communications Technologies (ICISCT), pp. 1–5. IEEE (2019)
4. Zhang, S.-X., Yang, C., Zhu, X., Yin, X.-C.: Arbitrary shape text detection via boundary transformer. IEEE Trans. Multimedia (2023). https://doi.org/10.1109/TMM.2023.3286657
5. Ye, M., Zhang, J., Zhao, S., et al.: Deepsolo: Let transformer decoder with explicit points solo for text spotting. In: Proceedings of the IEEE/CVF Conference on Computer Vision and Pattern Recognition, pp. 348–357 (2023)
6. Tian, S., Pan, Y., Huang, C., Lu, S., Yu, K., Tan, C.L.: Text flow: a unified text detection system in natural scene images. In: Proceedings of the IEEE International Conference on Computer Vision, pp. 4651–4659 (2015)

7. Zhang, Z., Shen, W., Yao, C., Bai, X.: Symmetry-based text line detection in natural scenes. In: Proceedings of the IEEE Conference on Computer Vision and Pattern Recognition, pp. 2558–2567 (2015)

8. Sun, L., Huo, Q., Jia, W., Chen, K.: A robust approach for text detection from natural scene images. Pattern Recogn. **48**(9), 2906–2920 (2015)

9. Yin, X.-C., Yin, X., Huang, K., Hao, H.-W.: Robust text detection in natural scene images. IEEE Trans. Pattern Anal. Mach. Intell. **36**(5), 970–983 (2013)

10. Ma, J., et al.: Arbitrary-oriented scene text detection via rotation proposals. IEEE Trans. Multimedia **20**(11), 3111–3122 (2018)

11. Liao, M., Shi, B., Bai, X.: Textboxes++: a single-shot oriented scene text detector. IEEE Trans. Image Process. **27**(8), 3676–3690 (2018)

12. Zhou, X., et al.: East: an efficient and accurate scene text detector. In: Proceedings of the IEEE conference on Computer Vision and Pattern Recognition, pp. 5551–5560 (2017)

13. Wang, W., et al.: Shape robust text detection with progressive scale expansion network. In: Proceedings of the IEEE/CVF Conference on Computer Vision and Pattern Recognition, pp. 9336–9345 (2019)

14. Wang, W., et al.: Efficient and accurate arbitrary-shaped text detection with pixel aggregation network. In: Proceedings of the IEEE/CVF International Conference on Computer Vision, pp. 8440–8449 (2019)

15. Liu, Y., Chen, H., Shen, C., He, T., Jin, L., Wang, L.: ABCNet: real-time scene text spotting with adaptive Bezier-curve network. In: Proceedings of the IEEE/CVF Conference on Computer Vision and Pattern Recognition, pp. 9809–9818 (2020)

16. Zhu, Y., Chen, J., Liang, L., Kuang, Z., Jin, L., Zhang, W.: Fourier contour embedding for arbitrary-shaped text detection. In: Proceedings of the IEEE/CVF Conference on Computer Vision and Pattern Recognition, pp. 3123–3131 (2021)

17. Dai, P., Zhang, S., Zhang, H., Cao, X.: Progressive contour regression for arbitrary-shape scene text detection. In: Proceedings of the IEEE/CVF Conference on Computer Vision and Pattern Recognition, pp. 7393–7402 (2021)

18. He, K., Zhang, X., Ren, S., Sun, J.: Deep residual learning for image recognition. In: Proceedings of the IEEE Conference on Computer Vision and Pattern Recognition, pp. 770–778 (2016)

19. Karatzas, D., et al.: ICDAR 2015 competition on robust reading. In: Proceedings of 13th International Conference on Document Analysis and Recognition (ICDAR), pp. 1156–1160. IEEE (2015)

20. Ch'ng, C.K., Chan, C.S.: Total-text: a comprehensive dataset for scene text detection and recognition. In: Proceedings of the 14th IAPR International Conference on Document Analysis and Recognition (ICDAR), vol. 1, pp. 935–942. IEEE (2017)

21. Najibi, M., Singh, B., Davis, L.S.: Autofocus: Efficient multi-scale inference. In: Proceedings of the IEEE/CVF International Conference on Computer Vision, pp. 9745–9755 (2019)

22. Gupta, A., Vedaldi, A., Zisserman, A.: Synthetic data for text localisation in natural images. In: Proceedings of the IEEE Conference on Computer Vision and Pattern Recognition, pp. 2315–2324 (2016)

23. Tian, Z., Huang, W., He, T., He, P., Qiao, Y.: Detecting text in natural image with connectionist text proposal network. In: Leibe, B., Matas, J., Sebe, N., Welling, M. (eds.) Computer Vision – ECCV 2016. Lecture Notes in Computer Science(), vol. 9912, pp. 56–72. Springer, Cham (2016). https://doi.org/10.1007/978-3-319-46484-8_4

24. Shi, B., Bai, X., Belongie, S.: Detecting oriented text in natural images by linking segments. In: Proceedings of the IEEE Conference on Computer Vision and Pattern Recognition, pp. 2550–2558 (2017)

25. Nabati, R., Qi, H.: RRPN: radar region proposal network for object detection in autonomous vehicles. In: Proceedings of the IEEE International Conference on Image Processing (ICIP), pp. 3093–3097. IEEE (2019)
26. Long, S., Ruan, J., Zhang, W., He, X., Wu, W., Yao, C.: Textsnake: A flexible representation for detecting text of arbitrary shapes. In: Ferrari, V., Hebert, M., Sminchisescu, C., Weiss, Y. (eds.) Computer Vision – ECCV 2018. Lecture Notes in Computer Science(), vol. 11206, pp. 20–36. Springer, Cham (2018). https://doi.org/10.1007/978-3-030-01216-8_2
27. Hung, P.D., Loan, B.T.: Automatic Vietnamese Passport recognition on android phones. In: Dang, T.K., Küng, J., Takizawa, M., Chung, T.M. (eds.) Future Data and Security Engineering. Big Data, Security and Privacy, Smart City and Industry 4.0 Applications. FDSE 2020. Communications in Computer and Information Science, vol. 1306, pp. 476–485. Springer, Singapore (2020). https://doi.org/10.1007/978-981-33-4370-2_36
28. Duy, L.D., Hung, P.D.: Adaptive graph attention network in person re-identification. Pattern Recogn. Image Anal. **32**, 384–392 (2022)
29. Su, N.T., Hung, P.D., Vinh, B.T., Diep, V.T.: Rice leaf disease classification using deep learning and target for mobile devices. In: Al-Emran, M., Al-Sharafi, M.A., Al-Kabi, M.N., Shaalan, K. (eds.) Proceedings of International Conference on Emerging Technologies and Intelligent Systems. ICETIS 2021. Lecture Notes in Networks and Systems, vol. 299. Springer, Cham (2022). https://doi.org/10.1007/978-3-030-82616-1_13
30. Hung, L.Q., Tuan, T.D., Hieu, N.T., Hung, P.D.: Cervical spine fracture detection via computed tomography scan. In: Nguyen, N.T., et al. (eds.) Recent Challenges in Intelligent Information and Database Systems. ACIIDS 2023. Communications in Computer and Information Science, vol. 1863. Springer, Cham (2023). https://doi.org/10.1007/978-3-031-42430-4_38

Fake Face Recognition on Images Generated by Various Deepfakes Tools

Anh Bao Nguyen Le, Hien Thanh Thi Nguyen, Anh Kim Su,
and Hai Thanh Nguyen[✉]

Can Tho University, Can Tho, Vietnam
anhb1910611@student.ctu.edu.vn, {ntthien,sukimanh,nthai.cit}@ctu.edu.vn

Abstract. In the era of rapid technological advancement, the emergence of Deepfake technology has transformed our interaction with digital content. Deepfakes are sophisticated synthetic media created using deep learning techniques that alter or replace visual and audio elements in images, videos, and audio recordings. While Deepfakes offer potential benefits in entertainment and training, they also raise ethical, social, and security concerns. Many people have been victims of deepfake tools that are widely available online. Such tools can cheat image recognition algorithms. Therefore, an assessment of the dangers of these tools is necessary so that researchers can focus on novel strategies for anti-deepfake. This study evaluates the ability of four famous deepfake tools, namely Deepfakes, Face2Face, Face Swap, and Neural Textures, to cheat deep learning architectures in fake/real face recognition in images. Experimental results show that the Neural Textures tool is the most sophisticated in creating fake faces, which is the most challenging for the considered fake image detection algorithms. In addition, we propose an architecture that can obtain better performance in fake/real face detection with fewer parameters.

Keywords: Deepfake detection · Convolutional Neural Network · deepfakes tools

1 Introduction

Deepfake technology has revolutionized how we perceive and interact with digital content in the era of rapid technological advancement. Deepfakes [1], a portmanteau of "deep learning" and "fake", refer to highly sophisticated synthetic media that convincingly alter or replace existing visual or audio elements in images, videos, and audio recordings. Deepfake technology offers a range of positive applications [2,3]. In the realm of entertainment, it enables filmmakers to seamlessly resurrect historical figures or rejuvenate aging actors, granting unprecedented creative freedom. Deepfakes offer remarkable potential in various fields, including entertainment and creative expression; however, their widespread use raises significant ethical, social, and security concerns. Despite its potential benefits, Deepfake technology poses substantial risks. Malicious actors can exploit

M. H. Hà et al. (Eds.): CSoNet 2023, LNCS 14479, pp. 51–62, 2024.
https://doi.org/10.1007/978-981-97-0669-3_5

Deepfakes for identity theft, defamation, and political manipulation. Deepfake-generated content can propagate misinformation and disinformation, eroding trust in visual media. Furthermore, the line between reality and fabrication becomes increasingly blurred, challenging our ability to discern genuine information from sophisticated fakes.

Deepfakes leverage deep learning algorithms, particularly Generative Adversarial Networks (GANs) [4], to create hyper-realistic simulations. GANs consist of two neural networks—the generator and the discriminator—that engage in a continual adversarial process. The generator generates synthetic content while the discriminator evaluates its authenticity. Through iterative refinement, the generator produces content that progressively becomes more indistinguishable from genuine media. Deepfake technology can manipulate facial expressions, voice, gestures, and even entire contexts, culminating in compelling simulations.

Detecting deepfakes presents an intricate challenge due to their remarkable fidelity and ever-evolving sophistication. Researchers strive to develop robust methods to identify manipulated media. These approaches include analyzing inconsistencies in facial features, unnatural blinking patterns, and subtle artifacts left by the deepfake generation process. Detection models are trained on large datasets of both real and synthesized media, utilizing machine learning algorithms to learn distinctive features that set deepfakes apart. These models are designed to adapt as deepfake techniques evolve continuously, ensuring effective recognition continuously. Creating reliable models for deepfake recognition demands a multifaceted approach. Researchers explore both traditional computer vision techniques and advanced machine learning algorithms. One approach involves examining the correlation between eye movements and facial expressions, as deepfake-generated faces may exhibit unnatural blinking patterns. Another strategy is identifying artifacts introduced during synthesis, such as inconsistent lighting or irregular skin textures. End-to-end deepfake detection systems incorporate convolutional neural networks (Proposed s) and more attention mechanisms to analyze intricate visual patterns. These models are trained on comprehensive datasets containing diverse deepfake variations and genuine media. The training process involves fine-tuning and iterative refinement to enhance accuracy and robustness.

While significant progress has been made in deepfake detection, the cat-and-mouse game with malicious actors persists. As detection techniques evolve, so do the tactics employed by creators of deepfakes. Continuous research and collaboration across academia, industry, and regulatory bodies are crucial to staying ahead of these evolving challenges. As deepfake technology advances, society must navigate the delicate balance between its potential benefits and inherent risks. At the same time, researchers and experts work tirelessly to develop robust mechanisms for its detection and regulation. The evolution of deepfake technology underscores the need for ongoing vigilance and 4 to safeguard the integrity of digital media and uphold the trust of global audiences.

The objective of this research is to develop a fake face recognition model with high accuracy, provide and evaluate the calculated indices from the model training. The following are the key contributions:

- Compare the model's accuracy with samples from fake image generation methods and determine which method is the most difficult to detect.
- Some machine learning-based architectures were leveraged during the implementation, and the findings were to the appropriate architecture, including MobileNet.
- Information about datasets, data pre-processing and classification, environment settings, and metrics for comparison calculations
- Results when testing machine learning models in recognizing fake faces in images

The rest of the article is divided into five sections. Section 1 begins with an introduction and explanation of the problem. Section 2 will then present similar works. Section 3 will next demonstrate the implementation process. The outcomes of the experiments are shown in Sect. 4. Finally, Sect. 5 is followed by the conclusion.

2   Related Work

In the realm of cutting-edge technological advancements, a pioneering study unveiled a revolutionary deepfake detection methodology that harnessed the prowess of deep learning [5]. This avant-garde research introduced the utilization of the XGBoost approach as the cornerstone of its investigative framework. Notably, the study embarked on a multifaceted journey by ingeniously extracting facial regions from video frames employing the sophisticated YOLO [6] face detector alongside the potent convolutional neural network and the Inception Res-Net techniques. The synthesis of these methodologies underscored the study's ingenuity and fortified the robustness of its deepfake detection mechanism. To bolster the foundation of knowledge upon which their innovation rested, the researchers delved into datasets, anchoring their model-building and training endeavors upon the renowned CelebDF and FaceForencics++ datasets [5]. These veritable data reservoirs facilitated the cultivation of a deep-learning model that thrived on the input of meticulously extracted facial features. These features, meticulously harvested from the visages within the datasets, seamlessly interfaced with the XGBoost framework, heralding a paradigm shift in the efficacy of deepfake detection [5]. An astonishing feat marked the pinnacle of this pioneering journey. This resounding 90% accuracy score attested to the prowess of the proposed methodology in the face of the intricate challenge of video deepfake detection.

The evolution of deep learning techniques has facilitated automatic deepfake video classification [7]. The synergistic deployment of MobileNet and Xception architectures enabled a remarkable classification accuracy range between 91% and 98% [7]. These results underscore the capacity of deep neural networks to discern minute differentials within synthetic videos, reinforcing the pivotal role of comprehensive datasets like FaceForensics++.

Diving into the physiological realm, a novel approach capitalized on human eye blinking patterns for deepfake recognition [8]. DeepVision, an innovative framework, adeptly deciphered deepfake deception through the analysis of ocular dynamics. A curated dataset of static eye-blinking images culled from video frames led to an impressive 87% accuracy score, showcasing the potential of physiological indicators in deepfake detection. In the domain of image detection, the synthesis of DenseNet and fake feature networks heralded a novel deepfake pattern (DFP) approach [9]. This approach, leveraging VGG16 and convolutional neural network architecture hybridization, achieved a commendable 90% accuracy score*. Furthermore, an exploration into medical deepfake image detection yielded an 80% accuracy score utilizing annotated CT-GAN datasets [10]. Distinctively, this paper presents a novel optimized hybrid model for deepfake detection [10]. Integrating lessons from preceding studies, this model architecture strategically emphasizes complexity reduction and data processing efficiency. Representing an avant-garde approach in cybersecurity, this architecture offers a new horizon in the fight against deepfake deception, substantiating the pivotal role of model architecture in enhancing detection capabilities.

In conclusion, the rapid evolution of deepfake detection methodologies showcases the dynamic nature of scientific inquiry in the face of emerging challenges. From deep learning ensembles to physiological indicators, these methodologies collectively unravel the intricate tapestry of deepfake detection. With each study contributing a unique facet, the pursuit of accuracy and robustness persists, redefining the boundaries of cybersecurity and ensuring the authenticity of digital content in an era dominated by synthetic media.

3   Methods

3.1   Overall Workflow

Fig. 1 shows the implementation of machine learning and counterfeit mold classification. The steps will be displayed in arrow order from the "Start" button to the "End" button. The first step is "Data Collection". This step is the step of collecting data to conduct research. The FaceForensics++ dataset [11] is used in this study because of its effectiveness in previous studies. Then, in the Data Preprocessing step, because the dataset has samples that are videos, we proceed to cut the face image frames on those videos. Details of this step will be mentioned in Sect. 3.4. The output is the images. The corresponding set includes samples that are images. From here, we prepare for the two scenarios this study experiments on. In scenario 1, we study the accuracy when detecting samples from state-of-the-art methods to see which counterfeit method is the most difficult to recognize. In this scenario, the dataset is divided into five corresponding classes, using holdout to divide the train set by 80% and the test set by 20%. The second scenario is to identify the optimality of the proposed model with a different architecture. Here, we will combine 4 data corresponding to the "state-of-the-art method" into one. That dataset will be called Fake, and the set corresponding to the original set will be called Real set. These two sets will proceed. Practice modeling according to the second scenario. The Test model and evaluate metrics step is the next step, where after training, the models will be tested for accuracy, loss, followed by comparison and evaluation.

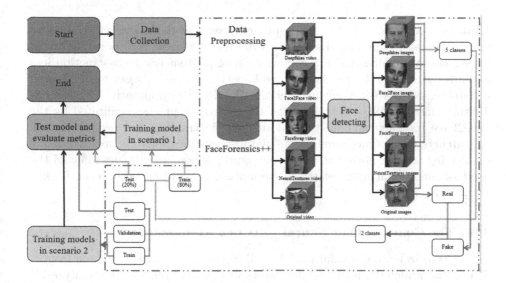

Fig. 1. The overall workflow for fake face recognition

3.2   Tools for Fake Face Generation

Deepfakes: [11] Deepfake is a popular term, but in this study, the word "Deepfake" is used to show the Faceswap tool [12]. However, another tool is the same as the "Faceswap" tool, so to separate, this study uses the word "Deepfake" to present. Deepfake is an open-source application that can convert faces or identify, crop, and align images. This method is based on autoencoders with a shared encoder trained to reconstruct the original face to a target face using an image edit technique called Poisson.

Face2Face [11,13]. Face2Face is a facial reenactment system that transfers the expressions of a source video to a target video while maintaining the identity of the target person. This method is implemented based on input videos and requires manual frame selection. These frames are used to create faces with different lighting and expressions. Researchers of the FaceForensics++ dataset have adapted the Face2Face method to reproduce entirely automatically.

Face Swap [11,14]. Face Swap is a method used to convert faces from source video to target video. This method uses "landmarks" points on the face to extract that face area, and then, based on these points, a 3D modeling method uses the blend shapes technique to project back. On the target image, it minimizes the difference between the original image's landmarks points and the target image's "landmarks" points. In the end, an edited product will be created.

Neural Textures. [11,15] This approach leverages the source video data to train a neural texture model specific to the target person, incorporating a rendering network trained using a combination of photometric reconstruction loss and adversarial loss. Researchers of the FaceForensics++ dataset have adopted a patch-based GAN-loss inspired by the Pix2Pix [16] approach. The Neural-Textures method relies on tracked facial geometry, a process facilitated by the Face2Face tracking module, utilized during the training and testing phases. Researchers of the FaceForensics++ dataset modifications are focused solely on altering facial expressions within the mouth region, allowing us to avoid the need for conditional input related to eye movement, as observed in scenarios like Deep Video Portraits.

3.3   The Convolutional Neural Network Architecture

We propose to use a Convolutional Neural Network that was conducted from [1]. The network includes many hidden layers designed to process and analyze 2D images by convolving them with filters to produce desired outputs, as shown in Fig. 2 with details. The network receives the input of $299 \times 299 \times 3$. The network uses Batch Normalization to normalize the output values from the previous layer, ensuring stable mean and variance distributions in the data. Conv2D (16 filters, kernel size: 3×3, activation: ReLU, padding: same): The first convolutional layer with 16 filters of size 3×3 and ReLU activation. "Padding: same" ensures the output size matches the input size. MaxPooling2D (pool size: 2×2): A pooling layer with a 2×2 window size, reducing the spatial dimensions of the data. Dropout (dropout rate: 0.1): A dropout layer randomly deactivates some neurons during training to prevent overfitting. Conv2D and subsequent Max-Pooling2D, Batch Normalization, and Dropout layers: These layers have similar purposes but with different numbers of filters and sizes. Their goal is to extract features from the image and reduce data size. GlobalAveragePooling2D: This layer performs global average pooling over the entire feature map output from the previous layer, reducing the output to a vector before entering the fully connected layers. Dense (48 neurons, activation: ReLU): A fully connected layer with 48 neurons and ReLU activation. It is used to learn complex relationships between the extracted features. Dropout (dropout rate: 0.5): Another dropout layer is used after this fully connected layer to reduce overfitting. Dense: The final fully connected layer with two neurons (for Scenario 2), five neurons (for

---

[1] https://www.kaggle.com/code/pratikshakya/custom-model-dense48.

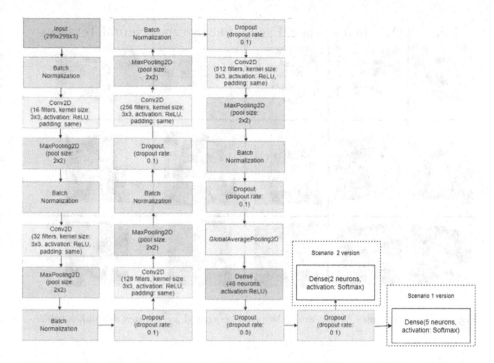

Fig. 2. The proposed architecture.

Scenario 1) and softmax activation is typically used for classification tasks. Compared with the proposed network, we leverage MobileNet, a compact architecture that usually performs highly in image classification.

3.4   Dataset

Datas Description. FaceForensics++ [11] is a dataset of facial forgeries that enables researchers to train deep-learning-based approaches in a supervised fashion. The dataset contains manipulations created with four methods, namely, Face2Face, FaceSwap, DeepFakes, and NeuralTextures, as some examples shown in Fig. 3.

Data Pre-processing. In this study, the dataset is divided into five various datasets, in which one dataset contains original videos which are collected on YouTube, and the remaining four ones are made by four state-of-the-art methods, including Face2Face, FaceSwap, DeepFakes, and NeuralTextures. Every dataset has 1000 videos.

Real	Deepfakes	Face2Face	FaceSwap	Neural Textures

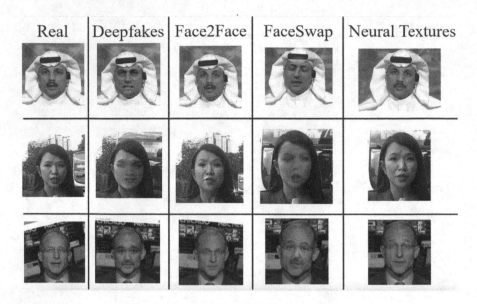

Fig. 3. Some examples of real and fake faces generated by various deepfakes tools.

In the data pre-processing stage, the first step is to cut face photos from videos. A video had many photos corresponding to each frame in the video. Then the best-quality frames are filtered. All photos have the same size 299×299. Next, these photos are put on the sets. Totally, 1600 videos are used, which is shown in Table 1

Table 1. Dataset Pre-processing

Type	Quantity (video)	Detail
Original	800	Video 000–799
Deepfakes	200	Video 000–199
Face2Face	200	Video 200–399
FaceSwap	200	Video 400–599
NeuralTextures	200	Video 600–799

Classification. At this step, the classification task has experimented with two scenarios. The first scenario is to divide the photo datasets like the original datasets. Samples in datasets are managed through the data pre-processing stage before. It was shown in Table 2, in which the train set and test set are divided with the ratio 80/20 for all datasets.

The second scenario combines four sets of Deepfakes, Face2Face, FaceSwap, and NeuralTexture, into a single set, namely the Fake set. However, the original

Table 2. The dataset with various types used in scenario 1

Real	Deepfakes	Face2Face	FaceSwap	NeuralTextures
6757	1109	1672	2631	2271

set is like the one in the first scenario, the Real set. It is shown in table 3, in which the train set, validation set, and test set are divided with a ratio of 80/10/10.

Table 3. The dataset used in scenario 2

Real	Fake
6757	7683

4 Experimental Results

4.1 Environmental Settings and Metrics

Environment settings for this study are shown in Table 4. We train the model in 20 epochs with a batch size of 32.

Table 4. Environmental setting

CPU count	4
Logical CPU count	8
CPU Frequency (MHz)	2304.0
Total Ram (GB)	8
Total GPU memory (GB)	4
Python Version	Python 3.11.3
Python Environment	Anaconda

Loss Calculation: The loss function measures the discrepancy between the predicted values and ground truth labels. It quantifies how well the model's predictions align with the true values. The loss value indicates how much error the model is making on the test data.

Accuracy Calculation as shown in Eq. 1: For classification tasks, the accuracy is calculated by comparing the model's predicted class labels with the true class labels from the test dataset. The accuracy is the ratio of correctly predicted samples to the total number of samples in the test dataset. It provides an understanding of how well the model performs regarding correct classification.

$$Accuracy = \frac{\text{Number of Correct Predictions}}{\text{Total Number of Predictions}} \tag{1}$$

4.2 Scenario 1: The Ability to Make Fake Faces by the Considered Tools

Figure 4 shows the ability to make fake faces in every tool. The results show that the proposed model made the highest percentage (99%) in identifying real faces. When detecting fake faces on data generated from 4 deep fake tools, it shows that the DeepFakes tool has the highest identification percentage at about 95.5%, the second one is Face2Face tool at 94%, the third one is FaceSwap(93.9%), the last one is Neural Textures (90.4%).

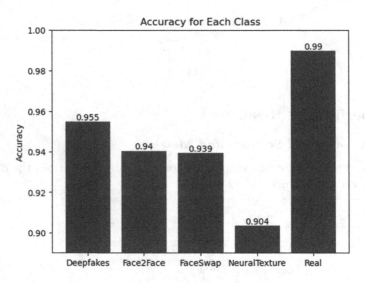

Fig. 4. The recognition accuracy on fake images generated by various tools against the real ones.

4.3 Scenario 2: The Comparison Between the Proposed Architecture and MobiletNet

The testing result of the second scenario is shown in Table 5. The results show that the proposed model is more significant than MobileNet. On the training set, the accuracy percentage of the proposed model is 99.3%, while that of the MobileNet model is 96.5%, The loss value of the proposed model is lower than

Table 5. The classification result

Model	Training Set		Validation Set		Test Set		#Params
	Accuracy	Loss	Accuracy	Loss	Accuracy	Loss	
Proposed model	0.993	0.019	0.992	0.022	0.998	0.0048	1,601,534
MobileNet	0.9648	0.0849	0.9738	0.0707	0.843	0.4168	2,422,210

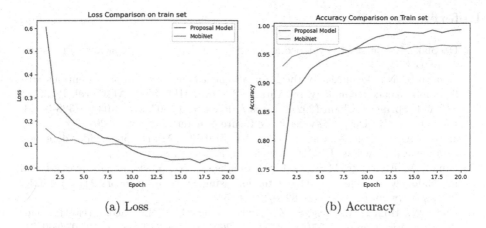

(a) Loss   (b) Accuracy

Fig. 5. The performance during the learning through epochs

that of MobileNet (1.9% and 8.49%, respectively). On the validation set, the accuracy percentage of the proposed model is 99.2%, while that of the MobileNet model is 97.3%, The loss value of the proposed model is lower than that of MobileNet (2.2% and 7.1%, respectively). When tested in the test set, the accuracy of the proposed model is 99.8%, much higher than the MobiNet model of 84.3%, the loss value of Proposed model reaches 0.0048, lower than the MobiNet model which is 0.4168

Training processes of both models are present in Fig. 5a and Fig. 5b. The Proposed model's loss curve (Blue Curve) in Fig. 5a starts high but gradually decreases over epochs; MobiNet's curve (Orange Curve) begins to decrease moderately and steadily but is still not lower than the proposed Model at the last epoch. The accuracy curve of the Proposed Model (Blue Curve) in Fig. 5b starts low but gradually increases over the stages. MobiNet's curve (Orange Curve) starts to increase moderately and steadily but is still not higher than the Model proposed in the last epoch. This shows that the learning ability of the proposed model is better than that of MobileNet.

5   Conclusion

This study evaluates the danger of various deepfake tools in generating fake face images. The results from the above two scenarios show that the most complex facial fake method to detect is using Neural Textures when the testing accuracy is the lowest compared to the other three methods. This method does not swap the entire face of the source video to the target video but only adjusts certain areas. In addition, the proposed architecture can be more effective when used to detect fake faces. By comparison to MobileNet, with more than 50% of parameters, the architecture model's loss index, and accuracy are superior.

Further work can be done to investigate numerous tools for deep comparison. Some deep architectures should also attempt to improve the performance.

References

1. Deepfake. Kaspersky Encyclopedia. https://encyclopedia.kaspersky.com/glossary/deepfake/
2. Caporusso, N.: Deepfakes for the good: a beneficial application of contentious artificial intelligence technology. In: Ahram, T. (ed.) AHFE 2020. AISC, vol. 1213, pp. 235–241. Springer, Cham (2021). https://doi.org/10.1007/978-3-030-51328-3_33
3. Usukhbayar, B.: Deepfake videos: the future of entertainment (2020)
4. Jadhav, A., Patange, A., Patel, J., Patil, H., Mahajan, M.: Deepfake video detection using neural networks. IJSRD - Int. J. Sci. Res. Dev. **8**(1) (2020)
5. Ismail, A., Elpeltagy, M.S., Zaki, M., Eldahshan, K.: A new deep learning-based methodology for video deepfake detection using XGBoost. Sensors **21**(16) (2021). https://www.mdpi.com/1424-8220/21/16/5413
6. Chen, W., Huang, H., Peng, S., Zhou, C., Zhang, C.: YOLO-face: a real-time face detector. Vis. Comput. **37**(4), 805–813 (2021). https://doi.org/10.1007/s00371-020-01831-7
7. Pan, D., Sun, L., Wang, R., Zhang, X., Sinnott, R.O.: Deepfake detection through deep learning. In: 2020 IEEE/ACM International Conference on Big Data Computing, Applications and Technologies (BDCAT), pp. 134–143 (2020)
8. Jung, T., Kim, S., Kim, K.: Deepvision: deepfakes detection using human eye blinking pattern. IEEE Access **8**, 83144–83154 (2020)
9. Hsu, C.C., Zhuang, Y.X., Lee, C.Y.: Deep fake image detection based on pairwise learning. Appl. Sci. **10**(1) (2020). https://www.mdpi.com/2076-3417/10/1/370
10. Solaiyappan, S., Wen, Y.: Machine learning based medical image deepfake detection: a comparative study. Mach. Learn. Appl. **8**, 100298 (2022). https://www.sciencedirect.com/science/article/pii/S2666827022000263
11. Rössler, A., Cozzolino, D., Verdoliva, L., Riess, C., Thies, J., Nießner, M.: Faceforensics++: learning to detect manipulated facial images (2019)
12. Faceswap (deepfakes) github repository https://github.com/deepfakes/faceswap
13. Thies, J., Zollhofer, M., Stamminger, M., Theobalt, C., Niessner, M.: Face2face: real-time face capture and reenactment of RGB videos. In: Proceedings of the IEEE Conference on Computer Vision and Pattern Recognition (CVPR) (2016)
14. Faceswap github repository https://github.com/MarekKowalski/FaceSwap/
15. Thies, J., Zollhöfer, M., Nießner, M.: Deferred neural rendering: image synthesis using neural textures. ACM Trans. Graph. **38**(4) (2019). https://doi.org/10.1145/3306346.3323035
16. Isola, P., Zhu, J.Y., Zhou, T., Efros, A.A.: Image-to-image translation with conditional adversarial networks. In: Proceedings of the IEEE Conference on Computer Vision and Pattern Recognition (CVPR) (2017)

Multi-scale Aggregation Network for Speech Emotion Recognition

An Dang[1]([✉])[iD], Ha My Linh[2][iD], and Duc-Quang Vu[3][iD]

[1] Phenikaa University, Hanoi, Vietnam
an.dangthithuy@phenikaa-uni.edu.vn
[2] VNU University of Science, Hanoi, Vietnam
halinh.hus@gmail.com
[3] Thai Nguyen University of Education, Thai Nguyen, Vietnam
quangvd@tnue.edu.vn

Abstract. Speech emotion recognition (SER) is a challenging task due to its difficulty in finding efficient representations of emotion in speech. Most conventional speech feature extraction methods tend to be highly sensitive to factors that are emotionally irrelevant, such as the speaker, speaking styles, and background noise, rather than capturing the underlying emotional nuances. The most efficiently used feature extraction method for SER is deep convolutional neural networks (CNN), which can extract high-level features from low-level features from speech signals. However, the majority of CNN-based approaches primarily leverage single-scale features extracted from the final network layer, often falling short of adequately encapsulating the diverse spectrum of emotional characteristics inherent in speech. This paper introduces a multi-scale feature aggregation (MSA) network based on a fully convolutional neural network of the feature pyramid network (FPN) family for SER. This network aggregates multi-scale features from different layers of the feature extractor via a top-down pathway and lateral connections. This methodology empowers our proposed network to encompass a more comprehensive and nuanced understanding of emotional information embedded in spoken language. Additionally, in light of the challenges posed by limited data and data imbalances inherent in speech emotion recognition, we adopt data augmentation techniques to generate supplementary training data samples. Our experimental evaluation conducted on the interactive emotional dyadic motion capture (IEMOCAP) dataset demonstrates the efficacy of the proposed model, revealing its capacity to significantly enhance the performance of SER.

Keywords: SER · MSA · data augmentation

1 Introduction

Speech emotion recognition (SER) is the task that uses the speaker's voice to recognize the emotional state of humans such as happiness, sadness, and anger.

© The Author(s), under exclusive license to Springer Nature Singapore Pte Ltd. 2024
M. H. Hà et al. (Eds.): CSoNet 2023, LNCS 14479, pp. 63–73, 2024.
https://doi.org/10.1007/978-981-97-0669-3_6

SER is a critical research field that plays a key role in diverse fields, for example in health care [1,2], vehicle assistance applications [3], and computer games [4].

Speech Emotion Recognition (SER) remains a difficult task, primarily owing to the intricate nature of emotional expressions and the myriad factors influencing speech, including speaker attributes, speaking styles, gender, age, and cultural nuances. The efficacy of SER systems is profoundly contingent upon the extraction and judicious selection of emotionally discriminative features. Moreover, the existing datasets available for SER are often characterized by limited sample sizes and an imbalanced number of samples across different emotional states. Therefore, the proposed system requires an efficient feature extraction framework capable of robustly characterizing emotional information embedded within spoken language and concurrently mitigating the data imbalance issues.

In recent years, the field of SER has witnessed a surge in research endeavors aimed at enhancing efficiency and performance [5–8]. [5] developed a deep CNN architecture to extract discriminative features from spectrograms. In a similar vein, [6] proposed an efficient and lightweight CNN model designed to acquire profound frequency-based features conducive to SER. Meanwhile, [7] designed a system that recognizes emotional states directly from raw speech signals by utilizing a convolutional long short-term memory recurrent neural network. Additionally, [8] proposed to use a CNN to learn emotional features from the spectrogram, and then enhance by the integration of two bidirectional Long Short-Term Memory (LSTM) layers to capture contextual information in spoken utterances. However, all these approaches exploit only single-scale features from the last layer of the CNN feature extractor, which may not be optimal for characterizing emotional information in speech.

For the limited data and data imbalance problems, [9–11]have proposed efficient data augmentation methods aimed at generating additional data samples for sparse emotional classes. Specifically, [9] employed the Vocal Tract Length Perturbation (VTLP) algorithm to oversample the least represented classes of the dataset, namely, happiness and anger. In a similar way, [10,11] introduced the incorporation of noise and musical elements from the MUSAN corpus for data augmentation. Despite improving SER performance, these methods however do necessitate signal-level modifications, thereby incurring increased computational complexity and storage requirements.

In this study, we propose efficient methodologies for the extraction of salient emotional features from speech data. To begin, we introduce a multi-filter convolutional neural network (MFCNN), designed to effectively capture both temporal and spectral characteristics inherent in emotional spectrograms. Additionally, we introduce a Multi-Scale Feature Aggregation (MSA) network architecture for SER that incorporates a feature pyramid network (FPN) [12,23]. Within this architectural framework, we extract high-level semantic feature maps across multiple scales, harnessing the inherent feature hierarchy while minimizing information loss. Furthermore, we propose a spectrogram augmentation technique, which operates at the spectrogram level, enabling the generation of additional data samples. With the aid of data augmentation, we efficacy mitigate the limited data and data imbalance problems in SER. Finally, we elaborate on the design of a specialized loss function that addresses class imbalance issues during the training process, focusing on the learning of difficult samples. The subsequent sections of this report are structured as follows: Sect. 2 provides a comprehensive overview of our proposed methodologies, including the MFCNN network, the MSA network, our novel data augmentation approach, and the specialized loss function. Section 3 is dedicated to the presentation of experimental results and in-depth analysis. Finally, in Sect. 4, we offer concluding remarks and insights drawn from our work.

2   Proposed Methodology

A general overview of our CNN-based approach is described in Fig. 1. Firstly, each speech utterance is standardized to a uniform length of 3 s, with utterances shorter than 3 s being padded with zeros. We then extract 32-dimensional Mel-Frequency Cepstral Coefficients (MFCC) features from each utterance segment, employing a window size of 2048 samples and a hop size of 512 samples. The resulting spectrogram is represented as a 94×32 matrix. Secondly, the MFCC features are fed into the MFCNN to extract three distinct types of representations. Thirdly, these three extracted information representations are fed into the MSA network to learn more efficient fusion representations. Ultimately, the acquired efficient fusion representations are forwarded to a Fully Connected Layer (FCN) for the final emotion prediction.

In this section, we present the architectural components of our proposed model. This encompasses a detailed examination of the Multi-Filter Convolutional Neural Network (MFCNN), the Multi-Scale Feature Aggregation Network (MSA), our data augmentation techniques, and the specialized loss function.

2.1   Multi-filter Convolutional Neural Network (MFCNN)

Traditional CNN approaches-based SER systems are typically employed with small squared filter shapes to learn local correlations in time and frequency dimensions of input spectrograms. In SER, the emotional characteristics of speakers are generally distributed sparsely and spread during a long utterance. Therefore, extracting relevant global information in each time and frequency dimension of emotional spectrograms is so important to designing effective emotional representations for speech segments. In this paper, we develop three distinct convolutional layers, each equipped with specialized filters (referred to as Conv_time, Conv_freq, Conv_inter) to facilitate the creation of three specific representations: time-specific representation, frequency-specific representation, and interaction representation, as shown in Fig. 1. Specifically, the Conv_time represents the convolution in the time-domain. It is designed to learn temporal information from spectrograms, comprising a convolutional layer featuring 10 temporal filters, followed by batch normalization and ReLU activation functions. In contrast, the Conv_freq presents the convolution in the frequency-domain.

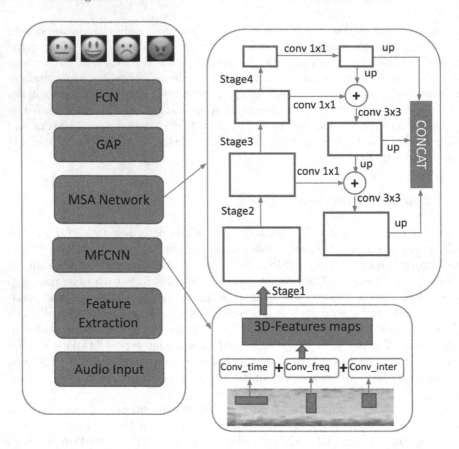

Fig. 1. The proposed MSA network architecture for speech emotion recognition.

It is designed to learn frequency-related features and consists of a convolutional layer with 8 frequency filters, followed by batch normalization and ReLU activation. Conv_inter, meanwhile, employs squared-shaped convolution kernels to concurrently learn both temporal and frequency characteristics. After these processes, we fuse the outputs of these three representations through element-wise addition, yielding 3-D feature maps that are subsequently input into the MSA model.

2.2   Multi-scale Feature Aggregation (MSA) Network

As shown in Fig. 1, our MSA network adopts the architecture of a feature-pyramid CNN model. The model extracts and aggregates emotional information from 3D feature maps across different stages in the hierarchy. The model aims to create multi-scale features that have high-level emotional information at all layers. Particularly, the MSA model consists of two branches: a backbone branch and a top-down aggregation branch.

Backbone Branch. We utilize DenseNet121 pre-trained on ImageNet to extract features. We remove the final fully connected layer and classification layer. More specifically, there are four stages in the DenseNet backbone branch, where each one has a time-frequency resolution of $\frac{1}{2}, \frac{1}{4}, \frac{1}{8}, \frac{1}{16}$ with respect to 3D input features. After we extract features from stage 1 to stage 4, a 1×1 convolution is performed on the output of each stage to generate equal feature channels for integration. Then these features are transmitted to top-down aggregation branches by a lateral connection.

Top-Down Aggregation Branch. The top-down aggregation branch is designed to aggregate the outputs from stage 2 to stage 4. Since the output of each stage has a different time-frequency resolution, we first utilize a bilinear interpolation operation to up-sample the output of the higher stages to match the output resolution of the lower stages. The up-sampled feature maps are then merged with features from the lower stages by element-wise addition. The merged feature maps are fed into a 3×3 convolution layer to reduce the aliasing effect of upsampling. Finally, the output feature maps of stages 2, 3, and 4 are concatenated along the channel axis. After concatenation, output embeddings are generated by global average pooling (GAP) followed by a fully connected layer to predict emotional states.

2.3   Data Augmentation Methods

To increase the size of the training set and mitigate the risk of overfitting, we use Mixup [13] as a data augmentation method. Furthermore, in the IEMO-CAP dataset, the neutral emotion dominates the overall dataset, thus rendering the emotion distribution imbalanced. During the training phase, we have observed instances where emotions like happiness, anger, and sadness are prone to being misclassified as neutral emotions. To rectify this imbalance and diminish the influence of neutral emotions on model recognition results, we implement a strategy consistent with our prior work [24] wherein we randomly pair utterances expressing neutral emotions with those conveying other emotions such as happiness, sadness, excitement, and anger within the batch. Subsequently, we apply the Mixup [13] technique to these paired instances. Specifically, we denote X_N to represent utterances expressing neutral emotions, while X_E to express other emotions as happy, sad, excited, and angry. We construct training examples as follows:

$$X_{ENmix} = \alpha X_{Ei} + (1 - \alpha)X_{Nj},$$
$$Y_{ENmix} = Y_{Ei}, \tag{1}$$

where X_{Ei} is the $i - th$ non-neutral emotion input and X_{Nj} is the $j - th$ neutral emotion input of the data samples, X_{ENmix} represent the mixed data samples by combining a pair of non-neutral emotion sample X_{Ei} and neutral emotion sample X_{Nj}, α is a randomly uniform selection from a range $(0.5, 1)$. Y_{Ei} is the label of X_{Ei} sample. Y_{ENmix} is the label of the X_{ENmix} sample. X_{ENmix} and X_N samples then are fed into the Mixup technique.

2.4   Loss Function

We train the network with the focal loss [14], which was previously used for object detection. The loss function is an extension of Cross Entropy (CE) loss, which solves class imbalance encountered during training and focuses learning on difficult samples. Since the neutral emotion covers a majority of the IEMOCAP dataset and leads to the misclassification of other emotions as happy, or sad. The focal loss diminishes this problem by reducing the contribution of well-classified samples and paying more attention to difficult and misclassified samples. The focal loss (FL) is defined as follows:

$$FL(p_t) = -\alpha(1 - p_t)^\gamma log(p_t), \tag{2}$$

where α is the balance parameter, γ is the focusing parameter, and p_t is the prediction score. Following [52], we set $\alpha = 0.25$ and $\gamma = 2$.

3   Experiments

3.1   Datasets

We conduct experiments on the IEMOCAP dataset [15] to assess the performance of the proposed model. This dataset encompasses a diverse collection of improvised and scripted multimodal dyadic conversations involving ten speakers (comprising 5 males and 5 females). Notably, the dataset spans approximately 12 h of speech data, meticulously annotated with emotion labels by three independent annotators. The entirety of the speech data is organized into five distinct sessions, and the speakers in the sessions are non-overlapping.

We design both speaker-dependent and speaker-independent experiments to evaluate the effectiveness of our proposed method. For the sake of consistency and comparability, we exclusively employ audio data and adopt the baseline experimental setup across all experimental configurations.

Speaker-Dependent Experiment. In this experiment, we conduct two separate experiments. One experiment only uses audio tracks of the improvised set and classifies four categorical emotions: angry (289 utterances), happy (284 utterances), neutral (1099 utterances), and sad (608 utterances). Another experiment uses both improvised and scripted sets and predicts five categorical emotions: angry, happy, excited, neutral, and sad. We combine happy and excited categories as happy categories. The final dataset contains 5,531 utterances in total (1,636 happy, 1,084 sad, 1,103 angry, and 1,708 neutral). The dataset is split randomly at 80:20 for the training set and testing set for two experiments. All the results are reported on five-fold cross-validation.

Speaker-Independent Experiment. In this experiment, we also use both improvised and scripted sets and predict five categorical emotions: angry, happy, excited, neutral, and sad. The estimation performances are compared by leave-one-speaker-out (LOSO) cross-validation; the 8 speakers are used for training, one speaker is used for validation, and another for testing.

In our evaluation, we employ two primary metrics: Weighted Accuracy (WA) and Unweighted Accuracy (UA) to report our experimental findings. WA provides a comprehensive classification accuracy measurement across all test utterances, while UA represents the average recall performance across various emotion categories. Additionally, we conduct two ablation experiments to systematically examine the effect of the top-down aggregation strategy and the data augmentation methods on the enhancement of SER accuracy.

3.2 Experimental Results and Analysis

Performance Comparison. Tables 1, 2, and 3 present a comparative analysis of the results obtained through our proposed method against several prior studies, encompassing both speaker-dependent and speaker-independent scenarios. In Table 1, we compare the results with the evaluation strategy used in [16] which conducts experiments only on the improvised IEMOCAP dataset within the speaker-dependent context. In [16], the authors used multi-head attention (MHA) and applied multi-task learning (MTL) with the auxiliary task of gender recognition to improve SER performance. Remarkably, our proposed model MSA outperforms the state-of-the-art system [16], achieving the best performance metrics with 77.4% in WA and 72.5% in UA. Table 2 extends our comparative analysis to encompass several recent studies that conduct experiments on both improvised and scripted IEMOCAP datasets, focusing on speaker-dependent context. The results emphatically affirm the power of our proposed MSA model overall baseline methods, achieving 69.5% in WA and 70.3% in UA accuracy. Table 3, conversely, delves into the outcomes of the speaker-independent experiment. In this context as well, our proposed model exhibits prominent performance in comparison with other benchmark approaches. Collectively, the meticulous comparisons featured in Tables 1, 2, and 3 demonstrate the efficacy of our proposed model.

Table 1. Accuracy comparison with previous SER results for Speaker-dependent experiment on improvised set.

Approaches	Weighted Accuracy[%]	Unweighted Accuracy[%]
MHA [16]	74.1	64.1
MHA + MTL [16]	76.4	70.1
MSA Network(proposed)	**77.4**	**72.5**

Ablation Study. In this section, we undertake two ablation experiments aimed at investigating the impact of (1) the top-down aggregation strategy and (2) the data augmentation methods in improving SER accuracy. Note that all the experiments are reported on an improvised IEMOCAP dataset for speaker-dependent context.

Table 2. Accuracy comparison with previous SER results for Speaker-dependent experiment on both improvised and scripted sets.

Approaches	Weighted Accuracy[%]	Unweighted Accuracy[%]
ProgNet [17]	-	65.7
Semi-supervised AAE [18]	-	68.8
Audio-BRE [19]	64.6	65.2
TFCNN_attention + BLSTM [20]	65.8	-
Self attention_BLSTM [21]	66.8	67.0
MSA Network(proposed)	**69.5**	**70.3**

Table 3. Accuracy comparison with previous SER results for Speaker-independent experiment on both improvised and scripted sets.

Approaches	Weighted Accuracy[%]	Unweighted Accuracy[%]
Self attention_BLSTM [21]	55.7	57.0
Multi-CRNN [22]	57.5	58.0
CNN-BLSTM [9]	56.41	57.1
MSA Network(proposed)	**60.5**	**61.3**

Top-down branch and without top-down branch: In this ablation experiment, we aim to explore the effect of the top-down aggregation branch on the enhancement of SER accuracy. As reported in Table 4, the MSA network with the top-down branch yields substantially superior results compared to the MSA network lacking this component. Specifically, the MSA network with the top-down branch manifests a noteworthy improvement, contributing to an increase of 4.3% in WA and 3.7% in UA.

Table 4. Result of ablation experiments on the top-down aggregation strategy.

Approaches	Weighted Accuracy[%]	Unweighted Accuracy[%]
MSA without top-down branch	73.1	68.8
MSA with top-down branch	**77.4**	**72.5**

Study on the contribution of the data augmentation methods: This experiment aims to assess the impact of the introduced data augmentation methods, which prove instrumental in enhancing SER performance. Table 5 reported the ablation results on the IEMOCAP dataset using two augmented settings: MSA+Mixup [13] and MSA+ENmix+Mixup [13]. The experimental results show that by combining ENmix and Mixup, the MSA model improves the performance from 70.9% to 72.5% in UA accuracy. Furthermore, we export two confusion matrices to find which emotion class can be improved more when using both ENmix and Mixup. As shown in Fig. 2 (left), after applying ENmix, our model exhibits heightened sensitivity towards the "Happy" emotion, achieving an absolute increment of 13%.

Table 5. Result of ablation experiments on the data augmentation methods.

Approaches	Weighted Accuracy[%]	Unweighted Accuracy[%]
MSA + Mixup	77.9	70.9
MSA + ENmix + Mixup	77.4	**72.5**

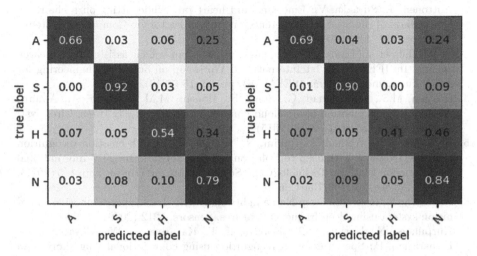

Fig. 2. The confusion matrices of two augmented settings: (left) MSA+ENmix+Mixup and (right) MSA+Mixup for 4 emotions: Angry(A), Sad(S), Happy(H) and Neutral(N).

3.3   Conclusions

In this research paper, we propose a Multi-Scale Feature Aggregation (MSA) network that integrates the principles of pyramid networks for speech emotion recognition. The network strategically fuses high-level features from top layers to bottom layers to improve the SER performance. Furthermore, we propose a data augmentation technique named ENmix that creates new samples by random mixing of neutral utterances with other emotional utterances and then applying the Mixup technique to diversify training data samples. The effectiveness of our proposed system is thoroughly assessed through distinct experimental configurations, and we provide a comparative analysis against recent studies in the field. Additionally, we conduct two ablation studies to empirically ascertain the influence of both the top-down aggregation strategy and the data augmentation methods on improving SER accuracy. Experimental results on the IEMOCAP dataset demonstrate the superiority of our model compared to state-of-the-art networks in SER.

References

1. Huang, Z., Epps, J., Joachim, D.: Speech landmark bigrams for depression detection from naturalistic smartphone speech. In: ICASSP 2019–2019 IEEE International Conference on Acoustics, Speech and Signal Processing (ICASSP), pp. 5856–5860 (2019)
2. Anttonen, J., Surakka, V.: Emotions and heart rate while sitting on a chair. In: Proceedings of the SIGCHI Conference on Human Factors in Computing Systems, ACM, pp. 491–499 (2005)
3. Vogel, H.J., et al.: Emotional awareness for intelligent vehicle assistants: a research agenda. In: IEEE/ACM 1st International Workshop on Software Engineering for AI in Autonomous Systems (SEFAIAS), pp. 11–15 (2018)
4. Hossain, M.S., Muhammad, G., Song, B., Hassan, M.M., Alelaiwi, A., Alamri, A.: Audio-visual emotion-aware cloud gaming framework. IEEE Trans. Circ. Syst. Video Technol. **25**, 2105–2118 (2015)
5. Badshah, A.M., Ahmad, J., Rahim, N., Baik, S.W.: Speech emotion recognition from spectrograms with deep convolutional neural network. In: 2017 International Conference on Platform Technology and Service (PlatCon) (Busan), pp. 1–5 (2017). https://doi.org/10.1109/PlatCon
6. Anvarjon, T., Kwon, S.: Deep-Net: a lightweight CNN-based speech emotion recognition system using deep frequency features. Sensors, 5212 (2020)
7. Kurpukdee, N., Koriyama, T., Kobayashi, T., Kasuriya, S., Wutiwiwatchai, C., Lamsrichan, P.: Speech emotion recognition using convolutional long short-term memory neural network and support vector machines. In: 2017 Asia-Pacific Signal and Information Processing Association Annual Summit and Conference (APSIPA ASC), pp. 1744–1749 (2017)
8. Satt, A., Rozenberg, S., Hoory, R.: Efficient emotion recognition from speech using deep learning on spectrograms. In: Proceedings of the INTERSPEECH, pp. 1089–1093 (2017)
9. Etienne, C., Fidanza, G., Petrovskii, A., Devillers, L., Schmauch, B.: CNN+ LSTM architecture for speech emotion recognition with data augmentation. arXiv preprint arXiv:1802.05630 (2018)
10. Pappagari, R., Wang, T., Villalba, J., Chen, N., Dehak, N.: X-vectors meet emotions: a study on dependencies between emotion and speaker recognition. In: ICASSP 2020–2020 IEEE International Conference on Acoustics, Speech and Signal Processing (ICASSP), pp. 7169–7173 (2020)
11. Lakomkin, E., Zamani, M.A., Weber, C., Magg, S., Wermter, S.: On the robustness of speech emotion recognition for human-robot interaction with deep neural networks. In: 2018 IEEE/RSJ International Conference on Intelligent Robots and Systems (IROS). IEEE, pp. 854–860 (2018)
12. Lin, T.Y., Dollár, P., Girshick, R., He, K., Hariharan, B., Belongie, S.: Feature pyramid networks for object detection. In: 2017 IEEE Conference on Computer Vision and Pattern Recognition (CVPR), Honolulu, HI, USA, pp. 936–944 (2017)
13. Zhang, H., Cisse, M., Dauphin, Y.N., Lopez-Paz, D.: mixup: Beyond empirical risk minimization. arXiv preprint arXiv:1710.09412 (2017)
14. Lin, T.Y., Goyal, P., Girshick, R., He, K., Dollár, P.: Focal loss for dense object detection. In: 2017 IEEE International Conference on Computer Vision (ICCV), pp. 2999–3007 (2017)
15. Howard, A.G., et al.: MobileNets: efficient convolutional neural networks for mobile vision applications. ArXiv abs/1704.04861 (2017)

16. Nediyanchath, A., Paramasivam, P., Yenigalla, P.: Multi-head attention for speech emotion recognition with auxiliary learning of gender recognition. In: ICASSP 2020–2020 IEEE International Conference on Acoustics, Speech and Signal Processing (ICASSP) (2020)
17. Keren, G., Schuller, B.: Convolutional RNN: an enhanced model for extracting features from sequential data. In: Proceedings of the IEEE IJCNN, pp. 3412–3419 (2016)
18. Xie, Y., Liang, R., Liang, Z., Zhao, L.: Attention-based dense LSTM for speech emotion recognition. In: IEICE Trans. Inf. Syst. 1426–1429 (2019)
19. Ma, X., Wu, Z., Jia, J., Xu, M., Meng, H., Cai, L.: INTERSPEECH, pp. 3683–3687 (2018)
20. Chen, M., He, X., Yang, J., Zhang, H.: 3-D convolutional recurrent neural networks with attention model for speech emotion recognition. IEEE Signal Process. Lett. 1440–1444 (2018)
21. Lee, J., Tashev, I.: High-level feature representation using recurrent neural network for speech emotion recognition. In: INTERSPEECH (2015)
22. Peng, Z., Lu, Y., Pan, S., Liu, Y.: Efficient speech emotion recognition using multi-scale CNN and attention. In: ICASSP (2021)
23. Vu, T.H., Dang, A., Wang, J.C.: Learning to remember beauty products. In: Proceedings of the 28th ACM International Conference on Multimedia (2020)
24. Dang, A., Vu, T.H., Wang, J.C.: EMIX: a data augmentation method for speech emotion recognition. In: ICASSP 2023–2023 IEEE International Conference on Acoustics, Speech and Signal Processing (ICASSP). IEEE (2023)

ViEcomRec: A Dataset for Recommendation in Vietnamese E-Commerce

Quang-Linh Tran[1]([✉])[iD], Binh T. Nguyen[2], Gareth J. F. Jones[1][iD], and Cathal Gurrin[1]

[1] ADAPT Centre, School of Computing, Dublin City University, Dublin 9, Ireland
linh.tran3@mail.dcu.ie, {gareth.jones,cathal.gurrin}@dcu.ie
[2] University of Science, Ho Chi Minh City, Vietnam
ngtbinh@hcmus.edu.vn

Abstract. Recent years have seen the increasing popularity of e-commerce platforms which have changed the shopping behaviour of customers. Valuable data from products, customers, and purchases on such e-commerce platforms enable the delivery of personalized shopping experiences, customer targeting, and product recommendations. We introduce a novel Vietnamese dataset specifically designed to examine the recommendation problem in e-commerce platforms, focusing on face cleanser products with 369,099 interactions between users and items. We report a comprehensive baseline experimental exploration into this dataset from content-based filtering to attribute-based filtering approaches. The experimental results demonstrate an enhancement in performance, with a 27.21% improvement in NDCG@10 achieved by incorporating a popularity score and content-based filtering, surpassing attribute-based filtering. To encourage further research and development in e-commerce recommendation systems using this Vietnamese dataset, we have made the dataset publicly available at https://github.com/linh222/face_cleanser_recommendation_dataset.

Keywords: Vietnamese datasets · e-commerce recommendation · content-based filtering

1 Introduction

With the development of the Internet and technological devices, e-commerce platforms have become hugely popular in recent years. The revenue generated through e-commerce continues to increase rapidly, showing significant growth during the COVID-19 pandemic, which imposed limitations on social interactions. Recommendations play a crucial role in this development to enhance customers' shopping experience and increase revenue from selling more products. While there is extensive research exploring methods for achieving reliable and effective recommendations, there are local features associated with the individual languages and markets of specific territories.

M. H. Hà et al. (Eds.): CSoNet 2023, LNCS 14479, pp. 74–82, 2024.
https://doi.org/10.1007/978-981-97-0669-3_7

While there are a number of datasets available recording purchases and user behavior on e-commerce platforms such as Amazon[1] and other international e-commerce platforms [2], the availability of such datasets specific to Vietnamese remains limited for public use. The Vietnamese language poses challenges due to its complicated grammar structure and diverse word forms, making it difficult to analyze and process. Furthermore, the available resources for Vietnamese are limited and primarily focused on sentiment analysis [13,15] and question answering [3]. Consequently, this paper introduces a novel dataset encompassing products, customers, and purchases from a Vietnamese e-commerce platform.

As well as describing this new dataset, we also report initial studies using this dataset. Content-based filtering [8] and attribute-based filtering is applied to run some initial experiments. In addition, the popularity of a product to customers is generally a significant factor influencing customers' purchase decisions. To assess its impact, an experiment is conducted to compare the performance by incorporating a popularity score.

2 Related Work

The recommendation problem has received significant attention from researchers due to its wide application in various domains, including food [14], and particularly e-commerce [10]. In e-commerce, the problem of recommendation has developed over the past few decades, starting with Ben Schafer's analysis [12] of six e-commerce platforms using recommender systems and the creation of a taxonomy of recommender systems in e-commerce.

Over time, more research has been conducted on recommendation systems in e-commerce, resulting in several benchmark datasets, especially in English-based e-commerce. The Amazon product reviews dataset [6] is one such benchmark dataset, consisting of customer reviews and ratings on Amazon from 1996 to 2014. Ahmed et al. [10] employed a context and attribute-aware cross-attention model to address next-item recommendations on four Amazon sub-datasets and achieved superior performance compared to previous systems. Other recommendation systems built upon this dataset, such as SSE-PT [17] proposed by Wu et al., utilized personalized transformers.

While there are numerous datasets recording activities for e-commerce platforms in English, the availability of datasets specific to Vietnamese e-commerce remains limited. Truong et al. [16] developed a recommendation database that incorporated customer preferences, purchase history, and 2,000 Vietnamese comments for employing opinion mining in recommendations. Nguyen et al. [9] examined the impact of online product recommendation systems on customer behavior on Vietnamese e-commerce websites. However, these studies did not introduce a suitable dataset for the recommendation problem in Vietnamese e-commerce.

Content-based filtering [8] is a classic recommendation algorithm. Numerous studies have employed content-based filtering in diverse domains.

---

[1] https://www.amazon.com/.

The e-commerce platforms, with their extensive product content, also present a promising application area for content-based filtering. Ruining et al. [2] highlighted the importance of product attributes, demonstrating that an attribute-aware recommendation system outperforms previous approaches.

3 Dataset

3.1 Dataset Crawling

In this study, data on face cleanser products is crawled from Shopee[2], a large e-commerce platform in Vietnam. Face cleansers attract significant attention from both men and women, resulting in many purchases on Shopee. We use Beautiful Soup[3] and Selenium[4] written in Python to crawl the face cleanser product information first and get the total number of 2244 items. From the information of items, we continue crawling the reviews indicating the interaction between users and items. It is worth noting that Shopee only allows customers to review products only after making a purchase. We recorded 369,099 reviews from 304,708 users collected with several attributes, including reviews, ratings, and date-time information.

3.2 Attribute Extraction

The descriptions of items are long paragraphs describing the content of products and other information. We perform an attribute extraction stage to get the useful attributes from the products. We extract 9 attributes from the description: item name, ingredient, product_feature, skin_type, capacity, design, brand, expiry, and origin. These attributes cover all of the aspects that users may typically want to know when purchasing an item. InstructGPT [7] released by OpenAI is a powerful tool that can automate a wide range of tasks and is used to extract the attribute from the description in this study. We provide some examples of extracted attributes from the descriptions first and give them to InstructGPT, and then ask it to perform the attribute extraction on all 2244 items. An annotator will double-check the extracted attributes from InstructGPT to ensure extraction accuracy and correct any wrong extraction. All the extracted and preprocessed data is published on the same repository.

4 Methodology

4.1 Problem Definition

A **next-item recommendation problem** comprises of a set of users $\mathcal{U} := \{1, 2, ..., U\}$, a set of items $\mathcal{I} := \{1, 2, ..., I\}$, and a sequence of users past interactions $\mathcal{D} := ((u_1, i_1), (u_2, i_2), ..., (u_{N-1}, i_{N-1}), (u_N, i_N) \in (\mathcal{U} \times \mathcal{I}))$ of pairs of a

---

[2] https://shopee.vn/.
[3] https://www.crummy.com/software/BeautifulSoup/bs4/doc/.
[4] https://www.selenium.dev/.

user and items. Given the purchased items i_1 to i_{N-1}, the objective is to predict the next item i_N that user u_N is likely to purchase. The input and output of the recommendation can be formulated as follows:

- **Input**: A set of users $\mathcal{U}$, a set of items $\mathcal{I}$, and the set of past interactions $\mathcal{D}$.
- **Output**: A ranked list of items $\mathcal{L}$ for a user sorted by the probability that the user will purchase.

Content-based filtering is combined with a popularity score, it is referred to as the 'content-based filtering with popularity score' problem. In this case, we have an embedded-description matrix $\mathcal{C} \in \mathbb{R}^{\mathcal{I} \times j}$ containing item description vectors, where j represents the dimension of the embedding matrix. On the other hand, the 'attribute-based filtering' problem involves an attribute matrix $\mathcal{A} \in \mathbb{R}^{\mathcal{I} \times j}$ containing item attribute vectors, with j representing the number of attributes associated with each item.

4.2   Content-Based Filtering with Popularity Score

Content-based filtering [8] (CB) is a conventional recommendation algorithm that leverages information obtained from previously purchased items to provide recommendations to customers. In this research, item descriptions are collected and preprocessed prior to performing content-based filtering. To overcome the challenges associated with processing Vietnamese reviews, this study adopts several preprocessing techniques proposed in [15], as their effectiveness has been demonstrated.

In this study, we employ four pre-trained models to extract embeddings from processed item descriptions. These models include TF-IDF, BLIP [4], PhoBERT [5], and OpenAI Ada2[5]. TF-IDF converts item descriptions into a matrix by assessing a term's importance based on its frequency in a specific description (TF) and rarity across the entire corpus (IDF). PhoBERT is a cutting-edge Vietnamese language model known for its strong performance in various natural language processing (NLP) tasks, including sentiment analysis [15]. BLIP is a multi-modal model capable of understanding both visual and textual information. Since descriptions contain valuable product information, utilizing BLIP can get meaningful embeddings for measuring item similarity. Ada2 is an embedding model developed by OpenAI, known for its advanced NLP applications such as ChatGPT, making it a reliable source for generating rich semantic embeddings. Once the descriptions are embedded, a cosine similarity calculation is performed between the embeddings of candidate items and purchased items to generate a ranked list of candidates.

Item popularity can significantly influence customer decisions, which the study [1] addresses biases from the popularity of products. We investigate the impact of item popularity on the content-based filtering recommendation system, by applying the popular score (number of sold products) to calculate the final

---

[5] https://platform.openai.com/docs/guides/embeddings.

relevance score using the formula 1 with adjustable experimental parameters α and β.

$$Relevance\_score = \alpha * Cosine\_Similarity + \beta * Popularity\_Score \qquad (1)$$

4.3   Attribute-Based Filtering

Attribute-based filtering suggests items by extracting specific attributes from purchased items to identify similar items that share similar attributes. We utilize the extracted attribute in Sect. 3.2 to perform the attribute-based filtering.

Attribute-based filtering is performed using Elasticsearch[6], an open-source search engine. Two approaches of attribute-based filtering are employed: text-based and embedding-based. In the text-based approach, the textual attributes of all items are indexed within Elasticsearch. Subsequently, the attributes of purchased items are fed to Elasticsearch to calculate the BM25 score [11] to perform searches on each attribute. The scores obtained from these searches are then combined through a weighted average, generating a list of similar items and their relevance scores.

Embedding-based attribute filtering is similar to content-based filtering described in Sect. 4.2. The textual attributes undergo an embedding process using the OpenAI Ada2[7] language model, chosen for its superior performance in content-based filtering. To perform recommendations based on purchased items, cosine similarity calculations are carried out between the attribute embeddings of the purchased items and those of all candidate items. The cosine similarities for each attribute are then combined using a weighted average approach, resulting in a ranked list of candidate items.

5   Experiment

5.1   Experimental Settings

We use the leave-one-out protocol for training, validation, and testing the recommendation systems, which has been widely used in previous research [2,10,17]. Each customer's two most recent interactions are withheld for validation and testing purposes, while the remaining previous interactions are utilized for training. Table 1 presents statistics on the three sets: training, validation, and testing.

In this study, the values of α and β in formula 1 are set to 0.7 and 0.3, respectively. These parameters are selected based on the weight-turning experiment. In attribute-based filtering, the weights assigned to different attributes are determined as follows: 0.7 for the item name, 0.5 for the ingredient and product_feature, and 0.5 for the other attributes. These parameter settings are chosen through a grid-search evaluation process.

---

[6] https://www.elastic.co.
[7] https://platform.openai.com/docs/guides/embeddings.

Table 1. Dataset Statistics

Dataset	Users	Items	Interactions
Train	304708	2244	358591
Validation	3592	900	5254
Test	3592	862	5254

Table 2. Content-based filtering versus Content-based filtering with the Popularity score

Model	R@10	MRR@10	NDCG@10
CB-TFIDF	0.1196	0.0586	0.2152
CB-Phobert	0.063	0.0377	0.1278
CB-BLIP	0.0786	0.0397	0.1426
CB-Ada2	0.1209	0.0535	0.2041
CB-TF-IDF+Popularity	0.1411	0.0661	0.2391
CB-Phobert+Popularity	0.0969	0.0415	0.1501
CB-BLIP+Popularity	0.1004	0.0451	0.1673
CB-Ada2+Popularity	**0.1644**	**0.0742**	**0.2721**

To assess the performance of the recommendation system on the new dataset, three metrics are utilized: Recall top K, Normalized Discounted Cumulative Gain (NDCG), and Mean Reciprocal Rank (MRR). The ranked list is truncated at a threshold value of 10, as this is a typical length for rank lists in various recommendation system studies [10].

5.2 Experimental Results

The results of four embedding models (TF-IDF, PhoBERT, BLIP, and Ada2) in the context of content-based filtering on the test set are presented in Table 2. Notably, PhoBERT and BLIP embeddings yield inferior results compared to TF-IDF and Ada2. Despite being trained on a large amount of data, PhoBERT and BLIP may struggle due to the generalization of embeddings and their lack of domain-specific knowledge. By contrast, TF-IDF and Ada2 perform well across the test set, achieving NDCG@10 scores of 21.52% and 20.41% for content-based filtering and 23.91% and 27.21% for content-based filtering with the inclusion of popularity scores, respectively. This demonstrates a significant improvement over PhoBERT and BLIP. Furthermore, adding the popularity score to content-based filtering noticeably enhances performance, leading to an increase of up to 7% in NDCG@10. From the experimental results, it becomes apparent that the dataset poses challenges in accurately recommending the next item, as evidenced by the highest R@10 score of only 16.44% and an NDCG@10 of 27.21%. We can conclude that content-based filtering performs moderately on the dataset for

Table 3. Text-based (TB) vs Embedding-based (EB) Attribute filtering with the Popularity score

Model	Recall@10	MRR@10	NGCD@10
TB + All attributes	0.1305	0.0638	0.2282
TB + All attributes except name	0.1029	0.0549	0.1934
TB + All attributes except product_feature	0.1310	0.0607	0.2245
TB + All attributes except ingredient	0.1376	0.0661	0.2372
TB + All attributes except design & expiry	0.1305	0.0622	0.2249
TB + Item name, ingredient and product_feature	0.1181	0.0574	0.2062
EB + All attributes	**0.1368**	**0.0759**	**0.2595**
EB + All attributes except name	0.1128	0.0534	0.1927
EB + All attributes except product_feature	0.1371	0.0583	0.2209
EB + All attributes except ingredient	0.1432	0.0612	0.2291
EB + All attributes except design & expiry	0.1449	0.0620	0.2297
EB + Item name, ingredient, and product_feature	0.1093	0.0521	0.1811

Table 4. Experimental results of different recommendation systems on the dataset

Model	Recall@10	MRR@10	NDCG@10
Random	0.0045	0.0014	0.0061
Top Popular	0.0812	0.0224	0.089
CB-Ada2	0.1209	0.0535	0.2041
CB-Ada2+ Popularity	**0.1644**	0.0742	**0.2721**
Text-based Attribute Filtering	0.1376	0.0661	0.2372
Embedding-based Attribute Filtering	0.1368	**0.0759**	0.2595

the next-item recommendation, with results varying depending on the chosen embedding model. The results demonstrate that incorporating the popularity score significantly improves the performance of all content-based models.

To compare the performance of text-based and embedding-based attribute filtering, we conducted an experiment and performed an ablation study on the attributes. The results are presented in Table 3. Embedding-based attribute filtering outperforms text-based filtering in all metrics. This can be because embeddings with cosine similarity carry more meaningful information than text-based BM25 similarity. However, the difference between the two approaches is relatively small, with an NDCG@10 improvement of only around 2%. When we selectively remove certain attributes to assess their importance in the overall performance, it becomes evident that the item name is the most important attribute. Removing the item name attribute in text-based and embedding-based attribute filtering results in a decrease in NDCG@10 of 3.48% and 6.68%, respectively.

A comprehensive experiment was conducted on attribute-based filtering using the dataset. The results of all recommendation models are presented in Table 4. The content-based filtering with a popularity score achieves the highest performance with 16.44% Recall@10, 7.42% MRR@10 and 27.21% NDCG@10. The embedding-based attribute filtering achieved the best performance among the attribute-based filtering approaches, with a Recall@10 of 13.68%, MRR@10 of 7.59%, and NDCG@10 of 25.95%. Although the Recall@10 and NDCG@10 scores of attribute-based filtering are not as high as those of content-based filtering, the MRR@10 score of attribute-based filtering is slightly better. Attribute-based filtering is not as effective as content-based filtering. This suggests that the entire description contains more information and has a stronger influence on attracting customers to purchase than extracting specific attributes.

6   Conclusions and Future Work

In this paper, we introduced a novel dataset designed to recommend face cleansers on a Vietnamese e-commerce platform. The dataset comprises 369,099 reviews from 304,708 customers, covering 2,244 unique products. An attribute extraction phase is conducted to extract valuable information from the product descriptions, which enables item recommendation based on attributes.

Baseline experimental results using this dataset indicate that content-based filtering, when combined with the popularity score, achieves the highest performance with an NDCG@10 of 27.21%. Additionally, attribute-based filtering is applied to the new dataset, and a comparative analysis is conducted between text-based and embedding-based attribute filtering approaches.

In the future, we want to continue improving the performance of recommendation systems on the dataset by utilizing additional data and advanced recommendation algorithms.

Acknowledgements. This research was conducted with the financial support of Science Foundation Ireland at ADAPT, the SFI Research Centre for AI-Driven Digital Content Technology at Dublin City University [13/RC/2106_P2]. For the purpose of Open Access, the author has applied a CC BY public copyright license to any Author Accepted Manuscript version arising from this submission.

References

1. Abdollahpouri, H., Burke, R., Mobasher, B.: Managing popularity bias in recommender systems with personalized re-ranking (2019)
2. He, R., McAuley, J.: VBPR: visual Bayesian personalized ranking from implicit feedback. In: Proceedings of the Thirtieth AAAI Conference on Artificial Intelligence, AAAI 2016, pp. 144–150. AAAI Press (2016)
3. Le, K., Nguyen, H., Le Thanh, T., Nguyen, M.: VIMQA: a Vietnamese dataset for advanced reasoning and explainable multi-hop question answering. In: Proceedings of the Thirteenth Language Resources and Evaluation Conference, pp. 6521–6529, Marseille, France (2022). European Language Resources Association

4. Li, J., Li, D., Xiong, C., Hoi, S.: Bootstrapping language-image pre-training for unified vision-language understanding and generation, Blip (2022)

5. Nguyen, D.Q., Nguyen, A.T.: PhoBERT: pre-trained language models for Vietnamese. In: Findings of the Association for Computational Linguistics: EMNLP 2020, pp. 1037–1042 (2020). Association for Computational Linguistics

6. Ni, J., Li, J., McAuley, J.: Justifying recommendations using distantly-labeled reviews and fine-grained aspects. In: Proceedings of the 2019 Conference on Empirical Methods in Natural Language Processing and the 9th International Joint Conference on Natural Language Processing (EMNLP-IJCNLP), pp. 188–197, Hong Kong, China (2019). Association for Computational Linguistics

7. Ouyang, L., et al.: Training language models to follow instructions with human feedback (2022)

8. Pazzani, M.J., Billsus, D.: Content-based recommendation systems. In: Brusilovsky, P., Kobsa, A., Nejdl, W. (eds.) The Adaptive Web. LNCS, vol. 4321, pp. 325–341. Springer, Heidelberg (2007). https://doi.org/10.1007/978-3-540-72079-9_10

9. Nguyen, P., Tho L.D.: The effect of online product recommendation system on consumer behavior: Vietnamese e-commerce websites **10**, 1–24 (2021)

10. Rashed, A., Elsayed, S., Schmidt-Thieme, L.: Context and attribute-aware sequential recommendation via cross-attention. In: Proceedings of the 16th ACM Conference on Recommender Systems, RecSys 2022, pp. 71–80, New York, NY, USA (2022). Association for Computing Machinery

11. Robertson, S., Zaragoza, H.: The probabilistic relevance framework: Bm25 and beyond. Found. Trends Inf. Retriev. **3**, 333–389 (2009)

12. Schafer, J.B., Konstan, J., Riedl, J.: Recommender systems in e-commerce. In: Proceedings of the 1st ACM Conference on Electronic Commerce, EC 2099, pp. 158–166, New York, NY, USA (1999). Association for Computing Machinery

13. Tran, L.Q., Van Duong, B., Nguyen, B.T.: Sentiment classification for beauty-fashion reviews. In: 2022 14th International Conference on Knowledge and Systems Engineering (KSE), pp. 1–6 (2022)

14. Tran, Q.L., Lam, G.H., Le, Q.N., Tran, T.H., Do, T.H.: A comparison of several approaches for image recognition used in food recommendation system. In: 2021 IEEE International Conference on Communication, Networks and Satellite (COMNETSAT), pp. 284–289 (2021)

15. Tran, Q.L., Le, P.T. D., Do, T.H.: Aspect-based sentiment analysis for Vietnamese reviews about beauty product on E-commerce websites. In: Proceedings of the 36th Pacific Asia Conference on Language, Information and Computation, pp. 767–776, Manila, Philippines (2022). De La Salle University

16. Truong, Q.-D., Thi Bui, T.D., Nguyen, H.T.: Product recommendation system using opinion mining on Vietnamese reviews. In: Phuong, N.H., Kreinovich, V. (eds.) Soft Computing: Biomedical and Related Applications. SCI, vol. 981, pp. 313–325. Springer, Cham (2021). https://doi.org/10.1007/978-3-030-76620-7_27

17. Wu, L., Li, S., Hsieh, C.J., Sharpnack, J.: SSE-PT: sequential recommendation via personalized transformer. In: Proceedings of the 14th ACM Conference on Recommender Systems, RecSys 2020, pp. 328–337, New York, NY, USA (2020). Association for Computing Machinery

Untargeted Code Authorship Evasion
with Seq2Seq Transformation

Soohyeon Choi[1]([✉]), Rhongho Jang[2], DaeHun Nyang[3], and David Mohaisen[1]

[1] University of Central Florida, Orlando, USA
soohyeon.choi@ucf.edu
[2] Wayne State University, Detroit, USA
[3] Ewha Womans University, Seoul, South Korea

Abstract. Code authorship attribution is the problem of identifying authors of programming language codes through the stylistic features in their codes, a topic that recently witnessed significant interest with outstanding performance. In this work, we present SCAE, a code authorship obfuscation technique that leverages a Seq2Seq code transformer called STRUCTCODER. SCAE customizes STRUCT-CODER, a system designed initially for function-level code translation from one language to another (*e.g.*, Java to C#), using transfer learning. SCAE improved the efficiency at a slight accuracy degradation compared to existing work. We also reduced the processing time by $\approx 68\%$ while maintaining an 85% transformation success rate and up to 95.77% evasion success rate in the untargeted setting.

Keywords: Code Authorship Identification · Program Stylistic Features · Machine Learning Identification · Software Forensics · Code Authorship Evasion Attack

1 Introduction

Code authorship attribution identifies the author(s) of a source code written in a particular programming language [3, 13]. Several studies have been introduced to address this task, exploiting that code often contains the programmers' stylistic patterns, extracted as distinguishing code features uniquely identifying the code author. Such features may include the style and structure of the code, comments, variable names, and function names and have shown great success in identifying single and multiple authors of the same piece of code [3, 4, 13]. However, code authorship attribution can be abused. For instance, it would be undesirable that the code authorship attribution technique would not withstand a misleading attempt by attributing the same code to multiple authors [17]. An adversary capable of false attribution will overcome the forensics effort and defeat malware origin tracking and cyber threat profiling [6, 7, 18].

To defeat the attribution techniques, Quiring *et al.* [21] proposed misleading authorship attribution with automatic code transformations (we refer to their approach by MAA). They applied various types of transformation to the source code (*e.g.*, changes to control flow, APIs, declarations, etc.) and then used Monte-Carlo Tree Search (MCTS)

M. H. Hà et al. (Eds.): CSoNet 2023, LNCS 14479, pp. 83–92, 2024.
https://doi.org/10.1007/978-981-97-0669-3_8

to choose the optimal transformed code that is syntactically correct, semantically equivalent to the original code, and likely to be misattributed by authorship attribution methods. However, this approach has various limitations. Most noticeably, it has significant memory-compute requirements for finding the optimal solutions among many possibilities. This issue is a fundamental limitation because of the brute-force nature of MCTS in attempting many different options to find the most optimal among them.

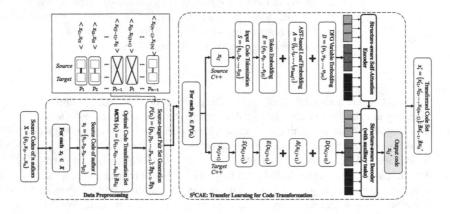

Fig. 1. An illustration of SCAE's pipeline.

Inspired by MAA [21] and to overcome some of its limitations, we propose a code authorship obfuscation with an automated sequence-to-sequence (Seq2Seq) model that avoids searching for the best transformation. Our approach utilizes a Seq2Seq-based code authorship evasion technique called SCAE. We exploited the advantages of Seq2Seq models by customizing STRUCTCODER [25], a recently proposed model with state-of-the-art performance in code translation. STRUCTCODER is designed and trained for code translation tasks, *i.e.,* to translate code written in one programming language to another programming language (*e.g.,* Java to C#), and is not meant to transform a source code to a target code in the same language. Therefore, we extended STRUCTCODER's capabilities to "transform" the code in one language to another code in the same language. In doing so, we build a source-target dataset for code transformation tasks formulated as a transfer learning task [26].

SCAE's evaluation showed that it reduced the processing time by ≈68% (from ≈11,500 min to ≈3,600 min) and achieved 85% of transformation success and 95.77% of evasion rates, significantly reducing resources usage and processing time while achieving competitive transformation and evasion performance.

Contributions. Our contributions are summarized as follows: (1) Our source-target pair dataset is built using codes from the code transformation method with MCTS to train a machine learning-based Seq2Seq model. (2) SCAE, utilizing a pretrained Seq2Seq model called STRUCTCODER, is customized for code transformation, fine-tuned with our source-target pair dataset, and formulated as a transfer learning task for generating transformed codes that are syntactically correct and semantically equivalent to the original code. The produced codes are misclassified by the attribution method at a high rate. (3) SCAE's evaluation, showing it reduced the processing time and resource usage compared to the existing work while maintaining (or improving) the performance.

Organization. The organization of the rest of this paper is as follows. The preliminaries are presented in Sect. 2. Our work's challenges, overview, and technical details are introduced in Sect. 3. Our results and analysis are presented in Sect. 4. Finally, our conclusions are drawn in Sect. 5.

2 Our Approach: Building Blocks

We aim to utilize the Seq2Seq model, STRUCTCODER [25], to transform source code into target code in a way that misclassifies the code author. This requires training STRUCTCODER with source-target code pairs, traditionally obtained through manual transformations, which is challenging (*e.g.,* prone to errors and laborious). To simplify this process, we employ MCTS as an oracle to generate training data, focusing on producing syntactically and semantically correct code variants with distinct programming styles. This allows us to train and fine-tune STRUCTCODER for code transformation instead of just translation. For evaluation, we rely on Abuhamad *et al.*'s work [3] as our primary code authorship attribution method due to its strong performance on large-scale datasets previously used for assessing MCTS. As a result, we will explain the three methods which we employed in this work in more detail in this section.

Code Authorship Attribution. The code authorship attribution problem is defined as the task of identifying the programmer [3] or group of programmers [4] who wrote a piece of code. Programming languages (*e.g.,* C++, Java) often contain various stylistic patterns of programmers [8]—*e.g.,* a programmer may prefer using a for loop instead of a while loop or generating an output in files instead of printing them on the terminal. These patterns can be used as features to identify authors of source codes, and this task is known as code authorship attribution.

Abuhamad *et al.* [3] proposed a system called Deep Learning-based Code Authorship Identification System (DL-CAIS). In the data preprocessing phase of their system, features are extracted from source codes using a Term Frequency - Inverse Document Frequency (TF-IDF) vectorizer. These features are then used to train a deep learning model with three recurrent neural networks (RNNs) and three fully connected layers (FCLs) to capture distinctive code features. To address the challenge of identifying authors in cases with numerous authors, deep representations are employed to build a robust random forest (RF) model for author classification. As a result, DL-CAIS achieved an accuracy of 92.3% with over 8.9K authors and was used to identify authors of four different programming languages, C, C++, Java, and Python.

Misleading Authorship Attribution. Authorship attribution poses a privacy risk by potentially revealing an author's identity, making it a concern for those seeking anonymity. Conversely, it can also be exploited to falsely assign credit or blame for code creation. For instance, attackers might use such techniques to shift focus away from their involvement in code development by attributing a bug or vulnerability to someone else. These diverse possibilities have driven research into misleading authorship attribution.

Quiring *et al.* [21] proposed misleading authorship attribution with automatic code transformations. MAA performed a series of semantics-preserving code transformations to deceive DL-CAIS. Quiring *et al.* [21] considered the code transformation as a game against the code authorship attribution and utilized MCTS to guide the transformation in the feature space to find a short sequence of transformations. With MCTS, the transformer can find a transformed code that is syntactically correct and semantically equivalent to the original code by minimal modification. However, MCTS can be computationally intensive, as it requires simulating many possible moves and evaluating their outcomes. Thus, the authors attempted to decrease computation time by limiting the number of transformations, implementing an early stop technique, etc. Despite their efforts, this method still requires more resources compared to others.

Table 1. Baseline attribution accuracy.

Method	Accuracy
Abuhamad *et al.* [3]	84.98%
Caliskan-Islam *et al.* [13]	90.5%

Seq2Seq Model: STRUCTCODER. Machine learning is widely used to analyze, understand, and generate natural language [9, 10, 14, 16, 19]. However, utilizing machine learning methods for programming languages presents difficulties due to factors such as syntax and organization, terminology, and the surrounding context. Programming languages have strict rules for syntax and structure (*e.g.,* ";" of C families and indentations of Python language), and even small errors can cause a program to fail. The vocabulary of a programming language is typically much smaller than the vocabulary of a natural language. This means that there is less data available for training machine learning models, which can be a challenge. The context in which a piece of code is used can have a significant impact on its meaning. This can make it more difficult to analyze code and understand its purpose. Despite these challenges, researchers have been developing machine learning techniques that can be applied to programs for various tasks [5, 20, 25].

Most recently, Tipirneni *et al.* [25] proposed a transformer-based encoder-decoder model called STRUCTCODER, a structure-aware transformer for text-to-code generation and code translation. They used a structure-aware self-attention framework for their model and pretrained it using a structure-based denoising autoencoding task. As a result, the model is trained to generate a source code based on a given text or translate a source code into a different language (*e.g.,* Java ↔ C#). In addition, STRUCTCODER uses the T5 transformer [22], augmented for modeling code structure, source syntax, and data flow when given a source code and generates a code that is syntactically correct and semantically equivalent to the source code. To apply this structure-aware transformer for code translation, the authors trained their model with 10K samples, tested with 1K samples, and achieved an 88.41 CodeBLEU score in Java $\rightarrow$ C# translations, which is the highest score on a code translation task with CodeXGLUE benchmark [11].

3   SCAE: Putting it Together

We transfer the MCTS task to Seq2Seq learning for fast and efficient code authorship evasion. The proposed SCAE extracts the functional behavior of the MCTS model and then transfers the knowledge to a lightweight Seq2Seq-based programming language processing (PLP) model for code transformation. In the following, we first provide a high-level overview of SCAE's architecture. Then, we explain the technical details for extending a PLP model's capacity from code translation (different languages) to code transformation (the same language).

Challenges and Overview. Figure 1 illustrates the architecture of SCAE. Given a source code, SCAE leverages a transfer learning accelerated PLP model, STRUCT-CODER, to transform (not translate) the code without retaining authors' discriminative features. We note that STRUCTCODER is designed for translating code to a different language. Thus, we extend the model to code transformation within the same language, leveraging a transfer learning technique and parameters fine-tuned. As we can see in the transfer learning stage in Fig. 1, the authorship misleading performance of SCAE is guaranteed by summarizing the functional behavior of MCTS via retrieving source-target code pairs, and then fine-tuning the STRUCTCODER model with the code pairs. As such, SCAE significantly reduces the training and code transformation costs.

Data Preprocessing. To construct source-target pairs, we used the outputs of MAA [21]. Given a set of code samples from n authors, each author's code (x_i) is transformed with MCTS and produces $n - 1$ transformed codes with different stylistic patterns. We note that x_{ii} is a code that is transformed with the author's own stylistic patterns and, thus, is excluded, *i.e.*, $|\mathsf{MCTS}(x_i)| = n - 1$. All transformed codes are functionally equivalent to the original code x_i, but with minimal changes in stylistic patterns to deceive the authorship attribution method. We built a source-target dataset with the transformed code set. The source-target pairs ($\mathsf{P}(x_i)$) of a source code x_i are characterized by the following: $\mathsf{P}(x_i) = \{< x_{i1}, x_{i2} >, < x_{i2}, x_{i3} >, \cdots, < x_{i(n-1)}, x_{in} > \}; \nexists < x_{x(i-1)}, x_{ii} >, \nexists < x_{ii}, xi(i+1) >$, where $< x_{ij}, x_{i(j+1)} >$ denotes two adjacent codes in the transformed set as a pair. We note that two pairs that involve x_{ii} are excluded, and thus $|\mathsf{P}(x_i)| = n - 2$, where n is the number of stylistic patterns.

Transfer Learning with Pretrained Model. We fine-tuned the pre-trained STRUCT-CODER model with our new dataset for transfer learning [26]. This allows us to transfer STRUCTCODER's function from code translation to code transformation, with a relatively small amount of data. The success of the technique has been verified in image recognition tasks, *e.g.*, using visual geometry group (VGG) [15] or residual networks (ResNet) [23] as the foundation to identify a specific object. The pretrained STRUCT-CODER, used in our work, was trained with 10K samples for Java-C# translation [24].

Tokenization and Embedding. After tokenizing a code input sequence, the code tokens are embedded in $\mathbb{R}^d$, among special tokens. The leaf (l) of the code is embedded with the path from the root of the leaf in an abstract syntax tree (AST), and data flow graph (DFG) variables that follow the default embedding will be used for structure-aware self-attention encoding. We note that the tokenization and embedding processes for source and target codes are identical. In SCAE, however, we feed the encoder and decoder pipelines with source and target codes with the same programming language and different stylistic features for "teaching" the decoder the code transformation task.

Fine-Tuning: Encoder and Decoder. Because STRUCTCODER was originally designed to translate Java to C# (or C# to Java) and takes the structural information of a code, such as AST and DFG, the encoder/decoder parsers should be modified to extract the AST information for C++ codes correctly. As such, we customized an open-source *tree-sitter-cpp* parser [1]. Moreover, we modified and added the DFG structure to the C++ code format for both the encoder and decoder. To optimize the performance, we fine-tuned the maximum length of the source input, DFG, and AST, and the maximum depth of AST. Unlike STRUCTCODER, which deals with a small piece of code (*i.e.,* functions), SCAE's training goal is to work with the whole program at once. This requires not only increasing the maximum input and output length of the T5 model to 1024 but also increasing the maximum lengths of the AST and DFG to 1000 to keep pace.

Table 2. A performance comparison: MAA vs. SCAE.

	MAA [21]	SCAE
Number of samples	320	Training: 640 & Testing: 320
Number of outputs	320	320
Processing time	$\approx 11{,}500$ mins	Training: $\approx 3{,}600$ mins & Testing: 58 mins
Transformation success rate	97.5%	85%

4   Evaluation

We evaluate the performance of SCAE on code obfuscation for misleading code authorship attribution and compare it with MAA [21]. In the following, we first explain the experiment setup, dataset, and goals. Then, we compare the processing time and transformation success rate of SCAE with MAA. In addition, we examine the evasion success rates for both Abuhamad *et al.* [3] and Caliskan-Islam *et al.* [13] methods. Finally, we provide a detailed analysis of syntax and semantic errors that we encountered.

4.1   Experimental Setup and Goal

Experiment Setup. We conducted our experiment on a workstation equipped with Nvidia RTX A6000 48GB GPU, Intel Core i7-8700K CPU, and Ubuntu 20.04.5 LTS.

Dataset. We used the same dataset from Quiring *et al.* [21], which consisted of C++ files from the 2017 Google Code Jam (GCJ) programming competition [2]. This dataset contains a total of 204 authors and eight challenges (C++ codes) per author (a total of 1,632). The GCJ competition features multiple rounds with multiple participants solving the same programming challenges, allowing us to train a classifier for attribution that concentrates on stylistic patterns rather than artifacts from different challenges. Moreover, for each challenge, there are test sample inputs that can be used to validate the program semantics and sample outputs.

Untargeted Transformation. The untargeted transformations generate codes predicted as written by any author other than the original author. For evasion, we consider the untargeted transformations due to the structure of SCAE. This transformation is defined as follows: $f\left(\text{STRUCTCODER}(< x_{ij}, x_{i(j+1)} >)\right) = y^*$ where y^* is anyone other than the original author y^s ($y^* \neq y^s$).

4.2 Results and Analysis

To evaluate the performance of our model against MAA [21], we implemented MAA, Abuhamad *et al.* [3], and Caliskan-Islam *et al.* [13]'s methods. To implement those methods, we utilized the same codes that Quiring *et al.* [21], available on their GitHub [12].

Processing Time. We measured the processing time for each method, showing that MAA had a drawback, as it took $\approx$11,500 min (or 8 d) to generate 320 transformed codes in comparison to SCAE's $\approx$ 3,600 min (or 2.5 d) for training and 58 min for testing, resulting in a 68% reduction as shown in Table 2. In addition to reducing processing time, SCAE also has the advantage of not requiring retraining when new features appear. This means that once the model is trained, it can generate 320 transformed codes within only one hour, making it a more efficient and practical solution for misleading code authorship attribution. Moreover, the reduction in processing time not only saves computational resources but also allows for a more efficient and flexible workflow, as it reduces the time required to generate transformed codes and makes it possible to perform misleading code authorship attribution on larger datasets and more complex problems.

Table 3. List of syntax errors.

Error	Count	Percentage
Undeclared variable	10	50%
Re-declared variable	5	12%
Missing ; or }	4	10%
Return statement	3	8%
Others	8	20%
Total	40	

Table 4. List of semantic errors.

Error	Count	Percentage
Misused variable	3	37%
Output statement	4	50%
Input statement	1	13%
Total	8	

Transformation Success Rate. We analyzed the transformation success rate of both methods. In this context, transformation success rate refers to the percentage of transformed codes that are semantically equivalent to the original code and syntactically correct. Our experiment showed that the MAA had a 97.5% transformation success rate for 320 samples, with 2.5% (8) instances of semantic errors. On the other hand, our proposed model performed slightly lower with an 85% (272) transformation success rate as shown in Table 2. We found 12.5% (40) syntax errors and 2.5% (8) semantic errors in the outputs from our method. However, it is important to note that while SCAE's success rate was lower than MAA's, it still achieved high accuracy while using significantly fewer computational resources. Moreover, the SCAE's syntax errors and semantic errors were minor, with the potential to improve SCAE's performance by fine-tuning and using a larger dataset. In summary, SCAE is practical since it achieves comparable results while saving computational resources and maintaining performance stability over different settings.

Syntax Error. Most of the errors we encountered were syntactical errors. However, fortunately, these errors were generally minor and could be easily corrected. The syntax errors we encountered consisted of five types: undeclared variables (10), re-declared variables (5), missing semicolons or curly braces (4), incorrect placement of return statements (3), and other errors (8) as shown in Table 3.

Semantic Error. We encountered a small portion of semantic error compared to the syntax error. This produces different outputs with the original code under the same input and this error consists of two types of error: misused variable (3), and missing input (or out) statement (1, 4) as shown in Table 4. It is important to note that semantic errors are more difficult to detect than syntax errors, as they do not break the code, but they can change the output of the code. In this experiment, we found that semantic errors were much less than syntax errors. However, semantic errors are still important to consider, as they can significantly change the output of the code, even if the code appears to run without any errors.

Table 5. Evasion attack success rate of MAA and SCAE for Abuhamad *et al.* and Caliskan-Islam *et al.* methods under untargeted transformation scenario.

Method	MAA [21]	SCAE
Abuhamad *et al.* [3]	99.1%	95.77%
Caliskan-Islam *et al.* [13]	99.2%	88.74%

Evasion Attack Success Rate. The success rate of evasion attacks is calculated as the percentage of instances where the attribution method assigns an incorrect label to a given code. To evaluate the effectiveness of SCAE and MAA's, we start by presenting the baseline accuracies of Abuhamad *et al.* [3] and Caliskan-Islam *et al.* [13] in Table 1. However, the list of authors that Quiring *et al.* used for their work and the authors who were randomly selected by their program for our experiment are different. Therefore, the accuracy that we got from our experiments is slightly different from the results stated in their paper [21]. SCAE recorded a success rate of 95.77% for Abuhamad *et al.*'s and 88.74% for Caliskan-Islam *et al.*'s methods. Meanwhile, the success rate of the MAA's was 99.1% and 99.2% for Abuhamad *et al.*'s and Caliskan-Islam *et al.*'s, respectively. The evasion attack success rate results are presented in Table 5.

5 Conclusion

In this paper, we presented a practical approach for obscuring code authorship attribution by using a machine learning-based Seq2Seq model, called STRUCTCODER. We chose this method as the current approach to using MCTS, although it is reliable, has limitations in terms of resource management. Thus, we utilized STRUCTCODER to mislead code authorship attribution while reducing resource usage and processing time as well as preserving the performance of the code transformation. As a result, our findings showed that STRUCTCODER which was fine-tuned with our dataset significantly reduced processing time while preserving transformation performance.

References

1. Abuhamad, M., AbuHmed, T., Mohaisen, A., Nyang, D.: Tree-sitter-CPP (2021). https://github.com/tree-sitter/tree-sitter-cpp
2. Abuhamad, M., AbuHmed, T., Mohaisen, A., Nyang, D.: Google Code Jam (2023). https://codingcompetitions.withgoogle.com/codejam/archive
3. Abuhamad, M., AbuHmed, T., Mohaisen, A., Nyang, D.: Large-scale and language-oblivious code authorship identification. In: Proceedings of the ACM SIGSAC Conference on Computer and Communications Security, CCS, pp. 101–114 (2018). https://doi.org/10.1145/3243734.3243738
4. Abuhamad, M., AbuHmed, T., Nyang, D., Mohaisen, D.: Multi-χ: identifying multiple authors from source code files. Proc. Priv. Enhanc. Technol. **2020**(3), 25–41 (2020). https://doi.org/10.2478/popets-2020-0044
5. Ahmad, W.U., Chakraborty, S., Ray, B., Chang, K.: Unified pre-training for program understanding and generation. In: Proceedings of the Conference of Human Language Technologies, NAACL-HLT, pp. 2655–2668 (2021). https://doi.org/10.18653/v1/2021.naacl-main.211
6. Alasmary, H., et al.: Soteria: detecting adversarial examples in control flow graph-based malware classifiers. In: 40th IEEE International Conference on Distributed Computing Systems, ICDCS, pp. 888–898. IEEE (2020)
7. Alasmary, H., et al.: Analyzing and detecting emerging internet of things malware: a graph-based approach. IEEE Internet Things J. **6**(5), 8977–8988 (2019)
8. Allamanis, M., Barr, E.T., Bird, C., Sutton, C.: Learning natural coding conventions. In: ACM SIGSOFT International Symposium on Foundations of Software Engineering, FSE, pp. 281–293 (2014). https://doi.org/10.1145/2635868.2635883
9. Aone, C., Okurowski, M.E., Gorlinsky, J.: Trainable, scalable summarization using robust nlp and machine learning. In: Annual Meeting of the Association for Computational Linguistics, COLING-ACL, pp. 62–66 (1998). https://aclanthology.org/P98-1009/
10. Ayanouz, S., Abdelhakim, B.A., Benahmed, M.: A smart chatbot architecture based NLP and machine learning for health care assistance. In: ACM International Conference on Networking, Information Systems & Security, NISS, pp. 78:1–78:6 (2020). https://doi.org/10.1145/3386723.3387897

11. CodeXGLUE, M.: General Language Understanding Evaluation benchmark for CODE (2023). https://microsoft.github.io/CodeXGLUE/
12. code imitator: Github:code-imitator. https://github.com/EQuiw/code-imitator
13. Islam, A.C., et al.: De-anonymizing programmers via code stylometry. In: USENIX Security Symposium, pp. 255–270 (2015). https://www.usenix.org/conference/usenixsecurity15/technical-sessions/presentation/caliskan-islam
14. Khan, W., Daud, A., Nasir, J.A., Amjad, T.: A survey on the state-of-the-art machine learning models in the context of NLP. Kuwait J. Sci. 43(4) (2016). https://journalskuwait.org/kjs/index.php/KJS/article/view/946
15. Rangarajan, A.K., Purushothaman, R.: Disease classification in eggplant using pre-trained VGG16 and MSVM. Sci. Rep. 10(1), 1–11 (2020). https://www.nature.com/articles/s41598-020-59108-x
16. Le Glaz, A., et al.: Machine learning and natural language processing in mental health: systematic review. JMIR 23(5), e15708 (2021). https://www.ncbi.nlm.nih.gov/pmc/articles/PMC8132982/
17. Li, Z., Chen, Q.G., Chen, C., Zou, Y., Xu, S.: RoPGen: towards robust code authorship attribution via automatic coding style transformation. In: IEEE/ACM International Conference on Software Engineering, ICSE, pp. 1906–1918 (2022). https://doi.org/10.1145/3510003.3510181
18. Mohaisen, A., Alrawi, O., Mohaisen, M.: AMAL: high-fidelity, behavior-based automated malware analysis and classification. Comput. Secur. 52, 251–266 (2015)
19. Oliinyk, V., Vysotska, V., Burov, Y., Mykich, K., Fernandes, V.B.: Propaganda detection in text data based on NLP and machine learning. In: Proceedings of the International Workshop on Modern Machine Learning Technologies and Data Science, MoMLeT+DS (2020). http://ceur-ws.org/Vol-2631/paper10.pdf
20. Phan, L.N., et al.: CoTexT: multi-task learning with code-text transformer. CoRR abs/2105.08645 (2021). https://arxiv.org/abs/2105.08645
21. Quiring, E., Maier, A., Rieck, K.: Misleading authorship attribution of source code using adversarial learning. In: 28th USENIX Security Symposium (USENIX Security 19), pp. 479–496 (2019)
22. Raffel, C., et al.: Exploring the limits of transfer learning with a unified text-to-text transformer. J. Mach. Learn. Res. 21, 140:1–140:67 (2020). http://jmlr.org/papers/v21/20-074.html
23. Rezende, E.R.S.D., Ruppert, G.C.S., Carvalho, T., Ramos, F., de Geus, P.L.: Malicious software classification using transfer learning of ResNet-50 deep neural network. In: International Conference on Machine Learning and Applications, ICMLA, pp. 1011–1014 (2017). https://doi.org/10.1109/ICMLA.2017.00-19
24. StructCoder: Github:structcoder. https://github.com/reddy-lab-code-research/StructCoder
25. Tipirneni, S., Zhu, M., Reddy, C.K.: StructCoder: structure-aware transformer for code generation. CoRR (2022). https://doi.org/10.48550/arXiv.2206.05239
26. Torrey, L., Shavlik, J.: Transfer learning. In: Handbook of Research on Machine Learning Applications and Trend, pp. 242–264 (2010). https://ftp.cs.wisc.edu/machine-learning/shavlik-group/torrey.handbook09.pdf

Mining the Potential Temporal Features Based on Wearable EEG Signals for Driving State Analysis

Ling Wang⬤, Fangjie Song⬤, Tie Hua Zhou(✉)⬤, Chunxu Yang⬤,
and Wanlin Zhang⬤

Department of Computer Science and Technology, School of Computer Science,
Northeast Electric Power University, Jilin, China
{smile2867ling,2202101005,thzhou,2202201003,2202201016}@neepu.edu.cn

Abstract. Fatigue driving is considered to be one of the main factors causing traffic accidents, so fatigue driving detection technology has an important role in road safety. Currently, EEG-based detection is one of the most intuitive and effective means for fatigue driving. We introduce a model known as EFDD (EEG-based Fatigue Driving Detection Model), in our study, by analyzing EEG signals, we extract time-domain and frequency-domain features respectively, explore the potential of different temporal EEG features for fatigue driving detection, Classification using LightGBM machine learning models, and then realize fatigue driving detection. Experiments demonstrate that our extracted features perform well in fatigue driving detection. Meanwhile, our study provides technical support for the feasibility of applying portable detection devices in the future.

Keywords: Fatigue Driving Detection · EEG Signal Processing · Feature Fusion · Temporal Analysis · Machine Learning

1 Introduction

Research has shown that traffic accidents are mostly caused by fatigued drivers, as it significantly affects the driver's ability to operate, which can have serious consequences for both passengers and the driver themselves. When a driver is tired, his reaction speed and judgment are significantly reduced, so it is crucial to accurately detect fatigue driving. Among many research methods, fatigue detection based on EEG signals has become one of the main methods.

Detecting fatigue based on drivers' EEG signals is categorized into the following two groups according to the research methods: one uses machine learning algorithms to study EEG signals, Qin, Xueb et al. first preprocessed the EEG signals and then extracted the relevant features. Next, classification analysis is performed using Support Vector Machines (SVM), which can ultimately determine the driver's fatigue state [1]. Wang, Fei et al. A brain functional network-based method for driving fatigue detection was proposed. Four graphical features

M. H. Hà et al. (Eds.): CSoNet 2023, LNCS 14479, pp. 93–101, 2024.
https://doi.org/10.1007/978-981-97-0669-3_9

were used for fatigue detection using SVM as a classifier [2]. Qin, Yingmei et al. proposed a method for analyzing electroencephalogram (EEG) signals using the directional transfer function, and their results show that there is a significant difference between the awake state and the driving fatigue state [3]. Wang, Jie et al. introduced an improved transformer architecture called GLU-Oneformer, where the combination of NHB EEG configuration and GLU-Oneformer model for one-dimensional feature vector classification, which can effectively support driving fatigue detection [4]. Wang, Li et al. extraction of EEG features using the CSP method. Support Vector Machines (SVMs) are used as classifiers for machine learning algorithms [5]. Zhang, Tao et al. The sample entropy approach quantifies the complexity of EEG signals. High classification accuracy was achieved using SampEn features and a cubic support vector machine classifier (SCS model) [6]. Fang, Zhaoguo et al. converting EEG data from two states into multispectral maps, including awake and fatigued states that maintain topology and input the accompanying percentage of eyelid closure (PERCLOS) labels into a trained deep recursive convolutional neural network inspired by image-based classification [7].

Deep learning algorithms study drivers' EEG signals. Ding, Xiangman et al. proposed a strategy based on deep learning (ResNet3D modeling) detecting fatigue using three channels of EEG data [8]. Xu, Tao et al. proposed a unified framework, E-Key, that utilizes convolutional neural network and attention (CNN-Attention) structures to perform personal identification (PI) and driving fatigue detection simultaneously [9]. Jia, Zhaoguo et al. proposed to transform fatigue and normal state EEG data into a series of multispectral images that maintain topology and input the accompanying percentage of eyelid closure (PERCLOS) labels into a trained deep recursive convolutional neural network inspired by image-based classification. Neural network [10]. Jia, Huijie et al. Features are extracted from EEG using MATCN and processed using GT. Experimentally, this model exhibits excellent performance [11].

In this paper, we introduce a model known as EFDD (EEG-based Fatigue Driving Detection Model), which we use only two-channel EEG signals, and use the model to deeply explore the features of EEG, combined with advanced machine learning frameworks, in order to achieve fast and accurate fatigue driving detection with a small amount of information, and to provide a certain research basis for the development of portable detection devices.

2   EEG-Based Fatigue Driving Detection Model

The EFDD model is consists of two parts, one for feature extraction and the other for model training and optimization, with the goal of extracting features in EEG signals and using a machine learning model to differentiate these features for the purpose of identifying driver fatigue. To detect the fatigue state of the driver, we input the raw electroencephalogram (EEG) signals into our model, which ultimately produces information about the driver's state. The overall framework is illustrated in Fig. 1.

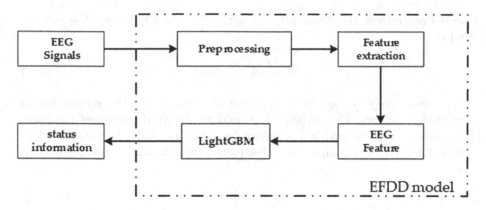

Fig. 1. Framework flowchart

2.1   Feature Extraction

Before feature extraction, pre-processing operation of the EEG is required to remove the high frequency and low frequency noise using a 0.5–40 Hz band pass filter, and to remove the interference from the power line using a 50 Hz filter. Minute-by-minute data cut into 60 segments. In order to fully understand the characteristics of the EEG signal, entropy features and frequency domain features were extracted from our EEG signal analysis, and the features are shown in the Table 1 below:

Table 1. Features extracted from EEG signals.

Features	Interpretations
Fuzzy Entropy	Measuring time series data complexity
Sample Entropy	Measures the probability of similar subsequences in the data
Spectral Entropy	Analyzing the uniformity or disorder of the signal spectrum
approximate Entropy	Measuring the probability of similar patterns in time series data
Delta Wave	The frequency range is between 0.5–4 (Hz)
Theta Wave	The frequency range is between 4–7 (Hz)
Alpha Wave	The frequency range is between 8–13 (Hz)
Beta Wave	The frequency range is between 13–40 (Hz)

Fuzzy entropy and sample entropy are used to measure irregularity nonlinear features in EEG signals. Fuzzy entropy mainly analyzes the randomness of the signal and is calculated using the following formula. The expression $C(X + 1, l)$ represents the count of repeated patterns in the signal with a length of $X + 1$ and a difference less than or equal to l. Similarly, $C(x, l)$ denotes the count of repeated patterns in the signal with a length of x and a difference less than or equal to l.

$$- ln\frac{C(X+1,l)}{C(x,l)} \tag{1}$$

Sample entropy is used to analyze the complexity of EEG signals and is calculated as follows, The variable A is used to signify the count of comparable subsequence pairs having a sequence length of m, while B is employed to represent the count of comparable subsequence pairs with a sequence length of $m+1$.

$$- ln\frac{A}{B} \tag{2}$$

Use spectral entropy to analyze the complexity and the characteristics of information distribution of EEG signals in the frequency domain. $P(f)$ represents the spectral power density of the signal at the frequency f.

$$- (P(f) * ln\,(P(f))) \tag{3}$$

Use approximate entropy to measure the repetitive and regular features in EEG signals. $C(m)$ stands for the count of pattern occurrences with a sequence length of m, while $C(m+1)$ stands for the count of pattern occurrences with a sequence length of $m+1$.

$$- ln\frac{C(m+1)}{C(m)} \tag{4}$$

For the extraction of frequency domain features, the fast Fourier transform (FFT) is applied to convert the EEG signal from the time domain into a frequency domain signal. This transformation enables us to analyze the distribution of the signal across various frequency domains, as depicted in Fig. 2.

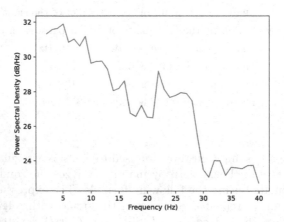

Fig. 2. Power spectral density map

The trapezoidal based numerical integration method is used to calculate the energy in a particular frequency band using the following formula.

$$\frac{b}{2} * [f(a_0) + 2f(a_1) + \ldots + 2f(a_{n-1}) + 2f(a_n)] \tag{5}$$

2.2   Model Training and Optimization

Our EFDD model utilizes the LightGBM machine learning framework, an integrated learning method based on gradient boosting trees, known for its high performance and low memory footprint. Here are some steps of our model training process: We will extract features from the raw data for normalization to make sure they are on the same scale, and the processed feature data will be divided into two main parts: partly for training, partly for testing. We also need to define the LightGBM model which will affect the training and performance of the model, some common LightGBM parameters include: type of tree, number of leaf nodes in the tree, learning rate, etc. Using the training set and the defined LightGBM parameters, we train the model. Iteratively enhance the performance of the model in multiple iterations. After the model training is completed, in order to improve its performance, we need to perform hyper-parameter tuning. This is a critical step, which can be achieved by explicitly defining a range of values for a series of hyperparameters. In order to systematically search for the optimal hyperparameter combinations, we combine the value ranges of these hyperparameters into a parameter dictionary for subsequent grid search algorithms. During the hyperparameter tuning process, we try different parameter combinations and evaluate the performance of each combination. Our goal is to find the best combination of model parameters that can have better generalization ability on new data. This process helps us find the optimal hyperparameter configurations to make our models perform better on new and unseen data.

3   The Experimental Analysis

To validate the effectiveness of our proposed model, a series of experiments were conducted. In our experiments, we used a computer equipped with a Xeon 2620 processor (2.1 GHz) and an NVIDIA GTX 1080 Ti GPU, and used the Anaconda software environment to conduct our experiments. Our experimental dataset is from a publicly available dataset [12], the dataset comprises raw electroencephalogram (EEG) data from 12 healthy participants, including two states: fatigue and wakefulness.

We processed the acquired dataset by first performing a series of preprocessing operations, which included noise reduction to ensure the quality and consistency of the data. Next, we performed a feature extraction step, a process aimed at extracting eight previously defined important features from the raw data. Subsequently, we partitioned the extracted features into two parts: We allocated 80% of the dataset as a training set to train the model, while the remaining 20% served as a test set for assessing the model's performance.

Our experimental results show that by combining our proposed eight features with the EFDD model, we achieve excellent performance in fatigue driving detection. This model achieves a precision of about 93.49% and a recall of about 88.09%, which are metrics that show the model's excellent performance in both accuracy and coverage. The test classification report show in Table 2 and the confusion matrix is shown in Fig. 3, which provides more detailed information about the performance.

Table 2. Test Classification Report.

	Precision	Recall	F1-score
0	0.93	0.88	0.91
1	0.88	0.94	0.91
accuracy			0.91
macro avg	0.91	0.91	0.91
weighted avg	0.91	0.91	0.91

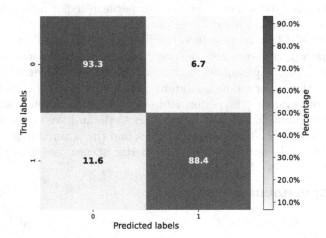

Fig. 3. Confusion matrix.

These experimental results strongly support the validity and superiority of our proposed model and provide a solid experimental foundation for our research work. During our experiments, we also found that each of the eight features we extracted contributes to the predictive performance of the model to varying degrees. Beta and spectral entropy show the largest contributions on both channels (T4 and T3), as shown in Fig. 4.

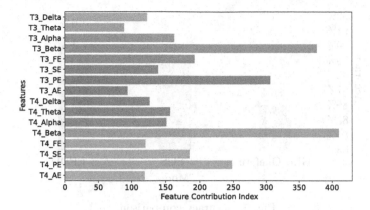

Fig. 4. Feature Contribution Index.

We also conducted comparative experiments with traditional SVM classifiers and LR logistic regression models, and the results show that the LightGBM model we selected exhibits superior performance. The experimental results are illustrated in Fig. 5.

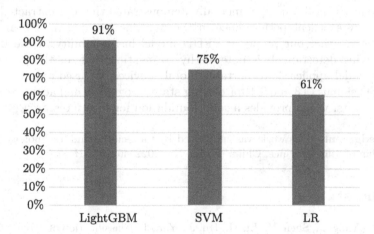

Fig. 5. Feature performance using different classifiers.

Meanwhile, we compared our proposed EFDD model with other models, including the GLU-Oneformer model [5] and the SCS model [6]. These comparative experiments were conducted to assess the performance of each model using the dataset [12]. After the experimental comparison, our EFDD achieves 91% accuracy in the detection of fatigued driving. The comparative experimental results are plotted in Fig. 6.

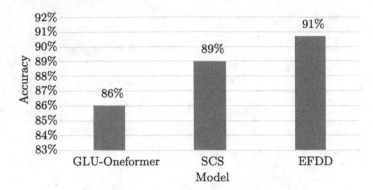

Fig. 6. Accuracy comparison.

4   Conclusion

Research on detecting driver fatigue based on electroencephalogram (EEG) signals has been extensively conducted. However, the use of multiple electrodes for collecting EEG signals in most devices may cause discomfort to drivers, potentially affecting their driving experience. To address this issue, we propose the EFDD model. It has been experimentally demonstrated that our extracted EEG features show excellent performance in the machine learning model, and this result indicates that our proposed EFDD model has reliability in the field of fatigue driving detection. It is noteworthy to mention that for the purpose of make the model applicable to portable mobile devices, we used only two channels of EEG signals (T3 and T4)for driving state recognition and achieved highly accurate results, which provides a solid foundation for future research.

Acknowledgment. This work was supported by the Science and Technology Development Plan of Jilin Province, China (Grant No. 20220402033GH).

References

1. Qin, X., Yang, P., Shen, Y., Li, M., Hu, J., Yun, J.: Classification of driving fatigue based on EEG signals. In: 2020 International Symposium on Computer, Consumer and Control (IS3C 2020), pp. 508–512. IEEE; IEEE Power Electronics Society; Institute of Science and Technology; Intelligent Living Technology Associates, Taiwan (2021)
2. Wang, F., Wu, S., Ping, J., Xu, Z., Chu, H.: EEG driving fatigue detection with PDC-based brain functional network. IEEE Sens. J. **21**(9), 10811–10823 (2021)
3. Qin, Y., et al.: Directed brain network analysis for fatigue driving based on EEG source signals. Entropy **24**(8), 1093 (2022)
4. Chen, C., Ji, Z., Sun, Y., Bezerianos, A., Thakor, N., Wang, H.: Self-attentive channel-connectivity capsule network for EEG-based driving fatigue detection. IEEE Trans. Neural Syst. Rehabil. Eng. **31**, 3152–3162 (2023)

5. Wang, J., et al.: Driving fatigue detection with three non-hair-bearing EEG channels and modified transformer model. Entropy **24**(12), 1715 (2022)

6. Wang, L., Johnson, D., Lin, Y.: Using EEG to detect driving fatigue based on common spatial pattern and support vector machine. Turk. J. Electr. Eng. Comput. Sci. **29**(3), 1429–1444 (2021)

7. Zhang, T., Chen, J., He, E., Wang, H.: Sample-entropy-based method for real driving fatigue detection with multichannel electroencephalogram. Appl. Sci.-Basel **11**(21), 10279 (2021)

8. Ding, X., et al.: Driving fatigue detection with three prefrontal EEG channels and deep learning model. In: 2023 15TH International Conference on Advanced Computational Intelligence (ICACI 2023), Seoul, South Korea (2023)

9. Xu, T., et al.: E-key: an EEG-based biometric authentication and driving fatigue detection system. IEEE Trans. Affect. Comput. **14**(2), 864–877 (2023)

10. Fang, Z., Dongl, E., Tong, J., Sung, Z., Duan, F.: Classification of EEG signals from driving fatigue by image-based deep recurrent neural networks. In: 2022 Proceedings of the 19th IEEE International Conference on Mechatronics and Automation (IEEE ICMA 2022), pp. 1773–1777 (2022). Electrical Network

11. Jia, H., Xiao, Z., Ji, P.: End-to-end fatigue driving EEG signal detection model based on improved temporal-graph convolution network. Comput. Biol. Med. **152**, 106431 (2023)

12. figshare. https://figshare.com

VN-Legal-KG: Vietnam Legal Knowledge Graph for Legal Statute Identification on Land Law Matters

Duc Nguyen[1], Thien Huynh[1(✉)], Thang Phung[1], Thu Bui[1], Phuong Thai[1], Long Huynh[1], Ty Nguyen[1], An Nguyen[1], Huu Pham[1], and Tho Quan[2,3]

[1] ADAI LAB, 2nd Floor, Mitech Center, No. 75 Road 2/4, Nha Trang, Vietnam
hnthien.1190@indivisys.jp
[2] Faculty of Computer Science and Engineering, Ho Chi Minh City University of Technology (HCMUT), Ho Chi Minh City 700000, Vietnam
[3] Vietnam National University, Ho Chi Minh City 700000, Vietnam
https://adai-lab.com

Abstract. *Legal Statute Identification* (LSI) is a critical task within the realm of law, involving the identification of relevant statutory laws based on the natural language descriptions found in legal documents. Traditionally, this challenge has been approached as a single-class text classification problem. However, due to the inherent complexity of legal information, characterized by intricate connections and associations between various legal entities and concepts, we propose that a graph-based representation offers a more suitable and informative solution. In response to this need, our paper introduces VN-Legal-KG, an innovative Legal Statute Identification Knowledge Graph tailored to meet the specific requirements of Vietnamese users seeking clarity on Land Law matters. Leveraging cutting-edge graph neural network techniques, we also present a link prediction mechanism integrated into VN-Legal-KG, which addresses the LSI task as a multi-label classification problem, better aligning with real-world legal practices. Through experimentation with real-world data, our approach demonstrates favorable performance when compared to previous models reported in the literature.

Keywords: Legal Statute Identification · Multi-Label Classification · Deep Learning · Knowledge Graph · Graph Neural Networks · Heterogeneous Graph · Graph Attention Network

1 Introduction

Legal Statute Identification (LSI) is a specific judicial task of classifying legal statutes to describe facts or evidence of a legal scenario. Legal documents or facts are described in different forms and formats, distinguishing each other in length and legal context. This has raised many challenges for recent research to find an approach for a model to fully wrap up the whole juridical content [12]. The existing methods need to make the most of the relationship between judicial documents and facts, which is a considerable source of knowledge for estimating legal document similarity [7].

© The Author(s), under exclusive license to Springer Nature Singapore Pte Ltd. 2024
M. H. Hà et al. (Eds.): CSoNet 2023, LNCS 14479, pp. 102–110, 2024.
https://doi.org/10.1007/978-981-97-0669-3_10

Example 1. *In a real conversation concerning the legal matter of land business, a user expresses a concern.* "Tôi đang thực hiện giao dịch mua đất của Ông A, hiện tại đã ký xong hợp đồng chuyển nhượng có công chứng. Nay tôi được công chứng viên báo là ông A đang bị khởi tố vì tội lừa đảo chiếm đoạt tài sản và có thể giao dịch mua đất của tôi sẽ bị tạm dừng do tài sản của ông A sẽ bị phong toả? Xin hỏi công chứng viên nói như vậy có đúng không? Xin cảm ơn!" *("I am currently executing the purchase transaction of land from Mr. A. The transfer contract has been signed and notarized. Today, the notary public informed me that Mr. A is under investigation for the offense of fraudulent misappropriation of assets, and as a result, the land purchase transaction may be temporarily suspended due to the possibility of asset freezing against Mr. A. May I inquire if the notary public's statement is accurate? Thank you!").*

Ideally, to support legal readers in self-exploring their case, an LSI system would provide legal consultation by retrieving articles within the Vietnam Land Law 2013 that are relevant or similar to the reader's scenario. Specifically, the system will answer this question by giving the content of Article 188 (Nói về điều kiện thực hiện quyền chuyển nhượng quyền sử dụng đất - Regarding the conditions for executing the right to transfer the land use rights), Article 168 (Nói về thời điểm được thực hiện các quyền của người sử dụng đất - Regarding the timing of executing the rights of land users) from the Vietnam Land Law 2013.∎

Despite knowing the legal documents' similarity, an attempt has yet to be made to utilize the legal network for the LSI task [7]. Initially, LSI is considered a single-class classification [7], which could be more practical for real users' concerns. With Example 1 above, the concern would require two articles (188, and 168) for lawyers or readers to fully address the whole scenario context.

On the other hand, it's crucial to acknowledge that legal is a sophisticated domain that requires suitable linguistic resources, particularly in terms of legal terminology. Global researchers [2,6] identified some basic ontology design patterns regularly used to model legal norms. i) Agent-role-time [2]; ii) Event-time-place-jurisdiction [6]; iii) Agent-action-time [8]; iv) Object-document [8]; v) Legal deontic ontology [6,11]. These patterns, combined with linguistic taxonomies, could provide a good solution for creating a bridge between the variants of the legal definitions and the conceptualization level [5]. However, this knowledge base of legal has yet to be researched and widely explored.

Different from computer experts' view of a legal document as just a linguistic document, when a lawyer reads a legal document, the lawyer first pays attention to key phrases (legal terminology), extracting legal entities, legal relations, the object of impact, and the time of the legal event, thereby identifying which laws and provisions can be used to process a legal document. A graph structure built by legal entity nodes (person, legal entity, organization) and legal relationship nodes by extracting verbs (Example *mua_bán* - buy_sell: legal relationship commercial agent) is a great prompt for us to consider applying a graph-based approach to solve this problem. Our contributions are as follows.

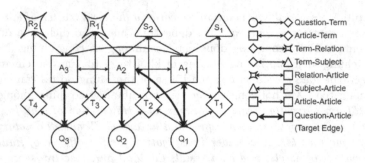

Fig. 1. The graph architecture of VN-Legal-KG. Our target training edge is Question-Article.

- We introduce the *Vietnam Legal Knowledge Graph* (VN-Legal-KG), which represents the elements of the land-related Legal Statute Identification challenge as a knowledge graph in the domain of land affairs.
- We present an approach towards link prediction for multi-label classification on the VN-Legal-KG to address the given problem.
- We have empirically evaluated our proposed approach on the Vietnam Land Law 2013 dataset, using real-world Land-Related Legal Statute Identification challenges gathered from the community.

2 Vietnam Legal Knowledge Graph

In this section, we present VN-Legal-KG to represent knowledge in the field of Vietnam Land Law. To build VN-Legal-KG, we use the following data sources:

- *Legal Dictionary*: This comprises 6700 legal terms with definitions selected from the Vietnamese Law Dictionary [4] by legal experts.
- *Vietnam Land Law 2013* [1]: A digital and structured version of the Vietnamese Land Law comprising 212 articles. Only relevant articles are used in this study.
- *Legal Question-Answering Knowledge Base*: It contains 5498 records gathered from legal forums, including questions, answers, summaries, and tags. These tags are classified by experts to indicate the related articles, clauses, and points the questions address. Additionally, annotations categorize words into subjects and verbs with a legal relationship. There are 12 legal subjects and 19 legal relations. These annotations facilitate efficient inference of related articles. The study uses question tags as inputs and article tags as labels for multi-label classification. Listing 1 shows that the record of the question in Example 1 is structured in JSON format. This study will use the question tag as an input and the article tag as a label for the multi-label classification problem.

Based on the above data, we construct VN-Legal-KG as a heterogeneous graph $G = (V, E)$, illustrated in Fig. 1. V is the set of vertices, and E is the set of edges.

Set V has five types of vertex, $\Phi = \{Q, A, T, S, R\}$:

{"id":"92",
"**question**":"Tôi đang thực hiện giao dịch mua đất của Ông A, hiện tại đã ký xong
hợp đồng chuyển nhượng có công chứng. Nay tôi được công chứng viên báo là ông A
đang bị khởi tố vì tội lừa đảo chiếm đoạt tài sản và có thể giao dịch mua đất của
tôi sẽ bị tạm dừng do tài sản của ông A sẽ bị phong toả? Xin hỏi công chứng viên
nói như vậy có đúng không? Xin cảm ơn! ",
"**legal**":[{"doctype":"Luật","legislation":"Luật Đất đai 2013", "**article**":"**188**",
"clause":"Không xác định","point":""}, {"doctype":"Luật","legislation":"Luật Đất đai 2013",
"**article**":"**168**", "clause":"1","point":""}],
"**subjects**":{"nguoiDuNangLucHanhViDanSu":["công chứng viên"], "nguoiThanhNien": ["ông"]},
"**relations**":{"danSuLaoDongQuanHeLaoDong":["công chứng","hợp đồng","thực hiện"],
"danSuQuanHeNhanThan":["ký","lừa đảo"],
"danSuQuanHeTaiSanHopDongDoiTuongTaiSan":["chuyển nhượng","giao dịch"],
"hanhChinhBienPhapPhongNguaNganChanHanhChinh":["phong tỏa"],
"hinhSuToiPham":["chiếm đoạt","lừa đảo","phong tỏa"],
"thuongMaiCacHoatDongThuongNhan":["giao dịch","mua"],
"toTungTrinhTuThuTuc":["khởi tố"]}}

Listing 1. Sample of a Legal Question-Answering Knowledge Base record.

- Node Q_i represents the ith question of Legal Question-Answering Knowledge Base, represented by the embedding vector h_{Q_i} from the text of this question.
- Node A_i represents the ith article of Vietnam Land Law 2013, represented by the embedding vector h_{A_i} from the text of this article.
- Node T_i represents the ith term from the Legal Dictionary, represented by the embedding vector h_{T_i} of this term.
- Node S_i represents the ith legal subject (or subject), represented by the embedding vector h_{S_i} from the text content of this legal subject.
- Node R_i represents the ith legal relation (or relation), represented by the embedding vector h_{R_i} from the text content of this legal relation.

To create the embedding vector for nodes Q_i, A_i, T_i, S_i, and R_i, we use the architecture of the BERT [11] model. The embedding vector h_{T_i} of T_i combines with BERT embedding with word type encoding. However, we do not use BERT's pre-trained model but train from scratch this model based on the text contents collected from Legal Dictionary, Legal Question-Answering Knowledge Base, and Vietnam Land Law 2013.

The set E consists of edges representing the following relationships.

- *Question-Term* association will be created if the question corresponding to Q_j contains the term T_i. The attribute of the edge will be represented by the *term frequency-inverse document frequency* (TF-IDF) of the T_i corresponding to the Q_j.
- *Article-Term* association will be created if the article corresponding to A_j contains the term T_i. The attribute of the edge will be represented by the TF-IDF of T_i corresponding to the A_j.
- *Question-Article* association will be created if the record corresponding to Q_i is labeled with the article corresponding to A_j in the Legal Question-Answering Knowledge Base. The attribute of the edge will be represented by the cosine-similarity score between two embedding vectors, Q_i and A_j.

– *Article-Article* association will be created if articles corresponding to Ai and Aj are labeled for the same record in the Legal Question-Answering Knowledge Base. The attribute of the edge will be represented by the normalized co-occurrence value between Ai and Aj.

– *Term-Subject* association will be created if the term T_i belongs to the legal subject S_j.

– *Term-Relation* association will be created if the term T_i belongs to the legal relation R_j.

– *Subject-Article* association will be created if S_i related to A_i based on legal annotation, which helps identify the relevant articles.

– *Relation-Article* association will be created if R_i related to A_i based on legal annotation, which helps identify the relevant articles.

Edge attributes are derived from the training dataset. VN-Legal-KG is used for multi-label classification in Legal Statute Identification. When a user raises a new question or issue represented as Q_{new}, we predict associated A_i nodes. Our network architecture optimally propagates and updates information between nodes, aiding in identifying relevant articles for new questions. We avoid explicitly designing Question-Question associations to reduce model complexity; instead, these associations are indirectly inferred from Question-Term associations.

3   Link Prediction for Multi-label LSI Prediction

To solve the problem of multi-label LSI prediction, we simulate this problem into link prediction on VN-Legal-KG. For a new question, we represent this question as a Q_{new} node and predict the node articles might be associated with it. We apply Graph Neural Network to process graph-structured data of VN-Legal-KG. The model we use is the *Graph Attention Network* (GAT) [10], trained and inferred as follows.

3.1   GAT Training with VN-Legal-KG

We train the link prediction model in the form of contrastive learning. Figure 2 illustrates the training process. VN-Legal-KG defines a graph's core knowledge as collecting all terms, articles, subjects, and relations. We randomly sample B questions in the training dataset for each training step. Together with the core knowledge edge and the sampled question set, we create a subgraph to train the model. Then, we use the GAT with two layers to propagate this subgraph. After obtaining the nodes embedding, we create positive and negative Question-Answer association edges for each question. Then, we calculate the score of each created link between Q_i and A_j, illustrated in Fig. 3.

$$score_{Q_i A_j} = h_{Q_i}^{l+1} \cdot h_{A_j}^{l+1} \tag{1}$$

where $h_{Q_i}^l$ and $h_{A_j}^l$ are the node embedding of the training questions and articles at the lth GAT layer. These embeddings are calculated based on the attention

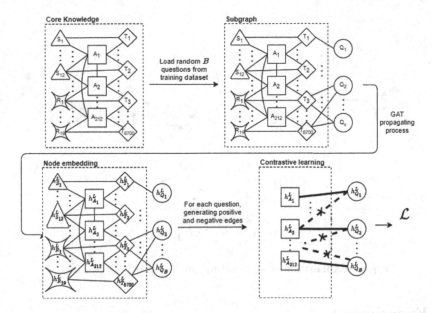

Fig. 2. Link Prediction Training Process.

mechanism, with α_{ij}^{Φ} as the attention score of node j to node i for each node type Φ. GAT projects the graph structure into the mechanism by performing masked-attention, which means we only compute α_{ij}^{Φ} for node $j \in \mathcal{N}_i^{\Phi}$, where $\mathcal{N}_i^{\Phi}$ is the typed based neighbors of node i. With positive and negative scores, we train the model with contrastive loss, described as follows.

$$\mathcal{L} = -\frac{1}{B} \sum_{i \in idList} \sum_{p \in positiveDict[i]} h_{Q_i}^L \cdot h_{A_p}^L$$

$$+ \frac{1}{B} \sum_{i \in idList} \log \left(\sum_{n \in negativeDict[i]} \exp\left(h_{Q_i}^L \cdot h_{A_n}^L\right) \right) \tag{2}$$

where $idList$ is a list of sampled questions, $positiveDict[i]$ is a list of relevant articles of Q_i, $negativeDict[i]$ is a list of relevant articles of Q_i, $h_{Q_i}^L$ is the node embedding of training questions, $h_{A_p}^L$ is the node embedding of positive articles, $h_{A_n}^L$ is the node embedding of negative articles, and L is the number of GAT layers.

3.2   Link Prediction for a New Question

For the new question, we create a Q_{new} node corresponding to this question. We connect Q_{new} with the corresponding terms T for each word in the question. Then, the message-passing process is performed similarly to the training process to obtain embedding vectors for all nodes. We calculate the score of connections between Q_{new} and all articles in the graph. Then, we take the top five articles with the highest score as the result. The above steps are described in Fig. 4.

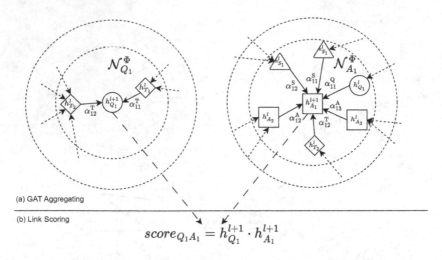

$$score_{Q_1 A_1} = h_{Q_1}^{l+1} \cdot h_{A_1}^{l+1}$$

Fig. 3. Explanation of aggregating process and Link Scoring.

4 Experiments

4.1 Dataset

We use the Legal Question-Answering Knowledge Base as the dataset to evaluate the model. Our dataset is highly imbalanced, with an imbalance ratio of 1058. Considering multi-label tasks, each question has about 2 related articles on average. Since we simulate the multi-label LSI prediction problem into a link prediction problem between question Q and article A, the training set and test set will not contain overlapped questions to ensure the model's generalization.

4.2 Training and Evaluating Protocol

Before training the graph neural network, we train the BERT model using Masked Language Modeling with legal documents. The pre-trained model from our previous work is called LegaRBERT [9]. While training the language model, we focus on masking terms from the Legal Dictionary to help the model learn many law-related features. Then, BERT pre-training is used to create embedding vectors for the nodes.

We use conventional metrics such as precision, recall, and F1-score. Furthermore, we introduce the *Usefulness* metric, described as follows.

Definition 1 (Usefulness). *The Usefulness of an article set A returned by the prediction model over a query Q is considered true (e.g. A is useful), if A consists at least one article matching the labeled ground-truth of Q.* ∎

4.3 Baselines

The baselines are described as follows.

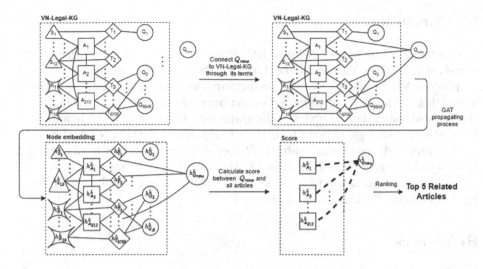

Fig. 4. Inference Process.

- *LegaRBERT-FC*: We encode questions into embedding vectors. Then, there is a *Fully Connected Layer* (FC) with a sigmoid function to predict which articles are related to the question.
- *LegaRBERT-XGBoost*: Instead of using FC, we use XGBoost [3] to perform the multi-label classification problem.
- *VN-Legal-KG Model*: We use a model with two GAT layers to process the graph structure of VN-Legal-KG.

Table 1 shows that the VN-Legal-KG Model significantly outperforms machine learning models with the top five results. We choose the top five articles with the highest probability because exploiting other articles related to the user's question is possible. VN-Legal-KG Model has promising results with the weighted average recall of 0.6 and the samples average recall of 0.69. Considering the Usefulness metric, the VN-Legal-KG Model has higher results than the remaining models. A minimum of one related article for delving deeper into clauses and points is guaranteed in 82% of the prediction results by VN-Legal-KG Model, while additional articles can be seen as extra material for reference.

The experiment highlights the value of leveraging entity relationships for accurate predictions and mitigating article omissions. Meanwhile, models like LegaRBERT-FC and LegaRBERT-XGBoost, relying solely on text content, require assistance learning term-to-article and question-to-article associations.

Table 1. Experimental Results.

Baselines	Weighted Avg. Recall	Samples Avg. Recall	Usefulness
LegaRBERT-FC	0.54	0.60	0.73
LegaRBERT-XGBoost	0.21	0.24	0.77
VN-Legal-KG Model	0.60	0.69	0.82

5   Conclusion

In this paper, we propose VN-Legal-KG, which contains entities and legal relationships related to Vietnam Land Law. Furthermore, we designed the model to process VN-Legal-KG to help predict articles related to users' questions. Through experiments, our proposed model outperforms machine learning models. We also tested the sensitivity of the graph with different settings. In addition, annotations from legal experts have been easily applied with VN-Legal-KG. In the future, we will explore more about VN-Legal-KG with answers from the Legal Question-Answering Knowledge Base. At the same time, we further research the connection between nodes to increase the ability to query articles and related legal documents in this legal network.

References

1. Vietnamese land law (2013). https://thuvienphapluat.vn/van-ban/Bat-dong-san/Luat-dat-dai-2013-215836.aspx (In Vietnamese)
2. Boella, G., Di Caro, L., Leone, V.: Semi-automatic knowledge population in a legal document management system. Artif. Intell. Law **27**, 227–251 (2019)
3. Brownlee, J.: XGBoost with Python: Gradient Boosted Trees with XGBoost and scikit-learn. Machine Learning Mastery (2016)
4. Diep, N.N.: Vietnamese Law Dictionary. The Gioi Publisher. https://www.sachluat.com.vn/sach-luat-d0n/tu-dien-phap-luat-viet-nam-luat-gia-nguyen-ngoc-diep/ (In Vietnamese)
5. Palmirani, M., Bincoletto, G., Leone, V., Sapienza, S., Sovrano, F.: PrOnto ontology refinement through open knowledge extraction. In: Legal Knowledge and Information Systems, pp. 205–210. IOS Press (2019)
6. Palmirani, M., Martoni, M., Rossi, A., Bartolini, C., Robaldo, L.: Pronto: Privacy ontology for legal compliance. In: Proceedings 18th Europe Conference Digital Government (ECDG). pp. 142–151 (2018)
7. Paul, S., Goyal, P., Ghosh, S.: LeSICiN: a heterogeneous graph-based approach for automatic legal statute identification from Indian legal documents. In: Proceedings of the AAAI Conference on Artificial Intelligence, vol. 36, pp. 11139–11146 (2022)
8. Peroni, S., Palmirani, M., Vitali, F.: UNDO: the united nations system document ontology. In: d'Amato, C., et al. (eds.) ISWC 2017. LNCS, vol. 10588, pp. 175–183. Springer, Cham (2017). https://doi.org/10.1007/978-3-319-68204-4_18
9. Thien, H.N., et al.: Legar: A legal statute identification system for Vietnamese users on land law matters. In: Communications in Computer and Information Science, vol. 1949–1950 (2023)
10. Veličković, P., Cucurull, G., Casanova, A., Romero, A., Lio, P., Bengio, Y.: Graph attention networks. arXiv preprint arXiv:1710.10903 (2017)
11. Wyner, A., Casini, G.: Legal Knowledge and Information Systems: Jurix 2017: the Thirtieth Annual Conference, vol. 302. IOS Press (2017)
12. Zhu, G., Hao, M., Zheng, C., Wang, L.: Design of knowledge graph retrieval system for legal and regulatory framework of multilevel latent semantic indexing. Comput. Intell. Neurosci. 2022 (2022)

CombiGCN: An Effective GCN Model for Recommender System

Loc Tan Nguyen[iD] and Tin T. Tran[✉][iD]

Faculty of Information Technology, Ton Duc Thang University,
Ho Chi Minh city, Vietnam
51900375@student.tdtu.edu.vn, trantrungtin@tdtu.edu.vn

Abstract. Graph Neural Networks (GNNs) have opened up a potential line of research for collaborative filtering (CF). The key power of GNNs is based on injecting collaborative signal into user and item embeddings which will contain information about user-item interactions after that. However, there are still some unsatisfactory points for a CF model that GNNs could have done better. The way in which the collaborative signal are extracted through an implicit feedback matrix that is essentially built on top of the message-passing architecture of GNNs, and it only helps to update the embedding based on the value of the items (or users) embeddings neighboring. By identifying the similarity weight of users through their interaction history, a key concept of CF, we endeavor to build a user-user weighted connection graph based on their similarity weight.

In this study, we propose a recommendation framework, CombiGCN, in which item embeddings are only linearly propagated on the user-item interaction graph, while user embeddings are propagated simultaneously on both the user-user weighted connection graph and user-item interaction graph graphs with Light Graph Convolution (LGC) and combined in a simpler method by using the weighted sum of the embeddings for each layer. We also conducted experiments comparing CombiGCN with several state-of-the-art models on three real-world datasets.

Keywords: Recommender System · Collaborative Filtering · Collaborative signal · Graph Convolution Network · Embedding Propagation

1 Introduction

Recommendation systems play an important role in online businesses because of the economic benefits they bring by suggesting suitable products or services to customers. That motivation has driven research to improve algorithms to offer powerful recommendation engines, typically collaborative filtering (CF). Concurrent with the rise of deep learning, especially the use of GNNs to learn representations of users and items (as known as embeddings), many recent studies have focused on enriching embeddings by encoding them with collaborative signals, which carry information about user-item interactions [1–5]. These signals

M. H. Hà et al. (Eds.): CSoNet 2023, LNCS 14479, pp. 111–119, 2024.
https://doi.org/10.1007/978-981-97-0669-3_11

are extracted through the message-passing architecture of GNNs. More specifically, considering a user u as a node in the graph whose embedding is e_u, at each propagation time this user node will adjust its embedding by aggregating all embeddings of neighboring items. During the aggregation progress, each embedding e_i from a neighboring node item i will be multiplied by a coefficient $p_{ui} = 1/\sqrt{|\mathcal{N}_u||\mathcal{N}_i|}$, where $\mathcal{N}_u$ and $\mathcal{N}_i$ denote the first-hop neighbors of user u and item i, so the updated embedding value e_u not only carries information about neighboring items, it also reflects the mutual importance between user u and item i through the p_{ui} coefficient.

However, GNN models only help each user or item embedding in the user-item interaction graph to be similar to neighboring nodes without regard to the weights of the links between nodes during the entire propagation process. There has been some research on adding weights to the embedding encoding process, such as [4,5]. These studies construct a user-user graph where each connection between two users is the number of items shared by them. Aiming at addressing this problem, we have normalized the user-user graph based on Jaccard similarity and integrated these weights, which improves the quality of the extracted collaborative signal over each propagation and produces satisfactory embeddings for CF. Combining embedding propagated from two graphs has also been conducted through many studies [3–5]. SocialLGN has proven that their proposed graph fusion operation is a state-of-the-art combination embeddings from the two graph method [3]. Their results are more accurate than results from graph fusion operations based on GCN methods [6] or GraphSage [7].

In this paper, we propose a model named CombiGCN based on Light Graph Convolution (LGC) [2] to propagate user and item embeddings on the user-item interaction graph; in the meantime, user embedding is also propagated on the user-user weighted connection graph. To fuse two user embeddings obtained after each propagation into an integrated embedding, instead of using the fusion graph operation of SocialLGN, we simply use the weighted sum of the embeddings. We demonstrate the superior performance of CombiGCN by comparing it with state-of-the-art recommendation models on three real-world datasets that we preprocessed to avoid cold-start and over-fitting.

2 Related Work

2.1 Graph Convolution Networks

Due to its superior ability to model graph-structured data, Graph Neural Networks (GNNs) have become the state-of-the-art technology for recommendation systems. A graph convolution network (GCN) is a special type of GNNs that uses convolution aggregations. Spatial GCNs based on 1-hop neighbor propagation and in each layer GCN neighborhood aggregations are required and thus the computational cost is significantly reduced. In the recommended context, spatial GCN contains NGCF [1], WiGCN [4] and GCMC [8]. A recent study [2] developed Light Graph Convolution (LGC) based on the GCN architecture but eliminates trainable matrices and non-linear activation functions in GCN. The experiment reported in [2] also shows that LGC outperform GCN. Today's most modern CF models [2, 3, 5] also use LGC instead of traditional GCN.

2.2 Multi-layer Perceptron and Backpropagation

In machine learning models involving Neural Networks like GNNs, learning the trainable parameters includes forward-propagation and back-propagation. The forward-propagation stage calculates the embedding value of each node in the neural network with trainable parameters. In matrix form, these parameters include the trainable matrices W^k and embeddings E^k in the k-th layer. In addition, non-linear activation functions such as $ReLU$ and $tanh$ are also applied to the results. The calculations in forward-propagation produce the prediction result in the last layer. To train the model, an optimization function to this result and propagate back to adjust the trainable parameters $[E, W]$. When training neural networks, forward-propagation and back-propagation depend on each other. For the recommendation problem using GNNs also follows this rule. However, a recent study [2] has demonstrated the redundancy of the trainable matrices W^k and non-linear activation functions in recommendation models, the reason being that the embeddings mapped from user and item IDs are not many features, so using too many trainable parameters makes the model heavy and ineffective.

3 Our Proposed Method

We proposed our model, which includes a method to pre-process data set and the CombiGCN model, in this chapter. CombiGCN will explores the user and item interaction and weighted similarity matrix as the input, and make prediction at the output as recommendations. The overview of CombiGCN model is illustrated in Fig. 1.

3.1 Pre-processing Data

Algorithm 1 brings two main benefits in the learning process of the recommendation model: **1) Avoid over fitting**, the dataset obtained from Algorithm has the most common features in the original dataset, so there will be little information about the typical interactions that cause the over fitting; **2)Remove noisy-negative interactions in implicit feedback** [15], in the first step we have determined the set of items I_c and throughout the next steps when collecting users we only collect interactions with items contained in set I_c. This will limit unpopular interactions, which are likely to be noisy-negative interactions.

3.2 Adjacent Graph and Weighted References Matrix

In this article, we use two graphs as the data sources including the user-item interaction graph and the user-user weighted connection graph denote by G_R and

---

Algorithm 1. Inference for data pre-processing

Input: $\mathcal{U} \times \mathcal{I}$ ▷ Interaction between users and items in original dataset
      r ▷ ratio between users and items you want to obtain
Output: $R = U \times I \subseteq \mathcal{U} \times \mathcal{I}$
    for each item $i \in \mathcal{I}$ **do**
       $set_i \leftarrow$ list of users that interact with item i
       $len_i =$ total number of users in set_i
    end for
    $\widetilde{m} \leftarrow$ cardinality of set I
    $I_c \leftarrow$ m items have highest len_i
    $\widetilde{n} \leftarrow \widetilde{m} \times r$
    for each user $u \in \mathcal{U}$ **do**
       $set_u \leftarrow$ list of items interacted by user u
       $sim_u =$ Jaccard distance between$I_c$and set_u
    end for
    $U_c \leftarrow \widetilde{n}$ users have highest sim_u
    $U \leftarrow n$ users from $\widetilde{n}$ users of set U_c have more than 10 interactions with items
    $I \leftarrow m$ items have interacted by users in set U
    return $R = U \times I$

G_W, $U = [u_1, \ldots, u_n](|U| = n)$ denotes the user nodes across both G_R and G_W and and $I = [i_1, \ldots, i_m](|I| = m)$ denotes the item nodes in G_R. $R \in \mathbb{R}^{n \times m}$ is the binary matrix with entries only 0 and 1 that represent user-item interactions in G_R.

In WiGCN [4], matrix $W_u = RR^T \in \mathbb{R}^{n \times n}$ accumulates the paths connecting two user via shared items. However, the matrix W_u only shows the number of intersections between the two sets of items I_i of user u_i and I_j of user u_j, but has not recorded the influence of couple of users i, j to all interaction data. We build the weight users matrix W to represent the user-user weighted connection graph through the matrix W_u.

$$W = W_u \odot (D_R J + (D_R J)^T - W_u)^{-1} \tag{1}$$

where, $D_R \in \mathbb{R}^{n \times n}$ is a diagonal matrix with each entry $D_{R_{ii}}$ represents the number of neighboring items of user i, $J \in \mathbb{R}^{n \times n}$ is the matrix of ones (or all-ones matrix) and $\odot$ denote element-wise product. From a mathematical perspective, each element of W_u represents the intersection while $(D_R J + (D_R J)^T - W_u)$ represents the union of two list items of two users u_i and u_j. Therefore Eq. 1 calculates the similarity between the pair of users i, j based on Jaccard Similarity. To avoid over-fitting the model when using both matrices W and R during the propagation process, we mapping the values of W to a number of discrete values in the interval $[0, 1]$ where value 0.0 represents no correlation between these two users while value 1.0 represents very high correlation.

3.3 CombiGCN

The general design of the proposed model is shown in Fig. 1, our model including three components - **1) Embeddings layer** that use the unique identifiers of users and items to create embedding, **2) Propagation layers**, which propagate the representations of users and items in LGC architecture and, **3) Prediction layer**, that predicts the score between users and items pair based on final embeddings obtained after L propagation layers.

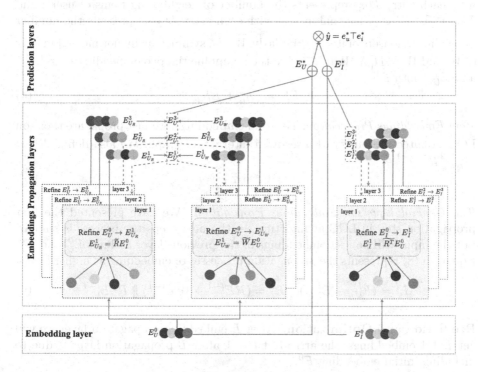

Fig. 1. The architecture of the CombiGCN model

Embedding Layer. Following the mainstream well-known models [1,2,4], we initialize user and item embeddings by map unique its ID into the latent space, and obtain dense vectors $e_u^{l=0} \in \mathbb{R}^d (e_i^{l=0} \in \mathbb{R}^d)$. Where l denote the number of layer propagation. The dimension of embeddings is denoted by d. We denote $E^l \in \mathbb{R}^{(n+m) \times d}$ is the set of all embeddings during propagation, i.e. E^l contains the set of n user embeddings and m item embeddings at l-th layer.

$$E^l = E_U^l \parallel E_I^l = [e_{u_1}^l, \dots, e_{u_n}^l, e_{i_1}^l, \dots, e_{i_m}^l]$$ (2)

Propagation Layers. In order to clearly introduce the embedding propagation process, we will first show this propagation process in the first layer of LGC architecture, and then show the general formula in the higher propagation layers.

User Embeddings Propagation. The input of first layer is embedding E_U^0, we will propagate this user embedding in two graphs, user-item interaction graph G_R and user-user weighted connection graph G_W respectively to obtain two user embeddings $E_{U_R}^1$ and $E_{U_W}^1$.

$$E_{U_R}^1 = \widetilde{R} E_I^0; E_{U_W}^1 = \widetilde{W} E_U^0 \tag{3}$$

We further define $\widetilde{R} = D_R^{-1/2} R D_{R^T}^{-1/2}$, where $D_R \in \mathbb{R}^{n \times n}$ is a diagonal matrix with each entry $D_{R_{ii}}$ represents the number of neighboring items of user i and $D_{R^T} \in \mathbb{R}^{m \times m}$ is a diagonal matrix with each entry $D_{R_{jj}^T}$ represents the number of neighboring users of item j. Similarly, $\widetilde{W}$ is a symmetrically normalized matrix of W and $\widetilde{W} = D_W^{-1/2} W D_W^{-1/2}$. We then combine the two embedding users $E_{U_R}^1$ and $E_{U_W}^1$ into E_U^1.

$$E_U^1 = E_{U_R}^1 + E_{U_W}^1 \tag{4}$$

Item Embeddings Propagation. For item embeddings, we just propagate them on LGC architecture only with user-item interaction graph. We also define $\widetilde{R^T} = D_{R^T}^{-1/2} R^T D_R^{-1/2}$.

$$E_I^1 = \widetilde{R^T} E_U^0 \tag{5}$$

The General Equation Embeddings Propagation. We have presented the first propagation step in LGC architecture, in the next steps the process is similar, but the input will be user embeddings of the previous layer and not E_U^0 and E_I^0. Equation (8) represents the propagation processes of embedding at higher levels.

$$E^l = (E_{U_R}^l + E_{U_W}^l) \parallel E_I^l = (\widetilde{R} E_I^{l-1} + \widetilde{W} E_U^{l-1}) \parallel \widetilde{R^T} E_U^{l-1} \tag{6}$$

Prediction and Optimization. After L embedding propagation layer we will get $L + 1$ embeddings, the arrival of $L + 1$ after L propagation layer is due to including initial embedding E^0.

$$E^* = \alpha_0 E^0 + \alpha_1 E^1 + \ldots + \alpha_L E^L \tag{7}$$

where $\alpha_l = 1/(L + 1)$, that mentioned in [2] denotes the importance of the l-th layer embedding in constituting the final embedding. To perform model prediction, we conduct the inner product to estimate user preference for the target.

$$\hat{y}_{ui} = e_u^{*T} e_i^* \tag{8}$$

To learn parameters $\Phi = [E_U^0, E_I^0]$, CombiGCN have been applied Bayesian Personalized Ranking (BPR) [9]. BPR assumes observed interactions have higher preferences than an unobserved interactions. To optimize the prediction model we use mini-batch Adam [10] and minimize the BPR loss.

$$Loss_{bpr} = \sum_{\Omega_{ui}^+} \sum_{\Omega_{uj}^-} -ln\sigma(\hat{y}_{ui} - \hat{y}_{uj}) + \lambda \parallel \Phi \parallel_2^2 \tag{9}$$

4 Experiments

4.1 Datasets Description

We make experiments with our proposed model on three well-known datasets, which are Ciao, Epinions, and Foursquare. Each dataset is being pre-processed and divided into two sets: 80% for training and 20% for testing.

- **Ciao** [11,12]: The Ciao dataset is an online shopping dataset containing the ratings given by users on a larger number of items.
- **Epinions** [11,12]: Epinions is a popular online consumer review website.
- **Foursquare** [13,14]: The Foursquare dataset record check-in data for different cities in the world.

4.2 Experimental Settings

Setting Parameters. To ensure that the experimental results are fair, we set the parameters to be the same across all models. Specifically, the learning rate is 0.001, the coefficient of L2 normalization is 0.00001, and the number of layers of LGC is 3, with each layer having an embedding size of 64. We also use the same early stop strategy as NGCF and LightGCN; specifically, if in 50 consecutive epochs, the recall at 20 on the test result does not increase, the model will be stopped.

Baseline. We use the same datasets and repeat the experiments on all the following baseline models to demonstrate the result:

- **BPR-MF** [9] is matrix factorization optimized by the Bayesian personalized ranking (BPR) loss, which exploits the user-item direct interactions only as the target value of interaction function.
- **GCMC** [8] adopts GCN encoder to generate the representations for users and items, where only the first-order neighbors are considered. Hence one graph convolution layer, where the hidden dimension is set as the embedding size.
- **WiGCN** [4] is developed on top NGCF and add the connection between each user-user and item-item pair in the interaction graph by the number of shared items or users.
- **NGCF** [1] conducts propagation processes on embeddings with several iterations. The stacked embeddings on output contains high-order connectivity in interactions graph. The collaborative signal is encoded into the latent vectors, making the model more sufficient.
- **LightGCN** [2] focus on the neighborhood aggregation component for collaborative filtering. This model uses linearly propagating to learn users and items embeddings for interaction graph.

4.3   Experiment Results

Table 1. Overall Performance Comparisons

Dataset	Ciao			Epinions			Foursquare		
	precision	recall	ndcg	precision	recall	ndcg	precision	recall	ndcg
BPR-MF	0.01047	0.03182	0.02221	0.00087	0.00613	0.00330	0.01923	0.02479	0.02721
GCMC	0.01439	0.04785	0.03484	0.00097	0.00825	0.00460	0.02066	0.03102	0.03006
NGCF	0.01596	0.05170	0.03825	0.00120	0.00955	0.00506	0.02094	0.03177	0.03107
WiGCN	0.01606	0.05317	0.03985	0.00147	0.01088	0.00683	0.02424	0.03433	0.03592
LightGCN	0.01673	0.05674	0.04294	0.00184	0.01219	0.00663	0.02612	0.03602	0.03778
CombiGCN	0.01730	0.05845	0.04406	0.00204	0.01398	0.00720	0.02621	0.03801	0.03818

The overall performance comparison is shown in Table 1. The results clearly show that our model consistently achieves the best performance in all three metrics and all three datasets. Further, MF performance is much inferior to that of GNN-based models because it cannot capture collaborative signals. Although GCMC uses GCN, it only captures neighborhood information in the first layer, so it is less effective than the NGCF and WiGCN. WiGCN has better accuracy than NGCF because it introduces information about the weights of users and items during embedding propagation, which makes the WiGCN model more efficient in capturing collaborative signals. LightGCN is an LGC-based model that has removed components that have been shown to negatively affect the model training process, so the results of LightGCN are very good, only worse than those of CombiGCN.

5   Conclusion

In this work, we attempted to improve the embedding quality by adding connection weights between users based on their interaction history. To do that, we introduce the CombiGCN model, which implements embedded functions on two graphs: a user-item interaction graph and a user-item weighted connection graph based on the Light Graph Convolution architecture. The key to CombiGCN lies in its ability to combine embedding functionality across multiple graphs in a simple and effective way. We provide three preprocessed datasets with our algorithm to reduce cold start, over-fitting, and data noise problems for evaluation experiments. The results of experiments with state-of-the-art models are a valuable demonstration of the success of weight addition and the multi-graph combination architecture of CombiGCN.

References

1. Wang, X., He, X., Wang, M., Feng, F., Chua, T.: Neural graph collaborative filtering. In: Proceedings of the 42nd International ACM SIGIR Conference on Research and Development in Information Retrieval (2019)
2. He, X., Deng, K., Wang, X., Li, Y., Zhang, Y., Wang, M.: LightGCN: simplifying and powering graph convolution network for recommendation. In: Proceedings of the 43rd International ACM SIGIR Conference on Research and Development in Information Retrieval, pp. 639–648 (2020)
3. Liao, J., et al.: SocialLGN: light graph convolution network for social recommendation. Inf. Sci. **589**, 595–607 (2022)
4. Tran, T., Snasel, V.: Improvement graph convolution collaborative filtering with weighted addition input. In: Nguyen, N.T., Tran, T.K., Tukayev, U., Hong, T.P., Trawinski, B., Szczerbicki, E. (eds.) ACIIDS 2022. LNCS, vol. 13757, pp. 635–647. Springer, Cham (2022). https://doi.org/10.1007/978-3-031-21743-2_51
5. Yu, J., Yin, H., Gao, M., Xia, X., Zhang, X., Viet Hung, N.: Socially-aware self-supervised tri-training for recommendation. In: Proceedings of the 27th ACM SIGKDD Conference On Knowledge Discovery & Data Mining, pp. 2084–2092 (2021)
6. Kipf, T., Welling, M.: Semi-supervised classification with graph convolutional networks (2017). https://arxiv.org/abs/1609.02907
7. Hamilton, W., Ying, R., Leskovec, J.: Inductive representation learning on large graphs. In: Proceedings of the 31st International Conference on Neural Information Processing Systems, pp. 1025–1035 (2017)
8. Berg, R., Kipf, T., Welling, M.: Graph convolutional matrix completion (2017). https://arxiv.org/abs/1706.02263
9. Rendle, S., Freudenthaler, C., Gantner, Z., Schmidt-Thieme, L.: BPR: Bayesian personalized ranking from implicit feedback. In: Proceedings of the Twenty-Fifth Conference on Uncertainty in Artificial Intelligence, pp. 452–461 (2009)
10. Kingma, D., Ba, J.: Adam: a method for stochastic optimization (2017). https://arxiv.org/abs/1412.6980
11. Tang, J., Gao, H., Liu, H.: mTrust: discerning multi-faceted trust in a connected world. In: Proceedings of the Fifth ACM International Conference on Web Search and Data Mining, pp. 93–102 (2012)
12. Tang, J., Liu, H., Gao, H., Das Sarmas, A.: eTrust: understanding trust evolution in an online world. In: Proceedings of the 18th ACM SIGKDD International Conference on Knowledge Discovery and Data Mining, pp. 253–261 (2012)
13. Yang, D., Qu, B., Yang, J., Cudre-Mauroux, P.: Revisiting user mobility and social relationships in LBSNs: a hypergraph embedding approach. In: The World Wide Web Conference, pp. 2147–2157 (2019)
14. Yang, D., Qu, B., Yang, J., Cudré-Mauroux, P.: LBSN2Vec++: heterogeneous hypergraph embedding for location-based social networks. IEEE Trans. Knowl. Data Eng. **34**, 1843–1855 (2022)
15. Gao, Y., et al.: Self-guided learning to denoise for robust recommendation. In: Proceedings of the 45th International ACM SIGIR Conference on Research and Development in Information Retrieval. (2022)

Unveiling Sentiments in Vietnamese Education Texts: Could Large Language Model GPT-3.5-turbo Beat PhoBERT?

Nguyen Ngoc Long⬦, Ngo Doan Kien⬦, Nguyen Thi Hong Hanh⬦,
Nguyen Thi Kieu Nhung⬦, Nguyen Son Tung⬦, and Tuan Nguyen(✉)⬦

National Economics University, Hanoi, Vietnam
nttuan@neu.edu.vn

Abstract. Text classification in general, and sentiment analysis specifically is a major branch of Natural Language Processing with various uses and challenges. Classifying sentiments from Vietnamese text presents numerous challenges as Vietnamese is inherently and linguistically dissimilar to English. Therefore, there urges measures to recognize subtleties in Vietnamese texts and accurately categorize them into suitable labels. In this work, we leverage the power of the pre-trained model PhoBERT to classify a collected dataset of education-related texts into three separate classes, namely positive, negative, and neutral. It is expected that the model will have positive social implications by bringing people updated information on the current education system and ensuring their comprehension of educational policies, thus accordingly adapting itself towards more progressive growth. The model is first trained on two datasets VLSP 2019 and ViHSD. We then use the fine-tuned model to train on our data gathered from Vietnam online news sites and social media platforms. The input is either a sentence or a paragraph and the expected output is among the three aforementioned labels. Through testing and fine-tuning different models including Large Language Models (LLMs) with one-shot and few-shot approaches, our model consistently outperformed them in sentiment classification tasks with an accuracy of up to 94%.

Keywords: Classification · Sentiment analysis · Vietnamese text · Pho-BERT · Education

1 Introduction

Sentiment analysis in Natural Language Processing involves the process of extrapolating sentiments from analyzing textual data and categorizing texts into three categories positive, negative, and neutral. Staying up-to-date with the news provides a gateway for people to understand current affairs and gain more knowledge. Vietnam, in seeking a well-rounded development, is increasingly prioritizing education and hence the prevalence of education news and education-related

Supported by National Economics University.

content on sites visited daily by Vietnamese people. Simply scrolling through any social media platforms and news sites, people can see that content posted regarding education earns the hot topic title. Staying informed of educational content brings forward several benefits. For educators, exposure to the latest information means a thorough comprehension of the current state of the education system thus bringing in appropriate instructional resources to facilitate students' attainment of knowledge. Students' awareness of relevant educational content is synonymous with better acquisition of knowledge paving the way for their future careers. Society as a whole through educational-related information can gear itself better towards state-of-the-art and progressive educational development.

As educational news is of importance to society, in this study, we developed a sentiment analysis system to assist people in accessing and understanding suitable and informative information. The model can automatically classify texts regarding education into three classes: positive, negative, and neutral. Initially, the process of building our dataset involves crawling education-related texts from Facebook and multiple online news sites such as Lao Dong and Thanh Nien. In total, we process 3015 data points either in the form of a paragraph or a sentence playing the role of either presenting news on education or expressing people's opinions on educational topics. Then, we consulted linguistic professionals in labeling each data point, classifying them into three mentioned categories. In terms of training, we utilized the efficiency of PhoBERT [1] trained on pre-labeled and cleaned datasets VLSP 2019 [2] and ViHSD [3] to obtain suitable hyperparameters for the model. The model was subsequently trained on our collected dataset to produce the expected result. After testing, we obtained a higher accuracy rate than our base model and other tested architectures such as GPT [4].

The paper has made the following contributions:

1. Proposed an optimal deep learning approach to deal with sentiment classification of Vietnamese educational documents.
2. Presenting a dataset containing 3015 data points cleaned and labeled suitably with the help of linguists.
3. Discuss experimental results of BERT-based language models and Large Language Model (LLM) approach in the task of sentiment classification task particularly for Vietnamese texts.

The rest of the paper is organized as follows. Section 2 reviews the related work, Sect. 3 presents the proposed model, Sect. 4 discusses the dataset and results and Sect. 5 concludes the works.

2 Related Works

In seeking to extract sentiments from Vietnamese texts, numerous papers have been published in English. In 2022, Nursat Japhan Prottasha' [5] et al. tested the effectiveness of a Bert-based transfer learning approach in sentiment analysis of the Bangla language. They discovered that combining Bangla-BERT and LSTM leads to an accuracy of 94.15%. Long Mai and Bac Le [6] in 2020 suggested a novel system to automatically collect, filter, and analyze Vietnamese comments on Youtube regarding a certain product. A joint process was introduced, combining sentence and aspect-level sentiment analysis to finally analyze the sentiment of the comments. Utilizing the benefit of fine-tuning pre-trained models, a BERT-based model surpassed BGRU-CRF-ELMO [7] with a performance of 91.45% on SSA(Sentence-level Sentiment Analysis) and 81.78% on ASA(Aspect-level Sentiment Analysis). On JSA(Joint approach for Sentiment Analysis), BERT was also the optimal model. Dang Van Thin et al. [8] in 2022 proposed a joint multi-task architecture based on neural network models that aim to address the tasks of Aspect Category Detection(ACD) and Aspect Category with Polarity(ACP) in datasets of whole documents. The model trains the two tasks in parallel and obtains the final representation by combining the information feature of the two tasks, which effectively predicts the aspect categories as well as the sentiment of the comments. The model consists of the ACD component, taking advantage of the Bi-GRU layer and concatenating from the attention, max pooling, and mean pooling to get the final representation. The ACP component has a Bi-GRU layer followed by a 3-layer CNN architecture to attain the representation, which is then concatenated from the ACD representation to get the final one. Compared to other state-of-the-art models, the introduced architecture performed better on the VLSP [2] and UIT_ABSA [9] datasets. Also in the topic of transfer learning are results brought forward by Ngoc C. Le et al. [10] through applying the pre-trained model BERT for Aspect Detection on the VLSP Hotel dataset and Aspect Polarity on the VLSP Restaurant dataset. Regarding the former task, they used BERT-based and a preprocessing step by re-annotating sentences split from the review and summing them up again. On testing, their method achieved an F1 score of 0.7966 and a precision score of 0.7972. In sentiment classification in general, Kian Long Tan et al. [11] achieved competitive results experimenting with a hybrid deep learning model last year. The ensemble model is a combination of three models based on RoBERTa namely RoBERTa-LSTM, RoBERTa-BiLSTM, and RoBERTa-GRU. The final classification class is obtained by fusing the predictions of these three architectures with averaging ensemble and majority voting. The model also solves the problem of an unbalanced dataset by taking advantage of pre-trained GloVe [12] word embedding in data augmentation. On testing, the model outclassed other models in comparison with a reported accuracy of 94.9% on the IMDB sentiment analysis dataset [13], 91.77% on the Twitter US Airline Sentiment dataset [14], and 89.81% on the Sentiment140 dataset [15], respectively. In our work, the benefit of transfer learning was optimized. Our model was based on the PhoBERT base model by VinAI, which has already been trained on Vietnamese text datasets. The pre-trained model was then trained and fine-tuned using our custom dataset to produce predictions.

3 Proposed Model

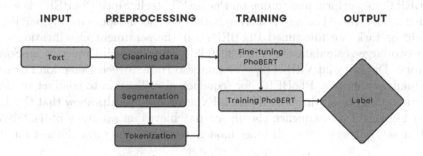

Fig. 1. Proposed system

3.1 PhoBERT Pre-trained Model and Fine-Tuning for Specified Task

In Fig. 1 we illustrate the proposed approach, which consists of various steps in natural language processing and the application of deep learning algorithms. Firstly, due to the carefully selected and relatively clean sources of data, we applied fundamental data-cleaning methods. Since Vietnamese uses Unicode encoding, NFC normalization was applied uniformly across the entire dataset. Additionally, we removed HTML tags, date formats, emojis, and special characters. The initial and one of the most crucial steps that significantly impact the results of the model is preprocessing Vietnamese text. Unlike English, where words are separated by spaces, Vietnamese text presents a more challenging segmentation task. According to Professor Nguyễn Văn Lợi's statistics in "Tiếng," [16] approximately 70% of Vietnamese words consist of two or more syllables, such as "cửa sổ" (window), "máy tính" (computer), and "bí thư' (secretary). If we segment these words using only spaces, there is a risk of incorrectly separating them, leading to entirely different meanings. For example, "bí" and "thư" are separated from "bí thư," resulting in "pumpkin" and "letter" instead of "secretary." Consequently, models that perform well with English data exhibit significantly reduced performance with Vietnamese data. Therefore, when training NLP models for Vietnamese data, correct word segmentation is essential.

To address this challenge, we employ a tool for segmenting Vietnamese words, namely RDRsegmenter [17] from VnCoreNLP [18], a well-known and powerful package for Vietnamese natural language processing. After segmentation, we obtain words consisting of two or more syllables connected by the "_" symbol. For example, the sentence "Đó là một câu chuyện cảm động" is transformed into "Đó là một câu_chuyện cảm_động." Next, we tokenize the sentences in the dataset because deep learning models can only understand numerical inputs. For this purpose, we use the Byte-pair encoding [19,20] (BPE) which is the tokenizer that the pre-trained model PhoBERT also uses. The dataset is now ready to be used as input for deep learning models.

We then utilize the state-of-the-art model PhoBERT [1] for a classification task on the Vietnamese language. Before initiating the training process with PhoBERT, we perform fine-tuning on PhoBERT itself. Since PhoBERT is a pre-trained model trained on a large corpus without a specific focus on any particular domain or task, we fine-tuned PhoBERT on the sentiment classification task using two large-scale datasets: VLSP2019 [2] - Hate Speech Detection on Social Networks Dataset and ViHSD [3] - Vietnamese Hate Speech Detection Dataset.

Finally, we employ PhoBERT for sequence classification to conduct training and evaluation on an education dataset. Experimental results show that the fine-tuned PhoBERT for sequence classification achieves an accuracy of 94.28% on the test set, outperforming all other models tested on the same dataset for this task.

3.2   Other Tested Models Including Variants of BERT and Large Language Model (GPT-3.5)

In addition to the proposed approach, we conducted experiments with several other models, including different versions of BERT such as the BERT base model, RoBERTa base model, BERT multilingual base model, XLM-RoBERTa [24], and PhoBERT base model. Furthermore, we also evaluated the well-known Large Language Model, GPT-3.5-turbo. For the models that are variants of BERT, we employed a similar pipeline to the proposed system, with the exception of fine-tuning using the hate-speech dataset.

Since the LLM GPT-3.5-turbo is open to use by giving the model-specified prompt, we simply use the test set data which is identical to one of the other tested models. Our task involves providing prompts to the Large Language Model (LLM) to return labels for each sample. The following are the steps of the process: Data Cleaning: Similar to other tested models, the data underwent a standard cleaning process. Prompt Generation: A prompt was formulated to describe the task that the model was expected to perform, and the desired output format was specified. The prompt needed to clearly indicate that the model was required to classify the sentiment of educational text segments into 3 labels [positive, negative; neutral]. The assignment of each label had to be explicitly explained with specific examples, and it was necessary to request output in a structured format such as JSON. Furthermore, the maximum number of tokens that the model can accept as input is limited to 4096 tokens, which is approximately equivalent to 2000 Vietnamese words (words were not segmented and they are separated by spaces only). As some data samples exceed this maximum token limit, we have truncated the end portion of those samples. All samples retain only the initial 2000 tokens. Through numerous experiments, this was found to be the most suitable token count for our dataset. The writing of the prompt strictly adhered to the guidelines provided in the course "ChatGPT Prompt Engineering for Developers" by OpenAI. The entire prompt which consists of all 5 components will be sent through the OpenAI API of get-3.5-turbo. The obtained result will be in JSON format, for example: {"label": "positive"}.

4 Result

4.1 Dataset

To conduct this study, we collected 3015 educational Vietnamese paragraphs from various sources, including university websites, electronic publications like "giaoducthoidai.vn", "laodong.vn" and "thanhnien.vn", as well as Facebook posts from education-focused groups like "Giáo dục Việt Nam", "Tin Giáo dục Hà" and other news/blog sources. Due to the study's narrow focus, data acquisition was limited and labor-intensive. Scraping text from websites was relatively straightforward, but associating content with the appropriate label required extensive work and domain expertise in Vietnamese literature. We enlisted the assistance of specialists with domain experience to aid in the data labeling process, as arbitrary classification would significantly impact the model's accuracy and the overall significance of the study. Our dataset comprises 1001 positive texts, 1012 negative texts, and 1002 neutral texts. In addition, it's important to address potential ambiguous cases in sentiment classification within the dataset. Ambiguous cases may include instances where language is unclear <*Giáo viên*>, mixed sentiments are present <*Môn học này rất thú vị, nhưng*> or sarcasm is used <*Chắc chắn, việc học suốt ngày là niềm vui*>. Handling such cases requires a nuanced approach to ensure the accuracy of sentiment labels.

Here is our annotation guideline:

Positive: Label text segments as "Positive" if they express favorable opinions or emotions about education. This includes content that supports, praises or emphasizes the benefits of education.

Negative: Label text segments as "Negative" if they express unfavorable opinions or emotions about education. This encompasses content that criticizes, opposes, or highlights issues related to education.

Neutral: Label text segments as "Neutral" if they do not express clear positive or negative opinions or emotions about education. This includes informative, factual, or unrelated content without strong emotional language or opinions.

4.2 Experimental Result

We compare seven deep-learning models to obtain the best architecture for the task of sentiment classification. The proposed model, PhoBERT-finetune-hatespeech, is based on the PhoBERT model from VinAI, which is a model already pretrained on two datasets VLSP and ViHSD. The performance in categorizing three classes in XLM-RoBERTa, BERT base model, BERT multilingual base model, RoBERTa base model, PhoBERT-finetune-hatespeech, and GPT-3.5 is shown as follows.

Table 1. Models accuracy on test set

Model	Accuracy
BERT base model	0.82
RoBERTa base model	0.82
GPT-3.5 turbo	0.85
BERT multilingual base model	0.87
XLM-RoBERTa	0.90
PhoBERT base	0.91
PhoBERT-finetune-hatespeech	**0.94**

Table 1 demonstrates accuracy in testing the models' abilities to infer sentiment from a piece of text in our dataset. BERT and RoBERTa base models shared the same rate of accuracy with 0.82. Performing slightly better was the BERT multilingual base model, predicting the correct class with an accuracy of 0.87. It can be seen that XLM-RoBERTa, PhoBERT base, and PhoBERT-finetune-hatespeech all achieved above-90 rate in prediction. Experimenting with LLM - calling the GPT API key and writing prompts yielded no better result with only 0.85 in testing accuracy. However, PhoBERT-finetune-hatespeech pretrained on Vietnamese datasets had the highest accuracy rate of 0.94, surpassing its base model by 0.3.

Throughout our experiments, the PhoBERT model, when fine-tuned, consistently surpassed the performance of the large language model (LLM) based on the GPT-3.5 architecture in sentiment analysis tasks. The primary reasons for this may be due to several factors. Firstly, the inherent design of GPT-3.5, which encompasses a vast multilingual dataset, offers broad versatility but potentially sacrifices the depth of specialization provided by monolingual models. PhoBERT, being trained exclusively on Vietnamese text, is deeply attuned to the language's nuances, idiomatic expressions, and intricacies, leading to a more refined accuracy in tasks specific to the Vietnamese context. Secondly, despite the fact that base pre-trained models like GPT-3.5 are unquestionably powerful due to their diverse training data, they might not be perfectly suited for specific domains. In contrast, our approach of fine-tuning PhoBERT using hate speech data from VLSP and ViHSD imbued the model with a profound understanding of sentiments within the Vietnamese educational domain, consequently boosting its performance.

5   Conclusion

Our work focuses on sentiment analysis in educational texts and aids readers in comprehending pertinent and practical information in educational documents. In order to support informed decision-making in education, we provide an efficient sentiment categorization tool for Vietnamese literature. Due to the exceptional circumstances inherent to our research context, characterized by the analysis of educational texts, we found it imperative to construct our own dataset comprising a comprehensive educational corpus. The development of this dataset was executed with the invaluable contributions of domain experts. There are 1001 positive texts, 1012 negative texts, and 1002 neutral texts in the dataset. They underwent preprocessing to be cleaned and standardized, after which they were put into the deep learning models, which are variants of BERT. Additionally, we experimented with applying prompting techniques using the renowned GPT-3.5-turbo model, a Large Language Model, to evaluate the responses received in a classification task. According to experimental findings, the PhoBERT-finetune-hatespeech model achieves the best result in terms of accuracy (0.94) and outstanding f1 score, which indicates the model works effectively on classifying all classes, especially the highest f1 score (0.93) in the negative class, which outperformed the remaining models. Overall, this performance on the education documents is a positive sign in our work of analyzing the sentiment of the educational corpus as positive, negative, or neutral. However, we will continue to implement different hyperparameters or training strategies and experiment to see if we can achieve even better results, as there is always room for improvement. As OpenAI releases GPT-4 recently and notes that it has more powerful capabilities, it is encouraged to experiment with different GPT versions, prompts, and few-shot learning strategies. In later work, we plan to add more examples to the dataset, update it, and tune some model parameters for further work and exploration.

References

1. Nguyen, D.Q., Nguyen, A.T.: PhoBERT: pre-trained language models for Vietnamese. arXiv:2003.00744
2. VLSP 2019 | Association for Vietnamese Language and Speech Processing. https://vlsp.org.vn/vlsp2019
3. Luu, S.T., Van Nguyen, K., Nguyen, N.L.-T.: A large-scale dataset for hate speech detection on Vietnamese social media texts. https://doi.org/10.1007/978-3-030-79457-6_35
4. Brown, T., et al.: Language models are few-shot learners
5. Prottasha, N.J., et al.: Transfer learning for sentiment analysis using Bert-based supervised fine-tuning, MDPI. https://www.mdpi.com/1424-8220/22/11/4157 (2022)
6. Mai, L., Le, B.: Joint sentence and aspect-level sentiment analysis of product comments. https://doi.org/10.1007/s10479-020-03534-7
7. Wei, H., et al.: A multichannel biomedical named entity recognition model based on multitask learning and contextualized word representations. https://doi.org/10.1155/2020/8894760
8. Dang Van, T., Lac Si, L., Minh Nguyen, H., Luu-Thuy Nguyen, N.: A joint multi-task architecture for document-level aspect-based sentiment analysis in Vietnamese, IJMLC **12**(4)
9. Van Thin, D., Nguyen, N.L.-T., Truong, T.M., Le, L.S., Vo, D.T.: Two new large corpora for Vietnamese aspect-based sentiment analysis at sentence level. ACM Trans. Asian Low-Resour. Lang. Inf. Process. **20**(4), 1–22 (2021). https://doi.org/10.1145/3446678

10. Le, N.C., Lam, N.T., Nguyen, S.H., Nguyen, D.T.: On Vietnamese sentiment analysis: a transfer learning method. https://doi.org/10.1109/rivf48685.2020.9140757
11. Tan, K.L., Lee, C.P., Lim, K.M., Anbananthen, K.S.M.: Sentiment analysis with ensemble hybrid deep learning model. IEEE Access **10**, 103694–103704 (2022). https://doi.org/10.1109/access.2022.3210182
12. Pennington, J., Socher, R., Manning, C.: Glove: global vectors for word representation. https://doi.org/10.3115/v1/d14-1162
13. Maas, A., Daly, R.E., Pham, P.T., Huang, D., Ng, A.Y., Potts, C.: Learning word vectors for sentiment analysis
14. Pre-Labeled Datasets. https://www.crowdflower.com/data-for-everyone
15. Go, A., Bhayani, R., Huang, L.: Twitter sentiment classification using distant supervision
16. Nguyen Van, L.: <Processingraph />. Vietnam Education Publishing House Limited Company
17. Nguyen, D.Q., Nguyen, D.Q., Vu, T., Dras, M., Johnson, M.: A fast and accurate Vietnamese word segmenter
18. Vu, T., Nguyen, D.Q., Nguyen, D.Q., Dras, M., Johnson, M.: VnCoreNLP: a Vietnamese natural language processing toolkit. https://doi.org/10.18653/v1/N18-5012
19. Sennrich, R., Haddow, B., Birch, A.: Neural machine translation of rare words with subword units. https://doi.org/10.18653/v1/p16-1162
20. Kudo, T., Richardson, J.: SentencePiece: a simple and language independent subword tokenizer and detokenizer for neural text processing
21. Devlin, J., Chang, M.-W., Lee, K., Toutanova, K.: BERT: Pre-training of deep bidirectional transformers for language understanding
22. Liu, Y., et al.: RoBERTa: a robustly optimized BERT pretraining approach. https://arxiv.org/abs/1907.11692
23. Tran, K., Nguyen, A., Hoang, P., Duc Luu, C., Do, T.-H., Nguyen, K.: Vietnamese hate and offensive detection using PhoBERT-CNN and social media streaming data
24. Conneau, A., et al.: Unsupervised cross-lingual representation learning at scale. arXiv:1911.02116

Portfolio Construction Based on Time Series Clustering Method Evidence in the Vietnamese Stock Market

The Nguyen Manh$^{(\boxtimes)}$ and Hoan Bui Quoc

National Economics University, Hanoi, Vietnam
{thenm,buiquochoan}@neu.edu.vn

Abstract. Portfolio optimization is indeed a crucial and highly pertinent topic in finance. During the process of constructing an investment portfolio, investors typically face with two important decisions on portfolio selection and portfolio allocation. This article aims to delve into the realm of portfolio optimization by applying the time series clustering method to historical data of stock returns on the Vietnamese stock market. The VNIndex (VNINDEX) from January 2, 2013, to December 31, 2022 was collected for analysis. About methodology, we utilize hierarchical clustering, which can be applied to a single time series (UTS) or multiple time series (MTS). The resulting portfolio was constructed by selecting stocks from these clusters based on their Sharpe ratio, a measure that finely makes balance between the risk and return. Afterward, we determine the optimal portfolio weights using the Markowitz's Mean - Variance model, enabling us to create two distinct portfolios: MV_UTS and MV_MTS. Furthermore, our analysis encompasses dynamic evaluation using a rolling window, shedding light on how different methods respond to events impacting financial markets, such as crises. This study provides valuable insights into the application of clustering techniques in portfolio optimization and elucidates the performance and sensitivity of these methods under diverse market conditions.

Keywords: portfolio optimization · mean - variance model ·
Hierarchical clustering · machine learning

1 Introduction

Constructing an effective investment portfolio is a significant objective for both individual investors and financial institutions or investment funds. In 1952, Harry Markowitz introduced the modern portfolio theory [6], which presented a mathematical framework known as mean-variance analysis for building an asset portfolio. This framework addresses one of two optimization problems: the first is to minimize portfolio variance while achieving a specified level of expected return or minimum required return, and the second is to maximize portfolio expected return while maintaining a certain level of expected variance or maximum acceptable variance.

© The Author(s), under exclusive license to Springer Nature Singapore Pte Ltd. 2024
M. H. Hà et al. (Eds.): CSoNet 2023, LNCS 14479, pp. 129–137, 2024.
https://doi.org/10.1007/978-981-97-0669-3_13

Markowitz demonstrated that we could minimize risk through portfolio diversification. It's crucial to acknowledge that most investors aim to balance their portfolios, avoiding overconcentration in a few individual stocks ("putting all their eggs in one basket") and ensuring diversification. However, maintaining a well-diversified portfolio can be challenging, as too many stocks may lead to increased management time and fees. Consequently, the challenge lies in constructing an optimal portfolio with limited stocks. Therefore, recently, there has been a growing interest in limiting the number of stocks under consideration, often based on clustering techniques. It is important to note that clustering is vital in exploratory data mining, especially in unsupervised machine learning. There are two stock clustering approaches: static data and time series data. Static data clustering relies on fixed attributes that do not change over time. On the other hand, time series data clustering is based on the dynamic characteristics of the data. For example, when analyzing a stock's returns, if we use the average return value for clustering, that value remains constant. It does not change over the entire period, representing a static approach. In contrast, using time series data involves examining the daily fluctuations in the stock's return values, capturing the dynamic nature of the data.

In the context of static data clustering, Nanda et al. employed clustering algorithms including K-Means, Self-Organizing Maps, and Fuzzy C-Means to categorize Indian stocks into different clusters [9]. Subsequently, they developed portfolios based on these clusters using various financial indicators such as the rate of return, price-to-earnings ratio, price-to-book value,... as well as short-term and long-term returns. The findings indicated that the K-Means method outperformed fuzzy C-Means and SOM. Similarly, Marvin and Bhatt utilized clustering techniques based on financial variables like revenues divided by assets or income divided by assets. They then constructed portfolios with a manageable number of stocks using the Sharpe index. The results of their study affirmed the utility of cluster analysis [8].

To effectively group assets, time series clustering techniques are commonly employed. Early research in time series clustering involved measures of interdependence between asset returns, such as Pearson or Spearman cross-correlation coefficients [5]. Marcos López de Prado proposed the Hierarchical Risk Parity method (HRP) as a risk parity allocation algorithm with robust out-of-sample [10]. Additionally, Raffinot introduced an asset allocation approach based on hierarchical clustering, leveraging concepts from network theory and machine learning techniques. His experimental findings demonstrated that portfolios generated through hierarchical clustering were stable, genuinely diversified, and exhibited superior risk-adjusted performance compared to traditional optimization methods [11]. Furthermore, the empirical study of Gubu et al. reported that portfolios constructed using time series clustering and MV portfolio model outperformed portfolios created using other approaches [3].

In our research, experimental results show that the time series clustering and mean-variance method outperform the VN-Index in achieving a much better value of the Sharpe ratio and a comparably smaller value of the corresponding standard deviation.

This paper continues as follows: Sect. 2 presents data and explains the proposed method, Sect. 3 describes the experiment with real data and shows its results, and finally, Sect. 4 gives conclusions, and further work opportunities.

2   Data and Methodology

2.1   Data

In this research, we employ the log daily returns of the HOSE stock market covering 2013 to 2022. In each sub-period, the stocks were not fully traded in the training window (used to build the portfolio), and the testing window (used to validate the portfolio) will be omitted. The stock quantities during the periods changed, ranging from a minimum of 255 to a maximum of 274 stocks. And Vietnam's 10-year government bond represented the risk-free rate.

2.2   Methodology

Our approach involves employing a clustering method to group of stocks into clusters where stocks within each cluster display strong correlations with each other. Specifically, we will utilize the hierarchical clustering method with an Agglomerative strategy. This method involves iteratively merging pairs of clusters based on complete linkage criteria. To quantify the distance between two stocks, we will calculate the Pearson distance. In the case of univariate time series, each stock is represented by a single feature. However, in the case of multivariate time series, each stock is represented by two features. In both scenarios, each feature is a time series. This approach allows us to effectively capture the temporal relationships and similarities between stocks, regardless of whether they are represented by one or two features.

Once the stocks are grouped into clusters, we will apply the Sharpe ratio to identify the top-performing stocks within each cluster. Stocks with high Sharpe ratios will be prioritized, as they indicate that, given the same level of risk, investing in these stocks is likely to yield better returns compared to those with lower ratios [3, 8].

Finally, we will determine the optimal portfolio weights using the Markowitz model with the primary objective of minimizing risk. The results will be compared to the benchmark portfolio, the VN-Index, to assess the performance of our portfolio allocation strategy. We adopt a rolling sample methodology, similar to the approach used by DeMiguel et al [1], to evaluate and compare the out-of-sample performance of the asset allocation strategies. In general, transaction costs are disregarded and the risk-free rate is set equal to zero.

The process of determining optimal portfolio based on clustering is shown in Fig. 1.

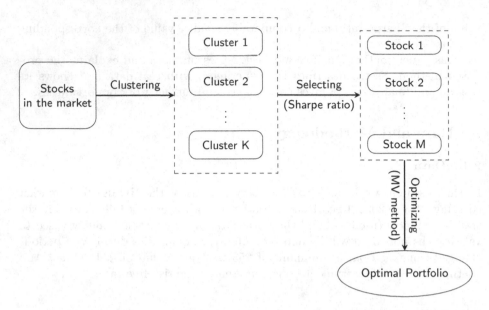

Fig. 1. Flowchart of portfolio selection method. This method will consist of three steps. The first step groups stocks based on time series information to group similar stocks together. The second step will select stocks from the clusters created in Step 1, and in Step 3, the optimization algorithm will be applied to the stocks selected from Step 2 to determine the optimal portfolio.

Hierarchical Clustering Methods model data in the form of a hierarchy of clusters [12]. The Agglomerative strategy, also known as the bottom-up approach, is employed to construct this hierarchy. Initially, all observations are placed in their own individual clusters. Subsequently, pairs of clusters are merged in a recursive manner. The Complete distance between clusters A and B is defined as the biggest distance among element pairs in which one comes from cluster A and another one comes from cluster B:

$$d(A, B) = \max_{x,y}\{d_{Corr}(x, y) \mid x \in A, y \in B\} \tag{1}$$

Here, the Pearson correlation distance is defined as:

$$d_{Corr}(x, y) = \sqrt{2(1 - \rho(x, y))} \tag{2}$$

In Eq. (2), $\rho(x, y)$ represents the Pearson correlation coefficient between x series and y series, with a range from -1 to 1. A coefficient close to 0, 1, or -1 signifies uncorrelated, correlated, or anti-correlated behavior, respectively.

In the context of multivariate time series, each data point is represented in the form of (x, y), where x and y typically denote two different features of the data. Specifically, the data is structured as $\{(x_1, y_1), \ldots, (x_N, y_N)\}$ where

$x_i = (x_{i1}, x_{i2}, \ldots, x_{iT}); \; y_i = (y_{i1}, y_{i2}, \ldots, y_{iT}), \; i = 1, \ldots, N.$ The distance between the elements (x_i, y_i) and (x_j, y_j) is defined as:

$$d^*((x_i, y_i), (x_j, y_j)) = \frac{1}{2} d_{Corr}(x_i, x_j) + \frac{1}{2} d_{Corr}(y_i, y_j) \tag{3}$$

The optimal number of clusters examine the within-cluster dissimilarity W_k, with W_k can be defined as the pooled within-cluster sum of squares around the cluster means

$$W_k = \sum_{j=1}^{k} \frac{1}{2|C_j|} \sum_{x,y \in C_j} d(x, y) \tag{4}$$

where, C_j is the j-th cluster and $|C_j|$ is the number of elements in it.

Yue et al [15] introduced an alternative function for the Gap method [14] when determining the optimal number of clusters. This alternative function is based on the maximization function, which is defined as:

$$\max_k \{W_k - 2W_{k+1} + W_{k+2}\} \tag{5}$$

$$\text{s. t.} \quad 1 \leq k \leq \sqrt{n}$$

When working with univariate time series, the primary feature of interest is the return series. However, when dealing with multivariate time series, the analysis includes not only the return series but also the calculation of conditional volatility. This volatility is determined using a GARCH $(1, 1)$ model.

The return of stock i at day t is determined by the formula:

$$r_{i,t} = \ln p_{i,t} - \ln p_{i,t-1} \tag{6}$$

where $p_{i,t}$ and $p_{i,t-1}$ are the close price of stock i at day t and day $t - 1$, respectively.

The intraday stock price volatility of stock i is determined using a GARCH$(1, 1)$ model:

Mean equation: $r_{i,t} = \mu_t + \sigma_{i,t}\varepsilon_{i,t}, i = 1, 2, \ldots, N_t$

Variance equation: $\sigma_{i,t}^2 = \alpha_0 + \alpha(r_{i,t-1} - \mu_t)^2 + \beta\sigma_{i,t-1}^2$ with $\alpha_0 > 0, \alpha > 0, \beta > 0$ and $\alpha + \beta < 1$.

Sharpe ratio aims to expand the risk-return measure so that portfolio volatility can be considered. The goal of investors is to get the best possible risk-adjusted return. The Sharpe ratio is calculated by the following formula [13]:

$$SR = \frac{E[r - r_f]}{\sigma(r - r_f)} \tag{7}$$

where r and r_f are return of portfolio and risk-free rate, respectively.
A positive Sharpe number indicates profitable risk-taking, and a negative one indicates unprofitable risk-taking.

We have set the historical observation period to 248 trading days, approximately one year. The choice of 248 trading days was made for practical reasons,

ensuring that each year considered in the analysis had the same number of trading days. This specific length of training data aligns with the research conducted
by Fastrich et al. [2] and Husmann et al. [4]. We select two stocks with the highest
Sharpe ratio from each cluster, similar to that employed by Marvin and Bhatt [8]
and Gubu et al. [3]. The aim is to simplify management and limit transaction
fees.

In Markowitz's (1952) original work, he framed portfolio selection as the
challenge of identifying a minimum variance portfolio from the available assets
in the investment universe, aiming to achieve a target return (R) of expected
return. This mathematical formulation can be expressed as follows:

$$\min_{\mathbf{w}} \mathbf{w}^T \Sigma \mathbf{w} \tag{8}$$
$$\text{s. t.} \quad \mathbf{w}^T \mathbf{1} = 1$$
$$\mathbf{w}^T \mu \geq R$$
$$\mathbf{w} \geq 0$$

where $\mathbf{w}$ is the weight of the assets in the portfolio and Σ is the covariance
matrix of the assets.

3   Empirical Analysis and Results

In this paper, we have conducted portfolio optimization utilizing a combination
of time series clustering and the mean-variance method. We have constructed
two portfolios, one based on univariate time series clustering procedures and
another based on multivariate time series clustering procedures. The performance of these optimal portfolios has been compared to that of portfolios built
using the HRP method, considering all stocks within the market as well as the
VN-Index. We backtest the out-of-sample performance of the proposed methods with a rolling window procedure, where $\tau = 248$ in-sample observations
(corresponding to one year of market data) are used to form a portfolio. The
optimized portfolio allocations are then kept unchanged for the subsequent 21
trading days (corresponding to 1 month of market data) and the out-of-sample
returns are recorded. After holding the portfolios unchanged for 1 month, the
time window is moved forward, so that the formerly out-of-sample days become
part of the in-sample window and the oldest observations drop out. The updated
in-sample window is then used to form a new portfolio, according to which the
funds are reallocated. The $T = 2,494$ observations allow for the construction of
107 portfolios with the corresponding out-of-sample returns (Fig. 2).

Out-of-sample series returns are used to evaluate the portfolio's performance
and presented in Table 1. According to Table 1, we can observe that the MV
portfolio achieves the best performance in terms of average returns. However,
the HRP portfolio's return series has the smallest standard deviation, resulting
in the highest Sharpe ratio. To compare MV_MTS with VNIndex, we observe
that the former has a slightly higher standard deviation than the latter, but

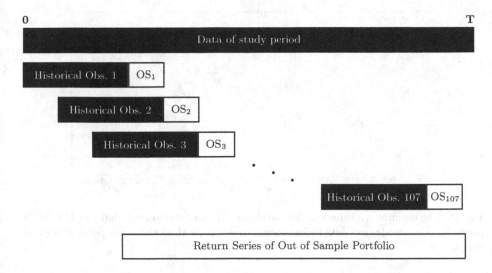

Fig. 2. The rolling window procedure

Table 1. Comparison of all of the evaluated allocation methods based on different performance measures. The bold numbers represent the best result for each performance measure.

	MV_UTS	MV_MTS	HRP	VNIndex
Mean	0.00031	**0.00040**	0.00039	0.00031
Variance	0.01289	0.01274	**0.00655**	0.01171
Sharpe ratio	0.01363	0.02063	**0.03926**	0.01484
Min/Max Num. Stocks	**3/16**	4/17	255/374	255/374
Average Num. Stocks	**6.92**	7.30	304.94	304.94

its average return is more than 30%. On the other hand, UTS, which uses just one series, exhibits a higher standard deviation but a lower average return when compared to VNIndex. The number of stocks in the portfolios utilizing clustering techniques is small, making them suitable for individual investors. The MV_UTS and MV_MTS portfolios have a similar number of stocks.

According to Fig. 3, we can see that, between 2013 and 2018, the Vietnam Stock Market exhibited stability, and our proposed method generated slightly better results than the HRP method. However, our strategy needs improvement during the market downturn from November 2021 to February 2023, resulting in performance levels below VNIndex's. The reason can be the inappropriate use of data calibrated for stable market conditions in portfolio determination, revealing its ineffectiveness when confronted with market shocks.

Fig. 3. The cumulative values of the portfolios. It can be observed that the MV_MTS portfolio consistently exhibits higher cumulative values than the other portfolios at all times.

4   Conclusion

In this paper, we have conducted portfolio optimization utilizing a combination of time series clustering and the mean-variance method. We have constructed two portfolios, one based on univariate time series clustering procedures and another based on multivariate time series clustering procedures. The performance of these optimal portfolios has been compared to that of portfolios built using the traditional mean-variance method, considering all stocks within the market as well as the VN-Index.

We backtest the out-of-sample performance of the proposed method with the rolling window method, where the overall trading period is split into many trading sub-periods. In each sub-period, the optimal portfolio from the former training dataset is used for trading. The resultant portfolio, MV_MTS, which originated from clustering multivariate time series and HRP model, exhibits extraordinary outperformance compared to the VNIndex benchmark, calculated as the accumulated value. The experimental results show that the MV_MTS portfolio is better regarding average returns and accumulated value but not in the Sharp ratio with the HRP portfolio.

The portfolio returns achieved by combining the mean-variance method with a clustering approach tend to exhibit higher volatility than portfolios constructed using the HRP method. However, this approach offers distinct advantages for investors, particularly in achieving higher average returns and creating more compact portfolios. These benefits can translate into reduced management costs and align better with real-world investment scenarios.

The study needs to improve its examination of the matter across short and long-term portfolio holding periods, such as one week or two months. Additionally, there is an opportunity for further research to explore additional features. Moreover, exploring alternative methods for selecting stocks within clusters is crucial, aiming to enhance the overall effectiveness of the mean-variance model.

References

1. DeMiguel, V., Garlappi, L., Uppal, R.: Optimal versus Naive diversification: how inefficient is the 1/N portfolio strategy? Rev. Finan. Stud. **22**(5), 1915–1953 (2007). https://doi.org/10.1093/rfs/hhm075
2. Fastrich, B., Paterlini, S., Winker, P.: Constructing optimal sparse portfolios using regularization methods. CMS **12**(3), 417–434 (2015). https://doi.org/10.1007/s10287-014-0227-5
3. Gubu, L., Rosadi, D.: Time series clustering for robust mean-variance portfolio selection: comparison of several dissimilarity measures. Paper presented at the Journal of Physics Conference Series (2021)
4. Husmann, S., Shivarova, A., Steinert, R.: Sparsity and stability for minimum-variance portfolios. Risk Manage. **24**(3), 214–235 (2022). https://doi.org/10.1057/s41283-022-00091-0
5. Kaufman, L., Rousseeuw, P.J.: Finding Groups in Data: An Introduction to Cluster Analysis. John Wiley & Sons, Hoboken (2009)
6. Markowitz, H.: Portfolio selection. J. Finan. **7**(1), 77–91 (1952). https://doi.org/10.2307/2975974
7. Markowitz, H.M.: Front matter. In: Portfolio Selection, pp. i–vi. Yale University Press (1959)
8. Marvin, K., Bhatt, S.: Creating diversified portfolios using cluster analysis. Princeton University (2015)
9. Nanda, S.R., Mahanty, B., Tiwari, M.K.: Clustering Indian stock market data for portfolio management. Expert Syst. Appl. **37**(12), 8793–8798 (2010). https://doi.org/10.1016/j.eswa.2010.06.026
10. de Prado, M.L.: Building diversified portfolios that outperform out-of-sample. J. Portf. Manag. (2016). https://doi.org/10.3905/jpm.2016.42.4.059
11. Raffinot, T.: Hierarchical clustering-based asset allocation. J. Portfolio Manage. **44**(44), 89–99 (2017). https://doi.org/10.3905/jpm.2018.44.2.089
12. Rokach, L., Maimon, O.: Clustering methods. In: Maimon, O., Rokach, L. (eds.) Data Mining and Knowledge Discovery Handbook, pp. 321–352. Springer, Boston (2005). https://doi.org/10.1007/0-387-25465-x_15
13. Sharpe, W.F.: The sharpe ratio. J. Portfolio Manage. **21**(21), 49–58 (1994). https://doi.org/10.3905/jpm.1994.409501
14. Tibshirani, R., Walther, G., Hastie, T.: Estimating the number of clusters in a data set via the gap statistic. J. Roy. Stat. Soc. Ser. B: Stat. Methodol. **63**(2), 411–423 (2001). https://doi.org/10.1111/1467-9868.00293
15. Yue, S., Wang, X., Wei, M.: Application of two-order difference to gap statistic. Trans. Tianjin Univ. **14**(3), 217–221 (2008). https://doi.org/10.1007/s12209-008-0039-1

An Approach for Web Content Classification with FastText

Huong Hoang Luong[1], Lan Thu Thi Le[1], and Hai Thanh Nguyen[2]([✉])

[1] FPT University, Can Tho, Vietnam
lanltt11@fe.edu.vn
[2] Can Tho University, Can Tho, Vietnam
nthai.cit@ctu.edu.vn

Abstract. Nowadays, with the Internet infrastructure and nearly global access, the amount and diversity of data are increasing rapidly. Many tasks require information retrieval and data collection for machine learning, research, and survey reports in various fields such as meteorology, science, geography, literature, and more. However, manual data collection and classification can be time-consuming and prone to errors. Additionally, AI assistants used for drafting or writing can sometimes be corrected regarding writing style and inappropriate language for the given context. Faced with these needs, In this article, Vietnamese documents are classified using the TF-IDF method, TF-IDF combined with SVD, and FastText at three levels: word level, n-gram level, and character level. For this approach, 15 categories were gathered from various online news sources. The dataset was preprocessed and trained using machine learning models such as SVM, Naive Bayes, Neural Network, and Random Forest to find the most effective method. The Random Forest combined with the FastText method was highly evaluated, achieving a success rate of 82% when measured against essential evaluation criteria of accuracy, precision, and F1 score.

Keywords: Content classification · FastText · TF-IDF · Vietnamese document

1 Introduction

The rapid growth of digital information and textual data on the web has posed significant challenges in extracting and searching information. Automatic classification of text and web content plays a crucial role in addressing these challenges, enabling efficient information retrieval, sentiment analysis, document categorization, and spam detection, among other applications. In recent years, researchers have explored various techniques to improve the performance of text classification systems, focusing on robust feature representation and modeling approaches. Among these techniques, the TF-IDF (Term Frequency-Inverse Document Frequency) method [1], TF-IDF combined with Singular Value Decomposition (SVD), and FastText [2] have emerged as powerful and widely adopted approaches.

M. H. Hà et al. (Eds.): CSoNet 2023, LNCS 14479, pp. 138–146, 2024.
https://doi.org/10.1007/978-981-97-0669-3_14

The TF-IDF (Term Frequency-Inverse Document Frequency) method [1] has been widely utilized in information retrieval and text mining. It measures the importance of terms by considering their frequency within a document and rarity across the entire corpus. TF-IDF provides a solid foundation for feature representation, effectively capturing the discriminative power of terms for classification tasks. In addition to TF-IDF and SVD, FastText has gained attention for its ability to capture sub-word information. FastText [1] represents words as bags of character n-grams, enabling it to handle morphologically rich languages and improve the treatment of out-of-vocabulary words. By considering sub-word units, FastText enriches the feature representation and captures more fine-grained semantic and syntactic information, thereby improving classification accuracy.

This study proposes a novel approach combining the TF-IDF method, TF-IDF combined with SVD, and FastText for automatically classifying text and web content. We aim to leverage these techniques' strengths to enhance the classification process's accuracy and efficiency. We hypothesize that the integration of TF-IDF, TF-IDF combined with SVD, and FastText will provide a comprehensive representation of textual data, capturing both local term frequencies, global term rarity, latent semantic structures, and information. To evaluate the effectiveness of our combined approach, we will conduct experiments on various text classification tasks using benchmark datasets.

This paper consists of five sections. The first section introduces and poses the problem. Related works will be presented in the next section (Sect. 2). The third section (Sect. 3) is the implementation methodology. The next is the experiments in Sect. 4. Moreover, Section 5 is the conclusion.

2   Related Works

In the last three years, many articles have used machine learning to combine the TF-IDF method, TF-IDF combined with SVD, and FastText.

The research in [3] aimed to improve the capability of text classification beyond what conventional text classification algorithms offer. Each document is represented as a sequence of vectors preserving the positional information of words within the document while incorporating the flexibility of combining semantic information from GloVe vectors, arousal ratings, and sentiment information from SentiWordNet. The use of LSTM with GloVe vectors achieves a high accuracy of 85.3%. Another research in [4] presented approaches to detect signs of depression using social media text. They explored three different strategies to address the challenge, and their best solution, based on knowledge graph and textual representations, was 4.9% behind the best model in Macro F1 and only 1.9% behind in Recall.

In this study [5], a taxonomy of digital investment management systems is presented, categorizing them based on the extent of decision automation and delegation throughout the investment management process. The research reveals that the level of automation is influenced by factors such as decision frequency, urgency, and algorithm accuracy. Interestingly, it is observed that many providers restrict their investments to a predetermined subset of funds chosen by humans, which may hinder the potential efficiency gains. Using this taxonomy, the study identifies archetypical system designs, which serve as a foundation for exploring the perception and adoption of digital investment management systems. This research contributes to understanding how automation and delegation impact investment management, providing valuable insights for practitioners and researchers alike.

This paper [6] addressed the challenges of feature selection and extraction in text categorization and aims to identify the main topics within a document. The study utilizes a Twitter dataset and applies an Uncapacitated P-Median Problem (UPMP) to cluster the tweets. Another research in [7] focused on analyzing COVID-19 conspiracies through public tweets. The study involved filtering tweets related to COVID-19 disease, symptoms, and general discussions, specifically targeting conspiracy-related tweets. The analysis identifies three conspiracy classes and COVID-19 tweets that do not involve conspiracies.

3   Methods

Our proposed approach is shown in Fig. 1 with steps as follows.

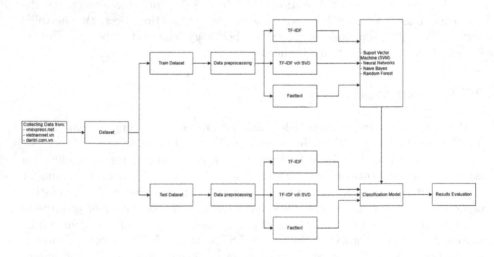

Fig. 1. Our proposed approach.

– **Step 1 - Data Split:** Divide the initial dataset into two subsets, typically using an 80/20 split, where 80% of the data is used for training and 20% for testing. This ensures that the models are trained on sufficient data while allowing for independent evaluation.

- **Step 2 - Data Preprocessing:** Perform preprocessing steps on the data, such as removing stopwords, tokenization, stemming, or lemmatization, depending on the requirements of the text evaluation methods that will be applied. This ensures that the data is in a suitable format for the models.
- **Step 3 - Text Representation Methods:** Use various text representation methods to represent the textual data, such as Bag-of-Words (BoW), Term Frequency-Inverse Document Frequency (TF-IDF), or Word Embeddings (e.g., Word2Vec, GloVe). Apply these methods to the data and observe their impact on the performance of the models.
- **Step 4 - Text classification:** Train different machine learning models on the preprocessed training data. Some commonly used models for text classification include Support Vector Machines (SVM), Naive Bayes, Random Forest, and Neural Networks. Each model has strengths and characteristics that may suit specific tasks or datasets. After training the models, evaluate their performance on the preprocessed testing data. Measure metrics such as accuracy, precision, recall, and F1 score to assess the effectiveness of each model.
- **Step 5 - Comparison and Evaluation:** Compare the results obtained from the different models and text representation methods. Analyze the models' accuracy, computational efficiency, and interpretability to determine which combination performs best for the given text classification task.

3.1   Data Preprocessing

Data preprocessing involves several tasks to prepare the data for further analysis or modeling. In text data, the preprocessing steps typically include: (1) Converting text to a consistent format: lowercase to handle and analyze. (2) Remove special characters such as punctuation marks, symbols, and other non-alphanumeric characters. These characters do not contribute much to the text's meaning and can introduce noise or interfere with subsequent analysis steps. (3) Tokenization: helps to break down the text into its basic components, making it easier to analyze and extract meaningful information. Tokenization can be performed using various techniques, such as splitting white spaces or special characters. (4) Representation using the TF-IDF and FastText methods. TF-IDF represents the importance of each word in a document relative to the entire corpus. The representation can be done at different levels, including word, n-gram, and character. These representations allow for further analysis and modeling of the text data. These preprocessing tasks transform the text data into a consistent and structured format for tasks such as analysis, topic modeling, text classification, or information retrieval. TF-IDF [1] is a statistical measure that evaluates the relevance of a word to a document in a given collection of documents. TF represents the frequency of a word's occurrence in a document, while IDF is used to estimate the importance of that word. FastText [2] proposes a subword embedding method where each central word is represented as a set of subwords. In FastText, for a word w, we consider the set of all its subwords with

lengths ranging from 3 to 6, including special subwords denoted as G_w. Therefore, the dictionary consists of a collection of subwords for all words. Assuming
the vector for subword g in this dictionary is z_g, the vector for the central word
u_w in the skip-gram model can be represented in 1:

$$u_w = \sum_{g \in G_w} z_g \tag{1}$$

The remaining part of the processing in FastText is consistent with the skip-
gram model. The FastText dictionary is larger than the skip-gram model, resulting in more model parameters. Additionally, computing the vector for a word
requires summing all the subword vectors, leading to higher computational complexity. However, we can obtain better vectors for complex and less common
words, including words not present in the dictionary, by referencing other words
with similar structures.

3.2 Text Classification

This article proposes using SVM, Naive Bayes, Random Forest, and Neural Network models on a preprocessed dataset in the TF-IDF format with SVD and
FastText at the word, n-gram, and character levels. The objective is to select
the best model for text and web content classification tasks.

4 Experiments

4.1 Dataset

The dataset consists of texts collected from popular Vietnamese news websites,
including vnexpress.net vietnamnet.vn, dantri.com.vn. These texts have been
pre-classified into 16 topics and stored as TXT files. The dataset contains 3,295
Vietnamese documents, offering a substantial corpus for analysis and research
purposes. Each text is associated with a specific topic, enabling researchers to
explore various aspects of Vietnamese news content across different domains.
The dataset covers various subjects, reflecting the diverse nature of news coverage in Vietnam. These topics include football, lifestyle, travel, entertainment,
education, science, business, vehicle, law, digitalization, health, personal stories,
world news, and sports. They are described in the Table 1.

The dataset will be divided into two subsets, typically using an 80/20 split,
where 80% of the data is used for training and 20% for testing. This ensures
that the models are trained on sufficient data while allowing for independent
evaluation.

4.2 Scenario 1: Text Classification with TF-IDF

In this experiment, we performed text representation using TF-IDF. The dataset
was modeled as a matrix containing the TF-IDF values of the words. The text

Table 1. Dataset of television channels in Vietnam

No.	Topic code	Topic in English	Amount
1	bong-da	Football	216
2	doi-song	Lifestyle	190
3	du-lich	Travel	95
4	giai-tri	Entertainment	395
5	giao-duc	Education	114
6	khoa-hoc	Science	132
7	kinh-doanh	Business	430
8	oto-xe-may	Vehicle	124
9	phap-luat	Law	194
10	so-hoa	Digitalization	310
11	suc-khoe	Health	177
12	tam-su	Personal Stories	101
13	the-gioi	World News	369
14	the-thao	Sports	122
15	thoi-su	Current Affairs	241
16	y-kien	Opinions	85

was represented and trained at three different levels: word level, n-gram level, and character level: (1) **Word Level:** At this level, each word in the text is treated as a separate unit. The TF-IDF values are calculated based on the frequency of individual words in the corpus. This level captures the semantic meaning of individual words and their importance in the text. (2) **N-gram Level:** N-grams are contiguous sequences of n words. At this level, we consider n-grams as the units of representation. For example, a 2-gram level representation considers pairs of consecutive words. This level captures the individual words and the contextual information word sequences provide. (3) **Character Level:** The text is treated as a sequence of individual characters at the character level. The TF-IDF values are calculated based on the frequency of characters in the corpus. This level captures fine-grained text details, including spelling variations and punctuation. The results of the training models for TF-IDF at different levels are shown in Tables 2. In which (1) is precision, (2) is present for recall, (3) is accuracy, and F1-Score is (4).

Table 2. TD-IDF with different levels

Models	Word level				2-gram level				character level			
	(1)	(2)	(3)	(4)	(1)	(2)	(3)	(4)	(1)	(2)	(3)	(4)
SVM	0.74	0.76	0.76	0.74	0.73	0.71	0.71	0.70	0.73	0.74	0.74	0.72
Naive Bayes	0.54	0.5	0.5	0.41	0.58	0.55	0.55	0.58	0.31	0.33	0.33	0.23
Random Forest	0.70	0.69	0.69	0.66	0.60	0.54	0.54	0.48	0.47	0.49	0.49	0.46
Neural Network	0.23	0.27	0.27	0.23	0.19	0.25	0.25	0.19	0.01	0.13	0.13	0.03

Table 2 shows that the SVM model performed well compared to the other models in the experiment. The SVM model was trained using a linear kernel function, a common choice for text classification tasks. The linear kernel allows the SVM to separate the data points by finding a linear decision boundary in the feature space. The default hyper-parameter values were used during the training of the SVM model. These default values are often a good starting point and can provide satisfactory performance. However, it is worth noting that the performance of the SVM model can be further optimized by tuning its hyperparameters, such as the regularization parameter (C) or the kernel coefficient (gamma), based on the specific dataset and problem at hand. Overall, the results suggest that the SVM model, with its linear kernel and default settings, performed relatively well in this experiment for the text classification task.

4.3 Scenario 2: Text Classification with TF-IDF with SVD

In this experiment, we performed text representation using TF-IDF, where the dataset was transformed into a matrix containing the TF-IDF values of the words. The text was represented and trained at three levels: word, n-gram, and character. The results of the training models for TF-IDF at different levels are shown in Table 3. In which (1) is precision, (2) is present for recall, (3) is accuracy, and F1-Score is (4). As shown, SVM performs better than other experimental models. Machine learning SVM was trained with a linear multiplier and other values as default.

Table 3. TD-IDF with SVD

Models	Word level				2-gram level				character level			
	(1)	(2)	(3)	(4)	(1)	(2)	(3)	(4)	(1)	(2)	(3)	(4)
SVM	0.74	0.74	0.74	0.73	0.66	0.64	0.64	0.61	0.73	0.72	0.72	0.70
Naive Bayes	0.48	0.34	0.34	0.27	0.27	0.28	0.28	0.18	0.33	0.37	0.37	0.26
Random Forest	0.62	0.63	0.63	0.62	0.6	0.6	0.6	0.59	0.52	0.53	0.53	0.50
Neural Network	0.02	0.13	0.13	0.03	0.02	0.13	0.13	0.03	0.01	0.13	0.13	0.03

4.4 Scenario 3: Text Classification with FastText

We conducted text representation in this experiment using FastText, where the dataset was modeled as vectors. The results of the trained models using FastText are shown in the Table 4. After training and testing, the comparative results show that the Random Forest model with FastText achieved the best performance with an accuracy of 0.82 and an F1 score of 0.81.

Table 4. FastText training model at the word level

Models	Precision	Recall	Accuracy	F1
SVM	0.66	0.69	0.69	0.62
Naive Bayes	0.67	0.70	0.70	0.65
Random Forest	0.82	0.82	0.82	0.81
Neural Network	0.50	0.57	0.57	0.52

4.5 Evaluate the Experimental Results

The above experimental results show the following graph 2. The comparison results on the chart 2 show that the Random Forest model with FastText gives the best results with accuracy and F1 measure of 0.82 and 0.81, respectively.

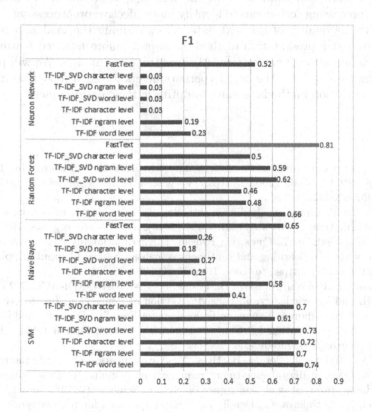

Fig. 2. Different text representation methods in F1-Score

5   Conclusion

In this paper, we presented an approach for text classification using various machine learning models. We implemented different text representation methods, such as TF-IDF and FastText. For each method, we performed representation at different levels, including word, n-gram, and character levels for TF-IDF. Additionally, we applied the SVD technique to reduce the dimensionality of the feature space for evaluation and comparison with other methods, such as TF-IDF without SVD and FastText. We trained different models, including SVM, Random Forest, Neural Network, and Naive Bayes, to validate and evaluate the results. The dataset consisted of 3,295 texts belonging to 16 different topics. The experiments revealed that the Random Forest model combined with FastText performed significantly better than the other models, achieving an accuracy of 0.82 and an F1 score of 0.81.

Further work can continue with the following approaches: (1) Search for better preprocessing techniques to identify more effective preprocessing methods to improve the quality of the text data before training the models. (2) Apply alternative text representation methods to capture more nuanced features and semantic information from the text. (3) Fine-tuning of models: We will perform fine-tuning to search for the best hyperparameters for each model on different text representation methods, aiming to optimize their performance.

References

1. Aizawa, A.: An information-theoretic perspective of TF-IDF measures. Inf. Process. Manage. **39**(1), 45–65 (2003). https://www.sciencedirect.com/science/article/pii/S0306457302000213
2. Bojanowski, P., Grave, E., Joulin, A., Mikolov, T.: Enriching word vectors with sub-word information. CoRR abs/1607.04606 (2016). http://arxiv.org/abs/1607.04606
3. Huan, J.L., Sekh, A.A., Quek, C., Prasad, D.K.: Emotionally charged text classification with deep learning and sentiment semantic. Neural Comput. Appl. **34**(3), 2341–2351 (2022). https://doi.org/10.1007/s00521-021-06542-1
4. Tavchioski, I., Koloski, B., Škrlj, B., Pollak, S.: E8-IJS@LT-EDI-ACL2022 - BERT, AutoML and knowledge-graph backed detection of depression. In: Proceedings of the Second Workshop on Language Technology for Equality, Diversity and Inclusion, pp. 251–257. Association for Computational Linguistics, Dublin (2022). https://aclanthology.org/2022.ltedi-1.36
5. Rühr, A., Streich, D., Berger, B., Hess, T.: A classification of decision automation and delegation in digital investment management systems. In: Proceedings of the 52nd Hawaii International Conference on System Sciences (2019)
6. Eligüzel, N., Çetinkaya, C., Dereli, T.: A novel approach for text categorization by applying hybrid genetic bat algorithm through feature extraction and feature selection methods. Expert Syst. Appl. **202**, 117433 (2022). https://www.sciencedirect.com/science/article/pii/S0957417422007709
7. Zeshan, K., Umar, N., Muhammad, A.T.: Short text classification using TF-IDF features and fast text learner. In: Working Notes Proceedings of the MediaEval 2021 Workshop (2021)

Optimization

Continuous Length-Bounded Paths Interdiction

Raed Alharbi[1], Lan N. Nguyen[2], and My T. Thai[2(✉)]

[1] Saudi Electronic University, Riyadh 11673, Saudi Arabia
ri.alharbi@seu.edu.sa
[2] University of Florida, Gainesville, FL 32611, USA
{lan.nguyen,mythai}@ufl.edu

Abstract. Network vulnerability assessment, in which a communication between nodes is functional if their distance under a given metric is lower than a pre-defined threshold, has received significant attention recently. However, those works only focused on discrete domain while many practical applications require us to investigate in the continuous domain. Motivated by this observation, we study a **Length-bounded Paths Interdiction in Continuous Domain** (cLPI) problem: given a network $G = (V, E)$, in which each edge $e \in E$ is associated with a function $f_e(x)$ in continuous domain, and a set of target pairs of nodes, find a distribution $\mathbf{x} : E \to \mathbb{R}^2$ with minimum $\sum_{e \in E} \mathbf{x}(e)$ that ensures any path p, connecting a target pair, satisfies $\sum_{e \in p} f_e(\mathbf{x}(e)) \geq T$. We first propose a general framework to solve cLPI by designing two oracles, namely *Threshold Blocking* (TB) oracle and *Critical Path Listing* (CPL) oracle, which communicate back and forth to construct a feasible solution with theoretical performance guarantees. Based on this framework, we propose a bicriteria approximation algorithm to cLPI. This bicriteria guarantee allows us to control the solutions's trade-off between the running time and the performance accuracy.

1 Introduction

Components of a network never have the same important level. There always exists a group of nodes or edges which plays more critical role than the others on determining networks' performance. Literature has spent significant effort on studying and identifying such group both theoretically and practically. The very first efforts mostly were invested for the connectivity metric, in which a connection between two nodes is functional if there exists a path connecting them. This metric could be found in the Multicut problem [3,5,12,13], Multiway problem [22], or Graph Partitioning [2,15].

However, as modern networks are evolving, connectivity is no longer sufficient on guaranteeing networks' functionality or quality of services. Instead of removing, a slight change on components' behavior can downgrade the whole

R. Alharbi and Lan N. Nguyen—Equal contribution.

system's performance. For example, a congestion or traffic jams [6,7] on some roads can damage a delivery business; or a change on priority level [1] of packet types on some routers can significantly delay communication between end systems, downgrading their quality of services.

Motivated by these observations, many recent researches turn the attention on network malfunction without damaging connectivity. For example, Kuhnle et al. [17] studied the problem of LB-MULTICUT: given a weighted network, a set of pairs of nodes and a threshold T, their work aims to identify a minimum set of edges whose removal cause the distance between a pair exceed T. By discarding the "remove" flavour, Nguyen et al. [20] extended this concept to introduce QoSD problem, in which an edge weight can be varied with an amount of efforts and the problem asks for a minimum amount of efforts for the same objective as in LB-MULTICUT. Other works can be found in [8–10,18]. However, those works share the same trait that they are all discrete problems, thereby leaving the continuous domain largely opened.

Indeed, many applications require us to investigate the above problem in the continuous domain. For example, in information and telecommunication engineering, a channel capacity in communication network is theoretically measured by the signal-to-interference-plus-noise ratio (SINR) [14] with wireless communication and signal-to-noise ratio (SNR) [16] with wired channel. Such measurements are related to the power of the interfering signal and noises, which consists of continuous variables. The information transfer between two systems, thus, is determined by the delays on propagation channels, which can be modified by those variables. Another example can be seen in diffusion protocol [11] in Bitcoin P2P network, in which a node u relays a message to its neighbors with an independent, exponential delay rate λ_u. Increasing some values of λ_us can delay the packet propagation between major miners, damaging the network consensus.

Motivated by these applications, in this paper, we extend the QoSD problem into continuous domain by introducing the cLPI problem as follows: Given a directed network $G = (V, E)$, a set S of target pairs of nodes and a threshold T, an edge $e \in E$ is associated with a continuous and monotone increasing function $f_e : \mathbb{R}^{\geq} \to \mathbb{R}^{\geq}$, the cLPI problem asks for a distribution $\mathbf{x} : E \to \mathbb{R}^{\geq}$ with minimum $\sum_{e \in E} \mathbf{x}(e)$ such that any path p, connecting a pair in S, satisfies $\sum_{e \in p} f_e(\mathbf{x}(e)) \geq T$. For simplicity, we write $\mathbf{x}$ under a vector form $\{x_e\}_{e \in E}$ where $x_e = \mathbf{x}(e)$, thus $\sum_{e \in E} \mathbf{x}(e) = \|\mathbf{x}\|$ (Again for simplicity, we use notation $\|\cdot\|$ to indicate norm 1 of a vector). Another presentation of cLPI's objective is to find $\mathbf{x}$ with minimum $\|\mathbf{x}\|$ that guarantees there exists no T-length-bounded multi-commodity flow on G. A T-length-bounded multi-commodity flow is a flow between the target pairs that can be decomposed into flow paths of length at most T. The solution $\mathbf{x}$ of cLPI can be used as a metric to measure the network's functionality: large $\|\mathbf{x}\|$ indicates the network is resilient to external interference or noises and able to maintain quality of service under extreme environment. Furthermore, a value of x_e indicates the important level of e to the network desired functionality.

Related Work and Challenges. Since cLPI is a new problem, it does not have much related work. Indeed, solving cLPI with bounded performance guarantee is challenging. First, a simple solution, which discretizes functions f_e and directly adopts the solutions of QoSD, actually has a problem. The discretization of f_e is simply a work of taking an integer x and returning the value $f_e(x \cdot \delta)$, where δ is called discretizing step. If δ is too large, the returned solution will be far from optimal due to discretization error; otherwise small δ creates significantly large inputs for QoSD, causing a burden on memory usage and undesirable running time. Therefore, a solution, which can directly applied into continuous domain, is more desired. Second, f_es could be any function, thus a typical Convex Optimization [4,19] solution cannot be applied. Also, any solution for Constrained Optimization can easily fall into local optima with complicated f_es, so no performance ratio is guaranteed. Furthermore, enumerating all constraints, each is corresponding to a path in the network, is intractable as the number of paths can be upto $\sum_{k=2}^{n} \binom{n}{k} k!$ where n is number of nodes in the network.

Our Contributions. This paper introduces and investigates the cLPI problem. Accordingly, we propose a general framework for solving cLPI, separating tasks into two different oracles, called *Critical Paths Listing* (CPL) and *Threshold Blocking* (TB). CPL's job is to restrict the amount of paths considered for finding feasible solution of cLPI. TB deals with the task of finding $\mathbf{x}$ in continuous domain, guaranteeing all paths, returned by CPL, have length exceed a certain threshold. We next propose Threshold Expansion for the TB oracle and Feasible Set Construction to for CPL. Finally, we show that our solution obtain an approximation ratio which allows a user to control the trade-off between running time versus accuracy.

2 Preliminaries

2.1 Problem Formulation

We abstract a network using a directed graph $G = (V, E)$ with $|V| = n$ nodes and $|E| = m$ directed edges. Each edge e is associated with a function $f_e : \mathbb{R}^{\geq} \to \mathbb{R}^{\geq}$ which indicates the weight of e w.r.t a budget distributed for e. In another word, if we spend x on edge e, the weight of edge e will become $f_e(x)$. f_e is monotonically increasing for all $e \in E$.

A budget distribution contains budget for each edge. Thus, given an arbitrary order of edges $E = \{e_1, ...e_m\}$, we denotes a budget distribution under the form of a vector $\mathbf{x} = \{x_1, ...x_m\}$ where x_i is a budget spent on the edge e_i. For simplicity, we use the notation e to present an edge in E and its index in E also. So x_e means the budget spent on edge e, and the entry in $\mathbf{x}$ corresponding to e also. The overall budget on all edges, therefore, is $\|\mathbf{x}\| = \sum_{e \in E} x_e$.

A path $p = \{u_0, u_1, ...u_l\} \in G$ is a sequence of vertices such that $(u_{i-1}, u_i) \in E$ for $i = 1, .., l$. A path can also be understood as the sequence of edges $\{(u_0, u_1), (u_1, u_2), ...(u_{l-1}, u_l)\}$. In this work, a path is used interchangeably as a sequence of edges or a sequence of nodes. A *single path* is a path that there exists no node who appears more than one in the path. Under a budget vector $\mathbf{x}$, the length of a path p is defined as $\sum_{e \in p} f_e(x_e)$. cLPI is formally defined as follows:

Definition 1. Length-bounded Paths Interdiction in Continuous Domain (cLPI). *Given a directed graph $G = (V, E)$, a set $f = \{f_e : \mathbb{R}^{\geq} \to \mathbb{R}^{\geq}\}$ of edge weight functions and a target set of pairs of nodes $S = \{(s_1, t_1), ...(s_k, t_k)\}$, determine a budget distribution $\mathbf{x}$ with minimum budget $\|\mathbf{x}\|$ such that under $\mathbf{x}$, any path connecting a pair of S has length at least T.*

For each pair $(s, t) \in S$, we call s a *start node* and t a *end node*. Let $\mathcal{P}_i$ denote a set of simple paths connecting the pair $(s_i, t_i) \in S$, whose initial length do not exceed T, i.e. $\sum_{e \in p} f_e(0) < T$ for all $p \in \mathcal{P}_i$. Let $\mathcal{F} = \cup_{i=1}^k \mathcal{P}_i$, we call a path $p \in \mathcal{F}$ a *feasible path* and $\mathcal{F}$ is a set of all feasible paths in G. A non-feasible path either connects no pair in S or has initial length exceed T.

Before going further, we now look at several notations, mathematical operators on vector space $\mathbb{R}^m$, which are used along the theoretical proofs of our algorithms. Given $\mathbf{x} = \{x_1, ...x_m\}, \mathbf{y} = \{y_1, ...y_m\} \in \mathbb{R}^m$, we have:

$$\mathbf{x} + \mathbf{y} = \{x_1 + y_1, ...x_m + y_m\}$$
$$\mathbf{x} \setminus \mathbf{y} = \{\max(x_1 - y_1, 0), ... \max(x_n - y_n, 0)\}$$

Moreover, we say $\mathbf{x} \leq \mathbf{y}$ if $x_i \leq y_i$ for all $i \in [1, m]$, the similar rule is applied to $<, \geq, >$.

Node version of the problem. The node version of cLPI asks for the minimum budget to increase node weights (rather than edge weights) in the problem definition above. Our solution can be easily adapted to the node version and keep the same theoretical performance guarantee.

2.2   General Model of Our Solutions

In this part, we present an overview model of our solutions, including a general framework and its performance guarantee.

About performance guarantees, given the problem instance with a threshold T, denote OPT as an optimal solution. We call a budget distribution $\mathbf{x}$ is ε-**feasible** to cLPI iff under $\mathbf{x}$, the distance between each target pair is at least $T - \varepsilon$. Our algorithms are bicriteria approximation algorithms, returning a ε-feasible solution $\mathbf{x}$ whose overall budget is bounded within a factor $A(G, \varepsilon^{-1})$ of OPT, where $A(G, \varepsilon^{-1})$ depends on structure of the input graph and is monotone increasing with ε^{-1}. ε is treated as a trade-off between the algorithms' accuracy and running time. To be specific, the smaller ε is, the closer pairs' distances are to T but the longer it takes for the algorithms to finish. ε is adjustable, allowing users to control running time versus accuracy as desired.

About general framework, our solutions contain two separate oracles, called *Threshold Blocking* (TB) and *Critical Paths Listing* (CPL). These two oracles communicate back and forth with the other to construct a solution to cLPI, given an input instance of cLPI and a parameter ε. These two oracles are proposed to tackle two challenges of cLPI as stated before, to be specific:

- *Threshold Blocking* - a primary role of TB is to solve a sub-problem of cLPI: Given a target set $\mathcal{P}$ of single paths and a threshold $T_u \leq T$, TB aims to find a minimum additional budget on edges in order to make each path in $\mathcal{P}$ has length exceeding T_u. For simplicity, we call this task TB problem.
- *Critical Paths Listing* - this oracle restricts the number of paths which need to be considered in the algorithm, thus significantly reducing the searching space and burdens on algorithms' running time and memory for storage.

Separating into two oracles allows us to design different solutions to each of the oracles. Assume if there exists one solution for each oracle, the flow of our solution is as follows:

1. The algorithm starts with $x_e = 0$ for all $e \in E$ (i.e. $\mathbf{x} = \{0\}_e$).
2. Given the current state of $\mathbf{x}$, by using a technique to restrict searching space, CPL oracle searches for a set of critical paths, who are feasible paths and shorter than a pre-determined threshold $T_u \leq T$.
3. Then those paths along with a current state of $\mathbf{x}$ are given as an input for the TB oracle, which then finds an additional budget $\mathbf{v}$ for $\mathbf{x}$ to make all input paths' length exceed T_u.
4. The additional budget $\mathbf{v}$ is then used for CPL to check the feasibility. If adding $\mathbf{v}$ makes $\mathbf{x}$ ε-feasible, the algorithm returns $\mathbf{x} + \mathbf{v}$ and terminates. Otherwise, $\mathbf{v}$ is used to drive the searching space of CPL and find a new value for $\mathbf{x}$ and T_u; then step (2) is repeated.

Due to the space limit, we only present one solution to each oracle.

3   Threshold Blocking Oracle

In this section, we present our solution to the Threshold Blocking (TB) Oracle, called *Threshold Expansion* (TE).

3.1   Requirements of TB

To recap, TB receives a set $\mathcal{P}$ of critical paths from CPL, the current budget $\mathbf{x}$ and an upper threshold T_u. The objective of TB is to find an additional budget vector $\mathbf{v} = \{v_1, ...v_m\}$ with minimum $\sum_e v_e$ such that under the budget $\mathbf{x} + \mathbf{v} = \{x_e + v_e\}_e$, each path in $\mathcal{P}$ has length exceeding T_u, i.e. $\sum_{e \in p} f_e(x_e + v_e) \geq T_u$ for all $p \in \mathcal{P}$. Another information that TB gets is $T_l \geq 0$, which is a lower bound of each path's length, i.e. $\sum_{e \in p} f_e(x_e) \geq T_l$ for all $p \in \mathcal{P}$. Without lost of generality, we assume that each path in $\mathcal{P}$, under $\mathbf{x}$, has length in range $[T_l, T_u)$.

The bicriteria guarantee of our algorithms originates from the TB algorithms. The desired accuracy ε is given to the TB oracle so the TB algorithm guarantees each path in $\mathcal{P}$ has length at least $T_u - \varepsilon$. To do so, an objective function of TB is defined as follows:

$$b_{\mathcal{P},\mathbf{x}}(\mathbf{v}) = \sum_{p\in\mathcal{P}} \min\Big(\sum_{e\in p} f_e(x_e + v_e), T_u\Big)$$

Trivially, a budget vector $\mathbf{v}$ satisfies TB's objective iff $b_{\mathcal{P},\mathbf{x}}(\mathbf{v}) = |\mathcal{P}| \times T_u$. $b_{\mathcal{P},\mathbf{x}}(\cdot)$ can be seen as a function with $m = |E|$ variables. Let's take more insight into $b_{\mathcal{P},\mathbf{x}}(\cdot)$ as it is important for devising algorithms in the TB oracle. Define:

$$l_{p,\mathbf{x},e}(x) = \sum_{e'\in p \& e'\neq e} f_{e'}(x_{e'}) + \mathbf{1}_{e\in p}f_e(x_e + x)$$

$$r_{\mathcal{P},\mathbf{x},e}(x) = \sum_{p\in\mathcal{P}}\Big(\min\big(T_u, l_{p,\mathbf{x},e}(x)\big) - \min\big(T_u, l_{p,\mathbf{x},e}(0)\big)\Big)$$

Basically, $r_{\mathcal{P},\mathbf{x},e}(\cdot)$ measures the increasing value of $b_{\mathcal{P},\mathbf{x}}(\{0\})$ by adding a budget of x into entry e. It is easy to see that $r_{\mathcal{P},\mathbf{x},e}(x)$ is a monotone increasing function w.r.t x.

Assuming $\{p_1,...p_l\} \subseteq \mathcal{P}$ are paths containing e and are sorted in descending order w.r.t to their length under $\mathbf{x}$. Define a_i as a minimum additional budget on edge e to make path p_i's length exceed T_u, i.e. $a_i = \arg\min_x \big\{l_{p_i,\mathbf{x},e}(x) \geq T_u\big\}$. Let $a_0 = 0$. $\{a_i\}$ are in ascending order. $r_{\mathcal{P},\mathbf{x},e}(x)$ can be rewritten as:

$$r_{\mathcal{P},\mathbf{x},e}(x) = i\cdot T_u + \sum_{j>i} l_{p_j,\mathbf{x},e}(x) - Q_{\mathcal{P},\mathbf{x},e} \text{ with } a_i \leq x \leq a_{i+1} \qquad (1)$$

where $Q_{\mathcal{P},\mathbf{x},e} = \sum_{p;e\in p}\sum_{e'\in p} f_{e'}(x_{e'})$, which does not depend on either x or i. Equation (1) allows us to discard the min term in the original $r_{\mathcal{P},\mathbf{x},e}(\cdot)$ to exploit the function's property within each range $[a_i, a_{i+1}]$.

3.2 Threshold Expansion

In a nutshell, our Threshold Expansion algorithm, TE, is a threshold greedy algorithm which aims to tackle the continuous domain challenges, especially when the objective function is not concave. TE starts with setting a sufficient large value of M, which is the upper bound of $\frac{r_{\mathcal{P},\mathbf{w},e}(x)}{x}$ for all $e \in E$, $x \geq 0$ and $\mathbf{w} \geq \mathbf{x}$. To find M, the algorithm utilizes the fact that $f_e(\cdot)$ is continuous and differentiable everywhere for all $e \in E$ as the following lemma.

Lemma 1. *By setting* $M = |\mathcal{P}| \times \max_{x\geq 0, e\in E, f_e(x)\leq T_u} \frac{\partial f_e}{\partial x}$, *the* TE *algorithm guarantees*

$$M \geq \frac{r_{\mathcal{P},\mathbf{w},e}(x)}{x} \text{ for all } \mathbf{w} \geq \mathbf{x}, e \in E, x \geq 0$$

We omit this proof due to space limit.

The algorithm works on top of the $\mathbf{x}'$ vector, which is just a copy of $\mathbf{x}$ initially. This step is to separate the work on $\mathbf{x}$ between the TB and CPL oracle, e.g. CPL

Algorithm 1. Threshold Expansion

Input

- $G = (V, E)$ - the input graph
- $f_e : \mathbb{R}^{\geq} \to \mathbb{R}^{\geq}$ for all $e \in E$
- $\mathcal{P}$ - the set of paths
- T_u - target threshold
- ϵ - the performance parameter of TE
- ε - the accuracy parameter
- $\mathbf{x}$ - current budget vector

Output: $\mathbf{v}$ - an additional budget vector to $\mathbf{x}$ to make each path in $\mathcal{P}$ has length exceeding $T_u - \varepsilon$

1: Sort E in an arbitrary order
2: $\mathbf{v} = \{0\}$, $\mathbf{x}' = \mathbf{x}$
3: $M = |\mathcal{P}| \times \max_{x \geq 0, e \in E, f_e(x) \leq T_u} \frac{\partial f_e}{\partial x}$
4: $e \leftarrow$ the first edge in E
5: **while** $\exists p \in \mathcal{P}$ that p's length $< T_u - \varepsilon$ **do**
6: $\quad \hat{x} = \arg\max_x \left\{ \frac{r_{\mathcal{P}, \mathbf{x}', e}(x)}{x} \geq M \right\}$
7: $\quad \mathbf{l} =$ a vector with $\hat{x}$ at entry e and 0 elsewhere
8: $\quad \mathbf{x}' = \mathbf{x}' + \mathbf{l}$, $\mathbf{v} = \mathbf{v} + \mathbf{l}$
9: $\quad$ **if** e is the last edge in E **then**
10: $\quad\quad M = (1 - \epsilon)M$
11: $\quad\quad e \leftarrow$ start over with the first edge
12: $\quad$ **else**
13: $\quad\quad e \leftarrow$ the next edge.

Return v

---

may not accept the result of TB (which is shown in the CPL section). Edges in E are sorted in an arbitrary order. TE considers edges sequentially in that order and for each edge e, TE finds a maximum addition budget $\hat{x}$ for e such that $\frac{r_{\mathcal{P}, \mathbf{x}', e}(\hat{x})}{\hat{x}} \geq M$ and add $\hat{x}$ into e.

Different to previous work in the discrete domain and submodular maximization, the function $\frac{r_{\mathcal{P}, \mathbf{x}', e}(\hat{x})}{\hat{x}}$ is not monotone increasing. Thus the technique of using binary search as in [21] is no longer applicable. To find $\hat{x}$, we utilize Eq. (1) by identifying local extreme points of $\frac{r_{\mathcal{P}, \mathbf{x}', e}(x)}{x}$ within each range $[a_i, a_{i+1}]$ using the function's first derivative and exploiting the increasing/decreasing traits of the function. Note that there could be a case that $\hat{x}$ cannot be found, if so we set $\hat{x} = 0$ and no budget is added into the considered edge. After adding $\hat{x}$ into e, the algorithm considers the next edge.

After the algorithm has considered the last edge in E in the order as stated, it means the algorithm has finished a round of edges, TE reduces M by a factor of $1 - \epsilon$ and starts over with the first edge in the order. Whenever TE adds a budget into an edge, the algorithm constantly checks whether **v** is sufficient to make each path's length exceed $T_u - \varepsilon$ and terminates whenever this condition is satisfied. The pseudo-code of TE is presented in Algorithm 1.

The adaptation into the continuous domain of TE can be seen as in the way the algorithm works. We now turn our attention to TE's performance guarantee. From now on, for simplicity, when we analyze the performance of the algorithm at a certain moment when it is running, we refer M, **v** and **x′** as their values at that moment.

Let's consider at a certain moment, denote $\mathbf{v}^o = \{v_e^o\} = \mathbf{v}^* \setminus \mathbf{v}$. We have the following lemma.

Lemma 2. $v_e^o = 0$ or $\frac{r_{\mathcal{P},\mathbf{x}',e}(v_e^o)}{v_e^o} < \frac{M}{1-\epsilon}$ for all $e \in E$.

We omit this proof due to space limit.

Therefore, even the edge weight functions are not concave or $\frac{r_{\mathcal{P},\mathbf{x}',e}(\hat{x})}{\hat{x}}$ is not monotone increasing, the selection of $\hat{x}$ and Lemma 2 allow us to bound the performance guarantee of TE, which is shown in the following theorem.

Theorem 1. *Given the information* $G, f_e, \mathcal{P}, T_u, T_l, \varepsilon, \mathbf{x}$, *if* **v** *is the budget returned by TE and* $\mathbf{v}^*$ *is the minimum additional budget to make each path in* $\mathcal{P}$ *has length exceeding* T_u, *then:*

$$\|\mathbf{v}\| \leq \frac{\ln\left(|\mathcal{P}|(T_u - T_l)\varepsilon^{-1}\right) + 1}{1 - \epsilon}\|\mathbf{v}^*\|$$

Proof. Let's assume edge e is being considered and $\hat{x}$ is the selected amount to add into e. Again, denote $\mathbf{v}^o = \{v_e^o\} = \mathbf{v}^* \setminus \mathbf{v}$. Without lost of generality, let $\hat{x} > 0$. From Lemma 2, we have:

$$\frac{r_{\mathcal{P},\mathbf{x}',e}(\hat{x})}{\hat{x}} \geq (1 - \epsilon)\frac{r_{\mathcal{P},\mathbf{x}',e}(v_{e'}^o)}{v_{e'}^o}$$

for all $e' \in E$ that $v_{e'}^o > 0$

Denote $\mathbf{x}' = \{x_e\}_{e \in E}$, $\mathbf{h}_e = \{x_{e'} + 1_{e'>e}v_{e'}^o\}_{e' \in E}$. As $\mathbf{h}_e \geq \mathbf{x}'$ but they have the same value at entry e, we have:

$$r_{\mathcal{P},\mathbf{h}_e,e}(v_e^o) \leq r_{\mathcal{P},\mathbf{x}',e}(v_e^o)$$

Therefore,

$$b_{\mathcal{P},\mathbf{x}'}(\mathbf{v}^o) - b_{\mathcal{P},\mathbf{x}'}(\{0\}) = \sum_{e \in E} r_{\mathcal{P},\mathbf{h}_e,e}(v_e^o) \leq \sum_{e \in E} r_{\mathcal{P},\mathbf{x}',e}(v_e^o)$$

$$\leq \sum_{e' \in E} \frac{v_{e'}^o}{\hat{x}(1 - \epsilon)}r_{\mathcal{P},\mathbf{x}',e}(\hat{x}) \leq \frac{\|\mathbf{v}^*\|}{\hat{x}(1 - \epsilon)}r_{\mathcal{P},\mathbf{x}',e}(\hat{x})$$

Note that $b_{\mathcal{P},\mathbf{x}'}(\mathbf{v}^o) = |\mathcal{P}| \times T_u$.

Now, let's assume the algorithm terminates after adding budget into edges L times, denote $\hat{x}_1, ...\hat{x}_L$ as an added budget at each times ($\|\mathbf{v}\| = \sum_{i=1}^{L} \hat{x}_i$). Also, denote $\mathbf{x}'_t$, $\mathbf{v}_t$ as $\mathbf{x}'$, $\mathbf{v}$ before adding $\hat{x}_t$ at time t. We have:

$$|\mathcal{P}| \times T_u - b_{\mathcal{P},\mathbf{x}}(\mathbf{v}_t) = |\mathcal{P}| \times T_u - b_{\mathcal{P},\mathbf{x}'_t}(\{0\}) \leq \frac{\|\mathbf{v}^*\|}{\hat{x}_t(1-\epsilon)} r_{\mathcal{P},\mathbf{x}'_t,e}(\hat{x}_t)$$

$$= \frac{\|\mathbf{v}^*\|}{\hat{x}_t(1-\epsilon)} \left(b_{\mathcal{P},\mathbf{x}}(\mathbf{v}_{t+1}) - b_{\mathcal{P},\mathbf{x}}(\mathbf{v}_t) \right)$$

Thus:

$$|\mathcal{P}| \times T_u - b_{\mathcal{P},\mathbf{x}}(\mathbf{v}_{t+1}) \leq \left(1 - \frac{\hat{x}_t(1-\epsilon)}{\|\mathbf{v}^*\|} \right) \left(|\mathcal{P}| \times T_u - b_{\mathcal{P},\mathbf{x}}(\mathbf{v}_t) \right)$$

Therefore, we have:

$$|\mathcal{P}| \times T_u - b_{\mathcal{P},\mathbf{x}}(\mathbf{v}_{L-1}) \leq \prod_{t=1}^{L-1} \left(1 - \frac{\hat{x}_t(1-\epsilon)}{\|\mathbf{v}^*\|} \right) \left(|\mathcal{P}| \times T_u - b_{\mathcal{P},\mathbf{x}}(0) \right)$$

$$\leq \left(1 - \frac{\sum_t^{L-1} \hat{x}_t(1-\epsilon)}{\|\mathbf{v}^*\|(L-1)} \right)^{L-1} |\mathcal{P}|(T_u - T_l) \leq e^{-\frac{\|\mathbf{v}^{L-1}\|}{\|\mathbf{v}^*\|}(1-\epsilon)} |\mathcal{P}|(T_u - T_l)$$

After $L - 1$ updates, there should exist at least a path in $\mathcal{P}$ whose length is shorter than $T_u - \varepsilon$ (otherwise the algorithm should terminate after $L - 1$ updates). Thus $|\mathcal{P}|T_u - b_{\mathcal{P},\mathbf{x}}(\mathbf{v}_{L-1}) \geq \varepsilon$, which means:

$$\|\mathbf{v}_{L-1}\| \leq \|\mathbf{v}^*\| \frac{\ln\left(|\mathcal{P}|(T_u - T_l)\varepsilon^{-1} \right)}{1-\epsilon}$$

Now, let consider the final update, we have:

$$\hat{x}_L \leq \frac{\|\mathbf{v}^*\|}{1-\epsilon} \cdot \frac{b_{\mathcal{P},\mathbf{x}}(\mathbf{v}_L) - b_{\mathcal{P},\mathbf{x}}(\mathbf{v}_{L-1})}{|\mathcal{P}| \times T_u - b_{\mathcal{P},\mathbf{x}}(\mathbf{v}_{L-1})} \leq \frac{\|\mathbf{v}^*\|}{1-\epsilon}$$

Finally, we have:

$$\|\mathbf{v}\| = \|\mathbf{v}_{L-1}\| + \hat{x}_L \leq \|\mathbf{v}^*\| \frac{\ln\left(|\mathcal{P}|(T_u - T_l)\varepsilon^{-1} \right) + 1}{1-\epsilon}$$

which completes the proof.

4   Critical Path Listing Oracle

Algorithm 2. Feasible Set Construction
___
Input

- $G = (V, E)$ - the input graph
- $f_e : \mathbb{R}^2 \to \mathbb{R}^2$ for all $e \in E$
- T - target threshold
- ε - accuracy parameter
- S - set of target pairs
- TB - threshold blocking oracle

Output x

1: $\mathcal{P} = \emptyset, \mathbf{x} = \mathbf{v} = \{0\}$
2: **while** $\exists (s, t) \in S$ that $d(s, t) < T - \varepsilon$ in G **do**
3:      Construct shortest path trees for all start nodes
4:      $\mathcal{L} = \emptyset$
5:      **for** each pair $(s, t) \in S$ **do**
6:          $H \leftarrow$ a copy of shortest path tree with root s
7:          $X = \emptyset$
8:          **while** $d(s, t) < T - \varepsilon$ in H **do**
9:              $p \leftarrow$ the shortest path from s to t in H
10:              $\mathcal{L} = \mathcal{L} \cup \{p\}$
11:              Randomly pick $e = (u, v) \in p$ and put into X
12:              Reconstruct H without edges of X
13:      $\mathcal{P} = \mathcal{P} \cup \mathcal{L}$
14:      $\mathbf{v} =$ run TB oracle with input $G, f_e, \mathcal{P}, T, \varepsilon, \mathbf{x}$
15:      Set edge e's weight to be $f_e(v_e)$ for all $e \in E$

Return v

In this section, we present *Feasible Set Construction* (FC) for the CPL oracle. The role of the CPL oracle is to reduce the searching space when constructing the returned solution $\mathbf{x}$. It works as a backbone for the overall process of finding $\mathbf{x}$. It is the one receiving the input information of the cLPI problem, then communicating back and forth with TB to construct $\mathbf{x}$ and return $\mathbf{x}$ when $\mathbf{x}$ guarantees that a distance between each target pair exceeds $T - \varepsilon$.

In general, FC (shown in Algorithm 2) aims to construct a set $\mathcal{P}$ of candidate paths, which is a subset of $\mathcal{F}$ but, if being used as an input for TB with a threshold $T_u = T$, can return $\mathbf{v}$ that is a ε-feasible solution of cLPI. $\mathcal{P}$ is constructed in order to avoid fully listing all paths in $\mathcal{F}$ when $\mathcal{F}$ is significantly large. FC starts with $\mathcal{P} = \emptyset$ and then builds it incrementally and iteratively. For each iteration, the algorithm uses the TB oracle to find a budget vector $\mathbf{x}$ to make each path in $\mathcal{P}$ has length exceeding $T - \varepsilon$. Then, the length of an edge e is set to be $f_e(x_e)$.

Next, FC checks whether $\mathbf{x}$ is ε-feasible. If not, the algorithm adds a set $\mathcal{L}$ of feasible paths into $\mathcal{P}$ where $\mathcal{L}$ contains paths, each of whom has length shorter than $T - \varepsilon$ ($\mathcal{L} \cap \mathcal{P} = \emptyset$); then reset all edges' length (i.e. the length of e turns back to $f_e(0)$). If yes, the algorithm returns $\mathbf{x}$ and terminates.

To optimize the number of iterations, after updating e's length to be $f_e(x_e)$ for all $e \in E$, FC builds shortest-path trees, a root of each tree is a *start node* of a target pair. Each pair $(s,t) \in S$ is then associated with a copy H of the shortest-path tree rooted at s and a set X of edges, which is initially set to be empty. For each pair $(s,t) \in S$, the algorithm works in an iterative fashion:

1. FC adds the shortest path $p \subseteq H$ from s to t into $\mathcal{L}$.
2. Then FC randomly picks an edge $e = (u, v) \in p$ and put e into X.
3. A sub-tree of H rooted at u is re-constructed with the condition that H contains no edge in X.
4. If there still exists a path from s to t in H with length shorter than $T - \epsilon$, the algorithm is back to step (1).

We have the following theorem.

Theorem 2. *The approximation guarantee of FC equals to the approximation guarantee of the algorithm used in the TB oracle.*

Proof. This Theorem uses a similar concept as Lemma 4.1 [20], in which we observe that: Since $\mathcal{P}$ is a subset of $\mathcal{F}$, the optimal budget $\|\mathbf{x}^*\|$ to cLPI is at least the optimal budget $\|\mathbf{x}^o\|$ to make all paths' length of $\mathcal{P}$ exceed T. Denote α as an approximation guarantee of the TB oracle, i.e. $\|\mathbf{x}\| \leq \alpha \|\mathbf{x}^o\|$. As $\mathbf{x}$ is guaranteed to be ε-feasible to the cLPI instance, α is also the approximation guarantee of FC to cLPI.

Combining Theorems 1 and 2, our solution to cLPI has a bicriteria approximation ratio of $\left(\ln(|\mathcal{P}_{\mathrm{TE}}| \cdot T \cdot \varepsilon^{-1}) + 1 \right)(1 - \epsilon)^{-1}$, where $\mathcal{P}_{\mathrm{TE}}$ is the final sets $\mathcal{P}$ of candidate paths using TE.

5   Conclusion

In this paper, we introduced the cLPI problem, which allows us to better assess the modern network vulnerability. To tackle the challenges of cLPI, we developed a solution framework that consists of two oracles, namely *Threshold Blocking* (TB) oracle and *Critical Path Listing* (CPL) oracle, which communicate back and forth to construct a feasible solution with theoretical performance guarantees. We further devised a bicriteria approximation algorithm to cLPI, of which we offer one solution to each oracle. For future work, we may consider different variants of cLPI. For example, an edge could be associated with multiple functions, serving for multiple objectives of networked functionality. Also, each function can have multiple variables and each variable could appear on more than one functions, making the problem become much more complicated. A solution, which can balance multiple objectives, is desirable. Furthermore, another perspective considering network flows is of interest, which we aim to modify edge weights to guarantee the max flow of the network is at most a certain threshold.

Acknowledgements. This work was supported in part by NSF CNS-1814614 and NSF IIS-1908594.

References

1. Priority packet (2019). https://www.sciencedirect.com/topics/computer-science/priority-packet. Accessed 18 July 2019
2. Andreev, K., Racke, H.: Balanced graph partitioning. Theory Comput. Syst. **39**(6), 929–939 (2006)
3. Birge, J.R., Louveaux, F.V.: A multicut algorithm for two-stage stochastic linear programs. Eur. J. Oper. Res. **34**(3), 384–392 (1988)
4. Boyd, S., Vandenberghe, L.: Convex Optimization. Cambridge University Press, Cambridge (2004)
5. Chawla, S., Krauthgamer, R., Kumar, R., Rabani, Y., Sivakumar, D.: On the hardness of approximating multicut and sparsest-cut. Comput. Complex. **15**(2), 94–114 (2006)
6. Checkoway, S., et al.: Comprehensive experimental analyses of automotive attack surfaces. In: USENIX Security Symposium, pp. 77–92, San Francisco (2011)
7. Chen, Q.A., Yin, Y., Feng, Y., Mao, Z.M., Liu, H.X.: Exposing congestion attack on emerging connected vehicle based traffic signal control. In: Network and Distributed Systems Security (NDSS) Symposium 2018 (2018)
8. Dinh, T.N., Thai, M.T.: Precise structural vulnerability assessment via mathematical programming. In: 2011-MILCOM 2011 Military Communications Conference, pp. 1351–1356. IEEE (2011)
9. Dinh, T.N., Thai, M.T.: Assessing attack vulnerability in networks with uncertainty. In: 2015 IEEE Conference on Computer Communications (INFOCOM), pp. 2380–2388. IEEE (2015)
10. Dinh, T.N., Thai, M.T.: Network under joint node and link attacks: vulnerability assessment methods and analysis. IEEE/ACM Trans. Netw. **23**(3), 1001–1011 (2015)
11. Fanti, G., Viswanath, P.: Deanonymization in the bitcoin p2p network. In: Advances in Neural Information Processing Systems, pp. 1364–1373 (2017)
12. Garg, N., Vazirani, V.V., Yannakakis, M.: Approximate max-flow min-(multi) cut theorems and their applications. SIAM J. Comput. **25**(2), 235–251 (1996)
13. Garg, N., Vazirani, V.V., Yannakakis, M.: Primal-dual approximation algorithms for integral flow and multicut in trees. Algorithmica **18**(1), 3–20 (1997)
14. Jeske, D.R., Sampath, A.: Signal-to-interference-plus-noise ratio estimation for wireless communication systems: methods and analysis. Naval Res. Logist. (NRL) **51**(5), 720–740 (2004)
15. Johnson, D.S., Aragon, C.R., McGeoch, L.A., Schevon, C.: Optimization by simulated annealing: an experimental evaluation; part i, graph partitioning. Oper. Res. **37**(6), 865–892 (1989)
16. Keiser, G.: Optical fiber communications. Wiley Encyclopedia of Telecommunications (2003)
17. Kuhnle, A., Crawford, V.G., Thai, M.T.: Network resilience and the length-bounded multicut problem: reaching the dynamic billion-scale with guarantees. Proc. ACM Meas. Anal. Comput. Syst. **2**(1), 4 (2018)
18. Lee, E.: Improved hardness for cut, interdiction, and firefighter problems. arXiv preprint arXiv:1607.05133 (2016)

19. Nesterov, Y.: Lectures on Convex Optimization. SOIA, vol. 137. Springer, Cham (2018). https://doi.org/10.1007/978-3-319-91578-4
20. Nguyen, L.N., Thai, M.T.: Network resilience assessment via QoS degradation metrics: an algorithmic approach. Proc. ACM Meas. Anal. Comput. Syst. 3(1), 1 (2019)
21. Soma, T., Yoshida, Y.: Maximizing monotone submodular functions over the integer lattice. Math. Program. 172(1–2), 539–563 (2018)
22. Svitkina, Z., Tardos, É.: Min-max multiway cut. In: Jansen, K., Khanna, S., Rolim, J.D.P., Ron, D. (eds.) APPROX/RANDOM -2004. LNCS, vol. 3122, pp. 207–218. Springer, Heidelberg (2004). https://doi.org/10.1007/978-3-540-27821-4_19

A* Search Algorithm for an Optimal Investment Problem in Vehicle-Sharing Systems

Ba Luat Le[1] , Layla Martin[2] , Emrah Demir[3] , and Duc Minh Vu[1(✉)]

[1] ORLab and Faculty of Computer Science, Phenikaa University, Hanoi, Vietnam
minh.vuduc@phenikaa-uni.edu.vn
[2] Department of Industrial Engineering and Eindhoven AI Systems Institute, Eindhoven University of Technology, Eindhoven, The Netherlands
[3] Cardiff Business School, Cardiff University, Cardiff, UK

Abstract. We study an optimal investment problem that arises in the context of the vehicle-sharing system. Given a set of locations to build stations, we need to determine *i*) the sequence of stations to be built and the number of vehicles to acquire in order to obtain the target state where all stations are built, and *ii*) the number of vehicles to acquire and their allocation in order to maximize the total profit returned by operating the system when some or all stations are open. The profitability associated with operating open stations, measured over a specific time period, is represented as a linear optimization problem applied to a collection of open stations. With operating capital, the owner of the system can open new stations. This property introduces a set-dependent aspect to the duration required for opening a new station, and the optimal investment problem can be viewed as a variant of the Traveling Salesman Problem (TSP) with set-dependent cost. We propose an A* search algorithm to address this particular variant of the TSP. Computational experiments highlight the benefits of the proposed algorithm in comparison to the widely recognized Dijkstra algorithm and propose future research to explore new possibilities and applications for both exact and approximate A* algorithms.

Keywords: Autonomous Mobility on-demand · vehicle-sharing · traveling salesman problem · A* algorithm

1 Introduction

Mobility on demand (MoD) is a rapidly growing market[1]. With the advanced technology of autonomous vehicles, Autonomous Mobility on demand (AMoD) is becoming increasingly popular because it alleviates some operational difficulties of MoD. The global market for autonomous mobility is projected to grow from 5 billion USD (in 2019) to 556 billion USD (in 2026)[2], promising safety (94% of accidents caused by human factors), increased performance, improved efficiency, and more affordable services.

---

[1] https://www.alliedmarketresearch.com/mobility-on-demand-market.
[2] https://www.alliedmarketresearch.com/autonomous-vehicle-market.

© The Author(s), under exclusive license to Springer Nature Singapore Pte Ltd. 2024
M. H. Hà et al. (Eds.): CSoNet 2023, LNCS 14479, pp. 162–173, 2024.
https://doi.org/10.1007/978-981-97-0669-3_16

Although auto manufacturers and major technology firms have the resources to quickly establish an AMoD system, smaller operators of shared mobility and public authorities may encounter challenges in securing enough initial capital to launch the service with a sufficient fleet[3]. Consequently, small companies start to operate in a smaller region, as studied in the literature on optimal service region design, e.g., [7,8]. As operators accumulate profits, they can gradually acquire more vehicles and expand their active sites. This research considers such a *refinancing* model of the AMoD system, where the operator aims to achieve the desired service area and the size of the fleet as quickly as possible.

The existing literature covers a spectrum of topics related to AMoD systems, including aspects such as vehicle-sharing system operations, strategic decision-making, and regulatory and subsidy considerations. Relevant sources can be found in works such as [3,5–7]. To the best of our knowledge, the question of what is the optimal investment sequence to build an AMoD has not been addressed yet. In this research, we consider an AMoD with a target service area, as well as a current set of open stations. The operator decides on the sequence in which they open the stations. The more profit they make, the faster they can open new stations.

In the following sections, we address the above questions and then analyze the performance of our proposed algorithm. To do so, we review publications close to our research in Sect. 2. Next, we present the problem statement and related formulations in Sect. 3. Section 4 presents our solution approach based on the A* search algorithm. Numerical experiments and some promising results are presented and analyzed in Sect. 5. Finally, Sect. 6 concludes and points out further research directions based on the current research.

2 Literature

This section provides a brief literature review on AMoD systems. Research into the operation and planning of AMoD systems encompasses a range of questions. However, its main emphasis lies in optimizing an existing vehicle-sharing network. Regarding fleet optimization, we can refer to [5,6,10,12]. George and Xia [6] study a fleet optimization problem in a closed queue network. This work suggests basic principles for the design of such a system. Nair and Miller-Hooks [13] use the equilibrium network model to find the optimal configuration of a vehicle-sharing network. The solutions to the model explain the correctness of the equilibrium condition, the trade-offs between operator and user objectives, and the insights regarding the installation of services. Freund et al. [5] address how to (re-)allocate dock capacity in vehicle-sharing systems by presenting mathematical formulations and a fast polynomial-time allocation algorithm to compute an optimal solution. Lu et al. [10] consider the problem of allocating vehicles to service zones with uncertain one-way and round-trip rental demand.

Regarding policies, Martin et al. [11] conclude that the use of driverless vehicles and human-driven vehicles can improve profits and operators can gain new unprofitable markets for them. The authors propose a model and an algorithm to find maximum profit

---

[3] https://www.weforum.org/agenda/2021/11/trends-driving-the-autonomous-vehicles-industry/.

while considering driverless and human-driven vehicles. Hao and Martin [7] present a model that studies the impact of regulations on the decisions of vehicle-sharing operators and measures the efficiency and effectiveness of these regulations. The results show that the interdependencies between regulations and societal welfare indicators are non-trivial and possibly counterintuitive.

To conclude, we observe that all the research so far has tried to address different questions with the goal of optimizing an already established vehicle-sharing network. However, the question of how to establish new stations and acquire new vehicles has not been addressed yet. In the following, we introduce an optimization problem aimed at identifying the optimal sequence for station establishment and the fleet size required to reach the end state where all stations are operational in the shortest possible time.

3   Problem Statement and Formulation

We study an optimal investment strategy for an AMoD (Autonomous Mobility-on-Demand) operator to increase their fleet size and operating area. The AMoD operator's business area comprises stations, $(\mathcal{R} : \{1, ..., R\})$. "Station" can also refer to a virtual location, e.g., the center of a region in a free-floating system. The operating station i incurs an initial cost c_i^b related to construction, permits, or marketing. Some stations are already open, and profits will be collected from already open stations to increase the budget for new stations. The operator incrementally grows the fleet to reach the optimal size promptly while ensuring acceptable service levels within a gradually expanding operating area.

At a given open station i, customers begin their journeys to a different station j. When a station is not operational, customers intending to start or complete their journeys there can opt for a neighboring station. Customer arrivals are modeled by a Poisson distribution with an arrival rate denoted as λ_{ij}, and 0 when at least on of the stations is closed. The travel times between the stations are exponentially distributed, with an average of $1/\mu_{ij}$, where μ_{ij} denotes the return rate. These arrival and return rates remain constant and are determined solely by whether stations i and j are open.

The operator determines the fleet size n at any given time, allowing it to grow during expansion. Each new vehicle acquisition comes with a procurement cost of c^p. The fleet size must be large enough to serve at least a fraction α of all customers, meeting the minimum service level requirement for the AMoD system. Throughout the development of the AMoD service, it is crucial to keep the service level constant to offset the potential learning effects that could deter customers from using the service [4]. To maintain the service level, the operator can rebalance vehicles between stations, incurring a cost of c_{ij}^r. The operator receives a contribution margin of δ_{ij} for each served customer traveling from station to station, representing the payoff minus direct operating costs such as fuel and periodic repairs.

Consequently, this problem involves two decision-making components: establishing the optimal investment plan, which includes timing, locations, and quantity for opening new stations and vehicle acquisition, and overseeing fleet operations, which includes vehicle rebalancing. The model for determining the optimal fleet size and an algorithm for determining investment sequence are introduced in the subsequent sections.

3.1 Semi-Markov Decision Process for Determining the Optimal Fleet Size

We see the optimal investment scheduling problem of AMoD operators as a semi-Markov decision process (SMDP) due to the nature of the investment problem. In an SMDP, the system's state evolves according to a semi-Markov process, and the decision-maker selects actions based on the current state.

States. Each state $s \in S$ describes the current fleet of size n and the currently open stations, given by $x_i = 1$ if station $i \in \mathcal{R}$ is open, 0 otherwise.

$$s = \langle n, x_1, \ldots, x_R \rangle$$

Each state s is associated with an operational profit $p(s)$ per period, which is calculated by subtracting the rebalancing costs from the contribution margins and an acquisition cost $c(s)$ related to the procurement cost of all vehicles and the cost incurred due to the opening of the station. Apparently, we only need to consider states with positive operational profit in our investment scheme. Regarding this point, the set of states with positive operational profit and the starting state is denoted as S. Also, if a state s' contains all open stations in a state s, we can easily see and prove that $p(s') \geq p(s)$. For referencing the fleet size and open stations of a specific state s, the notation $n(s)$ and $x_i(s)$ are utilized, respectively. Then, the value of $c(s)$ is determined as follows:

$$c(s) = n(s) \cdot c^p + \sum_{i \in \mathcal{R}} x_i(s) c_i^b$$

Actions. Actions refer to the operator's procurement decision, resulting in a state transition to the target state $t \in S$. Every state $s \in S$ allows transitions to all other states such that no stations are being closed, that is, $s \to t$ exists if $x_i(s) \leq x_i(t)\ \forall i$.

The time $\tau(s,t)$ necessary for a state transition from state s to a state t depends on the operational profit $p(s)$ and the necessary investment volume $C(s,t)$ where

$$C(s,t) = c(t) - c(s) = (n(t) - n(s)) \cdot c^p + \sum_{i \in \mathcal{R}} (x_i(t) - x_i(s)) \cdot c_i^b.$$

Given that we do not consider partial states (e.g., a state without optimal fleet size), this means that $p(s)$ is considered the maximum profit corresponding to state s, and the optimal decision is to transition to the next state as soon as possible. Thus, $\tau(s,t) = \frac{C(s,t)}{p(s)}$.

We notice that if $|t| \geq |s| + 2$, it is more advantageous to transition to an immediate state s' where $|s| < |s'| < |t|$ because $\frac{C(s,t)}{p(s)} \geq \frac{C(s,s')}{p(s)} + \frac{C(s',t)}{p(s')}$ due to the fact that $p(s) \leq p(s')$ and $C(s,t) = C(s,s') + C(s',t)$. Therefore, we only need to consider actions between two consecutive states in any optimal investment scheme.

3.2 A Model for Calculating Optimal Profit and Minimum Acquisition Cost

To compute the operational profit $p(s)$ per state $s \in S$, we formulate the rebalancing problem as an open-queueing network (in line with, e.g., [3,7,8,11]), and optimize over it to maximize operational profits. Given a set of available stations, the model determines the necessary size of the fleet to reach the level of service and rebalance. Since we want to maximize profit and minimize the corresponding acquisition cost, our objective function is hierarchical since we optimize the second objective after minimizing the first objective.

To start, we denote f_{ij}, e_{ij} $(i \neq j)$ as the number of occupied and empty vehicles traveling from i to j and e_{ii} as the number of idle vehicles currently parked at station i. To determine the maximum operational profit per period for state s, we solve (1) - (7) for all opening stations in $R_s = \{i \in \mathcal{R} | x_i(s) = 1\}$. The mathematical formulation is expressed as follows:

$$P(obj_1, obj_2) = \Big(\max \ \alpha \Big(\sum_{i \in R_s} \sum_{j \in R_s} \lambda_{ij} \delta_{ij}$$

$$- \sum_{i \in R_s} \sum_{j \in R_s} c^r_{ij} \mu_{ij} e_{ij}\Big), \min \Big(n \cdot c^p + \sum_{i \in R_s} c^b_i\Big)\Big) \quad (1)$$

subject to

$$\lambda_{ij} = \mu_{ij} f_{ij}, \qquad\qquad \forall i, j \in R_s \quad (2)$$

$$\sum_{j \in R_s \setminus \{i\}} \mu_{ji} e_{ji} \leq \sum_{j \in R_s \setminus \{i\}} \lambda_{ij}, \qquad \forall i \in R_s \quad (3)$$

$$\sum_{j \in R_s} \lambda_{ij} + \sum_{j \in R_s} \mu_{ij} e_{ij} = \sum_{j \in R_s} \mu_{ji} e_{ji} + \sum_{j \in R_s} \lambda_{ji}, \qquad \forall i \in R_s \quad (4)$$

$$\frac{\alpha}{1 - \alpha} \leq e_{ii}, \qquad\qquad \forall i \in R_s \quad (5)$$

$$\sum_{i,j \in R_s} (e_{ij} + f_{ij}) = n, \qquad\qquad (6)$$

$$e_{ij}, f_{ij} \geq 0, \qquad\qquad \forall i, j \in R_s \quad (7)$$

The objective function (1) maximizes profit by dividing the contribution margin of all served customers by rebalancing costs, multiplied by availability α, and minimizing set-up fees. Constraints (2) - (4) linearize flow constraints in queueing networks, almost directly follow from [3] and requiring the system to achieve a service level of at least α, eliminating any upper bound on demand, unlike [3]. Constraints (5) set the required safety stock, following the fixed population mean approximation in open queueing networks due to [14]. Constraints (6) bound fleet size, and constraints (7) defined the domain.

4   Solution Approach

It is important to note that in our problem, the optimal time for opening a new station depends on profits from existing stations, resulting in a set-dependent cost. The exponential growth of these sets makes mathematical representations potentially too complex, making contemporary solvers unsuitable for modeling and solving this formulation.

We can consider the investment problem as a variant of the well-known Traveling Salesman Problem (TSP) with set-dependent travel costs. Taking into account a permutation $(u_1, u_2, .., u_n)$ that presents an order that the stations are opened. Each subpath $(u_1, u_2, .., u_i)$ is assigned a state s_i where $x_k(s_i) = 1$ if $u_j = k$ for some $j = 1..i$. The cost between two consecutive states, s_i and s_{i+1}, is calculated using the formulations in Sect. 3.1, which depend on the set of open stations in s_i. In other words, it is a set-dependent cost function. While there is much research for TSP in general and several studies on level-dependent travel cost TSP [1,2] in particular (the cost associated with each city depends on the index of that city in the solution), our cost function makes the problem cannot be modeled with formulations similar to the ones for TSPs.

4.1 Heuristic Strategy for A* Algorithm

We model our investment problem as a shortest path problem. Consider a graph $G = (V, A)$ where each node $n_s \in V$ corresponds to the state s. Each arc $(n_s, n_{s'}) \in A$ corresponds to a feasible action between two consecutive states s and s' with cost $C(s, s')$. Finding the shortest investment time is equivalent to finding the shortest path from node n_{s_0} to node n_{s_f} where s_0 and s_f are the initial state and the final state, respectively. Since we can define a 1–1 mapping between s and n_s, we subsequently use s instead of n_s to simplify the notation.

To solve this shortest-path problem, we rely on the A* algorithm. Given a state s, unlike the classic Dijkstra algorithm, which only evaluates the cost of the shortest path $g(s)$ from the source s_0 to s, A* also evaluates the cost $h(s)$ from s to the final state s_f, and the cost for each node s is then $f(s) = g(s) + h(s)$ instead of $g(s)$. The A* algorithm can always find the shortest path from s_0 to s_f if $h(s)$ does not exceed the cost of the shortest path from s to s_f for any s. Otherwise, A* becomes a heuristic algorithm.

Simple Heuristic for A*. We start with some of the simplest heuristics for A*. Given that the current, next, and final states are s, s' and s_f, the cost of the shortest path from n_0 to s', $g(s')$, is $g(s') = g(s) + \frac{c(s')-c(s)}{p(s)}$. Several simple ways to calculate $h(s')$ are as follows (where eh and ah denote exact and approximate heuristics, respectively):

$$eh_1(s') = \frac{c(s_f) - c(s')}{P_{R-1}} \tag{8}$$

$$ah_1(s') = \frac{c(s_f) - c(s')}{p(s')} \tag{9}$$

Heuristic functions (8), (9) underestimate and overestimate the shortest time of the optimal path from s_0 to s_f that passes through s'. Here, P_{R-1} denotes the maximum profit for any state that has $R - 1$ open stations. Using a linear combination, we obtain other heuristics where $\gamma \in [0, 1]$ is a parameter that can be a fixed constant or dynamically adjusted during the execution of the algorithm. We aim to test whether we can obtain simple heuristics that may not be optimal but can quickly find reasonable solutions.

$$ah_2(s') = \gamma eh_1(s') + (1 - \gamma)ah_1(s') \tag{10}$$

Stronger Lower Bound Heuristics for A*. Assume that $s = s_1$ is the current state. Let $s_1, s_2, .., s_k$ be a sequence of states where s_{i+1} is obtained from s_i by adding a new station and $s_k = s_f$ be the final state where all stations are open. The total transition time from state s_1 to state s_k, $\tau(s_1, .., s_k)$, is:

$$\tau(s_1, .., s_k) = \frac{c(s_2) - c(s_1)}{p(s_1)} + \frac{c(s_3) - c(s_2)}{p(s_2)} + \ldots + \frac{c(s_k) - c(s_{k-1})}{p(s_{k-1})} \tag{11}$$

We denote $\underline{\Delta_c}(s_i)$ as a lower bound of the difference of the acquisition cost $c(s_{i+1}) - c(s_i)$ between two consecutive states s_i and s_{i+1}. Let P_m be a state with the maximum profit among all states with m opening stations. We can find the value of P_m by solving the model which is an extended version of (1)–(7) (see online Appendix [9]), which aims to maximize the profit and minimize the corresponding acquisition cost given a fixed number of stations that can be opened. Then, we obtain $p(s_i) \leq P_{|s_i|}, \forall i = 1, \ldots, k$. The values of $P_{|s_i|}$ define an increasing sequence since we open more stations. Therefore, we have $p(s_i) \leq P_{|s_i|} \leq P_{|s_{k-1}|} = P_{R-1}, \forall i = 1, \ldots, k-1$. Given that $c(s_{i+1}) - c(s_i) \geq \underline{\Delta_c}(s_i)$ or $c(s_{i+1}) - c(s_i) - \underline{\Delta_c}(s_i) \geq 0$, therefore, $\forall i = 1, \ldots, k-1$ we have the following.

$$\frac{c(s_{i+1}) - c(s_i)}{p(s_i)} = \frac{\underline{\Delta_c}(s_i) + (c(s_{i+1}) - c(s_i) - \underline{\Delta_c}(s_i))}{p(s_i)} \tag{12}$$

$$= \frac{\underline{\Delta_c}(s_i)}{p(s_i)} + \frac{c(s_{i+1}) - c(s_i) - \underline{\Delta_c}(s_i)}{p(s_i)} \tag{13}$$

$$\geq \frac{\underline{\Delta_c}(s_i)}{P_{|s_i|}} + \frac{c(s_{i+1}) - c(s_i) - \underline{\Delta_c}(s_i)}{P_{R-1}} \tag{14}$$

and consequently:

$$\tau(s_1, \ldots, s_k) \geq \left(\sum_{i=1}^{k-1} \frac{\underline{\Delta_c}(s_i)}{P_{|s_i|}} \right) + \frac{c(s_k) - c(s_1) - \sum_{i=1}^{k-1} \underline{\Delta_c}(s_i)}{P_{R-1}} \tag{15}$$

Inequality (15) gives us a more robust lower bound than the simple one presented in (8).

Evaluating the Lower Bound $\underline{\Delta_c}(s_1)$. From (6), we see that with each state S, the optimal number of vehicles n is equal to $\sum_{i,j \in S}(e_{ij} + f_{ij})$. Following obj_2, when we open a new station, the acquisition cost includes the cost of station setup and the new vehicle acquisition cost. We assume that the difference in acquisition cost between two consecutive states depends on the values f_{ij}, e_{ij} of the new station i. With this assumption, the minimum acquisition cost of opening station i from a given state S ($i \notin S$) to obtain maximum profit is determined by $\Delta_c(S, i)$. In other words, $\Delta_c(S, i)$ presents the lower difference in acquisition cost between two consecutive states in which the next state is reached by opening station i from the state S.

$$\Delta_c(S, i) = \sum_{j \in S}(e_{ij} + e_{ji} + f_{ij} + f_{ji})c^p + c_b^i \quad \forall i \notin S \tag{16}$$

Then, $c(s_{i+1}) - c(s_i) \geq \min_{o \notin s_i} \Delta_c(s_i, o) \quad \forall i = 1, 2, \ldots, k-1$.

Next, we show how to obtain the lower bound $\Delta_c(s_i, o)$ using Eq. (16). Assuming $T \subset \mathcal{R}$ be the state with any t stations not in S, $t < R - |S|$, $S \cap T = \emptyset$. Let $o \notin S \cup T$, and we evaluate $\Delta C(S, t, i)$ - the minimum acquisition cost difference when building a new station i starts from state $S \cup T$ with any state T such that $|T| = t$.

Underestimate Acquisition Cost. We rewrite $\Delta C(S, t, i)$ using equation (16) as follows:

$$\Delta C(S, t, i) = \min_{T \subset \mathcal{R}, |T|=t} \sum_{j \in S \cup T} (e_{ij} + e_{ji} + f_{ij} + f_{ji})c^p + c_i^b \tag{17}$$

and since e_{ij}, e_{ji} and c^p are non-negative, we have

$$\Delta C(S, t, i) \geq \min_{T \subset \mathcal{R}, |T|=t} \sum_{j \in S \cup T} (f_{ij} + f_{ji})c^p + c_i^b \tag{18}$$

Since $c_i^b + \sum_{j \in S}(f_{ij} + f_{ji})c^p$ is a constant, we will develop a lower bound for the sum $\sum_{j \in T}(f_{ij} + f_{ji})c^p$. Apparently, $\sum_{j \in T}(f_{ij} + f_{ji})c^p$ cannot be smaller than the sum of $|T|$ smallest values of $(f_{ij} + f_{ji})c^p$ where $j \notin S \cup \{i\}$. Therefore, we developed the Algorithm 1 to evaluate a lower bound of $\Delta C(S, t, i)$.

Algorithm 1. Lower bound evaluation of acquisition cost

Require: S, i, t
Ensure: A lower bound of $\Delta C(S, t, i)$
1: Let $\alpha \leftarrow c_i^b + \sum_{j \in S}(f_{ij} + f_{ji})c^p$
2: Sort $(f_{ij} + f_{ji})_{j \in \mathcal{R} \setminus (S \cup \{i\})}$ increasingly.
3: Let $(f_{ij_1} + f_{j_1 i}) \leq (f_{ij_2} + f_{j_2 i}) \leq \ldots \leq (f_{ij_k} + f_{j_k i}) \leq \ldots$ be the array after sorting.
4: Let $\beta \leftarrow \sum_{k=1}^{t}(f_{ij_k} + f_{j_k i})c^p$
5: **Return** $\alpha + \beta$

Using Algorithm 1, we have that

$$\Delta_c(s_i, o) \geq \Delta C(s_1, i - 1, o) \geq c_o^b + \sum_{j \in s_1}(f_{oj} + f_{jo})c^p + \sum_{k=1}^{i-1}(f_{oj_k} + f_{j_k o})c^p \tag{19}$$

and consequently,

$$c(s_{i+1}) - c(s_i) \geq \min_{o \notin s_i} \Delta_c(s_i, o) \tag{20}$$

$$\geq \min_{o \notin s_i} \left(c_o^b + \sum_{j \in s_1}(f_{oj} + f_{jo})c^p + \sum_{k=1}^{i-1}(f_{oj_k} + f_{j_k o})c^p \right) \tag{21}$$

Use $\underline{\Delta_c}(s_i) = \min_{o \notin s_i} \left(c_o^b + \sum_{j \in s_1}(f_{oj} + f_{jo})c^p + \sum_{k=1}^{i-1}(f_{oj_k} + f_{j_k o})c^p \right)$ in inequality (15), we obtain a lower bound heuristic for A*, called eh_2, which is stronger than the simple one eh_1. However, we need to solve it online.

We obtain a weaker lower bound version of eh_2 by fixing s_1, e.g., to the initial state s_0. Still, this strategy may reduce the total running time since the value of $\underline{\Delta_c}(s_i)$ needs to be calculated only once, while with eh_2, we will calculate $\underline{\Delta_c}(s_i)$ for each extracted state $s = s_1$ from the queue. Let eh_3 be this lower bound heuristic.

5   Numerical Experiments

In this section, we present the numerical design and then report the experiment results of exact and heuristic algorithms to find an optimal schedule investment. The algorithm and formulations were written in C++, and the MILP models were solved by CPLEX 22.1.1. The experiments were run on an AMD Ryzen 3 3100 machine with a 4-core processor, 3.59 GHz, and 16 GB of RAM on a 64-bit Windows system.

5.1   Numerical Design

We conducted experiments on randomly generated datasets, following a similar approach as Martin et al. [7]. To model the real-world transportation network structure, our datasets vary in size ($R \in \{7, 9, 16, 19, 25\}$ and geographic distributions of station locations, including circular (C), hexagonal (H), and quadratic (Q) layouts. The methodology for generating data and configuring model parameters is elucidated in the online Appendix [9].

The investment starts with a set of initially open stations. We assume that initially, there is a budget of $B = 10000$, optimally utilized to construct the initial stations to maximize the initial profit. With smaller instances (less than 10 stations), we use a dynamic budget of $500 \times R$ to avoid opening too many stations in the initial state. We simulate this process through a formulation which is an extended version of (1)–(7) with additional budget constraints, detailed in online Appendix [9]. With this budget, the initial state has $5 - 7$ open stations for larger instances and 2–3 for instances with fewer than 10 stations. Then, the A* algorithm will find an optimal investment plan starting from the initial state with a certain number of already opened stations obtained from the formulations.

5.2   Results

In the following, we assess the following two points:

1. We compare the performance of the exact A* heuristics and Dijkstra algorithm based on the execution time, the number of states explored, and the number of states remaining in the priority queue.
2. We compare the performance of approximate A* heuristics in terms of optimal gap and execution time.

Table 1 analyzes the performance of the exact A * algorithms and the Dijkstra algorithm by reporting their running time in seconds (column Time (s)), the number of nodes extracted by the A* algorithm (column Exp.), and the number of nodes still in the queue (column Rem.) with the optimal value (column Opt.) obtained from all exact algorithms.

The experiments show that datasets with imbalanced arrival rates take longer to open stations due to decreased profit margins. The strongest lower bound heuristic, eh_2, has the shortest running time, number of expanded nodes, and number of remaining nodes among all exact methods, detailed in Table 1. Using the A* algorithm

Table 1. Results of exact A* heuristic and Dijkstra algorithms

Instance	Opt.	Dijkstra	A* + eh_1			A* + eh_2			A* + eh_3		
		Time (s)	Exp.	Rem.	Time (s)	Exp.	Rem.	Time (s)	Exp.	Rem.	Time (s)
C-7-BAL	1563.19	<1	17	144	<1	12	10	<1	12	12	<1
H-7-BAL	1524.71	<1	17	13	<1	11	9	<1	12	12	<1
Q-9-BAL	435.53	<1	33	31	<1	14	25	<1	20	25	<1
Q-16-BAL	420.87	1	392	173	1	227	236	1	243	231	1
Q-16-IMB	723.69	1	340	176	1	150	208	1	170	195	1
C-19-BAL	1054.83	14	2733	2060	12	1453	2234	9	1603	2156	9
C-19-IMB	1681.48	14	2292	1473	11	902	1421	7	1103	1378	7
H-19-BAL	1028.32	13	2303	1710	11	903	1568	7	1149	1656	8
H-19-IMB	1833.02	14	1812	1720	10	592	1299	5	888	1385	6
Q-25-BAL	711.31	1313	140878	119407	1032	35068	84174	452	44551	90771	508
Q-25-IMB	1185.37	1311	124532	105743	978	18440	55015	328	24975	61453	372

with eh_2 significantly reduces computation time and vertice exploration compared to underestimating the optimal path's shortest time eh_1. The exact heuristic eh_3 also provides computational stability without online updates.

We observe that the number of visited vertices and execution time increases exponentially with the number of stations. To find a suitable investment schedule, the researchers experimented with various heuristic approximation approaches in the A* search algorithm. Results in Table 2 showed that larger values of γ resulted in better objective values and longer running time. Although these approaches achieve excellent time efficiency and small gaps, they are highly dependent on data and can become less effective when parameter ranges are modified.

Finally, we report the performance of weighted A* variants in Table 3, which multiply the values of eh_2 and eh_3 by 1.05 or 1.1. The best solutions ensure a gap between optimal and best solutions of at most 5% or 10%. Although slower than the ones mentioned in Table 2, it ensures an optimal gap that the approximate heuristics cannot. The results show that the optimal gap obtained by these approximation algorithms is very small, highlighting the effectiveness of both heuristics.

Table 2. Non-bounded approximation algorithms with simple heuristics.

Instance	Opt.	A* + ah_1		A* + $ah_2 (\gamma = 0.3)$		A* + $ah_2 (\gamma = 0.5)$		A* + $ah_2 (\gamma = 0.7)$	
		Gap (%)	Time (s)	Gap (%)	Time (s)	Gap (%)	Time (s)	Gap (%)	Time (s)
C-7-BAL	1563.19	9.01	<1	4.34	<1	0.00	<1	0.00	<1
H-7-BAL	1524.71	8.85	<1	4.37	<1	4.37	<1	0.00	<1
Q-9-BAL	435.53	4.63	<1	1.29	<1	1.29	<1	0.00	<1
Q-16-BAL	420.87	7.18	<1	3.86	<1	1.78	<1	0.00	1
Q-16-IMB	723.69	6.00	<1	3.82	<1	1.47	<1	0.00	1
C-19-BAL	1054.83	12.76	<1	7.78	<1	0.94	<1	0.00	3
C-19-IMB	1681.48	17.25	<1	9.62	<1	0.33	<1	0.00	3
H-19-BAL	1028.32	6.40	1	2.11	<1	1.20	<1	0.00	2
H-19-IMB	1833.02	11.98	<1	9.19	<1	4.48	<1	0.00	1
Q-25-BAL	711.31	15.10	1	10.08	1	6.84	1	0.53	39
Q-25-IMB	1185.37	11.87	1	7.28	1	3.39	1	1.26	15

Table 3. Bounded approximation algorithms based on stronger lower-bound heuristic

Instance	Opt.	A* + 1.1 * eh_2		A* + 1.1 * eh_3		A* + 1.05 * eh_2		A* + 1.05 * eh_3	
		Gap (%)	Time (s)	Gap (%)	Time (s)	Gap (%)	Time (s)	Gap (%)	Time (s)
C-7-BAL	1563.19	0.00	<1	0.00	<1	0.00	<1	0.00	<1
H-7-BAL	1524.71	0.00	<1	0.00	<1	0.00	<1	0.00	<1
Q-9-BAL	435.53	0.67	<1	0.67	<1	0.00	<1	0.00	<1
Q-16-BAL	420.87	0.17	1	0.13	1	0.13	1	0.13	1
Q-16-IMB	723.69	0.73	1	0.00	1	0.00	1	0.00	1
C-19-BAL	1054.83	0.40	6	0.09	6	0.09	7	0.09	8
C-19-IMB	1681.48	0.10	4	0.04	5	0.04	5	0.04	6
H-19-BAL	1028.32	0.24	3	0.07	4	0.07	5	0.01	6
H-19-IMB	1833.02	0.27	4	0.07	4	0.14	4	0.00	5
Q-25-BAL	711.31	0.26	194	0.08	241	0.04	306	0.03	370
Q-25-IMB	1185.37	0.43	117	0.09	135	0.10	181	0.00	241

To conclude the section, we observe that for those benchmark instances, exact methods can provide optimal solutions in a reasonable amount of time for those benchmark instances. The proposed lower bound heuristic eh_2 beats simple heuristic eh_1 and the Dijkstra algorithm. The simple approximate A* heuristic can give quite good results with a small computation time, while the weighted A* heuristic based on the best lower bound heuristic can reduce the computation time and maintain a small optimal gap.

6 Conclusion

We have studied an investment problem that arises in the context of autonomous mobility on demand systems. Given some already open stations, the question is to determine the optimal sequence of opening the remaining stations to minimize the total opening time. We modeled this investment problem as a Semi-Markov Decision Process and viewed this problem as a variant of the TSP problem, where the cost between two vertices s and t depends on the set of already visited vertices belonging to the path from the source vertex to vertex s. This special cost function makes the problem impossible to model and solve with current mixed-integer solver technology. We then developed and solved this new variant using the A* algorithm. The experiment results show that the A* algorithm can reduce by half the running time of the Dijkstra algorithm and a simple, exact A* algorithm. Regarding the approximate A* search, the result shows that we can obtain reasonable solutions with a small computation effort.

It is still a challenging task to solve larger problems. Therefore, we are developing and testing more robust lower-bound heuristics for exact A* search. Also, we are testing new approximate heuristics for A* search that take ideas from the lower bound heuristics. The initial results show that we can solve larger instances in a shorter time using both methods. Also, the approximate A* heuristic gives similar results to those returned by the exact A* heuristic in many problem instances.

Acknowledgement. The work has been carried out partly at the Vietnam Institute for Advanced Study in Mathematics (VIASM). The corresponding author (Duc Minh Vu) would like to thank VIASM for its hospitality and financial support for his visit in 2023.

References

1. Alkaya, A.F., Duman, E.: Combining and solving sequence dependent traveling salesman and quadratic assignment problems in PCB assembly. Discret. Appl. Math. **192**, 2–16 (2015)
2. Bigras, L.P., Gamache, M., Savard, G.: The time-dependent traveling salesman problem and single machine scheduling problems with sequence dependent setup times. Discret. Optim. **5**(4), 685–699 (2008)
3. Braverman, A., Dai, J.G., Liu, X., Ying, L.: Empty-car routing in ridesharing systems. Oper. Res. **67**(5), 1437–1452 (2019)
4. DeCroix, G., Long, X., Tong, J.: How service quality variability hurts revenue when customers learn: implications for dynamic personalized pricing. Oper. Res. **69**(3), 683–708 (2021)
5. Freund, D., Henderson, S.G., Shmoys, D.B.: Minimizing multimodular functions and allocating capacity in bike-sharing systems. Prod. Oper. Manag. **27**(12), 2346–2349 (2018)
6. George, D.K., Xia, C.H.: Fleet-sizing and service availability for a vehicle rental system via closed queueing networks. Eur. J. Oper. Res. **211**(1), 198–207 (2011)
7. Hao, W., Martin, L.: Prohibiting cherry-picking: regulating vehicle sharing services who determine fleet and service structure. Transp. Res. Part E: Logist. Transp. Rev. **161**, 102692 (2022)
8. He, L., Mak, H.Y., Rong, Y., Shen, Z.J.M.: Service region design for urban electric vehicle sharing systems. Manuf. Serv. Oper. Manage. **19**(2), 309–327 (2017)
9. Le, B.L., Martin, L., Demir, E., Vu, D.M.: A* search algorithm for an optimal investment problem in vehicle-sharing systems (2023). https://arxiv.org/abs/2311.08834
10. Lu, M., Chen, Z., Shen, S.: Optimizing the profitability and quality of service in carshare systems under demand uncertainty. Manuf. Serv. Oper. Manage. **20**(2), 162–180 (2018)
11. Martin, L., Minner, S., Pavone, M., Schiffer, M.: It's all in the mix: technology choice between driverless and human-driven vehicles in sharing systems (2021). Available at SSRN 4190991
12. Nair, R., Miller-Hooks, E.: Fleet management for vehicle sharing operations. Transp. Sci. **45**(4), 524–540 (2011)
13. Nair, R., Miller-Hooks, E.: Equilibrium network design of shared-vehicle systems. Eur. J. Oper. Res. **235**(1), 47–61 (2014)
14. Whitt, W.: Open and closed models for networks of queues. AT&T Bell Lab. Techn. J. **63**(9), 1911–1979 (1984)

The Matheuristic for Building Cost-Constrained Decision Trees with Multiple Condition Attributes

Hoang Giang Pham$^{(\boxtimes)}$ [iD]

ORLab, Faculty of Computer Science, Phenikaa University, Hanoi, Vietnam
giang.phamhoang@phenikaa-uni.edu.vn

Abstract. Cost factors are frequently essential in many real-world applications. Many previous studies in machine learning included costs, particularly when creating decision tree models. This research also takes into account a cost-sensitive decision tree construction problem, with the premise that test costs must be spent in order to get the values of the decision attribute and that a record must be categorized without surpassing the expenditure cost threshold. Furthermore, our problem handles records with multiple condition attributes. A mathematical programming heuristic based on Variable Neighborhood Descent (VND) is introduced to compare to the existing approach in the literature. The experimental results show that our approach not only satisfactorily handles small and medium datasets with multiple condition attributes under different cost constraints but also outperforms the existing method.

Keywords: Classification decision tree · Cost-sensitive learning · Multiple condition attributes · Variable Neighborhood Descent (VND)

1 Introduction

Decision trees have been one of the most widely used algorithms for interpretable machine learning since its inception some decades ago. They are frequently used in a variety of practical applications ranging from revenue management to medicine to bioinformatics. The vast majority of decision tree approaches are designed to categorize data using a single condition feature. In real-world applications, however, we must define multiple condition attributes per record. For example, the doctor must identify as many distinct ailments as possible based on blood test findings and patient symptoms. A bank must not only examine a customer's credit rating but also predict his or her likelihood of seeking a loan in the near future. In both circumstances, the values of multiple condition attributes must be predicted based on a given set of decision attributes.

In actuality, the problem of multiple condition attributes may be individually solved by making a decision tree for each condition attribute. These decision trees contain certain common decision attributes, which are unfortunate since

M. H. Hà et al. (Eds.): CSoNet 2023, LNCS 14479, pp. 174–185, 2024.
https://doi.org/10.1007/978-981-97-0669-3_17

they can violate a total budgetary restriction. Choosing how much of the budget to spend on each decision tree might be challenging. Even if it were possible, the cost limits would also make it difficult to identify the best classification method because the decision trees would have to be small to stay within the budget.

These difficulties motivate us to develop a MILP model to explore the optimal cost-constrained decision trees to classify multiple condition attributes in our previous study [11]. Although the proposed MILP model can create the optimal tree for small datasets, the performance of the mathematical formulation can be improved by several extensions in this study.

The remainder of this paper is organized as follows. We first review some related works in Sect. 2. In Sect. 3, we formalize the problem and introduce the proposed MILP formulation in [11] with several improvements. The matheuristic framework is implemented in Sect. 4. The data preprocessing and the performance evaluation are presented in Sect. 5. Our conclusion and suggestion for future works are discussed in Sect. 6.

2   Literature

Many algorithms have been introduced for conducting decision trees. In most of these methods, the purpose is to maximize classification accuracy without consideration of cost, such as well-known greedy algorithms: ID3, C4.5, CART, exact methods: OCT [2], DL8.5 [1], ... Since the early 1990s, various decision tree-based cost-sensitive machine learning models have been addressed in [9,10,14]. In recent years, the construction of cost-sensitive decision trees have been an interesting topic for researchers, see [4,6,7,12,16].

In literature, [3] is the first consideration of a cost-constrained decision tree with multiple condition attributes and is most related to our study. In this research, four different methods are implemented to evaluate the performance of the decision tree with multiple condition attributes. The first method is sequentially building a decision tree for each condition attribute by C4.5 without a cost constraint. The second one is sequentially building a decision tree for each condition attribute by C4.5 with the budget equally allocated among all condition attributes. The third one is the same as the second but with the difference that the condition attributes which have been predicted can be incorporated as decision attributes with test cost 0. The final is a greedy algorithm based on multi-dimensional information gain to build a cost-constrained decision tree with multiple condition attributes.

Although the final approach in [3] successfully creates the cost-constrained decision tree with multiple condition attributes and outperforms other algorithms, there is still no exact method to solve this problem. With the incredible increase in the computational power of MILP solvers, in our previous study [11], we formulate the problem as a mathematical optimization model which not only allows flexibility in modeling different learning objectives and additional constraints but also can provide such optimality guarantees. Because it is difficult to efficiently consider multi-dimensional attributes in mathematical formulation, that study focuses on the exact method for the induction of the binary decision tree with multiple condition attributes under the effect of the cost factors. In this research, the formulation in [11] is extended to consider group cost of decision attributes provided in [14]. Additionally, another mathematical formulation followed by a matheuristic algorithm is introduced to speed up the solution exploration.

3   Problem Statement and Existing Formulation

In this section, we reintroduce the problem proposed in [11] and its mathematical formulation. Afterward, we implement some modifications in the formulation in order to create a new model used together with a heuristic framework to find solutions to the original formulation.

The problem in [11] considers a full binary tree decision tree with a given depth H. Assume that N and L are a set of internal nodes and a set of leaves in the tree. Let D and C be the set of decision attributes and condition attributes, respectively. Denote that d is the index of the decision attribute in D and c is the index of the condition attribute in C. Let D_k^d and C_j^c respectively be kth thresholds in each decision attribute D^d and jth label in each condition attribute C^c. In [11], the author also introduces parameter $\phi_{D_k^d}^i$ as checkpoint related to threshold D_k^d. All labels of datapoint $i \in I$ are presented by the parameter $\psi_{C_j^c}^i$. If the set of i's condition attributes contains condition attribute C_j^c, the value of $\psi_{C_j^c}^i$ is set to C_j^c, otherwise $\psi_{C_j^c}^i = null$.

Binary variables $x_{nD_k^d}$ and $y_{nC_j^c}$ define the allocation of threshold k of decision attribute D^d and label j of condition attribute C^c to node n. The decision attributes must be assigned to the internal node, thus, for each $n \in N$, $x_{nD_k^d}$ equals 1 if the threshold $k \in D^d$ is branched at n, otherwise $x_{nD_k^d}$ equals to 0. The condition attributes must be assigned to the leaves of the tree and also can be allocated in the internal node. Therefore, for each $n \in N \cup L$, $y_{nC_j^c}$ is set to 1 if label $j \in C^c$ is assigned, 0 otherwise. In addition, let P_l be the path from the root to leaf $l \in L$ and two sets of binary variables, z_l^i and c_l^i, the ability that data i can traverse on the path P_l and can be correctly classified by path P_l or not. We have the objective function (1), which is to maximize the number of correctly classified datapoints, as follow:

$$\max \sum_{l \in L} \sum_{i \in I} c_l^i \tag{1}$$

In [11], the process of creating the tree must satisfy constraints formulated as follows:

$$\sum_{d \in D} \sum_{k \in D^d} x_{nD_k^d} \leq 1 \qquad \forall n \in N \tag{2}$$

$$\sum_{j \in C^c} y_{nC_j^c} \leq 1 \qquad \forall n \in N \cup L, c \in C \tag{3}$$

$$\sum_{c \in C} \sum_{j \in C^c} y_{nC_j^c} + \sum_{d \in D} \sum_{k \in D^d} x_{nD_k^d} \leq \|C\| \qquad \forall n \in N \cup L \tag{4}$$

$$\sum_{n \in P_l} \sum_{j \in C^c} y_{nC_j^c} = 1 \qquad \forall l \in L, c \in C \tag{5}$$

$\forall n \in N \cup L:$

$$\sum_{d \in D} \sum_{k \in D^d} x_{pr(n)D_k^d} \leq \sum_{d \in D} \sum_{k \in D^d} x_{nD_k^d} + \sum_{c \in C} \sum_{j \in C^c} y_{nC_j^c} \tag{6}$$

where: $pr(n)$ is the parent node of node n.

$$\|C\| \sum_{d \in D} \sum_{k \in D^d} x_{pr(n)D_k^d} \geq \sum_{d \in D} \sum_{k \in D^d} x_{nD_k^d} + \sum_{c \in C} \sum_{j \in C^c} y_{nC_j^c} \tag{7}$$

$$\sum_{n \in P_l} x_{nD_k^d} \leq 1 \qquad \forall d \in D, k \in D^d \tag{8}$$

$$\sum_{n \in P_l} y_{nC_j^c} \leq 1 \qquad \forall c \in C, j \in C^c \tag{9}$$

$\forall l \in L, n \in P_l:$

$$\sum_{d \in D} \sum_{k \in D^d} x_{nD_k^d} + \sum_{c \in C} \sum_{j \in C^c} y_{nC_j^c} \leq \|C\|(\|C\| - \sum_{n' \in P_{pr(n)}} \sum_{c \in C} \sum_{j \in C^c} y_{n'C_j^c}) \tag{10}$$

where: P_n is the path from the root to node n.

$$\sum_{l \in L} z_l^i \geq 1 \qquad \forall i \in I \tag{11}$$

$$\sum_{l \in L} c_l^i \leq 1 \qquad \forall i \in I \tag{12}$$

$$z_l^i \geq c_l^i \qquad \forall i \in I, l \in L \tag{13}$$

$\forall l \in L, i \in I:$

$$\sum_{n \in P_l} \sum_{d \in D} \sum_{k \in D^d} |\phi_{D_k^d}^i - \omega_{nP_l}| x_{nD_k^d} \leq (H-1)(1 - z_l^i) \tag{14}$$

$\forall l \in L, i \in I:$

$$\sum_{n \in P_l} \sum_{c \in C} \sum_{j \in C^c : \psi_{C_j^c}^i = C_j^c} y_{nC_j^c} \geq \|C\| c_l^i \tag{15}$$

$$\sum_{d \in D} \sum_{k \in D^d} x_{nD_k^d} + c_{ll}^i \geq c_{rl}^i \qquad \forall ll \in L \tag{16}$$

where: $ll, rl \in L$ and ll is left sibling of rl.

In [14], the author introduces several cost-constrained datasets wherein the features are divided into groups based on their characteristics. In each group, the first feature used in the classifier consumes the highest cost, and then other features consume a lower cost. For example, in a group of blood tests, the first test must contain an extra cost of $2.10 for collecting blood and the remaining tests consume a nominal cost of $1.00. In a different way, we can understand that all tests in that group share the common cost of $2.10, and this cost is paid when at least one test is taken. In this research, we replace the cost constraint in [11] by constraints (17) and (18) in order to adapt the benchmark instance provided by [14].

Constraints (17) present the budget limit in the case of using the group cost.

$$\sum_{g \in G} \eta_g e_l^g + \sum_{n \in P_l} \sum_{d \in D} \sum_{k \in D^d} \delta_{D^d} x_{nD_k^d} \leq B \qquad \forall l \in L \qquad (17)$$

where: η_g is the common cost of the group g in the set of groups G, and binary variable $e_l^g = 1$ if at least one decision $d \in g$ is assigned to path P_l, otherwise $e_l^g = 0$. The definition of variables e_l^g is presented as follows:

$$He_l^g \geq \sum_{n \in P_l} \sum_{d \in g} \sum_{k \in D^d} x_{nD_k^d} \geq e_l^g \qquad \forall g \in G, l \in L \qquad (18)$$

4 The Matheuristic Approach

Since optimizing the complete model $(\mathcal{F})$ may be too expensive, we propose a mathematical programming heuristic based on VND (see [5,8,15]) to speed up the exploration of solutions. The concept behind VND is a local search technique that involves systematically changing neighborhood structures in order to explore the solution space. The overall method operates as follows: a MILP formulation is implemented to create an initial solution $\hat{x}$ in which only decision attributes are considered. After that, the solution $\hat{x}$ is used in the VND local search, where a part of $\hat{x}$ are fixed and the remaining part and other variables, including y, z, c and e, are optimized by the model $(\mathcal{F})$ presented previously.

4.1 The MILP Formulation for Assigning Decision Attributes

Aforementioned in the previous sections, the multiple-condition-attribute decision tree creation can be presented by a series of discrete decisions: which internal node to assign a decision attribute, which threshold to split on; and discrete outcomes: which inner node or leaf a condition attribute should be assigned to, which label to choose, whether a datapoint is correctly classified. Among those questions, the decision attribute assignment plays an essential role because the decision attributes determine the path and the leaf node a datapoint falls into. Thus, a constructive formulation is introduced to generate a set of initial trees, including only decision attributes, with the given depth H. This formulation aims to create as many different trees as possible besides satisfying the cost constraints and temporarily ignoring condition attributes and datapoints.

Let $t_{D^d} \in [0,1]$ be the variable presenting the appearance of the decision attribute D^d in the decision tree. A decision attribute is used for constructing the decision tree when the value of the variable t_{D^d} is greater than 0. The constraints defining those variables are established as follows:

$$\sum_{n \in N} \sum_{k \in D^d} x_{nD_k^d} \geq t_{D^d} \qquad \forall d \in D \qquad (19)$$

$$\sum_{n \in N} \sum_{k \in D^d} x_{nD_k^d} \leq \beta \|N\| \qquad \forall d \in D \qquad (20)$$

Constraints (19) ensure that the value of t_{D^d} equals to 0 if and only if there is no threshold of decision attribute D^d assigned to any node n. Otherwise, the value of t_{D^d} is freely decided by the formulation. Constraints (20) restrict the maximum number of thresholds of decision attributes assigned to the tree. We introduce the parameter β used to create the diversity of solutions. For the same dataset, the value of β is randomly generated in $[0.5, 1]$ to create an "elite" set of different solutions.

Let $sub(n_l)$ and $sub(n_r)$ be the subtrees wherein n's left child and n's right child are their roots, respectively. We observe that if n contains a threshold D_k^d, every internal node in the $sub(n_l)$ should not be assigned a threshold $D_{k'}^d$: $D_{k'}^d \gtrsim D_k^d$ because the datapoints traversing the left branch of n obviously satisfy the threshold $\phi_{D_{k'}^d}^i$. Similarly, the $sub(n_r)$ should not contain the threshold $D_{k'}^d : D_{k'}^d \lesssim D_k^d$.

Denote that $\|sub(n_l)\|$ and $\|sub(n_r)\|$ are the number of internal nodes in the subtree $sub(n_l)$ and $sub(n_r)$. These constraints are formulated as follows:
$\forall n \in N, d \in D; k \in D^d$:

$$\|sub(n_l)\|(1 - \sum_{d \in D} \sum_{k \in D^d} x_{nD_k^d}) \geq \sum_{n' \in sub(n_l)} \sum_{d \in D} \sum_{k' \in D^d : D_{k'}^d \gtrsim D_k^d} x_{n'D_{k'}^d} \qquad (21)$$

$$\|sub(n_r)\|(1 - \sum_{d \in D} \sum_{k \in D^d} x_{nD_k^d}) \geq \sum_{n' \in sub(n_r)} \sum_{d \in D} \sum_{k' \in D^d : D_{k'}^d \lesssim D_k^d} x_{n'D_{k'}^d} \qquad (22)$$

The MILP model for the decision attribute assignment is presented as follows:

($\mathcal{F}x$):

Objective function:

$$\max \gamma \sum_{n \in N} \sum_{d \in D} \sum_{k \in D^d} x_{nD_k^d} + (1 - \gamma) \sum_{d \in D} t_{D^d} \qquad (23)$$

s.t.

$$(2), (17), (18), (19)-(22)$$

$$\sum_{d \in D} \sum_{k \in D^d} x_{pr(n)D_k^d} \geq \sum_{d \in D} \sum_{k \in D^d} x_{nD_k^d} \qquad (24)$$

The objective function is to maximize the total number of thresholds D_k^d and decision attributes D^d used in the decision tree. The complexity parameter γ is randomly generated in $[0.1, 0.9]$ to increase the diversity of the "elite" set. The new constraints (24), which replace constraints (6) and (7) in the formulation $(\mathcal{F})$, guarantee that an "empty" node does not have children. Thus, the output tree $\mathcal{T}'$ of the formulation $(\mathcal{F}x)$ can be used later as a part of the solution of the formulation $(\mathcal{F})$, wherein the constraints (6) and (7) are mandatory, to construct a complete multiple-condition-attribute decision tree $\mathcal{T}$.

From the "elite" set, the best candidate $\hat{x}$ is selected to search for the near-optimal solution in the matheuristic approach. The process archiving $\hat{x}$ is presented in the Algorithm 1. While the function $solve\_decisions()$ is used to generate the solution x_i of the formulation $(\mathcal{F}x)$ related to each pair of (β, γ), the function $solve\_fixed\_decisions()$ finds the optimal solution of the formulation $(\mathcal{F})$ with the given x_i. The function $calculate\_accuracy()$ estimates the accuracy of the decision tree (number of correctly classified datapoints) obtained by each pair (x_i, y_i) on the test set. Then this result is compared to 0 to determine whether the decision tree is overfitting on the training set or not. Thus, the solution of $solve\_fixed\_decisions()$ is acceptable for the further step.

Algorithm 1. Assigning Decision Attributes

Input: I, C, D, H, N, L
Output: $\hat{x}$
$maxObj \leftarrow 0$; $acc \leftarrow 0$; $\beta \leftarrow 0.5$; $\gamma \leftarrow 0.1$; $i \leftarrow 0$
while $\beta \leq 1$ **do**
> **while** $\gamma \leq 0.9$ **do**
> > $\bar{x}_i \leftarrow solve\_decisions(\mathcal{F}x, \beta, \gamma)$
> > $x_i \leftarrow \bar{x}_i$
> > $(\mathcal{O}_i, x_i, y_i) \leftarrow solve\_fixed\_decisions(\mathcal{F}, x_i)$
> > $acc \leftarrow calculate\_accuracy(x_i, y_i)$
> > **if** $maxObj < \mathcal{O}_i$ **and** $acc > 0$ **then**
> > > $maxObj \leftarrow \mathcal{O}_i$; $\hat{x} \leftarrow x_i$
> >
> > **end**
> > $\gamma \leftarrow \gamma + 0.1$; $i \leftarrow i + 1$
>
> **end**
> $\beta \leftarrow \beta + 0.1$
end
return $\hat{x}$

4.2   The MILP-Based Algorithm: VND

The basic idea of the VND algorithm is the steepest descent consisting of choosing an initial solution $\hat{x}$, finding a direction of the steepest descent from $\hat{x}$, within a neighborhood $\mathcal{N}(\hat{x})$, and moving to the minimum (maximum) of the objective function within $\mathcal{N}(\hat{x})$ along that direction. If there is no direction of descent, the heuristic stops and otherwise it is iterated. In our study, VND local search is constructed by solving the formulation $(\mathcal{F})$ from a solution wherein a part is fixed and the remaining part is "warm-started" from the current best solution.

The matheuristic contains the following parameters: h indicates the time limit for running the algorithm, l limits the runtime of each local search (time for solving the formulation $(\mathcal{F})$). Algorithm 2 shows the pseudo-code for our approach.

Algorithm 2. VND Algorithm

Input: $I, C, D, H, N, L, \hat{x}, \mathcal{N}, h, l$
Output: $(\mathcal{O}, x, y)$
$st \leftarrow time()$
$\mathcal{N} \leftarrow shuffle(); k \leftarrow 1; ft \leftarrow time(); et \leftarrow ft - st$
while ($k \leq \|\mathcal{N}\|$ **and** $et \leq h$) **do**
$\quad$ $x^* \leftarrow create\_neighbor(\hat{x}, \mathcal{N}_k)$
$\quad$ $(\mathcal{O}, x) \leftarrow solve(\mathcal{F}, x^*, l)$
$\quad$ **if** $maxObj < \mathcal{O}$ **then**
$\quad\quad$ $maxObj \leftarrow \mathcal{O}; \hat{x} \leftarrow x; k \leftarrow 1$
$\quad\quad$ $\mathcal{N} \leftarrow shuffle(\mathcal{N})$
$\quad$ **else**
$\quad\quad$ $k \leftarrow k + 1$
$\quad$ **end**
$\quad$ $ft \leftarrow time()$
$\quad$ $et \leftarrow ft - st$
end
return $\hat{x}$

Several neighborhoods have been designed to be employed in that fix-and-optimize strategy. Each neighborhood defines a set of subproblems wherein some variables x are fixed and the remaining will be optimized by the formulation $(\mathcal{F})$. A VND algorithm is implemented to explore these neighborhoods in random order. In Algorithm 2, the function $create\_neighbor(\hat{x}, \mathcal{N}_k)$ fixes some variables of the solution $\hat{x}$ and optimizes the others. Let $\mathcal{N}_k$ be the kth subset in the set of all neighborhoods $\mathcal{N}$. The set $\mathcal{N}_k$ is constructed by one of the following techniques:

- Set of neighborhoods $\mathcal{N}_1$: assigns decision attributes to the inner nodes at two consecutive levels of the tree.
- Set of neighborhoods $\mathcal{N}_2$: considers all inner nodes at the same level of the tree except the level of the root node.
- Set of neighborhoods $\mathcal{N}_3$: assigns decision attributes to the inner nodes of a sub-tree (the root node is not considered).
- Set of neighborhoods $\mathcal{N}_4$: considers an inner nodes and its children. The inner nodes at the two lowest levels are not chosen because these nodes do not have inner-node children or are considered in Neighborhood $\mathcal{N}_3$.

– Set of neighborhoods $\mathcal{N}_5$: assigns decision attributes to all inner nodes in a path from the root to a leaf.
– Set of neighborhoods $\mathcal{N}_6$: considers several inner nodes which are randomly chosen. The maximum number of considered nodes is $\|N\|/4$.

The list $\mathcal{N}$ contains all neighborhoods mentioned above. The algorithm shuffles this list so that there is no priority for searching first in one neighborhood relative to another. This strategy is inspired by [15] and [13], where several neighborhood orders are tested in a VND algorithm and the randomized order provides better solutions. When the incumbent solution is updated, the list is reshuffled and the algorithm starts exploring it from the beginning.

5   Numerical Experiments

In [3], the experiment shows that when the number of condition attributes increases, the predicted accuracies decrease. In our study, we focus on building the binary decision tree, therefore, the accuracies can significantly decrease compared to the method in [3] because the assignment of the condition attributes is limited. Although the MILP formulation and the VND algorithm can handle multiple-condition-attribute datasets, we restrict our experiment to the case of building the two-condition-attribute binary decision tree to ensure that the accuracies of the decision trees are considerable.

The models are written in C++ and sent to the optimization solver CPLEX, which runs on an AMD Ryzen machine with 24 GB of RAM. Each dataset is divided into 5 pairs of training and test sets at random, with a ratio of 75% and 25%. The complete formulation ($\mathcal{F}$) is solved in 3600 s on a single core of memory for each training set. The total runtime limit of the VND algorithm is also set to 3600 s and the maximum runtime of the function $solve(\mathcal{F}, x^*, l)$ is 180 s ($l = 180$). We use 6 datasets provided by [11] to compare the performances of the original MILP formulation and the matheuristic. Besides that dataset, we also examine our model on the *BUPA liver disorders, heart disease* and *Pima Indians diabetes* dataset (presented in Table 1) where the cost and the budget are given in [14]. Additionally, the features in [14] are divided into groups, thus, we assume that our randomly generated costs are in the same group. In Table 1, the first column presents the names of 3 UCI datasets in [14]. The second column contains the number of datapoints in each dataset. We use the same technique introduced in [11] to create the set of thresholds of decision attributes and the second condition attribute for these datasets. The number of thresholds of each decision attribute used in the experiment is shown in the third column. The fourth column presents the number of each label. The fifth column includes the costs of decision attributes and the groups containing decision attributes are shown in the brackets.

Our approaches are tested with the depth $H = \{2, 3, 4, 5\}$. The average value of objective, runtime, and accuracy is calculated for each dataset after running on different training sets five times and validating by test sets. The performances

Table 1. Data presentation

dataset	Description				
	$\|I\|$	$\|D\|$ $\|D^d\|$	$\|C\|$ $\|C^c\|$	δ_{D^d}	B
BUPA liver disorders	345	4 16, 24, 16, 14	2 2, 2	7.27(A), 7.27(A), 7.27(A), 9.86(A)	31.67
Pima Indians diabetes	768	7 7, 22, 15, 12, 16, 28, 15	2 2, 3	1(B), 17.61(A), 1(B), 1(B), 22.78(A) 1(B), 1(B)	45.39
heart disease	303	12 14, 1, 1, 10, 9, 1, 1, 14, 1, 9, 1, 3	2 4, 2	1(B), 1(B), 1(B), 1(B), 7.27(A), 5.2(A), 15.5(B) 102.9(C), 87.3(D), 87.3(D) 87.3(D), 100.9(B)	366.8

of the two approaches are evaluated based on the number of condition attributes, the value of cost, and the budget B.

In Table 2, the column "$\mathcal{O}/\|N\|$" presents the average ratio of correctly classified datapoints ($\mathcal{O}$) to the number of datapoints in the training sets (N). The column "Acc" contains the average accuracy of the MILP formulation and the VND algorithm on the test sets. We should note that the accuracy and runtime in the Table 2 are the average values of 5 runs for each dataset, thus, there are some cases that the MILP runs faster than the VND but provides worse accuracy because there exists a running time without optimal solution. In the [11], the author argues that the accuracy archived can be low because of the consideration of multiple condition attributes and cost. For example, the mean out-of-sample accuracy of single condition attribute data sets *car evaluation* provided by 2 methods are greater than 77%, while the average accuracy in case of multiple condition attributes are lower than 33%. The experiment shows that the VND algorithm provides acceptable objective value and accuracy in the cases of small datasets, such as *acute-inflammations-1, acute-inflammations-2, BUPA liver disorders, heart, Pima Indians diabetes, votes,* and *zoo.* The result of single condition attribute presented in Table 2b proves that our approach is flexible for solving both single and multiple condition attributes. The VND can solve to optimal more single-condition-attribute datasets and perform better objective values and accuracies than the case of multiple condition attributes.

The experiment results also show that the VND algorithm is slightly better than the MILP in both single-condition and multiple-condition datasets. In Table 2a, the VND algorithm provides 21 better objective values (shown in bold) compared to 3 values of the MILP formulation. The number of better accuracies performed by the VND is 15 while the value of the MILP is 11. For the case of single-condition datasets in Table 2b, the numbers of better objective values of the VND and the MILP are 16 and 8, respectively, and the numbers of better accuracies are 13 and 11.

Table 2. The results of the MILP formulation and the VND

(a) Two condition attributes

dataset	H	MILP formulation O/‖N‖	Acc	Runtime	VND algorithm O/‖N‖	Acc	Runtime
car evaluation	2	0.337	**0.322**	3600.070	**0.342**	0.306	2325.220
	3	0.334	**0.306**	3600.150	0.346	0.290	3439.590
	4	0.332	**0.314**	3600.370	0.351	0.280	3495.700
	5	0.295	**0.306**	3600.800	**0.362**	0.238	3493.810
acute inflammations 1	2	0.678	0.667	0.304	0.678	0.667	4.921
	3	0.678	0.667	1.058	0.678	0.667	4.972
	4	0.678	0.667	37.038	0.678	0.667	4.575
	5	0.678	0.667	1173.350	0.678	0.667	187.034
acute inflammations 2	2	0.756	0.733	0.289	0.756	0.733	2.116
	3	0.756	0.733	0.859	0.756	0.733	1.822
	4	0.756	0.733	7.887	0.756	0.733	140.083
	5	0.756	0.733	41.384	0.756	0.733	271.432
heart disease	2	0.597	0.550	3600.050	**0.604**	**0.561**	2545.080
	3	0.626	0.555	3600.090	**0.645**	**0.566**	3412.680
	4	0.644	0.534	3600.200	**0.710**	**0.574**	3477.210
	5	0.715	0.511	3600.460	**0.741**	**0.532**	3484.060
tic-tac-toe	2	**0.343**	0.322	3600.050	0.341	**0.336**	2110.320
	3	0.356	0.335	3600.100	**0.388**	**0.376**	3163.120
	4	0.361	0.330	3600.200	**0.431**	**0.378**	3522.040
	5	0.375	0.339	3600.450	**0.469**	**0.428**	3540.650
votes	2	0.791	0.786	70.175	0.791	0.786	111.173
	3	0.810	0.717	3600.050	0.810	**0.734**	431.925
	4	0.828	**0.724**	3600.080	**0.838**	0.703	1120.940
	5	0.833	**0.710**	3600.150	**0.848**	0.700	1346.500
zoo	2	0.629	0.546	1.940	0.629	0.546	7.618
	3	**0.779**	**0.585**	381.934	0.763	0.577	36.374
	4	0.819	**0.592**	3600.040	**0.827**	0.585	247.838
	5	**0.811**	**0.577**	3600.070	0.797	0.569	333.623
BUPA liver disorders	2	0.529	0.454	3600.050	**0.531**	**0.470**	1912.230
	3	0.560	**0.485**	3600.120	0.560	0.467	3506.790
	4	0.595	0.440	3600.280	**0.610**	0.458	3479.740
	5	0.619	0.463	3600.590	**0.643**	**0.472**	3454.500
Pima Indians diabetes	2	0.616	**0.589**	3600.130	**0.622**	0.588	2907.810
	3	0.623	0.593	3600.310	**0.653**	**0.607**	3483.670
	4	0.602	0.559	3600.770	**0.650**	**0.595**	3464.850
	5	0.325	0.515	3601.680	**0.681**	**0.580**	3528.850

(b) Single condition attribute

dataset	H	MILP formulation O/‖N‖	Acc	Runtime	VND algorithm O/‖N‖	Acc	Runtime
car evaluation	2	0.776	0.777	38.910	0.776	0.777	106.946
	3	**0.818**	0.812	2320.370	0.815	**0.813**	240.933
	4	0.824	0.822	3600.320	0.824	**0.823**	905.932
	5	**0.803**	**0.806**	3600.710	0.797	0.781	1060.100
acute inflammations 1	2	1.000	1.000	0.231	1.000	1.000	1.398
	3	1.000	1.000	2.094	1.000	1.000	2.712
	4	1.000	1.000	4.295	1.000	1.000	3.438
	5	1.000	1.000	16.394	1.000	1.000	5.261
acute inflammations 2	2	1.000	1.000	0.262	1.000	1.000	0.743
	3	1.000	1.000	1.587	1.000	1.000	0.892
	4	1.000	1.000	2.409	1.000	1.000	1.982
	5	1.000	1.000	18.842	1.000	1.000	5.727
heart disease	2	0.802	0.729	3600.080	**0.804**	**0.739**	1146.610
	3	0.812	0.761	3600.180	**0.864**	**0.763**	3330.120
	4	0.869	0.784	3600.430	**0.887**	0.734	3489.750
	5	0.841	0.739	3600.930	**0.916**	**0.766**	3506.950
tic-tac-toe	2	0.705	**0.688**	3600.050	**0.707**	0.680	1709.700
	3	0.716	0.698	3600.110	**0.766**	**0.735**	3179.510
	4	0.718	0.683	3600.240	**0.819**	**0.810**	3519.870
	5	0.689	0.652	3600.590	**0.816**	**0.772**	3490.290
votes	2	0.972	0.962	5.948	0.972	0.962	9.742
	3	**0.986**	0.917	966.861	0.980	**0.952**	27.080
	4	**0.991**	**0.941**	2269.400	0.990	0.931	228.701
	5	**0.992**	**0.924**	1980.860	0.991	0.910	301.834
zoo	2	0.827	**0.731**	3600.050	0.827	0.723	0.882
	3	**0.957**	0.754	34.666	0.939	0.746	6.521
	4	**0.997**	0.731	421.990	0.995	0.731	45.379
	5	0.987	0.754	2305.040	**0.997**	0.754	143.381
BUPA liver disorders	2	0.666	0.611	3600.050	0.662	0.595	1962.190
	3	0.698	0.591	3600.190	**0.702**	**0.595**	3395.770
	4	0.734	**0.591**	3600.390	**0.751**	0.566	3497.220
	5	0.701	**0.595**	3600.790	**0.802**	0.591	3474.720
Pima Indians diabetes	2	0.772	0.721	3600.140	**0.784**	**0.730**	2812.060
	3	0.772	**0.739**	3600.350	**0.794**	0.711	3509.890
	4	0.705	0.690	3600.870	**0.820**	**0.725**	3475.700
	5	0.392	0.615	3602.010	**0.830**	**0.732**	3521.210

6   Conclusion

In this research, we re-introduce the problem of constructing the cost-constrained decision tree with multiple condition attributes. A matheuristic based on the VND framework is implemented based on the existing MILP formulation to speed up the solution exploration. The findings demonstrate that the proposed technique is effective in handling small datasets and offers satisfactory solution quality for a number of larger datasets. These results provide comprehensive evidence that the optimal decision tree creation problem can lead to significant improvements over heuristic methods, even if in the case that the cost factors are included and multiple condition attributes are considered.

Future development should take a number of expansions and enhancements into consideration. For instance, the issue may be seen via the perspective of robust optimization when the cost factors are uncertain. Planning should be made to take into account any enhancements to the solution approach that might significantly lessen the reliance of the number of integer variables on the size of training sets, such as modifying or verifying the current formulation, and implementing decomposition, ...

References

1. Aglin, G., Nijssen, S., Schaus, P.: Learning optimal decision trees using caching branch-and-bound search. In: Proceedings of the AAAI Conference on Artificial Intelligence, vol. 34, pp. 3146–3153 (2020)
2. Bertsimas, D., Dunn, J.: Optimal classification trees. Mach. Learn. **106**, 1039–1082 (2017)
3. Chen, Y.L., Wu, C.C., Tang, K.: Building a cost-constrained decision tree with multiple condition attributes. Inf. Sci. **179**, 967–979 (2009)
4. Chen, Y.L., Wu, C.C., Tang, K.: Time-constrained cost-sensitive decision tree induction. Inf. Sci. **354**, 140–152 (2016)
5. Fischetti, M., Fischetti, M.: Matheuristics. In: Martí, R., Panos, P., Resende, M. (eds.) Handbook of Heuristics, pp. 1–33. Springer, Cham (2016). https://doi.org/10.1007/978-3-319-07153-4_14-1
6. Kao, H.P., Tang, K.: Cost-sensitive decision tree induction with label-dependent late constraints. INFORMS J. Comput. **26**, 238–252 (2014)
7. Lomax, S., Vadera, S.: A survey of cost-sensitive decision tree induction algorithms. ACM Comput. Surv. (CSUR) **45**, 1–35 (2013)
8. Mladenović, N., Hansen, P.: Variable neighborhood search. Comput. Oper. Res. **24**(11), 1097–1100 (1997)
9. Mookerjee, V.S., Dos Santos, B.L.: Inductive expert system design: maximizing system value. Inf. Syst. Res. **4**, 111–140 (1993)
10. Murphy, C.K., Benaroch, M.: Adding value to induced decision trees for time-sensitive data. INFORMS J. Comput. **9**, 385–396 (1997)
11. Pham, H.G.: The mixed-integer linear programming for cost-constrained decision trees with multiple condition attributes. In: 14th IEEE International Conference on Knowledge and Systems Engineering (KSE 2022) (2022)
12. Qiu, C., Jiang, L., Li, C.: Randomly selected decision tree for test-cost sensitive learning. Appl. Soft Comput. **53**, 27–33 (2017)
13. Souza, M., Coelho, I., Ribas, S., Santos, H., Merschmann, L.: A hybrid heuristic algorithm for the open-pit-mining operational planning problem. Eur. J. Oper. Res. **207**(2), 1041–1051 (2010)
14. Turney, P.D.: Cost-sensitive classification: empirical evaluation of a hybrid genetic decision tree induction algorithm. J. Artif. Intell. Res. **2**, 369–409 (1994)
15. Vilas Boas, M.G., Santos, H.G., Merschmann, L.H.D.C., Vanden Berghe, G.: Optimal decision trees for the algorithm selection problem: integer programming based approaches. Int. Trans. Oper. Res. **28**(5), 2759–2781 (2021)
16. Wu, C.C., Chen, Y.L., Tang, K.: Cost-sensitive decision tree with multiple resource constraints. Appl. Intell. **49**, 3765–3782 (2019)

Fast Bicriteria Approximation Algorithm for Minimum Cost Submodular Cover Problem

Canh V. Pham[1]([✉]), Quat V. Phu[2], and Dung T. K. Ha[2]

[1] ORLab, Faculty of Computer Science, Phenikaa University, Hanoi, Vietnam
canh.phamvan@phenikaa-uni.edu.vn
[2] Faculty of Information Technology, VNU University of Engineering
and Technology, Hanoi, Vietnam
{20025030,20028008}@vnu.edu.vn

Abstract. This paper studies the Minimum Cost Submodular Cover
(MCSC) problem over the ground set of size n, which aims at finding
a subset with the minimal cost required so that the utility submodular
function exceeds a given threshold. The issue has recently attracted a lot
of attention due to its applications in various domains of artificial intelligence and combination optimization. However, the best approximation
algorithm for the problem requires an expensive query complexity of
$O(n^2)$ that may become infeasible for some applications with large data.

In this work, we propose a bicriteria approximation algorithm that
keeps the performance guarantees of the state-of-the-art but reduces
the required number of queries to $O(n \log n)$. Besides the theoretical, the
experiment results on two applications, Twitter feed threshold summarization, and threshold influence in social networks, further show the
superiority of our algorithm with the state-of-the-art in terms of both
solution quality and query complexity.

Keywords: Submodular Cover · Approximation Algorithm

1 Introduction

A utility function $g : 2^V \mapsto \mathbb{R}^+$, defined on all subsets of a ground set V sized n
is submodular iff it satisfies *the diminishing return property*, i.e., for $S \subseteq T \subseteq V$
and $e \notin T$:

$$g(S \cup \{e\}) - g(S) \geq g(T \cup \{e\}) - g(T).$$

There are a lot of applications of submodular optimization in the fields of artificial intelligence, such as information diffusion [6,9,11,12,19], optimal allocation [22], recommendations [10], data summarization [15,16], and active set
selection [18] taking the form of the Minimum Cost Submodular Cover (MCSC)
problem, defined as follows:

Definition 1 (MCSC problem). *Given a group set V, a monotone and submodular function $g : 2^V \mapsto \mathbb{R}^+$ and a threshold $T, 0 < T \leq g(V)$, the problem
asks to find a subset $S \subseteq V$ with minimal cost so that $g(S) \geq T$.*

M. H. Hà et al. (Eds.): CSoNet 2023, LNCS 14479, pp. 186–197, 2024.
https://doi.org/10.1007/978-981-97-0669-3_18

In the literature, MCSC has attracted much effort in fast-finding comparative approximate solutions. Besides, the explosion of data in MCSC applications (e.g., the number of users via social networks) also motivates researchers to propose efficient approximation algorithms available to scale up to massive data. A simple but efficient way to address the aforementioned problems is designing fast algorithms to reduce query complexity since it dominates the running time of algorithms [1,12,14]. We refer to the *query complexity* as the number of oracle calls to the function g.

To the best of our knowledge, Greedy algorithms are the best approach to this problem in terms of guarantees of solutions [5,9,22,23]. These algorithms repeatably select which element has the maximum density gain, i.e., the ratio of marginal gain over the cost, into the partial solution until the value of the utility function exceeds T. A representative greedy algorithm in [9] can return the best approximation ratio of $1 + \log(1/\epsilon)$ with the value of utility function is at least $(1 - \epsilon)T$, where ϵ is an input. Unfortunately, the greedy algorithm requires an expensive query complexity of $O(n^2)$ that may be infeasible for some applications with large data. This raises an open and interesting question: *How do we reduce the query complexity but keep the theoretical guarantee of the greedy algorithm?* To address the above question, we propose a fast algorithm that can keep the theoretical guarantees of the greedy algorithm while reducing the query complexity to $O(n \log n)$.

Our detailed contributions are as follows:

- We propose FBA, a $((1 + \epsilon)(1 + \log(\frac{1}{\delta})), 1 - \delta)$-bicriteria approximate algorithm for the MCSC problem, where ϵ, δ are pre-fixed accuracy parameters. Our algorithm returns an approximation ratio arbitrarily close to the Greedy algorithm by [9] while keeping the value of the utility function at least $(1-\delta)T$. FBA takes $O(\frac{n}{\epsilon^2} \log(\frac{n}{\epsilon}) \log(\frac{1}{\delta}))$ query complexity that may better than that of the greedy algorithm by the factor of $\Omega(\log n)$.
- We further investigate the performance of our algorithm with the state-of-the-art algorithm. The experiment results reveal that our algorithm has significantly fewer queries, from dozens to hundred times, and runs from several up to dozens of times faster than state-of-the-art.

Our Techniques. One obstacle for solving MCSC is that one can not bound the $\rho(V)$, where $\rho(V) = \frac{\max_{e \in V} c(e)}{\min_{e \in V} c(e)}$ by a polynomial of n and therefore it may be arbitrarily large. Our algorithm first adapts the idea in [20] to filter the major set V' from the original ground set, and one can bound $\rho(V')$ by $O(n^3)$. We then find the near-optimal solution over V' by making multiple guesses for the objective value. For each guess, we adapt the greedy threshold method of [1] to filter new elements in a partial solution. Finally, the algorithm returns the best one among candidate solutions.

Organization. The rest of the paper includes Sect. 2, which reviews some related works. The notations are presented in Sect. 3. Section 4 presents our algorithms and theoretical analysis. The experiment of our algorithm and state-of-the-art algorithms are marked in Sect. 5. Finally, we conclude the paper in Sect. 6.

2   Related Works

The serious difficulty of MCSC is that it is an NP-hard problem [8] and can not be approximated with a ratio of $1 - o(1)$ unless $NP \subset DTIME(O^{\log \log n})$. First, people used the greedy strategy, which steply selected an element with the largest marginal gain into a solution to address the problem. Wolsey *et al.* [24] first proposed a $1 + \ln(\max_{e \in V} f(e)/\beta)$-approximation algorithm where β was the smallest non-zero marginal gain of any element added by the greedy and g was integer-valued. Wan *et al.* [23] considered the cost function c was submodular and proved that the greedy algorithm provided an approximation ratio of $\rho \ln T$, where $\rho = \min_{S \subseteq V} \sum_{e \in S} c(e)/c(S)$ was the curvature of c. Still, this approximation ratio only held when g was integer-valued. Another authors [9] developed another greedy algorithm for a special instance of MCSC, Minimum Target Selection, but can be adapted to any monotone and submodular utility function. Their algorithm provided a solution with the total cost at most $1 + \log(1/\epsilon)$, and the value of the objective was at least $(1 - \epsilon)T$. Thus, it is the best approximation algorithm because it can handle the real-valued utility and return a constant ratio related to the cost of the optimal solution while the utility value is almost larger than T. Nonetheless, the drawback of the greedy lies in sequentially adding an element to the partial solution, which makes the query complexity $\Omega(n|S|)$ and may reach $O(n^2)$ for the solution S. Besides, the greedy strategies were also popularly applied to expand the ground set over integer lattice [22] and the submodularity of cost function [6].

Another work of Crawford *et al.* [5] proposed an efficient evolutionary algorithm that could provide a $(1 + \log(1/\epsilon), 1 - \epsilon)$-bicriteria approximation solution. However, in expectation, the number of queries could be at most $O(n^3)$. The authors in [20] focused on efficient parallel algorithms, but they needed an expensive query complexity of $\Omega(n \log(nT) \log^2 T)$ and was only valid for the integer-valued function [20]. Besides, some studies focused on the Set Cover (SC), a special version of the MCSC with uniform cost [2,7,15].

Recently, streaming fashion has been an effective tool for submodular optimization problems to deal with big data. Norouzi-Fard *et al.* [17] introduced the first streaming for SC problem that made single-pass, used M memories and provided a $(2\ln(1/\epsilon), 1 - \frac{1}{\ln(1/\epsilon)})$-bicriteria approximation solution, where M was required memory. Crawford *et al.* [4] proposed a streaming algorithm for solving the MCSC problem with a non-monotone utility function. That algorithm returned a weak performance guarantees of $((1+\epsilon)(1+\frac{4}{\epsilon^2}), \frac{1-\epsilon}{2})$ bicriteria approximation ratio and needed a $O(\frac{n}{\epsilon} \log \frac{opt}{c_{min}})$ query complexity. Note that the query complexity depends on $\frac{1}{c_{min}}$ that is not a constant and may be arbitrarily large.

From the background of these works, we realized these algorithms required a large number of queries to find an approximate solution. Hence, it will be quite difficult to solve the problem with big input data. The proposed new algorithm reduces the query complexity to sub-linear with $O(n \log(n))$ queries. Moreover, it can reach the approximation ratio of the best one [9], which gave the ratio of $1 + \log(1/\epsilon)$. The proposed algorithm is a type of bicriteria approximation that provides the ratio of $(1 + \epsilon)(1 + \log(1/\delta))$ the optimal with $\epsilon > 0, \delta > 0$ are accuracy parameters.

3   Preliminaries

In this section, we introduce some notations used throughout the paper. Given a ground set $V = \{e_1, \ldots, e_n\}$ of size n, the utility function $g : 2^V \mapsto \mathbb{R}^+$ measures the quality of a subset $S \subseteq V$. We assume g normalized, i.e., $g(\emptyset) = 0$. *The marginal gain* (also called the contribution gain) of an element e to a set $S \subseteq V$ is defined $g_S(e) = g(S \cup \{e\}) - g(S)$. We also define $g_S(T) = g(S \cup T) - g(T)$ for any set $T \subseteq V$. It is assumed that there exists an oracle query, which, when queried with the set S, returns the value $g(S)$.

The function g is monotone iff for $A \subseteq B \subseteq V$, we have $g(A) \leq g(B)$ and g is submodular iff for any $e \in V \setminus B$, $g_A(e) \geq g_B(e)$.

An instance of the problem MCSC is presented by a tuple (V, g, T). Given an instance of MCSC with cost function c additive, i.e., $c(S) = \sum_{e \in S} c(e)$, we define $c_{min} = \min_{e \in V} c(e)$, $c_{max} = \max_{e \in V} c(e)$, and O is the optimal solution and the optimal cost $\mathsf{opt} = c(O)$.

We call an algorithm is an (δ_1, δ_2)-**bicriteria approximation** for MCSC problem if it returns a solution S satisfying $g(S) \geq \delta_2 \cdot T$ and $c(S) \leq \delta_1 \cdot \mathsf{opt}$, where $\delta_1, \delta_2 > 0$.

4   Proposed Algorithms for the Problem

In this section, we introduce our Fast Bicriteria Greedy Algorithm (FBA) that provides $((1 + \epsilon)(1 + \log \frac{1}{\delta}), 1 - \epsilon)$ bicriteria approximation solution within $O(n \log n)$ number of queries. For an easy following, firstly, we present a simplified version assuming that an estimation v of the objective value is known, i.e., $(1 - \epsilon)\mathsf{opt} \leq v \leq \mathsf{opt}$. Besides, the theoretical performance for this case is established. We then present the main version of our algorithm after removing the assumption, which contains two key steps. First, we find a "good" bound of c_{max}/c_{min} and the "major" set to find candidate solutions by adapting the method of dividing ground set [20]. We next make multiple guesses for objective value and adapt the simple version to get the final solution.

4.1   Proposed Algorithm with Known opt

The algorithm takes an instance (V, g, T), accuracy parameters $\epsilon, \delta > 0$ and an estimation v so that $(1 - \epsilon)v \leq \mathsf{opt} \leq v$ as inputs. It contains a main (**for**) loop that consists of at most $O(\log(1/\delta)/\epsilon)$ iterations. In each iteration, the algorithm establishes the threshold $\theta = (1-\epsilon)(T-f(S))/v$ and adapts the greedy threshold algorithm in [1] to filter every element with high density ratio, i.e., the ratio of its marginal gain over its cost, where $f(\cdot) = \min\{g(\cdot), T\}$. We note that $f(\cdot)$ is also monotone and submodular. Accordingly, the algorithm will keep every element with the density ratio over the threshold θ and eliminate the others. The algorithm terminates if it meets the conditions in Line 7 or the number of iterations reaches $\lceil \ln(1/\delta)/\epsilon \rceil$. The detailed descriptions of the algorithm are presented in Algorithm 1.

Algorithm 1: FBA algorithm with knowing opt

Input: An instance (V, g, T), $\epsilon \in (0, 1/2), \delta > 0, v$
Output: A solution S.
1: $S \leftarrow \emptyset$, $f(\cdot) = \min\{T, g(\cdot)\}$
2: **for** $l = 1$ **to** $\lceil \ln(1/\delta)/\epsilon \rceil$ **do**
3: $\quad$ $\theta \leftarrow (1 - \epsilon)(T - f(S))/v$
4: $\quad$ **foreach** $e \in V \setminus S$ **do**
5: $\quad\quad$ **if** $\frac{f_S(e)}{c(e)} \geq \theta$ **then**
6: $\quad\quad\quad$ $S \leftarrow S \cup \{e\}$
7: $\quad$ **if** $f(S) \geq (1 - \delta)T$ **then return** S

8: **return** S

We show the performance guarantees of 1 in Theorem 1.

Theorem 1. *For $\delta, \epsilon \in (0, 1/2)$ and $(1 - \epsilon)v \leq \text{opt} \leq v$, the Algorithm 2 runs in at most $\frac{n}{\epsilon} \log(\frac{1}{\delta})$ queries and returns a solution S satisfying $g(S) \geq T(1 - \delta)$ and $c(S) \leq (1 + 6\epsilon)(1 + \ln(\frac{1}{\delta}))\text{opt}$.*

Proof. Algorithm 1 consists of two loops. The outer loop includes $\frac{1}{\epsilon} \log(\frac{1}{\delta})$ iterations and each of them takes n queries to f. Therefore, the total number of queries of the Algorithm is at most $\frac{n}{\epsilon} \log(\frac{1}{\delta})$. We prove the approximation guarantee by dividing it into the following cases.

Case 1. If the main loop terminates at iteration $l = \frac{1}{\epsilon} \ln(\frac{1}{\delta})$. Denote by S_i S after end iteration $i, 1 \leq i \leq l$ of the main loop. We note that $f(\cdot)$ is a monotone and submodular function. Every element, which is not selected at the iteration i, has the density gain less than θ, therefore,

$$T - f(S_i) \leq f(O) - f(S_i) \tag{1}$$

$$\leq f(O \cup S_i) - f(S_i) \text{ (By the monotoncity of } f) \tag{2}$$

$$\leq \sum_{e \in O \setminus S_i} f_{S_i}(e) \text{ (By the submodularity of } f) \tag{3}$$

$$\leq \sum_{e \in O \setminus S_i} c(e)\theta \leq \frac{\text{opt}}{v}(1 - \epsilon)(T - f(S_{i-1})) \tag{4}$$

$$\leq (1 - \epsilon)(T - f(S_{i-1})). \tag{5}$$

By continuously applying the above inequality, we have:

$$T - f(S_l) \leq (1 - \epsilon)^l T \leq e^{-\epsilon l} T \leq \delta T. \tag{6}$$

Thus $g(S_l) \geq f(S_l) \geq (1 - \delta)T$. In this case, the algorithm does not meet the condition in Line 7 at iteration $l - 1$, which implies that $f(S_{l-1}) < (1 - \delta)T$. On the other hand, by the selection rule of new elements into S_i, we have

$$f(S_i) - f(S_{i-1}) \geq \sum_{e \in S_i \setminus S_{i-1}} f_{S_{i-1}}(e) \geq \sum_{e \in S_i \setminus S_{i-1}} c(e) \cdot \theta \tag{7}$$

$$= c(S_i \setminus S_{i-1}) \frac{(1 - \epsilon)}{v} (T - f(S_{i-1})). \tag{8}$$

Re-arranging the last inequality gives

$$T - f(S_i) \leq (1 - \frac{(1 - \epsilon)c(S_i \setminus S_{i-1})}{v})(T - f(S_{i-1})) \tag{9}$$

$$\leq e^{-\frac{(1-\epsilon)c(S_i \setminus S_{i-1})}{v}} (T - f(S_{i-1})). \tag{10}$$

By continuously applying the above inequality, we have

$$\delta T < T - f(S_{l-1}) \leq e^{-\frac{(1-\epsilon)c(S_l \setminus S_{l-1})}{v}} (T - f(S_{l-1})) \tag{11}$$

$$\leq e^{-\frac{(1-\epsilon)c(S_l \setminus S_{l-1})}{v}} e^{-\frac{(1-\epsilon)c(S_{l-1} \setminus S_{l-2})}{v}} (T - f(S_{l-2})) \tag{12}$$

$$= e^{-\frac{(1-\epsilon)c(S_l \setminus S_{l-2})}{v}} (T - f(S_{l-2})) \tag{13}$$

$$\dots \leq e^{-\frac{(1-\epsilon)c(S_{l-1})}{v}} T \leq e^{-\frac{(1-\epsilon)c(S_{l-1})}{\mathsf{opt}}} T. \tag{14}$$

Hence $c(S_{l-1}) \leq \frac{\mathsf{opt}}{(1-\epsilon)^2} \ln(\frac{1}{\delta})$. From (8) and the definition of $f(\cdot)$, we have the bound of $c(S_l \setminus S_{l-1})$, that is

$$c(S_l \setminus S_{l-1}) \leq \frac{f(S_l) - f(S_{l-1})}{T - f(S_{l-1})} \frac{v}{1 - \epsilon} \leq \frac{\mathsf{opt}}{(1 - \epsilon)^2}. \tag{15}$$

Therefore,

$$c(S_l) = c(S_{l-1}) + c(S_l \setminus S_{l-1}) \leq (1 + \ln(\frac{1}{\delta})) \frac{\mathsf{opt}}{(1 - \epsilon)^2} \tag{16}$$

$$\leq (1 + 6\epsilon)(1 + \ln(\frac{1}{\delta}))\mathsf{opt}. \tag{17}$$

The last inequality is due to $\frac{1}{1-\epsilon} \leq 1 + 2\epsilon$, for $\epsilon \in (0, 1/2)$.

Case 2. If the main loop terminates at iteration $l < \frac{1}{\epsilon} \ln(\frac{1}{\delta})$, i.e., the algorithm meets the condition in Line 7 at iteration l. We must have $f(S_l) \geq (1 - \delta)T$ and $f(S_{l-1}) < (1 - \delta)T$. By the similar transform from (11) to (14), we also have $c(S_{l-1}) \leq \frac{\mathsf{opt}}{(1-\epsilon)^2} \ln(\frac{1}{\delta})$ and by the similar argument of (15), we obtain $c(S_l \setminus S_{l-1}) \leq \frac{\mathsf{opt}}{(1-\epsilon)^2}$. Thus we get (17). Combining two cases, we finish the proof. $\qquad\square$

4.2 Main Algorithm

We now introduce our main algorithm FBA by discarding the assumption of known opt. The core of FBA lies in two steps. At the first one, it adapts the idea for carefully selecting the "main" subset V' from the original ground set V by [20]. It first sorts $V = \{e_1, e_2, \ldots, e_n\}$ in non-decreasing cost order and find the smallest number j so that $g(\{e_1, \ldots, e_j\}) \geq T$. The algorithm then finds the subset V' contains elements with the cost fall in an internal $(\epsilon c(e_j)/n, jc(e_j))$.

At the second, the algorithm finds candidate solutions over set V' by trying to find estimations of the optimal value opt' over the instance $(V', g_{V_0}(\cdot), T - g(V_0))$, where $V_0 = \{e \in V : c(e) \leq \epsilon c(e_j)/n\}$. For each estimation, it calls the Algorithm 1 multiple times to find a set of candidate solutions (Lines 7-9). Finally, the algorithm returns the best solution S' in Line 10 and returns $S' \cup V_0$ as the final solution. Details of FBA are illustrated in Algorithm 2.

Algorithm 2: Fast Bicriteria Approximation (FBA) Algorithm

Input: An instance (g, V, T), $\epsilon \in (0, 1/2), \delta > 0$.
Output: A subset S
1: $S \leftarrow \emptyset$, $\epsilon' \leftarrow \epsilon/7$
2: Sort $V = \{e_1, e_2, \ldots, e_n\}$ in non-decreasing cost order
3: $j \leftarrow \min\{i : g(\{e_1, e_2, \ldots, e_i\}) \geq T\}$
4: $c'_{min} \leftarrow \epsilon' c(e_j)/n$, $c'_{max} \leftarrow jc(e_j)$
5: $V_0 \leftarrow \{e \in V : c(e) < c'_{min}\}$, $V_1 \leftarrow \{e \in V : c(e) > c'_{max}\}$, $V' \leftarrow V \setminus (V_0 \cup V_1)$
6: $T' \leftarrow T - g(V_0)$, $g'(\cdot) \leftarrow g_{V_0}(\cdot)$, $c_0 = \min_{e \in V'} c(e)$
7: **for** $i = 0$ to $\lceil \log_{1/(1-\epsilon')}(c(V')/c_0) \rceil$ **do**
8: $\quad v_i = c_0/(1-\epsilon')^i$
9: $\quad S(i) \leftarrow$ Result of Algorithm 1 with a tuple input $(V', g', T', \epsilon', \delta, v_i)$
10: $S' \leftarrow \arg\min\{c(S(i)) : g(S(i)) \geq T'(1-\delta), i = 0, \ldots, \lceil \log_{1/(1-\epsilon')}(c(V')/c_0) \rceil\}$
11: **return** $S' \cup V_0$

The query complexity and theoretical bound of the solution of FBA are shown in Theorem 2.

Theorem 2. *For $\delta \in (0, 1)$ and $\epsilon \in (0, 1/2)$, the Algorithm 2 runs in $O(\frac{n}{\epsilon^2} \log(\frac{n}{\epsilon}) \log(\frac{1}{\delta}))$ queries and returns a solution S satisfying $g(S) \geq T(1-\delta)$ and $c(S) \leq (1+\epsilon)(1 + \ln(\frac{1}{\delta}))$opt.*

Proof. The algorithm first finds the number j in Line 3 with $O(n)$ queries. The algorithm then contains a main loop within $\lceil \log_{1/(1-\epsilon')}(c(V')/c_0) \rceil$ iterations, each calls Algorithm 1 as a subroutine. Combine with Theorem 1, we have the query complexity of Algorithm 2 is:

$$n + \frac{n}{\epsilon} \log(\frac{1}{\delta}) \lceil \log_{1/(1-\epsilon')} (\frac{c(V')}{c_0}) \rceil \leq n + \frac{n}{\epsilon} \log(\frac{1}{\delta}) (\log_{1/(1-\epsilon')} \frac{jn^2}{\epsilon'} + 1) \quad (18)$$

$$\leq n + \frac{n}{\epsilon} \log(\frac{1}{\delta}) (\log_{1+\epsilon/2} \frac{n^3}{\epsilon'} + 1) \leq n + \frac{n}{\epsilon} \log(\frac{1}{\delta}) (\frac{\log \frac{n^3}{\epsilon'}}{\log(1 + \epsilon/2)} + 1) \quad (19)$$

$$= O(\frac{n}{\epsilon^2} \log(\frac{n}{\epsilon}) \log(\frac{1}{\delta})). \quad (20)$$

We now show the approximation guarantee. From the proof of Theorem 13 in [20], we have: $c(e_j) \leq \text{opt} \leq jc(u_j)$ and thus we have $c(V_0) \leq nec(e_j)/n \leq \epsilon \text{opt}$. Denote by O' the optimal solution of the MCSC over the instance (V', g', T') and $\text{opt}' = c(O')$. Denote $v_i = \frac{c'_{min}}{(1-\epsilon')^i} = \frac{\epsilon c(e_j)}{n(1-\epsilon')^i}$. Since i varies from 0 to $\log_{1/(1-\epsilon)}(c(V')/c_0)$ and $c_0 \leq \text{opt}' \leq c(V')$, there exists an iteration i of the main loop that $v_i(1 - \epsilon') \leq \text{opt}' \leq v_i$. By Theorem 1, we have $c(S(i)) \leq (1 + 6\epsilon')\text{opt}'$. By the submodularity and the monotonicity of g, we have:

$$g'(O) = g_{V_0}(O) = g(O \cup V_0) - g(V_0) \geq T'$$

thus O is a feasible solution of the instance (V', g', T'). Therefore $\text{opt}' \leq \text{opt}$. By Theorem 1 and the selection of the candidate solution $S(i)$, we have:

$$c(S(i) \cup V_0) = c(V_0) + c(S(i)) \leq \epsilon' \text{opt} + (1 + 6\epsilon')(1 + \log(\frac{1}{\delta}))\text{opt}'$$

$$\leq (1 + 7\epsilon')(1 + \log(\frac{1}{\delta}))\text{opt} \leq (1 + \epsilon)(1 + \log(\frac{1}{\delta})).$$

We also have $g_{V_0}(S(i)) \geq T'(1 - \delta)$ which implies

$$g(S(i) \cup V_0) = g_{V_0}(S(i)) + g(V_0) = g'(S(i)) + g(V_0)$$
$$\geq T'(1 - \delta) + g(V_0) = (T - g(V_0))(1 - \delta) + \delta g(V_0) \geq T(1 - \delta).$$

The proof is completed.

5   Empirical Evaluation

In this section, we demonstrate the empirical performance of FBA outperforms the Greedy version of [9] for the metrics of the total cost, number of queries, and time consumption of two applications of MCSC: Twitter feed Threshold Summarization (TS) and Threshold Influence (TI). We used a variety of network topologies from two publicly available datasets: the Stanford Large Network Dataset Collection [13] and the Network Repository [21].

Implementation and Environment. We inherited the implementation in [3]. We conduct experiments by Python with Ubuntu 20.04.5 OS and run on Intel Core i7-11800H @ 2.30 GHz processor.

Parameters. We setup $\epsilon = 0.5$ and $\delta = 0.1$ for all test cases. With element cost, two different configurations were a random uniform distribution in $(0, 1)$

194   C. V. Pham et al.

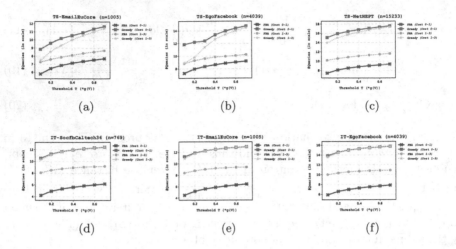

Fig. 1. Evaluation of total queries

and a random uniform distribution in $(1,3)$. The threshold T was chosen from $0.1 * g(V)$ to $0.7 * g(V)$ for each application to explore the behavior of each algorithm across a broad range of instance sizes. **Results and Discussions.** Figures from 1 to 4 illustrate the results of these algorithms on TS and TI. As can be seen, the lines of Greedy have significant increasing trends when T increases, while FBA trends keep the linear steady or slightly upward. Only in case Fig. 2(a), the trend is a little different. This is a normal thing because it's an objective experiment.

For more detail, FBA is more efficient than the Greedy in terms of both the number of queries and the running time. It uses significantly fewer queries, from

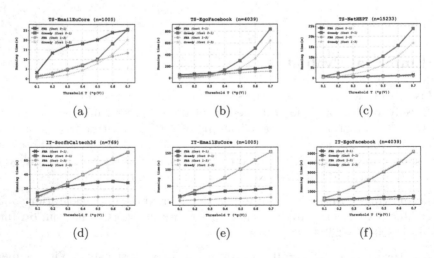

Fig. 2. Evaluation of running time

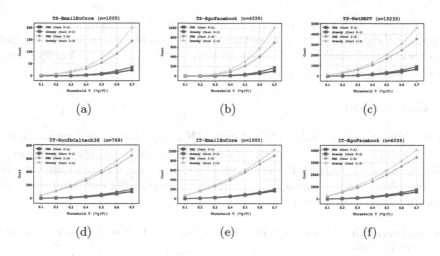

Fig. 3. Evaluation of total cost

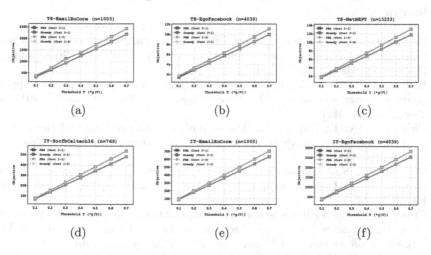

Fig. 4. Evaluation of the objective

9 to 200 times, and runs from 1.6 up to 16 times faster. Additionally, FBA gives results with lower total cost from 10% to 40% while ensuring that the objective is at least $T(1-\delta)$. We can see that the number of queries of Greedy can be higher, from dozens to millions, than that of FBA (Fig. 1). Reversely, the query numbers of FBA most are horizontal and slightly above zero with different T. According to the time consumption with TS-EmailEuCore, the time of FBA (cost 0–1) marks the highest values than others, while Greedy (cost 1–3) hits the lowest points when $T \leq 0.5$. However, these numbers seem to change when T grows in which the time of Greedy (cost 0–1) grows fast, followed by Greedy (cost 1–3), whereas FBA (cost 0–1) and FBA (cost 1–3) gradually increase. Nonetheless, for the remaining results, Greedy wastes more time than FBA, especially with small

costs and large T. It comes back to the general trend, like query and total cost. Regarding the total cost, we can see these results look like query results. Overall, the experimental results were consistent with the theory and FBA outperforms the aforementioned Greedy version.

6   Conclusion

For the Minimum Cost Submodular Cover (MCSC) problem, we proposed a fast bicriteria approximation algorithm, FBA, which is available for real-valued f within $O(n \log(n))$ queries. For the approximation ratio, our algorithm can give the equivalent ratio to the best one. For query complexity, our algorithm may reduce a factor of $\Omega(\log(n))$.

Acknowledgment. This research is funded by Phenikaa University under grant number PU2023-1-A-01.

References

1. Badanidiyuru, A., Vondrák, J.: Fast algorithms for maximizing submodular functions. In: Proceedings of the Twenty-Fifth Annual ACM-SIAM Symposium on Discrete Algorithms, pp. 1497–1514. SIAM (2014)
2. Blelloch, G.E., Peng, R., Tangwongsan, K.: Linear-work greedy parallel approximate set cover and variants. In: Proceedings of the 23rd ACMSPAA 2011, pp. 23–32. ACM (2011)
3. Chen, Y., Dey, T., Kuhnle, A.: Best of both worlds: practical and theoretically optimal submodular maximization in parallel. In: Neural Information Processing Systems (2021)
4. Crawford, V.: Scalable bicriteria algorithms for non-monotone submodular cover. In: International Conference on Artificial Intelligence and Statistics, pp. 9517–9537. PMLR (2023)
5. Crawford, V.G.: An efficient evolutionary algorithm for minimum cost submodular cover. In: Kraus, S. (ed.) Proceedings of the Twenty-Eighth International Joint Conference on Artificial Intelligence, pp. 1227–1233. ijcai.org (2019)
6. Crawford, V.G., Kuhnle, A., Thai, M.T.: Submodular cost submodular cover with an approximate oracle. In: Proceedings of the 36th International Conference on Machine Learning, vol. 97, pp. 1426–1435. PMLR (2019)
7. Fahrbach, M., Mirrokni, V.S., Zadimoghaddam, M.: Submodular maximization with nearly optimal approximation, adaptivity and query complexity. In: Proceedings of the Thirtieth Annual ACM-SIAM Symposium on Discrete Algorithms, pp. 255–273. SIAM (2019)
8. Feige, U.: A threshold of ln n for approximating set cover. J. ACM **45**(4), 634–652 (1998)
9. Goyal, A., Bonchi, F., Lakshmanan, L.V.S., Venkatasubramanian, S.: On minimizing budget and time in influence propagation over social networks. Social Netw. Analys. Min. **3**(2), 179–192 (2013)
10. Guillory, A., Bilmes, J.A.: Simultaneous learning and covering with adversarial noise. In: Getoor, L., Scheffer, T. (eds.) Proceedings of the 28th International Conference on Machine Learning, ICML 2011, Bellevue, Washington, USA, June 28 - July 2, 2011, pp. 369–376. Omnipress (2011)

11. Kuhnle, A., Pan, T., Alim, M.A., Thai, M.T.: Scalable bicriteria algorithms for the threshold activation problem in online social networks. In: IEEE Conference on Computer Communications, pp. 1–9 (2017)
12. Kuhnle, A., Smith, J.D., Crawford, V.G., Thai, M.T.: Fast maximization of non-submodular, monotonic functions on the integer lattice. In: Dy, J.G., Krause, A. (eds.) Proceedings of the 35th International Conference on Machine Learning. Proceedings of Machine Learning Research, vol. 80, pp. 2791–2800. PMLR (2018)
13. Leskovec, J., Krevl, A.: SNAP Datasets: Stanford large network dataset collection. http://snap.stanford.edu/data (2014)
14. Mirzasoleiman, B., Badanidiyuru, A., Karbasi, A.: Fast constrained submodular maximization: personalized data summarization. In: Proceedings of the 33nd International Conference on Machine Learning. JMLR Workshop and Conference Proceedings, vol. 48, pp. 1358–1367. JMLR.org (2016)
15. Mirzasoleiman, B., Karbasi, A., Badanidiyuru, A., Krause, A.: Distributed submodular cover: succinctly summarizing massive data. In: Annual Conference on Neural Information Processing Systems, pp. 2881–2889 (2015)
16. Mirzasoleiman, B., Zadimoghaddam, M., Karbasi, A.: Fast distributed submodular cover: public-private data summarization. In: Annual Conference on Neural Information Processing Systems, pp. 3594–3602 (2016)
17. Norouzi-Fard, A., Bazzi, A., Bogunovic, I., El Halabi, M., Hsieh, Y.P., Cevher, V.: An efficient streaming algorithm for the submodular cover problem. In: Advances in Neural Information Processing Systems, vol. 29 (2016)
18. Norouzi-Fard, A., Bazzi, A., Bogunovic, I., Halabi, M.E., Hsieh, Y., Cevher, V.: An efficient streaming algorithm for the submodular cover problem. In: Annual Conference on Neural Information Processing Systems, pp. 4493–4501 (2016)
19. Pham, C.V., Phu, Q.V., Hoang, H.X., Pei, J., Thai, M.T.: Minimum budget for misinformation blocking in online social networks. J. Comb. Optim. 38(4), 1101–1127 (2019)
20. Ran, Y., Zhang, Z., Tang, S.: Improved parallel algorithm for minimum cost submodular cover problem. In: Proceedings of the Learning Theory. Proceedings of MLS, vol. 178, pp. 3490–3502. PMLR (2022)
21. Rossi, R.A., Ahmed, N.K.: The network data repository with interactive graph analytics and visualization. In: AAAI (2015)
22. Soma, T., Yoshida, Y.: A generalization of submodular cover via the diminishing return property on the integer lattice. In: Annual Conference on Neural Information Processing Systems, pp. 847–855 (2015)
23. Wan, P., Du, D., Pardalos, P.M., Wu, W.: Greedy approximations for minimum submodular cover with submodular cost. Comput. Optim. Appl. 45(2), 463–474 (2010)
24. Wolsey, L.A.: An analysis of the greedy algorithm for the submodular set covering problem. Comb. 2(4), 385–393 (1982)

Mixed Integer Linear Programming-Based Methods for the Optimal Time-Constrained Cost-Sensitive Decision Tree

Hoang Giang Pham[1]([✉])[iD] and Toan Tran Quang[2]

[1] ORLab, Faculty of Computer Science, Phenikaa University, Hanoi, Vietnam
giang.phamhoang@phenikaa-uni.edu.vn
[2] Faculty of Computer Science, Phenikaa University, Hanoi, Vietnam
toan.tranquang@phenikaa-uni.edu.vn

Abstract. Cost management and completion timelines are common classification problem requirements. For instance, a blood test requires human and equipment resources, costs money, and must be done quickly. To avoid major patient risks, medical diagnosis should minimize positive-to-negative misclassification. There has been extensive research on how to build a decision tree from training data that minimizes misclassification and test costs, but not on how to design an optimal decision tree with time constraints. A mixed-integer programming is implemented to create an optimal time-constrained cost-sensitive decision tree in this study. We adapt several existing approaches in the literature with time constraints, misclassification cost, and feature selection cost, and introduce new mathematical models designed for these problems. Our experiments compare all methods and examine how time and cost constraints affect optimal solution identification and demonstration.

Keywords: Optimal Decision Tree · Time-Constrained · Cost-Sensitive · Mixed Integer Programming

1 Introduction

Since their invention over 30 years ago, decision trees have become a popular interpretable machine learning method. Decision trees can classify a future point by traversing a split sequence and recording the leaf label. Extreme interpretation, computational efficiency, and understandable classification rules are decision tree capabilities. In classification tasks, it is the most well-known, used, and successful. In recent years and in prominent venues, mathematical formulations that guarantee optimality have received the most attention due to MIP solvers' incredible computational power. The mathematical optimization models can also model fairness, interpretation, and linear branching and leafing rules. A number of exact methods have recently been proposed in the literature

© The Author(s), under exclusive license to Springer Nature Singapore Pte Ltd. 2024
M. H. Hà et al. (Eds.): CSoNet 2023, LNCS 14479, pp. 198–209, 2024.
https://doi.org/10.1007/978-981-97-0669-3_19

[1–3,6,11,15–17]. These methods limit tree depth to control search space and use a MIP solver to find the optimal tree provided by the training procedure under well-defined constraints.

Recently, researchers have focused on building cost-sensitive decision trees [7,9]. The most studied costs are misclassification and test. Misclassifying a sick patient as healthy is more dangerous than misclassifying a healthy patient as sick. The cost of classification error may be highly imbalanced in some cases, unlike in normal classification tasks. Each test may require expensive procedures like blood tests or x-rays. Numerous studies examine misclassification costs [4,12, 13,18] and add test costs to classification problems [10,20]. The initial study on both types of costs is [14].

While cost optimization has been studied extensively, only [5] addresses the issue of balancing costs and time constraints. According to the literature review, time-constrained cost-sensitive decision tree induction is an interesting but rarely discussed topic. There is no exact method for finding the best decision tree for this research. The MIP models' heuristic solutions have benefits despite their limitations in solving complex problems to optimality (see [13]). We adapt time constraints and costs to the existing MIP formulations and introduce a new mathematical model specifically for the problem to compare the results.

The goal of optimal decision tree design is to choose features and labels for each branching node and leaf to maximize prediction accuracy or minimize prediction error. We use the powerful Mixed Integer Programming (MIP) solver CPLEX to find optimal decision trees in this research. Because decision trees involve discrete decisions and outcomes, the problem of creating an optimal decision tree is a MIP problem.

The paper is organized as follows. The literature is revised in Sect. 1. Section 2 introduces our basic notation, new mathematical models, and other optimal decision tree concepts. Time limit and feature cost adaptation in existing methods are presented in Sect. 3. Section 4 presents our MIP model experiments and compares them to others. Section 5 concludes and suggests future research.

2   Mathematical Formulation

This section describes our MIP formulation for learning traditional optimal classification trees of a given depth. Our decision tree construction must make discrete decisions, such as: each inner node can have a feature assigned or not; a feature value (split) must be chosen to branch on if an inner node assigns an attribute, otherwise it must be denied; when two paths share "empty" inner nodes, they must classify the same label, thus, the same datapoint must traverse them; labels must be assigned to leaves; finally, respect the tree structure by choosing which paths and leaves a training point will take.

Assume that a dataset I and a depth-$\mathcal{H}$ decision tree containing a set of inner nodes N and a set of leaves L are considered. Denote that $P_l, A(n)$ and $a(n)$ are a set of inner nodes on the path corresponding leaf l, a set of the ancestors of inner node n, and the parent of inner node n, respectively. Let F and K be a set of splits and sets of classes in dataset I. We create a set of parameters $\phi_f^i \in \{0,1\}$ and a set of parameters $\omega_{nP_l} \in \{0,1\}$ to direct the flow of datapoints in the decision tree.

Sets of binary decision variables b_{fn}, z_l^i, a_{lk} and c_l^i are introduced. If split $f \in F$ is branched at node $n \in N$, the value of b_{fn} is set to 1, otherwise $b_{fn} = 0$. If leaf $l \in L$ predicts class k, $a_{lk} = 1$, otherwise $a_{lk} = 0$. Related to the datapoint, variables z_l^i present the opportunity that datapoint i reaches leaf l ($z_l^i = 1$), while variables c_l^i equal 1 if data i is classified correctly when reaching leaf l, otherwise $c_l^i = 0$.

The new formulation of the traditional decision tree is presented as follows:

(1) PathOCT:

$$\max \ \alpha \sum_{i \in I} \sum_{l \in L} c_l^i - (1-\alpha) \sum_{f \in F} \sum_{n \in N} b_{fn} \tag{1a}$$

$$\text{s.t.} \ \sum_{f \in F} b_{fn} \leq 1 \qquad\qquad \forall n \in N \tag{1b}$$

$$\sum_{n \in P_l} b_{fn} \leq 1 \qquad\qquad \forall l \in L, f \in F \tag{1c}$$

$$\sum_{k \in K} a_{lk} = 1 \qquad\qquad \forall l \in L \tag{1d}$$

$$\sum_{l \in L} c_l^i \leq 1 \qquad\qquad \forall i \in I \tag{1e}$$

$$\sum_{l \in L} z_l^i \geq 1 \qquad\qquad \forall i \in I \tag{1f}$$

$$a_{lk} \geq c_l^i \qquad\qquad \forall l \in L, k \in K, i \in I : \lambda^i = k \tag{1g}$$

$$z_l^i \geq c_l^i \qquad\qquad \forall l \in L, i \in I \tag{1h}$$

$$1 - z_l^i \leq \sum_{n \in P_l} \sum_{f \in F} b_{fn} \cdot |\phi_f^i - \omega_{nP_l}| \qquad \forall i \in I, l \in L \tag{1i}$$

$$\sum_{n \in P_l} \sum_{f \in F} b_{fn} \cdot |\phi_f^i - \omega_{nP_l}| \leq \mathcal{H} \cdot (1 - z_l^i) \forall i \in I, l \in L \tag{1j}$$

$$\sum_{f \in F} b_{fn} \leq \sum_{f \in F} b_{fa(n)} \qquad\qquad \forall l \in L, n \in P_l \tag{1k}$$

$$\sum_{f \in F} b_{fn} \geq a_{l'k} - a_{lk} \quad \forall l, l' \in L, n \in P_l \cap P_{l'}, k \in K \tag{1l}$$

$$\sum_{f \in F} b_{fn} \geq a_{lk} - a_{l'k} \quad \forall l, l' \in L, n \in P_l \cap P_{l'}, k \in K \tag{1m}$$

$$b_{fn} \in \{0,1\} \qquad\qquad \forall n \in N, f \in F \tag{1n}$$

$$Variables'\ domains \tag{1o}$$

The objective function (1a) aims to maximize the number of datapoints classified correctly and minimize the number of splits assigned to the paths.

Regularization parameter α addresses the complexity of the resulting problem. Constraints (1b) ensure that each position on each path is assigned at most one split. Constraints (1c) guarantee that each split appears at most once on each path in order to avoid assigning unnecessary ones. Constraints (1d) ensure that each path classifies only one class. Constraints (1e) force each datapoint to traverse at most one path whose the label is assigned the same class as its. Constraints (1f) simply show that each datapoint must traverse at least one path. Constraints (1g), (1h) ensure that the datapoints are correctly classified iff the paths traversed by them are assigned to the same class. Constraints (1i) and (1j) choose the right path for each datapoint to traverse based on the bitwise presenting the path, the split of the chosen feature in each position on the path and the corresponding feature value of the considered datapoint. Constraints (1k), (1l) and (1m) allow to change inner nodes into leaves. Constraints (1k) guarantee that an inner node is not assigned a split if its ancestors node do not contain any split.

From the above formulation, we propose two mathematical models for optimal time-constrained cost-sensitive binary decision trees. We call them **BCS-PathOCT** for balanced trees and **ICS-PathOCT** for imbalanced trees. Time constraints and cost parameters modify the previous model. Classification errors also replace decision variables related to datapoint classification accuracy.

(2) BCS-PathOCT:

$$\min \alpha \sum_{i \in I} \sum_{k \in K: k \neq \lambda^i} e_k^i \cdot \psi_{\lambda^i k} + (1 - \alpha) \sum_{f \in F} \sum_{n \in N} b_{fn} \cdot \delta_f \tag{2a}$$

s.t. (1d),(1i),(1j)

$$\sum_{f \in F} b_{fn} = 1 \qquad\qquad \forall n \in N \tag{2b}$$

$$\sum_{l \in L} z_l^i = 1 \qquad\qquad \forall i \in I \tag{2c}$$

$$z_l^i + a_{lk} \leq 1 + e_k^i \qquad \forall l \in L, i \in I, k \in K : k \neq \lambda^i \tag{2d}$$

$$\sum_{k \in K: k \neq \lambda^i} e_k^i \leq 1 \qquad\qquad \forall i \in I \tag{2e}$$

$$\sum_{n \in P_l} \sum_{f \in F} b_{fn} \cdot \sigma_f \leq \sum_{k \in K} a_{lk} \cdot \rho_k \qquad \forall l \in L \tag{2f}$$

$Variables'\ domains$ (2g)

In the model above, assume that parameters ρ_k and δ_f denote the limited time of label k (a deadline for completing the classification task) and the time used to carry out a test of feature f (or the time spent for a result of a test), respectively. The correct class of datapoint i is denoted by λ^i. Parameters $\psi_{\lambda^i k}$ present the cost of misclassifying data i belonging to class λ^i to k. The total consuming time of all features on each path must be less than or equal to the label assigned to this path's limited time. Although the time-limited constraints and cost parameters are firstly considered in [5], there has been no mathematical formulation for the time-constrained cost-sensitive decision tree since then.

All inner nodes in a balanced decision tree must have features assigned to them. As a result, constraints (1b) are converted to equations. Furthermore, constraints (1c), (1k), and (1l) will be removed because the tree is not pruned. Because there is no pruning constraint, a feature with a short consuming time can be reused rather than choosing other features with longer consuming times. Thus, we allow the model to assign the same feature to multiple nodes on a path in order to reduce the possibility of no feasible solution being found. This can avoid the risk that there exists a path whose minimum value of total consuming time is greater than the limited times of all labels. To calculate the cost of misclassifying datapoints, variables c_l^i are replaced by variables e_k^i. Constraints (2d) and (2e) ensure that if a datapoint is misclassified, it is assigned to at most one incorrect label. Constraints (2f) establish limited times for labels assigned to paths. Because assigning attributes to all inner nodes on each path enforces each data point to traverse only one path, transferring the inequalities (1f) to equations (2c) is not unnecessary, but might restrict the search space of the problem.

The imbalanced time-constrained cost-sensitive formulation is nearly identical to the **Path-OCT** model, with the exception of decision variables e_k^i, cost parameters added, and additional limited time constraints. When the limited time of labels is tight, pruning constraints allow the model to have a diverse feature assignment. Instead of assigning several attributes that take less time and perform ineffectively, the formulation can choose to use one attribute that takes a long time but provides valuable classification.

(3) ICS-PathOCT:

Objective(2a)

s.t. (1b),(1c),(1d),(1f), (1i),(1j),(1k),(1l),(1m),(2d),(2e),(2f)

$Variables'\ domains$ (3a)

Constraints (1b) and (2f) consider additional limited times in both two cases wherein inner nodes contain features or not. On one hand, they ensure that if there exists some variables b_{fn} are equal to 1, the total of the consuming time σ_f of attributes f assigned to inner nodes n on path P_l must be smaller or equal the limited time ρ_k of the label k chosen at leaf l. On the other hand, the consuming times at node $n \in P_l$ are not taken into account when $\sum_{f \in F} b_{fn} = 0$.

3   The Adaptation of Limited Times and Costs of Features in Existing Models

In this section, we re-implement the existing formulations introduced in [1] and [3], then add costs and time constraints for further comparisons. These models only consider minimizing prediction errors or maximizing the number of correct classifications without taking into account which incorrect labels datapoints reach. Thus, we must consider new decision variables denoted the misclassification of a datapoint belonging class k to a class $k' \neq k$. Following that, the formulations necessitate the addition of new constraints that are used to define the boundaries of these variables. Furthermore, the time constraints are implemented and modified due to unique characteristics of each model. The **BCS-FlowOCT** and the **ICS-FlowOCT** formulations for growing balanced and imbalanced decision trees, respectively, as well as the **CS-BinOCT** for constructing balanced decision trees, are presented as time-constrained cost-sensitive variants. The sets of variables and parameters of **BCS-FlowOCT** and the **ICS-FlowOCT** are presented in Table 1, while the ones used in the **CS-BinOCT** are presented in Tables 2.

(4) BCS-FlowOCT:

Objective(2a)

s.t.(1d),(2b),(2e),(2f)

$$z^i_{a(n),n} = z^i_{n,l(n)} + z^i_{n,r(n)} \quad \forall n \in N, i \in I \tag{4a}$$

$$z^i_{a(n),n} = z^i_{n,t} \quad \forall n \in L, i \in I \tag{4b}$$

$$z^i_{s,1} \leq 1 \quad \forall i \in I \tag{4c}$$

$$z^i_{n,l(n)} \leq \sum_{f \in F: x^i_f = 0} b_{fn} \quad \forall i \in I, n \in N \tag{4d}$$

$$z^i_{n,r(n)} \leq \sum_{f \in F: x^i_f = 1} b_{fn} \quad \forall i \in I, n \in N \tag{4e}$$

$$\sum_{n \in L} z^i_{n,t} = 1 \quad \forall i \in I \tag{4f}$$

$$z^i_{n,t} + a_{nk} \leq 1 + e^i_k$$
$$\forall n \in L, i \in I, k \in K : k \neq \lambda^i \tag{4g}$$

$$Variables'\ domains \tag{4h}$$

Compared with the original version proposed by [1], the **BCS-FlowOCT** uses constraints (1d) to enforce each datapoint to reach the sink even though it is classified incorrectly. Similar to model (2) and (3), the limited time constraints (2f) calculate the sum of the consuming times σ_f of features f assigned to inner nodes $n \in P_l$ for any $b_{fn} = 1$ and compares this value to the deadline ρ_k of label in leaf $l \in L$ related to P_l for any $a_{lk} = 1$. Additionally, constraints (4g), which specify decision variables e^i_k, combine with constraints (1d) to determine prediction errors at the sink.

The model (5) below decides to choose a split or a leave at each inner node. Therefore, the limited time constraints must satisfy both two cases. Constraints (5h), which replace constraints (2f), guarantee that if an inner node becomes a leave, the sum of the consuming time of its ancestors must be smaller or equal to the time limit corresponding the label. If this node is assigned a split, the value of M ensures that the inequalities (5h) are correct for all $n \in P^{n'}_l$.

Table 1. Decision variables in FlowOCT

Variables	Definition
p_n	Equals 1 if inner node n predicts a label, 0 otherwise
$z^i_{a(n),n}$	Equals 1 if datapoint i is correctly classified and traverses the arc between inner node n and its ancestor $(a(n))$ on its way to the sink t, 0 otherwise
$z^i_{n,l(n)}$	Equals 1 if datapoint i is correctly classified and traverses the arc between inner node n and its left child node $(l(n))$ on its way to the sink t, 0 otherwise
$z^i_{n,r(n)}$	Equals 1 if datapoint i is correctly classified and traverses the arc between inner node n and its right child node $(r(n))$ on its way to the sink t, 0 otherwise
$z^i_{n,t}$	Equals 1 if datapoint i is correctly classified and traverses the arc between node $n \in L$ and sink t, 0 otherwise

(5) ICS-FlowOCT:

Objective(2a)

s.t.(4b),(4c),(4d),(4e),(4f)

$$(4g) \qquad \forall n \in N \cup L, i \in I, k \in K : k \neq \lambda^i$$

$$\sum_{f \in F} b_{fn} + p_n + \sum_{m \in A(n)} p_m = 1 \qquad \forall n \in N \quad (5a)$$

$$p_n + \sum_{m \in A(n)} p_m = 1 \qquad \forall n \in L \quad (5b)$$

$$z^i_{a(n),n} = z^i_{n,l(n)} + z^i_{n,r(n)} + z^i_{n,t} \qquad \forall n \in N, i \in I \quad (5c)$$

$$\sum_{n \in N \cup L} z^i_{n,t} = 1 \qquad \forall i \in I \quad (5d)$$

$$z^i_{n,t} \leq p_n \qquad \forall i \in I, n \in N \cup L \quad (5e)$$

$$\sum_{k \in K} a_{nk} = p_n \qquad \forall n \in N \cup L \quad (5f)$$

$$p_n \in \{0,1\} \qquad \forall n \in N \cup L \quad (5g)$$

$$\sum_{k \in K} a_{n'k} \cdot \rho_k + M \cdot (1 - p_{n'}) \geq \sum_{n \in P_l^{n'}} \sum_{f \in F} b_{fn} \cdot \sigma_f$$

$$\forall l \in L, n' \in N \cup l \quad (5h)$$

$$Variables'\ domains \qquad (5i)$$

where: $P_l^{n'}$ is set of inner nodes from the root of tree to parent of node n' on the path corresponding to leaf l, and $M = |P_l^{n'}| \cdot \max(\sigma_f : f \in F)$.

The formulation presented in [17] only addressed balanced decision trees. The authors' goal in this study is to minimize number of prediction errors at leaves of the tree. To implement time-constrained cost-sensitive version, we introduce new variables $e_{l,k,k'} \in \mathbf{N}$ that denote number of datapoints belonging class k and reaching leaf l wherein the label $k' \neq k$ is predicted. We also add the cost-sensitive term, which minimizes total cost of features used, to the original formulation. We should note that F in the **CS-BinOCT** model is set of features (columns) in the dataset, not the set of splits as in other mathematical formulations. The set of splits, as known as the set of thresholds in [17], is denoted by T.

Table 2. Decision variables, parameters and sets in BinOCT

Variables	Definition
$t_{n,t}$	Equals 1 if node n is assigned threshold t, 0 otherwise
Sets	
$bin(f)$	Feature f's binary encoding ranges
$li(b)$	Datapoints with values in b's lower range, $b \in bin(f)$
$ui(b)$	Datapoints with values in b's upper range, $b \in bin(f)$
$tl(b)$	$t_{n,t}$ variables for b's ranges, $b \in bin(f)$
$ll(b)$	Node n's leaves under the left branches, $b \in bin(f)$
$rl(b)$	Node n's leaves under the right branches, $b \in bin(f)$
T	Set of thresholds
Parameters	
$min_{t(f)}$	Feature f's minimum threshold value
$max_{t(f)}$	Feature f's maximum threshold value
M, M', M'', M'''	Minimized big-M value

(6) CS-BinOCT:

$$\min \alpha \sum_{l \in L} \sum_{k,k' \in k:k \neq k'} e_{l,k,k'} \cdot \psi_{kk'} + (1-\alpha) \sum_{n \in N} \sum_{f \in F} b_{fn} \cdot \delta_f \tag{6a}$$

s.t.(1d),(2b),(2c),(2f)

$$\sum_{i \in li(b)} \sum_{l \in ll(n)} z_l^i + \sum_{t \in tl(b)} M \cdot t_{n,t} - \sum_{t \in tl(b)} M \tag{6b}$$

$$\leq M \cdot (1 - b_{fn}) \qquad \forall n \in N, f \in F, b \in bin(f) \tag{6c}$$

$$\sum_{i \in ui(b)} \sum_{l \in rl(n)} z_l^i - \sum_{t \in tl(b)} M' \cdot t_{n,t}$$

$$\leq M' \cdot (1 - b_{fn}) \qquad \forall n \in N, f \in F, b \in bin(f) \tag{6d}$$

$$\sum_{max_{t(f)} < f(i)} \sum_{l \in ll(n)} z_l^i + \sum_{f(i) < min_{t(f)}} \sum_{l \in rl(n)} z_l^i$$

$$\leq M'' \cdot (1 - b_{fn}) \qquad \forall n \in N, f \in F \tag{6e}$$

$$\sum_{i \in I:\lambda^i=k} z_l^i + M''' \cdot (a_{lk'} - 1) \leq e_{l,k,k'}$$

$$\forall k, k' \in K : k \neq k', l \in L \tag{6f}$$

$$t_{n,t} \in \{0,1\} \qquad \forall n \in N, t \in T \tag{6g}$$

$$e_{l,k,k'} \in \mathbf{N} \qquad \forall l \in L, k, k' \in K : k \neq k' \tag{6h}$$

$$Variables' \ domains \tag{6i}$$

Constraints (6f) establish decision variables $e_{l,k,k'}$, which are modified due to the original variables determining prediction error in the formulation of [17]. In the **BCS-PathOCT** and the **BCS-FlowOCT** formulations, the variables e_k^i solely describe the prediction error of each datapoint i. In contrast to those, the variables $e_{l,k,k'}$ calculate the total number of datapoints that are classified incorrectly at each leaf l. Thus, the set of constraints (6f) requires additional parameter M'''. These big-M constraints guarantee that if leaf l is assigned class k' then all datapoints belonging to label $k \neq k'$ are taken into account as errors. Otherwise, these inequalities are completely correct because the left hand side are less than or equal to zero. How to calculate the values of M, M', M'', M''' for different constraints and the details of equations are described in [17].

4 Numerical Experiments

The optimization solver CPLEX on an AMD Ryzen machine with 16GB RAM processes C++ models. On nine UCI datasets, we test five models. One memory core runs for 60 min for each instance. The time consumption of features (σ_f) is randomly generated within a range (1,100). To determine the time limit for all labels, we run CART from scikit-learn 20 times with $train\_size = 90\%$ of each dataset and $max\_depth = 5$. Then, the time consumed by inner nodes in each path from root to leaf is added. The CART execution sets the time limit for the label with the most datapoints to R. This implementation is based on [5], who implemented a decision tree induction algorithm to determine feature consumption time on each path. We randomly generate time limits in the range $[0.8 \cdot R, 1.2 \cdot R]$ in this paper. To evaluate the impact of time limit constraints on models, we examine 50% and 80% time limits for each label.

Table 3. Dataset used

Dataset	# rows	# labels	# feature	# thresholds
car evaluation	1728	4	6	9
contraceptive method choice	1473	3	9	42
diabetes	768	2	8	194
diagnosis D1	120	2	6	6
diagnosis D2	120	2	6	6
heart	303	2	13	113
tic-tac-toe	958	2	9	17
voting	232	2	16	16
zoo	101	7	16	17

The misclassification costs are determined based on the distribution of class labels as in [5], [8] and [19]. To ensure that the cost is higher for misclassifying rare classes, we set the cost of misclassifying a datapoint (ψ_{ik}) belonging to label i to a datapoint belonging to label k as $\sqrt{|i|/|k|} \cdot \theta$ for cases of imbalanced datasets and $|i|/|k| \cdot \theta$ for cases of balanced datasets. Misclassification cost and total feature cost are used to evaluate the trade-off between misclassifying data and using features. The speed at which models find optimal solutions depends on the value of θ. For the per-case cost of misclassification, θ is set to 1 instead of 200 and 400 as in [5] and [19], without compromising generality. For instance, in the Diabetes dataset, the Healthy label ratio is 65%, nearly twice that of the Diabetes label. The cost of misclassifying a Healthy case to a Diabetes case is $1.857 \cdot \theta$, and the cost of misclassifying a Diabetes case to a Healthy case is $0.538 \cdot \theta$. The dataset is randomly split into 5 pairs of training and test sets, with a 75% and 25% ratio for each. An instance is a combination of training and test sets, along with their parameters. After that, each dataset has 120 instances with $H = \{2, 3, 4, 5\}$, $\alpha \in \{0.2, 0.5, 0.8\}$, and $\epsilon = \{0.5, 0.8\}$. To create splits (F), CART splits are collected and duplicate values are removed. Table 3 displays the number of feature splits used to test MIP models. In the objective function, feature costs (δ_f) are randomly generated in the range $(1, 10)$ for cost-sensitivity. We also set $\epsilon = \{0.5, 0.8\}$ and use datasets added time and cost factors, such as misclassification matrices, limited times of labels, consuming times, and costs of features.

Two proposed scenarios aim to minimize misclassification cost and cost of using features. While the first scenario contains two models: **ICS-PathOCT** and **ICS-FlowOCT**, the second one compares three models: **BCS-PathOCT**, **BCS-FlowOCT** and **CS-BinOCT**.

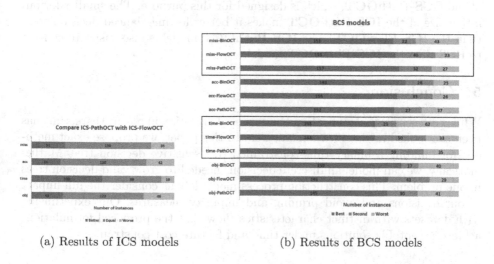

(a) Results of ICS models   (b) Results of BCS models

Fig. 1.

Results summaries for the first and second scenarios are shown in Figs. 1a and 1b. On the y-axis, the "miss, acc, time, obj" represent 4 terms of the comparison: misclassification cost and accuracy on the test set; run time and objective value on the training set. Figure 1a's x-axis displays the **ICS-PathOCT** model's better, same, or worse performance compared to the **ICS-FlowOCT** model, while Fig. 1b's x-axis displays each **BCS** model's best, worst, or equal performance. This analysis calculates the average objective function, run time, accuracy, and misclassification cost of 5 instances from the same dataset and parameters. Thus, each dataset has $24(=120/5)$ term values and 9 datasets have 216 values.

Figure 1a shows that in the first scenario, objective and accuracy values are similar $(122/216$ and $130/216)$, with the **ICS-PathOCT** offering slightly better values $(48/46$ and $44/42)$. The **ICS-PathOCT** has a lower misclassification cost $(51/35)$ than the **ICS-FlowOCT**. In particular, the **ICS-PathOCT** model runs faster than the **ICS-FlowOCT** $(108/19)$ because it has fewer constraints and variables.

Despite having the best objective, runtime, and accuracy, the **CS-BinOCT** model has the worst misclassification cost performance (see Fig. 1b). Misclassification cost weakens the original BinOCT model, which maximizes correct classified datapoints. The **BCS-FlowOCT** has the best runtime, as confirmed by our experiment [1]. This formulation is the most consistent and ranks second overall. The **BCS-PathOCT** has fewer best objective, accuracy, and runtime values than the **BCS-FlowOCT**. However, the **BCS-PathOCT** performs best in test set misclassification cost. The experiment also shows that the **BCS-FlowOCT** and the **CS-BinOCT** have reasonable runtime, but misclassification costs weaken them. These models outperform the **BCS-PathOCT** in accuracy, but their extra terms for computing misclassification costs are inferior to those of the **BCS-PathOCT**, which is designed for this purpose. The smaller formulation size of the **ICS-PathOCT** makes it better for imbalanced decision trees than the **ICS-FlowOCT**. The **ICS-PathOCT** model is also easier to convert to BCS than the **ICS-FlowOCT** model.

5   Conclusion

While cost-sensitive classification has garnered attention in recent years, time has been overlooked in classification research. In this paper, we propose exact methods for building a binary time-constrained cost-sensitive decision tree. Mathematically, we can model all discrete decisions needed to grow valid decision trees in one problem. This construction process model lets us consider the full impact of our decisions and avoid pruning and impurity measures. Our experiments with datasets with distinct characteristics show that the proposed formulations achieve acceptable solutions under time and feature cost constraints.

References

1. Aghaei, S., Gomez, A., Vayanos, P.: Learning optimal classification trees: strong max-flow formulations (2020)
2. Aglin, G., Nijssen, S., Schaus, P.: Learning optimal decision trees using caching branch-and-bound search. In: Proceedings of the AAAI Conference on Artificial Intelligence, vol. 34, no. 04, pp. 3146–3153 (2020)

3. Bertsimas, D., Dunn, J.: Optimal classification trees. Mach. Learn. **106**(7), 1039–1082 (2017)
4. Chen, Y.L., Wu, C.C., Tang, K.: Building a cost-constrained decision tree with multiple condition attributes. Inf. Sci. **179**(7), 967–979 (2009)
5. Chen, Y.L., Wu, C.C., Tang, K.: Time-constrained cost-sensitive decision tree induction. Inf. Sci. **354**, 140–152 (2016)
6. Firat, M., Crognier, G., Gabor, A.F., Hurkens, C., Zhang, Y.: Column generation based heuristic for learning classification trees. Comput. Oper. Res. **116**, 104866 (2020)
7. Kao, H.P., Tang, K.: Cost-sensitive decision tree induction with label-dependent late constraints. INFORMS J. Comput. **26**(2), 238–252 (2014)
8. Ling, C., Sheng, V., Yang, Q.: Test strategies for cost-sensitive decision trees. IEEE Trans. Knowl. Data Eng. **18**(8), 1055–1067 (2006)
9. Lomax, S., Vadera, S.: A survey of cost-sensitive decision tree induction algorithms. ACM Comput. Surv. **45**(16), 1–35 (2013)
10. Min, F., Hu, Q., Zhu, W.: Feature selection with test cost constraint. Int. J. Approximate Reason. **55**(1, Part 2), 167–179 (2014). special issue on Decision-Theoretic Rough Sets
11. Nijssen, S., Fromont, E.: Optimal constraint-based decision tree induction from itemset lattices. Data Min. Knowl. Disc. **21**(1), 9–51 (2010)
12. Pendharkar, P.C.: A misclassification cost risk bound based on hybrid particle swarm optimization heuristic. Expert Syst. Appl. **41**(4, Part 1), 1483–1491 (2014)
13. Pendharkar, P.C.: Linear models for cost-sensitive classification. Expert. Syst. **32**(5), 622–636 (2015)
14. Turney, P.D.: Cost-sensitive classification: empirical evaluation of a hybrid genetic decision tree induction algorithm. J. Artif. Intell. Res. **2**, 369–409 (1995)
15. Verhaeghe, H., Nijssen, S., Pesant, G., Quimper, C., Schaus, P.: Learning optimal decision trees using constraint programming. Constraints **25**(3), 226–250 (2020)
16. Verwer, S., Zhang, Y.: Learning decision trees with flexible constraints and objectives using integer optimization. In: Salvagnin, D., Lombardi, M. (eds.) CPAIOR 2017. LNCS, vol. 10335, pp. 94–103. Springer, Cham (2017). https://doi.org/10.1007/978-3-319-59776-8_8
17. Verwer, S., Zhang, Y.: Learning optimal classification trees using a binary linear program formulation. In: Proceedings of the AAAI Conference on Artificial Intelligence, vol. 33, no. 01, pp. 1625–1632 (2019)
18. Wang, J., Zhao, P., Hoi, S.C.H.: Cost-sensitive online classification. IEEE Trans. Knowl. Data Eng. **26**(10), 2425–2438 (2014)
19. Wu, C., Chen, Y., Tang, K.: Cost-sensitive decision tree with multiple resource constraints. Appl. Intell. **49**(10), 3765–3782 (2019)
20. Yi, W., Lu, M., Liu, Z.: Multi-valued attribute and multi-labeled data decision tree algorithm. Int. J. Mach. Learn. Cybern. **2**(2), 67–74 (2011)

Solving Time-Dependent Traveling Salesman Problem with Time Windows Under Generic Time-Dependent Travel Cost

Duc Minh Vu[1]($\boxtimes$)(iD), Mike Hewitt[2](iD), and Duc Duy Vu[3](iD)

[1] Phenikaa University and ORLab, Yen Nghia, Ha Dong, Vietnam
`minh.vuduc@phenikaa-uni.edu.vn`
[2] Loyola University Chicago, Chicago, USA
[3] University of Michigan - Flint, Flint, USA

Abstract. In this paper, we present formulations and an exact method to solve the Time Dependent Traveling Salesman Problem with Time Window (TD-TSPTW) under a generic travel cost function where waiting is allowed. A particular case in which the travel cost is a non-decreasing function has been addressed recently. With that assumption, because of both First-In-First-Out property of the travel time function and the non-decreasing property of the travel cost function, we can ignore the possibility of waiting. However, for generic travel cost functions, waiting after visiting some locations can be part of optimal solutions. To handle the general case, we introduce new lower-bound formulations that allow us to ensure the existence of optimal solutions. We adapt the existing algorithm for TD-TSPTW with non-decreasing travel costs to solve the TD-TSPTW with generic travel costs. In the experiment, we evaluate the strength of the proposed lower bound formulations and algorithm by applying them to solve the TD-TSPTW with the total travel time objective. The results indicate that the proposed algorithm is competitive with and even outperforms the state-of-art solver in various benchmark instances.

Keywords: time-dependent travel time · time-dependent travel cost · traveling salesman problem · dynamic discretization discovery

1 Problem Formulation

The TD-TSPTW is presented mathematically as follows. We let (N, A) denote a directed graph, wherein the node set $N = \{0, 1, 2, ..., n\}$ includes the depot (node 0) as well as the set of locations (node $1, ..., n$) that must be visited. Associated with each location $i \in N$ is a time window $[e_i, l_i]$ during which the location must be visited. A tourist must visit the city i within its time window. Note that the tourist may arrive at city $i \in N \setminus \{0\}$ before e_i, in which case he must wait until the time window opens. Because of waiting, he does not need to

© The Author(s), under exclusive license to Springer Nature Singapore Pte Ltd. 2024
M. H. Hà et al. (Eds.): CSoNet 2023, LNCS 14479, pp. 210–221, 2024.
https://doi.org/10.1007/978-981-97-0669-3_20

depart immediately after his visit. The time window associated with the depot means that the tour departs the depot at the time of at least e_0 and must return to the depot no later than l_0.

We define $A \subseteq N \times N$ as the set of arcs that present travel between locations in N. Associated with each arc $(i, j) \in A$ and time, t, at which travel can begin on the arc, is a travel time $\tau_{ij}(t)$. The FIFO property implies that for each arc $(i, j) \in A$ and times t, t' wherein $t \leq t'$, we must have $t + \tau_{ij}(t) \leq t' + \tau_{ij}(t')$. Thus, formally, the vehicle departs from node 0 at time $t \geq e_0$, arrives at each city $j \in N$ exactly once within its time window $[e_j, l_j]$ by traveling on arcs in A, and then returns to node 0 at time $t' \leq l_0$.

We formulate this tour as an integer program defined on a time-expanded network, $\mathcal{D} = (\mathcal{N}, \mathcal{A})$, with node set $\mathcal{N}$ and arc set $\mathcal{A}$. This formulation is based on the presumption that time may be discretized into a finite set of integer time points. As such, for each node $i \in N, t \in [e_i, l_0]$, $\mathcal{N}$ contains the node (i, t). $\mathcal{A}$ contains travel arcs of the form $((i, t), (j, t'))$ wherein $i \neq j, (i, j) \in A$, $t \geq e_i, t' = \max\{e_j, t + \tau_{ij}(t)\}$ (the vehicle cannot visit early), and $t' \leq l_j$ (the vehicle cannot arrive late). Note that, since waiting is allowed, we can depart from i to j at a time later than the time windows $[e_i, l_i]$ of location i. Finally, $\mathcal{A}$ contains arcs of the form $((i, t), (i, t + 1))$ presenting waiting at location i.

To formulate the integer program, for each arc $a = ((i, t), (j, t')) \in \mathcal{A}$, binary variable x_a represents whether the vehicle travels/waits along that arc. Let $c_a = c_{ij}(t)$ be the non-negative travel cost associated with arc a. If $i = j$ and $t' = t+1$, $c_{ii}(t)$ represents the waiting cost for one unit of time period, from time period t to time period $t+1$. Notations $\delta^+(i, t)$ and $\delta^-(i, t)$ present the set of incoming arcs and the set of outgoing arcs at the node $(i, t) \in \mathcal{N}$. The following formulation solves the TD-TSPTW with a generic travel cost function:

$$z = \text{minimize} \sum_{a \in \mathcal{A}} c_a x_a \tag{1}$$

subject to

$$\sum_{a=((i,t)(j,t'))\in \mathcal{A}|i\neq j} x_a = 1, \quad \forall i \in N, \tag{2}$$

$$\sum_{a \in \delta^+(i,t)} x_a - \sum_{a \in \delta^-(i,t)} x_a = 0, \quad \forall (i, t) \in \mathcal{N}, i \neq 0, \tag{3}$$

$$x_a \in \{0, 1\}, \quad \forall a \in \mathcal{A}. \tag{4}$$

Constraints (2) ensure that the vehicle arrives at each node exactly one time during its time window. Constraints (3) ensure that the vehicle departs every node at which it arrives. Finally, constraints (4) define the decision variables and their domains.

2   Literature Review

Due to the space, we refer [7] as a most recent review on TSP in general. Regarding time-dependent TSPTW literature, [6] propose a branch-and-cut algorithm while [1] extend the ideas described in [5] by using a branch-and-bound algorithm. [1] show that lower and upper bounds of time-dependent asymmetric TSPTW can be obtained from the optimal solution of a well-defined asymmetric TSPTW. [4] present the first application of the DDD method to solve the static TSPTW problem. Based on that work, [9] propose the first DDD method to solve the time-dependent TSPTW problem under the assumption of a non-decreasing travel cost function. The experiment results showed that the algorithm outperformed the state-of-art method for a particular problem of this class, the make-span problem [6]. [10] extend the DDD approach for solving TD-TSPTW to the Time-Dependent Minimum Tour Duration Problem and the Time-Dependent Delivery Man Problem, which, unlike TSPTW, have a scheduling element. Regarding how to refine the partial networks, [8] study path-based refinement strategy and compare results of various refinement strategies applied to TSPTW when using layer graph expansion. For a general discussion of Dynamic Discretization Discovery, readers can refer to [3] as a base source.

In this paper, we extend the ideas in [9,10] to solve the TD-TSPTW with a generic travel cost function. As far as we know, it is the first research for TD-TSPTW with generic travel costs. We propose lower-bound formulations, and extend the DDD algorithms to find optimal solutions for this generalized problem.

3   Partially Time-Expanded Network Formulation and Properties

To solve TD-TSPTW, we rely on the concept of the *partially time-expanded network* [2,9]. A *partially time-expanded network*, $\mathcal{D}_{\mathcal{T}} = (\mathcal{N}_{\mathcal{T}}, \mathcal{A}_{\mathcal{T}})$, is derived from a given subset of the timed nodes, $\mathcal{N}_{\mathcal{T}} \subseteq \mathcal{N}$. Given $\mathcal{N}_{\mathcal{T}}$, the arc set $\mathcal{A}_{\mathcal{T}} \subseteq \mathcal{N}_{\mathcal{T}} \times \mathcal{N}_{\mathcal{T}}$ consists of travel arcs and waiting arcs. A travel arc $((i,t),(j,t'))$, wherein $(i,t) \in \mathcal{N}_{\mathcal{T}}$, $(j,t') \in \mathcal{N}_{\mathcal{T}}$, $i \neq j$, and $(i,j) \in A$, models travel between locations i and j. We do not allow violations of time windows, so $t' \leq \max\{e_j, t + \tau_{ij}(t)\}$. An arc is *too short* if $t' < \max\{e_j, t + \tau_{ij}(t)\}$. A waiting arc $((i,t)(i,t+1))$ is in $\mathcal{A}_{\mathcal{T}}$ if both nodes (i,t) and $(i,t+1)$ are in $\mathcal{N}_{\mathcal{T}}$. For each arc $a = ((i,t),(j,t')) \in \mathcal{A}_{\mathcal{T}}$, we define $\underline{c}_{ij}(t)$ as the travel cost of arc a. We set these costs, $\underline{c}_{ij}(t)$, in such a manner that they under-estimate how the cost of such travel is presented in $\mathcal{D}$. Specifically, $\underline{c}_{ij}(t)$ is defined as $\underline{c}_{ij}(t) = \min\{\sum_{h=h'}^{h''-1} c_{ii}(h) + c_{ij}(h'') | t \leq h' \leq h'' \wedge h'' + \tau_{ij}(h'') \leq l_j\}$. The underestimated cost $\underline{c}_{ii}(t)$ for a waiting arc $((i,t)(i,t+1))$ is 0 since the waiting cost is taken into account while evaluating underestimated travel cost.

Given a partially time-expanded $\mathcal{D}_{\mathcal{T}}$ that meets Property 1–5, we establish the formulation TD-TSPTW($\mathcal{D}_{\mathcal{T}}$) defined by the objective function and constraints (5)–(8). We optimize this formulation with respect to the cost $\underline{c}_{ij}(t)$.

$$\text{TD-TSPTW}(\mathcal{D}_{\mathcal{T}}) : \min \sum_{a \in \mathcal{A}} \underline{c}_a x_a \qquad (5)$$

$$\sum_{a=((i,t)(j,t'))\in\mathcal{A}_\mathcal{T}|i\neq j} x_a = 1, \forall i \in N, \tag{6}$$

$$\sum_{a\in\delta^-((i,t))} x_a - \sum_{a\in\delta^+((i,t))} x_a = 0, \forall(i,t) \in \mathcal{N}_\mathcal{T} \tag{7}$$

$$x_a \in \{0,1\}, \forall a \in \mathcal{A}_\mathcal{T}. \tag{8}$$

Property 1. $\forall i \in N$, both nodes (i, e_i) and (i, l_i) are in $\mathcal{N}_\mathcal{T}$.

Property 2. $\forall(i,t) \in \mathcal{N}_\mathcal{T}, e_i \leq t$.

Property 3. If $(i,t) \in \mathcal{N}_\mathcal{T}$ and $(i,t+1) \in \mathcal{N}_\mathcal{T}$, the waiting arc $((i,t)(i,t+1))$ is in $\mathcal{A}_\mathcal{T}$.

Property 4. Underestimate travel-time arc: $\forall(i,t) \in \mathcal{N}_\mathcal{T}$ and arc $(i,j) \in A$, there is a travel arc of the form $((i,t)(j,t')) \in \mathcal{A}_\mathcal{T}$ if $t + \tau_{ij}(t) \leq l_j$. Furthermore, every travel arc $((i,t),(j,t')) \in \mathcal{A}_\mathcal{T}$ must have either (1) $t + \tau_{ij}(t) < e_j$ and $t' = e_j$, or (2) $e_j \leq t' \leq t + \tau_{ij}(t)$. Finally, there is no $(j,t'') \in \mathcal{N}_\mathcal{T}$ with $t' < t'' \leq t + \tau_{ij}(t)$.

Property 5. Underestimate travel cost of arc: $\forall((i,t)(j,t')) \in \mathcal{A}_\mathcal{T}, i \neq j$, the cost $\underline{c}_{ij}(t) = \min\{\sum_{h=h'}^{h''-1} c_{ii}(h) + c_{ij}(h'') | t \leq h' \leq h'' \wedge h'' + \tau_{ij}(h'') \leq l_j\}$. Underestimate waiting cost $\underline{c}_{ii}(t)$ takes value 0 for all i and t.

Property 1–5 ensure Lemma 1, 2 and 3. Since the non-decreasing property of $\underline{c}_{ij}(t)$, the algorithm proposed in [9] will converge to an optimal solution to the TD-TSPTW($\mathcal{D}$) but with the parameterized cost $\underline{c}_{ij}(t)$. Because $\underline{c}_{ij}(t)$ may be not equal $c_{ij}(t)$, we may not reach the optimal solution to TD-TSPTW($\mathcal{D}$). Also, using the result of Lemma 2, if all optimal solutions to TD-TSPTW($\mathcal{D}$) with the original cost have at least one waiting arc occurring after visiting some cities, then the current lower bound formulation, TD-TSPTW($\mathcal{D}_\mathcal{T}$), is not enough to find optimal solutions of TD-TSPTW($\mathcal{D}$).

Lemma 1. $\underline{c}_{ij}(t)$ is a non-decreasing function of t.

Lemma 2. If TD-TSPTW($\mathcal{D}_\mathcal{T}$) with the parameterized cost $\underline{c}_{ij}(t)$ is feasible, it always has an optimal solution without waiting arcs.

Lemma 3. TD-TSPTW($\mathcal{D}_\mathcal{T}$) with cost $\underline{c}_{ij}(t)$ is a lower bound of TD-TSPTW($\mathcal{D}$) with cost $c_{ij}(t)$.

As the first attempt to address the challenges, we extend the lower bound formulation TD-TSPTW($\mathcal{D}_\mathcal{T}$) (5)–(8) to take into account original travel cost function c. Conditions to determine whether we can evaluate an arc with its correct travel cost are presented. Then we introduce new algorithmic ideas and show how to adapt the algorithmic framework presented in [9] to find optimal solution to TD-TSPTW($\mathcal{D}$) using TD-TSPTW($\mathcal{D}_\mathcal{T}$). Let us state the conditions in which we can evaluate an arc with its correct travel cost.

Property 6. *An arc $a = ((i,t)(j,t')) \in \mathcal{D}_T$ can be evaluated with correct travel cost if and only if two following conditions are met:*

1. *The node (i,t) can be reached by a sequence of correct travel time arcs and waiting arcs from the depot $(0, e_0)$.*
2. *The waiting arc $((i,t)(i,t+1))$ is in $\mathcal{D}_T$.*

The first condition of Property 6 states that if an arc $a = ((i,t)(j,t'))$ can be evaluated with the correct travel cost, then it must be reached from the depot by a sequence of correct travel time arcs (including waiting arcs). With this condition, t is the correct arrival time at the location i. The second condition implies the possibility that we travel from location i at time t to another location with the correct travel cost, or we can wait and travel from i at time at least $t+1$ with underestimate travel cost. It is used to maintain the non-decreasing property of TD-TSPTW($\mathcal{D}_T$) when we update $\mathcal{D}_T$. Now, we present two new formulations satisfying Property 1–6.

4   New Lower Bound Formulations and Algorithm

4.1   Path-arc-based Formulation

We start with a path-arc-based formulation that allows us to evaluate arcs with their correct travel costs by using additional path variables representing paths with correct travel times. Let $p = ((u_0 = 0, t_0 = e_0) - (u_1, t_1) - (u_2, t_2) - ... - (u_m, t_m))$ be a path departing from the depot with correct travel times. We associate with p a binary variable x_p and with cost $c_p = \sum_{i=0}^{m-1} c_{u_i u_{i+1}}(t_i)$. Let denote $\mathcal{P}_T$ as a set of paths originated from the depot with correct travel times in $\mathcal{D}_T$. We denote $\mathcal{P}_T(i) \subseteq \mathcal{P}_T$ as a set of paths visiting the city i and $\delta_p^+(i,t)$ as a set of paths ending at (i,t). Let $\delta^+(i,t) = \{((j,t')(i,t)) \in \mathcal{A}_T | j \neq i\}$ denote of the set of travel arcs ending at (i,t). Let $\delta^+(i) = \{((j,t')(i,t)) \in \mathcal{A}_T | j \neq i\}$ denote of the set of travel arcs ending at city (i). Let $\mathcal{A}_T^= \subseteq \mathcal{A}_T$ be the set of arcs with correct travel times, and let $\mathcal{Q}_T \subseteq \mathcal{P}_T \times \mathcal{A}_T^=$ such that if $(p,a) \in \mathcal{Q}_T$ then $p \oplus a \in \mathcal{P}_T$. Here $p \oplus a = ((u_0 = 0, t_0 = e_0) - (u_1, t_1) - (u_2, t_2) - ... - (u_m = i, t_m = t), (j,t'))$, the path obtained by expanding the arc a to the end of p where $p \in \delta_p^+(i,t)$ and $a = ((i,t)(j,t')) \in \mathcal{A}_T^=$. The path-based formulation TD-TSPTW($\mathcal{D}_T, \mathcal{P}_T$) is:

$$\text{TD-TSPTW}(\mathcal{D}_T, \mathcal{P}_T) : \min \sum_{a \in \mathcal{A}_T} \underline{c}_a x_a + \sum_{p \in \mathcal{P}_T} c_p x_p \tag{9}$$

$$x_a + \sum_{p \in \mathcal{P}_T | a \in p} x_p \leq 1, \ \forall a \in \mathcal{A}_T^= \tag{10}$$

$$x_p + x_a \leq 1, \ \forall (p,a) \in \mathcal{Q}_T \tag{11}$$

$$\sum_{a \in \delta^+(i)} x_a + \sum_{p \in \mathcal{P}_T(i)} x_p = 1, \ \forall i \in N \tag{12}$$

$$\sum_{a\in\delta^+(i,t)} x_a + \sum_{p\in\delta_p^+(i,t)} x_p - \sum_{a\in\delta^-(i,t)} x_a = 0, \quad \forall (i,t)\in\mathcal{N}_{\mathcal{T}} \tag{13}$$

$$\sum_{((i,t)(i,t+1))\in\mathcal{A}_{\mathcal{T}}} x_{((i,t)(i,t+1))} = 0, \tag{14}$$

$$x_a, x_p \in \{0,1\}, \quad \forall a \in \mathcal{A}_{\mathcal{T}}, p \in \mathcal{P}_{\mathcal{T}}. \tag{15}$$

The objective function (9) estimates a lower bound of TD-TSPTW using paths with correct travel times and travel costs plus arcs with under-estimated travel costs. Suppose $p', p \in \mathcal{P}_{\mathcal{T}}$ and $p' = p \oplus a$ with some $a \in \mathcal{A}_{\mathcal{T}}^{=}$ then constraint set (11) forces to use p' instead of p and a to ensure that correct cost is used. However, if $p' \notin \mathcal{P}_{\mathcal{T}}$ and if p and a are selected, we will create p' and add p' to the formulation. Constraint set (12) ensures each city is visited exactly once (e.g. by an arc ending at (i,t) or by a path p passing through node (i,t)). Constraint set (13) ensures the balance of selected arcs at each node, either by arcs or by paths. Mathematically, if $x_a = 1$ for any $a \in \delta^+(i,t)$ in equation (12), then $\sum_{\mathcal{P}_{\mathcal{T}}(i,t)} x_p = 0$ and $\sum_{p\in\delta^+(i,t)} x_p = 0$ in (13). So there is an arc $a' \in \delta^-(i,t)$ with $x_{a'} = 1$, making the node (i,t) balanced. Otherwise, if $x_a = 0$ for all $a \in \delta^+(i,t)$, then $\sum_{\mathcal{P}_{\mathcal{T}}(i,t)} x_p = 1$. If $\sum_{p\in\delta^+(i,t)} x_p = 1$ then again there is an arc $a' \in \delta^-(i,t)$ with $x_{a'} = 1$, implying the node (i,t) balanced. Otherwise, $\sum_{p\in\delta^+(i,t)} x_p = 0$, so there is $p \in \mathcal{P}_{\mathcal{T}}\backslash\delta^+(i,t)$ such that $x_p = 1$. Because $p \notin \delta^+(i,t)$, there are exactly two arcs with correct travel time of form $((u,h)(i,t))$ and $((i,t)(j,t'))$ in p, making (i,t) balance. Constraint (14), which is used to strengthen the formulation by Lemma 3.2, eliminate waiting arcs with underestimated cost from the optimal solutions, in other words, waiting arcs (with correct travel costs) can only appear in paths in $\mathcal{P}_{\mathcal{T}}$. Finally, constraint (15) defines domains of the variables x and p.

We have the following results, which say that TSPTW$(\mathcal{D}_{\mathcal{T}}, \mathcal{P}_{\mathcal{T}})$ is always a lower bound of TD-TSPTW$(\mathcal{D})$ and explains when we find an optimal solution to TSPTW$(\mathcal{D})$.

Lemma 4. *TSPTW($\mathcal{D}_{\mathcal{T}}, \mathcal{P}_{\mathcal{T}}$) is a lower bound of TSPTW($\mathcal{D}$).*

Lemma 5. *If an optimal solution to TSPTW($\mathcal{D}_{\mathcal{T}}, \mathcal{P}_{\mathcal{T}}$) is a single tour prescribed by a path (variable), it is an optimal solution to TSPTW($\mathcal{D}$).*

4.2 Arc-Based Formulation

As we can see, there are two major disadvantages of the path-arc-based formulation TD-TSPTW$(\mathcal{D}_{\mathcal{T}}, \mathcal{P}_{\mathcal{T}})$ (9)-(15). First, the number of paths in $\mathcal{P}_{\mathcal{T}}$ can be an exponential number in terms of the number of nodes and arcs in $\mathcal{D}_{\mathcal{T}}$, making it impossible to solve the TD-TSPTW$(\mathcal{D}_{\mathcal{T}}, \mathcal{P}_{\mathcal{T}})$ by MIP solver. Second, given a sequence of correct travel time arcs in $\mathcal{D}_{\mathcal{T}}$, we cannot evaluate those arcs with correct travel costs unless there is a path including those arcs. We present another modeling approach to solve the two above issues. We associate with each arc $a \in \mathcal{A}_\mathcal{T}$ a variable z_a indicating whether this arc can be evaluated with correct travel cost or not. Let $\Delta_a = c_a - \underline{c}_a$ for $\forall a \in \mathcal{A}_\mathcal{T}$.

The following defines a new relaxation of TD-TSPTW($\mathcal{D}$) that allows evaluating any sequence of arcs with correct travel time from the depot with their correct travel cost when Property 1–6 are met. Let $\mathcal{N}_\mathcal{T}^W = \{(i,t) \in \mathcal{N}_\mathcal{T} | (i, t+1) \in \mathcal{N}_\mathcal{T}\}$ be the set of time nodes having waiting arcs, and $\mathcal{N}_\mathcal{T}^{NW} = \mathcal{N}_\mathcal{T} \backslash \mathcal{N}_\mathcal{T}^W$ be the set without this property. Let $\lambda_{(i,t)}^+$ be the set of correct travel time/correct travel cost arcs arriving at the timed node (i,t), and λ_i^+ be the set of correct travel time/correct travel cost arcs arriving at the node i.

$$\text{TD-TSPTW}(\mathcal{D}_\mathcal{T}, Z_{\mathcal{A}_\mathcal{T}}) : \min \sum_{a \in \mathcal{A}_\mathcal{T}} x_a \underline{c}_a + \sum_{a \in \mathcal{A}_\mathcal{T}} z_a \Delta_a \tag{16}$$

subject to constraints (6), (7) and

$$z_a \leq x_a, \forall a \in \mathcal{A}_\mathcal{T}, \tag{17}$$

$$z_a = x_a, \forall a \in \delta_{(0,e_0)}^- \text{ if } (0, e_0 + 1) \in \mathcal{N}_\mathcal{T}, \tag{18}$$

$$z_a = 0, \forall (i,t) \in \mathcal{N}_\mathcal{T}^{NW}, \forall a \in \delta_{(i,t)}^-, \tag{19}$$

$$z_a \geq x_a + \sum_{a' \in \lambda_{(i,t)}^+} z_{a'} - 1, \forall (i,t) \in \mathcal{N}_\mathcal{T}^W \backslash (0, e_0), \forall a \in \delta_{(i,t)}^-, \tag{20}$$

$$\sum_{a \in \lambda_{(i,t)}^+} z_a \geq \sum_{a \in \delta_{(i,t)}^-} z_a, \forall (i,t) \in \mathcal{N}_\mathcal{T} \backslash (0, e_0), \tag{21}$$

$$\sum_{a \in \lambda_{(i,t)}^+} z_a \geq x_{((i,t)(i,t+1))}, \forall (i,t) \in \mathcal{N}_\mathcal{T}^W \backslash (0, e_0) \tag{22}$$

$$x_a, z_a \in \{0,1\}, \forall a \in \mathcal{A}_\mathcal{T}. \tag{23}$$

The objective function (16) ensures that if x_a and z_a both take value 1 in a solution to TD-TSPTW($\mathcal{D}_\mathcal{T}, Z_{\mathcal{A}_\mathcal{T}}$), the cost associated to this arc in the objective function is exactly c_a. We are going to prove that given a solution $\{\bar{x}, \bar{z}\}$ to TD-TSPTW($\mathcal{D}_\mathcal{T}, Z_{\mathcal{A}_\mathcal{T}}$), for any $a = ((i,t)(j,t')) \in \mathcal{A}_\mathcal{T}$, $\bar{z}_a$ takes the value of 1 if and only if Property 6 is met.

Constraint set (17) ensures that an arc a is evaluated with its correct travel cost only if this arc is selected in a solution to the formulation. Next, constraint (18) implies that arcs representing departure from $(0, e_0)$ should be evaluated with correct travel costs if waiting arc $((0, e_0), (0, e_0+1)) \in \mathcal{A}_\mathcal{T}$. Next, constraint (19) enforces that if there is no waiting possibility at the node (i,t) in the current $\mathcal{D}_\mathcal{T}$, all arcs outgoing from this node cannot be evaluated with correct travel costs. Otherwise, constraint set (20) says that if $a = ((i,t)(j,t')) \in \mathcal{A}_\mathcal{T}$ is selected and if we can reach the node (i,t) by an arc $a' \in \mathcal{A}_\mathcal{T}^=$ which is also evaluated by its correct travel cost ($\sum_{a' \in \lambda^+_{(i,t)}} z_{a'} = 1$ or $z'_a = 1$ for some a'), this constraint forces a to be evaluated by its correct travel cost, or $z_a = 1$. Constraint (21) says that if we cannot reach (i, t) by a correct travel time and correct travel cost arc, no outgoing arc of this node can be evaluated with the correct travel cost. Precisely, if $\sum_{a' \in \lambda^+_{(i,t)}} z_{a'} = 0$, constraint (21) forces that any outgoing arc $a \in \delta^-_{(i,t)}$ will be evaluated with its underestimate cost since $z_a = 0$ for all $a \in \delta^-_{(i,t)}$). This constraint also forces $z_a = 0$ for any arc a in a sub-tour $((u_0, t_0), (u_1, t_1), ...,$ $(u_m, t_m), (u_0, t_0))$ where $u_i \neq 0$ for all i. W.r.t, we assume $t_0 \leq t_m$. Because the too short incoming arc $((u_m, t_m), (u_0, t_0)) \notin \lambda^+_{(u_0, t_0)}$ of the node (u_0, t_0) is selected, then the left-hand side of constraint (21) takes the value 0, consequently, $z_a = 0$ for all arcs a of the sub-tour $((u_0, t_0), (u_1, t_1), ..., (u_m, t_m), (u_0, t_0))$. Finally, constraint set (23) defines the domain of variables.

In conclusion, the set of constraints (17)–(23) ensures that if an arc is evaluated with correct travel cost, this arc must belong to the path from the depot node $(0, e_0)$ and all arcs in this path also must be evaluated with correct travel costs.

Aggregation formulation of TD-TSPTW$(\mathcal{D}_T, Z_{\mathcal{A}_T})$. Aggregating constraints (18)–(21) gives us constraints (24)–(27). λ^+_i and δ^-_i present the set of correct-travel-time inbound arcs to city i and set of outbound arcs from city i. The aggregated formulation TD-TSPTW-AGG$(\mathcal{D}_T, \mathcal{A}_T)$ includes the objective function (16), the constraints (6), (7), (17), (23) and the constraints

$$\sum_{a \in \delta^-_{(0, e_0)}} x_a = \sum_{a \in \delta^-_{(0, e_0)}} z_a \text{ if } (0, e_0 + 1) \in \mathcal{N}_T, \tag{24}$$

$$\sum_{(i,t) \in \mathcal{N}^{NW}_T} \sum_{a \in \delta^-_{(i,t)}} z_a = 0, \tag{25}$$

$$\sum_{a \in \delta^-_{(i,t)}} z_a \geq \sum_{a \in \delta^-_{(i,t)}} x_a + \sum_{a \in \lambda^+_{(i,t)}} z_a - 1, \forall (i, t) \in \mathcal{N}^W_T \setminus \{0, e_0\}, \tag{26}$$

$$\sum_{a \in \lambda^+_i} z_a \geq \sum_{a \in \delta^-_i} z_a, \forall i \in N \setminus 0. \tag{27}$$

Actually, while TD-TSPTW-AGG$(\mathcal{D}_T, Z_{\mathcal{A}_T})$ is the aggregated version of TD-TSPTW$(\mathcal{D}_T, Z_{\mathcal{A}_T})$, we can prove that they are equivalent (see online Appendix [11]). Similar to the results of the path-based formulation, we have:

Lemma 6. *If* $\mathcal{D}_T$ *satisfies Properties 1–5, then TD-TSPTW*$(\mathcal{D}_T, Z_{\mathcal{A}_T})$ *(or TD-TSPTW-AGG*$(\mathcal{D}_T, Z_{\mathcal{A}_T})$, *respectively) is a relaxation of TD-TSPTW*$(\mathcal{D})$.

Lemma 7. *An optimal solution to TD-TSPTW*$(\mathcal{D}_T, \mathcal{A}_T)$ *(or TD-TSPTW-AGG* $(\mathcal{D}_T, Z_{\mathcal{A}_T})$, *respectively) that has no too short arcs defines an optimal solution to TD-TSPTW*$(\mathcal{D})$

Algorithm 1. DDD-TD-TSPTW

Require: TD-TSPTW instance (N, A), e, l, τ and c, and optimality tolerance ϵ
1: Perform preprocessing, updating A, e and l.
2: Create a partially time-expanded network $\mathcal{D}_T$.
3: Set $\mathcal{P}_T \leftarrow \emptyset$, (or $\mathcal{A}_T^{=} \leftarrow$ the set of correct travel time arcs in $\mathcal{A}_T$)
4: Set $S \leftarrow \emptyset$
5: **while** not solved **do**
6:     Set $\bar{S} \leftarrow \emptyset$
7:     Solve primal heuristics, TD-TSPTW$(\mathcal{D}_T^1)$ and TD-TSPTW$(\mathcal{D}_T^2)$, with under-estimate cost $\underline{c}$, harvest integer solutions and add to $\bar{S}$.
8:     Solve TD-TSPTW$(\mathcal{D}_T)$, harvest integer solutions, $\bar{S}$, and lower bound, z.
9:     **for** $s \in \bar{S}$ **do**
10:         Let s' be a copy of s without waiting arcs.
11:         **if** s' can be converted to a feasible solution to TD-TSPTW$(\mathcal{D})$ **then**
12:             Solve R-TD-TSPTW$(\mathcal{D}, s')$ to find the best tour using travel arcs in s'.
13:             Update S with the solution returned by R-TD-TSPTW$(\mathcal{D}, s')$.
14:             Add a cut to exclude all copies of s' in TD-TSPTW$(\mathcal{D}_T)$.
15:         **else**
16:             Add cuts corresponding to sub-tours and infeasible paths in s' to TD-TSPTW$(\mathcal{D}_T)$
17:         **end if**
18:         Update $\mathcal{D}_T$, (and $\mathcal{P}_T$), and TD-TSPTW$(\mathcal{D}_T)$ by lengthening arcs in s.
19:     **end for**
20:     Compute gap δ between the best solution in S and lower bound, z.
21:     **if** $\delta \leq \epsilon$ **then**
22:         Stop: best solution in S is ϵ-optimal for TSPTW.
23:     **end if**
24: **end while**

4.3   Algorithm to Solve TD-TSPTW$(\mathcal{D}_T)$

Algorithm 1 shows how we solve the TD-TSPTW$(\mathcal{D})$ using proposed lower bound formulations. Readers can refer to [4,9,10] for additional reference of the components of the algorithm. In Algorithm 1, TD-TSPTW$(\mathcal{D}_T)$ refers to one of the lower bound formulations presented in Sect. 4. While it shares the main steps with the one mentioned in [9,10], there are differences. First, to check the feasibility of a solution s found by lower bound formulations, we check with the solution s' obtained from s excluding all waiting arcs (Line 10-11). It ensures that if s' is infeasible, s is always infeasible. If s' is feasible, we solve R-TD-TSPTW(D, s') to find the best tour using only travel arcs in s' (e.g. by adding waiting arcs to s', Line 12). R-TD-TSPTW(D, s') is a restricted formulation of TD-TSPTW(D) where only travel arcs in s' can be selected. If R-TD-TSPTW(D, s') is solved to optimality, we add a cut to exclude all copies of s' from TD-TSPTW$(\mathcal{D}_T)$. If s' is infeasible, we add cuts corresponding to sub-tours and infeasible paths extracted from s' to TD-TSPTW$(\mathcal{D}_T)$. The two primal heuristics in [9,10] are used to help find feasible solutions. We exclude all waiting arcs when solving those two primal heuristics (Line 7). Arcs in those primal heuristics are evaluated with under-estimate cost $\underline{c}_{ij}(t)$ and with basic formulation (5)-(8). We add cuts to exclude all tours corresponding to feasible solutions in S before solving those primal problems to force finding new feasible solutions. When updating $\mathcal{D}_{\mathcal{T}}$ (Line 18), given an arc $((i,t)(j,t'))$ to lengthen, we also add the node $(i,t+1)$ to $\mathcal{D}_{\mathcal{T}}$ to introduce waiting opportunities at (i,t) if $(i,t+1) \notin \mathcal{D}_{\mathcal{T}}$. To maintain Property 1-5, when a new node (i,t) is added to $\mathcal{D}_{\mathcal{T}}$, we also add arc $((i,t)(i,t+1))$ (or $((i,t-1)(i,t))$) if node $(i,t+1)$ (or $(i,t-1)$) existed in $\mathcal{D}_{\mathcal{T}}$. When the path-arc-based formulation is used, Algorithm ADD-PATHS (see online Appendix [11]) is employed to update $\mathcal{P}_{\mathcal{T}}$.

5   Experiments

The algorithm is implemented in C++ using Gurobi 8.0 as the MIP solver. All experiments were run on a workstation with an Intel(R) Xeon (R) CPU E5-4610 v2 2.30GHz processor running Ubuntu 14.04.3. One of the stopping conditions was a provable optimality gap of $\epsilon = 10^{-2}$. Two sets named "Set 1" and "Set w100" from [9] are used. Each set has 960 instances from 15 to 40 nodes with up to 73 travel time profiles. We set the cost $c_{ij}(t)$ be $\tau_{ij}(t)$, the travel time between i and j at time point t. We assess two points:

1. We compare the path-arc-based formulation (Path), the arc-based formulation (Z), and the aggregated arc-based formulation (Z-Agg) and the corresponding algorithms based on the number of instances solved.
2. We compare the strongest algorithm and formulation and the state-of-the-art solver, Gurobi, solving the problem with the full-time-expanded network formulation.

First, Table 1 reports the number of solved instances using the Path, Z, and Z-Agg formulation. In this experiment, we consider a setting in which waiting at site i after visiting i is not allowed, so $c_{ii}(t) = \infty$, or a very high value. Maximum running time for this setting is 1 h. This can happen for time-dependent scheduling problems where all jobs (cities) are performed without stopping. As we expect, the Z-Agg formulation is the most efficient and competitive formulation, while the Path formulation is the worst one. Using the Z-Agg formulation, we can solve 873 and 871 instances of Set 1 and Set w100 to optimality. It means the proposed algorithm is able to solve this particular variant.

Table 1. Number of instances solved optimally by each formulation.

	Set 1			Set w100		
n	Path	Z	Z-Agg	Path	Z	Z-Agg
15	240	240	240	240	240	240
20	239	239	240	226	228	231
30	214	218	224	192	230	232
40	147	149	169	115	167	188

Second, we consider the setting in which $c_{ii}(t) = 0$. This setting is harder because of the larger solution space, so we let 2 h of execution. We observe that while Gurobi can efficiently solve instances of Set w100, it struggles to find feasible solutions to instances of Set 1. Given two hours of computation time, it can only find feasible solutions to 596 over 960 instances of Set 1 (Table 2), while it is able to find feasible solutions to all instances of Set w100. Technically, while having the same number of nodes, instances of Set 1 have wider time windows, making the complete networks larger and harder to solve. The proposed algorithm finds feasible solutions for all instances.

Table 2. Feasible solutions: Gurobi versus Z-Agg (Set 1)

n	15	20	30	40
Gurobi	239	228	115	14
Z-Agg	240	240	240	240

Finally, Table 3 compares the number of ϵ-optimal solutions that Gurobi and the proposed algorithm find for instances of Set 1. Gurobi can prove optimality for 396 instances, while the proposed method with Z-Agg formulation can solve 712 instances. The average gap of unsolved instances is 7.37% (Gurobi) and 2.94% (the proposed algorithm). These preliminary results show that the proposed algorithm and formulations are promising for solving time-dependent TSPTW instances.

Table 3. Optimal solutions: Gurobi versus Z-Agg (Set 1)

n	15	20	30	40
Gurobi	218	145	29	4
Z-Agg	228	199	157	128

To conclude, the three lower bound formulations can be used to solve the time-dependent TD-TSPTW in which the aggregated formulation TD-TSPTW-AGG$(\mathcal{D}_T, \mathcal{A}_T)$ is the most effective one. It has fewer constraints than TD-TSPTW$(\mathcal{D}_T, \mathcal{A}_T)$, and therefore, makes it easier to solve with mixed-integer programming solvers. The proposed algorithm with the aggregated formulation performs better than the solver over benchmark instances.

6   Conclusion

In this paper, we study a generalized version of the time-dependent traveling salesman problem where travel cost is modeled as a generic function. We present three lower-bound formulations based on path and arc variables, and we introduce iterative exact algorithms based on the dynamic discrete discovery approach to solve the problems. The experiment results confirm the advantages of the proposed method over the state-of-art solvers when solving small- and medium-sized instances. Finally, our ongoing research shows that we can apply the proposed method in this paper to solve variants of the TSPTW including those with soft time windows. It confirms the strength and innovation of our proposed method.

Acknowledgement. The work has been carried out partly at the Vietnam Institute for Advanced Study in Mathematics (VIASM). The corresponding author (Duc Minh Vu) would like to thank VIASM for its hospitality and financial support for his visit in 2023.

References

1. Arigliano, A., Ghiani, G., Grieco, A., Guerriero, E., Plana, I.: Time-dependent asymmetric traveling salesman problem with time windows: properties and an exact algorithm. Dis. Appl. Math. **261**, 28–39 (2018)
2. Boland, N., Hewitt, M., Marshall, L., Savelsbergh, M.: The continuous-time service network design problem. Ope. Res. **65**(5), 1303–1321 (2017)
3. Boland, N.L., Savelsbergh, M.W.: Perspectives on integer programming for time-dependent models. TOP **27**, 147–173 (2019)
4. Boland, N., Hewitt, M., Vu, D.M., Savelsbergh, M.: Solving the traveling salesman problem with time windows through dynamically generated time-expanded networks. In: Salvagnin, D., Lombardi, M. (eds.) CPAIOR 2017. LNCS, vol. 10335, pp. 254–262. Springer, Cham (2017). https://doi.org/10.1007/978-3-319-59776-8_21
5. Cordeau, J., Ghiani, G., Guerriero, E.: Analysis and branch-and-cut algorithm for the time-dependent travelling salesman problem. Tra. Sci. **48**(1), 46–58 (2014)
6. Montero, A., Méndez-Díaz, I., Miranda-Bront, J.J.: An integer programming approach for the time-dependent traveling salesman problem with time windows. Comput. Oper. Res. **88**, 280–289 (2017)
7. Pop, P.C., Cosma, O., Sabo, C., Sitar, C.P.: A comprehensive survey on the generalized traveling salesman problem. Eur. J. Oper. Res. (2023)
8. Riedler, M., Ruthmair, M., Raidl, G.R.: Strategies for iteratively refining layered graph models. In: Blesa Aguilera, M.J., Blum, C., Gambini Santos, H., Pinacho-Davidson, P., Godoy del Campo, J. (eds.) HM 2019. LNCS, vol. 11299, pp. 46–62. Springer, Cham (2019). https://doi.org/10.1007/978-3-030-05983-5_4
9. Vu, D.M., Hewitt, M., Boland, N., Savelsbergh, M.: Dynamic discretization discovery for solving the time-dependent traveling salesman problem with time windows. Tran. Sci. **54**(3), 703–720 (2020)
10. Vu, D.M., Hewitt, M., Vu, D.D.: Solving the time dependent minimum tour duration and delivery man problems with dynamic discretization discovery. Eur. J. Oper. Res. **302**(3), 831–846 (2022)
11. Vu, D.M., Hewitt, M., Vu, D.D.: Solving time-dependent traveling salesman problem with time windows under generic time-dependent travel cost (2023). https://arxiv.org/abs/2311.08111

Improved Streaming Algorithm for Minimum Cost Submodular Cover Problem

Tan D. Tran[1], Canh V. Pham[2($\boxtimes$)], Dung P. Trung[2], and Uyen T. Nguyen[3]

[1] Faculty of Information Technology, VNU University of Engineering
and Technology, Hanoi, Vietnam
22027005@vnu.edu.vn
[2] ORLab, Faculty of Computer Science, Phenikaa University, Hanoi, Vietnam
{canh.phamvan,dung.phamtrung}@phenikaa-uni.edu.vn
[3] Institute of Engineering and Technology, Vinh University, Nghean, Vietnam
uyennt@vinhuni.edu.vn

Abstract. This paper introduces an efficient streaming algorithm for a well-known Minimum cost Submodular Cover (MSC) problem. Our algorithm makes $O(\log n)$ passes over the ground set, takes $O(n \log n)$ query complexity and returns a $(1/\epsilon, 1 - \epsilon)$-bicriteria approximation solution with the ground set of size n and the precise parameter $\epsilon > 0$. Therefore, it is better than the existing streaming algorithms in terms of both solution guarantees and query complexity. Besides the theoretical performance, the experiment results on two applications, Revenue Threshold and Coverage Threshold, further show the superiority of our algorithm with the state-of-the-art ones.

Keywords: Submodular Cover · Approximation Algorithm · Streaming Algorithm

1 Introduction

This paper considers the Minimum cost Submodular Cover problem (MSC). In the problem setting, we have a finite ground set V sized n, a monotone submodular set function $f : 2^V \to \mathbb{R}^+$, an additive cost function $c : 2^V \to \mathbb{R}^+$, and a positive threshold $T \leq f(V)$. Assume each element $e \in V$ assigned a positive cost $c(e) > 0$. The goal of the problem is to find a subset $S \subseteq V$ with the minimum cost such that $f(S) \geq T$, where the cost of S is $c(S) = \sum_{v \in S} c(v)$.

The problem has a wide range of applications in the areas of artificial intelligence, data mining, and combination optimization such as recommending systems [6], data summarization [12,18], social influence [10,16] and revenue maximization in social networks [9], maximum coverage [9,15], revenue threshold, coverage threshold, etc. The primary objective of revenue and coverage threshold

---

Canh V. Pham is a corresponding author.

M. H. Hà et al. (Eds.): CSoNet 2023, LNCS 14479, pp. 222–233, 2024.
https://doi.org/10.1007/978-981-97-0669-3_21

differs from typical maximization goals. Rather than solely seeking to maximize the solution, revenue and coverage threshold optimization focuses on identifying a solution in which the object value surpasses a specified threshold while minimizing costs. Although there has been a lot of work focused on designing efficient algorithms for the MSC problem [4,13,19,20], the exponential growth of data requires more efficient algorithms for both running time and memory usage. In this context, the streaming algorithm is an effective method to solve the above issues because it goes through the entire stream only once or a few times and uses a small amount of memory to get the solution with a theoretical bound.

Unfortunately, the proposed streaming algorithms for this problem still have weaknesses. The first work of this line [14] only focused on a special problem with uniform cost. Therefore, it could not be applied to the general MSC. Several streaming algorithms in [3] could work with non-monotone utility function, return a $(O(1/\epsilon^2), (1 - \epsilon)/2)$-bicriteria approximation solution but ran in $O(n \log \text{opt})/c_{min})$ query complexity, where opt was the cost of optimal solution and c_{min} was the smallest cost of an element. Note that the query complexity of this algorithm was not a polynomial since $1/c_{min}$ was not a constant, and it might become arbitrarily large.

Motivated by the above phenomena, in this paper, we propose an improved streaming algorithm that provides better approximation guarantees and query complexity for MSC problem. **Our contributions** are as following:

- We propose a streaming algorithm for the MSC problem, named (StrMSC) that provides a $(\frac{1}{\epsilon}, 1 - \epsilon)$-bicriteria approximation solution that takes $O(\frac{1}{\epsilon} \log \frac{n}{\epsilon})$ passes over the ground set, $O(n)$ memories and $O(\frac{n}{\epsilon} \log \frac{n}{\epsilon})$ query complexity, where $\epsilon > 0$ is a pre-defined accuracy parameter. Therefore, our algorithm is the first multi-pass and near-linear query complexity for MSC.
- We assess the practical performance of the StrMSC algorithm through an extensive experiment in two applications: Revenue Threshold and Coverage Threshold. Our comparison includes the the sate-of-the-art algorithms, MULTI and SINGLE, developed by Crawford et al. [3], as well as the non-streaming GREEDY algorithm by Goyal et al. [7]. Our algorithm consistently outperforms these benchmarked algorithms across various evaluation criteria, encompassing objective value, the number of queries, and memory utilization.

The core idea of our algorithm includes two components. The first component adapts the technique of splitting the ground set by [17] to find a major set within one pass over the ground set. The second one finds a good solution over the major set. For each pass, it establishes a threshold and limits the cost to select: (1) a new element to the partial solution if density gain is at least the threshold, and (2) a good singleton without violating the limited cost. Each pass returns the best candidate solution between the above candidates, and the algorithm terminates after at most $O(\log n)$ passes or the value of the utility function is at least $(1 - \epsilon)T$.

Organization. The rest of the paper is structured as follows. Section 2 provides the literature review on MSC problem. Section 3 presents notations and proprieties of studied problem. Section 4 introduces the proposed algorithm and theoretical analysis. Experimental computation is provided in Sect. 5. Finally, we conclude this work in Sect. 6.

2   Related Works

The MSC problem is an NP-hard problem [8]. One common approach to solving the problem is using greedy, which sequentially selects elements with maximal marginal gain into the partial solution and takes advantage of the submodular to derive the approximation bound. Wolsey *et al.* [20] first introduced a greedy version that had an approximation ratio of $1 + \ln(\alpha/\beta)$, where α was the maximum value of the objective over all the singletons, and β was the smallest non-zero marginal gain of the greedy algorithm. Then, Wan *et al.* [19] showed the greedy algorithm could return an approximation ratio of $1 + \ln(\alpha/\beta)$ for a special case of MSC problem. Another work of [7] proposed a greedy algorithm with a different stopping condition. It returned a $(\log(\frac{T}{\epsilon}), 1 - \epsilon)$-bicriteria approximation solution. Recently, Crawford *et al.* [4] proved that a greedy algorithm could provide another bound under noise models when one could only estimate the value of the utility function within a bias error. In general, greedy algorithms have $O(n^2)$ query complexity and make $O(n)$-passes through the data. Thus, they may be infeasible for some applications with large data. Besides, several works have focused on developing evolutionary algorithm [5] or parallel algorithm [17] for MSC. However, they needed expensive query complexity and required a polynomial number of passes through the data.

Streaming algorithms are effective for submodular optimization problems, especially in big data. Norouzi-Fard *et al.* [14] showed that a single pass streaming algorithm for MSC with an approximation ratio better than $n/2$ must use at least $O(n)$ memory. In the seminal work, they proposed an efficient algorithm for the Submodular Cover problem, a special case of MSC with uni-cost. Their algorithm made a single-pass, used M memories and provided $(2\ln(1/\epsilon), 1 - \frac{1}{\ln(1/\epsilon)})$-bicriteria approximation solution, where M was the required memory. More recently, Crawford *et al.* [3] proposed two bicriteria algorithms for solving MSC for the non-monotone case. The first one, called MULTI, returned $((1 + \epsilon)(1 + \frac{4}{\epsilon^2}), \frac{1-\epsilon}{2})$ bicriteria approximation ratio, made $O(\log(\mathsf{opt})/c_{min})$ passes, wasted $O(\frac{n}{\epsilon}\log(\mathsf{opt}/c_{min}))$ query complexity, and used $O(\mathsf{opt}/\epsilon^2)$ space complexity. The query complexity of MULTI depended on $1/c_{min}$ that was not a constant and might be arbitrarily large. Their second one, SINGLE, made a single pass and returned the same approximation bound but had a larger query complexity of $\Omega(n^2/c_{min})$.

3   Preliminaries

Given a ground set $V = \{e_1, \ldots, e_n\}$ of size n, the submodular set function $f : 2^V \mapsto \mathbb{R}^+$ measures the quality of a subset $S \subseteq V$. It is assumed that there exists an oracle query, which, when queried with the set S, returns the value $f(S)$. We assume f normalized, i.e., $f(\emptyset) = 0$. The marginal gain of an element e to a set $S \subseteq V$ is defined $f(e|S) = f(S \cup \{e\}) - f(S)$. We also define $f(S|X) = f(S \cup X) - f(X)$ for any set $X \subseteq V$. We simplify $f(\{e\})$ to $f(e)$.

The function f is monotone if for $A \subseteq B \subseteq V$, we have $f(A) \leq f(B)$. f is submodular if for any $A \subseteq B \subseteq V$, $e \in V \setminus B$, $f(e|A) \geq f(e|B)$.

An instance of the problem MSC is presented by a tuple (V, f, T). Given an instance of MSC with cost function c additive, i.e., $c(S) = \sum_{e \in S} c(e)$, we define $c_{min} = \min_{e \in V} c(e)$, $c_{max} = \max_{e \in V} c(e)$, and O is the optimal solution and the optimal cost $\mathsf{opt} = c(O)$.

We call an algorithm is a (x, y)-**bicriteria approximation** for MSC problem if it returns a solution S satisfying $f(S) \geq y \cdot T$ and $c(S) \leq x \cdot \mathsf{opt}$, where $x, y > 0$.

Streaming Algorithm. A streaming algorithm is an approximation algorithm that processes the data stream in which the input is presented as a sequence of elements and can be examined in only one or a few passes. These algorithms are designed to operate with limited memory, generally logarithmic in the size of the stream or in the maximum value in the stream.

4   Proposed Algorithm

This section introduces our streaming version StrMSC that provides a $(1 - \epsilon, \frac{1}{\epsilon})$-bicriteria approximation solution for MSC within $O(\log n)$ passes over the ground set V.

Algorithm Description. StrMSC consists of two phases. The first phase (lines 2-9) adapts a strategy of dividing the set V into reasonable subsets by [17], within one pass over the ground set V, to ensure the algorithm takes at most near-linear query complexity. Accordingly, it first sorts $V = \{u_1, u_2, \ldots, u_n\}$ in non-decreasing order and then finds the smallest j so that $f(u_1, u_2, \ldots, u_j) \geq T$. The algorithm divides V into three subsets: the first subset V_0 contains elements with the cost less than $c'_{min} \leftarrow \epsilon c(u_j)/n$, the second one V_1 contains elements with the cost greater than $c'_{max} \leftarrow jc(u_j)$, and the last one V' contains the rest. We call the set V' as the major set, and one may find the near-optimal solution of the problem over the ground V' instead of V. By the above division strategy, one can bound the ratio of $\frac{\max_{e \in V'} c(e)}{\min_{e \in V'} c(e)} = O(n^3)$ that helps the algorithm finds the solution in near-linear query complexity.

The second phase (lines 9-21) takes at most $O(\log_{1+\epsilon} n)$ passes over the major set V'. In each pass, the algorithm finds a candidate solution S_v by adding a new element e with the density gain, i.e., the ratio between $f'(e|S_v)$ and the cost $c(e)$, satisfies the condition in the line 13, where $f(\cdot) = f(\cdot|V_0)$. The algorithm then updates the element e_v with the highest utility value with the cost is at most $(1 + \epsilon)^{v+1}$. At the end of each pass, it finds the best solution among S_v and $\{e_v\}$ and terminates this phase if $f'(S'_v) \geq \frac{\alpha T'}{2}$.

Finally, the algorithm returns which set has a lower cost between candidate ones $S'_v \cup V_0$ and S^0.

Algorithm 1: Algorithm

Input: An instance (V, f, T), parameter $\epsilon > 0$
Output: A solution S
// Phase 1: Pre-processing
1: Within one passe over ground set V do:
2: Sort $V = \{u_1, u_2, \dots, u_{|V|}\}$ in non-decreasing cost order
3: Find $j \leftarrow \min\{i : f(\{u_1, u_2, \dots, u_i\}) \geq T\}$, $S^0 \leftarrow \{u_1, \dots, u_j\}$
4: $c'_{min} \leftarrow \epsilon c(u_j)/n$, $c'_{max} \leftarrow jc(u_j)$
5: $V_0 \leftarrow \{u \in V : c(u) < c'_{min}\}$
6: $V_1 \leftarrow \{u \in V : c(u) > c'_{max}\}$
7: $V' \leftarrow V \setminus (V_0 \cup V_1)$, $T' \leftarrow T - f(V_0)$, $f'(\cdot) \leftarrow f(\cdot|V_0)$
8: $c_0 \leftarrow \min_{e \in V'} c(e)$, $U = \{v \in [n] : c_0 \leq (1 + \epsilon)^v \leq c(V')\}$
9: $\alpha = 2(1 - \epsilon), \beta = \frac{(1+\epsilon)\alpha}{2-\alpha}$
// Phase 2: Main Streams
10: **foreach** $v \in U$ **do**
11: $\quad$ $S_v \leftarrow \emptyset, e_v \leftarrow \emptyset$
12: $\quad$ **foreach** $e \in V'$ **do**
13: $\quad\quad$ **if** $\frac{f'(e|S_v)}{c(e)} \geq \frac{\alpha T'}{\beta(1+\epsilon)^v}$ and $c(S_v \cup \{e\}) \leq \beta(1+\epsilon)^v$ **then**
14: $\quad\quad$ $\lfloor$ $S_v \leftarrow S_v \cup \{e\}$
15: $\quad\quad$ **if** $c(e_v) \leq (1+\epsilon)^{v+1}$ **then**
16: $\quad\quad$ $\lfloor$ $e_v \leftarrow \arg\max_{x \in \{e, e_v\}} f'(x)$
17: $\quad$ $S'_v \leftarrow \arg\max_{X \in \{S_v, e_v\}} f'(X)$
18: $\quad$ **if** $f'(S'_v) \geq \frac{\alpha T'}{2}$ **then**
19: $\quad\quad$ **break**
20: $\quad$ **else**
21: $\quad\quad$ $\lfloor$ Delete S'_v, e_v
22: **return** $\arg\min_{X \in \{S'_v \cup V_0, S^0\}} c(X)$.

Theoretical Analysis. In the following, we show the theoretical guarantees of StrMSC in Theorem 1.

Theorem 1. *Algorithm 1 is multi-pass streaming algorithm that*

- *Returns a solution S with $f(S) \geq (1 - \epsilon)T$ and $c(S) \leq \frac{1}{\epsilon}$opt.*
- *Takes $O(n)$ memories and makes at most $O(\frac{1}{\epsilon} \log(\frac{n}{\epsilon}))$-pass through V.*
- *Takes $O(\frac{n}{\epsilon} \log(\frac{n}{\epsilon}))$ query complexity.*

Proof. For ease of following, we first recap the proof of showing the bound c'_{min} and c'_{max} in [17]. Supposing that j is an integer number the algorithm finds in line 2 and $v_t = \max_{e \in O} c(e)$. If $c(v_t) < c(v_j)$, then $O = \{v_1, v_2, \dots, v_t\}$. By the monotoncity of f, we have $f(O) \geq T = f(\{v_1, v_2, \dots, v_t\})$ which contracts to the definition of j. Thus, $c(v_j) \leq c(v_t) \leq c(O)$. On the other hand, since the set $\{v_1, v_2, \dots, v_j\}$ is a feasible solution of (V, f, T), we have $c(O) \leq c(\{v_1, v_2, \dots, v_j\}) \leq jc(v_j)$.

Prove Approximation Guarantees. By the selection of V_0, we have $c(V_0) \leq |V_0|c'_{min} \leq \epsilon c(v_j) \leq \epsilon$opt. Denote by O' an optimal solution of the instance (V', f', T') and opt$' = c(O')$, where $f'(\cdot) = f(\cdot|V_0)$ and $T' = T - f(V_0)$. It is easy to see that $f'(\cdot)$ is a monotone and submodular function. Since $f'(O) = f(O \cup V_0) - f(V_0) \geq T - f(V_0)$, O is a feasible solution of the problem under the instance (V', f', T') and thus opt$' \leq$ opt. On the other hand, since $c'_{min} \leq c_0 \leq (1+\epsilon)^v \leq c(V')$, there exists an integer v so that $\frac{\text{opt}'}{1+\epsilon} < u = (1+\epsilon)^v \leq$ opt.

We provide the theoretical bound of S'_v and use it to obtain the proof. We consider two following cases:

Case 1. There exists an element $o \in O' \setminus S_v$ so that $c(S_v) + c(o) > \beta(1+\epsilon)^v$ and $\frac{f'(o|S_v)}{c(o)} \geq \frac{T'}{\beta(1+\epsilon)^v}$. By the selection of S_v, we have $f'(S_v) \geq \frac{c(S_v)\alpha T'}{\beta u}$. Therefore

$$f'(S_v \cup \{o\}) \geq f'(S_v) + \frac{\alpha c(o)T'}{\beta u} \geq \frac{c(S_v)\alpha T'}{\beta u} + \frac{\alpha c(o)T'}{\beta u} \qquad (1)$$

$$= (c(S) + c(o))\frac{\alpha T'}{\beta v} > \alpha T'. \qquad (2)$$

By the selection rule of e_v, we have $c(e_v) \leq (1+\epsilon)u >$ opt$'$, so $f(e_v) \geq \max_{o \in O'} f'(o)$. Combine this with the submodularity of f', we have

$$f'(S'_v) \geq \max\{f'(S_v), f(e_v)\} \geq \max\{f'(S_v), f'(o)\} \geq \frac{f'(S_v \cup \{o\})}{2} > \frac{\alpha T'}{2} \qquad (3)$$

and $c(S'_v) \leq \max\{c(S'_v), c(e_v)\} = \max\{\beta u, (1+\epsilon)u\} \leq \beta u \leq \beta$opt$'$.

Case 2. There is no such element $o \in O' \setminus S_v$, i.e., $c(S_v) + c(o) \leq \beta(1+\epsilon)^v$ and $\frac{f'(o|S_v)}{c(o)} \geq \frac{T'}{\beta(1+\epsilon)^v}$ for all $o \in O' \setminus S_v$. In this case, we also have $c(S'_v) \leq \beta$opt$'$. By the monotoncity and submodularity of f' with a note that $u = (1+\epsilon)^v > \frac{\text{opt}'}{1+\epsilon}$ we have:

$$f(O') - f(S_v) \leq f(O' \cup S_v) - f(S_v) \qquad (4)$$

$$\leq \sum_{o \in O' \setminus S_v} f(o|S_v) \qquad (5)$$

$$\leq \sum_{o \in O' \setminus S_u} c(o)\frac{\alpha T'}{\beta(1+\epsilon)^v} \leq \text{opt}'\frac{\alpha T'}{\beta u} \qquad (6)$$

$$< \frac{\alpha(1+\epsilon)T'}{\beta} \qquad (7)$$

which implies that

$$f(S_v) \geq f(O') - \frac{\alpha(1+\epsilon)T'}{\beta} \geq T' - \frac{\alpha(1+\epsilon)T'}{\beta} = (1 - \frac{(1+\epsilon)\alpha}{\beta})T'. \qquad (8)$$

Combine two case with choosing α, β in the algorithm, we have $f'(S'_v) \geq (1-\epsilon)T'$ and $c(S'_v) \leq \frac{1-\epsilon^2}{\epsilon}opt'$. Therefore, the algorithm must meet the condition in line 13 and return the final solution after at most v iterations. If the algorithm returns S'_v, recap that $c(V_0) \leq \epsilon \text{opt}$ and $\text{opt}' \leq \text{opt}$, we have:

$$c(S \cup V_0) \leq (\beta + \epsilon)\text{opt} \leq \frac{\text{opt}}{\epsilon}. \tag{9}$$

On the other hand,

$$f(S'_v \cup V_0) = f(S'_v \cup V_0) - f(V_0) + f(V_0) \tag{10}$$
$$= f'(S'_v) + f(V_0) \geq (1 - \epsilon)(T - f(V_0)) + f(V_0) \tag{11}$$
$$= (1 - \epsilon)T + \epsilon f(V_0) \geq (1 - \epsilon)T. \tag{12}$$

If the algorithm meets the condition in line 13 at the iteration $k < v$, we have $f(S'_k) \geq (1 - \epsilon)T'$ and thus $f(S'_k \cup V_0) \geq T$. Besides, $c(S'_k) \leq \beta(1 + \epsilon)^k < \beta(1 + \epsilon)^v = \beta\text{opt}'$, the approximation guarantees holds.

Prove Complexities. The algorithm makes one pass to finish the first phase and needs n memories to find S^0. For the second phase, the number of passes through V' is at most

$$\log_{1+\epsilon}(\frac{c(V')}{c_0}) < \log_{1+\epsilon}(\frac{nc'_{max}}{c'_{min}}) \leq \log_{1+\epsilon}(\frac{n^3}{\epsilon}) \tag{13}$$

$$= \frac{\log(\frac{n^3}{\epsilon})}{\log(1 + \epsilon)} \leq \frac{1}{\epsilon}\log(\frac{n^3}{\epsilon}) = O(\frac{1}{\epsilon}\log(\frac{n}{\epsilon})), \tag{14}$$

in which each pass takes at most n queries. Therefore the memories needed, the total number of passes and the query complexity are $O(n)$, $O(\frac{1}{\epsilon}\log(\frac{n}{\epsilon}))$ and $O(\frac{n}{\epsilon}\log(\frac{n}{\epsilon}))$, respectively. □

5 Experimental Evaluation

In this section, we provide a comparative analysis of our algorithm alongside MULTI, SINGLE [3] and GREEDY [7] for the MSC problem. We evaluate their performance on two specific applications: Revenue Threshold and Coverage Threshold. Our assessment primarily centers around four essential metrics: the oracle value of the objective function, the number of queries, cost value, and memory usage.

5.1 Applications and Datasets

Revenue Threshold. Given a social network represented by a graph $G = (V, E)$, where V denotes the set of users and E represents the set of user connections. Each edge (u, v) is assigned a weight $w_{(u,v)}$ that is non-negative. We follow [12] to define the advertising revenue of any node set $S \subseteq V$ as $f(S) = \sum_{u \in V} R_u(S)$. For this evaluation, we choose $R_u(S) = (\sum_{v \in S} w_{uv})^{\alpha_u}$, where α_u is chosen independently for each u uniformly in $(0, 1)$. The revenue objective $f(.)$ is monotone and submodular [9]. Different from the Revenue Maximization application defined by Kuhnle [9], the goal of Revenue Threshold is a solution S such that $f(S)$ exceeds a given threshold T such that the cost $c(S)$ is minimized. In this application, we utilized the ego Facebook dataset from [11]. This dataset consists of over 4K nodes and over 88K edges.

Coverage Threshold. Based on the Maximum Coverage described in [9], the Coverage Threshold can be described as follows: Considering a graph $G = (V, E)$, for any given subset $S \subseteq V$, we define S^I as the set comprising all vertices that share an incident edge with any vertex in S. Subsequently, we define the function $f(S)$ as the cardinality of S^I. It is worth noting that this objective function exhibits the properties of monotonicity and submodularity, as demonstrated in the work by Kuhnle [9]. The Coverage Threshold aims to find a solution S such that $f(S)$ exceeds a given threshold T such that the cost $c(S)$ is minimized. In our practical application, we employed datasets that consisted of an Erdős-Rényi (ER) random graph with 5000 nodes and an edge probability of 0.2. Additionally, the cost associated with each node, denoted as $c(u)$, was selected randomly and uniformly from the range between 0 and 1, following the methodology outlined in the study by Amanatidis *et al.* [1].

Experiment Settings. We compare our algorithms with the applicable state-of-the-art algorithms listed below:

- **MULTI**: The streaming algorithm, as presented in [3], boasts a bicriteria approximation guarantee of $((1 + \epsilon)(1 + \frac{4}{\epsilon^2}), \frac{1-\epsilon}{2})$. This algorithm conducts $O(\log(\text{opt})/c_{min})$ passes through the universe V, simultaneously retains elements with a total cost of $O(\text{opt})$, and makes $O(\frac{n}{\epsilon}\log(\text{opt}/c_{min}))$ queries to the function f when leveraging a linear-time algorithm for Unconstrained Submodular Maximization (USM) as a subroutine.
- **SINGLE**: The streaming algorithm, as introduced in [3], conducts a single pass through the universe V in an arbitrary order and provides an identical bicriteria approximation guarantee as MULTI. Nonetheless, it is worth noting that SINGLE requires a total number of queries to the function f that is within the order of $\Omega(n^2/c_{min})$.
- **GREEDY**: The greedy algorithm, as outlined in [7], achieves a bicriteria approximation guarantee of $(\log(\frac{T}{\epsilon}), 1 - \epsilon)$ for the minimum target set selection problem (MINTSS).

In each experiment, our analysis begins with the execution of the double greedy algorithm, as developed by [2] and denoted as USM, to establish an initial benchmark for comparison. We use the following symbols to represent the characteristics of the *USM* algorithm: c_0 for cost, f_0 for the f-value, q_0 for the number of queries, and m_0 for memory usage. In all the generated plots, the y-axis is dedicated to normalized f-values relative to the threshold T, while cost values are normalized with respect to c_0, memory usage is normalized with respect to m_0, and the threshold T is normalized in the relation to f_0. Within our experimental framework, we systematically vary the threshold within the range of 0.1

to 0.5, relative to the reference value f_0, following the configuration specified in
[3]. Additionally, we maintain a consistent setting of $\epsilon = 0.1$ for all algorithms
used in these experiments.

5.2 Experiment Results

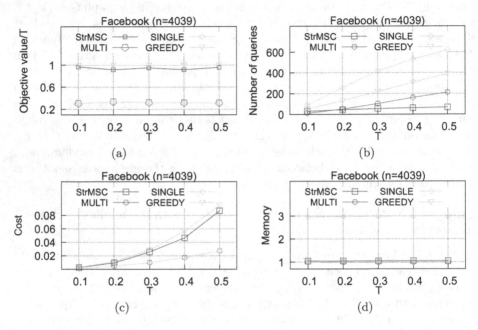

Fig. 1. Performance of algorithms for MSC on Revenue Threshold: (a) The objective
values, (b) The number of queries (c) The cost values (d) The allocated memory

The experimental results are depicted in Figs. 1 and 2. Specifically, Fig. 1 illustrates the results for the Revenue Threshold application, while Fig. 2 presents
the results for Coverage Threshold.

Firstly, our algorithm surpasses SINGLE and MULTI algorithms in terms
of the objective value in Revenue Threshold (Fig. 1a) and Coverage Threshold
(Fig. 2a) applications. This accomplishment is significant as our objective value
closely approaches the asymptotic objective value of the GREEDY and con-
verges in proximity to the threshold T. In stark contrast, the objective values
of the SINGLE and MULTI algorithms are confined to a mere one-third of the
threshold T.

Secondly, our algorithm demonstrates exceptional query efficiency (Fig. 1b,
Fig. 2b), with the number of queries consistently ranking among the lowest compared to other algorithms. A notable attribute is its capacity to maintain a

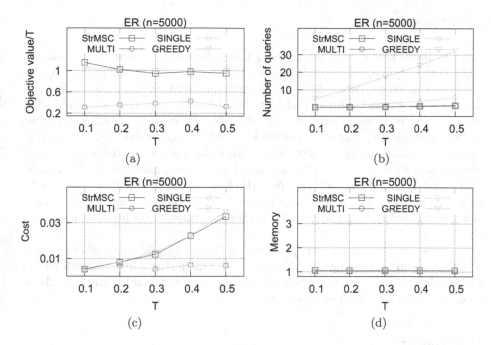

Fig. 2. Performance of algorithms for MSC on Coverage Threshold: (a) The objective values, (b) The number of queries (c) The cost values (d) The allocated memory

stable number of queries even as the threshold T increases, while other algorithms tend to experience significant increases in the number of queries under similar conditions.

Thirdly, with regard to the cost value analysis (Fig. 1c, Fig. 2c), our algorithm exhibits a higher cost value than the SINGLE and MULTI algorithms, yet it remains lower than that of the GREEDY. This cost disparity can be attributed to our algorithm's superior capacity to achieve a higher objective value. Nevertheless, it is crucial to emphasize that the assurance of a valid solution justifies this increased cost.

Lastly, concerning memory utilization (Fig. 1d, Fig. 2d), our StrMSC algorithm, along with the GREEDY and MULTI algorithms, exhibits similar memory usage patterns, closely aligning with the memory consumption of the USM algorithm. On the contrary, the SINGLE algorithm stands out due to its notably larger memory footprint, approximately three times that of the other algorithms.

In summary, our StrMSC algorithm excels in various evaluation criteria compared to the benchmarked algorithms. These criteria include objective value, number of queries, and memory utilization, all evaluated in the contexts of both Revenue Threshold and Coverage Threshold applications. While the cost value surpasses that of SINGLE and MULTI algorithms, it remains lower than that of GREEDY algorithm, which aligns with the observed differences in objective values.

6   Conclusion

In conclusion, this paper introduces a novel streaming algorithm designed to address the MSC problem. This algorithm yields a $(1 - \epsilon, \frac{1}{\epsilon})$-bicriteria approximation solution for MSC while maintaining computational efficiency with only $O(\log n)$ passes over the ground set V in the monotone case. To evaluate our algorithmic solutions, we conducted comprehensive experiments encompassing two diverse applications: Revenue Threshold and Coverage Threshold. The experimental outcomes unequivocally demonstrate the superior performance of our algorithms across various evaluation metrics when compared to MULTI, SINGLE, and GREEDY algorithms. Nevertheless, several open questions persist, igniting the spark for future research endeavors. Prominent among these questions is the pursuit of strategies to further minimize the solution's associated cost.

In summary, the algorithms proposed in this paper offer both efficiency and effectiveness in addressing the MSC problem. Our forthcoming research efforts will be dedicated to refining these algorithms and undertaking the formidable challenges that lie ahead in this domain.

References

1. Amanatidis, G., Fusco, F., Lazos, P., Leonardi, S., Reiffenhäuser, R.: Fast adaptive non-monotone submodular maximization subject to a knapsack constraint. In: Proceedings of Annual Conference on Neural Information Processing Systems (2020)
2. Buchbinder, N., Feldman, M., Seffi, J., Schwartz, R.: A tight linear time (1/2)-approximation for unconstrained submodular maximization. SIAM J. Comput. **44**(5), 1384–1402 (2015)
3. Crawford, V.: Scalable bicriteria algorithms for non-monotone submodular cover. In: Proceedings of The 26th International Conference on Artificial Intelligence and Statistics, pp. 9517–9537. PMLR (2023)
4. Crawford, V., Kuhnle, A., Thai, M.: Submodular cost submodular cover with an approximate oracle. In: Proceedings of the 36th International Conference on Machine Learning, pp. 1426–1435. PMLR (2019)
5. Crawford, V.G.: Faster guarantees of evolutionary algorithms for maximization of monotone submodular functions. In: Proceedings of the Thirtieth International Joint Conference on Artificial Intelligence, IJCAI 2021, Virtual Event / Montreal, Canada, 19–27 August 2021, pp. 1661–1667. ijcai.org (2021)
6. El-Arini, K., Guestrin, C.: Beyond keyword search: discovering relevant scientific literature. In: Proceedings of the 17th ACM SIGKDD International Conference on Knowledge Discovery and Data Mining, San Diego, CA, USA, 21–24 August 2011, pp. 439–447 (2011)
7. Goyal, A., Bonchi, F., Lakshmanan, L.V.S., Venkatasubramanian, S.: On minimizing budget and time in influence propagation over social networks. Soc. Netw. Anal. Min. **3**(2), 179–192 (2013)
8. Iwata, S.: Submodular function minimization. Math. Program. **112**, 45–64 (2008)

9. Kuhnle, A.: Quick streaming algorithms for maximization of monotone submodular functions in linear time. In: International Conference on Artificial Intelligence and Statistics, pp. 1360–1368. PMLR (2021)
10. Kuhnle, A., Crawford, V.G., Thai, M.T.: Scalable and adaptive algorithms for the triangle interdiction problem on billion-scale networks. In: 2017 IEEE International Conference on Data Mining, ICDM 2017, New Orleans, LA, USA, 18–21 November 2017, pp. 237–246 (2017)
11. Leskovec, J., Krause, A., Guestrin, C., Faloutsos, C., VanBriesen, J.M., Glance, N.S.: Cost-effective outbreak detection in networks. In: Proceedings of the 13th ACM SIGKDD International Conference on Knowledge Discovery and Data Mining, 2007, pp. 420–429 (2007)
12. Mirzasoleiman, B., Badanidiyuru, A., Karbasi, A.: Fast constrained submodular maximization: personalized data summarization. In: International Conference on Machine Learning. JMLR Workshop and Conference Proceedings, vol. 48, pp. 1358–1367 (2016)
13. Mitrovic, M., Kazemi, E., Zadimoghaddam, M., Karbasi, A.: Data summarization at scale: a two-stage submodular approach. In: Proceedings of the 33nd International Conference on Machine Learning, pp. 3593–3602 (2016)
14. Norouzi-Fard, A., Bazzi, A., Bogunovic, I., El Halabi, M., Hsieh, Y.P., Cevher, V.: An efficient streaming algorithm for the submodular cover problem. In: Advances in Neural Information Processing Systems, vol. 29 (2016)
15. Norouzi-Fard, A., Tarnawski, J., Mitrovic, S., Zandieh, A., Mousavifar, A., Svensson, O.: Beyond 1/2-approximation for submodular maximization on massive data streams. In: Proceedings of the 37th International Conference on Machine Learning Conference, vol. 80, pp. 3826–3835 (2018)
16. Pham, C.V., Pham, D.V., Bui, B.Q., Nguyen, A.V.: Minimum budget for misinformation detection in online social networks with provable guarantees. Optim. Lett. 16, 515–544 (2021)
17. Ran, Y., Zhang, Z., Tang, S.: Improved parallel algorithm for minimum cost submodular cover problem. In: Loh, P., Raginsky, M. (eds.) Conference on Learning Theory, 2–5 July 2022, London, UK. Proceedings of Machine Learning Research, vol. 178, pp. 3490–3502. PMLR (2022). https://proceedings.mlr.press/v178/ran22a.html
18. Tschiatschek, S., Iyer, R.K., Wei, H., Bilmes, J.A.: Learning mixtures of submodular functions for image collection summarization. In: Advances in Neural Information Processing Systems 27: Annual Conference on Neural Information Processing Systems 2014, 8–13 December 2014, Montreal, Quebec, Canada, pp. 1413–1421 (2014)
19. Wan, P.J., Du, D.Z., Pardalos, P., Wu, W.: Greedy approximations for minimum submodular cover with submodular cost. Comput. Optim. Appl. 45(2), 463–474 (2010)
20. Wolsey, L.A.: An analysis of the greedy algorithm for the submodular set covering problem. Combinatorica 2(4), 385–393 (1982)

Deletion-Robust Submodular Maximization Under the Cardinality Constraint over the Integer Lattice

Guangwen Zhou, Bin Liu$^{(\boxtimes)}$ (ID), and Yuanyuan Qiang

School of Mathematical Sciences, Ocean University of China, Qingdao, China
binliu@ouc.edu.cn

Abstract. Submodular optimization is a classical problem of combinatorial optimization. The objective functions of many combinatorial optimization problems are submodular functions and they also have significant applications in real life. Since some practical problems such as budget allocations that are hard to be modeled over set functions, submodular functions over the integer lattice have been widely and intensively studied subject to various classical constraints for decades. In this paper we study the robustness of maximizing a monotone diminishing return submodular function over the integer lattice under the cardinality constraint. We propose a robustness model over the integer lattice and design algorithms under this specific model by utilizing stochastic strategy combining with binary search approach. The algorithms we designed in centralized settings can achieve a $(1/2 - \delta)$-approximation and maintain robustness against deleting any d elements adversarially. While in streaming settings the algorithms we designed can still achieve the same approximation and be robust against deleting any d elements adversarially as well.

Keywords: Submodular maximization · Cardinality constraint · Robustness

1 Introduction

Submodular Optimization. Submodular function has been widely studied since it has a special property called the diminishing return property. The objective functions of many classical combinatorial optimization problems are submodular such as matroid rank functions [2] or the cut functions in the graphs [14]. Submodular functions also have significant applications in practical problems such as facility location [3] and document summarization [11]. Given a ground set V which is a finite set, a function $f : \mathbb{Z}^V \to \mathbb{R}$ is *submodular* if $f(A) + f(B) \geq f(A \cup B) + f(A \cap B)$ for any $A, B \subseteq V$. Its equivalent definition can also be expressed as follows: $f(A \cup \{e\}) - f(A) \geq f(B \cup \{e\}) - f(B)$ for any $A \subseteq B \subseteq V$ and $e \in V \setminus B$.

This work was supported in part by the National Natural Science Foundation of China (11971447), and the Fundamental Research Funds for the Central Universities.

M. H. Hà et al. (Eds.): CSoNet 2023, LNCS 14479, pp. 234–242, 2024.
https://doi.org/10.1007/978-981-97-0669-3_22

Maximizing submodular functions subject to various constraints already have abundant significant results. For the case that the objective function is monotone, the simple greedy algorithm designed by Nemhauser et al. [12] under the cardinality constraint can achieve a $(1 - 1/e)$-approximation. Sviridenko et al. [15] presented a $(1 - 1/e)$-approximation algorithm under the knapsack constraint. Nemhauser et al. [12] and Khuller et al. [8] respectively proved that unless $P = NP$ there is no polynomial time algorithm can achieve a approximation better than $(1 - 1/e)$ under the cardinality and knapsack constraint. Up to today, there are still massive related works on designing algorithms to study submodular optimization problems under different constraints, models and situations [4, 7, 10, 18].

Submodular Optimization Over the Integer Lattice. Since some practical problems such as budget allocation [1] are hard to be modeled on set functions, it's a natural idea that generalize the set functions to the integer lattice in which case each element can be selected repeatedly. Lattice submodular and DR-submodular functions are two kinds of submodular functions over the integer lattice. Given a ground set V which is a finite multiset, we say a function $f : \mathbb{Z}_+^V \to \mathbb{R}$ is *lattice submodular* if $f(\boldsymbol{x}) + f(\boldsymbol{y}) \geq f(\boldsymbol{x} \vee \boldsymbol{y}) + f(\boldsymbol{x} \wedge \boldsymbol{y})$ for any $\boldsymbol{x}, \boldsymbol{y} \in \mathbb{Z}_+^V$ and $f : \mathbb{Z}_+^V \to \mathbb{R}$ is *diminishing return submodular(DR-submodular)* if $f(\boldsymbol{x} + \chi_e) - f(\boldsymbol{x}) \geq f(\boldsymbol{y} + \chi_e) - f(\boldsymbol{y})$ for any $\boldsymbol{x}, \boldsymbol{y} \in \mathbb{Z}_+^V$, $\boldsymbol{x} \leq \boldsymbol{y}$. Note that only DR-submodular functions satisfy the diminishing return property over the integer lattice.

For maximizing the monotone lattice submodular functions, the algorithms designed by Soma et al. [17] under the cardinality constraint can achieve a $(1 - 1/e - \epsilon)$-approximation while the algorithms designed by Soma et al. [16] under the knapsack constraint achieved a $(1 - 1/e)$-approximation. For maximizing the monotone DR-submodular functions, the algorithms designed by Soma et al. [17] under the cardinality constraint and the knapsack constraint can both achieve a $(1 - 1/e - \epsilon)$-approximation. Similarly, submodular optimization problems over the integer lattice under different models, constraints and applications are still be widely studied in recent works such as in [5, 6, 19].

Robustness Models. With the rapid development of machine learning and the emergence of large data-sets in recent years, how to maintain the stability of the system has become an urgent need for optimization problems.

There can be various kinds of robustness models to evaluate the robustness of the system. Take the cardinality constraint for example, Orlin et al. [13] studied a robustness model in sensor placement to cover as much as areas with the sensors that some might be ineffective. They designed a 0.387-approximation algorithm when there at most $o(\sqrt{k})$ sensors we picked might be invalid. Kazemi et al. [9] studied a different robustness model to capture a two-phase problem. In this case some elements in the ground set may be deleted while we are unable to know the concrete deleting process at the beginning. They designed centralized and streaming algorithms that can both achieve a $(1/2)$-approximation against adversarially deletions.

Our Results. Although there are far-ranging previous works in studying the robustness over the submodular functions, most of the works focus on the set functions. In this paper we study the robustness of maximizing the monotone DR-submodular functions over the integer lattice under the cardinality constraint. We propose a robustness model based on a two-phase problem and design algorithms for this specific model. In centralized setting and streaming setting the algorithms we designed can both achieve a $(1/2-\delta)$-approximation. We apply the binary search approach and greedy strategy in the design of the algorithms to maintain robustness against any adversarially deletions and our results can be degenerated into the results of [9].

2   Preliminaries

Given a ground set V which is a finite multiset. We say that a function $f : \mathbb{Z}_+^V \to \mathbb{R}$ is *lattice submodular* if $f(\boldsymbol{x}) + f(\boldsymbol{y}) \geq f(\boldsymbol{x} \vee \boldsymbol{y}) + f(\boldsymbol{x} \wedge \boldsymbol{y})$ for all $\boldsymbol{x}, \boldsymbol{y} \in \mathbb{Z}_+^V$, where $(\boldsymbol{x} \vee \boldsymbol{y})(e) = \max\{\boldsymbol{x}(e), \boldsymbol{y}(e)\}$ and $(\boldsymbol{x} \wedge \boldsymbol{y})(e) = \min\{\boldsymbol{x}(e), \boldsymbol{y}(e)\}$. We say a function $f : \mathbb{Z}_+^V \to \mathbb{R}$ is *diminishing return submodular(DR-submodular)* if $f(\boldsymbol{x}+\chi_e)-f(\boldsymbol{x}) \geq f(\boldsymbol{y}+\chi_e)-f(\boldsymbol{y})$ for any $\boldsymbol{x} \leq \boldsymbol{y}$ and $e \in V$, where we denote χ_e the unit vector. Note that a lattice submodular function is DR-submodular if it is *coordinate-wise concave* which means $f(\boldsymbol{x}+2\chi_e)-f(\boldsymbol{x}+\chi_e) \leq f(\boldsymbol{x}+\chi_e)-f(\boldsymbol{x})$ for each $\boldsymbol{x} \in \mathbb{Z}_+^V$. We say a function $f : \mathbb{Z}_+^V \to \mathbb{R}$ is *monotone* if $f(\boldsymbol{x}) \geq f(\boldsymbol{y})$ for any $\boldsymbol{x} \leq \boldsymbol{y}$. To avoid symbol abusing, denote $f(\boldsymbol{x} \mid \boldsymbol{y}) = f(\boldsymbol{x} + \boldsymbol{y}) - f(\boldsymbol{y})$ for all $\boldsymbol{x}, \boldsymbol{y} \in \mathbb{Z}_+^V$ and $supp^+\{\boldsymbol{x}\} = \{e \mid \boldsymbol{x}(e){>}0\}$ for each $\boldsymbol{x} \in \mathbb{Z}_+^V$.

Given a vector $\boldsymbol{c} \in \mathbb{Z}_+^V$ and a monotone DR-submodular function $f \in F_c$ that each kind of elements $e_i \in V$ appears at most $\boldsymbol{c}(e_i)$ times, $j = 1, 2, \cdots, s$, where we acquiesce that V contains s kinds of elements totally. In this paper we study the robustness model as follows:

$$\boldsymbol{x}^* = \arg\max_{\boldsymbol{x} \in \mathbb{Z}_+^{V \setminus D}, \boldsymbol{x}(V) \leq k} f(\boldsymbol{x}),$$

where D is an adversarial multisubset of V and its cardinality does not exceed a positive integer d. Additionally, denote $f(\boldsymbol{x}^*) = \mathrm{OPT}_D$ according to each specific deleted multisubset D.

We still address this deletion-robust model in a two-phase problem. The deleting process occurs in a large-scale multiset V and we are unable to know the whole information at first. The specific information is given in two phases. In the first phase we are aware of the number of the elements that are going to be deleted. In the second phase, we are aware of the exact deleting set. Our goal is to maximize the monotone submodular function for any given deletion instance. We are expected to design a two-phase algorithm accordingly and the crucial idea is to extract the representative elements to scale down the size of V first. Denote this representative multisubset $A \subseteq V$ as a core-set of V and we are then expected to find a solution that still maintain a good approximation of this problem based on this core-set. Note that $\alpha \triangleq \min_D \frac{f(\boldsymbol{x}_A)}{\mathrm{OPT}_D}$ as the approximation ratio of the two-phase algorithm, where $\boldsymbol{x}_A$ is the output of the algorithm according to the specific deleted subset D. Define a notation as follows:

Definition 1 [9]. *We say $A \subseteq V$ is (β, d)-robust if for any $D \subseteq V$ and $|D| \leq d$, there always exists a vector $\boldsymbol{x} \in \mathbb{Z}_+^A$ such that $E[f(\boldsymbol{x})] \geq \beta \cdot \mathrm{OPT}_D$.*

3 Robustness Setting over the Integer Lattice

In this section we address the optimization problem in two robustness settings which are centralized and streaming settings and design algorithms respectively. In both settings an adversary may delete at most d elements in the ground set V while our goal is to maintain a good approximation after the deletion process. The robust model we study is based on a two-phase practical problem mentioned above where the ground set is a large data-set thus it requires us to scale down the ground set first.

In order to solve this two-phase optimization problem we first choose elements from the ground set V which is a multiset to constitute a representative multisubset called core-set in the first phase. Still we extract similar elements randomly from a big set to form a core-set A while these similar items can be seen as copies for each other and this approach serves as a quiet useful way to lower down the impact of the deletion process. An adversary cannot obtain the information about this randomness. In the second phase we select elements from the $A \setminus D$ by utilizing the thresholding framework combing with a binary search to achieve a good approximation. Note that the information of D is given in this stage. It can be proven that the core-set we obtained in the first phase is $(1/2 - \delta, d)$-robust which can maintain a $(1/2 - \delta)$-approximation against any deletion of arbitrary d elements.

3.1 Centralized Algorithm over the Integer Lattice

In this section we present Algorithm 1 called *Robust core-set over integer lattice* to construct the core-set and Algorithm 2 called *Robust-centralized over integer lattice* to output a solution which is robust against the adversarial deletion in centralized setting. The main idea of constructing a core-set is to select different kinds of elements that can be seen as copies of each other which means they have almost the same marginal value and we repeat this procedure in the decreasing thresholding framework. When an adversary delete elements in the core-set we can replace them with their copies immediately. While the set is large enough we uniform randomly pick one from these copies and add it to the current solution to lower down the impact of the deletion process. Then based on the core-set and the given deletion process we continue to select elements if they satisfy the thresholding condition.

We use the following four lemmas to prove the conclusion in Theorem 1:

Algorithm 1. Robust core-set over integer lattice

Require: V, $f \in F_c$ and the positive integers d, k

Ensure: a core-set that contains all the crucial elements of V

1: $\Delta_d \leftarrow$ the $(d+1)$-th largest value of $\{f(\chi_e) \,|\, e \in V\}$;

2: $V_d \leftarrow$ all the $(d+1)$ elements with the largest values of $\{f(\chi_e) \,|\, e \in V\}$;

3: $T = \{(1+\epsilon)^i - \frac{\Delta_d}{2(1+\epsilon)k} \le (1+\epsilon)^i \le \Delta_d\}$;

4: $V \leftarrow V \setminus V_d$;

5: for each $\tau \in T : a_\tau \leftarrow 0, b_\tau \leftarrow 0$;

6: **for** each $\tau \in T$ from the highest to the lowest **do**

7:     **while** $b_\tau(V) \ge \frac{\max l_{e_\tau}^*}{1-(1-\epsilon)^{1/d}} + d - 1$ for $b_\tau = \sum l_{e_\tau}^* \chi_e$ where

8:         $l_{e_\tau}^* = \max\{l_{e_\tau} \,|\, \tau \le \frac{f(l_{e_\tau}\chi_e \,|\, \sum_{\tau' \ge \tau} a_{\tau'})}{l_{e_\tau}} \le (1+\epsilon)\tau\}$

9:         with $BinarySearch(f, \sum_{\tau' \ge \tau} a_{\tau'}, c, k, \tau)$ **do**

10:            Uniform randomly pick $l_{e_\tau}^* \chi_e$ from b_τ and add it to a_τ, $b_\tau = b_\tau - l_{e_\tau}^* \chi_e$;

11:     **end while**

12: **end for**

13: $b = \vee b_\tau$;

14: Return b, V_d and all the a_τ

Lemma 1. *Define* $x^* = arg \max\limits_{x \in Z_+^{V \setminus D}} f(x)$ *and* $f(x^*) = \text{OPT}_D$, *then there exists a* $\tau^* \in T'$ *such that*

$$\tau^* \le \frac{\text{OPT}_D}{2k} \le (1+\epsilon)\tau^*.$$

Lemma 2. *Denote* $a = \sum\limits_{\tau \ge \tau^*} a_\tau$, $a' = \sum\limits_{\tau \ge \tau^*} a'_\tau$, *then*

$$E[f(a')] \ge (1-2\epsilon)E[f(a)].$$

Lemma 3. *It holds that*

$$E[f(x_{\tau^*})] \ge (1-2\epsilon)E[f(x_{\tau^*} \vee a)].$$

Lemma 4. *It can be concluded that*

$$f(x_{\tau^*} \vee a) \ge \frac{1}{2}(1-\epsilon)\text{OPT}_D.$$

Theorem 1. *By taking* $\epsilon = \frac{2}{3}\delta$ *for any* $\epsilon > 0$, *it holds* $E[f(x)] \ge (\frac{1}{2} - \delta)\text{OPT}_D$, *where* x *is the output by Algorithm 2. Algorithm 1 stores at most* $O(\frac{\log k}{\epsilon^2} d \max c(e) + k)$ *elements in core-set while the query complexity of Algorithms 1 and 2 are* $O(\frac{|V| \log^2 k}{\epsilon} + |V| k \log k)$ *and* $O(\frac{\log^3 k}{\epsilon^3} d \max c(e) + \frac{\log^2 k}{\epsilon} k)$.

Proof. Combining Lemmas 2 and 3 we have

$$E[f(x)] \ge E[f(x_{\tau^*})] \ge (1-2\epsilon)E[f(x_{\tau^*} \vee a)] \ge 1/2(1-3\epsilon)\text{OPT}_D \ge (1/2-\delta)\text{OPT}_D.$$

Algorithm 2. Robust-Centralized over the integer lattice

Require: a'_τ, V'_d and b' obtained by a_τ, V_d and b that have deleted all the elements in D

Ensure: a vector x satisfying the cardinality contraints

1: $\Delta'_0 \leftarrow$ the largest value of $\{f(\chi_e) - b'(e) > 0$ or $\vee a'_\tau(e) > 0$ or $e \in V'_d\}$;

2: $T' = \{(1+\epsilon)^i - \frac{\Delta'_0}{2(1+\epsilon)k} \le (1+\epsilon)^i \le \Delta'_0\}$;

3: **for** each $\tau \in T'$ from the highest to the lowest **do**

4:     $x_\tau \leftarrow \sum_{\tau' \ge \tau} a'_{\tau'}$;

5:     **for** all e where $b'(e) > 0$ or $e \in V'_d$ **do**

6:         **if** $\frac{f(l'_{e_\tau}\chi_e \mid x_\tau)}{l'_{e_\tau}} \ge \tau$ with $BinarySearch(f, x_\tau, c, k, \tau)$ for l'_{e_τ} **then**

7:             $x_\tau \leftarrow x_\tau + l'_{e_\tau}\chi_e$;

8:         **end if**

9:     **end for**

10: **end for**

11: Return $\arg\max_\tau f(x_\tau)$

For each threshold in T, b_τ stores at most $(\frac{\max l^*_{e_\tau}}{1-(1-\epsilon)^{1/d}} + d - 1)$ elements where this value can not exceed $O(\frac{\max c(e)}{\epsilon}d + d - 1)$. Thus the core-set stores at most $O(\frac{\log k}{\epsilon^2}d \max c(e) + k)$ elements. As for the query complexity, Algorithm 3 returns a coefficient with at most $O(\log k)$ evaluations, thus Algorithm 1 returns a core-set with at most $O(\frac{|V| \log^2 k}{\epsilon} + |V|k \log k)$ evaluations while Algorithm 2 returns an output with at most $O(\frac{k \log^2 k}{\epsilon} + \frac{\log^3 k}{\epsilon^3}d \max c(e))$ evaluations.   □

3.2 Streaming Setting over the Integer Lattice

In this section we present Algorithm 4 called *Robust core-set streaming over the integer lattice* and Algorithm 5 called *Robust-Streaming over the integer lattice* in the streaming setting. In this case each element arrives one by one which means we are unable to know the whole information at the beginning. We design algorithms pertinently by adjusting the previous framework above to fit it. Similarly we extract a representative subset called the core-set while based on this core-set and the specific deletion process we output a solution which has a good approximation and is robust against the adversarial deletion.

Lemma 5. *There exists a $\tau^* \in T'$ such that $\tau^* \le \frac{OPT_D}{2k} \le (1+\epsilon)\tau^*$.*

Theorem 2. *By taking $\epsilon = \frac{2}{3}\delta$ for any $\epsilon > 0$, it holds $E[f(x)] \ge (\frac{1}{2} - \delta)OPT_D$, where x is the output by Algorithm 5. Algorithm 4 stores at most $O(\frac{\log^2 k}{\epsilon^3}d \max c(e) + \frac{\log k}{\epsilon}k)$ elements in core-set while the query complexity of Algorithms 4 and 5 are $O(\frac{|V| \log^2 k}{\epsilon} + \frac{dk \log^3 k}{\epsilon^3} \max c(e))$ and $O(\frac{\log^4 k}{\epsilon^4}d \max c(e))$ respectively.*

Proof. The proof of the approximation is similar with Lemmas 2, 3 and Theorem 1, so we turn to calculate the memory and complexity. For each threshold, $b_{\tau,\tau'}$

Algorithm 3. BinarySearch$(f, \boldsymbol{x}, \boldsymbol{c}, k, \tau)$

Require: $f \in F_c, \boldsymbol{x}, \boldsymbol{c} \in \mathbb{Z}_+^V, k \in \mathbb{N}$ and $\tau \in \mathbb{R}_+$
Ensure: $l \in \mathbb{N}$
1: $l_l \leftarrow 1, l_r \leftarrow \min\{\boldsymbol{c}(e) - \boldsymbol{x}(e), k - \boldsymbol{x}(V)\}$;
2: **if** $\tau \le \frac{f(l_r \chi_e \mid \boldsymbol{x})}{l_r} \le (1 + \epsilon)\tau$ **then**
3:      return l_r;
4: **end if**;
5: **if** $f(\chi_e \mid \boldsymbol{x}) < \tau$ or $\frac{f(l_r \chi_e \mid \boldsymbol{x})}{l_r} \ge (1 + \epsilon)\tau$ **then**
6:      return 0;
7: **end if**;
8: **while** $l_r > l_l + 1$ **do**
9:      $m = \lfloor \frac{l_r + l_l}{2} \rfloor$;
10:      **if** $\tau \le \frac{f(m\chi_e \mid \boldsymbol{x})}{m} \le (1 + \epsilon)\tau$ **then**
11:          break and return m;
12:      **else if** $\frac{f(m\chi_e \mid \boldsymbol{x})}{m} > (1 + \epsilon)\tau$ **then**
13:          $l_r = m$;
14:      **else if** $\frac{f(m\chi_e \mid \boldsymbol{x})}{m} \le \tau$ **then**
15:          $l_l = m$;
16:      **end if**
17: **end while**

Algorithm 4. Robust core-set streaming over the integer lattice

---

Require: $f \in F_c$ and the positive integers d, k
Ensure: a core-set that contains all the crucial elements of V
1: $T = \{(1 + \epsilon)^i \mid i \in \mathbb{Z}\}$;
2: For each $\tau, \tau' \in T$: $\boldsymbol{a}_\tau \leftarrow \boldsymbol{0}, \boldsymbol{b}_{\tau,\tau'} \leftarrow \boldsymbol{0}$;
3: **for** every arriving element e_t **do**
4:      $\Delta_d \leftarrow$ the $(d+1)$-th largest values of $\{f(\chi_{e_1}), \cdots, f(\chi_{e_t})\}$;
5:      $\Delta_0 \leftarrow$ the largest value of $\{f(\chi_{e_1}), \cdots, f(\chi_{e_t})\}$;
6:      $V_d^t \leftarrow$ all the d+1 unit vectors with the largest values of $\{f(\chi_{e_1}), \cdots, f(\chi_{e_t})\}$;
7:      $T_t = \{(1 + \epsilon)^i - \frac{\Delta_d}{2(1+\epsilon)k} \le (1 + \epsilon)^i \le \Delta_d\}$;
8:      Delete all the $\boldsymbol{a}_\tau, \boldsymbol{b}_{\tau,\tau'}$ such that τ or $\tau' \notin T_t$;
9:      **for** $\tau \in T_t$ **do**
10:          **while** $\exists \tau'$ such that $\boldsymbol{b}_{\tau,\tau'}(V) \ge \frac{\max l_{e_t,\tau'}^*}{1 - (1-\epsilon)^{1/d}} + d - 1$ for $\boldsymbol{b}_{\tau,\tau'} = \sum l_{e_t,\tau'}^* \chi_{e_t}$
      where
11:          $l_{e_t,\tau'}^* = \max\{l_{e_t,\tau'} \mid \tau' \le \frac{f(l_{e_t,\tau'} \chi_{e_t} \mid \boldsymbol{a}_\tau)}{l_{e_t,\tau'}} \le (1 + \epsilon)\tau'\}$
12:          with $BinarySearch(f, \boldsymbol{a}_\tau, \boldsymbol{c}, k, \tau)$ **do**
13:              Uniform randomly pick $l_{e_t,\tau'}^* \chi_{e_t}$ from $\boldsymbol{b}_{\tau,\tau'}$ and add it to $\boldsymbol{a}_\tau$;
14:              Update and recompute the new $\{\boldsymbol{b}_{\tau,\tau''} \mid \tau'' \ge \tau\}$;
15:          **end while**
16:      **end for**
17: **end for**
18: **for** $\tau \in T_n$ **do**
19:      $\boldsymbol{b}_\tau \leftarrow \cup_{\tau' > \tau, \tau' \in T_t} \boldsymbol{b}_{\tau,\tau'}$;
20: **end for**
21: Return all the $\boldsymbol{a}_\tau$ and $\boldsymbol{b}_\tau$, V_d^n

---

stores at most $(\frac{\log k}{\epsilon}(\frac{\max l^*_{e_\tau}}{1-(1-\epsilon)^{1/d}}+d-1))$ elements where this value can not exceed $O(\frac{\log k}{\epsilon}(\frac{\max c(e)}{\epsilon}d+d-1))$, a_τ stores at most k elements. Consequently the core-set stores at most $O(\frac{\log^2 k}{\epsilon^3}d\max c(e) + \frac{\log k}{\epsilon}k)$ elements. As for the query complexity, the binary search returns a coefficient with at most $O(\log k)$evaluations, thus Algorithm 4 returns a core-set with at most $O(\frac{|V|\log^2 k}{\epsilon} + \frac{dk\log^3 k}{\epsilon^3}\max c(e))$ evaluations while Algorithm 5 returns an output with at most $O(\frac{\log^4 k}{\epsilon^4}d\max c(e))$ evaluations. $\qquad\qquad\square$

Algorithm 5. Robust-Streaming over the integer lattice

Require: a'_τ, b'_τ and $V^n_{d'}$ obtained by a_τ, b_τ and V^n_d that have deleted all the elements of D

Ensure: a vector x satisfying the cardinality constraint

1: $\Delta'_0 \leftarrow$ the largest value of $\{f(\chi_{e_t}) \mid l_t\chi_{e_t} \in \vee b'_\tau$ or $\vee a_\tau(e_t)>0\}$;
2: $T' = \{(1+\epsilon)^i - \frac{\Delta'_0}{2(1+\epsilon)k} \le (1+\epsilon)^i \le \Delta'_0\}$;
3: **for** $\tau \in T'$ **do**
4: $\quad x_\tau \leftarrow a'_\tau$;
5: $\quad$ **for** $b'_\tau(e_t)>0$ or $\chi_{e_t} \in V^n_{d'}$ **do**
6: $\qquad$ **if** $\frac{f(l_{t,\tau}\chi_{e_t} \mid x_\tau)}{l_{t,\tau}} \ge \tau$ with $BinarySearch(f,x_\tau,c,k,\tau)$ for $l_{t,\tau}$ **then**
7: $\qquad\qquad x_\tau \leftarrow x_\tau + l''_t\chi_{e_t}$;
8: $\qquad$ **end if**
9: $\quad$ **end for**
10: **end for**
11: Return $\arg\max_\tau f(x_\tau)$

---

4   Conclusion

In this paper we designed a specific robustness model over the integer lattice and got a $(1/2 - \delta, d)$-robust core-set for maximizing a monotone DR-submodular function under the cardinality constraint both in centralized and streaming settings. The model established in our works takes more consideration in the robustness aspects and we are expecting that it might be extended to more applicable scenarios.

References

1. Alon, N., Gamzu, I., Tennenholtz, M.: Optimizing budget allocation among channels and influencers. In: Proceedings of the 21st International Conference on World Wide Web, pp. 381–388. ACM, New York (2012)
2. Cunningham, W.H.: On submodular function minimization. Combinatorica **5**(3), 185–192 (1985)
3. Charikar, M., Khuller, S., Mount, D.M., Narasimhan, G.: Algorithms for facility location problems with outliers. In: Proceedings of ACM-SIAM Symposium on Discrete Algorithms, pp. 642–651. SIAM, Philadelphia (2001)

4. Feldman, M., Norouzi-Fard, A., Svensson, O., Zenklusen, R.: The one-way communication complexity of submodular maximization with applications to streaming
and robustness. ACM **70**(4), 1–52 (2023)

5. Gao, H., Xu, H., Vucetic, S.: Sample efficient decentralized stochastic Frank-Wolfe
methods for continuous DR-submodular Maximization. In: Proceedings of International Joint Conferences on Artificial Intelligence, pp. 3501–3507. AAAI Press,
Palo Alto (2021)

6. Gong, S., Nong, Q., Bao, S., Fang, Q., Du, D.Z.: A fast and deterministic algorithm
for knapsack-constrained monotone DR-submodular maximization over an integer
lattice. J. Global Optim. **85**(1), 15–38 (2023)

7. Ji, S., Xu, D., Li, M., Zhang, D.: Stochastic greedy algorithms for maximizing constrained submodular+ supermodular functions. Concurr. Comput. **35**(17), e6575
(2023)

8. Khuller, S., Moss, A., Naor, J.: The budgeted maximum coverage problem. Inform.
Process. Lett. **70**(1), 39–45 (1999)

9. Kazemi, E., Zadimoghaddam, M., Karbasi, A.: Scalable deletion-robust submodular maximization: data summarization with privacy and fairness constraints. In:
Proceedings of the 35th International Conference on Machine Learning, pp. 2544–
2553. ICML, Stockholm (2018)

10. Kothawade, S., Beck, N., Killamsetty, K., Iyer, R.: Similar: submodular information
measures based active learning in realistic scenarios. NIPS **34**, 18685–18697 (2021)

11. Lin, H., Bilmes, J.: Multi-document summarization via budgeted maximization of
submodular functions. In: Proceedings of the 2010 Annual Conference of the North
American Chapter of the Association for Computational Linguistics, pp. 912–920.
ACL, Stroudsburg (2010)

12. Nemhauser, G.L., Wolsey, L.A., Fisher, M.L.: An analysis of approximations for
maximizing submodular set functions. Math. Program. **14**(1), 265–294 (1978)

13. Orlin, J.B., Schulz, A.S., Udwani, R.: Robust monotone submodular function maximization. Math. Program. **172**(1–2), 505–537 (2018)

14. Queyranne, M.: Minimizing symmetric submodular functions. Math. Program. **82**,
3–12 (1998)

15. Sviridenko, M.: A note on maximizing a submodular set function subject to a
knapsack constraint. Oper. Res. Lett. **32**(1), 41–43 (2004)

16. Soma, T., Kakimura, N., Inaba, K., Kawarabayashi, K.: Optimal budget allocation:
theoretical guarantee and efficient algorithm. In: Proceedings of the International
Conference on Machine Learning, pp. 351–359. JMLR, New York (2014)

17. Soma, T., Yoshida, Y.: Maximizing monotone submodular functions over the integer lattice. Math. Program. **172**(1–2), 539–563 (2018)

18. Yang, R., Xu, D., Guo, L., Zhang, D.: Regularized two-stage submodular maximization under streaming. Sci. China Inf. Sci. **65**(4), 140602 (2022)

19. Zhang, Z., Guo, L., Wang, Y., Zhang, D.: Streaming algorithms for maximizing
monotone DR-submodular functions with a cardinality constraint on the integer
lattice. Asia. Pac. J. Oper. Res. **38**(05), 2140004 (2021)

Evolutionary Parameter Optimization: A Novel Control Strategy for Chaotic Environments

A. A. Musaev[1] and D. A. Grigoriev[2(✉)]

[1] ITMO University, Saint-Petersburg, Russia
[2] Center for Econometrics and Business Analytics (CEBA), St. Petersburg State University (SPBU), Saint-Petersburg, Russia
d.a.grigoriev@spbu.ru

Abstract. Efficient control of dynamic systems that interact with unstable immersions is of utmost importance across multiple domains, encompassing the stabilization of turbulent flows, generation of signals in radio engineering, and the optimization of asset management in capital markets. The primary challenge lies in the inherent unpredictability of deterministic chaos models, which engenders additional uncertainty. In order to assess the efficacy of control strategies, numerical methods represent the sole viable approach. The study is primarily concerned with the development of empirical algorithms aimed at identifying and forecasting local trends, with the ultimate objective of formulating extrapolation prediction techniques. The investigation centers specifically on speculative trading within currency markets, where stochastic chaos is a prominent characteristic. In contrast to physical and technical problems, currency markets are purely informational and devoid of inertia. Consequently, traditional prediction algorithms reliant on reactive control strategies have proved to be ineffectual. Accordingly, this study endeavors to rectify this efficiency deficiency by exploring control strategies that optimize evolutionary parameters sequentially while approximating the model structure of observation series.

Keywords: Stationarity · Evolutionary optimization · Asset allocation · Process dynamics prediction

1 Introduction

In currency markets, chaotic systems make it difficult to predict outcomes due to their inherent unpredictability [1–4]. However, ordered structures can still emerge within the market, presenting opportunities for skilled traders to identify and leverage them. These ordered formations can take the form of local trends or quasi-periodic fluctuations [5–7]. A minority of successful traders existence indicates the potential for developing effective control strategies.

Evolutionary optimization aims to select a control model that achieves the optimal solution based on a specified criterion, without requiring a precise mathematical model that corresponds to real data. Genetic algorithms have been reported to reduce computational workload by approximately 40% and perform well in handling noise. Control strategies can be modified through nonparametric mutations, selecting the structure and rules from a predefined knowledge bank. However, this approach limits the machine's ability to make arbitrary choices and hinders the discovery of unforeseen solutions. Allowing unrestricted random modifications can lead to meaningless decision rules, requiring significant time for a reasonable solution to emerge. The question of artificially generating control strategies remains open.

Evolutionary technology assumes experiment repeatability under unchanging or slowly changing conditions. Non-stationary or chaotic processes disrupt the optimality of statistical solutions, but chaos can also reduce uncertainty. Identifying and utilizing hidden patterns can lead to winning strategies. Evolutionary computational approaches help address the suitability of control strategies.

The research paper employs the fundamental evolutionary modeling algorithm detailed in reference [7]. The original version lacks additional constraints on variability mechanisms and offers a wide range of opportunities for formation. Adopting an evolutionary optimization computational scheme that adheres to traditional evolutionary modeling is reasonable in econometric models. It allows modifications to gene structures within the boundaries of common sense and market laws, using a well-established method for extracting random variables from permissible variations in genome parameters.

Past research conducted in [8, 9] has confirmed that chaotic processes have minimal or no inertia, making it impractical to rely on straightforward control strategies that rely on trend analysis. However, in practical situations, quasi-chaotic processes with a systemic component and weak order are common. By employing smoothing techniques, decision rules with slight positive balances can be derived, although their significance is limited. The possibility of developing a successful strategy using evolutionary modeling techniques was shown in [10]. However, the effectiveness of different approaches for constructing trend strategies remains unresolved. This paper discusses relevant research on this topic.

2 Approach and Execution

2.1 Trend Identification Strategies

Exploring 3 Control Strategies for Trend Analysis:

- Strategy S_1: Uses the K_1 criterion to determine increasing trends if the growth rate a_1 exceeds the critical value a_1^*. Conversely, decreasing trends are established when $a_1 < -a_1^*$.
- Strategy S_2: Incorporates the K_2 criterion with two linear approximations on sliding windows (w_1 and w_2). Increasing trends are identified when both slopes (a_{11} and a_{12}) exceed their critical values (a_{11}^* and a_{12}^*). Decreasing trends occur when $a_{11} < -a_{11}^*$ and $a_{12} < -a_{12}^*$.
- Strategy S_3: Applies a linear approximation on window w_1 and a quadratic approximation on window w_2. Trend presence (increasing or decreasing) is determined by whether $a_1 > a_1^*$ & $a_2 > a_2^*$ or $a_1 < -a_1^*$ & $a_2 < -a_2^*$. Parameters a_1 and a_2 represent speed and acceleration, while a_1^* and a_2^* are critical values.

The first two strategies estimate slope parameters using a least squares method (LSM). However, using higher degree polynomials with LSM can lead to degeneracy of the normal equations system, resulting in a less interpretable approximation. This limitation hinders the interpretation of polynomial coefficients as measures of speed or acceleration and makes trend visualization difficult. To preserve the meaningful aspects of criterion parameters, one can use incremental difference estimates for smoothed speed and acceleration using the following formula:

$$\hat{a}_1(i) = v(i) = \frac{Y_S(i) - Y_S(i - w_1)}{w_1} = \frac{\Delta Y_S(i)}{w_1};$$

$$\hat{a}_2(i) = a(i) = \frac{\Delta Y_S(i) - \Delta Y_S(i - w_2)}{w_2} = \frac{\Delta^2 Y_S(i)}{w_2},$$

where w - sliding window size, $\Delta Y_S(i)$ - first finite difference of the smoothed process Y_S (i.e. increment Y_S on the window w), $\Delta^2 Y_S(i)$ - second finite difference.

To estimate finite differences with a smoothed process, it is important to minimize susceptibility to random fluctuations and anomalies. This is achieved by using the simplest exponential filter, $Y_S(i) = \alpha Y(i) + (1 - \alpha) Y_S(i - 1)$, with $\alpha \in (0, 1)$. The parameter vector for the control strategy is supplemented by the value of α.

In some cases, using more complex smoothing filters may be advisable. These filters aim to balance the delay of the smoothed process ($Y_S(t)$) compared to the original process ($Y(t)$), while minimizing false alarms. This requires separate research.

The presented strategies are basic. Given specific situational contexts and additional conditions, it is feasible for strategy S_1 to manifest greater efficacy than strategy S_2, and for strategy S_2 to exhibit greater effectiveness than strategy S_3. As such, it is not possible to unequivocally assert that strategy S_3 can universally supplant the others and consistently showcase superior efficacy. Consequently, the concurrent application of all three strategies is essential to validate the findings of the research. The effectiveness of each strategy ($Eff(S_i)$) will be evaluated by calculating average gain values from a large sample size of retrospective observations. More details on this method can be found in [10].

2.2 Evolutionary Modeling for Optimal Control Strategies: A Profits-Based Approach

The evolutionary modeling method introduced in [11] is widely used in various applied problems, including modeling, forecasting, and optimization [12–16]. In [10], the method is applied to optimize control strategies.

Next steps of the program used to formulate an optimal control strategy using the evolutionary modeling method:

– Data input;
– Parent strategies initiation;
– Descendent/generation strategies formation;
– Strategies/time loop for strategies testing;
– New parent strategies selection;

– Best strategy choosing.

Each strategy is characterized by a set of parameters called the "genome". In this method, each parameter in parent strategy (PS) has a probability of varying. The resulting strategies are ranked based on effectiveness, as described in [10]. Random changes are made to the parent group of strategies, creating a group of descendant strategies (DS). By making r modifications to each PS, where the reproduction coefficient r is specified, $N_d = N_a r$ ("d" meaning "descendant") descendant strategies are formed. These descendant strategies, along with the parent strategies, form the first generation of size $N_g = N_a(1 + r)$ strategies ("g" meaning "generation").

Each strategy, labeled as S_i (where i ranges from 1 to N_g), is evaluated using the same retrospective data set to determine its effectiveness, $Eff(S_i)$, in terms of generated profits. The profitability of each strategy determines its ranking, which is crucial for selecting parent strategies for the next generation. Through iterations of modifying the parameters of the PS genome, new generations of strategies, DS (descendant strategies), and PS (parent strategies) are created.

The parent strategy genome is modified through the following methods:

1. Little Single Modifications (LSM): Small alterations are made to a single parameter in each parent strategy. The specific parameter to be modified is chosen randomly. These changes may relate to criterion K, determining the emergence of a trend, coefficients a and a^*, and it is also possible to modify individual coefficients specific to certain strategies S. If changes are made to all genes, each PS receives modifications equal to the genome size. The number of descendants with this modification type is $N_d^{(1)} = N_a m_g$ if m_g is the size of the gene and N_a is the number of variants retained. By making small random alterations to individual parameters within each parent strategy, LSM introduces exploration by allowing the algorithm to probe the neighborhood of the current solutions.

2. The second method of Little Group Modifications (LGM) entails a method similar to LSM, as it involves making changes to multiple parameters or genes simultaneously. However, in contrast to LSM, LGM focuses on making gradual adjustments to all PS parameters. This process results in the generation of $N_d^{(2)} = 4$ distinct versions of the descendant strategies. Essentially, LGM introduces controlled and incremental modifications to the entire set of parameters, leading to the creation of multiple evolved strategies based on these gradual changes. LGM provides a balance between exploitation and exploration by gradually adjusting multiple parameters or genes simultaneously. This gradual change allows for exploration within the parameter space while still retaining and building upon the existing knowledge embodied in the current solutions.

3. Strong Single Mutations (SSM): Randomly selects a PS and gene number for parametric mutations. The number of mutations is limited to a maximum of $N_d^{(3)} = 1 - 2$. SSM introduces an element of exploration by enabling random parametric mutations within the gene structures. By limiting the number of mutations and focusing on a single modified gene, it allows for exploration of new solutions while still maintaining some level of exploitation from the existing population.

4. Structural Nonparametric Mutations (SNM): Occurs with a small probability P_{nm} of switching to another game strategy variant. Ineffective mutations are common, but they provide opportunities for generating fresh, non-conventional solutions. This paper focuses on parametric modifications, while structural changes are left for future exploration.

In addition, we will add that LSM and LGM are complementary to crossover operations, as they introduce small and gradual changes that can fine-tune and adapt existing strategies. These operations can be considered in further research.

3 Experimental Procedures and Findings

3.1 Investigating Suboptimal Initial Threshold Values: Estimation and Analysis

In order to estimate non-optimal initial threshold values, it is necessary to conduct an analysis of the range and root mean square (RMS) deviation of approximation coefficients obtained from various observation windows using a polygon simulation. Data collected from 30-day observation intervals for the EURUSD currency pair quote, at 5-min intervals.

We will calculate the range of changes $\Delta(a_1)$ and the coefficient $\hat{\sigma}(a_1)$ for sliding windows of different durations: 30, 60, 90, 120, 150, 180, and 300 min. To approximate the data within these windows, we used least-squares minimization (LSM) fitting with a first-order polynomial model.

Table 1 showcases the ranges of variation $\Delta(a_1)$ and estimated standard deviation (SD) coefficients for the LSM approximation $\hat{\sigma}(a_1)$ using the first-order model. The $\Delta(a_1)$ range is indicated in the table by two values - the maximum value of coefficient a_1 (on the right side) and its corresponding minimum value (on the left side).

Expanding the duration of the observation window results in a noticeable amplification of the smoothing effect, offering both advantages and disadvantages in terms of strategic control.

When implementing second-order trend strategies, it is imperative to optimize the parameters of the decision rule, including those aforementioned. To acquire initial approximations, an analysis will be conducted on the range of modifications and coefficient values associated with diverse observation windows. The outcomes of a 30-day observation period, with a particular focus on the EURUSD currency instrument, are presented in Table 2. Table 2 aids in establishing the optimal range for selecting initial parameters of parent strategies. The differences in the initial parameters for various observation windows make it impractical to apply crossover for this specific research.

Table 1. Change ranges in estimates $\Delta(a_1)$ and $\hat{\sigma}(a_1)$ for the first order

w	$\Delta(a_1)$	$\hat{\sigma}(a_1)$
30	−6.81/4.80	0.5678
60	−3.39/2.71	0.3703
90	−1.96/1.89	0.3202
120	−1.93/1.88	0.2783
150	−1.21/1.22	0.2399
180	−1.12/0.94	0.2395
210	−0.99/0.86	0.2136
240	−0.94/0.83	0.1928
270	−0.84/0.83	0.1914
300	−0.78/0.80	0.1809

Table 2. Change ranges in Δv, Δa, standard deviations $\sigma(v)$, $\sigma(a)$

w	v_{min}	v_{max}	σ_v	a_{min}	a_{max}	σ_a
30	−1.856	1.392	0.260	−0.063	0.040	0.0065
60	−1.405	1.155	0.246	−0.025	0.021	0.0041
90	−1.159	1.045	0.234	−0.013	0.011	0.0029
120	−1.043	0.833	0.218	−0.010	0.007	0.0022
150	−0.850	0.821	0.200	−0.008	0.006	0.0017
180	−0.826	0.816	0.169	−0.007	0.004	0.0012
210	−0.713	0.802	0.158	−0.005	0.004	0.0011
240	−0.706	0.768	0.169	−0.004	0.003	0.0010
270	−0.554	0.708	0.152	−0.003	0.002	0.0008
300	−0.522	0.617	0.141	−0.003	0.002	0.0007

3.2 Implementation Details

Let's consider the application of basic evolutionary modeling algorithms within the frameworks of strategies S_1, S_2, S_3. The control algorithm's genome G comprises a set of variable parameters:

$$G = < w, a_n^*, TP, SL > .$$

In addition to the moving window w of observations and critical values a_n^*, the genome also utilizes parameters such as Stop Loss (SL) and Take Profit (TP) as pre-set values, which are used to prevent significant losses in case of errors in trend prediction.

The best 6 from the previous generation (24 descendants and 6 parents) were selected, resulting in 24 descendants. Changes in each ancestor's genome were determined probabilistically. Minor changes were applied to one parameter with a probability of 0.7 (LSM modification), while group changes were made to all parameters with a probability of 0.2 (LGM modification).

In this study, we used a modification technique called Strong Single Mutations to make significant changes to a single parameter. We randomly selected the specific parameter to be modified, ensuring a wide range of changes throughout the experiment. The critical slope parameter, a_n^*, depends on the window size w. To estimate this parameter, we created a function based on the observed empirical relationship with w.

We previously outlined the specific details of the correlation. To estimate the initial parameter value, we formulated a function that considered the observed empirical relationship between the parameter and the variable w. We then introduced random variations to add stochasticity to the estimation process.

"Small changes" refer to fluctuations within the standard deviation range of the average value, determined by the modified ancestor parameter. "Big changes" fall within 2 to 3 standard deviations. Physical limitations, such as angular inclination ($0\,0 < a_1^* < \pi/2$), must be considered.

3.3 Evolutionary Optimization in Control Strategy: Application, Modifications, and Parameter Estimation

For illustration purposes, let's explore how evolutionary optimization can be applied to control strategy S_1. In this case study, we analyzed ten days of one-minute observations for the EURUSD currency pair.

Evolutionary modeling naturally rejects pathological situations. The initial genome ($G_0 = < 180, 0.12, 75, 120 >$) underwent 50 generations to produce the functional genome ($G_{50} = < 102, 0.16, 117, 189 >$). Cumulative profit was 735 points with a success rate of 0.83. Figure 1 shows the gains across generations.

For control strategy S_2, initial genome $G_0 = < 180, 60, 0.12, 0.36, 75, 120 >$ evolved over 50 generations to produce terminal genome $G_{50} = < 168, 69, 0.10, 0.33, 85, 106 >$.

The cumulative profit reached 889 points with a success rate of 0.91. Figure 1 shows the temporal evolution of gains for the most successful gene-based strategies over 50 trading positions. For strategy S_3, the initial genome was $G_0 = < 0.02, 180, 0.18, 0.013, 75, 120 >$.

The genome in this case includes new parameters: the smoothing coefficient α and critical value a_2^* for the second coefficient of quadratic approximation. Figure 1 shows the growth of gain for strategy S_3. The final cumulative profit was 924 points with a success rate of 0.91 over a span of 10 trading days. The best genome is $G_{50} = < 0.038, 147, 0.129, 0.0017, 74, 123 >$. By estimating speed and acceleration on different sliding window sizes, it is possible to create strategy S_4.

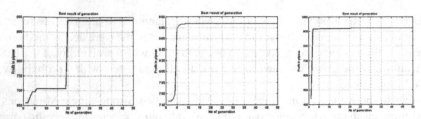

Fig. 1. The dynamics of the gain growth of the strategies S_1, S_2, S_3 in the process of its evolution

Table 3. The outcomes of the numerical assessment of the strategies S_1-S_3 effectiveness

Strategies/Days	1–100	101–200	201–300
S_1	1946/0.713	3051/0.711	2605/0.655
S_2	531/0.654	2521/0.762	1204/0.637
S_3	1188/0.741	3000/0.821	2644/0.819

4   Conclusion

This study aims to evaluate the effectiveness of three analyzed strategies using three 100-day (or 432000 min) intervals to observe EURUSD quote fluctuations. The evaluation involves 15 generations within the evolutionary framework. Results are presented in Table 3, showing winning values (in points) and win frequency.

In Table 3, the first and third strategies demonstrate higher potential effectiveness, but this may not hold true for all observation intervals due to the chaotic nature of the data. All trend strategies examined have the potential for positive outcomes, but it's uncertain if they'll maintain their winning characteristics in real-time with suboptimal parameters. Future research will explore methods for enhancing real-time evolutionary optimization and crossover operations. In trend strategies, simple methods can yield good results if the predictive mechanisms are accurate. This field is tied to adaptation and robustification, especially in uncertain environments. Adaptive methods work well in predictable environments but may struggle with chaotic behavior due to lack of inertia in the underlying information processes. This can limit responsiveness to sudden changes.

Robustification strategies, on the other hand, help manage fluctuations and develop better control strategies in uncertain environments. Traditional statistical methods might not be ideal for chaotic systems due to their unpredictability and lack of repeatability. This research area offers exciting opportunities, especially in developing methods that balance stability, adaptability, and robustness in uncertain and chaotic systems.

Acknowledgments. Dmitry Grigoriev research for this paper was supported by a grant from the Russian Science Foundation (Project No. 22–18-00588). The authors are grateful to participants at the Center for Econometrics and Business Analytics (ceba-lab.org, CEBA) seminar series for helpful comments and suggestions.

References

1. Peters, E.E.: Chaos and order in the capital markets: a new view of cycles, prices, and market volatility. Wiley, Hoboken (1996)
2. Gregory-Williams, J., Williams, B.M.: Trading Chaos: Maximize Profits with Proven Technical Techniques, vol. 161. Wiley, Hoboken (2004)
3. Musaev, A., Makshanov, A., Grigoriev, D.: Statistical analysis of current financial instrument quotes in the conditions of market chaos. Mathematics 10(4), 587 (2022)
4. Riva, A., et al.: Addressing non-stationarity in FX trading with online model selection of offline rl experts. In: Proceedings of the Third ACM International Conference on AI in Finance, pp. 394–402 (2022)
5. Ivancevic, T., Jain, L., Pattison, J., Hariz, A.: Nonlinear dynamics and chaos methods in neurodynamics and complex data analysis. Nonlinear Dyn. 56, 23–44 (2009)
6. Dinca, F., Zaharia, E., Baran, D.: An analysis of chaotic evolutions of dinamic systems. Revue Roumaine des Sciences Techniques-Mecanique Appliquee 49(1), 75–90 (2004)
7. Eigen, M., Schuster, P.: A principle of natural self-organization. Naturwissenschaften 64(11), 541–565 (1977)
8. Musaev, A., Makshanov, A., Grigoriev, D.: Numerical studies of channel control strategies for nonstationary immersion environments: EURUSD case study. Mathematics 10(9), 1408 (2022)
9. Musaev, A., Makshanov, A., Grigoriev, D.: The genesis of uncertainty: structural analysis of stochastic chaos in finance markets. Complexity (2023)
10. Musaev, A., Makshanov, A., Grigoriev, D.: Evolutionary optimization of control strategies for non-stationary immersion environments. Mathematics 10(11), 1797 (2022)
11. Fogel, D.B.: Artificial intelligence through simulated evolution, pp. 227–296. Wiley-IEEE Press (1998)
12. Lindgren, K.: Evolutionary phenomena in simple dynamics. Artif. Life II(10), 295–312 (1991)
13. Safarzyńska, K., van den Bergh, J.C.: Evolutionary models in economics: a survey of methods and building blocks. J. Evol. Econ. 20, 329–373 (2010)
14. Faber, A., Frenken, K.: Models in evolutionary economics and environmental policy: towards an evolutionary environmental economics. Technol. Forecast. Soc. Chang. 76(4), 462–470 (2009)
15. Bäck, T., Schwefel, H.P.: An overview of evolutionary algorithms for parameter optimization. Evol. Comput. 1(1), 1–23 (1993)
16. Whitley, D., Rana, S., Dzubera, J., Mathias, K.E.: Evaluating evolutionary algorithms. Artif. Intell. 85(1–2), 245–276 (1996)

Security and Blockchain

The Infrastructure Utilization of Free Contents Websites Reveal Their Security Characteristics

Mohamed Alqadhi[✉] and David Mohaisen

University of Central Florida, Orlando, USA
ay260080@ucf.edu

Abstract. Free Content Websites (FCWs) are a significant element of the Web, and realizing their use is essential. This study analyzes FCWs worldwide by studying how they correlate with different network sizes, cloud service providers, and countries, depending on the type of content they offer. Additionally, we compare these findings with those of premium content websites (PCWs). Our analysis concluded that FCWs correlate mainly with networks of medium size, which are associated with a higher concentration of malicious websites. Moreover, we found a strong correlation between PCWs, cloud, and country hosting patterns. At the same time, some correlations were also observed concerning FCWs but with distinct patterns contrasting each other for both types. Our investigation contributes to comprehending the FCW ecosystem through correlation analysis, and the indicative results point toward controlling the potential risks caused by these sites through adequate segregation and filtering due to their concentration.

Keywords: Web security · correlation analysis · free content websites

1 Introduction

The Web has revolutionized the way users spend their time online accessing various types of content, such as books, games, music, movies, and software. For example, many game websites offer users free or paid games. Generally, websites are grouped into two groups. 1. Website content is available for a fee, and these types of websites are known as premium content websites (PCW). 2. Website content for free, where they are known as free content websites (FCWs). Previous studies [8,9] reported that the FCWs tend to be riskier than PCWs in terms of user privacy and security features [4,6–10,17], although a clear understanding of what contributes to this risk is unclear. Given the popularity of these websites and the associated risk [6–8], we set out to investigate the network characteristics and the hosting patterns for these websites, including the network size, the cloud service provider (CSP), and the hosting country. We do so to identify the correlation between the security features of those websites and their characteristics in terms of hosting patterns.

Approach. For a complete characterization of the FCW hosting infrastructure and associated patterns, we continue to pursue the following. 1. We identify the size of networks these websites use for hosting in small, medium, and large sizes. 2. We identify and

© The Author(s), under exclusive license to Springer Nature Singapore Pte Ltd. 2024
M. H. Hà et al. (Eds.): CSoNet 2023, LNCS 14479, pp. 255–267, 2024.
https://doi.org/10.1007/978-981-97-0669-3_24

investigate the cloud service providers for these websites and their characteristics. 3. We study the main hosting countries of FCWs to provide a sufficient description of their hosting characteristics. 4 We perform a correlation analysis to distinguish the security and hosting patterns for FCWs compared to PCWs. 5. We provide a correlation analysis of the hosting patterns of FCW and PCW and their security assessment. In doing this correlation analysis, and in contrast to the PCWs, we hope to shed light on the features that contribute most to explaining such websites' security and privacy risks.

Revealing the correlations between the hosting countries with hosted FCWs and PCWs determines the appropriate action governments should take to improve hosting requirements. Revealing the correlations of malicious websites with the hosting countries will focus the efforts of governments to 1. evaluate their security standards, 2. take a step forward in implementing more stringent security standards to combat malicious websites, 3. and protect the end users by reviewing the privacy and security policies or mutual agreements that any website operating must adhere to in these countries.

Contributions. We used a data set that included 1,562 FCW and PCW obtained from the research work of Alabduljabbar *et al.* [5]. Using Pearson's correlation analysis, we examined the connections between FCW, PCW, network size, hosting CSP, and nations. We analyzed these correlations to find patterns and affinities related to various hosting arrangements. The links between website attributes, network size, hosting providers, and regional distribution are better understood due to this investigation. (**1**) **Full Comparison.** We provide a comprehensive understanding of the different characteristics of the FCW hosting pattern compared to PCW by studying their correlations with network size, hosting CSPs, and hosting countries. (**2**) **Systematic Analysis.** We provide a systematic security analysis for FCW and PCW. Analyze the correlations between FCW, PCW, and malicious or benign attributes of content categories. We study the correlations of malicious FCWs and PCWs with hosting infrastructures. (**3**) **Hosting Correlations** We provide a detailed discussion of different characteristics of the hosting pattern. Derived from the results of a correlation analysis between small, medium, and large sizes of the networks and malicious or benign websites. We provide correlation results of the top hosting CSPs and countries. We discuss whether a strong or weak correlation exists between hosting patterns for specific content categories or security behaviors.

Paper Organization. The rest of the paper reviews the related work Sect. 2, followed by research questions, data collection, and the analysis method described in Sect. 3. The results of the analysis are given in Sect. 4. The detailed discussion is provided in Sect. 5. Finally, the concluding remarks and the work summary are in Sect. 6.

2   Related Work

This work provided a detailed correlation analysis for FCWs and PCWs with their different networking hosting patterns and security aspects. Security analysis on FCWs has been established previously by Alabduljabbar *et al.* [5–8]. The cost of using FCWs has been investigated in [15, 16, 18, 24]. The correlation between FCW security and the use of a specific content management system has been introduced in [9], while other studies

Table 1. Network sizes and their characteristics. The maximum slash bit is 32 (IPv4). x represents the number of bits and y represents the number of addresses.

Size	Bits in CIDR	# Addresses
Small (SN)	$/24 < x \leq /32$	$2^8 > y \geq 2^0$
Medium (MN)	$/16 < x \leq /24$	$2^{16} > y \geq 2^8$
Large (LN)	$/8 < x \leq /16$	$2^{24} > y \geq 2^{16}$
Very Large (VLN)	$/0 < x \leq /8$	$2^{32} > y \geq 2^{24}$

performed a correlation analysis on website security, such as [11,13,19,20,23]. Taking into consideration the number of studies and the lack of space, we concentrate solely on a subset of relevant studies to this work and their results.

Security Analysis. Zhao *et al.* [25] investigated the impacts of user-generated content (UGC) and marketer-generated content (MGC) on free content consumption by integrating the literature with research on determinants of physical exercise. Drutsa *et al.* [12] investigated the utility of new data sources to predict video popularity without reliable data from video hosting services. Vasek *et al.* [14] examined the effectiveness of sharing abuse data with web hosting providers to mitigate malicious online activities. Mirheidari *et al.* [21] devised two attacks against web servers exploiting the improper isolation between files on shared web hosting servers. Also, in *et al.* [22] outlined a comprehensive overview of common attacks on shared Web servers.

Correlation Analysis. Several works performed a correlation analysis of the website's security. Visschers *et al.* [11] explores the cost of cybercrime and its relationship to the web security posture. Mezzour *et al.* [20] examines the relationship between social and technological factors and international variations in network-based attacks and hosting. Moreover, Mekovec *et al.* [19] found how user perceptions of security and privacy impact their evaluation of online services using correlation analysis.

Domestic Analysis. Goethem *et al.* [13] presents a large-scale security analysis of 22,851 websites originating in 28 European countries. Furthermore, Raponi and Di Pietro [23] analyzed the password recovery management mechanism of Alexa's top 200 websites, with domains registered in certain European countries. They found that more than 54% of the websites in France, 36% in Italy, 47% in Spain, and 33% in the UK were vulnerable in December 2017.

3 Methodology

3.1 Research Questions

This work aims to derive insightful results of FCW correlations and different hosting patterns compared to PCW. To achieve this goal, we have worked to provide valid answers to the following questions. **RQ1.** What are the main differences between the hosting patterns (networks, hosting CSPs, and countries) of FCWs compared to PCWs? **RQ2.** What type of correlation exists between hosting patterns (networks, hosting CSPs, and countries) and malicious FCWs or PCWs? **RQ3** What are the main correlations of the hosting patterns (networks, hosting CSPs, and countries) of content websites? **RQ4**. What are the implications of FCWs hosting patterns correlation analysis?

3.2   Data Collection Process

We comprehend the research questions by examining multiple datasets. 1. a main dataset of FCWs, PCWs, and their annotations, 2. complementary dataset for augmenting the analysis of the main dataset in terms of security (maliciousness detection), 3. network size classification and, 4. hosting patterns (network, CSP, and country) annotations. In the following, we review these datasets.

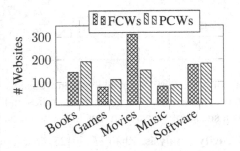

Fig. 1. FCWs vs. PCWs.

Free and Premium Websites. We use the dataset of Alabduljabbar *et al.* [6–8]. The main criteria for selecting the sample were determined based on popularity, main language, and activities. During the collection time, all selected websites were live. Data were collected using three search engines (Bing, DuckDuckGo, and Google). The classification of content type has been applied manually, whether the website is in FCW, PCW, or (book, game, movie, music, or software) content category.

Malicious Annotation. After collecting the data, the VirusTotal [2] API has been used to determine the security of each website, which is a tool that combines more than 70 scanning engines and is available online. VirusTotal enabled us to detect malicious IPs, domains, or URLs correlated with websites. We broadened the data collected according to the VirusTotal output. Since it gives multiple detection results, we take an entity, website, or IP as malicious if at least one of the returned scan results is at least.

Hosting Patterns Annotation. We analyze the scope of the network infrastructure associated with FCWs using the IP addresses connected to each domain as a feature for analysis. We rely on two major API services–ipdata [1] and IPSHU [3]–to gather pertinent information about the given IP address. The subnet mask is used to determine the size of each website's network. Using the CIDR (Classless Inter-Domain Routing) notation, we classified: small networks (/25 - /32), medium networks (/16 - /24), large networks (/8 -/15), and (anything below /7) very large networks as in Table 1.

The IPs of FCWs and PCWs are used to determine the hosting CSPs by querying ipdata [1] and IPSHU [3]. They give the CSP name for the hosting site and its longitude and latitude to determine the hosting country for each website. After refining the websites, we found that only 1,509 (96. 6%) websites are online, as appears in Fig. 1. Among the findings, 788 FCWs and 721 PCWs were grouped into five categories: books (144 free, 191 premium), games (78 free, 111 premium), movies (310 free, 152 premium), music (80 free, 86 premium), and software (176 free, 181 premium).

3.3   Correlation Analysis

We aim to determine whether there is a correlation between the distribution of malicious or benign FCWs and PCWs in different network sizes, CSPs, and counties. To quantify the strength of our correlation, we will use the Pearson correlation coefficient, which is calculated using the following formula: $\rho_{X,Y} = \frac{\text{cov}(X,Y)}{\sigma_X \sigma_Y}$ Here, X represents free, premium, malicious, or benign attributes. On the contrary, Y represents the characteristic being studied. The numerator of the formula represents the covariance between X and Y, while the denominator represents the product of their standard deviations.

In this study, we used the correlation analysis approach to recognize the patterns and differences between FCW and PCW, across various analysis dimensions. This study uses six main dimensions: Type of website (FCW or PCW), type of content category, maliciousness of websites, network size, CSP, and hosting country. In the following, we define each of those dimensions as appears in the workflow of this analysis in Fig. 2.

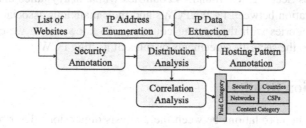

Fig. 2. The workflow of high-level representation of our data extraction.

Content Websites. This feature signifies the type of website, free (FCW) or paid (PCW), that correlates with a specific infrastructure entity (size, CSP, country), security attributes (malicious or benign) and content types. The paid feature of a website is determined by using different search engines, as described in the FCW and PCW data collection and annotation Sect. 3.2. We study the correlation of FCWs/PCWs with different infrastructure features, security features, or content categories to determine where to focus the development effort to improve the hosting of more secure FCWs or PCWs.

Content Categories. In this study, the content of the websites is categorized as (books, games, movies, music, and software). We study the correlation between content types and hosting infrastructure patterns. We study their correlation with FCWs/PCWs and their security attributes (malicious or benign). To know the weaknesses of hosting different content categories. Such as the correlation of malicious websites to a specific content type in a specific hosting infrastructure.

Security Attributes. This feature signifies the total association of malicious or benign websites with a specific infrastructure entity (size, CSP, or country). The results of the VirusTotal scan determine the maliciousness of a website as described in the security annotation process in Sect. 3.2. We study the correlation of malicious or benign websites with different types of content categories, the type of website (FCW, PCW), network sizes, CSPs, and countries. Inform hosting providers about the risks associated with FCW.

Network Size. The network size dimension represents the number of websites discovered within a specific size of the network (small, medium, large, and very large), as described in Sect. 3.2. We provide the results of the correlation analysis between FCWs and PCWs, the content categories of websites, and malicious associations with the size of the network. Investigating FCWs' networks is essential to know their weaknesses.

Cloud Service Provider. The CSP indicates the cloud service provider used to host FCW or PCW. We are studying the correlation between the top ten and the other 298 CSPs discovered during this study. We study the correlations of CSPs with the different content categories and security attributes. Determine the security policies of the CSPs that need to be investigated, altered, or improved.

Country. This feature represents the hosting countries obtained from the hosting patterns annotations Sect. 3.2. We found 44 countries with a heavy-tailed distribution. We study the correlation between FCWs/PCWs and their malicious association for different content categories with the hosting countries. To know where we can make any improvements to the security agreements or rules of hosting FCWs.

4   Correlation Results

We investigate the correlations between the analysis dimensions described in Sect. 3. Specifically, we examine the correlation between FCW and PCW with other characteristics, including network sizes, CSPs, and countries. We also study the malicious and benign classifications in their hosting infrastructures. Figures 3, 5, and 7, illustrate the correlation between FCW and PCW with various features of the infrastructure that indicate the five categories of content.

4.1   General Correlation Results

FCWs strongly correlate with malicious websites, and most FCWs reside in medium and small networks. PCWs are more prevalent in large networks. We also found a strong relationship between the top hosting CSPs and malicious FCWs. However, the relationship between the top countries and PCWs is more diverse. Interestingly, countries correlated with hosting FCWs are found to be more related to hosting malicious websites. The following are the most noticeable insights from the correlation analysis.

Malicious or Benign. We notice that FCWs are mostly correlated with the malicious attribute. As appears in Fig. 3, a negative correlation coefficient varies between 0.13 and 0.46. The strongest correlation is found on software websites. The weakest correlation is found on movie websites. Unlike the malicious website, we found a strong correlation between PCWs and benign attributes. The highest positive correlation coefficient is 0.46 on software websites, and the lowest was discovered on movie websites.

Network Correlation. Per Figs. 3 and 4, we observe a strong correlation between FCW and medium networks, especially in games, movies, and music websites. There is a weak correlation between small networks and FCWs. Compared to the large network that strongly correlates with PCWs. Noticeably, there are no correlations with very large networks. Moreover, benign attributes are correlated with large and small networks. The malicious attribute has a strong correlation with medium networks.

CSPs Correlations. The top ten CSPs strongly correlate with the FCWs. Although some CSPs show a strong correlation with premium websites, most CSPs correlate strongly with benign attributes. Only two of the top ten CSPs have a strong correlation with malicious websites. Some of the content categories in the top ten CSPs indicate a weak correlation with malicious websites, as we can see in Figs. 5, and 6.

Countries Correlations. The top hosting countries strongly correlate with benign websites. Similar to the other countries. In the opposite direction, some content categories indicate a strong correlation to malicious websites in several countries. Such as the games websites in the United States and Belgium as in Fig. 8. However, the FCWs strongly correlate with the United States, Germany, Australia, France, and other countries. Especially for the categories of books, movies, and software as in Fig. 7.

Furthermore, since we provided a summary of the most important findings of the results from the correlation analysis, the following will be a detailed analysis of the network size, CSPs, and countries' correlation to FCWs and PCWs.

Corr	(+)	(-)	SN	MN	LN	VLN
Books	0.02	−0.02	−0.08	−0.07	0.11	0.05
Games	0.32	−0.32	0.02	−0.2	0.21	0
Movies	0.13	−0.13	−0.01	−0.22	0.23	0
Music	0.24	−0.24	−0.01	−0.18	0.18	0
Software	0.46	−0.46	−0.13	−0.08	0.16	0
Overall	0.2	−0.2	−0.05	−0.14	0.17	0.03

Corr	SN	MN	LN	VLN
Books	−0.04	0.1	−0.09	−0.04
Games	−0.12	0.22	−0.19	0
Movies	−0.03	0.08	−0.08	0
Music	−0.07	0.17	−0.16	0
Software	−0.06	0.21	−0.2	0
Overall	−0.05	0.14	−0.13	−0.02

Fig. 3. General networks. Red and blue indicate a vital contribution FCWs and PCWs respectively. (Color figure online)

Fig. 4. The correlation of malicious vs. benign networks. Red for malicious and green for benign. (Color figure online)

4.2 Networks Correlations

General Networks. Figure 3 shows the relationship between FCWs and PCWs in different network sizes, indicating their correlation with various content categories. The results indicate a strong relationship between the book FCWs, predominantly hosted in small and medium networks. In contrast, large networks strongly correlate with PCWs. Unlike the book category, the games, movies and music categories show a weak correlation with small networks, which varies between FCWs and PCWs.

Figure 3 illustrates the associations between FCWs and PCWs with different networks. The correlation highlights the connections between FCWs and PCWs in different categories that use different network sizes and their malicious or benign classification. Reflecting the network correlation observed earlier in Fig. 3, malicious attributes emerge as a significant factor. However, the distinction here is the pronounced association between malicious attributes and FCWs, suggesting that medium and small networks are more strongly linked to malicious factors than other websites.

Malicious Networks. The heat map shown in Fig. 4 illustrates the associations between malicious websites and various characteristics of the size of the network. This correlation highlights the connections between malicious and benign websites in different categories and network sizes. For example, red indicates a high concentration of malicious websites and green represents predominantly benign content. On examination, we observe that most malicious websites are found in medium-sized networks, while small and large networks mainly consist of benign websites. Furthermore, there is a notable correlation between the malicious attribute and the category of games in medium networks, with similar patterns observed on music and software websites. On the contrary, the "Other" categories exhibit a weaker likelihood of maliciousness.

Corr	CF	AZ	LW	TR	GO	ST	LS	AK	FS	MS	Or
Books	-0.07	0.19	-0.16	-0.16	0.14	-0.14	-0.06	0.1	0.11	0.07	-0.04
Games	-0.2	0.26	-0.15	-0.09	0.12	0	-0.15	0.21	0.14	0.06	-0.07
Movies	-0.17	0.39	-0.2	-0.18	0.09	-0.16	-0.15	0.18	0.15	0.08	0.06
Music	-0.17	0.39	-0.05	-0.11	-0.01	-0.2	-0.08	0.11	0.06	0.04	-0.1
Software	-0.27	0.13	-0.18	-0.09	0.07	0	-0.17	0.13	0.07	0.16	0.2
Overall	-0.15	0.26	-0.18	-0.16	0.08	-0.15	-0.15	0.15	0.11	0.09	0.05

Fig. 5. Most used CSP's analysis. The color indication is similar to Fig. 3. The top hosting CSPs are, "Cloudflare"(CF), "Amazon"(AZ), "Liquid Web"(LW), "Trellian"(TR), "Google"(GO), "Sp-Team"(ST), "LeaseWeb"(LS), "Akamai"(AK), "Fastly"(FS), "Microsoft"(MS), Other CSPs(Or).

Corr	CF	AZ	LW	TR	GO	ST	LS	AK	FS	MS	Or
Books	0.58	-0.2	-0.02	-0.09	-0.06	-0.08	-0.03	-0.01	-0.08	0.12	-0.28
Games	0.7	-0.22	0.14	0.08	-0.13	0	0.06	-0.22	-0.15	-0.07	-0.44
Movies	0.11	-0.15	0.05	0.02	0.04	0.08	0.02	-0.05	-0.06	-0.02	-0.05
Music	0.52	-0.17	0.12	-0.07	-0.08	-0.05	-0.05	-0.07	-0.12	-0.08	-0.16
Software	0.58	-0.16	0.15	-0.01	-0.09	0	-0.04	-0.11	-0.1	-0.13	-0.38
Overall	0.48	-0.18	0.06	-0.03	-0.05	-0.01	-0.01	-0.08	-0.09	-0.04	-0.25

Fig. 6. Malicious vs. benign hosting CSPs. The colors are similar to Fig. 4.

4.3   Cloud Service Providers

General Correlations. Figure 5 illustrates the associations between FCWs and PCWs and the CSPs most commonly used in the top hosting countries. The correlation shows the connections between FCWs and PCWs over the top-used CSPs. Furthermore, we found that most PCWs are associated with CSPs that report the lowest malicious activity. We notice that FCWs are used primarily with the most malicious websites that host

CSPs, as appears in Fig. 6. In contrast, PCWs are used primarily with the least malicious websites hosting CSPs. Most PCWs, whose categories are games, movies, and music, are hosted by "Amazon", while "Cloudflare" hosts most FCWs of books and software FCWs. Finally, the general categories are highly distributed.

Malicious Correlations. Figure 6 shows the relationship between malicious websites and the top hosting CSPs. The correlation indicates the relation between malicious and benign websites on the most used CSPs. We notice that the highest concentration of malicious websites strongly correlates with the CSPs "Cloudflare" and "Liquid Web", while benign websites are primarily associated with the other CSPs. Interestingly, book websites exhibit a strong malicious relationship with "Microsoft" CSP, which is known to have one of the lowest reported percentages of malicious activity. The Movies also display multiple malicious correlations with the top six CSPs compared to the others.

4.4 Countries Correlation

General Correlations. Figure 7 shows the relationship between FCW and PCW in the top 10 hosting countries. The correlation indicates the relationship between FCW and PCW in the top hosting countries. For example, we noticed a strong relationship between PCWs in the movie category and the United States and fewer correlations with other categories. Moreover, we observed that most of the top hosting countries exhibit strong relationships with FCWs, especially those reported to be highly malicious. For example, countries such as China, the UK, Canada, and Ireland show weak relationships with PCWs, but surprisingly, it is more vital than their relationship with the FCWs. Furthermore, we noticed a high concentration of FCWs in the game and software categories in Belgium, which are reported to be the most malicious websites. Simultaneously, a strong association can be observed between FCWs in movies and music categories and Germany, which is reported to have a low level of malicious activity.

Corr	US	BE	NL	DE	AU	FR	CN	GB	CA	IE	Or
Books	0.03	−0.17	0.04	−0.17	−0.13	−0.06	0.13	0.11	0.11	0.08	−0.03
Games	0.1	−0.25	0.11	0	−0.02	0.03	0.03	0.09	0.09	0.09	−0.2
Movies	0.29	−0.16	−0.07	−0.22	−0.15	−0.07	0.15	0.09	0	0.16	−0.08
Music	0.14	−0.1	−0.04	−0.25	−0.05	0.04	0.11	0.13	−0.08	0.15	−0.07
Software	0.19	−0.29	−0.08	0.04	−0.05	0.01	0.07	−0.05	0.04	0.09	0.03
Overall	0.17	−0.19	−0.03	−0.16	−0.13	−0.02	0.11	0.07	0.05	0.12	−0.04

Fig. 7. Top hosting countries (Alpha-2). The colors are similar to Fig. 3.

Malicious Correlations. Figure 8 shows the correlation between malicious and benign websites with the top ten hosting countries. The correlation highlights the relationship between malicious and benign websites in the top hosting countries. The heat map reveals a strong relationship between the United States and Belgium that hosts malicious websites, particularly on books, games, and software websites. Most other countries have a strong connection to benign websites.

Corr	US	BE	NL	DE	AU	FR	CN	GB	CA	IE	Or
Books	0.11	0.12	−0.09	−0.13	−0.09	0.06	−0.01	0.02	0.02	−0.05	−0.08
Games	0.31	0.27	−0.17	−0.15	0.01	−0.04	−0.1	−0.16	−0.09	−0.09	−0.21
Movies	−0.06	0.05	0.01	0.02	0.01	0.04	−0.03	−0.04	−0.04	−0.06	0.08
Music	0.11	0.2	−0.09	0.03	−0.08	0.02	0.05	−0.08	−0.1	−0.1	−0.11
Software	−0.04	0.29	−0.08	−0.12	−0.03	0.05	−0.06	0.05	−0.11	−0.08	−0.1
Overall	0.05	0.2	−0.07	−0.07	−0.04	0.04	−0.03	−0.01	−0.05	−0.07	−0.06

Fig. 8. Malicious vs. benign hosting countries (Alpha-2). Colors are similar to Fig. 4.

5 Results Discussion

In this section, we will discuss the key insights of the correlation analysis. Highlighting the answers to the research questions. We will list the challenges we encountered during the study. Finally, we will shed light on the limitations and recommendations.

5.1 Results Takeaway

To sum up the key results of the correlation analysis, we will highlight the insights that provide detailed answers to the research questions as follows.

Free or Premium. The correlation analysis results answer **RQ1**.
1. We notice the difference in the hosting patterns of FCWs and PCWs in their common network size, the top CSPs, and most of the hosting countries. 2. FCWs have a weak correlation to small networks, whereas PCWs have no correlation to small networks. 3. FCWs have a strong correlation with "Cloudflare", "Liquid Web", "Trilian", "SP-Team", and "LeaseWeb" CSPs. Although PCWs seem to have a strong correlation with the other top ten hosting CSPs. 4. Some of the top hosting countries show a strong correlation with FCWs. On the contrary, the other top hosting countries have a strong correlation with PCWs. 5. The results of FCWs depict certain hosting patterns that are uniquely different from PCWs. Indicating the differences in their security behavior.

Malicious or Benign. The results also provide answers to **RQ2** where we find the network hosting patterns for malicious websites. 1. Malicious websites show a strong association with FCW, while benign websites strongly correlate with PCW. 2. In general, malicious websites have a strong correlation with the medium size of the networks. The benign websites are strongly correlated with large networks and weakly with small networks. 3. The top ten CSPs and the other hosting CSPs show a significant correlation to benign websites. Some of the top ten CSPs have a strong correlation with hosting malicious websites. 4. Hosting countries seem to have a significant correlation with benign websites. In the opposite direction, some of the content categories exhibit a strong correlation with malicious attributes. Especially in the top two hosting countries.

Hosting Patterns. The results of studying the different categories of website content in the different hosting patterns give significant answers to **RQ3**. 1. Different content categories show a different level of correlation to malicious and benign attributes. Games and software websites exhibit a strong correlation with malicious FCWs. 2. Small networks have a weak correlation with all FCW content categories. Medium networks have a strong correlation with FCW games, movies, and music websites. Large networks show a lower correlation with such categories in PCWs. 3. We notice the differences in the correlation with the top hosting CSPs. We found a strong correlation between all content categories and FCWs in the top hosting CSPs. Other top CSPs strongly correlate with PCWs. Such as "Amazon", "Akamai", "Fastly", and "Microsoft". 4. There is a weak correlation between all categories of PCWs and some of the top hosting countries. In contrast, we found a strong correlation of FCWs and categories hosted in "Belgium".

Results Implications. The implications of the previous findings provide answers to **RQ4**. 1. Isolation of FCWs that use small networks may be considered an applicable solution to mitigate FCW and PCW risks. 2. Addressing malicious environments within CSPs is one of the most effective solutions to reduce risk exposure. 3. Taking legal action to force such CSPs to improve their security could be a viable solution to secure the network. 4. FCWs and PCWs are concentrated in medium networks, the same as malicious content websites. This implies the need for a better solution than isolating these networks. 5. Games and software content are the most correlated with malicious websites. This implies the serious need to develop security scanning tools specialized in detecting malicious code that may be injected into software or game FCWs.

5.2 Limitations and Recommendations

Limitations. Initially, our main data set consisted of 1,562 FCW and PCW. However, after the network annotation process, we found that only 1,509 websites were operating, suggesting a decrease over time. Thus, longitudinal analysis is required to gain insight into changes in an operation performed on these websites. The top hosting CSPs discovered during this study are widely spread. Where some of these CSPs have different companies, we combined all of the companies of the same entity into one CSP. For example, "Amazon" CSPs provide their services regionally, such as Amazon Data Services Canada and Amazon Data Services France. Consequently, all these CSPs were aggregated into one entity "Amazon". For further analysis of their service distribution, it is imperative to conduct further investigation to ensure their security.

Recommendations. Based on the findings, our recommendations to system administrators are to apply stronger security protocols. To protect their networks from malicious activities. In particular, organizations must prioritize segmenting medium-sized networks as they are often malicious. Moreover, analyzing the CSPs used by FCWs and PCWs can aid in determining which CSPs have a higher number of malicious websites than good ones. This indicates where legal action need to be considered if necessary. General observation suggests that improvements should be made by developing these aspects, reducing malicious websites, and strengthening overall network security.

6 Conclusion

The correlations between FCWs, PCWs and their hosting habits in network size, CSP, and hosting countries have been revealed by this research. Our investigation has shown a significant association between FCWs and medium networks, suggesting that these networks tend to host malicious websites. Additionally, we have identified some CSPs that may need to increase their security requirements, as they are significantly correlated with hosting more malicious content categories. Furthermore, our research shows a notable association between the nations where FCWs are hosted, pointing to the need for more stringent laws and other countermeasures to address dangerous websites.

References

1. Akhawe, D., Barth, A., Lam, P.E., Mitchell, J.C., Song, D.: Reliable IP address Data (2022). Accessed 14 Dec 2022
2. Akhawe, D., Barth, A., Lam, P.E., Mitchell, J.C., Song, D.: Analyze suspicious files and URLs to detect types of malware automatically (2022). Accessed 14 Dec 2022
3. Akhawe, D., Barth, A., Lam, P.E., Mitchell, J.C., Song, D.: IP Address Lookup Tools (2023). Accessed 19 Jan 2023
4. Akhawe, D., Barth, A., Lam, P.E., Mitchell, J.C., Song, D.: Towards a formal foundation of web security. In: Proceedings of the 23rd IEEE Computer Security Foundations Symposium, CSF, pp. 290–304 (2010)
5. Alabduljabbar, A., Abusnaina, A., Ülkü Meteriz-Yıldıran, Mohaisen, D.: TLDR: deep learning-based automated privacy policy annotation with key policy highlights. In: ACM WPES, pp. 103–118 (2021)
6. Alabduljabbar, A., Ma, R., Alshamrani, S., Jang, R., Chen, S., Mohaisen, D.: Poster: measuring and assessing the risks of free content websites. In: NDSS (2022)
7. Alabduljabbar, A., Ma, R., Choi, S., Jang, R., Chen, S., Mohaisen, D.: Understanding the security of free content websites by analyzing their SSL certificates: a comparative study. In: CySSS@AsiaCCS, pp. 19–25 (2022)
8. Alabduljabbar, A., Mohaisen, D.: Measuring the privacy dimension of free content websites through automated privacy policy analysis and annotation. In: Companion of The Web Conference, WWW, pp. 860–867 (2022)
9. Alaqdhi, M., Alabduljabbar, A., Thomas, K., Salem, S., Nyang, D., Mohaisen, D.: Do Content Management Systems Impact the Security of Free Content Websites? CSoNet, A Correlation Analysis. In (2022)
10. Alrawi, O., Mohaisen, A.: Chains of distrust: towards understanding certificates used for signing malicious applications. In: Proceedings of the 25th International Conference on World Wide Web, (WWW), pp. 451–456 (2016)
11. Chen, P., et al.: The relationship between the cost of cybercrime and web security posture: a case study on Belgian companies. In: ACM ECSA, pp. 115–120 (2017)
12. Drutsa, A., Gusev, G., Serdyukov, P.: Prediction of video popularity in the absence of reliable data from video hosting services: utility of traces left by users on the web. CoRR abs/1611.09083 (2016)
13. van Goethem, T., Chen, P., Nikiforakis, N., Desmet, L., Joosen, W.: Large-scale security analysis of the web: challenges and findings. In: Holz, T., Ioannidis, S. (eds.) Trust 2014. LNCS, vol. 8564, pp. 110–126. Springer, Cham (2014). https://doi.org/10.1007/978-3-319-08593-7_8
14. Vasek, M., Weeden, M., Moore, T.: Measuring the impact of sharing abuse data with web hosting providers. In: Proceedings of the Workshop on Information Sharing and Collaborative Security, pp. 71–80. ACM (2016)
15. Hu, T., Tripathi, A.K.: Is there a free lunch? examining the value of free content on equity review platforms. In: 16th Workshop on e-Business Digital Transformation: Challenges and Opportunities, pp. 79–86 (2017)

16. Hu, T., Tripathi, A.K., Berkman, H.: The value of free content on social media: evidence from equity research platforms. In: Lang, K.R., et al. (eds.) WeB 2019. LNBI, vol. 403, pp. 123–130. Springer, Cham (2019). https://doi.org/10.1007/978-3-030-67781-7_12

17. Kosba, A.E., Mohaisen, A., West, A.G., Tonn, T., Kim, H.K.: ADAM: automated detection and attribution of malicious webpages. In: Rhee, K.H., Yi, J. (eds.) WISA 2014. LNCS, vol. 8909, pp. 3–16. Springer, Cham (2014). https://doi.org/10.1007/978-3-319-15087-1_1

18. Lee, D., Nam, K., Han, I., Cho, K.: From free to fee: Monetizing digital content through expected utility-based recommender systems. Inf. Manag. **59**(6), 103681 (2022)

19. Mekovec, R., Hutinski, Z.: The role of perceived privacy and perceived security in online market. In: IEEE MIPRO, pp. 1549–1554 (2012)

20. Mezzour, G., Carley, K.M., Carley, L.R.: Global variation in attack encounters and hosting. In: ACM Proceedings of the Hot Topics in Science of Security, pp. 62–73 (2017)

21. Mirheidari, S.A., Arshad, S., Khoshkdahan, S., Jalili, R.: Two novel server-side attacks against log file in Shared Web Hosting servers. In: Proceedings of The 7th International Conference for Internet Technology and Secured Transactions, ICITST IEEE, pp. 318–323 (2012)

22. Mirheidari, S.A., Arshad, S., Khoshkdahan, S., Jalili, R.: A comprehensive approach to abusing locality in shared web hosting servers. CoRR abs/1811.00922 (2018)

23. Raponi, S., Pietro, R.D.: A longitudinal study on web-sites password management (in)security: evidence and remedies. IEEE Access 52075–52090 (2020)

24. Roy, S.S., Karanjit, U., Nilizadeh, S.: A large-scale analysis of phishing websites hosted on free web hosting domains. CoRR abs/2212.02563 (2022)

25. Zhao, K., Zhang, P., Lee, H.: Understanding the impacts of user- and marketer-generated content on free digital content consumption. Decis. Support Syst. **154**(154), 113684 (2022)

Understanding the Utilization of Cryptocurrency in the Metaverse and Security Implications

Ayodeji Adeniran[✉], Mohammed Alkinoon, and David Mohaisen

University of Central Florida, Orlando, USA
ay260080@ucf.edu

Abstract. We present our results on analyzing and understanding the behavior and security of various metaverse platforms incorporating cryptocurrencies. We obtained the top metaverse coins with a capitalization of at least 25 million US dollars and the top metaverse domains for the coins, and augmented our data with name registration information (via whois), including the hosting DNS IP addresses, registrant location, registrar URL, DNS service provider, expiry date and check each metaverse website for information on fiat currency for cryptocurrency. The result from virustotal.com includes the communication files, passive DNS, referrer files, and malicious detections for each metaverse domain. Among other insights, we discovered various incidents of malicious detection associated with metaverse websites. Our analysis highlights indicators of (in)security, in the correlation sense, with the files and other attributes that are potentially responsible for the malicious activities.

Keywords: Metaverse · security · cryptocurrencies · data analysis

1 Introduction

Metaverse is a technology of the future with much anticipation and hype about its capabilities to alter the life of humans through online model values [4]. Several companies are energetically working on building the metaverse, including technology giants like Facebook and Microsoft, among others. The metaverse is still in its development phase, and the full realization of an interconnected virtual world is yet to be a reality. The metaverse holds the potential for various applications, such as entertainment, gaming, education, virtual commerce, virtual meetings, and more, and is expected to revolutionize how we socialize, work, learn, and interact with digital contents [2].

Although the metaverse is still developing, metaverse coins already amount to trillions of USD in value, and this trend is expected to persist as the technology reaches maturity [11]. However, as with any digital platform or online community [1], the possibility of malicious activities occurring in the metaverse cannot be ignored. As the metaverse concept evolves, it is essential to address potential security concerns, including detecting malicious activities within this

M. H. Hà et al. (Eds.): CSoNet 2023, LNCS 14479, pp. 268–281, 2024.
https://doi.org/10.1007/978-981-97-0669-3_25

virtual space. While the metaverse presents new opportunities for collaboration, interaction, and entertainment, it can also attract malicious actors who seek to exploit vulnerabilities or engage in harmful activities. The intent and motivation for carrying out the malicious activity could be to steal vital information or assets that can be translated into money. Since the metaverse represents the digital world, which involves buying and selling with either cryptocurrency or fiat currency, malicious activities cannot be uncommon.

This paper focuses on understanding malicious activities in the metaverse represented by various platforms and domains. The attackers are sophisticated and experienced with reported attacks on other online platforms, e.g., cryptocurrencies and social media platforms. One of the ways the cyber attackers operate is by sending malicious files to the intended targets to corrupt the system and enable them to access it. The cyber-attacks can be malware, denial-of-service (DOS) attacks, phishing, or code injections. Security analysis of the metaverse domains is the central focus of this paper, and we intend to analyze the files interacting with the domains to gain insight. We will discuss the possible security challenges and malicious activities in the metaverse.

Organization. In Sect. 2, we present the related work, including the research gap. In Sect. 3, we introduce the problem statement, including the research questions. In Sect. 4 we introduce our approach. In Sect. 5, we discussed the results. We discuss various aspects of our studies in Sect. 6 and conclude our work in Sect. 7.

2   Related Work

Several papers explored the security of the metaverse. Di Pietro and Cresci [6] explored the security and privacy concerns surrounding the metaverse by focusing on the security risks that metaverse users may face and how it could affect their privacy. Zhao et al. [21] also conducted a study on security in the metaverse, discussing the common security issues and how they can impact the metaverse. Choi et al. [5] examined the future of the metaverse, tackled similar security issues as the previous ones, and discussed the technology and structural frameworks associated with the realization of solutions.

Kurtunluoglu et al. [10] explored authentication in virtual reality and the metaverse, focusing on security and privacy concerns related to authentication methods. Aks et al. [3] also conducted a study on metaverse security, covering metaverse infrastructure, human interactions, and other interconnected virtual worlds aspects [8].

Tariq et al. [18] explored the security implications of deepfakes in the metaverse, the security challenges, authentication issues, and impersonation problems. Oosthoek et al. [12] researched the security threats to cryptocurrencies, particularly to Bitcoin exchanges—Bitcoin is one of the major cryptocurrencies used in the metaverse. Zaghloul et al. [20] also examined the security and privacy issues with Bitcoin and blockchain relevant to the metaverse. Giechaskiel et al. [7] examined Bitcoin security challenges and their impact when there is a security breach or exposure.

Rosenberg *et al.* [13] conducted a study on marketing in the metaverse and consumer protection. Rosenberg *et al.* [14] also studied marketing in the metaverse and the associated risks. Kshetri *et al.* [9] studied the economics of the metaverse and its impact on the global economy. Other works that explored the security of cryptocurrencies in general include those in [15–17]

The Research Gap. Our study is significantly different from other existing related studies. Our study examines the sources of security vulnerability in the metaverse and relates the findings to market capitalization. Unlike the prior work, our study conducts a thorough direct analysis of each metaverse token rather than focusing on general security concerns (e.g., human error, authentication issues, and other vulnerabilities). Our approach involves analyzing the top metaverse tokens, obtaining their domains and relevant information, and conducting a vulnerability scan to identify potential security issues that may lead to recommendations for this emerging application domain.

We note that our work is the first of its type in this space, as there is prior work that directly studied or measured the overlap between metaverse technologies and cryptocurrencies and how these cryptocurrencies are utilized within the metaverse.

3   Problem Statement and Research Questions

Both legal and illegal activities and transactions are expected in the metaverse. Metaverse is expected to become the digital center for gaming, entertainment, education, etc. Traffic to the metaverse will likely increase with millions of dollars in daily transactions. Security of assets, non-fungible tokens, cryptocurrency, and other technologies has become a challenge due to illegal activities associated with them in the metaverse.

To this end, this paper aims to tackle three crucial research questions related to identifying harmful behavior in the metaverse, particularly those associated with virtual tokens. Our analysis will be guided by these questions to ensure we provide accurate and self-contained answers. By scrutinizing various domains in the metaverse, we will obtain valuable insights that will aid our examination.

1. **RQ1: What are the prevalence of digital coins in the metaverse, and what are their associated threats?** We thoroughly scrutinize the correlation between the popularity and market capitalization of the metaverse and the plausible malicious threats. We analyzed the top forty metaverse coins with the highest market capitalization to accomplish this objective.
2. **RQ2: How significant are metaverse domain artifacts such as communication and referring files in determining the maliciousness of such domains?** To effectively identify malicious incursions in Metaverse domains, conducting a thorough analysis of critical artifacts is imperative. This includes communication files, referrer files, and Passive DNS artifacts, which all directly impact Metaverse domains. Therefore, a comprehensive assessment of their contribution is essential.

3. **RQ3: Is there any correlation between fiat currency to cryptocurrency and vice versa, and the maliciousness of metaverse applications?** It is imperative to recognize the imminent threat posed by cyber attackers who aim to steal money and assets, especially in the metaverse, where cryptocurrency reigns supreme. Our investigation will determine whether domains incorporating fiat currency are more susceptible to malicious activities than those solely relying on cryptocurrency.

4 Technical Approach

This study explored the level of malicious activities in the top metaverse tokens. We analyzed 44 metaverse tokens with a market capitalization of at least 25 million USD. We hypothesize that cybercriminals are likelier to target tokens with a high market capitalization. To test this, we first divided the metaverse tokens into their respective domains and mapped them to their IP addresses. Then, we used the "whois" tool to gather information about the DNS service provider, registrar location and URL, hosting DNS IP addresses, and content delivery network (CDN). We manually inspected all the metaverse websites we studied for transactions from fiat to cryptocurrency.

We thoroughly scanned the metaverse domains and associated IP addresses using virustotal.com. During the scan, we gathered *passive DNS*, communication files, and referrer files and identified malicious detections. We then analyzed the communication and referrer files to detect any malicious activities and identified the file types to locate the source of the malicious activities. We then cross-referenced the metaverse domains with the malicious detections in the communication and referrer files to verify their presence. Additionally, we compared domains with fiat currency and cryptocurrency to domains with malicious activity. Lastly, we examined the metaverse tokens to identify patterns between the top and low tokens based on their market capitalizations.

4.1 Dataset and Preprocessing

Websites and Their Attributes. For this study, we collected data on metaverse coins, their corresponding domains, and their IP addresses. Our first step was to manually select metaverse coins with a market capitalization of at least 25 million USD and then map them to their respective domains. For the initial set of domains, we utilized https://coinmarketcap.com, a website that specializes in tracking coins, their market caps, and associated domains of application. To extract infrastructure information and address the first research question we posed in Sect. 3, we used domain query tools to extract information such as the IP addresses and CDN providers and *manually* checked each webpage for the presence of fiat currency.

Security Data Attributes. We then scanned each metaverse domain and its associated IPs with virustotal.com. This scan provided information on Passive DNS, communication files, referrer files, and malicious detections. We further analyzed the communication files and referrer files to identify those with malicious detection and their types. The malicious detection was also categorized into different types with the number of occurrences for each type. Our primary focus was collecting data with malicious detection to explore the correlation between the different metaverse platforms, cryptocurrencies, artifacts, and associated malicious detection.

To gain a deeper understanding of file connections, especially those related to malicious activities, we thoroughly examined the interlinking between infected communication and referrer files and malware detections. Moreover, we meticulously tallied the frequency of each file type and its association with infected communication and referrer files. Our efforts to uncover malicious behavior were further amplified by our detailed analysis of every scan result and its correlation with malware detection in the scanned files and hosting metaverse platforms.

4.2 Analysis Dimensions

Our study explores the relationship between the metaverse domains and malicious activity and detection. We aim to identify the source and prevalence of such activity within the metaverse space. To do so, we analyzed various dimensions and provided answers to research questions. In the next section, we will focus on specific dimensions to uncover answers to our research questions in Sect. 3. Namely, the dimensions we cover with our analysis are (1) communication files and referrer files activities in the metaverse domain, (2) metaverse coins market capitalization, (3) malicious activities in Metaverse coins, and (4) metaverse coins with fiat currency to cryptocurrency.

5 Results and Findings

Our main results, which analyze and map the relationship between malicious detections in metaverse domains and other artifacts, will be presented in this section.

5.1 Communication and Referrer Files in the Metaverse Domain

The popularity of online platforms is determined by the number of visitors, transactions, and overall traffic. Facebook, for instance, boasts billions of registered users and experiences a significant amount of communication and transactions. These interactions are facilitated through manual website exploration, file exchanges, and website database access. However, it is important to exercise caution as autonomous programs such as bots can also interact with these systems. They can inject messages or code, store data in databases, and even remotely manipulate and hijack systems. Therefore, it is crucial to implement proper security measures to prevent unauthorized access and protect sensitive information. In the metaverse, communication files play a significant role. We have collected communication files from all domains and are studying their relationship with malicious activities. Our analysis aims to determine if the number of communication files is linked to malicious detections and identify the types of files responsible for such detections. This information will be crucial in developing preventive policies against malicious threats in the metaverse.

Observations. The heatmap in Fig. 1 displays the frequency of malicious detections in different file types across various domains in the metaverse. The Win32 EXE file type had the highest frequency of malicious detection, with 14 domains recording it. Android came in second, with 11 domains showing a malicious presence. The axieinfinity.com domain had the highest number of malicious detections at 483. Other file types with malicious activity included PDF, Javascript, Android, and MS Excel Spreadsheet. These file types were responsible for most malicious detections in the study. Additionally, Fig. 2 shows the frequency of referrer files with no detection. The figure displays a heatmap indicating the frequency of infected referrer file types in the metaverse domain. The number of occurrences for each file type is indicated.

The heatmap in Fig. 3 displays a significant number of communication files with malicious detections. It was discovered that metaverse domains that had malicious detections also had communication files with malicious detections. The Win32 EXE and Android file types were more commonly found than others. The Win32 EXE file type had more detections and was present in approximately 25 out of 31 metaverse domains with malicious detections. Figure 3 provides a visualization of the total occurrences of each file type in the metaverse domains, with Android and Win32 EXE file types following the same pattern as previously observed. These two file types are dominant and contribute significantly to the detections recorded in the metaverse domains.

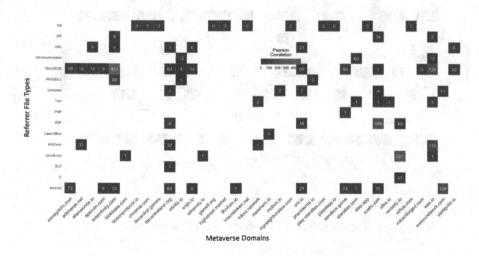

Fig. 1. Metaverse Domain with Infected Referrer Files

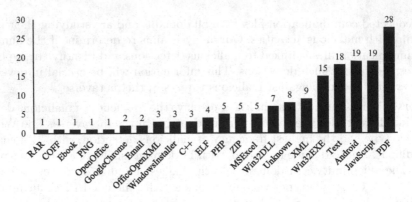

Fig. 2. Number of Referrer File Types

5.2 Metaverse Coins Market Capitalization

The market capitalization of each metaverse token is obtained from crypto.com[1]. It is important to note that this value is subject to fluctuations, as with other markets. The data provided in this paper reflects the value at a specific point in time and may have since changed. Despite being a futuristic technology, the metaverse already boasts a trillion-dollar market capitalization. The highest-valued token is worth over a billion USD, while the lowest is approximately one thousand USD (Fig. 4).

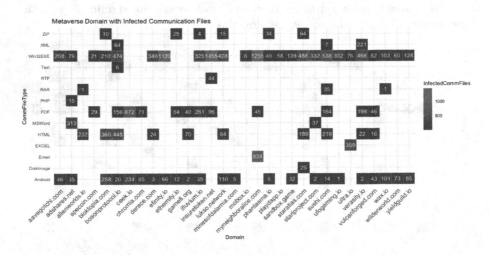

Fig. 3. Infected Communication File Per Site

---

[1] https://crypto.com/price/categories/metaverse.

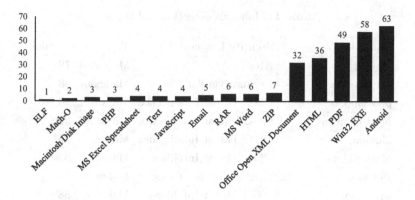

Fig. 4. Average Infected Communication File

Table 1 shows the list of metaverse tokens in descending order based on market capitalization for the domains with at least 25 million USD capitalization.

Observations. We analyzed the top metaverse token with at least a market capitalization of about 25 million USD for vulnerability and malicious activities by performing a scan with third-party software. The scan result reveals various malicious detections in 31 out of the 44 metaverse domains, representing about 70% of the domains under consideration as shown in Fig. 1 and Fig. 3. The malicious detections reported are those obtained from the scan of the metaverse domains, IP addresses, communication files, and referrer files associated with the domains.

5.3 Malicious Activities in Metaverse Coins

Using Virustotal.com, we conduct thorough scans of files, IP addresses, and domains using many security engines, each utilizing unique algorithms to detect any sign of malicious activity. It is important to note that these engines may classify results differently, which is why we meticulously scrutinize associated components such as passive DNS, communication files, and referrer files to determine the presence of any malicious activity accurately.

Table 2 displays the domains of the metaverse, their corresponding security engines, and the types of malicious detections they can identify. These findings are a result of scanning IP addresses that have been linked to their respective domains.

Table 1. Malicious detection and types

Domain	Security Engines	Type	# Files
playdapp.io	Abusix	Malicious	79
playdapp.io	Xcitium Verdict Cloud	Malicious	58
playdapp.io	CMC Threat Intelligence	Malware	46
bloktopia.com	CMC Threat Intelligence	Malware	210
illuvium.io	CMC Threat Intelligence	Malware	261
bloktopia.com	CMC Threat Intelligence	Malware	360
step.app	Xcitium Verdict Cloud	Malware	544
sushi.com	CMC Threat Intelligence	Malware	588
sushi.com	CMC Threat Intelligence	Malware	655
sushi.com	Criminal IP	Malicious	124
efinity.io	Xcitium Verdict Cloud	Malware	680
myneighboralice.com	Xcitium Verdict Cloud	Malware	822
myneighboralice.com	CMC Threat Intelligence	Malware	824
myneighboralice.com	Xcitium Verdict Cloud	Phishing	248
myneighboralice.com	Xcitium Verdict Cloud	Phishing	840
bosonprotocol.io	CMC Threat Intelligence	Malware	1220

Observations. We found eight domains to have malicious infections when the domain IP addresses were scanned. Some domains reported more than one type of malicious detection through different security engines used by virustotal.com. The malicious types in the results are shown in Table 2. Malware, malicious, and phishing are types of files found. The CMC Threat Intelligence security engine was more prevalent, appearing eight times. The table shows the relationship between the metaverse domain and communication files. Every domain that has malicious detection records corresponding communication files. The communications files have shown to have some files with malicious detection, and these files will invariably infect the host domain with malware, phishing, and other maliciousness.

5.4   Metaverse Coins with Fiat Currency to Cryptocurrency

Fiat currency in the metaverse refers to using government-issued currencies, such as traditional national currencies (e.g., USD, EUR, JPY) or digital representations of those currencies within virtual worlds or virtual reality environments.

Table 2. Security engines and Malicious types

Security Engines	Malicious Type	Count of Malware
CMC Threat Intelligence	Malware	7
Xcitium Verdict Cloud	Malware	3
Xcitium Verdict Cloud	Phishing	2
Xcitium Verdict Cloud	Malicious	1
Abusix	Malicious	1
CMC Threat Intelligence	Malware	1
Total		15

While virtual worlds primarily operate with their virtual currencies or tokens, some platforms or virtual marketplaces may support the integration of fiat currency as a means of exchange. This integration lets users purchase virtual assets or participate in economic activities using real-world currencies.

Cryptocurrency in the metaverse refers to using digital currencies, typically using blockchain technology, within virtual worlds or immersive virtual environments value [19]. Cryptocurrencies offer a decentralized and secure means of conducting transactions and can play a role in facilitating economic activities within the metaverse.

Categorizing metaverse domains into two groups is crucial for identifying which currency type is more susceptible to malicious activity. These groups include those using fiat currency and those using cryptocurrency. It is important to understand the vulnerabilities associated with each type of currency within these domains.

Observations. After analyzing 44 domains, it was found that 21 of them (48.84%) use fiat currency. Both classifications of domains showed evidence of malicious activity. It was observed that domains using fiat currency did not exhibit any distinct behavior from those using cryptocurrency, nor did it impact market capitalization. The exchange of fiat currency and cryptocurrency in the metaverse domain is considered a potential factor contributing to malicious activity, but the analysis revealed otherwise.

6 Discussion

Our analysis revealed several instances of malicious activity within metaverse domains. Interestingly, the location of the domains and the DNS and CDN service providers did not contribute to detecting these malicious activities. Our investigation revealed numerous communication and referrer files within the domains, many containing malware. This discovery was unsurprising, as communication and information exchange are common on metaverse web pages. Unfortunately, cyber infections within domains are quite common. Cyber criminals often select their targets based on reconnaissance activities or random selection.

Table 3. Metaverse Fiat to Cryptocurrency

Domain	Fiat Currency	Domain	Fiat Currency
apecoin.com	No	minesofdalarnia.com	Yes
decentraland.org	No	myneighboralice.com	Yes
axieinfinity.com	No	efinity.io	Yes
sandbox.game	No	insuretoken.net	Yes
enjin.io	No	bloktopia.com	Yes
wemixnetwork.com	No	yieldguild.io	Yes
sushi.com	No	staratlas.com	Yes
ont.io	No	virtua.com	Yes
illuvium.io	No	aavegotchi.com	Yes
wax.io	No	ufogaming.io	Yes
lukso.network	No	adshares.net	Yes
playdapp.io	No	gamefi.org	Yes
highstreet.market	No	starlproject.com	Yes
chromia.com	No	play.staratlas.com	Yes
vulcanforged.com	No	wilderworld.com	Yes
decentral.games	No	step.app	Yes
ceek.io	No	ethernity.io	Yes
mobox.io	No	bosonprotocol.io	Yes
raca3.com	No	derace.com	Yes
ultra.io	No	metahero.io	Yes
verasity.io	No	phantasma.io	Yes
alienworlds.io	No		

With ongoing cyber attacks on cryptocurrency domains and pools, we anticipate similar threats to emerge within metaverse tokens.

We have gathered communication files from 44 domains and found malicious activity in 31 of them. However, when we directly scanned the domains and their IP addresses, only 8 out of the 44 domains showed signs of malicious activity, as shown in Fig. 5. This means that the number of domains with malicious activity after a direct scan using virustotal.com is much smaller than reported from the communication files and referrer files. It's possible that the large number of communication files with malicious detection does not necessarily translate to domain infections. This could be due to various reasons, such as the domains having security checkpoints, anti-malware, firewalls, or policies that prevent infections from corrupt communication files. While our study doesn't dive deeply into communication files, we can conclude that the eight domains we identified also had communication files with malicious activity (Table 3).

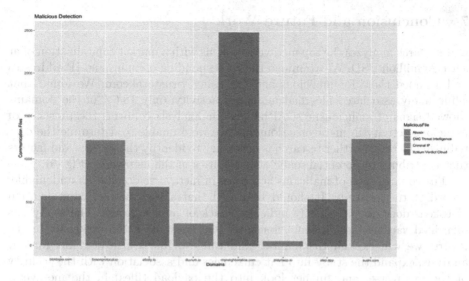

Fig. 5. Metaverse Domains with Malicious Detection Types

The website Virustotal.com has its own passive DNS service. We have noticed that the passive DNS results show many malicious detections. Passive DNS stores DNS queries for future analysis, which can help detect malicious networks or infrastructure. However, we cannot confirm if the malicious detections in passive DNS are directly linked to the malicious activities in the eight domains mentioned in Fig. 5. It is worth noting that these eight domains are also present in the passive DNS malicious results, as seen in communication files.

The body of the analysis is based on several scan results from virutotal.com.

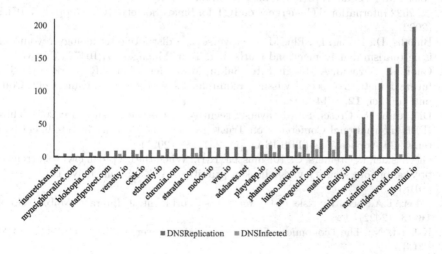

Fig. 6. Metaverse Domains with Malicious Detection Types

7 Conclusion and Future Work

Our research analyzes the top metaverse tokens with a market capitalization of at least 25 million USD. We examined the corresponding domains and IP addresses and scanned them for malicious activity using virustotal.com. We found that while many associated files had malicious activity, only 18.6% of the domains showed signs of maliciousness. Although our analysis confirms the presence of malicious activity in metaverse domains, we were unable to determine the contributing factors. Further research is necessary to identify the sources and factors that contribute to potential malicious activities in the metaverse (Fig. 6).

The confirmation of malicious activities in metaverse domains is undeniable, according to the study. It should be noted that a high market capitalization of tokens does not necessarily indicate a lack of maliciousness. The study has identified various forms of maliciousness that must be taken seriously. In the future, we will expand the number and range of metaverse domains for our analysis, expand the study into fiat currencies and association with the security of the metaverse, and further look into the payload (files) in the metaverse platform and their contribution to the security of such systems.

References

1. Adeniran, A., Mohaisen, D.: Measuring cryptocurrency mining in public cloud services: a security perspective. In: Dinh, T.N., Li, M. (eds.) CSoNet 2022. LNCS, vol. 13831, pp. 128–140. Springer, Cham (2023). https://doi.org/10.1007/978-3-031-26303-3_12
2. Akkus, H.T., Gursoy, S., Dogan, M., Demir, A.B.: Metaverse and metaverse cryptocurrencies (meta coins): bubbles or future? J. Econ. Financ. Account. 9(1), 22–29 (2022)
3. Aks, S.M.Y., et al.: A review of blockchain for security data privacy with metaverse. In: 2022 International Conference on ICT for Smart Society (ICISS), pp. 1–5. IEEE (2022)
4. Buhalis, D., Leung, D., Lin, M.: Metaverse as a disruptive technology revolutionising tourism management and marketing. Tour. Manage. 97, 104724 (2023)
5. Choi, M., Azzaoui, A., Singh, S.K., Salim, M.M., Jeremiah, S.R., Park, J.H.: The future of metaverse: security issues, requirements, and solutions. Hum.-Cent. Comput. Inf. Sci. 12, 1–14 (2022)
6. Di Pietro, R., Cresci, S.: Metaverse: security and privacy issues. In: 2021 Third IEEE International Conference on Trust, Privacy and Security in Intelligent Systems and Applications (TPS-ISA), pp. 281–288 (2021)
7. Giechaskiel, I., Cremers, C., Rasmussen, K.B.: When the crypto in cryptocurrencies breaks: bitcoin security under broken primitives. IEEE Secur. Priv. 16(4), 46–56 (2018)
8. Jaber, T.A.: Security risks of the metaverse world. Int. J. Interact. Mob. Technol. 16(13) (2022)
9. Kshetri, N.: The economics of the industrial metaverse. IT Prof. 25(1), 84–88 (2023)
10. Kürtünlüoğlu, P., Akdik, B., Karaarslan, E.: Security of virtual reality authentication methods in metaverse: an overview. arXiv preprint arXiv:2209.06447 (2022)

11. Momtaz, P.P.: Some very simple economics of web3 and the metaverse. FinTech **1**(3), 225–234 (2022)
12. Oosthoek, K., Doerr, C.: Cyber security threats to bitcoin exchanges: adversary exploitation and laundering techniques. IEEE Trans. Netw. Serv. Manag. **18**(2), 1616–1628 (2021)
13. Rosenberg, L.: Marketing in the metaverse and the need for consumer protections. In: 13th IEEE Annual Ubiquitous Computing, Electronics & Mobile Communication Conference, UEMCON, pp. 35–39. IEEE (2022)
14. Rosenberg, L.: Marketing in the metaverse: emerging risks. In: Arai, K. (ed.) FICC 2023. LNNS, vol. 651, pp. 41–51. Springer, Cham (2023). https://doi.org/10.1007/978-3-031-28076-4_5
15. Saad, M., Chen, S., Mohaisen, D.: SyncAttack: double-spending in bitcoin without mining power. In: ACM CCS, pp. 1668–1685. ACM (2021)
16. Saad, M., Khormali, A., Mohaisen, A.: Dine and dash: static, dynamic, and economic analysis of in-browser cryptojacking. In: APWG eCrime, pp. 1–12 (2019)
17. Saad, M., et al.: Exploring the attack surface of blockchain: a comprehensive survey. IEEE Commun. Surv. Tutor. **22**(3), 1977–2008 (2020)
18. Tariq, S., Abuadbba, A., Moore, K.: Deepfake in the metaverse: security implications for virtual gaming, meetings, and offices. CoRR abs/2303.14612 (2023)
19. Xu, H., Li, Z., Li, Z., Zhang, X., Sun, Y., Zhang, L.: Metaverse native communication: a blockchain and spectrum prospective. In: IEEE ICC Workshops, pp. 7–12. IEEE (2022)
20. Zaghloul, E., Li, T., Mutka, M.W., Ren, J.: Bitcoin and blockchain: security and privacy. IEEE Internet Things J. **7**(10), 10288–10313 (2020)
21. Zhao, R., Zhang, Y., Zhu, Y., Lan, R., Hua, Z.: Metaverse: security and privacy concerns. J. Metaverse **3**(2), 93–99 (2023)

Blockchain and IoT for Enhanced Traceability in Waste Treatment Processes: A Microservice and Brokerless Approach

N. Q. Hien[✉], M. N. Triet, T. D. Khoa, H. G. Khiem, L. K. Bang,
N. T. Phuc, H. V. Khanh[✉], and N. T. K. Ngan

FPT University, Can Tho, Vietnam
hiennqce172010@fpt.edu.vn, khanhvh@fe.edu.vn

Abstract. The management of medical waste, especially in developing countries, presents substantial challenges that have been further intensified by the Covid-19 pandemic. Traditional waste treatment methods often bypass the crucial step of segregating waste at the source, which results in environmental pollution and health hazards. To tackle these issues, we propose a model that leverages Hyperledger Fabric to establish a transparent, secure, and unalterable record of waste treatment processes, thereby ensuring data integrity, transparency, and traceability. The incorporation of Internet of Things (IoT) devices facilitates real-time data collection and control, thereby further enhancing the traceability of the medical waste treatment process. Our model adopts a microservice architecture, which provides several advantages over traditional approaches, including improved scalability, simplified maintenance and updates, and the flexibility to use different technologies for different services. This research makes a five-fold contribution to the field, namely i) presenting a robust and scalable solution based on the blockchain platform; ii) implementing a proof-of-concept via Hyperledger Fabric; iii) providing an integration of IoT devices for real-time data collection and control; iv) proposing the microservice architecture for medical waste treatment; and v) evaluating the effectiveness of the proposed model via the Round Trip Time and Hyperledger Caliper (i.e., data creation & query) test cases.

Keywords: Waste treatment · Blockchain · IoTs · Microservice · Hyperledger Fabric · Hyperledger Caliper

1 Introduction

Medical waste, a critical subset of domestic and industrial waste, is a significant concern for the economic development of a country [16], as well as a burden for the environment [2]. Developed countries have stringent processes for inspecting, classifying, and disposing of waste, including the conversion of hazardous waste

M. H. Hà et al. (Eds.): CSoNet 2023, LNCS 14479, pp. 282–294, 2024.
https://doi.org/10.1007/978-981-97-0669-3_26

into electricity via incineration plants [10]. However, in developing countries such as the Philippines and Vietnam, waste treatment has not been given the methodical attention it requires due to economic and population constraints.

Traditional waste treatment methods often neglect the crucial step of waste segregation at the source, such as residential areas, hospitals, or industrial sites [14]. This lack of pre-treatment and waste separation leads to unsorted waste being dumped directly into the environment, causing serious pollution. This waste is then collected and destroyed in a traditional manner, often without the treatment of smoke and odors, leading to further air and water pollution.

Medical waste, a critical subset of domestic and industrial waste, poses significant challenges for both the economic development of a country and the preservation of the environment [2, 16]. While developed countries have stringent processes for inspecting, classifying, and disposing of waste [10], developing countries like the Philippines and Vietnam face unique challenges due to economic and population constraints.

Traditional waste treatment methods often overlook the crucial step of waste segregation at the source, such as residential areas, hospitals, or industrial sites [14]. This lack of pre-treatment and waste separation results in unsorted waste being dumped directly into the environment, causing serious pollution. The Covid-19 pandemic has further highlighted these shortcomings, with unsafe medical waste handling procedures identified as a contributing factor to the spread of the virus [3].

To address these challenges, our paper proposes a novel approach that leverages Blockchain technology [8] and the Internet of Things (IoT) [13] for enhanced traceability in medical waste treatment processes. Specifically, we exploit Hyperledger Fabric to implement a transparent and secure record of waste treatment processes. This use of Blockchain technology ensures data integrity, transparency, and traceability, which are crucial for effective waste management.

Furthermore, we advocate for the use of a microservice architecture over the traditional client-server or sockets communication approach [22]. Microservices offer several advantages, including improved scalability, easier maintenance and updates, and the ability to use different technologies for different services [20]. This architectural style is particularly beneficial in the context of medical waste treatment processes, where different services may have distinct requirements [21].

The effectiveness of our proposed model is evaluated using Hyperledger Caliper, providing a robust assessment of its performance in a real-world context. Moreover, we evaluate the proposed IoT model for the Waste Treatment Processe by Round Trip Time (RTT) test scenarios.

The rest of the paper consists of parts. After the introduction is the related work section, which presents state-of-the-art with the same research problem. The next section (i.e., Sects. 3) present traditional and our proposed model for Blockchain and IoT-based medical waste treatment processes. To demonstrate our effectiveness, Sect. 4 presents our evaluation steps in different scenarios before making comments in Sect. 5. The 6 section summarizes and outlines the next steps for future work.

2   Related Work

Given the nascent nature of research in the intersection of blockchain technology, IoT, and microservices for the medical waste treatment processes, a scarcity of directly related studies exists. However, to broaden our understanding, we extend our consideration to encompass the general field of waste management where the application of blockchain technology has seen significant attention.

Research on the implementation of blockchain technology within waste management has surged over recent years. Bamakan et al. [1] delivered an exhaustive review of blockchain applications concerning hospital waste management. They provided a critical appraisal of the utilization of blockchain in various facets of waste management, including waste generation, segregation, packaging, storage, treatment, transportation, disposal, and employee training. In the same idea, Hrouga et al. [6] investigated the potential of uniting Blockchain technology and the Internet of Things (IoT) within the digital reverse supply chain. They focused on asbestos waste treatment and proposed two innovative conceptual models for both open and closed-loop digital reverse supply chains.

Laouar et al. [7] introduced a blockchain-based approach dedicated to waste tracking in urban planning, specifically targeting waste collection management. They advocated that implementing blockchain technology in the waste sector could ensure reliable, transparent, and secure documentation of all waste movements. A comprehensive review of waste management using blockchain was conducted by Sambare et al. [15]. They spotlighted the opportunities presented by blockchain technology in handling various types of waste, including Solid Waste, Electronic Waste, Medical Waste, and Industrial Waste.

A blockchain-based medical waste supervision model was proposed by Wang et al. [23]. By integrating the Ethereum blockchain with the decentralized storage of Interplanetary File Systems (IPFS), they aimed to securely fetch, store, and share data pertaining to the forward supply chain of COVID-19 medical equipment and its waste management. Besides, Musamih et al. [11] tackled the issue of COVID-19 vaccine waste due to overproduction and underutilization. They formulated a blockchain-based solution consisting of five core components: a smart contract, a decentralized application, a blockchain, a cloud-based database, and a user interface. Their solution is aimed at ensuring the traceability and transparency of the vaccine supply chain, thereby mitigating waste.

Our study contributes to this growing body of research by proposing a comprehensive blockchain-based waste management system that integrates all these aspects. Unlike previous studies, which focused on specific facets of waste management, our system offers a holistic solution encompassing the entire waste management process from generation to disposal. Furthermore, our system integrates advanced features such as smart contracts for automated waste handling operations and a decentralized application for real-time tracking and tracing of waste materials. This approach enhances waste management's efficiency and transparency and ensures compliance with environmental regulations and standards.

3   Approach

In many developing countries (e.g., Vietnam), the classification of general waste is not commonplace due to a lack of robust infrastructure and standardized protocols. However, the classification and management of medical waste are exceptions to this rule. The strict regulations surrounding medical waste, owing to its hazardous nature, mandate its proper classification and handling. This forms the basis for our focus on medical waste in our research.

In the upcoming architecture section, we present the two most common models for medical waste treatment. Firstly, we explore the Traditional Monitoring Approach, typically utilized in countryside settings, where waste management practices may not be as technologically advanced or robustly structured due to resource constraints. This approach often involves manual tracking and monitoring of waste, emphasizing the importance of strict protocols and thorough training for those involved in the process. Secondly, we delve into the Automated Control Approach, predominantly found in urban environments, where resources for sophisticated waste management systems are more readily available.

Lastly, we introduce our proposed approach (i.e., blockchain, IoT, and microservices structure), which integrates the improvement from both models and employs innovative technologies to enhance the traceability and transparency of medical waste treatment processes. We believe that our method provides a comprehensive solution that can be adapted to a variety of contexts [13], regardless of the available resources [10] and infrastructural constraints [4,5].

3.1   Traditional Monitoring Approach

This approach involves manually monitoring the waste treatment process and making adjustments based on observations and experience. It is a more reactive approach that makes changes in response to problems rather than proactively seeking to improve the process. The main advantage of this approach is that it is simple and does not require complex technology or data analysis. However, it is less effective at discovering hidden patterns and may not be as effective at improving the process. In practices, Fig. 1 shows the six main steps presenting below:

1. **Generation**: Medical waste is generated from various sources within a healthcare facility, such as patient care areas, laboratories, and pharmacies. The waste is typically segregated at the point of generation into different categories, such as general waste, infectious waste, hazardous waste, and radioactive waste.
2. **Segregation and Packaging**: The waste is then segregated according to its type and risk level. This is usually done using color-coded bags or containers. For example, infectious waste might be placed in red bags, while general waste might be placed in black bags. The waste is then packaged for safe handling and transportation.

3. **Storage**: Packaged waste is stored in a designated area within the health-care facility until it can be collected for treatment or disposal. The storage area should be secure and inaccessible to unauthorized personnel to prevent tampering or accidental exposure.

4. **Collection and Transportation**: The waste is collected from the storage area and transported to the treatment or disposal site. This is usually done by a licensed waste transporter. The waste should be transported in a way that prevents leaks or spills.

5. **Treatment or Disposal**: Depending on the type of waste, it may be treated to reduce its risk before disposal. This could involve methods such as auto-claving, incineration, or chemical disinfection. After treatment, the waste is disposed of in a safe and environmentally friendly manner, often in a sanitary landfill.

6. **Documentation and Record Keeping**: Throughout the process, records are kept of the amount and type of waste generated, how it was handled, and where it was disposed of. This documentation is important for regulatory compliance and for tracking and improving waste management practices.

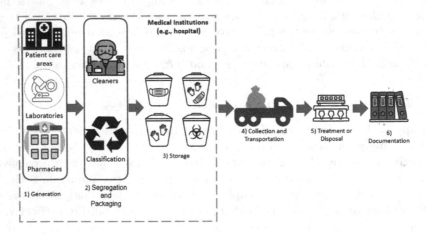

Fig. 1. Waste treatment model for the traditional monitoring and automated control approaches

According to the traditional approach, we have four main limitations, i.e., i) *Lack of Real-Time Tracking* it can be difficult to know exactly where a particular batch of waste is in the process at any given time; ii) *Manual Documentation* it relies heavily on manual documentation and record-keeping. This can be time-consuming, prone to human error, and can lead to inconsistencies or gaps in the data; iii) *Limited Transparency* it can be difficult for all stakeholders to have visibility into the waste management process; and iv) *Risk of Tampering* Paper-based records in a centralized database can be altered or falsified.

3.2   Automated Control Approach

This approach involves using automated systems to control the waste treatment process. These systems can make adjustments in real-time based on predefined parameters. The main advantage of this approach is that it can respond quickly to changes in the process and maintain a high level of consistency. However, like the traditional monitoring approach, it may not be as effective at discovering hidden patterns or insights. The automated control approach for medical waste management leverages the power of Internet of Things (IoT) and other technologies to streamline and optimize the entire process. This approach is almost the same processes of the medical institution area, but it has some difference in the collection, transportation, treatment, and disposal.

– **Collection**: IoT-enabled waste bins are a significant part of this approach. These smart bins are capable of monitoring their fill levels autonomously. When they reach full capacity, they send a signal to the waste management company. This automation ensures timely collection of medical waste and eliminates the need for manual monitoring, thus increasing efficiency.
– **Transportation**: The transportation of medical waste is also optimized in the automated control approach. Real-time monitoring of waste location is made possible through GPS tracking. Additionally, route optimization software is employed to ensure that the transportation of waste is carried out in the most efficient manner, reducing unnecessary travel and thus saving time and resources.
– **Treatment**: The treatment of medical waste is handled by automated waste treatment technologies, such as autoclaves and incinerators. These systems can be programmed to operate at specific times and to treat specific types of waste. This level of automation ensures effective and efficient treatment, reducing the risk of human error and increasing the overall safety of the process.
– **Disposal**: The disposal process is also streamlined through automation. Radio Frequency Identification (RFID) tags can be used to track waste as it is disposed of, providing a clear and accurate record of when and where disposal took place. This level of traceability enhances accountability and ensures compliance with waste disposal regulations.

3.3   Blockchain and IoT-Based Approach

This section proposes a novel model that integrates Blockchain and IoT technologies to address the limitations of both the "Traditional Monitoring" and "Automated Control" approaches in medical waste treatment. This model is an extension of two previous projects: the blockchain for medical problems presented in [9,18][1] and the microservices architechture which introduced in [12,19],

---

[1] https://github.com/Masquerade0127/medical-blockchain.

i.e., Microservice[2]; data collection[3]; and server[4]. Therefore, our proposed model is presented in Fig. 2. In particular, this model includes the three main components, namely Medical Institution area - (A) (i.e., Generation, Segregation and Packaging, and storage), IoT layer - (B) (i.e., Collection and Transportation, Treatment or Disposal), and Microservices architecture model - (C). We apply the Blockchain for the documentation process (i.e., Hyperledger Fabric).

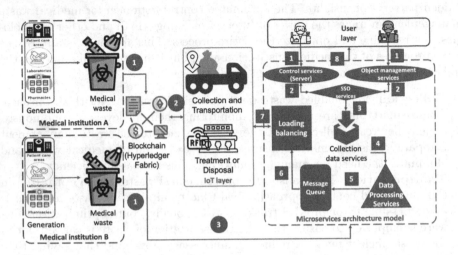

Fig. 2. Waste treatment model based on blockchain, IoT and microservices

In the medical treatment process at (A), each piece of waste generated is tagged with an IoT device (i.e., a piece can be a package after the segregation process). This device records essential information such as the type of waste, the time and place of generation, and the person responsible for packaging. This data is then automatically uploaded to the blockchain, creating an immutable record of the waste's generation, packaging, and storage (step-by-step).

In (B), once the waste is collected, it is transported to the treatment or disposal facility. During transportation, each waste package is tracked in real-time using GPS-enabled IoT devices. This provides a clear record of the waste's journey, including the route taken and the time of transportation. This data is automatically recorded on the blockchain, ensuring transparency and traceability. Upon reaching the treatment or disposal facility, the waste undergoes the appropriate treatment process, which could be incineration, autoclaving, or any other approved method. IoT devices are used to monitor the treatment process, recording data such as the time of treatment, the method used, and the person responsible for the treatment. This information is then added to the blockchain.

[2] https://github.com/thanhlam2110/bmdd-collection-service/tree/main/service.

[3] https://github.com/thanhlam2110/bmdd-collection-service/tree/main/collectionpb.

[4] https://github.com/thanhlam2110/bmdd-collection-service/tree/main/server.

If the waste is to be disposed of, each disposal action is also recorded. For instance, RFID tags can be used to track waste as it is disposed of, providing a clear record of when and where disposal took place. This data is also added to the blockchain, creating an immutable record of the disposal process.

In (C), we extend the IoHT model to continue the process of medical device after the time of usages (please follow our previous paper [19] for more details). In this point we balance between the data query and system loading via the Kafka message queue[5] and the dynamic access control for the authorization process [17,24] (i.e., Single Sign-On (SSO)). All the transaction are logged into the distributed ledger.

4   Evaluation

4.1   Evironment Setting

Our evaluation process focuses on two key technologies in our proposed model: the blockchain technology implemented through Hyperledger Fabric, and microservice architecture.

For the blockchain technology, we use Hyperledger Fabric, which is simulately deployed on a client node via our PC - UbuntuOS v. 22.4, a core i5 2.7Ghz processor, and 8GB RAM. This setup provides a robust environment for running and evaluating the blockchain component of our model. To evaluate the performance of the proposed model, we exploit Hyperledger Caliper[6], a blockchain benchmarking tool. We analyze several key parameters, including the number of successful and failed requests, the send rate (transactions per second, or TPS), maximum, minimum, and average latency (in seconds), and throughput (TPS). Our measurements are based on five scenarios, ranging from 1,000 to 5,000 requests per second. These scenarios allow us to evaluate the performance of our model under varying loads, simulating different real-world conditions.

For the microservice architecture, we utilize the Amazon EC2 platform[7], where each service is equivalent to a virtual machine with a configuration of 1GB RAM and 1 vCPU. This setup allows us to simulate a real-world environment where each microservice is isolated and can be independently scaled. For the IoT devices, we deploy data collection service (client) and control service (client) on the Raspberry Pi 3 model B+[8] module. This module, equipped with Broadcom BCM2837, ARMv8 (64bit) quad-core, 1.2 GHz, and 1 GB RAM, represents a typical IoT device in terms of processing power and memory. For the client node, we communicate Raspberry Pi 3 model B+ with our aforementioned PC (i.e., Ububtu OS v. 22.4).

---

[5] https://kafka.apache.org/.

[6] https://www.hyperledger.org/use/caliper.

[7] https://aws.amazon.com/.

[8] https://www.raspberrypi.org/products/raspberry-pi-3-model-b/.

4.2 Microservice Architecture Test Case

One of the key performance metrics in a distributed system like our proposed model is the Round Trip Time (RTT). RTT is the time taken for a signal to travel from a source to a destination and back. In the context of our model, it represents the time taken for a request to travel from an IoT device to a microservice and back. This metric is crucial as it directly impacts the responsiveness of the system and the user experience. In a medical waste treatment process, where timely and accurate data is critical, a lower RTT can significantly enhance the system's effectiveness. Table 1 presents the results of our RTT tests for microservice architecture. The tests were conducted with varying loads, ranging from 1,000 to 5,000 requests.

Table 1. Round Trip Time (RTT) test results

Factor	1,000	2,000	3,000	4,000	5,000
RTT(s)	3.04	3.35	3.69	3.75	3.92
Error(%)	0%	0%	0%	0%	0%

As shown in this table, the RTT stabilizes with the number of requests. For instance, with 1,000 requests, the RTT is 3.04 s, and this slightly increases to 3.92 s for 5,000 requests. This results is expected in a distributed system and indicates that our microservice architecture scales well with the number of requests. Importantly, the error rate remains at 0% across all tests, indicating that our system can handle a large number of requests without any loss of data. This is crucial for a medical waste treatment process, where data integrity is of utmost importance.

These results demonstrate the effectiveness of our proposed microservice architecture in handling a large number of requests with low latency and zero error rate, making it a suitable solution for enhancing traceability in medical waste treatment processes.

4.3 Hyperledger Caliper Test Case

In our study, we focus on two primary operations in the Hyperledger Fabric: data creation and data query. These operations are fundamental to our study as they represent the core functionalities of our system: recording medical waste data (data creation) and retrieving this data for traceability purposes (data query).

Data creation involves recording the medical waste data onto the blockchain. This data includes details about the waste's origin, type, quantity, treatment process, and final disposal. Recording this data accurately and efficiently is crucial for ensuring traceability and accountability in the medical waste treatment process. Table 2 presents the results of our data creation tests. The tests were conducted with varying loads, ranging from 1,000 to 5,000 requests.

Table 2. Data creation of medical waste

Name	Success	Fail	Send Rate (TPS)	Max Latency (s)	Min Latency (s)	Avg Latency (s)	Throughput (TPS)
1,000 request	26,192	14,327	145.0	1,683.22	0.77	712.23	21.1
2,000 request	29,108	15,270	143.6	1,652.17	1.22	684.21	20.3
3,000 request	27,601	19,102	139.9	1,523.32	1.23	735.59	22.4
4,000 request	28,512	19,468	140.1	1,602.21	4.64	735.62	24.2
5,000 request	31,108	16,145	137.8	1,596.24	4.55	768.12	25.8

Table 3. Data query of medical waste

Name	Success	Fail	Send Rate (TPS)	Max Latency (s)	Min Latency (s)	Avg Latency (s)	Throughput (TPS)
1,000 request	109,613	3,102	345.1	248.16	0.01	3.98	297.12
2,000 request	108,204	3,152	369.3	241.12	0.01	4.11	289.64
3,000 request	106,984	3,615	389.2	241.78	0.01	4.30	296.17
4,000 request	108,198	3,231	382.6	236.14	0.01	4.03	281.00
5,000 request	109,106	3,472	369.3	235.11	0.01	4.12	286.90

Data query, on the other hand, involves retrieving the recorded medical waste data from the blockchain. This operation is crucial for traceability purposes, allowing stakeholders to track the journey of the medical waste from its origin to its final disposal. The efficiency of data query operations directly impacts the system's responsiveness and the user experience. Table 3 presents the results of our data query tests. Similar to the data creation tests, these tests were conducted with varying loads, ranging from 1,000 to 5,000 requests.

As shown in the results, our system demonstrates robust performance in both data creation and data query operations under varying loads. This robustness, combined with the inherent security and transparency of the blockchain, makes our proposed model a promising solution for enhancing traceability in medical waste treatment processes.

5   Discussion

In the microservice architecture, the Round Trip Time (RTT) test results (Table 1) show that the system can handle up to 5,000 requests per second with no errors. This is a significant finding as it demonstrates the system's ability to scale and handle large volumes of data, a crucial requirement in real-world medical waste management scenarios where thousands of waste items are processed daily.

In the Hyperledger Fabric, the data creation and data query tests (Tables 2 and 3) show that the system can handle varying loads, from 1,000 to 5,000 requests, with a high success rate and reasonable latency. This demonstrates the system's robustness and responsiveness, which are key to providing a smooth user experience. Moreover, the Hyperledger Fabric usage provides the system with a high level of security and transparency. Each data entry is recorded on the blockchain, making it immutable and traceable. This enhances accountability in the medical waste treatment process, as each waste item can be tracked from its origin to its final disposal. The integration of IoT devices allows for real-time data collection and control, further enhancing the traceability of the medical waste treatment process. The use of Raspberry Pi 3 model B+ modules for data collection and control services demonstrates the feasibility of deploying our system on low-cost, widely available hardware.

6   Conclusion

This paper has presented a novel approach for enhancing traceability in medical waste treatment processes by leveraging Blockchain technology and the Internet of Things (IoT) within a microservice architecture. Our proposed model utilizes Hyperledger Fabric to create a transparent, secure, and immutable record of waste treatment processes. The integration of IoT devices in our model allows for real-time data collection and control, further enhancing the traceability of the medical waste treatment process. The use of a microservice architecture in our model offers several advantages over traditional approaches, including improved scalability, easier maintenance and updates, and the ability to use different technologies for different services.

Future work could explore further optimizations to improve the system's performance and investigate its applicability to other waste management scenarios. The integration of Blockchain technology, IoT, and a microservice architecture provides a robust and scalable solution that can significantly improve the management of medical waste, contributing to environmental preservation and public health protection.

References

1. Bamakan, S., et al.: Towards blockchain-based hospital waste management systems; applications and future trends. J. Clean. Prod. 131440 (2022)
2. Chisholm, J.M., et al.: Sustainable waste management of medical waste in African developing countries: a narrative review. Waste Manag. Res. **39**(9), 1149–1163 (2021)
3. Das, A.K., et al.: Covid-19 pandemic and healthcare solid waste management strategy-a mini-review. Sci. Total Environ. **778**, 146220 (2021)
4. Duong-Trung, N., et al.: On components of a patient-centered healthcare system using smart contract. In: Proceedings of the 2020 4th International Conference on Cryptography, Security and Privacy. p. 31–35 (2020)
5. Duong-Trung, N., et al.: Smart care: integrating blockchain technology into the design of patient-centered healthcare systems. In: Proceedings of the 2020 4th International Conference on Cryptography, Security and Privacy, pp. 105–109 (2020)
6. Hrouga, M., et al.: The potentials of combining blockchain technology and internet of things for digital reverse supply chain: a case study. J. Clean. Prod. **337**, 130609 (2022)

7. Laouar, M.R., et al.: Towards blockchain-based urban planning: application for waste collection management. In: Proceedings of the 9th International Conference on Information Systems and Technologies, pp. 1–6 (2019)

8. Le, H.T., et al.: Medical-waste chain: a medical waste collection, classification and treatment management by blockchain technology. Computers **11**(7), 113 (2022)

9. Le, H.T., et al.: Patient-chain: patient-centered healthcare system a blockchain-based technology in dealing with emergencies. In: Shen, H., et al. (eds.) Parallel and Distributed Computing, Applications and Technologies. PDCAT 2021. LNCS, vol. 13148, pp. 576–583. Springer, Cham (2022). https://doi.org/10.1007/978-3-030-96772-7_54

10. Moldovan, M.G., Dabija, D.C., Pocol, C.B.: Resources management for a resilient world: a literature review of eastern European countries with focus on household behaviour and trends related to food waste. Sustainability **14**(12), 7123 (2022)

11. Musamih, A., et al.: Blockchain-based solution for COVID-19 vaccine waste reduction. J. Clean. Prod. **372**, 133619 (2022)

12. Nguyen, L.T.T., et al.: BMDD: a novel approach for IoT platform (broker-less and microservice architecture, decentralized identity, and dynamic transmission messages). PeerJ Comput. Sci. **8**, e950 (2022)

13. Nguyen, T.T.L., et al.: Toward a unique IoT network via single sign-on protocol and message queue. In: Saeed, K., Dvorsky, J. (eds.) Computer Information Systems and Industrial Management. CISIM 2021. LNCS, vol. 12883, pp. 270–284. Springer, Cham (2021). https://doi.org/10.1007/978-3-030-84340-3_22

14. Salvia, G., et al.: The wicked problem of waste management: an attention-based analysis of stakeholder behaviours. J. Clean. Prod. **326**, 129200 (2021)

15. Sambare, S., et al.: Literature review on waste management using blockchain. In: Saraswat, M., Chowdhury, C., Kumar Mandal, C., Gandomi, A.H. (eds.) Proceedings of International Conference on Data Science and Applications. LNNS, vol. 551, pp. 495–510. Springer, Singapore (2023). https://doi.org/10.1007/978-981-19-6631-6_35

16. Singh, N., Ogunseitan, O.A., Tang, Y.: Medical waste: current challenges and future opportunities for sustainable management. Crit. Rev. Environ. Sci. Technol. **52**(11), 2000–2022 (2022)

17. Son, H.X., Dang, T.K., Massacci, F.: REW-SMT: a new approach for rewriting XACML request with dynamic big data security policies. In: Wang, G., Atiquzzaman, M., Yan, Z., Choo, KK. (eds.) Security, Privacy, and Anonymity in Computation, Communication, and Storage. SpaCCS 2017. LNCS, vol. 10656, pp. 501–515. Springer, Cham (2017). https://doi.org/10.1007/978-3-319-72389-1_40

18. Son, H.X., et al.: Toward an privacy protection based on access control model in hybrid cloud for healthcare systems. In: Martinez Alvarez, F., Troncoso Lora, A., Saez Munoz, J., Quintian, H., Corchado, E. (eds.) International Joint Conference: 12th International Conference on Computational Intelligence in Security for Information Systems (CISIS 2019) and 10th International Conference on European Transnational Education (ICEUTE 2019). CISIS ICEUTE 2019 2019. AISC, vol. 951, pp. 77–86. Springer, Cham (2019). https://doi.org/10.1007/978-3-030-20005-3_8

19. Thanh, L.N.T., et al.: IoHT-MBA: an internet of healthcare things (IoHT) platform based on microservice and brokerless architecture. Int. J. Adv. Comput. Sci. Appl. **12**(7) (2021)

20. Thanh, L.N.T., et al.: SIP-MBA: a secure IoT platform with brokerless and microservice architecture. Int. J. Adv. Comput. Sci. Appl. **12**(7) (2021)

21. Thanh, L.N.T., et al.: Toward a security IoT platform with high rate transmission and low energy consumption. In: Gervasi, O., et al. (eds.) Computational Science and Its Applications – ICCSA 2021. ICCSA 2021. LNCS, vol. 12949, pp. 647–662. Springer, Cham (2021). https://doi.org/10.1007/978-3-030-86653-2_47

22. Thanh, L.N.T., et al.: UIP2SOP: a unique IoT network applying single sign-on and message queue protocol. Int. J. Adv. Comput. Sci. Appl. **12**(6) (2021)

23. Wang, H., et al.: Research on medical waste supervision model and implementation method based on blockchain. Secur. Commun. Netw. **2022** (2022)

24. Xuan, S.H., et al.: Rew-XAC: an approach to rewriting request for elastic ABAC enforcement with dynamic policies. In: 2016 International Conference on Advanced Computing and Applications (ACOMP), pp. 25–31. IEEE (2016)

Towards a Management System of Blood and Its Products Based on Blockchain, Smart Contracts, and NFT: A Case Study in Vietnam

N. T. Anh[1]([✉]), T. D. Khoa[1], N. Q. Hien[1], L. K. Bang[1], T. B. Nam[1],
V. H. Khanh[1], N. T. K. Ngan[2], and M. N. Triet[1]([✉])

[1] FPT University, Can Tho, Vietnam
`anhntce160237@fpt.edu.vn, trietnm3@fe.edu.vn`
[2] FPT Polytecnic, Can Tho, Vietnam

Abstract. In today's healthcare landscape, the integration of science and technology has greatly impacted various aspects of patient care, particularly in the management and preservation of blood and its derivatives. This is of paramount importance as there exists no viable natural or artificial substitute for blood. With a high demand for blood and its products, the primary source of supply comes from voluntary donors. However, in regions like the Mekong Delta in Vietnam, the process of blood donation and preservation presents significant challenges. To address these challenges, this paper proposes an innovative solution utilizing blockchain technology, smart contracts, and Non-Fungible Tokens (NFTs). This work represents a groundbreaking approach that combines technical expertise, human collaboration, and organizational innovation to enhance the healthcare sector, particularly in blood management. Furthermore, it serves as a compelling case study that contributes to our understanding of the intricate relationship between collaboration and technology.

Keywords: Blood donation · Blockchain · blood products supply chain · Smart contract · NFT · Ethereum · Fantom · Polygon · Binance Smart Chain

1 Introduction

The management, security, and transportation of blood are currently overseen by medical staff with minimal technological support. This process is demanding due to the specific storage requirements of blood and its products, such as temperature, humidity, and shelf life [1]. Moreover, the equipment necessary for maintaining these conditions is costly [4]. In developing regions like Vietnam, only major cities have blood storage and preservation centers. For instance, the entire Mekong Delta region relies on a single hematology hospital for the storage and preservation of blood and its products[1]. Besides the above limitations, it is extremely difficult to determine the origin, type of blood and donor information [2], because all data related to the blood donation process is stored centrally at central server. This leads to other health care centers (i.e., in the provinces) having to contact the Hematology hospital in Ho Chi Minh City directly. Can Tho to ask for help when there is an anemic patient. Blood banks at major provincial hospitals (e.g., Ben Tre, Vinh Long) are also limited in supply and reserve due to the small number of blood donors [8]. According to our observations, local hospitals will hold blood donation sessions to call for volunteers to support. This amount of blood will be transferred to the Hematology hospital before taking it to other hospitals (i.e., when the patient needs it). An approach deemed appropriate for the blood supply chain management requirements of developing countries must meet facility limitations and other requirements related to regional isolation [3]. Specifically, these models must and are easy to deploy on existing systems in big cities (e.g., Hanoi, Ho Chi Minh City, Can Tho) but are also not too expensive to deploy in other cities. other provinces (e.g., Ben Tre, Vinh Long), where medical equipment and infrastructure are limited [7].

In addition to the above reasons, the verification of information of donors is also handled locally and affects the contact process when there are emergency cases[2]. Because of this, previous approaches have presented studies that support Blockchain and smart contracts for decentralized storage (i.e., distributed ledger storage) and increased transparency of stored data (i.e., based on consensus - proof-of-wook mechanism). We also present similar studies based on these two technologies [10,11].

In Vietnam, after each blood donation, donors will receive a certificate (with a small gift and a part of money) in paper form. These certificates not only act as a way to boost the spirit of the donor, they also support the donor to receive free blood (i.e., the same type and corresponding amount of blood) when the donor needs it (e.g., accidents, future blood diseases). However, in today's hospitals and blood donation centers, these certificates are stored in paper form - very difficult to maintain (i.e., due to natural problems such as floods, fires) and easily lost (e.g., owner's fault, lost during relocation - home, work). In addition, the centralized storage of this information cannot be applied due to the limitation of information sharing in medical facilities [2].

Our proposed solution, which combines blockchain technology, smart contracts, and NFTs, represents a novel approach to collaboration in the healthcare sector. By proposing a solution for the management of the blood supply chain, we provide a case study that explores the interplay between collaboration, technology, and healthcare. Our work also addresses the validation of our approach through prototyping and empirical tests, in line with the field's interest in multiple validation approaches. Moreover, our paper aligns with the focus on social

---

[1] This observation is we do the field assessment in November 2022.

[2] Due to the mobilization of blood donation volunteers. over the phone and the donor must wait at least for the red blood cell donation and 3 weeks for the platelet donor, respectively.

computing. By leveraging blockchain technology and smart contracts, our work explores how these technologies can facilitate social good by improving the blood donation process. The use of NFTs for issuing blood donation certificates also represents an innovative application of a recent development in social computing [13]. Therefore, our work contributes on four aspects. (a) Propose a mechanism to manage the supply chain of blood and its products based on blockchain technology and smart contract for the Vietnamese environment; (b) propose a model to generate blood donation certificates based on NFT tool; (c) implementing the proposed model based on smart contracts and the proposed model (i.e., proof-of-concept); and (d) deploying proof-of-concept on 4 supporting platforms (ERC721 - NFT of ETH) and EVM (deploying smart contract implemented in solidity language) including BNB Smart Chain, Fantom, Polygon, and Celo.[3]

2   Related Work

Kim et al. [5] proposed a blood supply chain management system based on the Hyperledger Fabric platform. The authors leveraged the privacy features of the Hyperledger Fabric platform to create a closed supply chain management system, covering the entire process from blood collection to distribution to hospitals/medical centers. Another study that utilizes the Hyperledger Fabric platform is conducted by Lakshminarayanan et al. [6]. They apply a blockchain model to increase transparency in the transportation of blood from donors to the receiving location. To facilitate recipient access to blood type information and related metadata (e.g., donor information, time, location), Toyoda et al. [12] propose a hybrid model of blockchain and RFID. Each blood unit is assigned an RFID tag after donation, enabling medical staff and recipients to easily access information related to blood donation, such as location, time, and the corresponding shipping process.

In the context of blood supply chain management systems on other platforms, such as Ethereum, Ccaugliyangil et al. [2] propose a decentralized solution based on Ethereum-based blockchain to empower certified blood donation centers (CBDCs) by allowing the deployment of smart contracts. For specific blood products, Peltoniemi et al. [9] discuss the use of decentralized blockchain for plasma monitoring and management. Donor-related information is recorded before plasma is separated from their blood, and the system performs plasma analysis to assess the quality of the blood.

3   Approach

3.1   Traditional Model of Blood Donation and Blood Management

We conducted a survey of hospitals in the provinces of the Mekong Delta to gather information about blood and blood product collection procedures.

---

[3] We do not deploy smart contracts on ETH because the execution fee of smart contracts is too high.

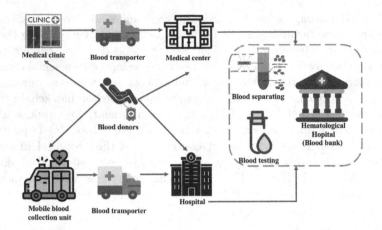

Fig. 1. Traditional model of blood donation and blood management

According to our records (conducted in November 2022), currently, all 12 provinces in the Mekong Delta have only one Hematology hospital located in Can Tho City, which serves as the capital of the Mekong Delta. This hospital is equipped with modern facilities for blood separation, preservation, and storage. Other hospitals within the same system must contact the hematology hospital to request the required amount of blood for treatments or in case of emergencies. Figure 1 illustrates the four procedures involved in blood collection from donors, followed by the separation of blood into respective components, such as red blood cells, white blood cells, platelets, and plasma, at the hematology hospital in Can Tho. These procedures include (a) medical clinics, (b) medical centers, (c) mobile blood collection units, and (d) hospitals. All collected blood is transported to large medical centers for preservation in provincial-city hospitals, or it is sent to the hematology hospital for separation and preservation. Our assessment reveals that a single hematology hospital in Can Tho is insufficient to meet the blood supply needs of the 12 provinces. As a result, the third blood donation process (mobile blood collection units) organizes flexible blood donation campaigns in areas where blood collection is challenging for other processes due to a lack of equipment and medical support. However, this approach is temporary and intermittent, typically conducted on weekends or holidays. Figure 4 illustrates the steps in creating NFTs to replace traditional paper-based blood donation certificates. These NFTs, accessible to donors, are tamper-resistant due to blockchain's transparency and decentralized storage. Donors and medical centers confirm the time and location of blood donations through mutually agreed-upon verification services. Electronic certificates with donor and event details are generated, assigned to NFTs, and updated on the distributed ledger via predefined methods in the smart contract (see Implementation for details).

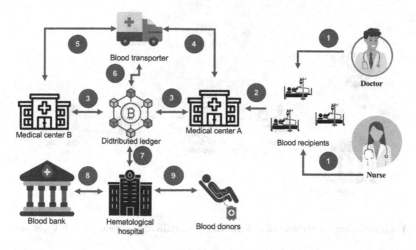

Fig. 2. Blood donation and blood management model based on blockchain technology, smart contracts, and NFTs

3.2 Blood Donation and Blood Management Model Based on Blockchain Technology, Smart Contracts, and NFTs

Figure 2 illustrates our approach, which consists of nine steps (the number of steps may vary depending on the context). We divide the approach into three possible cases within the Mekong Delta environment encompassing the 12 provinces/cities.

- Case one: The hospital treating the recipient's disease depletes its blood reserves (step 2).
- Case two: Hospitals within the same city run out of blood reserves (step 7).
- Case three: The hematology hospital in Can Tho depletes its blood reserves (step 8).

Under the assumption that all three situations occur simultaneously, the blood donation model entails nine steps. Initially, step 1 involves the doctor's examination and treatment process with their patients, the blood recipients. If a patient requires a blood sample for treatment, the request is forwarded to the hospital where the patient is receiving treatment (step 2). These requests are then updated in the distributed ledger (step 3). The system searches for other hospitals to identify the corresponding blood type if the target hospital is identified as the one contacting the blood donor (step 4). Step 5 depicts the carrier receiving blood from the target hospital, and all relevant data, such as time and location, are updated in the distributed ledger (step 6). As per the aforementioned assumption, step 7 involves contacting the hematology hospital to provide the necessary blood source. The hematology hospital checks its stock of blood reserves (step 8) and contacts donors in cases of emergencies or blood shortages (step 9).

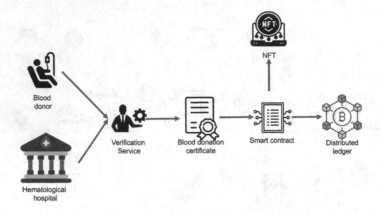

Fig. 3. Generating electronic blood donation certificates based on NFT technology

Figure 3 outlines the steps involved in creating NFTs to replace traditional paper-based blood donation certificates. These NFTs are easily accessible to donors and cannot be replaced or tampered with during use, owing to the transparency and decentralized storage offered by blockchain technology. Specifically, donors and medical centers must confirm the time and location of blood donations, respectively (this confirmation is mutually agreed upon by both parties through verification services). Subsequently, electronic blood donation certificates are generated, containing information related to the donors and the corresponding event (see Implementation for further details). These credentials are then assigned to the respective NFTs before being updated on the distributed ledger, with the entire operation performed based on predefined methods available in the smart contract.

4   Evaluation Scenarios

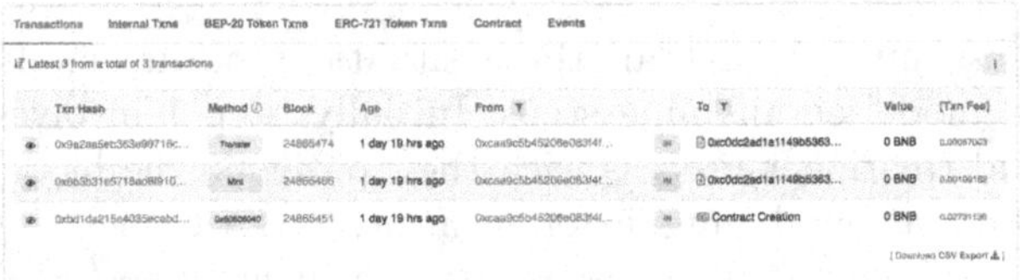

Fig. 4. Transaction info (e.g., BNB Smart Chain)

Since our proposed model focuses on generating blood donation certificates to incentivize donors for community service behavior, we implemented the recommendation model on EVM-enabled blockchain platforms instead of mining platforms belonging to the Hyperledger ecosystem. These platforms are easily extensible, leveraging existing platforms and systems. In addition, the system responsiveness assessments, such as the number of successful/failed requests and system latency (min, max, average), have been evaluated in our previous paper.

Fig. 5. NFT creation   **Fig. 6.** NFT transfer

In this paper, we select the suitable platform for our proposed model. Specifically, we install the recommendation system on four popular blockchain platforms that support Ethereum Virtual Machine (EVM): Binance Smart Chain (BNB Smart Chain)[4], Polygon[5], Fantom[6], and Celo[7]. Our implementations on these platforms also serve as contributions to this article, collecting transaction fees corresponding to the supporting coins of the four platforms: BNB[8], MATIC[9], FTM[10], and CELO[11]. Figure 4 provides detailed information on three successful installations on BNB Smart Chain (similar settings are provided for the other three platforms). We also evaluate the execution cost of the smart contracts, implemented in Solidity language, on the testnet environments of these platforms to choose the most cost-effective platform for deployment. Our detailed assessments focus on the cost of contract creation, NFT generation (see Fig. 5), NFT retrieval/transfer (i.e., updating NFT ownership address - see Fig. 6), and are presented in the respective subsections: i) Transaction Fee, ii) Gas Limit, iii) Gas Used by Transaction, and iv) Gas Price.

4.1 Transaction Fee

Table 1. Transaction fee

	Contract Creation	Create NFT	Transfer NFT
BNB Smart Chain	0.02731136 BNB ($8.37)	0.00109162 BNB ($0.33)	0.00057003 BNB ($0.18)
Fantom	0.009576826 FTM ($0.001860)	0.000405167 FTM ($0.000079)	0.0002380105 FTM ($0.000046)
Polygon	0.006840590024626124 MATIC ($0.01)	0.00028940500115762 MATIC ($0.00)	0.000170007500612027 MATIC ($0.00)
Celo	0.0070973136 CELO ($0.004)	0.0002840812 CELO ($0.000)	0.0001554878 CELO ($0.000)

---

[4] https://github.com/bnb-chain/whitepaper/blob/master/WHITEPAPER.md.

[5] https://polygon.technology/lightpaper-polygon.pdf.

[6] https://whitepaper.io/document/438/fantom-whitepaper.

[7] https://celo.org/papers/whitepaper.

[8] https://testnet.bscscan.com/address/0xc0dc2ad1a1149b5363d7f58c2cf7231d83925 c0c.

[9] https://mumbai.polygonscan.com/address/0xd20ae7123c4387d25d670a6fd74a6095f 4dcaa56.

[10] https://testnet.ftmscan.com/address/0xd20ae7123c4387d25d670a6fd74a6095f4dca a56.

[11] https://explorer.celo.org/alfajores/address/0xD20aE7123C4387d25d670a6fd74A60 95F4dCaa56/transactions.

Table 1 shows the cost of creating contracts on the four platforms. It is evident that the highest transaction fee among the three requirements is for contract creation on all four platforms. BNB Smart Chain has the highest cost, with 0.02731136 BNB ($8.37) for contract creation. The lowest cost is recorded by the Fantom platform, with less than 0.009576826 FTM ($0.001860) for contract creation. The cost for contract creation on Celo is lower than that of Polygon, with only $0.004 compared to $0.01. For the remaining two requirements (Create NFT and Transfer NFT), we observe that the cost of implementing them on Polygon, Celo, and Fantom is negligible (close to $0.00), while on BNB Smart Chain, it is 0.00109162 BNB ($0.33) for Create NFT and 0.00057003 BNB ($0.18) for Transfer NFT.

4.2   Gas Limit

Table 2. Gas limit

	Contract Creation	Create NFT	Transfer NFT
BNB Smart Chain	2,731,136	109,162	72,003
Fantom	2,736,236	115,762	72,803
Polygon	2,736,236	115,762	72,803
Celo	3,548,656	142,040	85,673

Table 2 shows the gas limit for each transaction. Our observations indicate that the gas limits of BNB, Polygon, and Fantom are roughly equivalent, with Polygon and Fantom having similar values for all three transactions. Celo has the highest gas limit among the platforms, with 3,548,656; 142,040; and 85,673 for contract creation, create NFT, and transfer NFT, respectively.

4.3   Gas Price

Table 3. Gas Price

	Contract Creation	Create NFT	Transfer NFT
BNB Smart Chain	0.00000001 BNB (10 Gwei)	0.00000001 BNB (10 Gwei)	0.00000001 BNB (10 Gwei)
Fantom	0.0000000035 FTM (3.5 Gwei)	0.0000000035 FTM (3.5 Gwei)	0.0000000035 FTM (3.5 Gwei)
Polygon	0.0000000002500000009 MATIC (2.500000009 Gwei)	0.000000000250000001 MATIC (2.50000001 Gwei)	0.0000000002500000009 MATIC (2.500000009 Gwei)
Celo	0.0000000026 CELO (Max Fee per Gas: 2.7 Gwei)	0.0000000026 CELO (Max Fee per Gas: 2.7 Gwei)	0.0000000026 CELO (Max Fee per Gas: 2.7 Gwei)

Table 3 shows the gas prices for the four platforms. BNB, Fantom, and Celo have the same gas price for all three transactions: 10 Gwei, 3.5 Gwei, and 2.7 Gwei, respectively. Polygon's gas price (MATIC) has the lowest value and fluctuates around 2.5 Gwei.

5 Conclusion

The paper introduces a model for blood management in Vietnam's Mekong Delta region, utilizing Blockchain, Smart Contracts, and NFTs. The proposed solution on the Ethereum platform addresses decentralized storage challenges. NFTs replace traditional certificates, enhancing security. Evaluating EVM-compatible platforms (Binance Smart Chain, Fantom, Polygon, Celo), Fantom emerged as the most cost-effective for contract creation, NFT creation, and transfer. The evaluation emphasizes economic factors, and while Fantom is favored, other considerations like regulatory compliance and governance should be weighed in the final platform selection.

References

1. Baek, E.J., Kim, H.O., Kim, S., Park, Q.E., Oh, D.J.: The trends for nationwide blood collection and the supply of blood in Korea during 2002 2006. Korean J. Blood Transfus. **19**(2), 83–90 (2008)
2. Çağlıyangil, M., et al.: A blockchain based framework for blood distribution. In: Hacioglu, U. (eds.) Digital Business Strategies in Blockchain Ecosystems, pp. 63–82. Contributions to Management Science. Springer, Cham (2020). https://doi.org/10.1007/978-3-030-29739-8_4
3. Chapman, J.: Unlocking the essentials of effective blood inventory management. Transfusion **47**, 190S-196S (2007)
4. Emmanuel, J.C.: The blood cold chain. WHO report (2017)
5. Kim, S., Kim, D.: Design of an innovative blood cold chain management system using blockchain technologies. ICIC Express Lett. Part B Appl. **9**(10), 1067–1073 (2018)
6. Lakshminarayanan, S., Kumar, P., Dhanya, N.: Implementation of blockchain-based blood donation framework. In: Chandrabose, A., Furbach, U., Ghosh, A., Kumar M., A. (eds.) Computational Intelligence in Data Science. ICCIDS 2020. IFIP AICT, vol. 578, pp. 276–290. Springer, Cham (2020). https://doi.org/10.1007/978-3-030-63467-4_22
7. Le Van, H., et al.: Blood management system based on blockchain approach: a research solution in Vietnam. IJACSA **13**(8) (2022)
8. Mellström, C., Johannesson, M.: Crowding out in blood donation: was titmuss right? J. Eur. Econ. Assoc. **6**(4), 845–863 (2008)
9. Peltoniemi, T., Ihalainen, J.: Evaluating blockchain for the governance of the plasma derivatives supply chain: how distributed ledger technology can mitigate plasma supply chain risks. Blockchain in Healthcare Today (2019)
10. Qu, Q., et al.: Enable fair proof-of-work (PoW) consensus for blockchains in IoT by miner twins (MinT). Futur. Internet **13**(11), 291 (2021)
11. Quynh, N.T.T., et al.: Toward a design of blood donation management by blockchain technologies. In: Gervasi, O., et al. (eds.) Computational Science and Its Applications – ICCSA 2021. ICCSA 2021. LNCS, vol. 12956, pp. 78–90. Springer, Cham (2021). https://doi.org/10.1007/978-3-030-87010-2_6
12. Toyoda, K., et al.: A novel blockchain-based product ownership management system (POMS) for anti-counterfeits in the post supply chain. IEEE Access **5**, 17465–17477 (2017)
13. Wang, F.Y., Qin, R., Yuan, Y., Hu, B.: Nonfungible tokens: constructing value systems in parallel societies. IEEE Trans. Comput. Soc. Syst. **8**(5), 1062–1067 (2021)

Secure Conversation: A View from Physical Layer

Hung Tran[1]([✉]), Pham Ngoc Hung[1], Van Nhan Vo[2], Xuan-Truong Quach[3], Tung Pham Huu[4], Nguyen Quoc Long[2], and Giang Quynh Le Vu[5]

[1] Phenikaa University, Yen Nghia, Ha Dong, Hanoi, Vietnam
{hung.tran,hung.phamngoc}@phenikaa-uni.edu.vn
[2] Duy Tan University, Da Nang 550000, Vietnam
vonhanvan@dtu.edu.vn, nguyenquoclong@duytan.edu.vn
[3] Thai Nguyen University of Information and Communication Technology, Thai Nguyen, Vietnam
qxtruong@ictu.edu.vn
[4] Hanoi University of Civil Engineering, Hanoi, Vietnam
tungph@huce.edu.vn
[5] National Academy of Education Management, Hanoi, Vietnam
giangvlq@niem.edu.vn

Abstract. In this paper, we investigate the performance of a two-way secure conversation among users under the threat of an eavesdropper. To be more specific, we assume that the source and destination engage in a conversation to exchange confidential information. An eavesdropper exists, seeking to exploit the conversation illicitly. The messages of sender are split into multiple packets and then delivered to the receiver via wireless channels. To ensure communication security, we introduce a new concept called the "secure conversation constraint" to analyze the trade-off between security and system performance. Most importantly, the proposed approach can be extended to the study of other wireless networks such as cognitive radio, non-orthogonal multiple access communication, and cooperative relay networks.

Keywords: Secure conversation · security constraint · packet transmission time

1 Introduction

Recently, the concept of physical layer security (PLS) has arisen as a highly promising solution for consolidating security in wireless communication systems. By capitalizing on the distinctive properties of wireless channels such as signal fading, interference, and noise, PLS offers an innovative approach to ensuring confidentiality, integrity, and availability of sensitive information transmitted over wireless links to provide security without relying solely on encryption. More specifically, the wiretap channel model, often used to conceptualize PLS scenarios [1,2]. This model encompasses legitimate communication between a sender and receiver, while considering potential eavesdroppers, leading to the design

M. H. Hà et al. (Eds.): CSoNet 2023, LNCS 14479, pp. 304–312, 2024.
https://doi.org/10.1007/978-981-97-0669-3_28

of strategies that reduce the risks of unauthorized interception. Techniques like beamforming [3–6] and artificial noise injection [7–9] are often used to enhance the security performance.

To measure the performance and security risk as wireless systems having unauthorized eavesdroppers, some performance indicators have been proposed such as secrecy capacity and intercept probability [10]. The secrecy capacity is a fundamental concept that quantifies the maximum rate at which confidential information can be reliably transmitted over a communication channel while keeping it hidden from unauthorized eavesdroppers [11,12]. If the secrecy capacity is greater than zero, there exists a possibility of security for the considered system.The intercept probability is defined as the probability that the signal-to-noise ratio (SNR) at the eavesdropper's location exceeds a certain threshold, enabling successful interception [13,14]. The lower the intercept probability, the more resistant the communication system is to unauthorized access [15–18].

Unlike previous publications, in this work, we consider a practical scenario where users have confident messages to exchange while an eavesdropper tries to exploit the information. The messages are splitted into multiple small packets to deliver them over wireless channel. If the eavesdropper accumulates a number of packets, it will have a high probability to understand the content of communication. To reduce the risk of information leakage, the sender and receiver should control their power to keep the leakage probability below a predefined threshold. Given the obtained power, the outage probability for the conversation is proposed to measure the system performance. Our major contribution is summerized as follows:

- A new concept called the outage probability for the secure conversation is proposed.
- A constraint to secure the two-way conversation between users is considered.
- Most importantly, this approach can be extended to study the secure conversation in different wireless networks such as cognitive radio networks, NOMA communication, cooperative communication and so on.

To the best of our knowledge, this is the first work studying the secure conversation in wireless network from the view of physical layer.

The remainder of this paper is organized as follows. In Sect. 2, the system model and objective function for the secure conservation are presented. In Sect. 3, numerical results and discussions are provided. Finally, conclusions are presented in Sect. 4.

2   System Model and Objective Function

2.1   System Model

Let us consider a system model as show in Fig. 1 in which the S and D communicate under the threat of an illegal eavesdropper. The message of S will be splitted into multiple packets with the same size L to sends to the S. Here, we assume

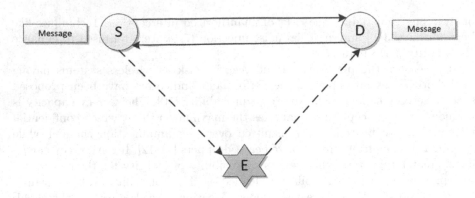

Fig. 1. The S communicates with the D by exchanging messages. There exists an E who is illegal listening the confident messages of both S and D by capturing packets over wireless channel.

that the channel does not change during the transmission of one packet but it may be various thereafter. The time to deliver one packet is defined as [19]

$$T_{S-D}^{(n)} = \frac{L}{B \log_2(1 + \gamma_{S-D}^{(n)})}, \tag{1}$$

in which $\gamma_{S-D}^{(n)}$ is the signal-to-noise ratio defined as

$$\gamma_{S-D}^{(n)} = \frac{P_{S-D} h_n}{N_0}, \tag{2}$$

where h_n, P_{S-D}, and N_0 are channel gain from S→D as it transmits n-th packet, transmit power of S, and noise power density, respectively.

To decode the confident message of the S successfully, the D needs to receive at least N packets before the timeout threshold t_{out}^{S-D}. Accordingly, the total time $T_{S-D}^{(total)}$ that needs to understand the message of the S can be formulated as

$$T_{S-D}^{(total)} = \sum_{n=1}^{N} T_{S-D}^{(k)} = \sum_{n=1}^{N} \frac{L}{B \log_2(1 + \gamma_{S-D}^{(n)})} \tag{3}$$

As the S sends packets to the D, the E also manages to capture the packets for the illegal purpose. To decode the S's message successfully, the E needs to receive at least K of packets, $K \leq M$, before the timeout threshold, t_{out}^{S-D}.

$$T_{S-E}^{(total)} = \sum_{k=1}^{K} T_{S-E}^{(k)} = \sum_{k=1}^{K} \frac{L}{B \log_2(1 + \gamma_{S-E}^{(k)})}, \quad K \leq N \tag{4}$$

where $\gamma_{S-E}^{(k)}$ is defined as

$$\gamma_{S-E}^{(k)} = \frac{P_{S-D} f_k}{N_0}, \tag{5}$$

f_k is the channel gain of the S→E link corresponding to each packet.

At the D, it also has messages to feedback the dialog of the S. Similar to the S→D direction, the message of the D is divided into M small packets with the same size L and the time taking to send one packet from the D to the S is expressed as

$$T_{D-S}^{(m)} = \frac{L}{B \log_2(1 + \gamma_{D-S}^{(m)})} \qquad (6)$$

Accordingly, the total time that S needs to receive M packets and then decode the message of the D may be formulated as

$$T_{D-S}^{(total)} = \sum_{m=1}^{M} T_{D-S}^{(m)} = \sum_{m=1}^{M} \frac{L}{B \log_2(1 + \gamma_{D-S}^{(m)})} \qquad (7)$$

in which $\gamma_{S-D}^{(m)}$ is the signal-to-noise ratio defined as

$$\gamma_{S-D}^{(m)} = \frac{P_{S-D} g_m}{N_0}, \qquad (8)$$

where g_m, P_{D-S}, and N_0 are channel gain from D→S as it transmits m-th packet, transmit power of D, and noise power, respectively.

Similarly, the E can decode the message of the D if it receives at least Q packets of the D before a timeout threshold.

$$T_{D-E}^{(total)} = \sum_{q=1}^{Q} T_{D-E}^{(q)} = \sum_{q=1}^{Q} \frac{L}{B \log_2(1 + \gamma_{D-E}^{(q)})}, \quad Q \leq M \qquad (9)$$

where $\gamma_{D-E}^{(q)}$ is defined as

$$\gamma_{D-E}^{(q)} = \frac{P_{D-S} u_q}{N_0}, \qquad (10)$$

and u_q is the channel gain of the D→E link corresponding to each packet.

Intuitively, the exchanged messages between the S and D are considered as safe and secure communication, if and only if the E cannot receive full packets. In other words, the probability that the E is able to receive full packets to decode messages of the S and D should be smaller than predefined threshold to guarantee the secure communication, i.e.,

$$O_E = \Pr \left\{ T_{S-E}^{(total)} \leq t_{out}^{S-E} \cap T_{D-E}^{(total)} \leq t_{out}^{D-E} \right\} \leq \epsilon \qquad (11)$$

Here, the S and D should have a reason power allocation policy to satisfy (11) to not reveal their messages to the E. To measure the performance of the S and D, we define the outage probability of communication as follows:

$$O_S = \Pr \left\{ T_{S-D}^{(total)} \geq t_{out}^{S-D} \cap T_{D-S}^{(total)} \geq t_{out}^{D-S} \right\} \qquad (12)$$

As for the wireless links between different users, we assume all channels are subject to independent but not necessarily identically distributed (i.n.i.d.) Nakagami-m block fading.

2.2   Performance Analysis

Intuitively, we can see that the transmit power of the S and D and channel conditions will affect the security and system performance. Thus, a reasonable optimal power allocation policy to satisfy the constraint (11) is important. Accordingly, the system performance of the considered system under the security constraint can be reformulated as follows:

$$O = \min_{P_{S-D}, P_{D-S}} \{O_S\} \tag{13}$$

$$Subject\ to:$$

$$O_E \leq \epsilon$$

$$P_{S-D} \leq P_{pk}$$

$$P_{D-S} \leq P_{pk}$$

3   Numerical Results

In this section, we present simulation results for the considered system. In particular, we study the impact of the S and D transmit power and number of packets on the leakage probability and outage probability, respectively. Unless otherwise stated, the following system parameters are used for both simulation and analysis:

- System bandwidth: $B = 1\,\text{MHz}$
- Packet size: $L_s = L_p = 224$ bits (28 bytes)
- Timeout: $t_{out}^{S-D} = t_{out}^{D-S} = 0.02$ s
- Timeout: $t_{out}^{S-E} = t_{out}^{D-E} = 0.01$ s
- Outage constraints: $\theta_{out}^{(p,1)} = \theta_{out}^{(p,2)} = 1\%$
- Number of packets that D needs to decode message from S $N = [4, 5, 6]$
- Number of packets that S need to decode the message from D $M = [3, 4, 5]$;
- Number of packets that the eavesdropper needs to decode the message from S $K = [2, 3, 4]$;
- Number of packets that eavesdropper needs to decode the message from D $Q = [1, 2, 3]$;
- $d_{SD} = [2, 10]$, $d_{SE} = 3$, $d_{DE} = 4$
- $P_{S-D} = [-15, 15]$

In Fig. 2, we plot the leakage probability as a function of the transmit power of S, P_{S-D} (11). It is clear to see that if the conversation between S and D will be leaked out if the transmit power is not constrained by $\epsilon = 0.01$. As the transmit power of the S is beyond -2.5 dB (without constraint), the leakage probability is reaching 1 is very fast. However, under the secure constraint, the leakage probability is always less than or equal $\epsilon = 0.01$. Moreover, as the S only need a small number of packets (K and Q) to decode the conversation, the leakage probability increases significantly. It illustrates that the eavesdropper is quite dangerous with powerful calculation.

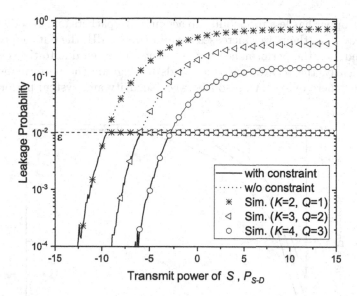

Fig. 2. The probability that the conversation between S and D is exploited with and without constraints.

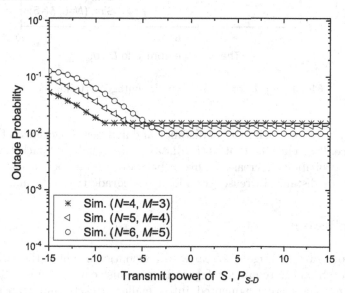

Fig. 3. Outage probability as a function of transmit power of S under the security constraint.

In Fig. 3, we plot the outage probability as a function of the transmit power of the S under the security constraint. It can be seen that the outage probability is decreased as the transmit power increases to −5 dB, and saturated in the high regime of the transmit power. It is due to the fact that at the low power level, the eavesdropper has less probability to accumulate packets and decode the message. However, as the power increases beyond the −5 dB, the outage probability is saturated, i.e., the performance has not been increased due to the secure constraint. Clearly, the secure constraint leads to degrade the performance of the system, i.e., there exists a trade-off between security and system performance.

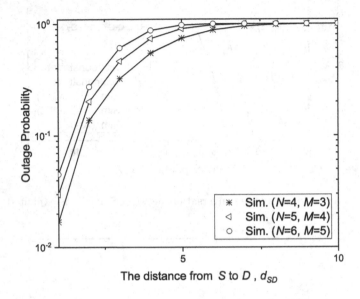

Fig. 4. Impact of distance on the outage performance.

In Fig. 4, we show the impact of distance and number of packets on the outage performance. It can be seen that as the distance and number of packets increases, the outage probability increases. This is because the number of packets being timeout as the distance increases, this lead to degrade the performance.

4   Conclusions

In this paper, we investigate a real-world scenario in which the communication between S and D requires safeguarding against eavesdropping. To achieve this, user messages are fragmented into smaller packets and transmitted to the receiver through wireless channels. A security constraint is implemented to ensure the protection of user conversations. Within this context, we introduce a novel concept known as the "secure conversation constraint" and "outage probability of secure conversation". These concept can serve as a valuable metric for evaluating communication in other wireless networks such as cooperative communication, cognitive radio networks, NOMA communication, and so on.

Acknowledgement. This work is partially supported by the Hanoi University of Civil Engineering.

References

1. Huu, P.N., Ho-Van, K., Bao, V.N.Q.: Secrecy outage analysis of energy harvesting two-way relaying networks with friendly jammer. IET Commun. **13**(13), 1877–1885 (2019)
2. Hui, H., Lee, S.A., Guobing, L., Junli, L.: Secure relay and jammer selection for physical layer security. IEEE Signal Process. Lett. **22**(8), 1147–1151 (2015)
3. Bloch, M., Barros, J., Rodrigues, M.R.D., McLaughlin, S.W.: Wireless information-theoretic security. IEEE Trans. Inf. Theory **56**(4), 2515–2534 (2008)
4. Keeth, J., Praneeth, J., Nandana, R., Matti, L.-A.: Secure beamforming design for physical layer network coding based MIMO two-way relaying. IEEE Commun. Lett. **18**(7), 1270–1273 (2014)
5. Haejoon, J., In-Ho, L.: Analog cooperative beamforming with spherically-bound random arrays for physical-layer secure communications. IEEE Commun. Lett. **22**(3), 546–549 (2018)
6. Wei, Z., Jian, C., Yonghong, K., Yuchen, Z.: Artificial-noise-aided optimal beamforming in layered physical layer security. IEEE Commun. Lett. **23**(1), 72–75 (2019)
7. Wang, L., Zhang, C., Wang, X., Han, Z.: 5G physical layer security: a survey. IEEE Access (6), 18 609–18 627 (2017)
8. Nien-En, W., Hsueh-Jyh, L.: Effect of feedback delay on secure cooperative networks with joint relay and jammer selection. IEEE Wirel. Commun. Lett. **2**(4), 415–418 (2013)
9. Jingchao, C., Rongqing, Z., Lingyang, S., Zhu, H., Bingli, J.: Joint relay and jammer selection for secure two-way relay networks. IEEE Trans. Inf. Forensics Secur. **7**(1), 310–320 (2012)
10. Shabnam, S., Nan, L., Sennur, U.: Towards the secrecy capacity of the gaussian MIMO wire-tap channel: the 2-2-1 channel. IEEE Trans. Inf. Theory **55**(9), 4033–4039 (2009)
11. Zhang, H., Cai, Y., Jiang, Y., Ding, Z.: Secrecy rate optimization for physical layer security in wireless networks. IEEE Trans. Commun. **66**(8), 3481–3495 (2018)
12. Lingxiang, L., Zhi, C., Jun, F.: On secrecy capacity of helper-assisted wiretap channel with an out-of-band link. IEEE Signal Process. Lett. **22**(9), 1288–1292 (2015)
13. Yunsung, C., Dongwoo, K.: Optimal power and rate allocation in superposition transmission with successive noise signal sharing toward zero intercept probability. IEEE Wirel. Commun. Lett. **7**(5), 824–827 (2018)
14. Yulong, Z., Gongpu, W.: Intercept behavior analysis of industrial wireless sensor networks in the presence of eavesdropping attack. IEEE Trans. Industr. Inf. **12**(2), 780–787 (2016)
15. Liu, W., Zhang, R., Zhang, J., Wang, X., Cui, S.: Physical layer security in wireless networks: a survey. IEEE Wirel. Commun. **27**(2), 32–39 (2020)
16. Jules, M., Walaa, H., Fambirai, T.: Intercept probability analysis of wireless networks in the presence of eavesdropping attack with co-channel interference. IEEE Access **6**, 41 490–41 503 (2018)
17. Nhan, V.V., et al.: Outage probability minimization in secure NOMA cognitive radio systems with UAV relay: a machine learning approach. IEEE Trans. Cogn. Commun. Netw. **9**(2), 435–451 (2023)

18. Nhan, V.V., Hung, T., Chakchai, S.-I.: Enhanced intrusion detection system for an EH IoT architecture using a cooperative UAV relay and friendly UAV jammer. IEEE/CAA J. Autom. Sinica **8**(11), 1786–1799 (2021)
19. Mehta, N.B., Sharma, V., Bansal, G.: Performance analysis of a cooperative system with rateless codes and buffered relays. IEEE Trans. Wireless Commun. **10**(4), 1069–1081 (2011)

MIDAS: A Multi-chain Interoperable Data and Access System for Healthcare

Bui Kim Ngan Nguyen[1]●, Binh Thuc Tram Nguyen[1]●,
Tuan-Dung Tran[1(✉)]●, Phan The Duy[2]●, and Van-Hau Pham[2]●

[1] Faculty of Computer Networks and Communications, University of Information
Technology, Vietnam National University, Ho Chi Minh City, Vietnam
{20520648,20520815}@gm.uit.edu.vn, dungtrt@uit.edu.vn
[2] Information Security Laboratory, University of Information Technology,
Vietnam National University, Ho Chi Minh City, Vietnam
{duypt,haupv}@uit.edu.vn

Abstract. The emergence of Blockchain technology has inaugurated
a transformative era by its multifaceted advantages and wide-ranging
applications across diverse industries. Nevertheless, while holding great
promise, Blockchain encounters a significant challenge in achieving interoperability within the complex landscape of multi-blockchain ecosystems.
The imperative necessity for seamless data and digital asset exchange is
evident, yet it is accompanied by the escalating complexities of managing
network entity identities dispersed across disparate systems resulting in
a stark dearth of cohesive connectivity and agile interaction. Henceforth,
in response to these challenges, we present 'MIDAS' as a captivating
research endeavor aimed at fostering seamless interoperability among
a multitude of blockchain networks. MIDAS acts as a key intermediary, skillfully facilitating cross-chain interactions, elevating user experience, and ensuring secure data access for authorized users. In order
to augmenting this architecture's prowess while also focusing on user-
centric data control, we introduce a pioneering decentralized identity
management system known as "Blockchain Interoperability Decentralized Identifier" (BIDI). BIDI offers a range of powerful features, including strict entity management, seamless connections, and customized data
access controls for authorized users, with a focus on user-centric and
data ownership. In other words, our framework is a significant step
towards improving the effectiveness and versatility of blockchain technology, breaking down barriers for harmonious coexistence among multiple
blockchains.

Keywords: Blockchain interoperability · Data access control ·
Decentralized identifiers · Sidechain · Healthcare

1 Introduction

Nowadays, blockchain has developed into a decentralized network system that
can satisfy several crucial security requirements, including reliability, transparency and consensus of each transaction; as the capacity to guarantee data

M. H. Hà et al. (Eds.): CSoNet 2023, LNCS 14479, pp. 313–322, 2024.
https://doi.org/10.1007/978-981-97-0669-3_29

integrity and resilience against cyber attacks. However, as per [1,2], 88% of blockchain applications involve several parties using the same blockchain network, 9% of them are cross-disciplinary, and 73% want to expand and strengthen their connections with new partners. As a result, the isolation of individual blockchains and the high degree of heterogeneity between them present a significant challenge for achieving interoperability, which is a major obstacle in the field of blockchain practical applications [3].

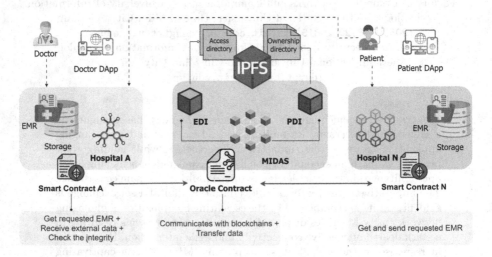

Fig. 1. The concept of MIDAS data transfer between multiple blockchains

In the pursuit of addressing the challenges of cross-chain interaction, our previous research introduced an innovative approach that leveraged a sidechain as an intermediary entity. The system was built as a decentralized oracle network, in which individual oracles undertook the pivotal role of facilitating seamless data transmission between the distinct blockchain systems involved. An oracle contract played a crucial role in ensuring smooth operation as it was enable robust communication with smart contracts across various blockchain networks. Despite advancements in prior systems, limitations persist in data access permissions and management within blockchain environments, especially in complex settings like hospital administration. A key challenge is the fragmentation of patient electronic medical records (EMRs) across diverse hospital blockchains, lead to hinder data linkage, management, and retrieving past EMRs faces obstacles from scattered data.

To address these limitations, this paper introduces a new architecture called Blockchain Interoperability Decentralized Identifier (BIDI). BIDI utilizes decentralized identifiers for blockchain entities to enhance data management and query efficiency across locations. It aims to improve data access permissions, eliminate administrative inefficiencies, and facilitate interoperability through streamlined data request, query, and transfer methods. The main contributions of our research are as follows:

- We propose a novel interchain system for transferring data named MIDAS.
- We implement the BIDI architecture to identify and manage entities in the system including people and data. We also integrate and store the BIDI on MIDAS for maximum efficiency for cross-chain interactive operations such as requesting, querying, and transporting data.
- We conducted practical testing to implement the proposed system, assessed the system's security, and evaluated its performance, cost, and latency.

2   Related Works

2.1   Cross-Chain Technology

In the recent study, [4] provided a comprehensive overview of cross-chain interoperability technologies, encompassing notary mechanisms, sidechains/relays, hash-locking, distributed private key control, and others. These technologies aim to enable the transmission of data and transactions between different blockchains, which is a critical requirement for the widespread adoption of blockchain technology. [5] proposed a quantum-secure notary scheme for resilient cross-blockchain transfers and [6] introduced a notary group mechanism providing enhanced security guarantees. [7] focuses on atomic cross-chain swaps via hash-locked contracts, enabling trustless asset exchange. Unique solution like Cosmos [8] connects heterogeneous chains via relay bridges, with collective validation by multiple parties for robust trust. While progress has been made, blockchain interoperability remains an open challenge. Constructing a multi-chain interoperable data system, especially for healthcare, faces several challenges. One key issue is integrating different blockchain structures, each with its unique rules. Ensuring security and privacy is crucial, aligning with healthcare regulations adds complexity. Another challenge is maintaining data integrity across various chains. For instance, patient records scattered in different hospital blockchains need an efficient system for better management. These challenges highlight the need for a robust and flexible multi-chain data system for effective healthcare applications.

2.2   Identity Management Systems and Decentralized Identifiers

Identity management (IdM) is defined as policies, rules, methods and systems that implement identity authentication, authorization management, access control, and operation audit based on digital identity [9]. The centralized identity model stands as the most traditional approach, however, this model carries inherent limitations, such as privacy concerns, escalating data volumes, and the growing ubiquity of online accounts that individuals must juggle, each demanding vigilant safeguarding [10]. The federated identity model has emerged as a salient solution to the quandary of managing numerous disparate accounts. Users can leverage identity credentials established within one security domain to gain access to various other sites and services. Notably, OAuth and OpenID Connect constitute instrumental standards within the realm of federated identity protocols and are widely used in today's web services [11]. Extensive efforts have been devoted to developing user-centric IdM, emphasizing improvements in both user experience and security. CardSpace, a product developed by Mircosoft, has applied the user-centric identity model. In consonance with this trajectory, Lenz et al. [12] proposed a lightweight model for user-centric and qualified identity information that facilitates selective disclosure and domain-specific altering of single identity attributes in order to protect the citizen's privacy.

Contemporary IdM paradigms often employ a centralized model, wherein specific organizations assume responsibility for issuing and managing user IDs, resulting in user dependency and limited control over identity data. Decentralized Identifiers (DIDs) have emerged as a promising alternative, offering users enhanced autonomy and control over their identity information, and reducing reliance on centralized identity providers. A seminal work in [13] delves into the profound impact of DIDs on the evolution of data exchanges, offering a comparative analysis that underscores the distinctions between DIDs and their centralized counterparts. The study conducted by [14] introduces a robust registration and authentication mechanism, ingeniously utilizing a double-layer blockchain architecture that seamlessly incorporates DIDs. [15] aligns with the World Wide Web Consortium (W3C) DID recommendation [16], signifying the growing adoption of DIDs as a critical element in the contemporary IdM landscape.

3   Proposed System

In the healthcare domain, hospitals have embraced blockchain networks for managing personnel, patients, and EMRs. However, a pressing need arises to enable seamless data exchange across disparate hospital networks, enhance identity management for hospital entities, establish connections between EMRs and their owners, and enable efficient data inquiries across multiple EMRs and hospitals. To address these challenges, we introduce MIDAS as the central component of our architectural paradigm (Fig. 1). MIDAS acts as a Sidechain, facilitating interoperability between heterogeneous blockchain networks. This architecture effectively fulfills the aforementioned requirements while prioritizing the security, efficiency, and confidentiality of personal information within participating blockchain networks. Assume that the Doctor belongs to Hospital A, and needs to access EMRs within the hospital or access other EMRs located inside or outside the patient's existing hospital. For Hospital N where the patient went and owns EMR in both Hospital A and N. The hospital system is implemented with the following roles: Doctor and Patient.

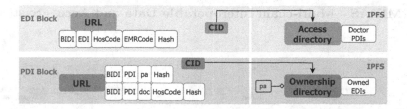

Fig. 2. The architecture for configuring and storing BIDI in MIDAS and IPFS.

3.1 BIDI - Blockchain Interoperability Decentralized Identifier

BIDI is designed to identity provisioning and enable smooth interactions between different blockchain networks, applicable and versatile across various subjects within our scope. Each participant in this system, including Doctors, Patients, and EMRs, possesses a distinct and unambiguous identification marker, represented by a URL-based identifier. The URL-based identifier consists of three essential components, as illustrated in Fig. 2.

1. **BIDI:** The fundamental prefix following it is types of BIDI encompassing EMR - EDI and Person - PDI.
2. **Specific Identifier Path:** As shown in Fig. 2, the structure of the Path is contingent upon *Type* of BIDI and *Role*. In the case of the EDI type, it comprises the following components: *HosCode*, signifying the unique identifier of the hospital to which the EMR is affiliated; *EMRCode*, representing the distinctive EMR code; and *Hash* string. Conversely, the PDI type encompasses distinct components, including roles such as *doctor* or *patient*. Additionally, *HosCode* is included if the role is doctor, signifying the hospital to where they belong. Finally, a *Hash* string, calculated from the Public and Private key pair.

BIDI directory is a dataset designed to encompass predefined information crucial for establishing data linkage management and automated data access control. It is linked to URLs associated with the same BIDI, with different types of BIDI having their distinct directory variants. For EDI-type BIDIs, each EDI possesses an Access directory. This Access directory contains PDIs, with the top and mandatory PDI corresponding to the URL of the patient who is the rightful owner of the corresponding EMR. Subsequent PDIs pertain to doctors sharing the same HosCode as the EDI, thereby granting them seamless access automatically to the EMR's contents. The management of the Access directory, encompassing tasks such as addition or removal of DocPDIs, is entrusted to the patient who is the owner of the EMR. Conversely, for PDI, only the patient role is endowed with an Ownership directory. Within this directory lies a comprehensive record of EDIs corresponding to EMRs owned by the patient, creating pivotal links between data entities and expediting data retrieval. As a result, an inventory of EMRs is curated, affording patients the discretion to select from this catalog for viewing or sharing with doctors.

3.2   MIDAS - Multi-chain Interoperable Data and Access System

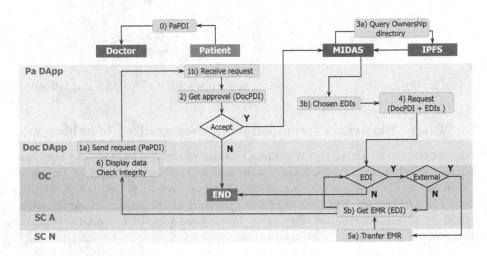

Fig. 3. EMR access request processing flows across multiple sources

MIDAS plays a role similar to that of Sidechain in cross-chain solutions, acts as an intermediary, facilitating communication between different blockchains. As a decentralized oracle network, MIDAS inherits and encapsulates the diverse capabilities of blockchain oracle technology. It establishes a bidirectional connection between smart contracts on the blockchain network and the external world. Additionally, MIDAS serves as the repository for BIDIs, and its organizational structure adheres to a designed schema. Each BIDI is stored in a distinct block, following the data model depicted in Fig. 2.

Owing to the inherent characteristics of MIDAS, which features an architecture akin to that of a blockchain and is ill-suited for the storage of mutable data such as BIDI directories, a strategic amalgamation with InterPlanetary File System (IPFS) has been orchestrated. The integration with IPFS serves as the repository for these dynamic datasets. To establish matching between the BIDI directory and its corresponding URL stored within MIDAS, a pivotal step necessitates affixing a unique IPFS hash (CID) to the URL. Consequently, when interfacing with a BIDI stored within MIDAS, users can seamlessly initiate queries that retrieve the associated directory from IPFS.

3.3   Data Authorization Mechanism

Algorithm 1. EMR access request procedure

1: $PaDApp \leftarrow$ SendEMRrequest $\leftarrow DocDApp$ ▷ Step 1
   $EMRreq(DocPDI) \leftarrow PaPDI$
2: **if** getApproval($DocPDI$) **then**   ▷ Step 2
3:     $ODir \leftarrow CID, PaPDI$ ▷ Step 3
4:     $ListEDIs \leftarrow ODir$
5:     $sum \leftarrow ChosenEDIs \leftarrow$ ChooseEMRs($ListEDIs$)
   create Fetch data Request $\leftarrow DocPDI, ChosenEDIs$ ▷ Step 4
6:     $i \leftarrow 0$
7:     **while** $i \neq sum$ **do**   ▷ Step 5
8:         $EDI \leftarrow ChosenEDIs[i]$
9:         **if** DocPDIHosCode $\neq$ EDIHosCode **then**
10:            Crosschain Data transfer $\leftarrow EDI, DocPDI$
11:        **end if**
12:            $i \leftarrow i + 1$
13:            Display data for doctor $\leftarrow$ getEMR(EDI)
14:     **end while**
15: **end if**
16: END

The data transfer activities within the system are depicted in Fig. 3. The process of a Doctor sending access requests to a patient's existing EMRs unfolds as follows: **Step 0)** Doctor first obtains the patient PDI. **Step 1)** Via the Doc DApp, Doctor specifies PaPDI and sends a data access request to DApp of patient. **Step 2)** Get the approval. **Step 3)** PaDApp retrieve the corresponding Ownership directory on IPFS. It compiles a list of EDIs from which the patient selects EMRs to share with the Doctor. **Step 4)** Create a query request and sends it to MIDAS. **Step 5)** Check EDI quantity, HosCode and then get the requested data. **Step 6)** Display EMRs to the Doctor and data integrity can be verified through URL hash string. The operation subsequently reverts to step 5. Also, Algorithm 1 provides a succinct representation of this operation sequence.

Algorithm 2 outlines the automated authorization process for granting data access permissions to Doctors. The process begins when the Doctor sends the EDI requiring access to the EMR. The DApp performs an initial verification by comparing the HosCode in the DocPDI with that of the requested EMR. Next, the DApp interfaces with MIDAS, creating an oracle contract to search for the corresponding EDI block. If the EDI block exists, a query is sent to the Ownership directory stored in IPFS. The query aims to confirm the presence of DocPDI within the directory, verifying the Doctor's authorization to access the specific EMR. If the verification process succeeds, the Doctor's access request is approved, and then transmit the required data to the Doctor.

Algorithm 2. Automatic data access control mechanism

1: SendEMRrequest ← $DocPDI, EDI$ ▷ Step 1
2: **if** DocPDIHosCode == EDIHosCode **then**
    create Oracle contract
3:     Query ADir ← EDI, CID ▷ Step 2
4:     **if** isDocPDIexist($DocPDI$) ← $ADir$ **then**   ▷ Step 3
5:         getAccess   ▷ Step 4
6:     **end if**
7: **end if**
8: END

4 Experiment Results

In this section, we evaluated the practical performance of the proposed system by implementing and deploying Quorum, Ethereum and MIDAS, also conducted experimental transactions including: Registering entities with the DApp, storing new EMRs in the hospital's IPFS storage, automating the EMR sharing process internally using BIDI and manually selecting EMRs to share. Table 1 provides a detailed breakdown of the specific activities of each transaction and presents time consumption and the cost results in terms of gas and USD for each of them. We also performed multiple measurements for each experimental transaction to ensure the maximum accuracy and reliability of the figures. Based on the obtained results, we evaluate the cost of sharing EMR data across the blockchain as relatively low, dependent on the complexity of the data. On the other hand, the cost of storing new BIDI is relatively higher due to the many complex steps involved, however, this process only needs to be done once. Importantly, the cost for the creation and update of the BIDI directory is quite low, demonstrating the efficiency of the system's permissions function. Overall, the experimental results we achieved are relatively favorable. Therefore, we assess that our proposed solution has shown positive results and further development potential.

Security is a paramount consideration in the architecture of our system, featuring notable focal points. Firstly, MIDAS is a decentralized oracle network, and each transaction is verified by all Oracles, ensuring transparency and preventing fraudulent activities. Secondly, BIDI provides identity and permission for entities in the blockchain, ensuring that only authorized individuals can access the data, thus making the system resilient against data breaches and ensuring data privacy. Notably, BIDI adopts a public URL format devoid of sensitive data, mitigating the risk of exposing personal information. Lastly, extends comprehensive data management and access capabilities to data subjects. Consequently, the system is adept at aligning with diverse healthcare regulations across global jurisdictions, and compliance with standards such as HIPAA (United States), GDPR (EU), and PHIPA (Canada). This adaptability becomes particularly salient when considering the system's prospective global deployment and application within the healthcare domain. Moreover, BIDI finds application in a myriad of healthcare scenarios, exemplified by real case applications such as EMR Management, Cross-Border Medical Consultation, Decentralized Clinical Trials, Collaborative Medical Research, and Emergency Patient Data Access.

Table 1. The average cost consumption of transaction

Transactions	Gas	USD	Seconds
Deploy Smart Contracts	2,365,536	227.13	
Register Doctor	111,476	10.70	1.62
Register Patient	202,711	19.46	1.82
Create new EMR	152,673	14.66	2.51
Internal automatic request	12,774	1.23	0.93
Overall Request	330,888	31.77	19.97

5   Conclusion

In this research, we have introduced MIDAS system integrated with our decentralized identity management solution, BIDI scheme. Our objective is to enhance the capabilities of the healthcare sector by overcoming traditional barriers to data management and access. The system provides a secure and efficient framework for cross-chain data transfer, enabling seamless interoperability. It also enables decentralized administration of entity identities, aligning with contemporary data governance practices. The BIDI directory is a breakthrough mechanism that grants autonomous data access control and establishes associations with rightful owners, enhancing user experience and query efficiency. We have rigorously tested the practical viability and effectiveness of our proposal through various scenarios, validating its robustness and foreseeing its promising applications in the healthcare domain. Moving forward, our future research endeavors will focus on fortifying the privacy and security measures surrounding medical data, while concurrently striving to optimize the cross-chain system by minimizing latency and cost.

Acknowledgment. This research is funded by the Faculty of Computer Networks and Communications, University of Information Technology, Vietnam National University Ho Chi Minh City, Vietnam.

References

1. Pang, Y.: A new consensus protocol for blockchain interoperability architecture. IEEE Access **8**, 153719–153730 (2020)
2. Hardjono, T., Lipton, A., Pentland, A.: Toward an interoperability architecture for blockchain autonomous systems. IEEE Trans. Eng. Manag. **67**(4), 1298–1309 (2019)

3. Harris, C.G.: Cross-chain technologies: challenges and opportunities for blockchain interoperability. In: 2023 IEEE International Conference on Omni-layer Intelligent Systems (COINS), pp. 1–6. IEEE (2023)
4. Wei, O., Huang, S., Zheng, J., Zhang, Q., Zeng, G., Han, W.: An overview on cross-chain: mechanism, platforms, challenges and advances. Comput. Netw. **218**, 109378 (2022)
5. Yi, H.: A post-quantum blockchain notary scheme for cross-blockchain exchange. Comput. Electr. Eng. **110**, 108832 (2023)
6. Xiong, A., Liu, G., Zhu, Q., Jing, A., Loke, S.W.: A notary group-based cross-chain mechanism. Digital Commun. Netw. **8**(6), 1059–1067 (2022)
7. Herlihy, M.: Atomic cross-chain swaps. In: Proceedings of the 2018 ACM Symposium on Principles of Distributed Computing, pp. 245–254 (2018)
8. Kwon, J., Buchman, E.: Cosmos whitepaper. A Netw. Distrib. Ledgers 27 (2019)
9. Cao, Y., Yang, L.: A survey of identity management technology. In: 2010 IEEE International Conference on Information Theory and Information Security, pp. 287–293. IEEE (2010)
10. Avellaneda, O., et al.: Decentralized identity: where did it come from and where is it going? IEEE Commun. Stand. Maga. **3**(4), 10–13 (2019)
11. Pöhn, D., Hommel, W.: An overview of limitations and approaches in identity management. In: Proceedings of the 15th International Conference on Availability, Reliability and Security, pp. 1–10 (2020)
12. Lenz, T., Krnjic, V.: Towards domain-specific and privacy-preserving qualified eid in a user-centric identity model. In: 2018 17th IEEE International Conference on Trust, Security and Privacy in Computing and Communications/12th IEEE International Conference on Big Data Science and Engineering (TrustCom/BigDataSE), pp. 1157–1163. IEEE (2018)
13. Fukami, Y., Shimizu, T., Matsushima, H.: The impact of decentralized identity architecture on data exchange. In: 2021 IEEE International Conference on Big Data (Big Data), pp. 3461–3465. IEEE (2021)
14. Li, X., Jing, T., Li, R., Li, H., Wang, X., Shen, D.: BDRA: blockchain and decentralized identifiers assisted secure registration and authentication for vanets. IEEE Internet Things J. (2022)
15. Garzon, S.R., Yildiz, H., Küpper, A.: Decentralized identifiers and self-sovereign identity in 6g. IEEE Netw. **36**(4), 142–148 (2022)
16. Reed, D., Sporny, M., Longley, D., Allen, C., Grant, R., Sabadello, M., Holt, J.: Decentralized identifiers (dids) v1. 0. Draft Community Group Report (2020)

Network Analysis

Leveraging GNNs and Node Entropy for Anomaly Detection: Revealing Misinformation Spreader on Twitter Network

Asep Maulana[✉] and Johannes Langguth

Simula Research Laboratory, 0164 Oslo, Norway
asep@simula.no

Abstract. The rapid growth of social media, misinformation propagation has become a critical challenge, especially on platforms like Facebook and Twitter. Detecting misinformation spreaders is vital to mitigate its harmful impact on users and society. This paper proposes an innovative approach to identify potential anomalous nodes of misinformation spreaders on Twitter networks by employing Graph Neural Networks (GNNs) and entropy-based method. Utilizing GNNs, we learn node embeddings that capture the intricate patterns of information diffusion and user attributes. Additionally, we analyze the entropy of node attributes on the embeddings to identify nodes exhibiting attribute distributions significantly deviating from the normal. Those anomalous nodes exhibit in the class of misinformation spreader will lead to detect potential of aggressive node in spreading further misinformation.

Through extensive experiments conducted on real-world Twitter datasets containing misinformation-related content, our novel approach showcases its efficacy in identifying potential anomalous nodes as misinformation spreaders across various categories. By harnessing the capabilities of Graph Neural Networks (GNNs) and integrating them with entropy-based techniques via node embeddings, our methodology offers a promising avenue for gaining deeper insights into the behavior of distinct misinformation spreaders and their potential influence on others.

Keywords: Graph neural network · Node embedding · Node entropy · Anomaly detection · Misinformation spreader · Twitter network analysis

1 Introduction

In the era of rapid social media expansion, the spread of misinformation, especially on platforms like Facebook and Twitter, has become a significant and intricate challenge. There is a growing need to identify and counteract the actions of agents disseminating misinformation due to its potentially harmful consequences for users and society at large [16,22]. This necessity extends to the development of specialized methods aimed at safeguarding or immunizing specific nodes

© The Author(s), under exclusive license to Springer Nature Singapore Pte Ltd. 2024
M. H. Hà et al. (Eds.): CSoNet 2023, LNCS 14479, pp. 325–336, 2024.
https://doi.org/10.1007/978-981-97-0669-3_30

within networks [9]. To address this issue, this paper presents a pioneering approach that focuses on identifying potential unusual nodes within Twitter networks, which serve as conduits for misinformation dissemination. This method
combines Graph Neural Networks (GNNs) with an entropy-based mechanism to
achieve its goals.

By leveraging GNNs, this approach efficiently condenses complex information diffusion patterns and user attributes into concise node embeddings. This
fusion of network structure and user traits provides a nuanced representation of
the intricate dynamics in information propagation. Additionally, this study pio-
neers attribute entropy analysis on these embeddings, enabling the detection of
nodes with significantly different attribute distributions, particularly within the
misinformation spreader category. These anomalous nodes have the potential to
act as indicators of nodes primed for aggressive misinformation dissemination.
The approach's effectiveness is rigorously demonstrated through extensive experiments on real Twitter datasets containing misinformation-related content. Its
ability to detect potential anomalous nodes across various categories highlights
its robustness and versatility. By combining node embeddings and entropy-based
techniques through GNNs, this approach emerges as a promising solution for
deciphering the behavior of distinct misinformation spreader archetypes, facilitating a comprehensive understanding of their influence and misinformation
propagation potential. Our proposed approach consists of the following steps:

1. We investigate a Twitter network comprising 1721 nodes, 3488 edges, which
   labeled within one of nine distinct categories. These labels are divided into
   three classes: class 1, class 2, and class 3. Our primary focus is on class labels 2
   and 3, specifically studying them as sources of misinformation across various
   topics. The nodes within this network are characterized by six features that
   are taken into consideration for generating node embeddings using Graph
   Neural Networks (GNNs).
2. Using the node embeddings generated by GNNs, we calculate node entropy
   to identify anomalous nodes. Anomalous nodes are defined as those with high
   entropy values.
3. In addition to entropy measurement, we assess node centrality using four centrality methods. We also tally the number of nodes that appear as spreaders
   of misinformation in various topic categories.
4. Finally, we utilize the outcomes of entropy, centrality, and the extent of
   involvement in diverse topics to evaluate the roles played by nodes in class 2
   and 3 in the dissemination and propagation of false information.

2   Related Literature

Graph Neural Networks (GNNs) have emerged as a transformative framework for
analyzing and learning from complex network data. Scarselli et al. [14] laid the
foundation for GNNs with their pioneering work on the Graph Neural Network
model for processing graph-structured data effectively [14,14]. Subsequently,
Hamilton et al. [3] advanced the field with Inductive Representation Learning on

Large Graphs. Building on this foundation, Velickovic et al. [17] provided a comprehensive review of GNNs in Graph Convolutional Networks: A Comprehensive Review, showcasing the wide-ranging applications and methodologies within the GNN landscape [17, 23].

In recent years, node entropy, derived from information theory, has become pivotal in complex network analysis, revealing the significance of individual nodes [2]. Lei and Cheong furthered this concept with a local structure entropy approach, considering neighborhood context [6], while Zhang et al. employed relative entropy to measure structure similarity among nodes [21]. Yu et al. explored node propagation entropy for identifying important nodes in information dissemination [19]. Zareie et al. applied entropy for influential node ranking, emphasizing nodes with diverse connections [20]. Additionally, Qiao et al. introduced a novel entropy centrality approach to identify the most powerful node [13]. These approaches collectively highlight node entropy's role in understanding complex network dynamics and identifying influential nodes.

Our research work related directly to previous work on misinformation spreader. Pogorelov et al. [10] introduced the Fakenews: Corona virus and conspiracies multimedia analysis task at MediaEval 2021, in other related study, (Pogorelov et al., [12]). Pogorelov et al. [11] explored the integration of tweets and connection graphs for fake news detection, emphasizing the importance of network structures in combating false information. Additionally, Langguth et al. [4] conducted a long-term observation of COVID-19 and 5G conspiracy theories, providing insights into how such misinformation persists over time. Moreover, regarding anomaly detection in social networks using diverse approaches have been investigated . For example, Akoglu et al. graph based anomaly detection and description [1] or Maulana et al. applied many-objective optimization for centrality-based anomaly detection in multi-layer networks [7, 8]. showcasing the adaptability of optimization techniques in addressing anomalies in complex network structures

3 Theoretical Framework and Approaches

3.1 Graph Neural Networks (GNNs) and Node Embeddings

Graph Neural Networks (GNNs) are specialized models designed to handle data structured as graphs. They have gained significant attention due to their outstanding performance in tasks such as node classification, link prediction, and graph-level prediction. In node classification, GNNs aim to assign labels or predict properties for individual nodes within a graph. They achieve this by iteratively learning informative node representations that consider both local neighborhood details and the broader graph structure. At the core of GNN theory is the concept of information propagation and aggregation. This iterative process involves nodes updating their representations by gathering information from neighboring nodes and incorporating it into their own. This enables nodes to effectively absorb information from nearby nodes and share it across the entire graph. The key components of a GNN model for node classification include

Node Features, Message Passing, Aggregation Function, Graph Convolutional Layer, and Readout Function. In summary, Graph Neural Networks excel in node classification tasks by efficiently capturing and utilizing information from both the local neighborhood and the overall graph structure inherent in graph-structured data.

Node embeddings, generated through unsupervised or semi-supervised techniques, compactly represent graph nodes, facilitating the application of traditional and deep machine learning methods to graph data. These embeddings capture node similarities based on attributes and neighborhood structures, benefiting tasks like visualization, clustering, link prediction, and anomaly detection in complex graphs. Graph neural networks (GNNs) frequently employ these embeddings as input, leveraging their rich representations to excel in node classification, link prediction, and various other graph-related tasks.

3.2 Node Entropy

The Node Entropy Theory (NET) is a concept that originates from information theory and is adapted to the context of networks [15]. It focuses on quantifying the uncertainty and information content of individual nodes within a network. The theory provides insights into how nodes contribute to the overall dynamics and functioning of the network. Node Entropy Theory finds applications in various fields, such as social network analysis, biological networks, and communication networks. In Node Entropy Theory, we are interested in the entropy associated with individual nodes within a network. Consider a network represented as a graph G = (V, E), where V is the set of nodes (vertices) and E is the set of edges connecting the nodes. For a specific node v in V, we define its Node Entropy H(v) as the Shannon Entropy of the probability distribution of the node's neighboring states.

Let's denote the set of neighboring nodes of v as N(v). For each neighbor u in N(v), there is an associated probability P(u) representing the likelihood of v being in the state represented by u

Then, the Node Entropy H(v) is given by:

$$H(v) = - \sum_{u \in N(v)} P(u) \log_2(P(u))$$

Where the summation is performed over all neighbors u of v. In some cases, the interactions between nodes may have different strengths or weights. To consider these weights in the Node Entropy calculation, we introduce a weight function w(u, v) that gives the weight of the edge between nodes u and v. The Weighted Node Entropy $H_w(v)$ is then calculated as follows:

$$H_w(v) = - \sum_{u \in N(v)} w(u, v) \cdot P(u) \cdot \log_2(P(u))$$

Where w(u, v) represents the weight of the edge between nodes u and v, and the summation is performed over all neighbors u of v.

Node entropy can be simplified as a measure of how unpredictable or varied a node's connections and interactions are within a network. Nodes with high entropy have a wide array of connections, possibly involving different topics or attributes. Conversely, nodes with low entropy have more consistent and limited connections

4 Study Framework and Investigative Methodology

4.1 Dataset

The dataset comprises a Twitter interaction network with approximately 1.6 million nodes and around 258 million edges. Each node represents a Twitter account, connected if one account retweeted the other. While the graph is naturally directed, we use the subgraph undirected version due to completeness. Among this graph, they consist of 1,721 nodes connected with 3,488 edges among them. The nodes labeled to indicate whether their tweets promote or discuss one of nine categories of conspiracy theories [4]. The dataset was originally created for the MediaEval 2022 evaluation challenge [11], and is based on the COVID Conspiracy (COCO) data set [5]. It uses the following categories of COVID-19 related conspiracy theories which are listed here with an abbreviated description of the narratives.

1. Suppressed Cures *COVID-19 cures exist, but are hidden by the nefarious actors, e.g. Big Pharma.*
2. Behavior Control *Powerful actors try to control the population either through fear or via hypothetical mind control technology.*
3. Anti Vaccination *COVID-19 vaccines serve a nefarious purpose and/or are intentionally harmful.*
4. Fake Virus *The Coronavirus is not real or the severity of the epidemic is vastly overblown.*
5. Intentional Pandemic *The pandemic was created by powerful nefarious actors.*
6. Harmful Radiation *The COVID-19 pandemic is connected to or caused by wireless technology, especially 5G* [4]
7. Depopulation *The COVID-19 pandemic is being used to intentionally reduce the global population or that of specific ethnic groups.*
8. New World Order *The COVID-19 pandemic is being used to establish some kind of new world order which is often described as socialist.*
9. Satanism *Secret nefarious elite satanic or pedophile societies are responsible for or benefit from COVID-19.*

In the COCO dataset, each thread was classified in each of the nine categories as *unrelated* (Class 1), *related* (Class 2), and *promoting* (Class 3). Here, related means that the tweet is discussing conspiracy content without believing or promoting it. An account is then labeled for each category by the maximum class among the tweets posted by that account. Thus, an account that has several Class 1 and one Class 3 tweet w.r.t.§ a category is labeled as *promoting* (Class 3) for that category. A tweet and, consequently, an account can be labeled as Class 3, i.e. spreading misinformation, in multiple categories.

All nodes have features derived from user profiles. Due to privacy concerns, the account description or e.g. BERT features thereof were not provided in the MediaEval2022 data [11], only the length of the description, i.e. the number of characters. In addition, a binary flag indicating verified accounts was provided. Note that this data was gathered before the changes to Twitter account verification introduced in 2023. Verification is rare, but typically constitutes a very powerful signal.

4.2   Experimentation and Result

Our experimental framework begins by ingesting graph data along with nodes characterized by six features, including verification status, description length, number of favorites, number of followers, and number of statuses. Subsequently, we employ Graph Neural Networks (GNNs) to structure the data in preparation for training. Specifically, we employ Graph Convolutional Networks (GCN) to generate node embeddings.

These node embeddings, in turn, serve as inputs for calculating node entropy within Class 2 and Class 3. Our experimental outcomes unveiled the presence of nodes with high entropy values, signifying their anomalous nature, within both of these classes. For instance, as demonstrated in Table 1, within Category 1, 2 out of 9 Class 2 nodes and 3 out of 29 Class 3 nodes exhibited elevated entropy values. Similarly, in Category 4, we observed that 22 out of 100 Class 2 nodes and 19 out of 144 Class 3 nodes displayed notably high entropy values. It's important to note that the determination of high entropy was based on a threshold set above the mean plus the standard deviation, which serves as a standard measure in statistical evaluation.

Our experiment proceeded by assessing four distinct centrality methods: Eigenvector, Degree, Closeness, and Betweenness centrality. To identify nodes with high centrality, we established a threshold, considering nodes with centrality values exceeding the respective mean centrality values in any of these measurements. In doing so, we identified nodes among the anomalous nodes based on entropy that exhibited high centrality, while others did not. As shown in Table 2, in Category 4, 19 out of 22 nodes in Class 2 and 13 out of 19 nodes in Class 3 met this criterion. Our analysis leads us to interpret that nodes with both high entropy and high centrality are indeed potential sources of concern, representing a significant risk in the dissemination of misinformation.

Furthermore, to ensure the robustness of our analysis, we extended our investigation to calculate the frequency with which nodes in Class 2 and Class 3, identified as misinformation spreaders, appeared across various topics when propagating false information. Our network data conveniently encompasses nine distinct categories, each representing a different topic. This allows us to assess the prevalence of these nodes acting as misinformation spreaders across different categories. This additional investigation enhances our evaluation of the potential risk posed by misinformation spreaders exhibiting both high entropy (anomalous behavior) and high centrality, while also accounting for their engagement in diverse topics.

Table 1. The count of misinformation spreader nodes in class 2 and class 3 across nine different categories, as well as the count of anomalous nodes characterized by high entropy in each category.

Category	Node as misinformation spreader		Node with high entropy (Anomalous)	
	Node class2	Node class3	Node class2	Node class3
Category1	9	29	2	3
Category2	88	66	17	9
Category3	109	94	23	10
Category4	100	144	22	19
Category5	71	186	14	26
Category6	37	25	6	3
Category7	31	106	8	11
Category8	18	112	3	12
Category9	35	53	5	8

Table 2. The count of anomalous nodes, referring to those with high entropy, and nodes with high entropy that also display high centrality.

Category	Node with high entropy (Anomalous)		Node with high entropy and high centrality	
	Node class2	Node class3	Node class2	Node class3
Category1	2	3	2	3
Category2	17	9	16	2
Category3	23	10	21	5
Category4	22	19	19	13
Category5	14	26	11	17
Category6	6	3	5	2
Category7	8	11	7	9
Category8	3	12	2	5
Category9	5	8	4	5

 This method allowed us to establish a comprehensive understanding of the danger posed by misinformation spreaders with high entropy, as those significantly deviating from the norm in terms of attribute values are likely to carry a higher risk compared to their counterparts exhibiting more typical characteristics. Furthermore, misinformation spreaders demonstrating the combination of high entropy, high centrality, and a broader range of multi-topics they engage with are deemed as extreme dangerous nodes in the context of disseminating false information. This approach enables a nuanced evaluation of the varying degrees of risk posed by different categories of misinformation spreaders in the network (Table 3).

Table 3. The count of nodes exhibiting both high entropy and involvement in multiple topics, as well as nodes characterized by high entropy, high centrality, and involvement in multiple topics.

Category	Node with high entropy and involved in multi-topics		Node with high entropy, high centrality and involved in multi-topics	
	Node class2	Node class3	Node class2	Node class3
Category1	2	1	2	1
Category2	15	7	14	1
Category3	20	10	18	5
Category4	11	7	8	3
Category5	7	12	4	8
Category6	3	1	2	0
Category7	6	6	5	4
Category8	2	7	2	5
Category9	1	5	1	3

4.3   Methodological Soundness and Justification

The primary objective of our methods in this paper is to identify and pinpoint specific nodes within the category of misinformation spreaders, particularly those with the highest potential for widespread dissemination of false information. We designate nodes as the most dangerous when they exhibit a combination of anomalous characteristics [1], including *high entropy*, *high centrality*, and *involvement in various topics* related to misinformation. This classification underscores their pivotal role as the most dangerous misinformation spreaders. Furthermore, our investigation delves into the intriguing question of whether nodes displaying anomalies in the form of *high entropy* and *high centrality*, or those with *high entropy* and participation in *multiple topics* as more divers topic involvement, continue to exert significant influence in the propagation of misinformation [18]. This inquiry broadens our comprehension of how different categories of anomalous nodes contribute to the dynamics of misinformation, recognizing that their threat may manifest in diverse and complex ways. The pursuit of answers to these questions is the driving force behind our research endeavors in this study (Fig. 1).

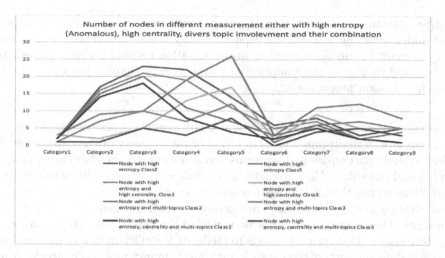

Fig. 1. Various node counts across nine distinct categories within the Twitter network, each associated with diverse metrics encompassing high entropy, high centrality, and presence in multiple topics

High Entropy and Appeared in Multi-topics Nodes: In intricate information networks, nodes displaying *high entropy and involvement in multiple topics* are influential actors. Their high entropy signifies active participation in diverse conversations, establishing them as information hubs. They engage across a broad spectrum of topics, becoming formidable actors in the misinformation landscape. Furthermore, they stand out for their involvement in various misinformation topics, disseminating false information across different narratives. Their ability to engage broadly and spread misinformation across multiple fronts makes them influential contributors to the spread of false information.

High Entropy and High Centrality Nodes: These nodes, characterized by *high entropy* and *high centrality*, play a pivotal role in information networks. Their high entropy indicates active involvement in numerous conversations, allowing them to gather and distribute a wealth of information. What distinguishes them is their high centrality, as they occupy central positions, bridging different network segments. These intermediaries facilitate information flow among various network communities. In the context of misinformation, they become potent agents of influence, rapidly disseminating false content and amplifying its reach. Addressing such nodes is crucial in combating misinformation's deceptive narratives and its impact on public opinion.

5   Discussion and Analysis

Given our ability to readily define nodes within the misinformation spreader class characterized by *high entropy, high centrality*, and *involvement in various misinformation topics*, our attention naturally shifts towards the exploration of two distinct definitions: Nodes with *high entropy and involvement in multiple topics* and nodes with *high entropy and high centrality*. These definitions are particularly relevant within the context of misinformation networks, where we seek to understand their respective implications and roles in shaping the dynamics of false information propagation.

Diversity of Engagement vs. Network Influence: Nodes with *high entropy and appeared in multi-topics* excel in terms of the diversity of their engagement. They actively participate in discussions across various topics, showcasing adaptability and versatility. Their strength lies in their ability to contribute to different narratives within the misinformation ecosystem. at the other hand, nodes with *high entropy and high centrality*, are primarily distinguished by their network influence. They occupy central positions within the network structure, acting as key connectors. Their primary role is to facilitate the efficient flow of information between different parts of the network, making them instrumental in accelerating the spread of misinformation.

Spread Across Topics vs. Network Bridging: Nodes with *high entropy* and *appeared in multi-topics* spread misinformation effectively across multiple topics. They are like disseminators who can adapt their messaging to suit various narratives, making them influential across a wide spectrum of subjects. while nodes with *high entropy* and *high centrality* act as bridges or hubs within the network. They don't necessarily engage in as many topics as the former category but play a crucial role in connecting different communities or clusters within the network. Their focus is on efficient information transfer rather than topic diversity.

Understanding these two categories of nodes, whether those with *high entropy and appeared in multi-topics* or *high entropy and high centrality*, provides critical insights into the mechanics of misinformation spread within networks. These nodes are not only actively engaged across a diverse range of topics but also have the ability to connect disparate parts of the network, making them key players in amplifying and disseminating false information. Tackling the challenges posed by these influential nodes requires a multidisciplinary approach that combines network analysis, information theory, and psychology to counteract their impact effectively. In summary, the key difference lies in their primary influence mechanisms: *high entropy and appeared in multi-topics* nodes excel at spreading misinformation across various topics due to their adaptability, while *high entropy and high centrality* nodes leverage their central positions to bridge gaps and efficiently disseminate misinformation within the network. Both categories are significant contributors to the spread of false information, but they operate in slightly different ways and have distinct strengths in the propagation of misinformation within the network.

6 Conclusion and Future Work

In today's rapidly evolving digital landscape, comprehending the complex dynamics of misinformation propagation is paramount. Our research addresses this challenge by uncovering the pivotal roles of specific nodes within misinformation networks. Leveraging node embeddings generated by Graph Neural Networks (GNNs) and guided by node entropy, our approach allows us to identify key nodes in the dissemination of misinformation.

In our investigation, our primary focus has been on identifying the most harmful nodes within the misinformation spreader category, those with the greatest impact in propagating false information. To this end, we can classify them as the nodes with *high entropy, high centrality* and *appeared in multi-topics*. Furthermore, our research has provided an additional unique perspective by examining two distinct types of nodes: those characterized by *high entropy and involvement in multiple topics* and those distinguished by *high entropy and high centrality*. Both categories, in their unique ways, significantly contribute to the spread of false information. Our findings have profound implications for mitigating and fighting against misinformation. By recognizing the distinct mechanisms through which these nodes operate, we can tailor our strategies to counteract their influence effectively. We classify nodes with *high entropy, high centrality, and involvement in multiple topics* as the most extreme and dangerous misinformation spreaders. Yet, nodes with *high entropy and involvement in multiple topics* or *high entropy and high centrality* remain dangerous actors in the propagation of false information in different way. In future work, we aim to scale our approach to larger datasets, diving deeper into misinformation dynamics. We also plan to incorporate a broader range of features from diverse resources.

Acknowledgment. This work is part of the *Enabling Graph Neural Networks at Exascale* (EGNE) Project and was funded by the Norwegian Research Council under contracts 303404 and has benefited from the Experimental Infrastructure for Exploration of Exascale Computing(eX3), which is financially supported by the Research Council of Norway under contract 270053

References

1. Akoglu, L., Tong, H., Koutra, D.: Graph based anomaly detection and description: a survey. Data Min. Knowl. Disc. **29**, 626–688 (2015)
2. Guo, C., Yang, L., Chen, X., Chen, D., Gao, H., Ma, J.: Influential nodes identification in complex networks via information entropy. Entropy **22**(2), 242 (2020)
3. Hamilton, W.L., et al.: Inductive representation learning on large graphs. In: Advances in Neural Information Processing Systems (NeurIPS) (2017)
4. Langguth, J., Filkuková, P., Brenner, S., Schroeder, D.T., Pogorelov, K.: Covid-19 and 5g conspiracy theories: long term observation of a digital wildfire. Int. J. Data Sci. Anal. **15**(3), 329–346 (2023)
5. Langguth, J., Schroeder, D.T., Filkuková, P., Brenner, S., Phillips, J., Pogorelov, K.: Coco: an annotated twitter dataset of covid-19 conspiracy theories. J. Comput. Social Sci. 1–42 (2023)

6. Lei, M., Cheong, K.H.: Node influence ranking in complex networks: a local structure entropy approach. Chaos, Solitons Fractals **160**, 112136 (2022)

7. Maulana, A., Atzmueller, M.: Centrality-based anomaly detection on multi-layer networks using many-objective optimization. In: 2020 7th International Conference on Control, Decision and Information Technologies (CoDIT), vol. 1, pp. 633–638, IEEE (2020)

8. Maulana, A., Atzmueller, M.: Many-objective optimization for anomaly detection on multi-layer complex interaction networks. Appl. Sci. **11**(9), 4005 (2021)

9. Maulana, A., Kefalas, M., Emmerich, M.T.: Immunization of networks using genetic algorithms and multiobjective metaheuristics. In: 2017 IEEE Symposium Series on Computational Intelligence (SSCI), pp. 1–8, IEEE (2017)

10. Pogorelov, K., Schroeder, D.T., Brenner, S., Langguth, J.: Fakenews: corona virus and conspiracies multimedia analysis task at mediaeval 2021. In: Multimedia Benchmark Workshop, vol. 67 (2021)

11. Pogorelov, K., Schroeder, D.T., Brenner, S., Maulana, A., Langguth, J.: Combining tweets and connections graph for fakenews detection at mediaeval 2022. In: Multimedia Benchmark Workshop (2022)

12. Pogorelov, K., Schroeder, D.T., Filkuková, P., Brenner, S., Langguth, J.: Wico text: a labeled dataset of conspiracy theory and 5g-corona misinformation tweets. In: Proceedings of the 2021 Workshop on Open Challenges in Online Social Networks, pp. 21–25 (2021)

13. Qiao, T., Shan, W., Zhou, C.: How to identify the most powerful node in complex networks? a novel entropy centrality approach. Entropy **19**(11), 614 (2017)

14. Scarselli, F., Gori, M., Tsoi, A.C., Hagenbuchner, M., Monfardini, G.: The graph neural network model. IEEE Trans. Neural Netw. **20**(1), 61–80 (2008)

15. Shannon, C.E.: A mathematical theory of communication. Bell Syst. Techn. J. **27**(3), 379–423 (1948)

16. Shu, K., Sliva, A., Wang, S., Tang, J., Liu, H.: Fake news detection on social media: a data mining perspective. ACM SIGKDD Explor. Newsl. **19**(1), 22–36 (2017)

17. Velickovic, P., et al.: Graph convolutional networks: a comprehensive review. IEEE Trans. Neural Netw. Learn. Syst. **34**(11), 2414–2440 (2023)

18. Wohn, D.Y., Min, S.J., Hoewe, J., Bowe, B.J.: The impact of online network diversity on familiarity and engagement with social issues news on facebook. J. Social Media Soc. **12**(1), 286–308 (2023)

19. Yu, Y., Zhou, B., Chen, L., Gao, T., Liu, J.: Identifying important nodes in complex networks based on node propagation entropy. Entropy **24**(2), 275 (2022)

20. Zareie, A., Sheikhahmadi, A., Fatemi, A.: Influential nodes ranking in complex networks: an entropy-based approach. Chaos, Solitons Fractals **104**, 485–494 (2017)

21. Zhang, Q., Li, M., Deng, Y.: Measure the structure similarity of nodes in complex networks based on relative entropy. Phys. A Stat. Mech. Appl. **491**, 749–763 (2018)

22. Zhang, X., Ghorbani, A.A.: An overview of online fake news: characterization, detection, and discussion. Inf. Process. Manag. **57**, 102025 (2020)

23. Zhou, J., et al.: Graph neural networks: a review of methods and applications. AI Open **1**, 57–81 (2020)

Air Transportation Network Backbone Extraction: A Comparative Analysis of Structural Filtering Techniques

Ali Yassin[1]($\boxtimes$), Hocine Cherifi[2], Hamida Seba[3], and Olivier Togni[1]

[1] Laboratoire d'Informatique de Bourgogne - Univ. Bourgogne - Franche-Comté, Dijon, France
aliyassin4@hotmail.com
[2] ICB UMR 6303 CNRS - Univ. Bourgogne - Franche-Comté, Dijon, France
[3] Univ Lyon, UCBL, CNRS, INSA Lyon, LIRIS, UMR5205, 69622 Villeurbanne, France

Abstract. In the age of advanced data collection tools, large-scale network analysis presents significant visualization and data processing challenges. Backbone-extracting techniques have emerged as crucial tools to tackle this challenge. They aim to reduce network size while preserving essential characteristics. One can distinguish two primary approaches: structural methods, which prioritize nodes and edges based on their topological properties, and statistical methods, which focus on their statistical relevance within the network data. This study investigates eight popular structural methods in an air transportation case study. Correlation analysis reveals that shortest path-based methods yield similar backbones, while Doubly Stochastic and H-backbone methods do not correlate with their alternatives. Interestingly, H-backbone retains high-weight edges, and High Salience Skeleton and Doubly Stochastic backbones capture diverse weight scales. We evaluate the original network information loss using the backbone's edge, node, and weight fraction. Doubly Stochastic and H-backbone methods keep substantially more edges compared to others. H-backbone, High Salience Skeleton, and Doubly Stochastic uncovered backbones fail to retain all nodes. Connectivity and transitivity comparisons indicate Primary Linkage Analysis, High Salience Skeleton methods disrupt the connectivity, and the Doubly Stochastic preserves the transitivity. This study sheds light on the strengths and weaknesses of these techniques, facilitating their application in real-world scenarios and inspiring future research directions in network analysis.

Keywords: Complex Networks · Backbone Extraction · Filtering Techniques · Network Compression · Graph Summarization · Sparsification

1 Introduction

In recent decades, networks have emerged as valuable tools for analyzing complex systems [1]. They provide a way to portray complex systems by using nodes to

M. H. Hà et al. (Eds.): CSoNet 2023, LNCS 14479, pp. 337–348, 2024.
https://doi.org/10.1007/978-981-97-0669-3_31

represent elements and edges to depict binary interactions between them. Common analyses involve detecting communities [2], identifying influential nodes [3], and exploring network formation [4]. Yet, in numerous systems, one can quantify the strength of these interactions. In such cases, we refer to these networks as weighted networks.

Processing and visualization of large-scale networks present challenges due to their complexity. Multiple backbone extraction methods have been developed to address this issue. Their goal is to reduce the network's size while retaining its essential features. One can classify backbone extraction methods into two groups: structural [5–7] and statistical [8] approaches. Structural techniques involve filtering edges and nodes based on the relevance of specific topological properties. In contrast, statistical methods evaluate the significance of edges using statistical tests and remove the least significant ones.

A prior study [9] compares six backbone extraction methods in the Southeast Asian intercity air transport network. It includes five structural methods (global weight thresholding, k-core decomposition, minimum spanning tree, primary linkage analysis, multiple linkage analysis) and a statistical technique (disparity filter). Their study evaluates the geographical and topological characteristics of the extracted backbones. It highlighted the suitability of each method for various transport research applications. For instance, the authors demonstrate the advantage of k-core decomposition for analyzing well-connected cores in multiplex networks. Additionally, primary linkage analysis proved effective for functional/nodal regions exploration and revealing hub-and-spoke structures.

In [10], we report a comparative analysis of the US-weighted air transportation network's seven statistical backbone extraction techniques. The methods under investigation are Disparity Filter, Polya Urn Filter, Marginal Likelihood Filter (MLF), Noise Corrected Filter, Enhanced Configuration Model (ECM) Filter, Global Statistical Significance (GLOSS) Filter, and Locally Adaptive Network Sparsification (LANS) Filter. The comparison encompasses elements such as the number of components, sizes, fractions of airport and edge types, and weights retained by each method. The findings showcase that the ECM Filter primarily revealed the infrastructure connecting regional spoke airports. In contrast, alternative filters like Disparity, Polya Urn, Marginal Likelihood, Noise Corrected, GLOSS, and LANS highlight the hub-and-spoke network structure typical of US airline organizations.

Another study [11] concerns a comparison of seven statistical backbone filtering methods within the World Air Transportation network. The methods include Disparity Filter, Polya Urn Filter, MLF, Noise Corrected Filter, ECM Filter, GLOSS Filter, and LANS Filter. The findings indicate that the Marginal Likelihood Filter, Disparity Filter, and LANS Filter assign greater significance to high-weight edges. Conversely, the other techniques emphasize both small and high-weight edges. The study demonstrates that filters grounded in a binomial distribution, such as Marginal Likelihood and Noise Corrected Filter, retain a substantial proportion of links and nodes. Apart from the ECM Filter, other filters demonstrate a more aggressive approach to edge removal for typical significance levels ($\alpha \leq 0.05$).

Over the past few decades, significant interest has been in analyzing transportation and urban networks [12,13]. Network backbone extraction techniques have emerged as valuable tools for faster analysis and more coherent visualization of these networks. These techniques aid in swiftly identifying critical spatial and topological structures within the network. Previous studies have compared both statistical and structural methods. However, it's important to note that statistical methods typically require a significance level for backbone extraction, while many structural methods lack tunability. This discrepancy presents a challenge in comprehensively comparing different method types. Consequently, our focus is solely on comparing non-tunable structural methods within the weighted air transportation network context.

Our approach involves several key steps. First, we extract the network backbones using the Netbone package [14]. We then assess the backbones' similarity by computing the Jaccard index of the various pair of extracted backbones. Next, we investigate the relationship between the presence of an edge in the backbone and its associated weight. Additionally, we quantify the information loss from filtering by comparing the basic topological properties of the extracted backbones, including edge, node, and weight fractions. Finally, we examine backbone connectivity and transitivity by evaluating the reachability, number of components, largest connected component size, and transitivity.

2   Structural Backbone Extraction Methods

Structural backbone methods operate on the network's topology to extract a backbone with specific topological properties. One can divide them into two categories. The first category includes techniques for extracting a single substructure from the network. They cannot be adjusted and typically result in a single backbone. The second category assigns scores to nodes or edges based on topological features. These methods can be tuned by setting a threshold β or selecting the top fraction of scores.

- **Maximum Spanning Tree Filter:** It extracts a subgraph that includes all the nodes connected without forming cycles with the maximum total edge weight.
- **h-Backbone Filter** [15]: It is inspired by the h-index and edge betweenness. First, using the edge weights, it extracts the h-strength network: h is the largest natural number such that there are h links, each with a weight at least equal to h. Then it extracts the h-bridge network similarly. A bridge of an edge is the edge betweenness divided by the number of all nodes. Finally, the h-backbone merges the two networks.
- **Metric and Ultrametric distance backbone filters** [6]: Both methods extract a subgraph consisting of the shortest paths in the network. Still, they diverge in their definitions of the shortest path length. Specifically, the Metric filter defines the shortest path length as the sum of the edge distances. In contrast, the Ultrametric filter defines it as the maximum distance among all edges in the path.

- **Planar Maximally Filtered Graph** [16]: It simply reconstructs the graph by adding edges with the highest weight iteratively as long as the resulting graph is still planar.
- **Primary Linkage Analysis** [17]: This method preserves the edge with the largest weight for each node.
- **Doubly Stochastic Filter** [18]: It transforms the network's adjacency matrix into a doubly stochastic matrix by iteratively normalizing the row and column values using their respective sums. Next, one sorts the edges in descending order based on their normalized weight. One adds the edges to the backbone sequentially until it includes all nodes in the original network as a single connected component. It is not always possible to transform the matrix into a doubly-stochastic one.
- **High Salience Skeleton Filter** [5]: It is based on the concept of edge salience. First, one constructs a shortest path tree for each node by merging all the shortest paths from that node to every other node in the network. Then the edge salience is computed as the proportion of shortest-path trees where the edge is present. The authors observed that edge salience follows a bimodal distribution near the boundaries 0 and 1. Consequently, they retain only the edges with salience near 1, eliminating the need to select an arbitrary threshold.

3 Data, Evaluation Measures, and Methods

In this section, we introduce the dataset under examination, outline the measures employed, and describe the methodology used for the comparative analysis.

3.1 Data

In the US Air Transportation Network [8], nodes represent airports in the continental US, and edges represent the routes between these airports. Edge weights correspond to the number of passengers for the year 2006. Table 1 lists the main topological properties of the network.

Table 1. The Topological features of the US Air Transportation network. N is the number of nodes. E is the number of edges. $< k >$ is the average degree. ρ is the density.

Network	N	E	$< k >$	ρ
US Air Transportation	380	9678	50.9	0.134

3.2   Evaluation Measures

This subsection defines the evaluation measures and the tools used in the experiments.

- **Node Fraction:** The node fraction in the backbone represents the proportion of nodes preserved from the original network.
- **Edge Fraction:** The edge fraction in the backbone represents the proportion of edges preserved from the original network.
- **Weigh Fraction:** The weight fraction in the backbone represents the proportion of edge weights preserved from the total weights of the original network.
- **Transitivity:** The transitivity is the ratio between the observed number of closed triplets and the maximum possible number of closed triplets in the network.
- **Jaccard score:** The Jaccard score [19] quantifies the similarity between two sets, A and B, by computing the ratio between the intersection's cardinality and the union's cardinality. This reads:

$$J = \frac{|A \cap B|}{|A \cup B|} \tag{1}$$

  The score ranges between 0 and 1. A value $J = 1$ indicates that A and B are identical, while a value $J = 0$ denotes that the sets have no overlap.
- **Reachability:** The Reachability [20] quantifies the connectivity between any pair of nodes in a network. It is defined as the fraction of node pairs that can communicate with each other. This reads:

$$R = \frac{1}{n(n-1)} \sum_{i \neq j \in G} R_{ij}. \tag{2}$$

  with n is the number of nodes and $R_{ij} = 1$ if path exists between node i and j and $R_{ij} = 0$ otherwise. The Reachability values are in the $[0,1]$ range. If any pair of nodes can communicate in a network, the reachability R becomes 1. If $R = 0$ it means all nodes are isolated from each other.

3.3   Methods

We conduct a series of four experiments to assess the performance of the backbone extraction techniques.

In the initial experiment, we employ the netbone package [14] to apply the backbone extraction methods. Subsequently, we employ the Jaccard Score to compare the sets of edges extracted from the extracted backbones. The aim is to gauge the level of similarity among these extracted backbones.

In the second experiment, we apply the backbone extraction methods and designate edges as "True" if included in the backbone, and "False" otherwise. We then create a pair plot, plotting these values against the corresponding edge weights. This step allows us to evaluate whether the techniques demonstrate bias against lower weights. An equitable treatment of small and large weights would ensure the preservation of hierarchies across all weight scales, yielding a more comprehensive representation of the network.

The third experiment compares basic topological properties, encompassing the network's fractions of edges, nodes, and weights. This aims to assess the extent of information loss following the filtering process.

Finally, in the fourth experiment, we investigate network connectivity in the backbones. It involves analyzing reachability, the number of connected components, and the size of the largest connected component. Additionally, we compare their transitivity. The ultimate goal is identifying which methods disrupt network connectivity and cycles.

4 Experimental Results

4.1 Investigating the Backbones Similarity

Most backbone extraction techniques under evaluation are not adjustable, leading to potential variations in the backbones size. Consequently, we calculate the Jaccard score between pairs of backbone edges to emphasize the differences between these methods. The Jaccard score is particularly suited for assessing similarity in this context, as it focuses on the presence or absence of edges within the backbones. Its score ranges between 0 and 1, quantifying the similarity between two sets of edges. A higher score indicates greater similarity between the backbones. Figure 1 is a heatmap of Jaccard scores, illustrating the relationships between the various pairs of backbones. One can observe that the Maximum Spanning Tree (MSP) and Ultrametric (UMB) extract the same backbones. They share over 99% of their edges with the Primary Link Analysis (PLAM) backbone. Moreover, the three previous methods share approximately 82% of their edges with the High Salience Skeleton (HSS) backbone.

In contrast, the H-backbone and Doubly Stochastic backbones manifest distinct patterns. The former shares a maximum of 23% of its edges with the other methods, whereas the latter's similarity is even lower, around 8%. Interestingly, these two distinctive backbones share 28% of their edges. The remaining pairs of backbones exhibit varying fractions of shared edges, spanning from 33% to 56%

4.2 Investigating the Relation Between Backbone Edges and Weights

The primary backbone extraction method selects all the edges with a weight above a given global threshold. It cannot preserve the original network's weight distribution as it truncates edge weights. Here, we examine the ability of the various techniques to keep the range of weights within the extracted backbones to assess the efficacy of different backbone extraction methodologies. Figure 2 illustrates pair plots corresponding to the various backbone extraction method.

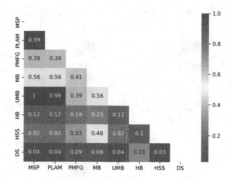

Fig. 1. A heatmap of the Jaccard scores computed between backbone couples. The MSP is the Maximum Spanning Tree. The PLAM is the Primary Linkage Analysis. The PMFG is the Planar Maximally Filtered Graph. The MB and UMB are the Metric and Ultrametric Backbone Methods. The HB is the H-backbone method. The HSS is the High Salience Skeleton. Finally, the DS is the Doubly Stochastic Method.

The horizontal axis represents edge labels, marked as "True" if the edge is part of the backbone and "False" otherwise. Meanwhile, the vertical axis represents the edge weights in a logarithmic scale. A distinct cut-off is evident in the H-backbone. Most edges within the H-backbone exhibit substantial weights, with only a couple displaying low values. Conversely, the Doubly Stochastic and Planar Maximally Filtered backbones show a well-distributed range of edge weights. Both backbones encompass weights spanning various scales, yet the former is more densely populated due to having a greater number of edges. The other backbones fall between these two extremes. The plots illustrate a concentration at the upper end where higher-weight scales are prominent, gradually fading as we move toward lower-weight.

4.3 Comparing Backbones Basic Properties

To assess how filtering affects the network's topology, we compare the basic topological properties of the extracted backbones with the original network's properties.

The edge fraction quantifies the ratio of remaining connections in the backbone compared to the original network, while the node fraction measures the proportion of non-isolated nodes. Meanwhile, the edge weight fraction measures the remaining strength of links. Table 2 reports the results. The Doubly Stochastic and H-backbones conserve 26% and 64% of the original network's edges, respectively. In contrast, the other methods keep less than 10%. However, they did not preserve the complete fraction of nodes within the backbone. Specifically, the H-backbone, High Salience Skeleton, and Doubly Stochastic backbones encompass only around 80% to 93% of the original nodes. In contrast, the other methods

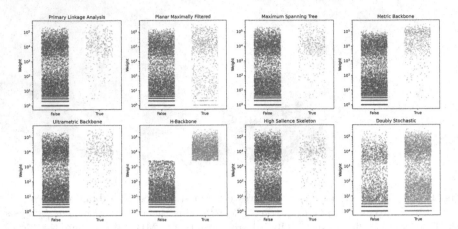

Fig. 2. The pair plots for each backbone extraction method. The horizontal axis represents edge labels, marked as "True" if the edge is part of the backbone and "False" otherwise. Meanwhile, the vertical axis represents the edge weights in a logarithmic scale.

retain all the nodes. The H-backbone retains 99% of the edge weights, followed by the Doubly Stochastic backbone with a score of 83%, and then the Metric backbone at 50%. In contrast, the other methods have an edge weights fraction ranging from 10% to 36%.

Table 2. The fraction of nodes, edges, and weights in the extracted backbones.

Backbone	Node Fraction	Edge Fraction	Weight Fraction
Maximum Spanning Tree	1.00	0.04	0.19
Primary Linkage Analysis	1.00	0.04	0.18
Planar Maximally Filtered	1.00	0.10	0.36
Metric Backbone	1.00	0.07	0.50
Ultrametric Backbone	1.00	0.04	0.19
H-Backbone	0.81	0.26	0.99
High Salience Skeleton	0.92	0.03	0.10
Doubly Stochastic	0.93	0.64	0.83

4.4   Comparing Backbones Connectivity and Transitivity

An ideal filtering technique maintains network connectivity. To evaluate this ability of the filtering techniques, we calculate metrics such as reachability, the number of connected components, and the size of the largest connected component. Furthermore, we examine the backbones transitivity, as this characteristic contributes to the emergence of network clusters or communities. Table 3 reports the results. We can distinguish two backbone categories. The first includes the Doubly Stochastic, Primary Linkage Analysis, and High Salience Skeleton. The second category contains all the other backbone extraction methods. Backbones in the second category are characterized by a reachability of 1. They have a unique component that retains all the nodes of the original network. In contrast, the backbones in the first category have multiple components and reachability below one. Indeed, reachability ranges from 0.99 to 0.1. It's important to note that a reachability of 1 indicates that any pair of nodes can communicate, while a reachability of 0 signifies complete isolation between nodes. With two components, a reachability of 0.99 and an LCC of 99%, the Doubly Stochastic is not far from the backbones of the second category. The Primary Linkage Analysis follows it with five components, a reachability of 0.38, and an LCC of 49%. The High Salience Skeleton is less effective with its 25 components, reachability of 0.10, and the smallest LCC. Transitivity decreases across all backbones. The Doubly Stochastic backbone demonstrates the lowest deviation from the original network, with a transitivity value 0.51. The Maximum Spanning Tree, Primary Linkage Analysis, Ultrametric, and High Salience Skeleton backbones are not transitive. For other backbones, the transitivity values range from 0.1 to 0.36. These findings provide valuable insights into the impact of different backbone extraction methods on network connectivity and transitivity.

Table 3. The reachability, number of connected components (# CC), size of the largest connected component (LCC Size), and the transitivity of the extracted backbones.

	Reachability	# CC	LCC Size	Transitivity
Original Network	1.00	1	1.00	0.55
Maximum Spanning Tree	1.00	1	1.00	0.00
Primary Linkage Analysis	0.38	5	0.49	0.00
Planar Maximally Filtered	1.00	1	1.00	0.12
Metric Backbone	1.00	1	1.00	0.10
Ultrametric Backbone	1.00	1	1.00	0.00
H-Backbone	1.00	1	1.00	0.36
High Salience Skeleton	0.10	25	0.21	0.00
Doubly Stochastic	0.99	2	0.99	0.51

5 Discussion

This investigation compares eight distinct structural backbone extraction methods using the Air Transportation network. First, we investigate the similarity of these backbones using the Jaccard Score. The results show that the H-backbone and Doubly Stochastic backbones are pretty different from the others. In contrast, the High Salience Skeleton, Maximum Spanning Tree, Metric, and Ultrametric backbones share at least 80% of their edges. Indeed, they all rely on the shortest paths in the network.

Second, we explore the relationship between the backbone's edge presence and weight. The diversity of weight scales is a desirable attribute in a backbone extraction technique, as it contributes to accurately representing the original network. The Doubly Stochastic and Planar Maximally Filtered methods retain the most diverse scales of weights. Conversely, the H-backbone predominantly includes high-scale weights.

Third, we evaluate the basic topological properties of the extracted backbones, encompassing the fractions of preserved edges, nodes, and weights. The Doubly Stochastic and H-backbone techniques are the most conservative filtering techniques concerning edges. Despite this, they retain a substantial fraction of edge weights. However, the H-backbone, Doubly Stochastic, and High Salience Skeleton backbones experience node loss.

Lastly, we investigate the connectivity and transitivity of the extracted backbones. Noteworthy is the Doubly Stochastic backbone's close alignment with the original network regarding transitivity. In contrast, the Maximum Spanning Tree, Primary Linkage Analysis, High Salience Skeleton, and Ultrametric backbones disrupt all cycles within their structures. Summarizing these discoveries, Table 4 synthesizes the key outcomes of this study.

Table 4. Summary of the properties of the backbone extraction methods.

Filtering Technique	Maintains Nodes	Maintains Connectivity	Breaks all Cycles	Other
Maximum Spanning Tree	Yes	Yes	Yes	Filters many edges
Primary Linkage Analysis	Yes	Not always	Yes	Filters many edges
Planar Maximally Filtered	Yes	Yes	No	Filters many edges
Metric Backbone	Yes	Yes	No	Filters many edges
Ultrametric Backbone	Yes	Yes	Yes	Filters many edges
H-Backbone	No	Yes	No	Maintains higher-scale weights
High Salience Skeleton	Not always	Not always	Yes	Maintains all scales of weights and Filers many edges
Doubly Stochastic	Not always	Yes	No	Maintains all scales of weights and the Transitivity

6 Conclusion

This exploration of network backbone extraction techniques unravels multiple insights into their behaviors. The backbone similarity analysis shows that the Maximum Spanning Tree (MSP) and Ultrametric (UMB) techniques extract identical backbones. Furthermore, it resembles the Primary Link Analysis (PLAM) and the High Salience Skeleton (HSS) backbones. In contrast, the H-backbone and Doubly Stochastic backbones manifest unique patterns with significantly lower edge overlap.

The Relationship analysis between Backbone Edges and Weights unveils the impact of these techniques on edge weight distribution. The H-backbone favors high-weight edges, whereas the Doubly Stochastic and Planar Maximally Filtered backbones displayed well-distributed weight ranges. This variation in weight handling underscores the importance of considering the method's impact on weight-related analyses.

Comparing Backbones' Basic Properties highlights variations in edge, node, and edge weight fractions across different techniques. For instance, the Doubly Stochastic High Salience Skeleton and H-backbones retain a substantial fraction of nodes with a diverse fraction of weights and links. In contrast, the others keep all the nodes with a comparable magnitude of edges. Understanding these trade-offs is crucial for preserving the structural integrity of networks during analysis.

Comparing Backbones' Connectivity and Transitivity demonstrates the diverse effects of backbone extraction methods on network connectivity and transitivity. Some techniques effectively maintained network connectivity, while others produced multi-component backbones. These observations underscore the importance of method selection to preserve specific network properties.

In conclusion, backbone extraction techniques are very sensitive to the networks characteristics. By leveraging the insights provided by our investigation, analysts can navigate the diverse landscape of network backbone extraction methods with greater precision and confidence. Future investigations will extend this preliminary study using multiple real-world networks to validate these findings.

Acknowledgment. This material is based upon work supported by the Agence Nationale de Recherche under grant ANR-20-CE23-0002.

References

1. Vespignani, A.: Twenty years of network science (2018)
2. Cherifi, H., Palla, G., Szymanski, B.K., Lu, X.: On community structure in complex networks: challenges and opportunities. Appl. Netw. Sci. **4**(1), 1–35 (2019)
3. Chakraborty, D., Singh, A., Cherifi, H.: Immunization strategies based on the overlapping nodes in networks with community structure. In: Nguyen, H., Snasel, V. (eds.) International Conference on Computational Social Networks, vol. 9795, pp. 62–73. Springer, Cham (2016). https://doi.org/10.1007/978-3-319-42345-6_6
4. Orman, G.K., Labatut, V., Cherifi, H.: Towards realistic artificial benchmark for community detection algorithms evaluation. arXiv preprint arXiv:1308.0577 (2013)
5. Grady, D., Thiemann, C., Brockmann, D.: Robust classification of salient links in complex networks. Nat. Commun. **3**(1), 864 (2012)
6. Simas, T., Correia, R.B., Rocha, L.M.: The distance backbone of complex networks. J. Complex Netw. **9**(6), cnab021 (2021)
7. Rajeh, S., Savonnet, E.L., Cherifi, H.: Modularity-based backbone extraction in weighted complex networks (2022)
8. Serrano, M.A., Boguna, M., Vespignani, A.: Extracting the multiscale backbone of complex weighted networks. Proc. Natl. Acad. Sci. **106**, 6483–6488 (2009)
9. Dai, L., Derudder, B., Liu, X.: Transport network backbone extraction: a comparison of techniques. J. Transp. Geogr. **69**, 271–281 (2018)

10. Yassin, A., Cherifi, H., Seba, H., Togni, O.: Exploring statistical backbone filtering techniques in the air transportation network. In: 2022 IEEE Workshop on Complexity in Engineering (COMPENG), Florence, Italy, pp. 1–8. IEEE (2022)
11. Yassin, A., Cherifi, H., Seba, H., Togni, O.: Air transport network: a comparison of statistical backbone filtering techniques. In: Cherifi, H., Mantegna, R.N., Rocha, L.M., Cherifi, C., Micciche, S. (eds.) Complex Networks and Their Applications XI, vol. 1078, pp. 551–564. Springer, Cham (2023). https://doi.org/10.1007/978-3-031-21131-7_43
12. Ducruet, C., Rozenblat, C., Zaidi, F.: Ports in multi-level maritime networks: evidence from the atlantic (1996–2006). J. Transp. Geogr. **18**, 508–518 (2010)
13. Liu, X., Derudder, B., Kang, W.: Measuring polycentric urban development in China: an intercity transportation network perspective. Reg. Stud. **50**, 03 (2015)
14. Yassin, A., Haidar, A., Cherifi, H., Seba, H., Togni, O.: An evaluation tool for backbone extraction techniques in weighted complex networks. Preprint (2023)
15. Zhang, R.J., Stanley, H.E., Ye, F.Y.: Extracting h-backbone as a core structure in weighted networks. Sci. Rep. **8**(1), 1–7 (2018)
16. Tumminello, M., Aste, T., Di Matteo, T., Mantegna, R.N.: A tool for filtering information in complex systems. Proc. Natl. Acad. Sci. **102**(30), 10421–10426 (2005)
17. Nystuen, J., Dacey, M.: A graph theory interpretation of nodal regions. In: Papers of the Regional Science Association, vol. 7, p. 01 (2005)
18. Slater, P.B.: A two-stage algorithm for extracting the multiscale backbone of complex weighted networks. Proc. Natl. Acad. Sci. **106**(26), E66–E66 (2009)
19. Jaccard, P.: The distribution of the flora in the alpine zone. 1. New Phytologist **11**(2), 37–50 (1912)
20. Sato, Y., Ata, S., Oka, I.: A strategic approach for re-organization of internet topology for improving both efficiency and attack tolerance, pp. 331–338 (2008)

Multiplex Network Approach for Modeling the Spread of African Swine Fever in Poland

Andrzej Jarynowski[1,2,4(✉)], Łukasz Czekaj[2], Alexander Semenov[3],
and Vitaly Belik[4]

[1] Interdisciplinary Research Institute, Wroclaw, Poland
ajarynowski@gmail.com
[2] Aidmed, Gdańsk, Poland
lczekaj@aimded.ai
[3] Herbert Wertheim School of Engineering, University of Florida,
Gainesville, FL, USA
asemenov@ufl.edu
[4] System Modeling Group, Institute of Veterinary Epidemiology and Biostatistics,
Freie Universität Berlin, Berlin, Germany
vitaly.belik@fu-berlin.de

Abstract. African swine fever (ASF) is a viral infection which causes acute disease in *Sus scrofa* - domestic pigs and wild boar. Although the virus does not cause disease in humans, the impact it has on the economy, especially via trade and farming disturbance, is substantial. We analyze 3487 ASF notifications of wild boars and pigs in Poland (infection events registered to World Animal Health Organization) from February 2014 to April 2019 comprising event time, longitude, latitude and administrative unit: county (poviat). We propose a spatial modeling approach incorporating phenomenological analysis of multiplex transmission networks due to: 1) domestic pig abundance, 2) disease vectors (wild boar) abundance, 3) human mobility related to disease propagation. We used a pseudo gravity model to simulate the future epidemic projection and calculated the most probable infection paths for all counties (poviats) as well as estimated the most likely disease arrival times with or without countermeasures such as border fencing and animals corridors blocking on the A1 motorway. According to our model, the ASF spread in Poland had been continuing and investigated jump in Autumn 2019 to wschowski poviat (Western Poland) 320 km from the closest previously affected area manifests its complex behavior. The proposed complex network approach promises to be useful for practitioners, farmers and veterinarians, helping them to choose the optimal mitigation strategies.

1 Introduction

African swine fever (ASF) "is probably the most serious animal disease the world has had for a long time, if not ever" according to Dirk Pfeifer, a renown veterinary epidemiologist [28]. The simultaneous human COVID-19 pandemic might

M. H. Hà et al. (Eds.): CSoNet 2023, LNCS 14479, pp. 349–360, 2024.
https://doi.org/10.1007/978-981-97-0669-3_32

only worsen the ASF situation, due to the attention distraction. Recent rapid propagation of ASF from East to West of Europe encouraged us to prepare risk assessment for Poland. We develop a predictive model for ASF spread based on empirical geographical data incorporating multiplex network of regions: human populations (vectors mobility), forests (wild boar density), swines (as theoretical organizational structure of the pork production supply chain). Results of the study could serve as a decision support system and as a tool for epidemiologists and veterinarians in charge [27]. We used available outbreak data from WOAH (World Animal Health Organization)[1] (Fig. 2) and regional information from Statistics Poland (GUS)[2] (Fig. 3). ASF is a highly contiguous viral infection. The pathogen was imported from Africa to Georgia in 2007 and spread from there via Russia, the Baltic States, Ukraine, Belarus to Poland, Romania, the Czech Republic, and Germany. The disease continues to spread in the wild boar and pigs populations of affected regions in Eastern Europe. ASF causes serious illness and is almost always fatal. However, there is no danger of infection for humans. Its further spread in Western Europe would have severe consequences for the health of wild boar and domestic pigs and strongly affect pork production industry. Although the understanding of its spread and transmission dynamics increased with time significantly, an integrative framework for Poland is still missing. There are several within or between pig farms models [16], ecological models for wild boars habitats [31,33] and risk assessment for pig and pork meat trade [24,36] even for Poland. However, one essential factor – human mobility [5] – was not integrated in these models. Quantitative statistical studies to explain the ASF spread for affected countries are rare (see e.g. Ref. [10] for Estonia). Moreover, predictive modeling tools are needed to address challenging objectives in ASF control [12] as it was proved during COVID-19 pandemic.

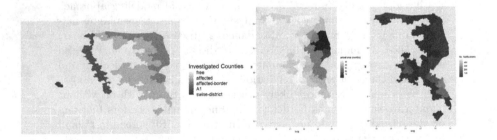

Fig. 1. Map of Poland with analyzed counties/poviats (left) and geographical distribution of notifications with arrival time (right). Situation up to April 2019 (59 months of epizootic).

Drastic containment strategies like building fences between countries, blocking animal corridors or obligatory sanitary inspections on the border have been suggested, but their possible long-term impact is unknown [37]. Moreover socio-cultural context of conflicting agencies of farmers, ecologists, hunters as well as

---

[1] https://www.oie.int/wahis_2/public/wahid.php/Diseaseinformation/.
[2] https://bdl.stat.gov.pl/BDL/start.

public and veterinary administration has a very complex landscape in Poland [20,29]. In this paper, alongside with statistical analysis of the ASF spread in Poland we want to assess theoretically a barrier effect of building a fence on the part of the Polish EU-border and blocking animals corridors on the A1 motorway by comparison of the disease arrival times to Polish "swine hot spot"/ "swine-district" - poviat gostyński and surroundings (Fig. 1).

1.1 ASF Epidemiology

ASFv (virus) causes massive economic losses (directly at least 100M EUR yearly) in Poland mainly due to trade restrictions (indirectly more than 300M EUR yearly) [1,19]. Only in Poland, after introduction in 2014, in some regions up to 97% of farms stopped pig production or were banned [13]. Nationwide pigs' heads reduced from 14 million in 2013 to 11 million in 2016. The transmission process is very complex (multiple routes, hosts and vectors); however, we identified 3 major factors [9,22] for Poland: i) habitat - Wild Boars (WB) can be a host and a biological vector in the form of carcasses, meat and hunting target; ii) domestic factor - Swine/domestic pig (denoted pig later on) can be a host and a vector as a living animal or pork product; iii) anthropocentric factor - humans and their equipment can be a mechanical vector.

Clinical signs of the disease manifest themselves in acute (animals die before producing antibodies) or subacute (animals die before showing specific clinical symptoms) forms. So far, there is no vaccine (even almost billion of euros are spent on research around the world [3]). There is no treatment and ASF leads to almost 100% animal mortality [7]. Thus prevention is the only mitigation strategy available for disease management. Infectious materials are blood, fat, nasal swabs, rectal and vaginal swabs.

One can identify possible infection routes [7,22] for Poland:

- WB and pig nose-nose and other (pig) contacts in farm;
- Feeding on carcasses (pig, but WB are not showing cannibalism in normal conditions and feed on other WB only if access to food/proteins is limited [10];
- Swills/Food scraps/Meat rest-overs and fecal-oral route (pig-WB via hum and pig-pig via hum who are feeding animals with contaminated swills);
- Fomites and contaminated environment (pigs directly or indirectly via humans);
- Mechanical vectors such as flies, rodents and predators;
- Pork supply chain (pig-pig via hum).

Long distance jumps to disease free territory (as release or entry to Warsaw and wschowski poviat) can be classified by exposure routes [22] (WB are unlike to be spread disease further faster than 20km by year [17,27]):

- Legal trade in live animals [35] and products of animal origin (which was already considered for Poland [24]);
- Illegal trade in live animals or products of animal origin (e.g. due to very low price of affected meat);

- Accidental introductions by formites (e.g. hunters because of wild boar hunting tourism; truck drivers because they travel long distances throughout Europe and migrant workers from affected areas who may inadvertently discard infected meat products);
- Intentional disease introductions.

Fig. 2. Registered ASF genotype II cases around the World (left) and around Poland (right) since introduction of the disease in Georgia in 2007 up to end of 2019.

The percentage of positive wild boars detected through passive surveillance (carcase searching) reached 73%, but through active (hunting) is at the level of 1% in 2018 in already affected areas [14]. Biosecurity in the context of ASF is a first choice strategy to decrease risks of ASF introduction to a farm or a region and is an important element of veterinary infection prevention, and other mitigation strategies. WB population reduction, trade restriction, border fencing or disconnecting animal corridors is only supplementary strategy [30,37].

2   Data Preparation, Methodology and Descriptive Analysis

We choose several spatial covariates to assess possible infections paths for each county (denoted by j) in Poland: P_j - normalized amount of pigs; F_j - coverage of forests serving as a proxy for WB density; H_j - normalized human population [Fig. 3].

2.1   Regressions

For descriptive data analysis we choose several regression models for each of three explained (dependent) variable for each affected until April 2019 county ($j = \overline{1,53}$): i) sum of notifications $N_j = \sum_T N_j(T)$; ii) number of cases cases

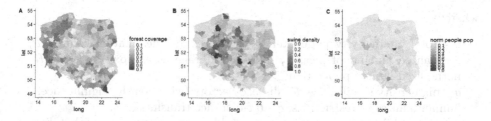

Fig. 3. Spatial covariates used as predictors in the model. Left: Forest Coverage (area fraction). Center: Amount of pig heads (normalized). Right: Human populations (normalized). Data source .

$C_j = \sum_T C_j(T)$ for each county; iii) the time of first arrival of ASF to a given county $t_j(E_0)$. As explanatory variables: numeric variables P_j, F_j, H_j, as well as categorical border indicator variable were used (B - border county, I - interior county).

In multiple regression models (Table 1) for 53 affected counties (j) till Apr 2019, we found strong relationship between pig population and moderate with forest density with outbreak observables: $t_j(E_0)$, N_j, C_j.

Table 1. Multiple linear regressions for different dependent variables. Geographical factors such as pig density, forest coverage and human population. Interior counties (I) were taken as a reference zero level in contrast to border counties (B), pig and human population were normalized to (0,1).

Dependent variable significance levels: *** p<0.01, ** p<0.05, * p<0.1	B/I (categorical variable)	Pig population (estimate)	Human population (estimate)	Forest coverage (estimate)
Arrival time (days) $t_j(E_0)$ (Multiple R)^2 =0.25	−41***	−129**	−8	−65*
Number of notifications N_j (Multiple R)^2 =0.21	32	280***	56	124*
Total number of cases C_j (Multiple R)^2 =0.25	43	654***	64	220

2.2 Network Representation

The main goal of spatial models is the time of introducing ASF into currently disease-free areas [18]. We run set of simulations of SIR model (where recovery rate is estimated to be zero) [8,32] for selected subspace of fitted parameters based on historical data. Probability of infection transmission to a new county is defined according to the so called gravity model [2,4,25,38]:

$$p_{ij} = \gamma \left(a \frac{P_i \cdot P_j}{1 + d_{ij}} + b \frac{F_i \cdot F_j}{1 + d_{ij}^2} + c \frac{H_i \cdot H_j}{1 + d_{ij}} \right), \ g_{ij} \sim p_{ij} \cdot d,$$

where:

- γ - total interactivity parameter, i, j - source and destination county, P_j - normalized amount of pigs, F_j - forest coverage as a proxy for WB; H_j - normalized human population;
- a - pig density significance; b - disease vectors (wild boards) significance; c - human failures to restrictions; d - far-distance transmissions;
- p_{ij} - probability of infection from a neighboring county; g_{ij} - probability of infection from a whole networks; d_{ij} - angular distance between centroids of counties.

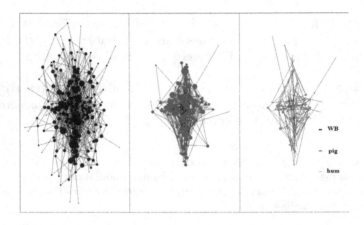

Fig. 4. Visualization of thresholded layers of the transmission network with edge weights due to: WB $\omega_{ij}^{\mathrm{WB}} \sim (F_i \cdot F_j)/\left(1 + d_{ij}^2\right)$, pigs $\omega_{ij}^{\mathrm{pigs}} \sim (P_i \cdot P_j)/(1 + d_{ij})$, humans $\omega_{ij}^{\mathrm{hum}} \sim (F_i \cdot F_j)/(1 + d_{ij})$ of 380 nodes (counties or poviats) for the ASF spreading model. For visualization purposes the fully connected network was thresholded on the level of $\left(\frac{380}{\sum_{ij} \omega_{ij}^{\mathrm{WB}}}, \frac{380}{\sum_{ij} \omega_{ij}^{\mathrm{pigs}}}, \frac{380}{\sum_{ij} \omega_{ij}^{\mathrm{hum}}} \right)$ for each layer.

Performing parameter estimation (the code is provided at Github[3]), and motivated by Ref. [6] we have obtained most likely arrival times for each county based on the historical propagation. We verify theoretically a barrier effect of building a fence on the part of the Polish EU-border and blocking animals corridors on the A1 motorway by comparison of the disease arrival times to Polish "swine hot spot" (poviat gostyński and surroundings) (Fig. 1) in Greater Poland to the baseline (no barrier interventions) scenario (most likely to be affected in 33.5 months around 04.2022 according to our model[4]).

---

[3] https://github.com/ajarynowski/ASF/_poland/.
[4] http://interdisciplinaryresearch.eu/index.php/asf/.

Modeling allows to test scenarios of most common measures [11,12]:

– Pork supply movements bans;
– Biosecurity levels in farms;
– Fences and intensive hunting;
– Active search for WB carcasses;
– Extended surveillance (in pigs and WB).

For both scenarios we start a set of simulations on 01.07.2019. To imitate fencing, we set all outgoing weights at WB-layer of selected border counties to zero ($\omega_{.j}^{WB}=0$ see Fig. 1). To imitate A1 blocking, we set all outgoing weights at WB layer of counties on Northern A1 to zero ($\omega_{.j}^{WB}=0$ see Fig. 1).

3   Results

3.1   Simulation Scenario: Border Fencing

There is only a small difference in the arrival time to swine hot spot district (most likely to be affected in 34.2 months - on average less than one month), because most of the dynamics is currently happening on the West of the border counties.

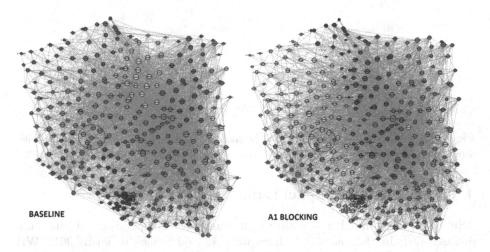

Fig. 5. Infection Paths in the baseline case (left) and A1 Blocking case (right). Detected communities marked by colors according to Louvain algorithm. We observe that "swine hot spot" (red oval) splitted into 2 communities. (Color figure online)

3.2   Simulation Scenario: A1 Blocking

To verify a possible effect of blocking animal corridors, we test a scenario in which all counties on A1 motorway are disconnected in the outgoing wild boars layer (Fig. 4). We aggregated infections paths and visualized the corresponding communities found via the Louvain algorithm on the map (Fig. 5). There is an important difference in the arrival time to the swine district (most likely to be affected in 39 months - on average half a year barrier). A1-blocking leads to splitting of "swine district" cluster (Fig. 5).

3.3 Arrival Times Without Intervention Before and After Wschowski Case

In November 2019, there was a jump of ASF epidemic to the wschowski poviat (just 30 km from the swine district) (Fig. 1) 320 km from the closest affected area (Fig. 2). Wschowski poviat, even having pig and human populations below the country average, was in top 15% percentile in Page Rank centrality according to propagation simulations (Fig. 6). Updated simulations with a epidemic seed in wschowski poviat resulted in the arrival time to swine district less than 12 months. Moreover, the disease might propagate faster that in Eastern Poland, due to larger weights $\omega_{ij}^{WB}, \omega_{ij}^{pig}$, and ω_{ij}^{hum} in Western Poland.

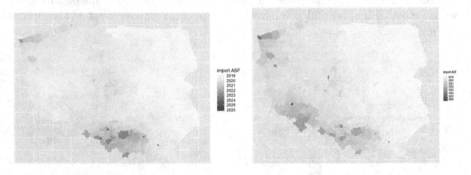

Fig. 6. Most likely ASF arrival times. Simulations based on data until Nov 2019 (with a new case in wschowski poviat) (left) and based on data until Apr 2019 (right).

4 Discussion and Conclusions

ASF is currently number one threat in veterinary epidemiology of emerging diseases [28]. In the year 2021 there were 124 outbreaks in farms 3018 WB notification (while in 2019 it was 2247 WB notifications and 48 outbreaks in farms [15]). Main impact of our project will be the improved and cost-effective disease mitigation strategy provided to institutional decision makers and individual stakeholders such as farmers. The main challenge for risk assessment and prediction of the ASF spread lies in the lack of adequate understanding of the human role in the process [5]. Spatio-temporal analysis and modeling of ASF notification events is crucial in understanding its spread. In our study control and mitigation strategies such as border fencing and animal corridors disconnecting at motorways were tested via extensive computational simulations. The most important conclusion form the analysis of dependent variables is, that pig heads strongly explain both time of the ASF introduction as well as the reported epidemic size (which is in contradiction to the Estonian study [10]). On the other hand, the forest coverage explains a little of the ASF arrival times (the same as in the Estonian study [10]). This might imply regional variation of the ASF spread in different parts of the EU (e.g. in Baltic States the ASF dominates in WB, in Romania in pigs, but in Poland it is well mixed). Thus, mitigation strategies must take into account regional specifics and universal solutions could not work properly, as we might have observed in Poland in massive protests[5].

A1 Blocking and Border Fencing: To compare mitigation scenarios (border fencing and corridor blocking), we measured the difference to the baseline case of various incoming centralities (proxies for arrival times) for a "swine hot spot" in Greater Poland in the network of infection paths. There is currently no vaccine, but extensive and moderately promising research is currently going on worldwide (e.g. [3]), so delay in the disease introduction to a production hub would allow to save up to few hundreds millions EUR per each delayed year, but in long perspective an effective mitigation strategy might be available. Moreover since November 2019 the ASF is already near to the "Polish swine hot spot" and jumped over A1, so any tested strategy probably could not stop this jump anymore. However, based on our simulations, we could conclude:

- by verifying a possible effect of the border fence, we indicate that there is only a small difference in the arrival time to the "swine district". Fencing would be necessary if Poland would be considering disease elimination, but it would not be possible in the next few years perspective at least.
- by verifying a possible effect of blocking animal corridors, we find an important difference in the arrival time to "swine district" as compared to the baseline. Besides, we observed separation of the swine district due to A1 blocking. This estimation seems to be in agreement with the observed propagation in the Baltic States (e.g. via Baltica and A1 in Lithuania [10]). Polish Authorities decided to block animal corridors on parts of A1, A2, A4, S3 and S4, however it happened in Fall/Winter 2019[6] (after jump to Western Poland), probably too late to achieve significant delays.

Our methodology captures only the upper limit of a theoretically perfect barrier in a simple static model and more analysis in realistic time-dependent scenario is required. Proactive approaches for ASF control in other country as Germany are being currently simulated and parameterised [23,34]. Fence between Germany and Poland was build in 2020 [21] while along the border with Belarus it converted in 2023 into a steel wall [26] disconnecting terrestrial animals corridors.

---

[5] http://naukawpolsce.pap.pl/sites/default/files/201901/Stanowisko%20PAN%20-%20ASF_15%20I%202019%20final.pdf.

[6] https://www.gddkia.gov.pl/pl/a/36253/Ustawiamy-prewencyjne-ogrodzenia-by-uniemozliwic-migracje-dzikow.

Jump to Wschowski Poviat: The spread of the disease to Western Poland accelerated the ASF spread, because after focal introduction of a new seed in wschowski poviat in November 2019, disease reached wolsztyński, głogowski and zielonogórski counties in less than a month (with comparison to few months according to our mathematical model (Fig. 6). In September 2020, ASF reached Germany [29].

The epidemiological situation in regards to ASF in Poland could be controlled to some extend by strengthening costly biosecurity measures [30], but further long-distance ASF spread in wild boar by human population (like jump to Warsaw or wschowski poviat (Fig. 2) are much more difficult to control, and even impossible to predict.

Codes and datasets used are available at the Github repository[7]. AJ and VB were partially supported by the German Federal Ministry for Education and Research for the OPTIMAGENT project (031L0299A), German Research Foundation for COVINT project (458528774), ASF-STOP (Cost Action CA15116), OpenMultiMed (Cost Action CA15120), Foundation for Polish-German Cooperation (PNFN 2019-21), BUA (Berlin University Alliance) "Flattening the curve" grant as well as computing time was granted by HPC ZEDAT at FU Berlin.

References

1. Agropolska: Koszty i zalozenia programu zwalczania asf w 2020 r (2020). https://www.agropolska.pl/produkcja-zwierzeca/trzoda-chlewna/koszty-i-zalozenia-programu-zwalczania-asf-w-2020-r-,2271.html. Accessed 27 May 2020
2. Balcan, D., Colizza, V., Gonçalves, B., Hu, H., Ramasco, J.J., Vespignani, A.: Multiscale mobility networks and the spatial spreading of infectious diseases. Proc. Natl. Acad. Sci. **106**(51), 21484–21489 (2009)
3. Barasona, J.A., et al.: First oral vaccination of eurasian wild boar against African swine fever virus genotype II. Front. Veter. Sci. **6** (2019). https://doi.org/10.3389/fvets.2019.00137
4. Belik, V., Brockmann, D.: Accelerating random walks by disorder. New J. Phys. **9**(3), 54 (2007)
5. Belik, V., Geisel, T., Brockmann, D.: Natural human mobility patterns and spatial spread of infectious diseases. Phys. Rev. X **1**(1), 011001 (2011). https://doi.org/10.1103/PhysRevX.1.011001
6. Brockmann, D., Helbing, D.: The hidden geometry of complex, network-driven contagion phenomena. Science **342**(6164), 1337–1342 (2013)
7. Cwynar, P., Stojkov, J., Wlazlak, K.: African swine fever status in Europe. Viruses **11**(4), 310 (2019). https://doi.org/10.3390/v11040310
8. Diekmann, O., Heesterbeek, H., Britton, T.: Mathematical Tools for Understanding Infectious Disease Dynamics, vol. 7. Princeton University Press, Princeton (2012)
9. EFSA_team, et al.: Epidemiological analyses of African swine fever in the European union (november 2017 until november 2018). EFSA J. **16**(11), e05494 (2018)
10. EFSA_team, et al.: Epidemiological analyses of African swine fever in the Baltic states and Poland: (update september 2016-september 2017). EFSA J. **15**(11), e05068 (2017)

---

[7] https://github.com/ajarynowski/ASF_poland/.

11. EFSA_team, et al.: Epidemiological analysis of African swine fever in the European union during 2022. EFSA J. **21**(5), e08016 (2023)
12. Ezanno, P., et al.: The African swine fever modelling challenge: model comparison and lessons learnt. Epidemics **40**, 100615 (2022)
13. Farmer: Byc moze gdzies wraca hodowla świn po asf - ale nie w bialej podlaskiej (2019). https://www.farmer.pl/prawo/przepisy-i-regulacje/byc-moze-gdzies-wraca-hodowla-swin-po-asf-ale-nie-w-bialej-podlaskiej,85344.html. Accessed 27 May 2020
14. Frant, M., Lyjak, M., Bocian, L., Barszcz, A., Niemczuk, K., Wozniakowski, G.: African swine fever virus (ASFV) in Poland: prevalence in a wild boar population (2017–2018). Veterinární medicína **65**(4), 143–158 (2020)
15. GIW: Asf w polsce (2020). https://www.wetgiw.gov.pl/nadzor-weterynaryjny/asf-w-polsce. Accessed 27 May 2023
16. Halasa, T., Bøtner, A., Mortensen, S., Christensen, H., Wulff, S.B., Boklund, A.: Modeling the effects of duration and size of the control zones on the consequences of a hypothetical African swine fever epidemic in Denmark. Front. Veter. Sci. **5** (2018). https://doi.org/10.3389/fvets.2018.00049
17. Iglesias, I., et al.: Spatio-temporal kriging analysis to identify the role of wild boar in the spread of African swine fever in the Russian federation. Spatial Stat. **28**, 226–235 (2018). https://doi.org/10.1016/j.spasta.2018.07.002
18. Jarynowski, A., Belik, V.: Modeling the asf (African swine fever) spread till summer 2017 and risk assessment for Poland. Konferencja zastosowan matematyki (2017)
19. Jarynowski, A., Belik, V.: Analiza kosztow rozprzestrzeniania sie afrykanskiego pomoru swin w polsce. Public Health Forum **V**(XIII), 72 (2019)
20. Jarynowski, A., Buda, A., Platek, D., Belik, V.: African swine fever awareness in the internet media in Poland-exploratory review. E-methodol. **6**(6), 100–115 (2019)
21. Jarynowski, A., Krzowski, Ł, Belik, V.: Afrykański pomór świń-epizootiologia, ekonomia i zarządzanie kryzysowe w kontekście naturalnego bądź intencjonalnego wprowadzenia. Studia Administracji i Bezpieczeństwa **11**(11), 129–153 (2021)
22. Jarynowski, A., Platek, D., Krzowski, Ł, Gerylovich, A., Belik, V.: African swine fever-potential biological warfare threat. Technical report, EasyChair-Preprint (2019)
23. Lentz, H.H., Bergmann, H., Conraths, F.J., Schulz, J., Sauter-Louis, C.: The diffusion metrics of African swine fever in wild boar. Sci. Rep. **13**(1), 15110 (2023)
24. Lu, Y., Deng, X., Chen, J., Wang, J., Chen, Q., Niu, B.: Risk analysis of African swine fever in Poland based on spatio-temporal pattern and latin hypercube sampling, 2014–2017. BMC Veter. Res. **15**(1) (2019). https://doi.org/10.1186/s12917-019-1903-z
25. Manitz, J., Kneib, T., Schlather, M., Helbing, D., Brockmann, D.: Origin detection during food-borne disease outbreaks-a case study of the 2011 EHEC/HUS outbreak in Germany. PLoS currents **6**(1) (2014)
26. Moll, Ł, et al.: Mobile commoning from the margins to the fore? hostipitality on the polish-belarusian and polish-ukrainian borders (2021–2022). Praktyka teoretyczna **46**, 129–160 (2023)
27. Mur, L., Martínez-López, B., Martínez-Avilés, M., Costard, S., Wieland, B., Pfeiffer, D.U., Sánchez-Vizcaíno, J.: Quantitative risk assessment for the introduction of African swine fever virus into the European union by legal import of live pigs. Transbound. Emerg. Dis. **59**(2), 134–144 (2012)
28. Normile, D.: African swine fever keeps spreading in Asia, threatening food security. Science (2019). https://doi.org/10.1126/science.aay0376

29. Oelke, J., Jarynowski, A., Belik, V.: Media discourses and social perception of asfrisk across overlapping interspecies (sus scrofa and human) and national (Germany Poland) borders (2023). http://politologia.uni.opole.pl/wp-content/uploads/2023/09/program-sessions3.pdf. Accessed 17 Sept 2023

30. Pejsak, Z., et al.: Przewidywany rozwój sytuacji epizootycznej w zakresie afrykańskiego pomoru świń w polsce. Życie Weterynaryjne **92**(04) (2017)

31. Pepin, K.M., Golnar, A.J., Abdo, Z., Podgórski, T.: Ecological drivers of African swine fever virus persistence in wild boar populations: insight for control. Ecol. Evol. **10**(6), 2846–2859 (2020)

32. Pfeiffer, D., et al.: Spatial Analysis in Epidemiology, vol. 142. Oxford University Press, Oxford (2008)

33. Podgórski, T., Borowik, T., Łyjak, M., Woźniakowski, G.: Spatial epidemiology of African swine fever: host, landscape and anthropogenic drivers of disease occurrence in wild boar. Prevent. Veter. Med. 104691 (2019). https://doi.org/10.1016/j.prevetmed.2019.104691

34. Reichold, A., Lange, M., Thulke, H.H.: Modelling the effectiveness of measures applied in zones dedicated to stop the spread of African swine fever in wild boar when bordering with a region of limited control. EFSA Support. Publ. **19**(5), 7320E (2022)

35. Schirdewahn, F., Colizza, V., Lentz, H.H., Koher, A., Belik, V., Hövel, P.: Surveillance for outbreak detection in livestock-trade networks. In: Masuda, N., Holme, P. (eds.) Temporal Network Epidemiology, pp. 215–240. Springer, Heidelberg (2017). https://doi.org/10.1007/978-981-10-5287-3_10

36. Taylor, R.A., Condoleo, R., Simons, R.R.L., Gale, P., Kelly, L.A., Snary, E.L.: The risk of infection by African swine fever virus in European swine through boar movement and legal trade of pigs and pig meat. Front. Veter. Sci. **6**, 486 (2020). https://doi.org/10.3389/fvets.2019.00486. https://www.frontiersin.org/article/10.3389/fvets.2019.00486

37. Vicente, J., et al.: Science-based wildlife disease response. Science **364**(6444), 943–944 (2019)

38. Zipf, G.K.: The P 1 P 2/D hypothesis: on the intercity movement of persons. Am. Sociol. Rev. **11**(6), 677–686 (1946)

Identification and Analysis of the Spread of {Mis}information on Social Media

Muhammad T. Khan, Rachel Gordon, Nimra Khan, Madeline Moran,
Mohammed Abuhamad, Loretta Stalans, Jeffrey Huntsinger, Jennifer Forestal,
and Eric Chan-Tin[✉]

Loyola University Chicago, Chicago, USA
{mkhan59,rgordon,nkhan21,mmoran11,mabuhamad,lstalan,jhuntsinger,
jforestal,dchantin}@luc.edu

Abstract. With unfolding crises such as the COVID-19 pandemic, it is essential that factual information is dispersed at a rapid pace. One of the major setbacks to mitigating the effects of such crises is misinformation. Advancing technologies such as transformer-based architectures that can pick up underlying patterns and correlational information that constitutes information provide tools that can be used to identify what is misinformation/information. To identify and analyze the spread of misinformation, this work performs a quantitative analysis that uses **X** (previously Twitter) as the data source and a BERT-based model to identify misinformation. The information of the posts, users, and followers was collected based on hashtags and then processed and manually labeled. Furthermore, we tracked the spread of misinformation related to COVID-19 during the year 2021 and determined how communities that spread information and/or misinformation on social networks interact from an analytical perspective. Our findings suggest that users tend to post more misinformation than information, possibly intentionally spreading misinformation. Our model showed good performance in classifying tweets as information/misinformation, resulting in an accuracy of 86%.

Keywords: BERT · Spread of Misinformation · Social Networks

1 Introduction

Misinformation is false or misleading information that is spread or shared through various channels such as social media, news outlets, or word-of-mouth. Misinformation can have dangerous consequences, as it can alter individuals' behavior, causing them to make decisions that can harm themselves, others, or society. It is essential to combat misinformation because its existence has a significant detrimental impact on individuals and society at large. Misinformation has the potential to spread fear, incite hate and violence, and has been shown to alter the behavior of individuals [9]. For example, during the COVID-19 pandemic, movements spreading misinformation on the efficacy of masks led to individuals refusing to wear masks; for at-risk populations, this created a very dangerous situation, because they were more likely to contract COVID-19 and have health complications. Combating this type of misinformation is essential to protecting public health. To effectively combat misinformation, it is essential to understand its root causes and why people share misinformation in the first place. People may share misinformation because it may align with their worldview or beliefs, they may want to influence public opinion, or for personal gain, but many also share misinformation because they do not know it is untrue. Understanding these different motivations allows us to find ways to combat misinformation without resorting to extreme measures such as speech censorship.

There are quite a few ways in which misinformation spreads on social media. There has been a lot of misinformation on the safety and efficacy of vaccines, such as those related to COVID-19, which can lead people to refuse vaccination. One post in our data set, which was shared 163 times, said: *"It's not a vaccine, stop calling it that. It's an experimental flu shot. It was created and released at the perfect time to undermine an election and funnel millions into Big Pharma. #WakeUpAmerica"*. There are also cases of fake news stories that are shared on the Internet usually without any fact-checking protocols. Another tweet from the dataset linked an article from a "doctor", stating *"Chinese military is responsible for the physical creation of the virus. The COVID mandate & vaxx passports fit into the CCP agenda by making the whole world accept and adopt the CCP's social control system"*. This tweet had more than 2,500 shares. Another way misinformation has spread is the use of manipulated images, graphs, and videos; this poses an additional threat to those who consume information on social networks because the posts look more similar to information.

Social media such as Twitter, Instagram, and Facebook have become an integral part of the lives of people; they allow us to interact with each other and the world as a whole. They are also a source of information for many individuals. Social networks use recommendation algorithms to engage users and determine what content to show in users' feeds. These algorithms are designed to maximize engagement and keep users on the platform as long as possible. Social media allow for rapid consumption of information because there is usually a character constraint, especially on **X**, forcing the conciseness of the information being conveyed. This means that an individual is capable of consuming large amounts of information (both factual and non-factual), and it is up to the individual to parse what is true and false. The algorithms mentioned earlier focus resources on increasing engagement rather than credibility and accuracy, further exacerbating the spread of misinformation. These algorithms can also create echo chambers for individuals based on their engagement, creating a cycle of media consumption that aligns with only their beliefs. An example of such an algorithm is the TikTok feed algorithm that suggests content to users based on their short-term interactions, such as videos they liked or shared, and also factors in the amount of time they spend watching certain types of content [23]. This creates custom filters that expose consumers to content that reinforces their beliefs and opinions and increases the possibility of spreading misinformation.

The purpose of this research is to better understand how misinformation pertaining specifically to the COVID-19 pandemic and the vaccine spreads on social media. We seek to classify posts that were collected from social media as either information or misinformation using a machine learning algorithm. To this end, we train and evaluate a BERT (Bidirectional Encoder Representations from Transformers) [8] model using our own collected and manually labeled dataset. We plan to publish the models and data to the public for research purposes. We use these classifications to look at how often users post and share misinformation as opposed to information, how communities of people share misinformation, and the proportions of information and misinformation posts coming from a single user. This analysis allows us to better understand the dynamics of how the sharing of misinformation on social media differs from the sharing of information, which in turn will allow us to make more informed decisions when attempting to combat the spread of misinformation.

One contribution of this paper is the successful utilization of the state-of-the-art transformer architecture, e.g., BERT, to classify posts on social networks as information or misinformation despite the nuances that come with misinformation, with an accuracy of 86%. Another contribution of this paper is the finding that the dissemination of both information and misinformation seems to occur only within communities that are already sharing primarily information or misinformation. Therefore, misinformation is more likely to spread within a community of users who follow each other and already primarily share misinformation, and it has a harder time spreading to users outside of that community.

2 Background

Twitter (now called **X**) is a social media platform that allows users to share short public messages called tweets, which have a character limit of 280 characters. On Twitter, users can follow other individuals, like content, retweet content (re-posting content), and comment on those tweets. Twitter has become a popular media platform for social and political discourse, hence its selection for this project. To obtain the data from Twitter, an Academic API (Application Programming Interface) license was obtained to gain robust access to historical tweets and real-time streaming data. The API provides a set of rules for how developers can interact with Twitter's platform and access the data. The license allowed the collection of up to 500,000 tweets per month, which were filtered by hashtags related to COVID-19. These hashtags were utilized to focus the search and obtain relevant posts related to COVID-19.

Misinformation is any information that is incorrect or misleading, regardless of intent, and can be spread through various forms of communication such as word-of-mouth, social media, and news outlets. Classification of information is based mainly on the factuality of the information. If there is no evidence that the information is true or factual, it is then classified as misinformation. If the spread of that misinformation is done with the intent to deceive others, it then becomes disinformation.

BERT, which stands for bidirectional transformer encoder representation, is a type of neural network that uses the Transformer architecture [8]. Transformer is a deep learning model that has a self-attention mechanism that allows it to capture the relationships between all elements of the sequence, regardless of their position. BERT is well suited for natural language processing tasks such as the classification of data as information or misinformation. We can use the pre-trained BERT model and train it on data that has been manually pre-labeled. This allows BERT to understand the patterns and relationships between information and misinformation, allowing it to learn how to classify new, unseen data based on those patterns. Due to resource limitations, we were unable to train the BERT model on the entirety of the data set, so we opted to construct a coreset for data-efficient training of the machine learning model. Data coreset is a technique that allows the selection of optimal data points that approximate the entirety of the data set. This is done based on importance sampling and on the Frank-Wolfe algorithm [7]. Using these two algorithms, we are able to capture information that is necessary for posterior inference via Bayesian probability. This then allows us to capture the data points that accurately reflect the entirety of the data set at a fraction of the size.

3   Methods and Experimental Design

Data Collection. We scraped data from Twitter from the year 2021 using 13 hashtags that are shown in Table 1. The table also shows the total number of tweets and retweets for each hashtag and the number of users who posted with that hashtag. Our entire data set contained a total of 6,168,735 unique tweets.

Table 1. Twitter data collected based on various #hashtags.

Hashtag	# Unique Tweets	# Retweets	# Users who Posted
#antivaccine	24,390	74,378	53,335
#antivax	47,451	35,575	43,107
#antivaxxer	29,762	19,237	23,803
#covid5g	77,484	79,202	101,228
#covidvaccinehoax	29,764	87,518	82,890
#ivermectin	176,757	313,757	140,819
#joerogan	822,634	899,432	1,026,368
#mercola	88,737	282,614	125,928
#misinformation	3,981,313	6,322,806	2,675,969
#RFKjr	4,039	4,367	5,259
#stoptheshot	9,019	21,006	10,750
#VAERS	772,467	415,789	217,386
#wakeupamerica	104,918	63,468	50,670
Total	6,168,735	8,619,149	3,303,015

Data Labeling. After the data was collected, 100 of the most popular (by number of likes and retweets) tweets per hashtag were hand-labeled as *misinformation*, *information*, or *ambiguous*. "Ambiguous" means that the data was neither information nor misinformation and the tweet could be ignored. Two examples of misinformation posts were shown in Sect. 1. To ensure that the labels were as accurate as possible while minimizing bias, three independent raters were used. Each rater used fact-checking sites and common knowledge for labeling – if they were unsure, the post was classified as "ambiguous". This allowed for a robust and rigorous labeling process that ensures the minimization of bias to create a high-quality training dataset. 1,345 tweets were manually labeled using this method, as follows: 456 (33.9%) misinformation, 215 (16%) information, and 674 (50.1%) ambiguous.

Data Cleaning. After scraping the data, we removed any duplicate posts as well as phone numbers, emails, URLs, special characters, and punctuation. We also converted all of the text to lowercase and tokenized the data using the regular expression tokenizer in Python. Stopwords were not removed due to their ability to alter the context of tweets. Finally, we removed unnecessary data, such as tweet ID, timestamp, and reference ID, and only kept the posts, user IDs, and post IDs for training the model. The posts are used by BERT to capture the contextual information, and the user ID and post ID are used for cross reference and follower analysis.

Bayesian Coresets. After cleaning the data, we constructed the training data set for BERT. Due to resource limitations, it was not feasible to train BERT on the typical data split of 70-15-15 or 80-10-10 (Train, Validate, and Test respectively). Recognizing this limitation, we chose to employ Bayesian inference via the Hilbert Coreset [4] algorithm that allows us to construct a training data set that is a fraction of the size but allows us to train the model as if we were training on 70%–80% of the dataset. The data points that were returned were then manually labeled as information, misinformation, or ambiguous. The independent rating protocol was used once again to ensure minimization of bias in the training data set. This training dataset was combined with the previously labeled tweets creating the complete dataset for model training. The training dataset consisted of 319 misinformation posts and 72 information posts. The testing dataset consisted of 137 misinformation posts and 65 information posts.

Training and Evaluating BERT. Once the BERT model was trained on the labeled data, it was used to classify a dataset that contained all tweets. Each tweet was classified as information or misinformation. Our final model had an accuracy of 86% and a confidence of 76% based on our testing dataset. Of the total data, 3,227,765 posts were classified as misinformation and 1,750,709 were classified as information.

4   Results and Analysis

Figure 1 shows the cumulative distribution function (CDF) of the number
of followers of users who post misinformation compared to the number of
followers of users who post information. Both lines follow a similar trend,
although information-posting users seem to have slightly more followers than
misinformation-posting users. On average, users who posted information had
1,431 followers, while users who posted misinformation had 1,680 followers.

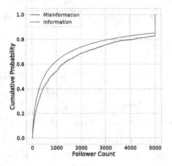

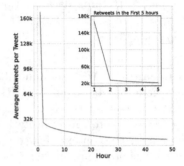

Fig. 1. CDF of followers of users posting   **Fig. 2.** Active tweets that have been
Information and Misinformation.   retweeted at least once per 48(/5) h.

Figure 2 shows the total number of active tweets remaining after each of the
first 48 h. A tweet is considered to be "active" if it is still being retweeted at
least once after that hour. The graph shows that there is a sharp decline after
the first two hours, so almost 80% of the tweets stopped being retweeted after
that time. Figure 2 also shows a close-up view of the first five hours. Hour 1
has more than 160,000 active tweets, which means there are 160,000 tweets that
are retweeted at least once after the initial posting. Hour 2 has about 30,000
active tweets, showing an 80% decline. This steep decline indicates that there is
a significant drop in engagement with the tweet after more than an hour. The
difference between Hour 1 and Hour 2 could be attributed to the fact that when
the tweet is initially posted, it only reaches the user's immediate followers, but as
the post reaches a wider audience there is a sharp decline in engagement because
they might not be the original target audience. This engagement difference could
be attributed to the fast nature of social media and user attention span where
typically posts see an initial boost in popularity but quickly become "old news"
as the constant flux of new content grabs a user's attention.

Figure 3 shows the total number of misinformation posts vs. the total number
of information posts per user. Most users only posted a few COVID-19 related
tweets, hence why the majority of data points are near the origin. The linear
$y = x$ line shows that many users posted about the same amount of information
and misinformation tweets. There is also a cluster of users along the x-axis,
indicating that these users posted much more misinformation than information

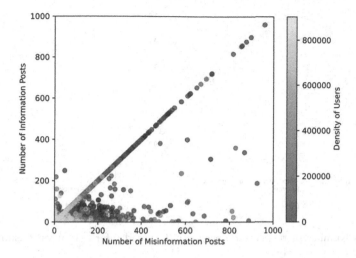

Fig. 3. Number of information posts vs. misinformation posts per user.

tweets. Users who post a similar amount of information and misinformation could think that they are posting information, but do not know that half of the posts contain misinformation. Another possibility is that these users post misinformation with a warning in order to educate others. The cluster of users along the x-axis post much more misinformation than information, and could possibly spread misinformation on purpose. These two different clusters in the graph show the harmful effects of rampant misinformation – even users who are posting information spread misinformation, and there is a large number of users who seem to be posting misinformation on purpose.

Figure 4(a) shows the number of retweets for information posts compared to misinformation posts. The trend for both lines is similar, but information posts seem to typically have more retweets than misinformation posts. This difference may be due to people being more likely to like posts that contain misinformation, but not wanting to retweet them if they are particularly controversial. Additionally, users who post information tend to have slightly more followers than users who post misinformation, so their posts may be more likely to be retweeted. Finally, information posts are helpful and informative by nature and people may be retweeting them because they want to spread the word and help others. Figure 4(b) is a cumulative distribution graph of the number of followers who also retweeted their respective following user's original posts. The graph shows that more than 95% of the users have fewer than 10 followers who retweet their posts. This tells us that there is little follower interaction with the user's post. However, followers tended to retweet posts that were information more than posts that were misinformation. The number of likes for information posts compared to misinformation posts was similar with 75% of all posts receiving at most 200 likes.

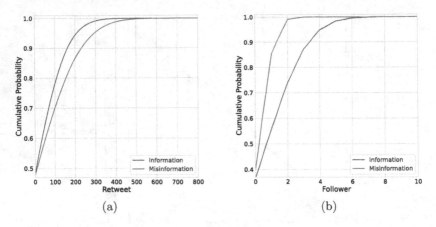

Fig. 4. (a) Number of retweets for users that spread information vs. misinformation and (b) for followers only.

Takeaways. 1) After the first two hours, almost 80% of the tweets stopped being retweeted after that time, showing a lack of consistent engagement with posts. 2) The spread of misinformation is a serious problem, since information and misinformation tweets have similar numbers of likes, and information tweets are only slightly more likely to be retweeted. 3) Users who post information tweets also post misinformation tweets, although misinformation posts are less likely to be retweeted.

5   Related Work

Misinformation on social media is a pressing topic and efforts to identify, understand, and even stop the spread of misinformation are continuing to be explored. Utilizing machine learning to classify misinformation on social media is also a growing area of interest and there has been a large amount of relevant work in these fields, specifically pertaining to COVID-19 misinformation.

For example, several people have utilized machine learning algorithms, natural language processing techniques, and deep neural networks such as CNNs to identify fake content during the COVID-19 pandemic on social media, including interesting additions to machine learning algorithms to detect such types of information [12,15,16,19,24]. Collectively, these works address aspects of misinformation on social media platforms with an emphasis on misinformation or COVID-19. Nistor and Zadobrischi [19] studied the detection of health-related misinformation on social media by proposing a model that combines topic characteristics (central-level features) and semantic and behavior traits (peripheral-level features). Using this approach, they are able to detect 85% of health misinformation. Our work has a similar goal and seeks to apply transformers to this task to obtain more accurate results [21,28]. Zhao et al. [28] is an example of using CNNs to detect fake news using user meta-data such as content and user profiles to detect misinformation. Furthermore, others have looked at keywords and hashtags related to COVID-19 on Twitter and quantified the amount of misinformation or unverifiable information associated with each keyword [13], which is very similar to our approach. It could also be interesting to compare the hashtags we chose with others and to look at other keywords that we did not include in our analysis.

In addition to classifying content as either misinformation or information, some work has been done to understand what factors influence the spread of misinformation [5,11] and to identify patterns in the content of misinformation specifically related to COVID-19. For instance, work has been done to identify factors that influence the sharing of fake news about COVID-19 on social media [2], including identifying how the theory of third-person perception applies to COVID-19 misinformation [27], as well as the content themes and writing strategies used in vaccine misinformation [18]. These studies provide a qualitative understanding of how misinformation spreads on social media and our work seeks to provide a more quantitative understanding by looking at how the number of posts, retweets, and other attributes of misinformation compare to that of information. Furthermore, much work has been done to identify and assess methods to stop the spread of misinformation, such as testing the effectiveness of infographics about COVID-19 myths [25]. Although our work is not focused on stopping misinformation but rather understanding how it spreads, it is interesting to consider methods to combat the spread of misinformation, and our analysis can contribute to identifying which methods may be the most effective [3,6,17].

Detecting misinformation as a whole is a challenge considering the sociopolitical and economic nuances that motivate individuals to spread misinformation. With more and more research into the realm of machine learning, we are increasingly able to detect such misinformation or "fake news" [1,10,20]. The detection of this misinformation on any platform requires the creation of robust data sets that can accurately capture the semantics that comprise misinformation. The data set that we created by manually labeling can be improved by providing the BERT model with more contextual information that constitutes misinformation as shown in [26]. With the added element of social media platforms like Twitter and their ability to rapidly spread information, especially in the case of COVID-19, it is imperative that the speed of its spread be quantitatively measured as is done in this paper, in addition to capturing the differences between those who spread information and those who spread misinformation [14,22].

6   Discussion

Although the results of this research provided interesting insights into how misinformation actually spreads on social media, it is important to recognize that there are also several limitations to this work. We included 13 hashtag, as seen in Table 1, which is not exhaustive of all potential topics related to COVID-19 and misinformation. Therefore, we may notice different patterns or results depending on the hashtags we chose.

Another limitation is the possibility of bias in the way that the data was labeled and its effects on the predicted value from BERT. There have been measures to limit as much bias as possible using the independent rating protocol, but researchers may share similar viewpoints or draw information from similar sources to determine whether something is factual or not, and this inadvertently may cause the model to reflect this behavior.

There is also the case that the data collected via the Twitter API is only limited to a certain time frame, which is from 2021, when the pandemic was at its peak, which introduces a temporal constraint on the data. This constraint limits our ability to accurately extrapolate the results to other years. However, this information can be combined with future research to determine how misinformation flows from year to year.

The focus of this research is information/misinformation related to COVID-19 which may not be enough to capture the true breadth of the spread of misinformation across various topics. The dynamics of the spread of information are influenced by many factors such as the platform, audience, time, and overall context. Taking this into account, generalizations made from this research must be done with caution as the trends in misinformation and dissemination may vary significantly depending on the topic.

Finally, despite the fact that the idea of creating the Hilbert coreset using Bayesian inference is theoretically sound, it is crucial to note that due to its various settings and algorithmic constraints, this data selection strategy may not be consistent. This means that the data set that was produced has the potential to either have too few data points to accurately capture the complexity of the collected data or too many data points that may lead to redundancy or unnecessary computational burden. It may introduce unforeseen bias or distortion to the data set due to the black-box nature of the construction.

7   Conclusion

The spread of COVID-19-related misinformation was a major concern during the pandemic, and its ability to reduce the effectiveness of government and health mandates cannot be overlooked. Knowing how this misinformation spreads enables and empowers future researchers to find solutions to combat such misinformation as future crises arise. Adapting current architecture to solve complex problems such as the spread of misinformation is novel, and this research paves the way to novel pathways that allow us to understand how misinformation spreads, how to detect it using natural language models, and how to effectively combat misinformation. Our analysis shows that misinformation posts are less likely to be re-posted by their respective followers than information posts. We found that there is a drop in consistent engagement in posts after two hours of being posted, which could be a result of newer posts that appear above the "older" posts. This could again be attributed to the fast-paced nature of social media where newer posts supersede older posts. Our final model achieved an accuracy of 86% and a confidence of 76% in classifying information/misinformation based on our testing dataset.

Future work could look at more hashtags, increase the training data size, and look at other topics than COVID-19.

Acknowledgments. We thank Spencer Johnston for his help with the Twitter API. This material is based upon work supported by the Dr. Scholl Foundation. Any opinions, findings, and conclusions or recommendations expressed in this material are those of the author(s) and do not necessarily reflect the views of the Dr. Scholl Foundation.

References

1. Aphiwongsophon, S., Chongstitvatana, P.: Detecting fake news with machine learning method. In: 15th International Conference on Electrical Engineering/Electronics, Computer, Telecommunications and Information Technology (ECTI-CON), pp. 528–531 (2018)
2. Apuke, O.D., Omar, B.: Fake news and covid-19: modelling the predictors of fake news sharing among social media users. Telematics Inf. **56**, 101475 (2021)
3. Bogale Gereme, F., Zhu, W.: Fighting fake news using deep learning: pre-trained word embeddings and the embedding layer investigated. In: Proceedings of the 2020 3rd International Conference on Computational Intelligence and Intelligent Systems, CIIS 2020, p. 24–29. Association for Computing Machinery, New York (2021)
4. Campbell, T., Broderick, T.: Automated scalable bayesian inference via hilbert coresets. arXiv (2019)
5. Chen, S., Xiao, L., Kumar, A.: Spread of misinformation on social media: what contributes to it and how to combat it. Comput. Human Behav. **141**, 107643 (2023)
6. Choraś, M., et al.: Advanced machine learning techniques for fake news (online disinformation) detection: a systematic mapping study. Appl. Soft Comput. **101**, 107050 (2021)
7. Clarkson, K.L.: Coresets, sparse greedy approximation, and the Frank-Wolfe algorithm. ACM Trans. Algor. **6**(4), 1–30 (2010)
8. Devlin, J., Chang, M.W., Lee, K., Toutanova, K.: Bert: pre-training of deep bidirectional transformers for language understanding. arXiv (2019)
9. Greene, C.M., Murphy, G.: Quantifying the effects of fake news on behavior: evidence from a study of covid-19 misinformation. J. Exp. Psychol. Appl. **27**(4), 773 (2021)
10. Hakak, S., Alazab, M., Khan, S., Gadekallu, T.R., Maddikunta, P.K.R., Khan, W.Z.: An ensemble machine learning approach through effective feature extraction to classify fake news. Future Gener. Comput. Syst. **117**, 47–58 (2021)
11. Halpern, D., Valenzuela, S., Katz, J., Miranda, J.P.: From belief in conspiracy theories to trust in others: Which factors influence exposure, believing and sharing fake news. In: Meiselwitz, G. (ed.) HCII 2019, vol. 11578, pp. 217–232. Springer, Heidelberg (2019). https://doi.org/10.1007/978-3-030-21902-4_16
12. Hunt, K., Agarwal, P., Zhuang, J.: Monitoring misinformation on twitter during crisis events: a machine learning approach. Risk Anal. **42**(8), 1728–1748 (2020)
13. Kouzy, R., et al.: Coronavirus goes viral: quantifying the covid-19 misinformation epidemic on twitter. Cureus **12**, e7255 (2020)

14. Lazer, D.M.J., et al.: The science of fake news. Science **359**(6380), 1094–1096 (2018)
15. Manzoor, S.I., Singla, J.: Fake news detection using machine learning approaches: a systematic review. In: 3rd International Conference on Trends in Electronics and Informatics (ICOEI) (2019)
16. Monti, F., Frasca, F., Eynard, D., Mannion, D., Bronstein, M.M.: Fake news detection on social media using geometric deep learning (2019)
17. Ngada, O., Haskins, B.: Fake news detection using content-based features and machine learning. In: 2020 IEEE Asia-Pacific Conference on Computer Science and Data Engineering (CSDE), pp. 1–6 (2020)
18. Ngai, C.S., Singh, R.G., Yao, L.: Impact of covid-19 vaccine misinformation on social media virality: content analysis of message themes and writing strategies. J. Med. Internet Res. **24**, e37806 (2022)
19. Nistor, A., Zadobrischi, E.: The influence of fake news on social media: analysis and verification of web content during the covid-19 pandemic by advanced machine learning methods and natural language processing. Sustainability **14**, 10466 (2022)
20. Reis, J.C.S., Correia, A., Murai, F., Veloso, A., Benevenuto, F.: Explainable machine learning for fake news detection. In: Proceedings of the 10th ACM Conference on Web Science, WebSci 2019, pp. 17–26. Association for Computing Machinery, New York (2019). https://doi.org/10.1145/3292522.3326027
21. Sahoo, S.R., Gupta, B.: Multiple features based approach for automatic fake news detection on social networks using deep learning. Appl. Soft Comput. **100**, 106983 (2021)
22. Shahi, G.K., Dirkson, A., Majchrzak, T.A.: An exploratory study of covid-19 misinformation on twitter. Online Social Netw. Media **22**, 100104 (2021)
23. Smith, B.: How tiktok reads your mind (2021). https://www.nytimes.com/2021/12/05/business/media/tiktok-algorithm.html
24. Tashtoush, Y., Alrababah, B., Darwish, O., Maabreh, M., Alsaedi, N.: A deep learning framework for detection of covid-19 fake news on social media platforms. Data **7**, 65 (2023)
25. Vraga, E.K., Bode, L.: Addressing covid-19 misinformation on social media preemptively and responsively. Emerg. Infect. Dis. **27**, 396 (2021)
26. Wang, W.Y.: "liar, liar pants on fire": a new benchmark dataset for fake news detection. arXiv (2017)
27. Yang, J., Tian, Y.: "Others are more vulnerable to fake news than i am": third-person effect of covid-19 fake news on social media users. Comput. Hum. Behav. **125**, 106950 (2021)
28. Zhao, Y., Da, J., Yan, J.: Detecting health misinformation in online health communities: incorporating behavioral features into machine learning based approaches. Inf. Process. Manag. **58**(1), 102390 (2021)

Modeling the Change of Public Opinion Caused by Opinion Posts' Dissemination in Social Networks

Liman Du[ID], Wenguo Yang[✉][ID], and Suixiang Gao

School of Mathematical Sciences, University of Chinese Academy of Sciences,
Beijing 100049, China
duliman18@mails.ucas.edu.cn, {yangwg,sxg}@ucas.ac.cn

Abstract. The various extensively used social platforms make it possible for the public to facilitate quick and easy sharing of information as well as express their views and opinions in real time, which can lead to the rapid outbreak of online public opinion. To simulate the change of online public opinion resulting from opinion posts' dissemination in social networks, this study proposes a more realistic and novel model named as Agent-Based Opinion Dissemination model. It provides the additional advantage to incorporate the effect of real-world characteristics from the perspective of outer interventions and individuals' attributes. The experimental results show that our model can simulate the evolution of public opinion, thus providing a clearer explanation of the law and causes of public opinion's evolution from the perspective of individual and media behavior.

Keywords: Social Networks · Online Public Opinion · Information Dissemination · Agent-Based Model

1 Introduction

Given a particular topic, public opinion is an aggregate of the individual views, attitudes, and beliefs expressed by a significant proportion of a community. By processing new information and interacting with others, opinions may change in time, contributing to the evolution of the public debate and society itself [8]. With the popularization and the fast development of social platforms, the Internet provides online space for users to vent, dissent, deliberate, and debate. Due to the rising importance of online public opinion, the government's attentiveness to understand, guide, manage, and channel online public opinion increases. At the same time, network media which aims to obtain popularity, reading volume, click rate, and other related topic indexes, may neglect of their reports' authenticity and objectivity and release opinion-inclined reports about public

Supported by the National Natural Science Foundation of China under Grant Numbers 12071459 and 11991022.

opinion topics And the provider of social platforms can also influence opinion dynamic by filtering rules and recommendation algorithms. So public opinion can be viewed as the result of the interaction from various social forces and its evolution is typically revealed by opinion dynamics models.

Government or authoritative media can be used to release information, solve the crisis of public opinion, and guide the positive development of public opinion. Recent years have witnessed the increasing of study focusing on government media and intervention in public opinion [1,2,6,7,10,11,16]. However, these studies are based on epidemic model and the influence of media are generally reflected by the transformation probability between various groups. Therefore, they assume that all individuals are homogeneous and the invention does not change. In fact, different individuals respond differently to intervention from different media, resulting in a large gap between the real situation and the simulation results of models based on classic epidemic model. And changing invention according to reality is more useful and meaningful. What's more, there are some factors that have been proved to owe the ability of influencing the opinion dynamic in social theories, and most existing related studies underestimate the importance of these factors.

To overcome these gaps, we propose a novel Agent-Based Opinion Dissemination (ABOD) model to simulate the dynamic of online public opinion in social networks. By applying the concept of multi-agent systems to the basic structure of simulation models, ABOD model regards each individual as an agent and simulates the spread of opinion post in waves. Some real-world characteristics in the form of novel agent and model parameters that are essential in the formation and update of individual opinion but are absent in the current literature are incorporated into the ABOD model. These factors include individuals' anti-interference capability, attitude-hide behavior, engagement and activeness in the network, self-persistence and intervention from different perspectives.

The remainder of this paper is organized as follows: Sect. 2 presents the design of our Agent-Based Opinion Dissemination (ABOD) model in detail. Section 3 outlines the simulation experiment conducted of the model followed by conclusion in Sect. 4.

2 Model Design

Given a following relationship in a social platform, define a followee as an individual who is being followed and a follower is someone who is doing the following. Then, most of online social networks can be regarded as networks formed by follower-followee relationships. And every social network can be abstracted as a weight directed network $G = (V, E, W)$ where every element in V represents a social platform's user while E is the set of follower-followee relationships. Inspired by the ABM that is proposed in [3] to model the influencer marketing campaign based on information spread in social networks, we propose a modified agent-based model which is named as Agent-Based Opinion Dissemination (ABOD) model to simulate the online public opinion dynamics caused by the spread of posts expressing certain views in various scenarios. Here, a post and the opinion it expresses can be regraded as a unit and defined as an opinion post. In other words, the concept of "opinion post" used in the ABOD model proposed in this paper is a piece of writing that expresses a particular point of view and is propagated between a pair of individuals with a social relationship in social networks. Therefore, from the perspective of the spread of opinion post, the Agent-Based Opinion Dissemination (ABOD) model seems like a extension of the classical IC model. Nevertheless, different from IC model, the ABOD model not only focuses on the behaviors of individuals but also takes the interventions of different medias into account to simulate the dynamics of online public opinion.

Abstract a social network as a directed social graph $G = (V, E)$. Every node $v \in V$ represents a individual in the social network. At the same time, every directed edge going from u to v, i.e.$\langle u, v \rangle \in E$ shows the following relationship between u and v. For each pair of users of social networks, v can receive the information shared by u if u is followed by v. ABOD model regards every node $v \in V$ as an agent and the whole social graph as a system. There are two main approaches by which users of social networks who participate in online discussions can express their opinion on a topic. One is post or reposting a post that agrees with their preferred viewpoint. And the other is reposting a post that disagrees with their opinion and refuting it. No matter which approach a followee takes, his followers will be able to understand his opinion. Once exposed to an opinion piece, an individual may be persuaded to change his or her point of view and have the opportunity to decide whether or not to repost it. Once an individual reposts the opinion post, his or her identity is changed from follower to followee and the opinion expressed by the article as well as his or her own opinion are available to their followers. In the process, when considering different social relationships, the identity of the same individual may be different. This is why we define followee and follower at the same time.

Given an opinion post, its dissemination happening in a social network will finally result in the change of online public opinion. There are many factors that can influence the spread of opinion posts and the dynamics of online public opinion. Given that online public opinion integrates everyone's opinion, and individual's opinion may change after receiving an opinion post, we divide all the factors that can result in the change of online public opinion into two categories: factors related to the spread of opinion posts and factors related to changes in opinions. In ABOD model, crucial real-world behaviors happening in the dynamic of online public opinion are modeled from two perspectives: media's interventions and individual's behaviors. The former one includes the influence of network media, government media and social platforms while the latter one considers the influence of some kinds of individual's attributes. All the factors considered in ABOD model and opinion post propagation are described in detail in the subsequent sections.

2.1   Model's Parameters and Individuals' Attributes

Model's Parameters

opinion post's label $l(m)$: In online discussion, an opinion post usually expresses the author's opinion on a particular topic. And each topic may consist of many different keywords. Given a sequence consisting of n keywords, for any opinion post m, its label $l(m)$ is an n-dimensional 0-1 vector used to show its keywords. That is for $i = 1, 2, \ldots$, if opinion post m's keyword contains the i-th element of the keyword sequence, then the i-th element of $l(m)$ is 1, otherwise $l(m)$'s i-th element is 0.

opinion post's opinion $o(m)$: For opinion post m, $o(m) \in [-1, 1]$ shows the leaning of the opinion expressed by opinion post m.

thresholds for outer behaviors θ_a, θ_n and θ_f: The ABOD model considers the following three types of outer behaviors: the intervention of authoritative media, the intervention of network media and the change of social platforms' filtering rules. And three thresholds, denoted as θ_a, θ_n and θ_f, are used to determine when these outer behaviors happens. When the opinion post expresses positive point of view and the proportion of individuals holding positive opinion at current time step is smaller than θ_a, the authoritative media may try to boost the probability with which individuals receive the opinion post. And authoritative media may try to limit the spread of an opinion post expressing a negative opinion when most of individuals holds negative opinion.

Individual's Attributes

label $l(v)$: For a given topic, an individual participating in the discussion may be interested in certain keywords of the topic and not in other keywords. And different individuals are interested in different keywords. Therefore, label $l(v)$ is used to show the keywords that individual v are interested in. The method to obtain label $l(v)$ of individual v is similar to that used to generate opinion post's label $l(m)$. For each opinion post m and individual v, the similarity of $l(m)$ and $l(v)$ can be calculated by their dot product and play an important role in the propagation of opinion post.

opinion $o(v)$: Similar to opinion post m's opinion $o(m)$, $o(v)$ represents individual v's opinion and its value is confined into $[-1, 1]$.

threshold for exiting the discussion $\theta_t(v)$: Human attention is a limited resource. And the ABOD model takes into account the limited attention bound of individuals, which can be user-specific [12]. In other words, individual v will exit the discussion when v receives the opinion post no less than $\theta_t(v)$ times.

probabilities of reacting to outer behaviors $\delta_a(v), \delta_n(v), \delta_f(v)$: Given that there are three types of out behaviors considered in ABOD model, whether these intervention and change can truly influence the probability with which an opinion post propagates in a social network is related to each individual's reactions to them. And $\delta_a(v) \in [0, 1]$ represents the probability with which individual v reacts to the intervention of authoritative media. If $\delta_a(v) > 0$, it means the intervention of authoritative is effective for v and the extent of effectiveness is $\delta_a(v)$. And the meaning of $\delta_n(v) \in [0,1]$ and $\delta_f(v) \in [0,1]$ are similar to that of $\delta_a(v)$.

engagement rate $e(v,m)$: The frequency of interaction between individual v and its followers is defined as engagement rate $e(v,m)$ [3,13]. If individual v who has a small number of followers, v can frequently interact with v's followers and these social interactions can be high quality. In addition, given an opinion post m, if m's keywords are highly consistent with the keywords that v are interested in, v may be more willing to interact with its followers. Hence, we assume that engagement rate $e(v,m)$ is related to both the number of v's followers and the degree of consistency between $l(m)$ and $l(v)$.

activeness degree $a(v,m)$: A follower's activeness reflects the frequency and quality of his or her interactions with a followee's other followers. Individuals whose activeness degree are high tend to be more likely to be influenced. And the theoretical basis is social identity theory introduced in [9]. Besides, the similarity between opinion post's label and individual's label also affects the value of activeness degree.

self-persistence degree $s(v,m)$: This attribute reflects the extent to which v insists on maintaining its own opinion. The "self-persistence" concept and some other concepts which have the similar meaning are mentioned in some studies about opinion dynamics [14,15]. In ABOM model, we assume that self-persistence degree is related to individual v's inner attribute and the difference between the opinion of individual v and opinion post m.

2.2 Opinion Post Propagation

As is introduced in Sect. 1, users of social networks can post or repost an opinion post. The main difference between post and repost is that post is defined as a behavior that an individual shares a original opinion post while repost is defined as a behavior that an individual shares an existing opinion post. Then, individuals who post an opinion post can be defined as initial publishers. And followers of initial publishers repost the opinion post to expose it to their own followers. However, because post and repost have the same role in the spread of opinion post, we do not distinguish them from the perspective of probability which represents people's willing to spread an opinion post. And we replace both "post" and "repost" with "share" in the following.

Definition 1. *For each node $v \in V$, the probability with which v shares the opinion post m is defined as*

$$p_s(v,m) = \min\left\{ l(v) \cdot l(m) \cdot \cos^2\left(\frac{\pi|o(v) - o(m)|}{2}\right), 1 \right\} \qquad (1)$$

where $o(v)$ and $o(m)$ are the opinion of individual v and opinion post m, respectively.

What should be emphasized is that under this configuration only when opinions of both individual v and opinion post m are extreme, i.e., $|o(v) - o(m)|$ is closer to 2, the probability with which v shares m reaches maximum. This definition is abstracted from two real-world scenarios in which individuals are more likely to share an opinion post with their friends. When individuals come across an opinion post that expresses an opinion similar to their own opinions, they tend to share the opinion post with their followers to show the correctness of their opinion. Besides, when an individual are exposed to an opinion post whose point of view opposes their own opinions, it is possible that they share the opinion post. But in this case, they may express their opinions by criticizing or refuting the view of the opinion post. In fact, to some extent, whether an individual v criticizes or refutes opinion whose tendency differs from that of v's opinion depends on the distribution of the current views of the individuals around v. According to [4], people might remain silent when there is a divergence between their own views and the opinion voiced in their surrounding environment. Therefore, the ABOD model assumes that when the tendency of opinion post m's opinion is inconsistent with that of the individual v's point of view and more than half of v's followers hold views similar to v's opinion, v expresses its own views while sharing the opinion post. Otherwise, the individual only shares the opinion post without any comment.

Once an individual shares an opinion post, whether he or she comments or not, the opinion post can be exposed to the individual's followers. In classic IC model, the probability with which information successfully spreads from an individual to another individual is denoted as the weight attached to the tie between them and reflects the influence between them. However, the ABOD model takes a further step: consider the influence of individual's attributes and the outer behaviors. Given an opinion post m, we first introduce how to calculate individual's engagement rate and activeness degree.

Table 1. the setting for engagement rate $e(v)$

Range of $d(v)$	$[0, 0.06)$	$[0.06, 0.12)$	$[0.12, 0.25)$	$[0.25, 0.5)$	$[0.5, 0.9)$	$[0.9, 1]$
$e(v)$	0.3	0.25	0.18	0.12	0.05	0.01

Denote $d^-(v)$ as the out-degree of node v, $d^-_{\max} = \max_{v \in V} d^-(v)$ and $d(v) = \frac{d^-(v)}{d^-_{\max}}$. Because engagement rate $e(v, m)$ is related to both the number of v's followers and the degree of consistency between $l(m)$ and $l(v)$, we define $e(v, m) = \frac{e(v)}{2} + \frac{l(v) \cdot l(m)}{2|l(v)|}$ where the value of $e(v)$ can be obtained from Table 1. As for individual v's activeness degree, denote $d^+(v)$ as the indegree of node v and define $a(v, m) = \frac{a(v)}{2} + \frac{l(v) \cdot l(m)}{2|l(v)|}$ where $a(v) = \frac{1}{d^+(v)}$. Besides, denote one kind of v's inner attribute which is related to $s(v, m)$ as $s(v)$, then v's self-persistence towards opinion post m can be calculated by $s(v, m) = s(v) \cdot \frac{|o(v) - o(m)|}{2}$.

Denote P^t as the set of individuals who hold positive opinion at time step t. Then, according to the introduction of threshold for authoritative media's intervention θ_a, we define

$$I_a(v,m) = \begin{cases} 1, & \text{if } \frac{|P^t|}{|V|} \leq \theta_a \text{ and } o(m) \geq 0 \\ -1, & \text{if } \frac{|P^t|}{|V|} > \theta_a \text{ and } o(m) < 0 \\ 0, & \text{otherwise} \end{cases} \tag{2}$$

Similarly, denote R^t as the set of individuals who successfully receive opinion post m at time step t and denote C^t as the set of individuals whose opinion are updated at time step t. Then, we have

$$I_n(v,m) = \begin{cases} 1, & \text{if } \frac{|R^t|}{|V|} < \theta_n \\ 0, & \text{otherwise} \end{cases} \tag{3}$$

and

$$I_f(v,m) = \begin{cases} 1, & \text{if } \frac{|C^t|}{|V|} < \theta_f \\ 0, & \text{otherwise} \end{cases} \tag{4}$$

Based on them, we define the probability $\Delta(v,m)$ with which $v \in V$ can successfully receive the opinion post m resulting from intervention of different medias and change of filtering rules as

$$\Delta(v,m) = I_a(v,m) \cdot \delta_a(v) + I_n(v,m) \cdot \delta_n(v) + I_f(v,m) \cdot \delta_f(v), \tag{5}$$

where $\delta_a(v)$, $\delta_n(v)$ and $\delta_f(v)$ present the probability of reacting to three types of out behavior.

Then, we propose the following definition.

Definition 2. *For each directed edge $(u,v) \in E$, the probability with which $v \in V$ can successfully receive the opinion post m shared by $u \in V$ is defined as*

$$p_r(u,v,m) = \min \{w_{u,v} \cdot (e(u,m) + a(v,m)) + \Delta(v,m), 1\} \tag{6}$$

where $w_{u,v}$ is the weight of directed edge (u,v) and represents the influence of u on v, $e(u,m)$ is u's engagement rate, $a(v,m)$ is v's activeness degree and $\Delta(v,m)$ is used to measure the influence of three types outer behavior.

If at least two neighbors want to spread m to v at the same time, their tries are independent. So the probability with which node v can not receive m can be calculated by $\prod_{u \in N_v'} (1 - p_r(u,v))$ where N_v' consists of all the v's neighbors who share opinion post m.

2.3   Individual's Opinion Update

As is mentioned in Sect. 2.2, when an individual shares a opinion post, he or she can also comment on it or not. Therefore, an individual may be exposed to at least two different opinions at the same time. And according to the condition under which an individual comments on the opinion post, once an followee receives both opinion post's opinion and follower's opinion, the tendency of these two opinions must be inconsistent. In this part, we first propose the following definition under the assumption that the probabilities of individuals being convinced and updating their opinions are not affected by the number and diversity of opinions they receive.

Definition 3. *For each individual v, the probability with which $v \in V$ are persuaded to update v's opinion is defined as*

$$p_c(v,m) = \min\left\{\frac{a(v,m)}{s(v,m)},1\right\}. \tag{7}$$

where $a(v,m)$ and $s(v,m)$ are v's activeness degree and self-persistence degree, respectively.

Denote $I_o^{t-1}(v)$ as the set of opinions received by individual v at time step $t-1$. Let $o^{t-1}(v)$ and $o^t(v)$ be the opinion of individual v at time step $t-1$ and t, respectively. Use $X(v, I_o^{t-1}(v))$ to show the direction of change of v's opinion that happens at time step t. Then, we introduce the definition of $X(v, I_o^{t-1}(v))$ in two different cases. *Case I:* $|I_o^{t-1}(v)| = 1$. Define

$$X(v, I_o^{t-1}(v)) = \begin{cases} 0, & o(m) = 0 \\ 1, & o(m) \neq 0 \wedge o(v) \cdot o(m) \geq 0 \\ -1, & o(v) \cdot o(m) < 0 \end{cases} \tag{8}$$

Cased II: $|I_o^{t-1}(v)| \geq 2$. In this case, individual v is exposed to the opinion $o(m)$ expressed by the opinion post m and opinions of its followers. Denote $o(u) = \arg\max_{o(i)\in I_o(v)} |o(i) - o(m)|$. Define

$$X(v, I_o^{t-1}(v)) = \begin{cases} 0, & o(m) + o(u) = 0 \\ 1, & (o(m) + o(u) > 0 \wedge o(u) \geq 0) \vee (o(m) + o(u) < 0 \wedge o(u) < 0) \\ -1, & (o(m) + o(u) < 0 \wedge o(u) \geq 0) \vee (o(m) + o(u) > 0 \wedge o(u) < 0) \end{cases} \tag{9}$$

Then we propose the definition of opinion update function as follows.

Definition 4. *For an individual v which is persuaded to update his or her opinion, the opinion update function is defined as*

$$o^t(v) = o^{t-1} + X(v, I_o^{t-1}(v)) \cdot \delta_c, \tag{10}$$

where $X(v, I_o^{t-1}(v))$ and δ_c show the direction and degree of opinion change, respectively.

2.4   Model Framework

The algorithm which propagates the opinion post and updates individuals' opinions in the manner discussed above is shown in Algorithm 1.

Algorithm 1. Opinion Post Propagation and Individual's Opinion Update

1: Initialize model parameters and individual's attributes.
2: Initialize q as a breadth first queue consisting of all the selected initial publishers.
3: Initialize $T(v) = 1$ if $v \in V$ is a selected initial publisher, otherwise $T(v) = 0$.
4: **while** q is not empty **do**
5:    $u \leftarrow q.\text{dequeue}()$ ▷ u is an node in the given social directed graph
6:    **for** $v \in N^-(u)$ **do**   ▷ $N^-(u)$ is the set of out neighbor nodes of u
7:        **if** $T(v) < \theta_t(v)$ **then**
8:            Calculate $p_s(u, m)$ by Equation 1.
9:            Calculate $p_r(u, v)$ by Equation 2.
10:           v receives opinion post m with probability $p_s(u, m) \cdot p_r(u, v)$.
11:           **if** v receives opinion post m **then**
12:               $T(v) = T(v) + 1$.
13:               Calculate $p_c(v)$ by Equation 3.
14:               Update v's opinion $o(v)$ with probability $p_c(v)$ based on Equation 4.

---

3 Simulation

In this section, experiments are conducted to validate the working of the ABOM model and study the effect of model parameters mentioned in Sect. 2. Three datasets are used for experimentation. MI (Moreno-Innovation [5]) data set is a directed network capturing innovation, shown as 1098 edges among 246 physicians. And PHH(Petster-Hamster-Household [5]) data set includes 921 nodes and 4032 edges. For each individual v, $l(v)$ is a 6-dimension vector and each component is randomly chosen from $\{0, 1\}$, $o(v) \in [-1, 1]$ is randomly generated and follows a distribution $N(0, 0.3)$, $\theta_t(v)$ is randomly chosen from $\{1, 2, 3, 4, 5, 6\}$, and $\theta_a(v), \theta_n(v), \theta_f(v), e(v), a(v) \in [0, 1]$ are randomly generated. The distributions of out-degree, in-degree and label of the datasets are shown in Fig. 1. Set the proportion of initial opinion post m's publishers to all individuals to be nearly 10%. The first series of experiments are conducted to investigate the influence of opinion post's opinion on public opinion. We assume that the opinion post's opinion $o(m)$ is chosen from $\{-0.9, -0.1, 0.1, 0.9\}$. Set $l_{\text{fixed}}(m) = [1, 1, 1, 1, 1, 1]$ which means that the opinion post m consists of all the given keywords and the similarity between opinion post m's label and each individual v' label reaches maximum. For each pair of bars, the left one shows the number of individual whose initial opinion are in the given interval and is regarded as the baseline for comparison. Based on Fig. 2, we can draw a conclusion that if different opinion posts have the same tendency, the distribution of individuals' opinion after the dissemination of opinion post are similar. And the extreme degree of opinion post's opinion can influence the specific number of individuals whose opinion are within a certain range. Then, we pay attention to the influence of $l(m)$. According to the label distribution of MI and PHH data sets, we assume that $l_{\min}(m) = [0, 0, 0, 1, 0, 0]$ for both MI and PHH data sets while $l_{\min}(m) = [0, 0, 1, 0, 0, 0]$ for MI data set and

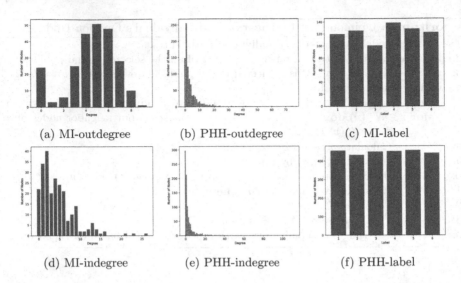

(a) MI-outdegree   (b) PHH-outdegree   (c) MI-label

(d) MI-indegree   (e) PHH-indegree   (f) PHH-label

Fig. 1. Out-degree, in-degree and label distribution of the datasets

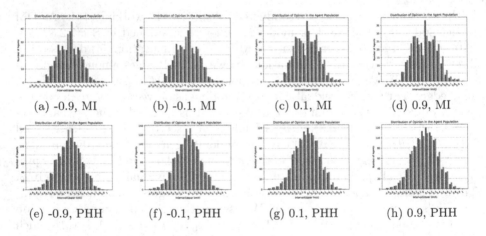

(a) -0.9, MI   (b) -0.1, MI   (c) 0.1, MI   (d) 0.9, MI

(e) -0.9, PHH   (f) -0.1, PHH   (g) 0.1, PHH   (h) 0.9, PHH

Fig. 2. the influence of $o(m)$ on opinion distribution of the datasets

$l_{\max}(m) = [1,0,0,0,0,0]$ for PHH data set. The experimental results are shown in Fig. 3. We find that the opinion distribution shown in Fig. 3c is different from those shown in Fig. 3a and Fig. 3b and the latter two are similar. In addition, it seems that the opinion distribution shown in Fig. 3d, Fig. 3e and Fig. 3f are nearly normal distribution while the average of the last one is smaller than those of the first two. These observations lead us to further study the ABOD model's parameters sensitivity in the future work.

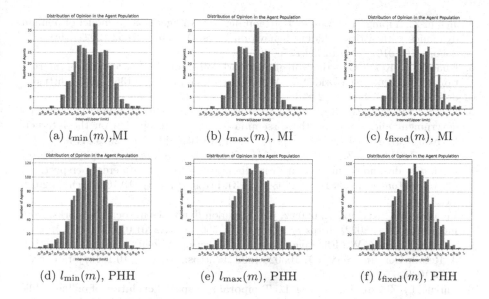

(a) $l_{\min}(m)$, MI   (b) $l_{\max}(m)$, MI   (c) $l_{\text{fixed}}(m)$, MI

(d) $l_{\min}(m)$, PHH   (e) $l_{\max}(m)$, PHH   (f) $l_{\text{fixed}}(m)$, PHH

Fig. 3. the influence of $l(m)$ on opinion distribution of the datasets

4 Conclusion

An agent-based model used for simulating the change of public opinion caused
by the propagation of opinion post in social networks is proposed in this paper.
It incorporates some realistic and important factors whose influence are under-
estimated by most scholars in the filed of opinion dynamic. From the perspective
of outer force, the intervention of both authoritative media and network media
as well as the change of filtering rules are considered to be variable during the
dissemination of opinion posts. And some individual's attributes that are related
to concepts and phenomenons studied in social science are introduced to make
the ABOD model more realistic. Two series of experiments conducted on two
data sets with different degree and label distribution are conducted and results
show the working of our proposed model. And the parameters sensitivity analysis
of ABOD model deserves a further study.

References

1. Baosheng, Z., He, H.: Research on evolution and control of network public opinion
   based on seir model with martial law mechanism. In: 2020 International Conference
   on Information Science and Education (ICISE-IE), pp. 272–276 (2020). https://
   doi.org/10.1109/ICISE51755.2020.00066
2. Dashuang, Z., Shaorong, S.: Public opinion dissemination and control of serious
   emergencies: based on epidemic model. Inf. Stud. Theory Appl. **41**(5), 104 (2018)
3. Doshi, R., Ramesh, A., Rao, S.: Modeling influencer marketing campaigns in social
   networks. IEEE Trans. Comput. Soc. Syst. **10**(1), 322–334 (2023). https://doi.org/
   10.1109/TCSS.2022.3140779

4. Jiefan, Z., Yiping, Y., Wenjie, T., Haoming, Z.: An agent-based model of opinion dynamics with attitude-hiding behaviors. Phys. A **603**, 127662 (2022). https://doi.org/10.1016/j.physa.2022.127662

5. Kunegis, J.: KONECT - the Koblenz network collection. In: Proceedings of International Conference on World Wide Web Companion, pp. 1343–1350 (2013). https://doi.org/10.1145/2487788.2488173

6. Lei, S., Yan-nan, Z.: Research on the impact of information interaction between government and media on the dissemination of public opinion on the internet. Heliyon **9**(6), e17407 (2023). https://doi.org/10.1016/j.heliyon.2023.e17407

7. Lixiao, G., Hongye, Z., Gaigai, Q., Lisha, G., Ke, W.: Online public opinion dissemination model and simulation under media intervention from different perspectives. Chaos Solitons Fractals **166**, 112959 (2023). https://doi.org/10.1016/j.chaos.2022.112959

8. Peralta, A.F., Kertész, J., niguez, G.I.: Opinion dynamics in social networks: from models to data (2022). https://doi.org/10.48550/arXiv.2201.01322

9. Samira, F., Fang, W.: Effective influencer marketing: a social identity perspective. J. Retail. Consum. Serv. **67**, 103026 (2022). https://doi.org/10.1016/j.jretconser.2022.103026

10. Shiyue, L., Zixuan, L., Yanling, L.: Temporal and spatial evolution of online public sentiment on emergencies. Inf. Process. Manag. **57**(2), 102177 (2020). https://doi.org/10.1016/j.ipm.2019.102177

11. Shuning, W.: Research on problems and countermeasures of government response to online public opinion in the era of self-media. In: The 2nd International Conference on Public Relations and Social Sciences (ICPRSS 2022), vol. 148, p. 03007 (2022). https://doi.org/10.1051/shsconf/202214803007

12. Shuyang, L., Qingbo, H., Fengjiao, W., Philip S., Y.: Steering information diffusion dynamically against user attention limitation. In: 2014 IEEE International Conference on Data Mining, pp. 330–339 (2014). https://doi.org/10.1109/ICDM.2014.131

13. Voorveld, H.A.M., van Noort, G., G. Muntinga, D., Bronner, F.: Engagement with social media and social media advertising: the differentiating role of platform type. J. Advert. **47**, 38–54 (2018)

14. Xu, H.Y., Luo, Y.P., Wu, J.W., Huang, M.C.: Hierarchical centralities of information transmissions in reaching a consensus. Phys. Lett. A **383**(5), 432–439 (2019). https://doi.org/10.1016/j.physleta.2018.11.013

15. Zhaogang, D., Xia, C., Yucheng, D., Francisco, H.: Consensus reaching in social network degroot model: the roles of the self-confidence and node degree. Inf. Sci. **486**, 62–72 (2019). https://doi.org/10.1016/j.ins.2019.02.028

16. Zhiying, W., Weikang, W., Chaolong, Y.: Model and simulation of interactive dissemination of multiple public opinion information under government interventio. J. Syst. Simul. **32**, 956–966 (2020)

Scalable Deep Metric Learning
on Attributed Graphs

Xiang Li[1]([✉]), Gagan Agrawal[2], Ruoming Jin[3], and Rajiv Ramnath[1]

[1] The Ohio State University, Columbus, OH 43210, USA
li.3880@osu.edu
[2] University of Georgia, Athens, GA 30602, USA
[3] Kent State University, Kent, OH 44242, USA

Abstract. We consider the problem of constructing embeddings of large attributed graphs and supporting multiple downstream learning tasks. We develop a graph embedding method, which is based on extending deep metric and unbiased contrastive learning techniques to 1) work with attributed graphs, 2) enabling a mini-batch based approach, and 3) achieving scalability. Based on a multi-class tuplet loss function, we present two algorithms – DMT for semi-supervised learning and DMAT-i for the unsupervised case. Analyzing our methods, we provide a generalization bound for the downstream node classification task and for the first time relate tuplet loss to contrastive learning. Through extensive experiments, we show high scalability of representation construction, and in applying the method for three downstream tasks (node clustering, node classification, and link prediction) better consistency over any single existing method.

Keywords: Attributed Graph · Deep Metric Learning · Graph Embedding · Graph Convolutional Network · Scalability

1 Introduction

Last several years have seen much interest in developing learning techniques on *attributed graphs*, i.e., graphs with features associated with nodes. Such graphs are seen in multiple domains such as recommendation systems [28], analysis of citation or social networks [11,22], and others. Of particular interest are the deep learning based graph embedding methods [6,21,29,31,32] that encode graph structural information and node features into low-dimensional representations for multiple downstream tasks. Current approaches use Graph Convolutional Networks (GCN) [32] or graph filters [6,29,31], but either way, the methods do not scale to large graphs. At a high level, these graph embeddings are designed with the primary objective of pulling examples with distinct labels apart from each other, while pushing the ones sharing the same label closer. It turns out that the spirit of deep metric learning [16,19] is also almost the same, though to date this idea has been primarily applied to learn visual representations [2,13,30].

© The Author(s), under exclusive license to Springer Nature Singapore Pte Ltd. 2024
M. H. Hà et al. (Eds.): CSoNet 2023, LNCS 14479, pp. 385–397, 2024.
https://doi.org/10.1007/978-981-97-0669-3_35

However, besides the challenges of tailoring these methods for attributed graphs, scalability is also a concern. Specifically, deep metric learning requires: 1) explicit sampling of tuplets such that one or more negative examples is against a single positive example [16], and 2) expensive search to increase negative hardness of samples, which is needed for enhanced learning power [7,15,19].

This paper addresses these problems in applying deep metric learning to attributed graphs in a scalable fashion. First, we employed an extended version of *multi-class tuplet loss* function [20] capable of working with multiple positive samples, building on a similar loss function has been discussed in [10] for image classification. Next, we use (approximate) Generalized PageRank (GPR) [3] as a scalable graph filter, which also leads to a compact node representation and, as we observe, increased negative sample hardness. Finally, we further achieve scalability by mini-batch training; specifically with each batch serving as a natural tuplet comprising multiple positive and negative samples; and eliminate the cost of sampling. With this basic framework, we build multiple algorithms, specifically, **D**eep **M**etric Learning with **M**ulti-class **T**uplet Loss (**DMT**) for semi-supervised learning and **DMAT-i** for unsupervised conditions.

To summarize the novelty of our contributions – we connect DMAT-i with an extensively applied contrastive loss [4] and theoretically establish how it leads to a bound on the generalization error of a downstream classification task. Equally important, our theoretical analysis explains why contrastive learning is successful for graph representation learning from a deep metric learning perspective. On the experimental side, we compare our methods with the state-of-the-art baselines in semi-supervised node classification, node clustering, and link prediction, and show more consistent level of accuracy as compared to any existing method, and state-of-the-art results in several cases. Finally, we also show greater scalability with our methods.

2   Preliminaries

Deep Metric Learning. We denote $x \in \mathcal{X}$ as the input data, with corresponding labels $y \in \mathcal{Y}$. Let $\mathcal{C}: \mathcal{X} \to \mathcal{Y}$ be the function of assigning these labels, i.e., $y = \mathcal{C}(x)$. In deep metric learning, we denote x^+ as a *positive sample* of x (i.e., $\mathcal{C}(x^+) = \mathcal{C}(x)$) and x^- as the *negative sample* (i.e., $\mathcal{C}(x^-) \neq \mathcal{C}(x)$). Define $p_x^+(x')$ to be the probability of observing x' as a positive sample of x and $p_x^-(x')$ the probability its being a negative sample. We assume the class probabilities are uniform such that probability of observing y as a label is τ^+ and probability of observing any different class is $\tau^- = 1 - \tau^+$. Then the data distribution can be decomposed as $p(x') = \tau^+ p_x^+(x') + \tau^- p_x^-(x')$.

Deep metric learning uses a neural network $f : \mathcal{X} \to \mathbb{R}^d$ to learn a d-dimensional nonlinear embedding $f(x)$ for each example x based on objectives such as tuplet loss [20] or triplet loss [19]. [20] proposed a $(\mathcal{N}+1)$-tuplet loss, where for a tuplet $(x, x^+, \{x_i^-\}_{i=1}^{N-1})$ we optimize to identify a single positive example from multiple negative examples as:

$$L_{\text{tuplet}}^{\mathcal{N}+1}(f) = \log \left(1 + \sum\nolimits_{i=1}^{\mathcal{N}-1} exp\{f(x)^\top f(x_i^-) - f(x)^\top f(x^+)\} \right) \quad (1)$$

This softmax function based objective is *hardness known* where the hard negative samples receive larger gradients [8].

Contrastive Learning. In fact, $L_{\text{tuplet}}^{\mathcal{N}+1}$ is mathematically equal to the ideal *unbiased contrastive loss* $\widetilde{L}_{\text{Unbiased}}^{\mathcal{N}+1}(f)$ proposed in [5], where they introduced:

$$\widetilde{L}_{\text{Unbiased}}^{\mathcal{N}+1}(f) = -\log \frac{exp\{f(x)^\top f(x^+)\}}{exp\{f(x)^\top f(x^+)\} + (\mathcal{N}-1)\mathbb{E}_{x^- \sim p_x^-} exp\{f(x)^\top f(x^-)\}} \tag{2}$$

In contrastive learning, the positive sample (and negative samples) are obtained through perturbation and mainly used in the unsupervised setting (where class label is not available). Thus, p_x^- is usually not accessible and negative samples x_i^- are generated from the (unlabeled) $p(x)$ [5]. Thus, the typical contrastive loss [4] now becomes:

$$\widetilde{L}_{\text{Contrast}}^{\mathcal{N}+1}(f) = -\log \frac{exp\{f(x)^\top f(x^+)\}}{exp\{f(x)^\top f(x^+)\} + (\mathcal{N}-1)\mathbb{E}_{x^- \sim p} exp\{f(x)^\top f(x^-)\}} \tag{3}$$

Since x_i^- is drawn from $p(x)$, it also has a probability of τ^+ of being a positive sample. Thus, the contrastive learning is closely related to, and can even be considered a variant of, deep metric learning, where the positive/negative samples are generated through different perturbation mechanisms. To facilitate our discussion, we use the notations $L_{\text{tuplet}}^{\mathcal{N}+1}$ and $\widetilde{L}_{\text{Unbiased}}^{\mathcal{N}+1}$ interchangeably in the rest of the paper. More related works are reviewed in appendix.

3 Methodology

3.1 Problem Statement

We are given an attributed graph $\mathcal{G} = (\mathcal{V}, \mathcal{E}, \widetilde{X})$, where $\mathcal{V} = \{v_1, v_2, \cdots, v_N\}$ and $\mathcal{E}$ represent node set and edge set, respectively, and $\widetilde{X}$ denotes the node attributes (i.e., each node is associated with a feature vector). Each vertex v_i belongs to a single class (or a cluster) and we apply all notations defined in deep metric learning to graph representations. The input data for deep metric learning $\mathcal{X}$ is calculated by a graph filter $\mathcal{H}$: $\mathcal{X} = \mathcal{H}(\widetilde{X}, A)$, where A is the adjacency matrix. Our objective is to learn an encoder $f : \mathcal{X} \to \mathbb{R}^d$ to obtain a d-dimensional embedding $f(\mathcal{X})$.

To develop deep metric learning (or contrastive learning) on graphs, we need to consider and address the following problems: (1) How to establish a unified approach to cover both semi-supervised and unsupervised settings for graphs? (2) How to scale the learning process for large-scale graphs by taking advantage of mini-batch training?

To elaborate on the second point, the existing contrastive learning for graph representation, particularly GCA [32], is built upon a GCN architecture and uses a typical contrastive loss [4]. It perturbs the graph topology and node attributes separately, which are fed to GCN to generate augmented views for contrasting. The transformation by GCN limits both accuracy (due to over-smoothing [12]) and scalability.

3.2   DMT Algorithm

We first propose the learning framework, **D**eep **M**etric Learning with **M**ulti-class **T**uplet (**DMT**), for semi-supervised node classification task. By applying a multiclass tuplet loss [10,20] which can recognize multiple positive samples from the tuplet, DMT addresses the aforementioned batch and scalability problem with the following distinguishing advantages: 1) high scalability and efficiency is achieved by using each shuffled node batch as a natural tuplet – this choice also alleviates the need for explicit (and expensive) sampling; 2) enhanced and faster representations construction through graph filtering, which we show later increases *negative sample hardness*.

Specifically, **DMT** employs a GPR-based graph smoothing filter $\mathcal{H}$ – as described earlier, the goal is to smooth node attributes $\widetilde{X}$ by graph structure via $\mathcal{X} = \mathcal{H}(\widetilde{X}, A)$ such that each $x \in \mathcal{X}$ contains information from its neighborhood as well. The details of this filtering, and how it can be done on large graphs, is presented in the appendix. This approach can also help increase negative sample hardness, a property that has been shown to accelerate training and enhance the discriminative power [7,15,19] - details again are captured in the appendix.

DMT employs an extended version of the multi-class tuplet loss from the deep metric learning [20]. Training is conducted in mini-batches and we consider each train batch $\mathcal{X}_B$ of size $\mathcal{B}$ as a $\mathcal{B}$-tuplet $(x, \{x_i^+\}_{i=1}^m, \{x_i^-\}_{i=1}^q)$ with m positive samples x^+ and q negative samples x^- of x respectively (m and q are batch dependent). Furthermore, we define $h(x, x'; f) = exp\{\frac{f(x)^T \cdot f(x')}{t}\}$, where we apply the cosine similarity as a metric distance such that each feature vector $f(x)$ is normalized before performing the Cartesian product. Temperature t is the radius of hypersphere where the representations lie [25] and can control penalty degree on hard negative samples as inspired by [24].

Now, the *multi-class tuplet loss* function is:

$$L_{\text{DMT}}^{m,q}(x; f) = -\log \frac{h(x, x; f) + \sum_{i=1}^m h(x, x_i^+; f)}{h(x, x; f) + \sum_{i=1}^m h(x, x_i^+; f) + \sum_{i=1}^q h(x, x_i^-; f)} \quad (4)$$

Here, x is counted as one positive sample of itself to avoid zero-value inside the *log* function. The loss function above shares a close mathematical form of supervised contrastive loss as proposed in [10] and enables us to create efficient mini-batch versions, while preserving the essential ideas behind metric or contrastive learning. One important aspect is because the function can work with varying m and q across batches, we can simply use all the positive and negative samples associated with any given batch.

3.3   DMAT-i Algorithm

In the unsupervised cases, $\{x_i^+\}$ and $\{x_i^-\}$ are no longer recognizable. To deal with this problem, we adopt the idea of contrastive learning, which includes multiple views of graph embeddings through *augmentation*, while assuming that the labeling still exists initially (thus, drawing from the deep metric learning framework). Then, we will show we can drop out the labels of the loss, which leads to the format of the contrastive learning loss.

Specifically, for one batch of samples $\mathcal{X}_B$ of size $\mathcal{B}$ together with their augmented counterparts, we have a $2\mathcal{B}$-tuplet $(x, \bar{x}, \{x_i^+\}_{i=1}^m, \{x_i^-\}_{i=1}^q)$ with m positive pairs and q negative pairs – here, $\bar{x}$ denotes the augmented counterpart (trivial positive sample) of x. Thus, we introduce an immediate DMAT tuplet loss $L_{\text{DMAT}}^{\text{m,q}}(x, \bar{x}; f)$ following the similar form of Eq. 4:

$$L_{\text{DMAT}}^{\text{m,q}}(x, \bar{x}; f) = -\log \frac{h(x, \bar{x}; f) + \sum_{i=1}^m h(x, x_i^+; f)}{h(x, \bar{x}; f) + \sum_{i=1}^m h(x, x_i^+; f) + \sum_{i=1}^q h(x, x_i^-; f)} \quad (5)$$

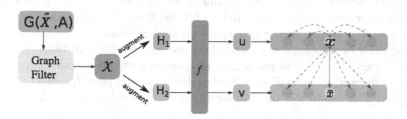

Fig. 1. Schematic of DMAT-i architecture. The graph filter generates smoothed node attributes $\mathcal{X}$ by incorporating graph structural information. A pair of views (H_1, H_2) of $\mathcal{X}$ are produced by augmentation and fed to the subsequent encoder f to generate latent representations $U = f(H_1)$ and $V = f(H_2)$. Metric distance measurement is performed on $U \bigcup V$. For each sample $x \in U$, its counterpart $\bar{x} \in V$ is the only recognizable positive sample.

Next, we extend DMAT to unsupervised cases where $\{x_i^+\}$ and $\{x_i^-\}$ are no longer recognizable. Here, the resulting method, DMAT-i, involves further simplification by extracting $\bar{x}$ as the only positive sample of x while ignoring all other positive ones. The loss function is (mathematically equal to Eq. 3):

$$L_{\text{DMAT-i}}^{\text{m,q}}(x, \bar{x}; f) = -\log \frac{h(x, \bar{x}; f)}{h(x, \bar{x}; f) + \sum_{i=1}^m h(x, x_i^+) + \sum_{i=1}^q h(x, x_i^-)} \quad (6)$$

Note $\{x_i^+\}_{i=1}^m$ and $\{x_i^-\}_{i=1}^q$ are explicitly denoted for ease of analysis, but they remain unknown during the training. Eq. 6 is in fact calculated without knowing any labels as:

$$L_{\text{DMAT-i}}^{\text{m,q}}(x, \bar{x}; f) = \log \left\{ \sum_{\substack{x' \in \mathcal{X}_B \\ x' \neq x}} h(x, x'; f) / h(x, \bar{x}; f) \right\}$$

Complete Algorithm: The general idea is illustrated in Fig. 1. Augmented views are generated on the fly from $\mathcal{X}$ by masking certain columns – the consequence is that the node features and structural information (encoded inside $\mathcal{X}$) are "distorted" simultaneously. A subsequent DNN based module can abstract information and perform metric similarity measurements (as in Eq. 6) between each pair of views. In real implementation, we use $\mathcal{X}$ as the anchor view and each augmented view as the counterpart to calculate an average of training loss. Thus, the encoder will be optimized to learn robust characteristics of representations across different views. The overall objective to be maximized is defined as the average agreement $L_{\text{DMAT-i}}(x, \bar{x}; f)$ over all interchangeable view pairs as follows:

$$\mathbf{J} = \frac{1}{2\mathcal{B}} \sum_{x \in \mathcal{X}_B} [L_{\text{DMAT-i}}^{\text{m,q}}(x, \bar{x}; f) + L_{\text{DMAT-i}}^{\text{m,q}}(\bar{x}, x; f)] \tag{7}$$

The entire training process is presented in Algorithm 1. As input, $\mathcal{X}$ is generated using random-walk based GnnBP (Graph neural network via Bidirectional Propagation [3]) as graph filtering. In line 3, multiple (n_{view}) augmented embedding will be generated from one batch of filtered feature $\mathcal{X}_B$ by masking certain columns in $\mathcal{X}_B$. In line 5, the generated graph embedding views will be input into the DNN based encoder f to produce the latent representations. The deep metric learning in line 6 is performed in batches between encoded representations u of the anchor view $\mathcal{X}_B$ and v of each augmented view H_B. The obtained embedding Z in line 8 will be used for the downstream learning tasks.

Algorithm 1. DMAT-i Training

Input data: GnnBP filtered attributes $\mathcal{X}$, Graph G, number of views: n_{view}

1: **for** $epoch = 1, 2, \cdots$ **do**
2:     **for** $\mathcal{X}_B$ in $\mathcal{X}$ **do**
3:         Generate n_{view} augmented views of $\mathcal{X}_B$: $\{H_B\}$
4:         **for** $i = 1, 2, \cdots$ **do**
5:             $u \leftarrow f(\mathcal{X}_B); v \leftarrow f(H_B^i)$
6:             Compute multi-class tuplet loss $\mathbf{J}$ (Eq.7)
7:         **end for**
8:         SGD update on f to minimize $\mathbf{J}$
9:     **end for**
10: **end for**
11: $Z \leftarrow f(\mathcal{X})$

---

4   Theoretical Analysis

DM(A)T and Contrastive Learning. $\widetilde{L}_{\text{Unbiased}}^{\mathcal{N}+1}(f)$ (Eq. 2) contrasts one positive sample against multiple negative samples and has been recognized as the ideal loss to optimize [5]. $L_{\text{DM(A)T}}^{\text{m,q}}(f)$ improves $\widetilde{L}_{\text{Unbiased}}^{\mathcal{N}+1}(f)$ by recognizing multiple positive samples at the same time. It turns out that it can be shown as a lower bound of $L_{\text{Unbiased}}^{\mathcal{N}+1}(f)$, specifically:

Lemma 1. *For any embedding f, given the same size of tuplets sharing one positive sample x_0^+, i.e. $(x, x_0^+, \{x_i^-\}_{i=1}^{N-1})$ for $L_{\text{Unbiased}}^{N+1}$ and $(x, x_0^+, \{x_i^+\}_{i=1}^{m}$, $\{x_i^-\}_{i=1}^{q})$ for $L_{\text{DM(A)T}}^{m,q}$, we have: $L_{\text{DM(A)T}}^{m,q}(f) \leq \widetilde{L}_{\text{Unbiased}}^{N+1}(f)$*

Now, as we know, both $\widetilde{L}_{\text{Unbiased}}^{N+1}(f)$ and $L_{\text{DM(A)T}}^{m,q}(f)$ require p_x^+ and p_x^-, which can only be accessed from training data (i.e., during supervised learning). For unsupervised conditions, our $L_{\text{DMAT-i}}^{m,q}$ considers $\bar{x}$ as the only available positive sample. Next, we will show how $L_{\text{DMAT-i}}^{m,q}$ contributes to a downstream learning task.

DMAT-i Generalization Bound on Node Classification. We relate $L_{\text{DMAT-i}}^{m,q}$ to a supervised loss and present how $L_{\text{DMAT-i}}^{m,q}$ leads to a generalization bound for a supervised node classification task. Consider a supervised node classification task with K classes, we fix the embedding $f(\mathcal{X})$ from DMAT-i representation learning and train a linear classifier $\psi(\mathcal{X}) = f(\mathcal{X})W^\top$ with the standard multiclass softmax cross entropy loss $L_{\text{Softmax}}(\psi)$. We define the supervised loss for the representation $f(\mathcal{X})$ as: $L_{\text{Sup}}(f) = \inf_{W \in \mathbb{R}^{K \times d}} L_{\text{Softmax}}(fW^\top)$

[5] has proved $\widetilde{L}_{\text{Unbiased}}^{N+1}(f)$ as an upper bound of $L_{\text{Sup}}(f)$. What we contribute here is to bound the difference between $\widetilde{L}_{\text{Unbiased}}^{N+1}(f)$ and $L_{\text{DMAT-i}}^{m,q}$.

Theorem 1. *For any embedding f and same size of tuplets,*

$$\left| \widetilde{L}_{Unbiased}^{N+1}(f) - L_{DMAT\text{-}i}^{m,q}(f) \right| \leq \sqrt{\frac{2(e^3 - e)(\tau^0)^2\pi}{m}} + \sqrt{\frac{2(e^3 - e)(\tau^-)^2\pi}{q}}$$

$$\tau^0 = \tau^+ \left(\frac{\left| \frac{1}{m}\sum_{i=1}^{m} h(x, x_i^+) - \mathbb{E}_{x^- \sim p_x^-} h(x, x^-) \right|}{\left| \frac{1}{m}\sum_{i=1}^{m} h(x, x_i^+) - \mathbb{E}_{x^+ \sim p_x^+} h(x, x^+) \right|} \right) \tag{8}$$

where $\sum_{i=1}^{m} h(x, x_i^+)$ represents the positive samples unrecognized by $L_{DMAT\text{-}i}^{m,q}$, i.e., false negative samples. Hence τ^0 covers the side effects from these false negatives and an empirical evaluation in appendix has shown reasonable small values of τ^0 for most samples across our experimental datasets.

In practice, we use an empirical estimate $\widehat{L}_{\text{DMAT-i}}^{m,q}(f)$ over N data samples $x \in \mathcal{X}$, each sample with a tuplet $(x, \bar{x}, \{x_i^+\}_{i=1}^{m}, \{x_i^-\}_{i=1}^{q})$. The optimization process learns an empirical risk minimizer $\widehat{f} \in \arg\min_{f \in \mathbb{F}} L_{\text{DMAT-i}}^{m,q}(f)$ from a function class $\mathbb{F}$. The generalization depends on the *empirical Rademacher complexity* $\mathcal{R}_{\mathcal{S}}(\mathbb{F})$ of $\mathbb{F}$ with respect to our data sample $\mathcal{S} = \{x_j, \bar{x}_j, \{x_{i,j}^+\}_{i=1}^{m}, \{x_{i,j}^-\}_{i=1}^{q}\}_{j=1}^{N}$. Let $f_{|\mathcal{S}} = (f_k(x_j), f_k(\bar{x}_j), \{f_k(x_{i,j}^+)\}_{i=1}^{m}, \{f_k(x_{i,j}^-)\}_{i=1}^{q})_{j \in [N], k \in [d]} \in \mathbb{R}^{(m+q+2)dN}$ be the restriction of f onto $\mathcal{S}$, using $[N] = \{1, \ldots, N\}$ and $[d] = \{1, \ldots, d\}$. Then $\mathcal{R}_{\mathcal{S}}(\mathbb{F})$ is defined as: $\mathcal{R}_{\mathcal{S}}(\mathbb{F}) := \mathbb{E}_\sigma \sup_{f \in \mathbb{F}} \langle \sigma, f_{|\mathcal{S}} \rangle$ where $\sigma \sim \{\pm 1\}^{(m+q+1)dN}$ are *Rademacher random variables*. We provide a data dependent bound from $L_{\text{DMAT-i}}^{m,q}(f)$ on the downstream supervised generalization error as follows.

Theorem 2. *With probability at least* $1 - \delta$, *for all* $f \in \mathbb{F}$ *and* $q \geq K - 1$,

$$L_{\text{Sup}}(\hat{f}) \leq L_{\text{DMAT-i}}^{\text{m,q}}(f) + \mathcal{O}\left(\tau^0 \sqrt{\frac{1}{m}} + \tau^- \sqrt{\frac{1}{q}} + \frac{\lambda \mathcal{R}_{\mathcal{S}}(\mathbb{F})}{N} + \Gamma \sqrt{\frac{\log \frac{1}{\delta}}{N}}\right)$$

where $\lambda = \frac{(m+q)e}{m+q+e}$ *and* $\Gamma = \log(m + q)$.

The bound states that if the function class $\mathbb{F}$ is sufficiently rich to contain embeddings for which $L_{\text{DMAT-i}}^{\text{m,q}}$ is small, then the representation encoder $\hat{f}$, learned from a large enough dataset, will perform well on the downstream classification task. The bound highlights the effects caused by the false negative pairs with the first term and also highlights the role of the inherent positive and negative sample sizes m and q per mini-batch in the objective function. The last term in the bound grows slowly with $m + q = 2\mathcal{B} - 2$, but the effect of this on the generalization error is small if the dataset size N is much larger than the batch size $\mathcal{B}$, as is common.

5   Experimental Results

Baselines: For the node clustering task, we compared the proposed DMAT-i model with multiple frameworks: 1) **KMeans** [9] (when applied to attributed graphs uses node attributes only); 2) **DeepWalk** [18], which uses topological information only, and seven recent frameworks that leverage both node attributes and graph structure: 3) **AGC (2019)** [29] that uses high-order graph convolution; 4) **DGI (2019)** [23] maximizes mutual information between patch representations and high-level summaries of graph; 5) **SDCN (2020)** [1] unifies an autoencoder module with a GCN module; 6) **AGE (2020)** [6] applies a customized Laplacian smoothing filter; 7) **SSGC (2021)** [31] is a variant of GCN that exploits a modified Markov Diffusion Kernel. 8) **GCA (2021)** [32] leverages a node-level contrastive loss between two augmented graph views to learn a graph representation; 9) **ProGCL (2022)** [26], on top of GCA, further proposed a more suitable measure for negatives hardness and similarity. To compare performance on node classification and link prediction, we select the most competitive graph embedding based frameworks correspondingly.

Scalability of Representation Construction. As in Fig. 2, all baselines hit specific ceilings as limited by the GPU memory capacity while DMAT-i can continuously scale with application of mini-batch training and use of random-walk to obtain approximate pagerank scores. Particularly, DMAT-i could handle 10^7 nodes, and no other frameworks could handle more than 10^6 nodes. The details of experimental settings are in appendix.

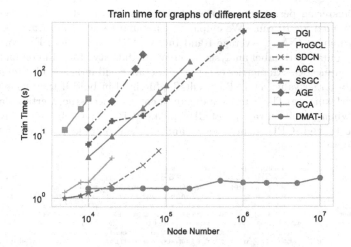

Fig. 2. Scalability of Different Frameworks: Training Time vs. No. of Nodes in Graph

5.1 Results on Downstream Tasks

DM(A)T is evaluated on performance of semi-supervised node classification while DMAT-i is evaluated for multiple tasks: node clustering, node classification, and link prediction. Our framework is compared with existing state-of-the-art appraoches on 8 real-world datasets (with details in appendix).

Node Clustering. We set the number of clusters to the number of ground-truth classes and perform K-Means algorithm [9] on resulting embedding Z from DMAT-i following previous efforts [1,6,17,31]. Table 1 summarizes clustering results. DMAT-i maintains either the state-of-the-art clustering results or is fairly close to the best. In particular, DMAT-i further reduced state-of-the-art accuracy gap between unsupervised learning and transductive supervised learning as presented later in Table 2 across datasets such as DBLP and Coauthor PHY. Not surprisingly, deep clustering methods that use both node attributes and graph structure appear to be more robust and stronger than those using either of them (KMeans and DeepWalk), although the latter shows good performance for certain datasets. Compared with GCN based methods like SDCN, DMAT-i shows significant performance gain due to solving over-smoothing issues through graph filtering. For clustering methods like AGC, SSGC or AGE with carefully designed Laplacian-smoothing filters, DMAT-i can still outperform them in most cases. The most competitive clustering performance comes from AGE on several datasets – however, it does not even converge for DBLP. DMAT-i achieves robust convergence across all real-word datasets – a detailed summary of convergence time across different datasets is presented in the appendix.

Table 1. Clustering performance on eight datasets (mean±std) where each experiment is performed for 10 runs. We employ six popular metrics: accuracy, Normalized Mutual Information (NMI), Average Rand Index (ARI), and macro F1-score are four metrics for ground-truth label analysis, whereas modularity [14] and conductance [27] are graph-level metrics. All metrics except conductance will indicate a better clustering output with a larger value. DMAT-i results highlighted in bold if they have the top 2 clustering performance. The asterisk indicates a convergence issue. Certain data points are missing when execution ran out of GPU memory. DGI can only handle five smaller datasets due to high GPU memory cost, and GCA also could not handle largest of these 8 datasets.

Dataset	Metric	KMeans	DeepWalk	SDCN	AGC	SSGC	AGE	DGI	GCA	ProGCL	DMAT-i
ACM	Accuracy ↑	66.62 ± 0.55	50.59 ± 4.27	89.63 ± 0.31	78.21 ± 0.00	84.43 ± 0.29	90.18 ± 0.13	90.17 ± 0.28	89.91 ± 0.46	89.18 ± 1.70	**91.60 ± 0.70**
	NMI ↑	32.41 ± 0.34	16.12 ± 4.96	66.74 ± 0.75	46.31 ± 0.01	56.15 ± 0.51	66.92 ± 0.30	67.84 ± 0.72	66.58 ± 0.91	64.64 ± 3.04	**70.95 ± 1.44**
	ARI ↑	30.22 ± 0.41	18.56 ± 5.80	72.00 ± 0.75	48.02 ± 0.00	60.17 ± 0.60	73.12 ± 0.31	73.28 ± 0.66	72.49 ± 1.08	70.72 ± 3.88	**76.72 ± 1.75**
	macro F1 ↑	66.83 ± 0.57	46.56 ± 4.43	89.60 ± 0.32	78.26 ± 0.00	84.44 ± 0.29	90.18 ± 0.13	90.12 ± 0.27	89.89 ± 0.46	89.16 ± 1.71	**91.59 ± 0.70**
	Modularity ↑	31.20 ± 0.50	38.57 ± 9.51	60.86 ± 0.16	59.44 ± 0.02	60.19 ± 0.05	60.93 ± 0.08	59.79 ± 0.19	60.05 ± 0.12	60.14 ± 0.43	57.92 ± 0.20
	Conductance ↓	30.96 ± 0.23	1.79 ± 0.59	3.07 ± 0.17	2.51 ± 0.01	2.54 ± 0.11	3.64 ± 0.19	3.87 ± 0.14	3.85 ± 0.18	4.06 ± 0.15	6.68 ± 0.27
DBLP	Accuracy ↑	38.65 ± 0.58	38.99 ± 0.02	69.08 ± 1.95	69.06 ± 0.06	68.66 ± 1.95	*62.49 ± 0.76	59.72 ± 4.68	77.69 ± 0.39	73.79 ± 1.70	**80.30 ± 0.60**
	NMI ↑	11.56 ± 0.53	5.91 ± 0.02	34.64 ± 1.94	37.00 ± 0.07	33.89 ± 2.08	*37.32 ± 0.50	26.90 ± 4.43	46.24 ± 0.57	41.54 ± 1.27	**51.00 ± 0.81**
	ARI ↑	6.95 ± 0.39	5.83 ± 0.02	36.31 ± 2.86	33.69 ± 0.13	37.30 ± 3.13	*34.60 ± 0.71	25.12 ± 4.76	50.46 ± 0.81	43.30 ± 2.99	**55.42 ± 1.08**
	macro F1 ↑	31.81 ± 0.53	63.87 ± 2.14	67.81 ± 3.46	68.59 ± 0.05	65.91 ± 2.19	*59.16 ± 0.83	59.31 ± 4.69	77.29 ± 0.37	72.96 ± 4.59	**74.94 ± 0.59**
	Modularity ↑	33.83 ± 0.47	64.05 ± 0.03	63.38 ± 1.87	68.77 ± 0.01	62.02 ± 1.64	*48.62 ± 0.87	50.16 ± 3.77	63.01 ± 0.28	64.62 ± 1.02	55.67 ± 0.71
	Conductance ↓	36.20 ± 0.51	4.03 ± 0.02	7.56 ± 0.54	5.29 ± 0.01	3.24 ± 0.52	*11.15 ± 0.15	13.84 ± 1.12	9.51 ± 0.16	9.53 ± 0.29	16.52 ± 0.53
Cora	Accuracy ↑	35.37 ± 3.72	63.87 ± 2.14	64.27 ± 4.87	65.23 ± 0.93	68.50 ± 1.98	74.34 ± 0.42	68.47 ± 1.43	69.24 ± 2.92	68.17 ± 4.67	**70.57 ± 1.28**
	NMI ↑	16.64 ± 4.21	44.11 ± 1.33	47.39 ± 3.49	50.05 ± 0.49	52.80 ± 1.03	58.11 ± 0.58	52.60 ± 0.88	54.48 ± 1.94	54.37 ± 2.71	53.59 ± 1.22
	ARI ↑	9.31 ± 2.14	39.64 ± 1.68	39.72 ± 5.53	40.23 ± 0.95	45.70 ± 1.28	50.87 ± 0.96	45.63 ± 1.44	46.63 ± 3.25	45.37 ± 5.04	**47.34 ± 2.41**
	macro F1 ↑	31.49 ± 4.58	57.98 ± 2.43	57.88 ± 6.99	58.93 ± 1.68	64.38 ± 2.71	70.37 ± 0.29	65.79 ± 1.53	68.10 ± 2.68	67.12 ± 4.85	**69.33 ± 1.00**
	Modularity ↑	20.77 ± 3.37	72.98 ± 0.79	62.59 ± 5.18	69.98 ± 0.46	73.71 ± 0.45	71.89 ± 0.14	69.86 ± 0.29	74.18 ± 0.51	74.36 ± 0.38	**74.19 ± 0.39**
	Conductance ↓	59.77 ± 5.31	7.88 ± 0.35	18.32 ± 2.26	11.08 ± 1.61	9.41 ± 0.55	8.23 ± 0.11	13.64 ± 0.69	10.27 ± 0.31	9.47 ± 0.54	10.04 ± 0.52
Citeseer	Accuracy ↑	46.70 ± 4.33	43.56 ± 1.03	63.42 ± 3.31	67.18 ± 0.52	67.86 ± 0.26	66.06 ± 0.78	68.68 ± 0.76	66.23 ± 1.00	66.43 ± 1.16	**67.46 ± 0.41**
	NMI ↑	18.42 ± 3.26	16.02 ± 0.56	37.28 ± 2.19	41.37 ± 0.70	41.86 ± 0.22	40.56 ± 0.88	43.22 ± 0.91	40.81 ± 1.15	41.41 ± 1.03	**41.75 ± 0.62**
	ARI ↑	18.42 ± 3.26	16.37 ± 0.66	37.40 ± 2.79	42.10 ± 0.87	42.95 ± 0.30	39.84 ± 0.75	44.53 ± 0.87	44.45 ± 1.40	41.73 ± 1.52	**42.48 ± 0.60**
	macro F1 ↑	44.47 ± 4.44	40.37 ± 0.97	56.16 ± 4.53	62.68 ± 0.48	63.61 ± 0.23	60.80 ± 0.75	64.41 ± 0.70	62.16 ± 0.95	62.53 ± 1.11	**62.83 ± 0.38**
	Modularity ↑	43.57 ± 2.67	76.44 ± 0.20	70.83 ± 2.77	77.57 ± 0.21	78.03 ± 0.12	71.88 ± 0.45	72.42 ± 0.38	73.14 ± 0.36	74.54 ± 0.44	**75.78 ± 0.23**
	Conductance ↓	37.21 ± 2.19	2.98 ± 0.12	7.98 ± 1.99	1.72 ± 0.04	1.75 ± 0.03	4.84 ± 0.13	7.19 ± 0.55	6.96 ± 0.58	5.57 ± 0.23	3.02 ± 0.22
Pubmed	Accuracy ↑	59.50 ± 0.02	69.98 ± 0.04	59.95 ± 1.00	61.54 ± 0.00	70.71 ± 0.00	69.66 ± 0.09	-	64.10 ± 2.11	-	**70.90 ± 0.20**
	NMI ↑	31.21 ± 0.10	29.09 ± 0.11	17.78 ± 0.91	29.11 ± 0.00	32.12 ± 0.00	29.06 ± 0.16	-	28.50 ± 2.41	-	**32.49 ± 0.28**
	ARI ↑	28.08 ± 0.08	31.81 ± 0.13	16.39 ± 1.16	26.16 ± 0.00	33.26 ± 0.00	31.26 ± 0.12	-	26.15 ± 2.46	-	**33.52 ± 0.36**
	macro F1 ↑	58.15 ± 0.02	68.51 ± 0.06	60.29 ± 1.02	60.28 ± 0.00	69.91 ± 0.00	68.68 ± 0.08	-	63.69 ± 2.34	-	**70.10 ± 0.20**
	Modularity ↑	34.92 ± 0.06	57.25 ± 0.26	55.53 ± 0.86	50.40 ± 0.00	57.73 ± 1.35	57.48 ± 0.10	-	53.90 ± 1.76	-	57.56 ± 0.44
	Conductance ↓	17.27 ± 0.04	4.67 ± 0.03	7.50 ± 0.58	8.65 ± 0.00	3.93 ± 0.00	4.75 ± 0.16	-	9.51 ± 0.80	-	**4.10 ± 0.20**
Amazon Photo	Accuracy ↑	27.86 ± 0.81	77.22 ± 2.48	60.42 ± 3.36	55.93 ± 0.09	56.16 ± 1.05	66.96 ± 3.00	61.05 ± 2.48	77.21 ± 0.72	78.27 ± 0.97	76.53 ± 1.32
	NMI ↑	13.78 ± 1.19	68.97 ± 1.96	50.08 ± 3.28	53.35 ± 0.05	51.74 ± 1.66	56.73 ± 2.62	52.93 ± 2.11	66.48 ± 1.23	70.11 ± 1.32	**66.94 ± 1.37**
	ARI ↑	5.62 ± 0.42	58.64 ± 2.81	40.08 ± 3.95	25.31 ± 0.10	33.86 ± 1.36	46.48 ± 3.37	39.59 ± 2.74	56.09 ± 0.92	61.30 ± 1.71	58.84 ± 1.07
	macro F1 ↑	23.78 ± 0.48	71.59 ± 2.47	53.13 ± 5.99	51.56 ± 0.06	52.00 ± 0.67	62.13 ± 3.33	59.60 ± 2.94	76.23 ± 0.71	72.35 ± 1.49	**70.05 ± 0.77**
	Modularity ↑	8.38 ± 0.51	73.18 ± 0.12	59.25 ± 4.04	57.69 ± 0.04	62.07 ± 1.88	64.07 ± 1.45	61.12 ± 1.39	67.76 ± 0.83	70.81 ± 0.47	**70.72 ± 0.19**
	Conductance ↓	76.38 ± 0.58	8.47 ± 0.23	20.17 ± 3.88	4.42 ± 0.00	8.37 ± 2.15	15.81 ± 1.49	22.14 ± 1.65	15.27 ± 1.11	10.46 ± 0.22	10.98 ± 0.67
Coauthor CS	Accuracy ↑	27.96 ± 1.09	67.10 ± 2.98	56.86 ± 3.40	62.24 ± 1.81	66.19 ± 1.19	76.35 ± 3.14	-	72.02 ± 2.54	-	**76.92 ± 1.26**
	NMI ↑	15.42 ± 2.25	66.67 ± 0.86	54.79 ± 2.44	65.22 ± 0.44	70.06 ± 6.67	76.75 ± 1.66	-	73.95 ± 1.02	-	**72.55 ± 0.41**
	ARI ↑	1.02 ± 0.74	53.66 ± 2.91	40.41 ± 4.52	46.96 ± 3.54	58.50 ± 0.17	71.27 ± 5.46	-	63.92 ± 3.21	-	**66.91 ± 1.38**
	macro F1 ↑	11.68 ± 1.56	63.36 ± 2.84	29.36 ± 3.22	51.42 ± 1.27	60.17 ± 1.94	71.10 ± 1.96	-	63.63 ± 3.28	-	**70.48 ± 3.13**
	Modularity ↑	9.61 ± 1.88	72.88 ± 0.41	68.50 ± 1.00	69.58 ± 0.14	71.82 ± 0.14	70.45 ± 1.71	-	69.91 ± 0.58	-	69.79 ± 0.40
	Conductance ↓	37.12 ± 4.10	17.09 ± 0.66	*23.09 ± 1.89	19.80 ± 0.24	19.76 ± 0.22	14.41 ± 0.32	-	21.96 ± 0.60	-	21.13 ± 0.66
Coauthor PHY	Accuracy ↑	56.19 ± 0.75	87.97 ± 0.01	64.65 ± 6.92	77.41 ± 0.00	55.70 ± 2.26	92.04 ± 0.06	-	-	-	**89.30 ± 0.70**
	NMI ↑	11.72 ± 1.92	69.13 ± 5.63	50.60 ± 3.71	62.11 ± 0.02	57.71 ± 1.31	75.84 ± 0.13	-	-	-	**72.54 ± 0.80**
	ARI ↑	8.25 ± 1.26	79.15 ± 0.03	48.76 ± 9.58	72.43 ± 0.02	44.91 ± 1.58	84.44 ± 0.16	-	-	-	**77.68 ± 1.61**
	macro F1 ↑	24.74 ± 2.11	83.32 ± 0.02	48.51 ± 4.68	62.09 ± 0.00	55.26 ± 2.30	88.90 ± 0.08	-	-	-	**86.65 ± 0.91**
	Modularity ↑	5.74 ± 0.83	47.96 ± 0.00	44.97 ± 3.16	45.31 ± 0.00	60.70 ± 0.39	47.69 ± 0.07	-	-	-	50.56 ± 0.27
	Conductance ↓	10.56 ± 1.47	5.99 ± 0.00	19.86 ± 7.16	5.80 ± 0.00	13.47 ± 0.07	5.73 ± 0.03	-	-	-	7.31 ± 0.31

Node Classification. For the transductive semi-supervised node classification task, we applied train-validation-test data split with fraction as train (10%), validation (10%), and test (80%). Following the experimental settings of SSGC [31] and GCA [32], we evaluate the classification performance of DM(A)T and DMAT-i by using a linear classifier to perform semi-supervised classification and report the accuracy. As shown in Table 2, the embedding generation methods are

Table 2. Accuracy for semi-supervised node classification task with different data usage for embedding generation: 1) using 10% of data with labels; 2) using all data without labels.

Data Usage	Method	Cora	Citeseer	Pubmed	ACM	DBLP	Amazon Photo	Coauthor CS	Coauthor PHY
train data (labeled)	DMT	84.30 ± 0.25	70.42 ± 0.33	86.46 ± 0.16	91.42 ± 0.36	77.59 ± 0.30	92.60 ± 0.42	93.30 ± 0.12	95.44 ± 0.03
	DMAT	83.92 ± 0.45	71.39 ± 0.38	86.19 ± 0.10	92.04 ± 0.16	79.80 ± 0.60	93.42 ± 0.11	93.44 ± 0.15	95.20 ± 0.04
	DMAT-i	81.99 ± 0.54	70.91 ± 0.27	83.52 ± 0.21	91.32 ± 0.38	78.39 ± 0.67	93.19 ± 0.19	92.90 ± 0.12	94.86 ± 0.07
all data (unlabeled)	DMAT-i	83.65 ± 0.71	72.40 ± 0.43	83.91 ± 0.25	92.55 ± 0.40	80.92 ± 0.50	92.97 ± 0.16	91.28 ± 0.17	94.66 ± 0.08
	SSGC	83.48 ± 0.06	68.15 ± 0.02	84.59 ± 0.01	89.71 ± 0.25	77.14 ± 0.12	89.80 ± 0.14	91.37 ± 0.03	94.88 ± 0.02
	GCA	83.89 ± 0.56	73.36 ± 0.34	83.38 ± 0.17	90.01 ± 0.27	79.73 ± 0.50	90.30 ± 0.47	90.91 ± 0.11	-
	ProGCL	85.04 ± 0.42	71.42 ± 0.39	-	88.98 ± 0.48	79.55 ± 0.41	92.13 ± 0.82	-	-
	AGE	83.78 ± 0.22	72.13 ± 0.92	80.18 ± 0.24	92.10 ± 0.18	80.02 ± 0.40	73.16 ± 2.53	91.40 ± 0.13	94.21 ± 0.08

Table 3. Link prediction performance.

Dataset	Metrics	DMAT-i	SSGC	AGE	GCA	ProGCL
Cora	AP	92.41 ± 0.28	93.24 ± 0.00	92.26 ± 0.30	92.95 ± 0.41	92.87 ± 0.28
	AUC	92.62 ± 0.29	92.14 ± 0.00	92.07 ± 0.21	92.95 ± 0.34	93.60 ± 0.13
Citeseer	AP	95.52 ± 0.26	96.14 ± 0.00	92.22 ± 0.48	93.38 ± 0.39	95.65 ± 0.28
	AUC	95.19 ± 0.26	95.29 ± 0.00	92.66 ± 0.44	92.57 ± 0.49	95.59 ± 0.24
Pubmed	AP	95.42 ± 0.08	97.53 ± 0.00	84.67 ± 0.09	92.65 ± 0.44	-
	AUC	95.18 ± 0.10	97.84 ± 0.00	86.70 ± 0.12	93.81 ± 0.37	-
ACM	AP	97.55 ± 0.17	82.33 ± 0.00	98.14 ± 0.10	92.61 ± 1.05	97.02 ± 0.23
	AUC	97.41 ± 0.17	81.15 ± 0.00	97.51 ± 0.18	94.19 ± 0.75	97.31 ± 0.18
DBLP	AP	95.50 ± 0.37	95.88 ± 0.00	92.68 ± 0.31	93.41 ± 0.61	95.99 ± 0.24
	AUC	95.50 ± 0.50	95.22 ± 0.00	90.96 ± 0.43	92.47 ± 0.59	95.38 ± 0.23
Amazon Photo	AP	92.73 ± 0.23	83.93 ± 0.00	91.65 ± 0.23	76.26 ± 1.39	93.43 ± 0.65
	AUC	93.89 ± 0.20	89.21 ± 0.00	93.12 ± 0.19	81.28 ± 1.34	95.66 ± 0.42
Coauthor CS	AP	94.76 ± 0.14	88.96 ± 0.00	93.96 ± 0.18	82.70 ± 0.98	-
	AUC	95.03 ± 0.12	93.56 ± 0.00	93.61 ± 0.15	83.54 ± 0.74	-
Coauthor PHY	AP	91.25 ± 0.20	93.92 ± 0.00	94.35 ± 0.08	-	-
	AUC	92.75 ± 0.15	96.57 ± 0.00	95.20 ± 0.06	-	-

categorized based on the availability of labels, where DM(A)T learns from train data (10% of all data) with labels and DMAT-i can proceed in an unsupervised way on all data samples. For comparison, we apply DMAT-i in both settings.

With labelled training data, DM(A)T turns out to achieve high quality of representations and shows superior results. DMAT-i, however, fails to recognize part of positive samples as compared with DMAT in this condition and lose some accuracy. When labels are completely unavailable, we can see that competitive results have been observed from DMAT-i compared to other advanced baselines under unsupervised setting. More importantly, DMAT-i generally achieves better performance when generating embedding in unsupervised condition than "partially-supervised" condition (with partial labels available). That is because much more samples i.e. all data, are included during tuplet loss optimization.

Link Prediction. To evaluate DMAT-i on this task, we remove 5% edges for validation and 10% edges for test while keeping all node attributes [6,17,21]. The reconstructed adjacency matrix $\hat{A}$ can be calculated as per the previous publication [21]: $\hat{A} = \sigma(ZZ^T)$, where σ denotes the sigmoid function. For comparison purposes, we report area under the ROC curve (AUC) and average precision (AP) following settings from previous works [6,17,21]. As shown in Table 3, DMAT-i is robust, i.e., produces high-quality link prediction (above 90% for both metrics for all datasets), whereas no other methods has a comparable consistency.

6   Conclusions

This paper has presented a scalable graph (node-level) learning framework. Employing a mutli-class tuplet loss function, we have introduced both semi-supervised learning and unsupervised algorithms. We have also established connections between tuplet loss and contrastive loss functions and also theoretically shown how our method leads to generalization error bound on the downstream classification task. The learned representation is used for three downstream tasks: node clustering, classification, and link prediction. Our extensive evaluation has shown better scalability over any existing method, and consistently high accuracy (state-of-the-art or very competitive in each case).

References

1. Bo, D., Wang, X., Shi, C., Zhu, M., Lu, E., Cui, P.: Structural deep clustering network. In: WWW (2020)
2. Chen, B., Li, P., Yan, Z., Wang, B., Zhang, L.: Deep metric learning with graph consistency. In: AAAI, vol. 35, pp. 982–990 (2021)
3. Chen, M., Wei, Z., Ding, B., Li, Y., Yuan, Y., Du, X., Wen, J.: Scalable graph neural networks via bidirectional propagation. In: NeurIPS (2020)
4. Chen, T., Kornblith, S., Norouzi, M., Hinton, G.: A simple framework for contrastive learning of visual representations. In: ICML (2020)
5. Chuang, C.Y., Robinson, J., Lin, Y.C., Torralba, A., Jegelka, S.: Debiased contrastive learning. In: NeurIPS (2020)
6. Cui, G., Zhou, J., Yang, C., Liu, Z.: Adaptive graph encoder for attributed graph embedding. In: KDD (2020)
7. Cui, Y., et al.: Fine-grained categorization and dataset bootstrapping using deep metric learning with humans in the loop. In: CVPR (2016)
8. Goodfellow, I., Bengio, Y., Courville, A.: Deep Learning. MIT Press, Cambridge (2016). http://www.deeplearningbook.org
9. Hartigan, J.A., Wong, M.A.: A k-means clustering algorithm. J. Roy. Stat. Soc. Ser. C (Appl. Stat.) 28(1), 100–108 (1979)
10. Khosla, P., et al.: Supervised contrastive learning. In: NeurIPS (2020)
11. Lazer, D., et al.: Life in the network: the coming age of computational social. Science 323 (2009)
12. Li, Q., Han, Z., Wu, X.: Deeper insights into graph convolutional networks for semi-supervised learning. In: AAAI (2018)
13. Meyer, B.J., Harwood, B., Drummond, T.: Deep metric learning and image classification with nearest neighbour gaussian kernels. In: ICIP (2018)

14. Newman, M.E.J.: Modularity and community structure in networks. Proc. Natl. Acad. Sci. **103**(23) (2006)
15. Norouzi, M., Fleet, D.J., Salakhutdinov, R.R.: Hamming distance metric learning. In: Advances in Neural Information Processing Systems, vol. 25 (2012)
16. Oh Song, H., Xiang, Y., Jegelka, S., Savarese, S.: Deep metric learning via lifted structured feature embedding. In: CVPR, pp. 4004–4012 (2016)
17. Park, J., Lee, M., Chang, H., Lee, K., Choi, J.: Symmetric graph convolutional autoencoder for unsupervised graph representation learning. In: ICCV (2019)
18. Perozzi, B., Al-Rfou, R., Skiena, S.: Deepwalk: online learning of social representations. In: KDD (2014)
19. Schroff, F., Kalenichenko, D., Philbin, J.: Facenet: a unified embedding for face recognition and clustering. In: CVPR (2015)
20. Sohn, K.: Improved deep metric learning with multi-class n-pair loss objective. In: Advances in Neural Information Processing Systems (2016)
21. Thomas, K.N., Max, W.: Variational graph auto-encoders. In: NIPS Workshop on Bayesian Deep Learning (2016)
22. Thomas, K.N., Welling, M.: Semi-supervised classification with graph convolutional networks. In: ICLR (2017)
23. Veličković, P., Fedus, W., Hamilton, W.L., Liò, P., Bengio, Y., Hjelm, R.: Deep graph infomax. In: ICLR (2019)
24. Wang, F., Liu, H.: Understanding the behaviour of contrastive loss. In: CVPR (2021)
25. Wang, T., Isola, P.: Understanding contrastive representation learning through alignment and uniformity on the hypersphere. In: ICML (2020)
26. Xia, J., Wu, L., Wang, G., Chen, J., Li, S.Z.: ProGCL: rethinking hard negative mining in graph contrastive learning. In: ICML (2022)
27. Yang, J., Leskovec, J.: Defining and evaluating network communities based on ground-truth. In: KDD. MDS 2012 (2012)
28. Ying, R., He, R., Chen, K., Eksombatchai, P., Hamilton, W.L., Leskovec, J.: Graph convolutional neural networks for web-scale recommender systems. In: KDD (2018)
29. Zhang, X., Liu, H., Li, Q., Wu, X.: Attributed graph clustering via adaptive graph convolution. In: IJCAI (2019)
30. Zhao, W., Rao, Y., Wang, Z., Lu, J., Zhou, J.: Towards interpretable deep metric learning with structural matching. In: Proceedings of the IEEE/CVF International Conference on Computer Vision (2021)
31. Zhu, H., Koniusz, P.: Simple spectral graph convolution. In: ICLR (2021)
32. Zhu, Y., Xu, Y., Yu, F., Liu, Q., Wu, S., Wang, L.: Graph contrastive learning with adaptive augmentation. In: WWW (2021)

Deep Learning Based Model for Stress Measurement in Online Social Networks

Akshat Gaurav[1], Brij B. Gupta[2,3(✉)], Kwok Tai Chui[4], and Varsha Arya[5]

[1] Ronin Institute, Montclair, NJ 07043, USA
akshat.gaurav@roninstitute.org

[2] Department of Computer Science and Information Engineering, Asia University,
Taichung City, Taiwan
gupta.brij@gmail.com

[3] Department of Electrical and Computer Engineering, Lebanese American
University, Beirut, Lebanon

[4] School of Science and Technology, Hong Kong Metropolitan University,
Kowloon, Hong Kong
jktchui@ouhk.edu.hk

[5] International Center for AI and Cyber Security Research and Innovations (CCRI),
Asia University, Taichung City, Taiwan

Abstract. Online Social Networks (OSNs) have become ubiquitous platforms for individuals to express their thoughts and emotions, making them valuable sources for studying mental health. This paper presents a novel Deep Learning-based approach for stress measurement in OSNs. We leverage a comprehensive dataset collected from Kaggle, specifically curated for stress analysis in social media. The proposed model demonstrates remarkable accuracy in identifying stress levels, paving the way for proactive mental health interventions and more targeted support systems in the digital age. This research contributes to the growing body of knowledge addressing mental health challenges in the online world, emphasizing the potential of AI and deep learning techniques in this critical domain.

Keywords: Stress Detection · Online Social Networks · Deep Learning · Reddit · Mental Health

1 Introduction

In the contemporary era, Online Social Networks (OSNs) have evolved into powerful platforms where individuals freely express their thoughts, emotions, and concerns. These platforms have become a digital mirror reflecting our society's multifaceted nature, offering valuable insights into the mental well-being of their users. Among the plethora of content shared on OSNs, the manifestation of stress is a subject of growing concern [17].

M. H. Hà et al. (Eds.): CSoNet 2023, LNCS 14479, pp. 398–406, 2024.
https://doi.org/10.1007/978-981-97-0669-3_36

However, Social media networks can have a significant impact on the stress levels of users. During events like the COVID-19 pandemic, social media platforms, such as Facebook, can create fear and panic among users. This fear and panic can be attributed to the dissemination of misinformation on social media, which contributes to increased stress levels [20,24]. Additionally, social media platforms can be used as a tool for detecting and predicting mental health issues, such as depression. Deep learning techniques have been employed to predict depression in social media users, highlighting the importance of social media information in identifying individuals at risk. Topic models have also been used to classify users with mental disorders, showing significant differences in expressions and emotions between ordinary users and those with mental disorders on social media platforms [1,2,4,8,25]. Furthermore, social media can be utilized for early detection and treatment of depression. A study developed a system to detect depression based on tweets and achieved high accuracy and f1 scores, indicating the potential of social media in identifying individuals in need of support [6,18].

Social media networks also play a role in influencing users' behaviors and social status. Influential nodes on social media platforms, identified based on social and behavioral characteristics, have been found to have a significant impact on other users [3,10,14,16]. These influential users can shape the opinions and actions of a large number of nodes on social networks. This influence can contribute to the stress experienced by users, as they may feel pressured to conform to certain behaviors or social expectations.

Hence, we can say that social media networks have a complex relationship with the stress levels of users. On one hand, the dissemination of misinformation and fear-inducing content on social media platforms can contribute to increased stress levels. On the other hand, social media can be used as a tool for detecting and predicting mental health issues, providing opportunities for early intervention and support. The influence of influential nodes on social media platforms can also contribute to the stress experienced by users. Further research is needed to fully understand the mechanisms through which social media networks affect the stress levels of users and to develop strategies for mitigating the negative impact of social media on mental well-being.

Our research harnesses a diverse dataset harvested from Reddit communities spanning a wide array of domains. With careful consideration, we have refined this dataset to 110 pertinent features, thus enabling precise stress analysis. Furthermore, we adopt rigorous preprocessing procedures, including data normalization, to facilitate the seamless integration of our data into a deep learning framework.

2 Related Work

Social media use has both positive and negative effects on psychological well-being [5,21,22]. Ostic et al. [13] found that social media use had an overall positive indirect impact on psychological well-being, mainly due to the positive effect of bonding and bridging social capital. Perry et al. [15], on the other hand, suggests that high usage of social media may act as a forum for negative behaviors and psychological detriments, such as feelings of exclusion or victimization. Keles et al. [9] conducted a systematic review and found that social media use correlated with depression, anxiety, and psychological distress in adolescents across all domains of social media use (time spent, activity, investment, and addiction). However, the review also noted methodological limitations of cross-sectional design, sampling, and measures. Overall, the papers suggest that social media use has complex effects on psychological well-being, and more research is needed to fully understand these effects.

Recently, researchers have suggested that deep learning and machine learning algorithms can effectively detect stress in social media posts. Illahi et al. [7] found that ensemble machine-learning approaches, such as boosting, bagging, and voting, outperformed classical machine-learning techniques like decision trees and support vector machines. Selvadass et al. [19] used supervised machine learning algorithms, such as BERT and TF-IDF, to identify stress in social media posts and achieved an accuracy of 75.80% with the Random Forest classifier. Nijhawan et al. [12] used natural language processing and machine learning algorithms, including a deep learning model called BERT, to detect stress based on social interactions and found that the models had a good detection rate. Lin et al. [11] used a deep neural network model to detect psychological stress from social media data and found that the model was effective and efficient. Overall, the papers suggest that ensemble machine learning approaches and deep neural network models are effective for detecting stress in social media posts.

3   Proposed Model

The proposed deep learning model is presented in Fig. 1 and is designed for stress measurement in online social networks. It consists of several layers, each with a specific function in processing and analyzing data to predict stress levels in users' online interactions.

- **Linear Layer 1**: The first layer takes input data and applies a linear transformation to it. It converts the input into a 32-dimensional vector. This transformation involves a set of weights and biases, which are learned during the training process to capture meaningful patterns in the data.
- **ReLU Activation 1**: After the first linear transformation, a Rectified Linear Unit (ReLU) activation function is applied element-wise to introduce non-linearity into the model. ReLU helps the model learn complex relationships and activations that linear transformations alone cannot capture.
- **Linear Layer 2**: The output of the first ReLU layer is then linearly transformed again into a 16-dimensional vector using a second set of weights and biases.
- **ReLU Activation 2**: Similar to the first activation, another ReLU activation is applied to the output of the second linear layer.

- **Linear Layer 3 (Output Layer):** Finally, the model reduces the 16-dimensional representation to a 2-dimensional vector, which represents the predicted stress levels. This output layer is essential for making stress predictions, and the model's parameters are fine-tuned during training to minimize prediction errors.

The model is trained on a labeled dataset, such as the Kaggle and Reddit dataset for stress analysis in social media, where the input data includes features extracted from social media posts, comments, or user profiles. The model learns to capture patterns and relationships between these features and stress levels during training.

```
====================================================================================
Layer (type:depth-idx)                    Output Shape              Param #
====================================================================================
DeepLearning                              [32, 2]                   --
├─Linear: 1-1                             [32, 32]                  3,552
├─ReLU: 1-2                               [32, 32]                  --
├─Linear: 1-3                             [32, 16]                  528
├─ReLU: 1-4                               [32, 16]                  --
├─Linear: 1-5                             [32, 2]                   34
====================================================================================
Total params: 4,114
Trainable params: 4,114
Non-trainable params: 0
Total mult-adds (M): 0.13
====================================================================================
Input size (MB): 0.01
Forward/backward pass size (MB): 0.01
Params size (MB): 0.02
Estimated Total Size (MB): 0.04
====================================================================================
```

Fig. 1. Model Architecture

4 Results and Discussion

4.1 Data Preprocessing

First, we prepare the dataset for the deep learning model; this involves cleaning and reducing the feature set, ensuring all data is on a consistent scale through normalization, and then converting the data into tensors suitable for deep learning. Finally, we set up data loaders to efficiently feed batches of data to our deep learning model during the training process, with each batch containing 32 data points. This preprocessing is essential for training a deep learning model effectively on your stress identification task.

- **Dataset Collection from Kaggle:** We initially collected dataset from Kaggle [23]. This dataset contains lengthy social media data from five different categories of Reddit communities and is intended for identifying stress. It consists of 116 features (attributes) and 2837 rows (data points).
- **Feature Selection:** We recognized that not all of the 116 features are relevant to our task. To streamline the dataset and potentially improve model performance, we performed feature selection. After this step, we were left with a reduced dataset containing 110 relevant features.
- **Data Normalization:** Data normalization is a crucial preprocessing step in machine learning and deep learning. It involves scaling the data to ensure that all features have the same range. This helps prevent some features from dominating the learning process. By normalizing your dataset, we've ensured that each feature's values are on a similar scale.

- **Tensor Conversion**: Deep learning models typically work with numerical data in the form of tensors. We converted our normalized dataset into tensors. Tensors are multi-dimensional arrays that can hold your data in a format suitable for feeding into a neural network.
- **Data Loader Creation**: In deep learning, training is typically done in batches to efficiently process large datasets. We created data loaders with a batch size of 32. Data loaders are responsible for managing how data is loaded and distributed to the model during training. Each batch consists of 32 data points, and the data loader takes care of iterating through the dataset, providing batches of data to the model for training.

4.2   Accuracy and Loss Curves

Using Cross-Entropy Loss and Stochastic Gradient Descent (SGD) optimisation over 100 iterations, the model was trained. The learning rate was 0.001. The loss and accuracy curves are represents in Fig. 2.

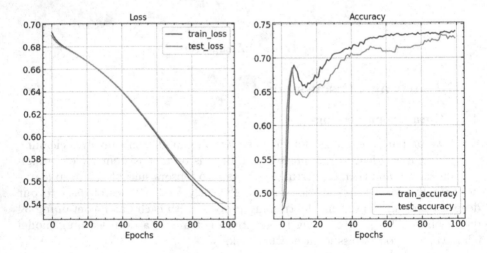

Fig. 2. Accuracy and Loss Curves

From Fig. 2, we can observe the model's progression in terms of training and testing accuracy and loss. In the initial epochs, both training and testing accuracy showed modest improvement, indicating that the model was learning patterns in the data. However, as training continued, the model's accuracy on the testing data began to plateau, suggesting that further training might not significantly improve its generalization. The loss curves displayed a similar pattern, initially decreasing but eventually reaching a minimum point. These curves provide essential insights into the model's learning dynamics and its ability to generalize to unseen data, aiding in the evaluation and potential fine-tuning of the model for better performance.

4.3   Classification Report

The classification report, represented in Fig. 3, offers a detailed evaluation of the model's performance, highlighting its ability to distinguish between "Normal" and "Stress" instances. Our model demonstrates reasonably good precision and recall, with room for potential improvements in classifying "Normal" instances. Overall, it achieves an accuracy of 73%, indicating its effectiveness in this binary classification task. The presented classification report provides a comprehensive evaluation of a binary classification model's performance on a dataset.

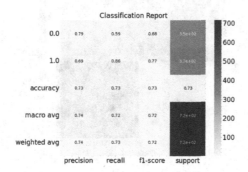

Fig. 3. Classification Report

- **Precision**: Precision is the degree to which a model is accurate in its positive predictions. The "Normal" class has a precision of 0.79, indicating that 79% of the time, the proper class was chosen. Accurately classifying 69% of cases as "Stress" yields an accuracy of 0.69 for this class.
- **Recall**: Model performance is evaluated by its recall, also known as sensitivity or true positive rate. The "Normal" class has a recall of 0.59, meaning that 59% of real-world "Normal" occurrences were correctly recognised by the model. The "Stress" class's recall is 0.86, indicating that 86% of real-world "Stress" occurrences were correctly recognised by the model.
- **F1-Score**: The F1-score balances accuracy and recall into a single number. It's a good compromise between accuracy and memory retention. The F1-scores for the "Normal" and "Stress" groups are 0.68 and 0.77, respectively.
- **Support**: The amount of data points that may be attributed to each class is represented by support. Of the total, 346 are "Normal" and 369 are "Stress."
- **Accuracy**: The model was able to accurately categorise 73% of all cases in the training data, giving it an overall accuracy of 0.73.
- **Macro Avg**: Accuracy, recall, and F1-score are summarised for both groups in this row. The average F1-score, recall, and accuracy across the board is 0.72.
- **Weighted Avg**: In this row, we provide the class-imbalanced weighted average of accuracy, recall, and F1-score. It thinks about how well each group is supported. F1-score is 0.72, recall is 0.73, and accuracy is 0.74 on average when weighted.

4.4   Confusion Matrix

The confusion matrix (Fig. 4) allows for a detailed assessment of the model's performance, particularly in terms of its ability to classify each class and identify errors correctly. It's a crucial tool for understanding where the model may need improvement and for evaluating its effectiveness in a binary classification problem.

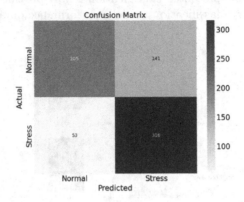

Fig. 4. Confusion Matrix

- **True Positives (TP)**: The model accurately identified 316 instances as "Stress," while the true category was "Stress."
- **True Negatives (TN)**: In 205 instances, the model accurately identified the true category as "Normal."
- **False Positives (FP)**: There are 141 instances that are actually "Normal," but the model incorrectly predicted them as "Stress." These are also known as Type I errors or false alarms.
- **False Negatives (FN)**: There are 53 instances that are actually "Stress," but the model incorrectly predicted them as "Normal." These are also known as Type II errors or misses.

5   Conclusion

This paper presents a deep learning-based model for stress measurement in online social networks, utilizing a multi-domain dataset from Reddit communities. Our model exhibited promising results, achieving an overall accuracy of 73%. While precision and recall varied between the "Normal" and "Stress" classes, the model's ability to identify stress-related content is notably robust. These findings underscore the potential of deep learning techniques in discerning stress indicators from social media data. However, further refinements to address class imbalances and overfitting are warranted. Overall, this research contributes to the ongoing exploration of mental health analysis in the digital age, offering valuable insights for proactive interventions and support systems in online social networks.

Acknowledgement. This research work is supported by National Science and Technology Council (NSTC), Taiwan Grant No. NSTC112-2221-E-468-008-MY3.

References

1. Al Sobbahi, R., Tekli, J.: Comparing deep learning models for low-light natural scene image enhancement and their impact on object detection and classification: overview, empirical evaluation, and challenges. Signal Process. Image Commun. 116848 (2022)
2. Chakar, J., Sobbahi, R.A., Tekli, J.: Depthwise separable convolutions and variational dropout within the context of YOLOv3. In: Bebis, G., et al. (eds.) ISVC 2020, pp. 107–120. Springer, Cham (2020). https://doi.org/10.1007/978-3-030-64556-4_9
3. Forouzandeh, S., Sheikhahmadi, A., Aghdam, A.R., Xu, S.: New centrality measure for nodes based on user social status and behavior on Facebook. Int. J. Web Inf. Syst. **14**, 158–176 (2018). https://doi.org/10.1108/ijwis-07-2017-0053
4. Gao, W., Gao, B.Y.W., Yang, Y., Wang, Y.: Depression detection in social media using XLNet with topic distributions. J. Comput. **33**, 095–106 (2022). https://doi.org/10.53106/199115992022083304008
5. Hasib, K.M., Towhid, N.A., Islam, M.R.: HSDLM: a hybrid sampling with deep learning method for imbalanced data classification. Int. J. Cloud Appl. Comput. (IJCAC) **11**(4), 1–13 (2021)
6. Hidayatullah, M.R., Maharani, N.W.: Depression detection on twitter social media using decision tree. Jurnal RESTI (Rekayasa Sistem Dan Teknologi Informasi) **6**, 677–683 (2022). https://doi.org/10.29207/resti.v6i4.4275
7. Illahi, M., Siddiqui, I.F., Ali, Q., Alvi, F.A.: Ensemble machine learning approach for stress detection in social media texts. Quaid-E-Awam Univ. Res. J. Eng. Sci. Technol. Nawabshah **20**(02), 123–128 (2022)
8. Jain, A.K., Gupta, B.: PHISH-SAFE: URL features-based phishing detection system using machine learning. In: Bokhari, M., Agrawal, N., Saini, D. (eds.) Cyber Security: Proceedings of CSI 2015, pp. 467–474. Springer, Singapore (2018). https://doi.org/10.1007/978-981-10-8536-9_44
9. Keles, B., McCrae, N., Grealish, A.: A systematic review: the influence of social media on depression, anxiety and psychological distress in adolescents. Int. J. Adolesc. Youth **25**(1), 79–93 (2020)
10. Lakhwani, K., et al.: Adaptive and convex optimization-inspired workflow scheduling for cloud environment. Int. J. Cloud Appl. Comput. (IJCAC) **13**(1), 1–25 (2023)
11. Lin, H., et al.: User-level psychological stress detection from social media using deep neural network. In: Proceedings of the 22nd ACM International Conference on Multimedia, pp. 507–516 (2014)
12. Nijhwan, T., Attigeri, G., Ananthakrishna, T.: Stress detection using natural language processing and machine learning over social interactions. J. Big Data **9**(1) (2022)
13. Ostic, D., et al.: Effects of social media use on psychological well-being: a mediated model. Front. Psychol. **12**, 678766 (2021)
14. Peñalvo, F.J.G., et al.: Mobile cloud computing and sustainable development: opportunities, challenges, and future directions. Int. J. Cloud Appl. Comput. (IJCAC) **12**(1), 1–20 (2022)

15. Perry, J., Devore, S.K., Pellegrino, C., Salce, A.J.: Social media usage and its effects on the psychological health of adolescents. NASN School Nurse 1942602X231159901 (2023)

16. Ramadan, Z.B., Farah, M.F.: Influencing the influencers: the case of retailers' social shopping platforms. Int. J. Web Based Communities **16**(3), 279–295 (2020)

17. Ren, P., et al.: A survey of deep active learning. ACM Comput. Surv. (CSUR) **54**(9), 1–40 (2021)

18. Sayour, M.H., Kozhaya, S.E., Saab, S.S.: Autonomous robotic manipulation: real-time, deep-learning approach for grasping of unknown objects. J. Robot. **2022** (2022)

19. Selvadass, S., Bruntha, P.M., Priyadharsini, K.: Stress analysis in social media using ml algorithms. In: 2022 4th International Conference on Smart Systems and Inventive Technology (ICSSIT), pp. 1502–1506. IEEE (2022)

20. Shankar, K., Perumal, E., Elhoseny, M., Taher, F., Gupta, B., El-Latif, A.A.A.: Synergic deep learning for smart health diagnosis of covid-19 for connected living and smart cities. ACM Trans. Internet Technol. (TOIT) **22**(3), 1–14 (2021)

21. Singh, A., Gupta, B.B.: Distributed denial-of-service (DDoS) attacks and defense mechanisms in various web-enabled computing platforms: issues, challenges, and future research directions. Int. J. Semant. Web Inf. Syst. (IJSWIS) **18**(1), 1–43 (2022)

22. Tembhurne, J.V., Almin, M.M., Diwan, T.: Mc-DNN: fake news detection using multi-channel deep neural networks. Int. J. Semant. Web Inf. Syst. (IJSWIS) **18**(1), 1–20 (2022)

23. Turcan, E., McKeown, K.: Dreaddit: a reddit dataset for stress analysis in social media. arXiv preprint arXiv:1911.00133 (2019)

24. Yas, H., et al.: The negative role of social media during the covid-19 outbreak. Int. J. Sustain. Dev. Plan. **16**, 219–228 (2021). https://doi.org/10.18280/ijsdp.160202

25. Zhang, Z., Sun, R., Zhao, C., Wang, J., Chang, C.K., Gupta, B.B.: Cyvod: a novel trinity multimedia social network scheme. Multimedia Tools Appl. **76**, 18513–18529 (2017)

Stress Expression Identification Model for Emotion-Driven Association Calculation over Social Network Blogs

Tie Hua Zhou[iD], Jinwei Wang[iD], Ling Wang[✉][iD], Haoyu Hao[iD],
and Tianshuo Bi[iD]

Department of Computer Science and Technology, School of Computer Science,
Northeast Electric Power University, Jilin, China
{thzhou,2202101007,smile2867ling,2202201020,2202200985}@neepu.edu.cn

Abstract. Emotion and stress expression are deeply intertwined. Analyzing blog data from social network platforms reveals that specific emotions often appear simultaneously with expressions indicating stress, and emotional expressions in different stress scenarios also display unique patterns. This paper introduces the Stress Expression Identification (SEI) model based on Emotion Sequence Pattern Analysis (ESPA), which can identify user stress accurately by exploring the corresponding rules between emotion and stress. We constructed a stress emotion dictionary, mined the pattern rules of emotion sequence under different stress scenarios, and established a stress emotion rule set, aiming at identifying and understanding stress more accurately. The experimental results show that this model achieved a higher accuracy rate in stress identification.

Keywords: Stress expression · Emotion sequence · Association rules · NLP · Data mining

1 Introduction

Emotion is an important indicator of stress analysis. Understanding the relationship between emotion and stress expression can reveal the interaction between them more deeply, which is of great significance for stress identification. The rapid development of social networking platforms has provided us with a large amount of data, providing new possibilities for objectively identifying stress. In particular, rapid advances in machine learning and artificial intelligence technologies allow us to extract useful information from large amounts of complex data, providing powerful computational tools for accurately identifying stress.

Social networking platforms have become a key source of data for sentiment analysis tasks. Shaw et al. [1] used a multi-channel CNN to automatically extract features to identify stressed text, achieving an accuracy of 97.5% on a Twitter dataset. Yang et al. [2] proposed a Knowledge Perception and Comparison network (KC-Net) for stress states to identify depressed and stressed users on the

M. H. Hà et al. (Eds.): CSoNet 2023, LNCS 14479, pp. 407–415, 2024.
https://doi.org/10.1007/978-981-97-0669-3_37

Dreaddit dataset. Prashanth et al. [3] used neighborhood blogs to solve the data sparsity problem caused by the limited number of blogs in pressure recognition, and achieved better performance. Singh et al. [4] transformed interview information and social networking site text data into scale factors of perceived stress scale for stress identification, and achieved good experimental results. In the field of emotion detection, a series of outstanding research has emerged. Prabhu et al. [5] used a multimodal approach of transfer learning to detect depression using emotions. Dheeraj et al. [6] proposed a model with bidirectional long short-term memory and a convolutional neural network multi-head attention model to extract various negative emotions.

However, considering the complexity of stress, only analyzing non-emotional factors or a limited number of emotions may not fully capture its details, which limits the interpretability of the model. Therefore, it is necessary to propose a more fine-grained stress identification model that uses more detailed classification of emotions and subtle changes between emotions under different stress scenarios to identify and interpret stress. This paper proposes an SEI model based on ESPA, which uses advanced algorithms and data processing techniques to conduct in-depth analysis of data on social networking platforms, establish rules, and train models to identify stress more accurately.

2   Emotion Sequence Pattern Analysis

This section introduces ESPA, which aims to mine representative rules between emotion and stress, and quantify these rules to form rule sets for subsequent stress identification tasks.

2.1   Stress Emotions Dictionary Construction

This section describes the process of building a stress dictionary. Data preprocessing includes removing urls from blogs, using the no slang dictionary to handle slang and abbreviations, and using NRC dictionaries to remove noise words. The list of emotion words is vectorized using the improved TF-IDF method, and then unsupervised clustering is performed using the Latent Dirichlet Allocation. We got a total of 18 emotional word themes, which are anxiety, fear, nervous, panic, tension, worry, depression, sadness, hopelessness, helplessness, guilt, shame, anger, frustration, overwhelm, confusion, excitement and optimism. Use the WordNet lexicon to expand our stress emotion dictionary. For each emotion, we iteratively obtain all synonyms based on the 20 most relevant words, and then remove duplicate words. The average similarity was calculated as the strength support of potential words under this emotion, and words with strength support less than 0.3 were removed. Finally, we obtained a 20,055 word dictionary of stress emotions.

2.2   Stress Emotion Sequence Intensity Quantification

The intensity of emotional sequence patterns mined under different stress scenarios was quantified using ESPA. ESPA is based on the stress dictionary, uses the FP-Growth algorithm to mine stress emotion sequences under stress situations, and considers the potential emotion sequence pattern conversion probability and intensity to generate $ERSet$. Table 1 lists the 8 parameters of the ESPA. The pseudocode of ESPA is shown in Algorithm 1.

Table 1. Parameters in ESPA

Parameter	Definition
fp_i	Frequent pattern set for scenario i
$ps_{(i,j)}$	Strength support of the j-th pattern in fp_i
aps_i	Average strength support for scenario i
$apa_{(i,j)}$	Antecedent of the j-th association pattern in scenario i
$apc_{(i,j)}$	Consequent of the j-th association pattern in scenario i
$ac_{(i,j)}$	Confidence of the j-th association pattern in scenario i
pp_i	Potential pattern for scenario i
pps_i	Strength support of the potential pattern for scenario i

Algorithm 1. ESPA

```
1:  Input: PssC , n              ▷ Stress scenarios corpus and number of scenarios labels
2:  Output: ERSet                        ▷ Stress emotion sequence pattern rule set
3:  Begin
4:  for i = 0 to n - 1 do
5:      Use FP-Growth to get the fpᵢ and association rules
6:      Calculate q and apsᵢ based on fpᵢ
7:      for j = 0 to q - 1 do
8:          if ps₍ᵢ,ⱼ₎ > apsᵢ then
9:              Add ps₍ᵢ,ⱼ₎ to ERSet
10:         end if
11:         if apa₍ᵢ,ⱼ₎ in ERSet then
12:             ppᵢ = apc₍ᵢ,ⱼ₎, ppsᵢ = ac₍ᵢ,ⱼ₎ × psₐₚₐ₍ᵢ,ⱼ₎
13:             Add ppᵢ and ppsᵢ to ERSet
14:         end if
15:         if apc₍ᵢ,ⱼ₎ in ERSet then
16:             ppᵢ = apa₍ᵢ,ⱼ₎, ppsᵢ = ac₍ᵢ,ⱼ₎
17:             Add ppᵢ and ppsᵢ to ERSet
18:         end if
19:     end for
20: end for
21: End
```

3   Stress Expression Identification Model

In this part, we propose a SEI model based on ESPA to identify user stress. We use machine learning methods to train our models. We choose Random Forest (RF) [7] as the model classifier, use Optuna for Bayesian optimization, and use stratified K-fold cross-validation to ensure that the label distribution of the training and validation data sets is similar, and the training set is trained multiple times until the parameter threshold meets the criteria. Figure 1 is the flow chart of SEI model. The parameters defined in SEI model are shown in Table 2. Definitions 1–4 describe the four key parameters in SEI model and give the calculation formula.

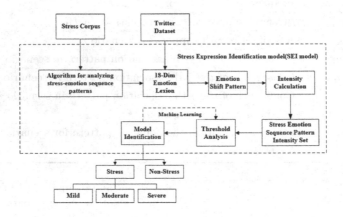

Fig. 1. SEI model Flow Chart

Table 2. Parameters in SEI model

Parameter	Definition
u_i	i-th user
ESP	Emotion Sequence Pattern detected by u_i
$rs_{(j,k)}$	Support strength of rule j in scenario k
mrs_j	Maximum support strength among matched rules for rule j
n	Number of Emotion Sequence Patterns matched detected by u_i
m	Number of distinct emotion types detected by u_i
sc_j	Score mapping for the corresponding rule of mrs_j
RoP	Rule matching rate of u_i
Edf	Emotional perception dimension of u_i
Dms	Degree of emotion fluctuation for u_i
$SoSL$	Stress level score of u_i
$RoPS$	Stress identification result for u_i

Definition 1. *Stress rule matching ratio RoP of u_i. RoP shows the matching degree between the emotion sequence calculated by ESPA in the actual data and the pattern rule set of emotion sequence.*

$$RoP = \frac{n}{ESP} \tag{1}$$

Definition 2. *The emotional feeling dimension Edf of u_i. In the same case, u_i with a larger Edf has a stronger ability to withstand, and the possibility of stress is less.*

$$Edf = \frac{m}{18} \tag{2}$$

Definition 3. *The degree of emotional fluctuation Dms of u_i. The greater the Dms value in a certain period of time, the more unstable emotions and the greater the possibility of stress.*

$$Dms = \frac{\sum_{i=1}^{n} Edf}{ESP} \tag{3}$$

Definition 4. *The stress level score SoSL of u_i. SoSL converts the rule pattern set into the LCU score in the SRRS scale, and after adjusting the score with Dms and Edf, calculates the overall stress score of the u_i over a period of time.*

$$SoSL = \sum_{i=1}^{n} sc_i \times (1 + \alpha \times Dms - \beta \times Edf) \tag{4}$$

For a given u_i, after obtaining its ESP, calculate the above parameters and send them to the trained model for judgment to obtain the final result. The pseudocode of SEI model is shown in Algorithm 2.

Algorithm 2. SEI model

1: **Input:** ESP_{u_i}, RoP, Edf, Dms, $SoSL$
2: **Output:** $RoPS$
3: **Begin**
4: Calculate the number of $ERSet$ as m
5: Calculate the length of ESP_{u_i} as n
6: **for** $i = 0$ to $n - 1$ **do**
7:    **for** $j = 0$ to $m - 1$ **do**
8:       **if** ESP_{u_i} in $ERSet$ **then**
9:         $rs_{(j,k)} = ps_{ESP_{u_i}}$
10:         **if** $rs_{(j,k)} < mrs_j$ **then**
11:           Determine ESP_{u_i} as the stress scene belonging to mrs_j
12:         **end if**
13:       **end if**
14:    **end for**
15:    Calculate RoP, Edf, Dms, and $SoSL$ based on the formula (1)-(4)
16:    $Sum_{SoSL} \mathrel{+}= SoSL$
17: **end for**
18: Use RoP, Edf, Dms, and $SoSL$ to identify stress with the model.
19: **if** stress exists **then**
20:    Determine the level of stress based on $SoSL$
21: **end if**
22: **return** $RoPS$
23: **End**

4   Experiment

This section evaluates the performance of the SEI model. The experiment used a dataset from twitter that contained 875,636 blogs related to stressful scenarios and 150,571 blogs related to stressed and non-stressed users.

4.1   Classification Algorithms Evaluation

To determine the classifier best suited for the SEI model, we integrated three mainstream machine learning classifiers: Logistic Regression (LR) [8], Support Vector Machine (SVM) [9], and RF [7]. To clearly differentiate and compare these three different implementations, we named each version of the SEI model as follows: SEI-LR (Version of the SEI model using LR), SEI-SVM (Version of the SEI model using SVM), SEI-RF (Version of the SEI model using RF). In the training process, the same data preprocessing method and feature construction engineering were adopted. Bayesian optimization method was used to find the best hyperparameters of each of the three versions, and four indexes of accuracy, precision, recall rate and F1 score were used to compare the performance of the three versions on the test set.

As shown in Fig. 2, the accuracy rate, precision rate and F1 value of SEI-RF are 87.12%, 93.54% and 86.09%, showing obvious advantages over SEI-LG and

SEI-SVM. Based on these results, we chose SEI-RF as the final version of the SEI model to ensure that the model can achieve the best performance in practical applications.

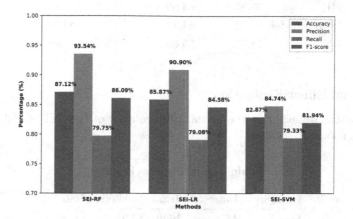

Fig. 2. Classification Algorithms Comparison

4.2 SEI Model Evaluation

This section uses DNN [10], ME [11], and hybrid models [12] to evaluate the performance of the SEI model. To comprehensively evaluate the performance of the model, we adopted four main evaluation metrics: accuracy, precision, recall, and F1-Score.

As shown in Table 3, our model achieved 87.12% accuracy, 93.54% precision, and performed better in the stress identification task. Compared with the four models, SEI model has the best comprehensive performance. The advantage of ME models and hybrid models is that they have a wide range of applications and perform well on multiple data sets. The SEI model is more accurate in stress detection, and uses more detailed classification of emotions and subtle changes between emotions under different stress scenarios to identify and interpret stress, with better overall performance. The excellent performance of the SEI model is largely dependent on the stress emotion dictionary we constructed, which contains the 18 types of emotions most commonly associated with stress and covers the emotional vocabulary in multiple stressful scenarios. Another key factor is the application of ESPA in the model, which not only digs deeply into the internal relationship between stress and emotion, but also quantifies the emotional rules that are mined to optimize the model's discriminating ability. The combination of these factors allows the SEI to accurately capture the emotional flow associated with stress in complex social network blogs, improving the accuracy of stress recognition.

Table 3. Model Comparison

Method	Accuracy%	Precision%	Recall%	F1-score%
SEI model	87.12	93.54	79.75	86.09
ME	80.54	83.89	75.62	79.54
hybrid model	84.52	84.13	88.55	84.79
DNN	76.57	75.63	78.58	77.08

4.3   Actual Effect Evaluation

In this section, we evaluate the actual performance of the SEI model, and the results are shown in Table 4.

Table 4. Identification Result

Category	Detected	Total	Prediction Rate
Stress	1375	1646	83.53%
Non-stress	1116	1179	94.66%
Total	2491	2825	88.18%

According to the experimental results in the table, the SEI model has a comprehensive prediction rate of 88.18%. This highlights the value of the model in practical applications. For non-stressed users, the model recognition accuracy was as high as 94.66%, accurately identifying users who were not affected by stress, which may be attributed to the relatively consistent and stable emotional patterns of normal users. However, for stressed users, the model predicted a relatively low accuracy of 83.53%, indicating that in some cases, the emotional patterns of stressed blogs are more complex and variable, or the differences between them and normal blogs are not obvious enough to make the model difficult to distinguish completely. This also shows that in the actual environment, there are obvious differences in the expression of stress, direct expressions of stress are less common, and implicit or vague expressions are more common.

5   Conclusion

In this research, we found that emotions often appear in a regular pattern in different stress scenarios. Based on this observation, we propose a SEI model based on ESPA to mine rules and identify stress according to the relationship between emotion and stress. Experiments show that this model has achieved good performance in stress identification.

Acknowledgment. This work was supported by the Science and Technology Development Plan of Jilin Province, China (Grant No. 20220402033GH).

References

1. Shaw, B., Saha, S., Mishra, S.K., Ghosh, A.: Investigations in psychological stress detection from social media text using deep architectures. In: 2022 26th International Conference on Pattern Recognition (ICPR), pp. 1614–1620. IEEE (2022)
2. Yang, K., Zhang, T., Ananiadou, S.: A mental state knowledge-aware and contrastive network for early stress and depression detection on social media. Inf. Process. Manag. **59**(4), 102961 (2022)
3. Kvtkn, P., Ramakrishnudu, T.: A novel method for detecting psychological stress at tweet level using neighborhood tweets. J. King Saud Univ.-Comput. Inf. Sci. **34**(9), 6663–6680 (2022)
4. Singh, A., Kumar, D.: Gauging stress, anxiety, depression in student during covid-19 pandemic. Scalable Comput. Pract. Exp. **23**(4), 159–170 (2022)
5. Prabhu, S., Mittal, H., Varagani, R., Jha, S., Singh, S.: Harnessing emotions for depression detection. Pattern Anal. Appl. 1–11 (2022)
6. Dheeraj, K., Ramakrishnudu, T.: Negative emotions detection on online mental-health related patients texts using the deep learning with MHA-BCNN model. Expert Syst. Appl. **182**, 115265 (2021)
7. Liu, K., Hu, X., Zhou, H., Tong, L., Widanage, W.D., Marco, J.: Feature analyses and modeling of lithium-ion battery manufacturing based on random forest classification. IEEE/ASME Trans. Mechatron. **26**(6), 2944–2955 (2021)
8. Wu, Y., et al.: Novel binary logistic regression model based on feature transformation of XGBoost for type 2 diabetes mellitus prediction in healthcare systems. Futur. Gener. Comput. Syst. **129**, 1–12 (2022)
9. Zhang, H., Zou, Q., Ju, Y., Song, C., Chen, D.: Distance-based support vector machine to predict DNA N6-methyladenine modification. Curr. Bioinform. **17**(5), 473–482 (2022)
10. Lin, H., et al.: User-level psychological stress detection from social media using deep neural network. In: Proceedings of the 22nd ACM International Conference on Multimedia, pp. 507–516 (2014)
11. Munoz, S., Iglesias, C.A.: A text classification approach to detect psychological stress combining a lexicon-based feature framework with distributional representations. Inf. Process. Manag. **59**(5), 103011 (2022)
12. Bharti, S.K., et al.: Text-based emotion recognition using deep learning approach. Comput. Intell. Neurosci. **2022** (2022)

Extended Abstracts

Analytics for an E-commerce: Demand Analysis and Prediction

Alexandr Karpovich(ID) and Lyudmila Gadasina(✉)(ID)

Saint Petersburg University, 7/9 Universitetskaya Nab, Saint Petersburg 199034,
Russian Federation
l.gadasina@spbu.ru

Keywords: E-commerce · Predictive model · Online retailer · Boosting · LightGBM · Elasticity of demand

The problem of balancing supply and demand in different market segments is one of the fundamental problems for an online retailer. The emergence of the e-commerce market is a natural evolution of the offline retail market. The growth rate of the online sales market is significantly overtaking offline sales. This has led to a dramatic increase in the number of sellers and products distributed, and thus a highly competitive environment.

Sales companies in highly competitive conditions need, on the one hand, to reach the largest possible number of customers, but on the other hand, to have tools to understand the factors affecting the demand for products. There are common factors, such as price, discount and segment-specific factors such as brand and seasonality. Development of interpretable demand prediction models for different segments can enable the formation of effective policies for its pricing.

This research considers the problem of predicting the demand for products of the kitchen knives category from the kitchen accessories segment in the Wildberries, the largest Russian online store. The dataset for this research is created using the sales information for 7918 products for 13 months from 01.01.2022 to 05.02.2023 of the specified segment. The main purpose of the study is to find out what factors are the most important and how they affect demand in a particular sales sector.

We consider demand as the volume of sales of a product in pieces in a certain period. A week is selected for the period. The model building approach consists of two steps. At the first step, models are built for the basic set of features then extracted features, which were identified through exploratory analysis are added. After that, comparisons of the obtained models are carried out and the best one is selected. To construct a prediction for weekly sales, aggregation was performed with the average values of data for weeks for input variables and the total value of sales per week for the output variable.

We use linear regression, LightGBM, Xgboost and CatBoost for creating predictive models. As a result of comparing the obtained indicators, the LightGBM model was chosen as a model for further research and improvement. It has the highest R^2 score and the smallest value of the target WAPE error metric.

M. H. Hà et al. (Eds.): CSoNet 2023, LNCS 14479, pp. 419–420, 2024.
https://doi.org/10.1007/978-981-97-0669-3

We expand the set of features to improve the values of the model and increase its accuracy. Buyers prefer to choose products from one specific price category, so we added features containing information about the number of products in a certain price segment and the proportion of products that were available on the day of purchase. Also, the price of the goods in the segment under consideration is important for buyers, so variables of the average price value and the standard deviation of the price were added to measure the distribution of prices in the segment.

In the data there is a relationship between the week and the month and the volume of product sales. These variables were added to the purchase date information as well.

In the studied product category, there are no customer comments on many products. The number of products that do not have comments is 49% of their total number. For products that have comments, the median of comments is equal to 6. We included a logical variable equal to 1 if the number of comments is greater than 6 and 0 otherwise. The number of comments and rating have a high impact on the fact of the purchase of the product, so the feature describing their interaction with each other was added.

Table 1 shows the values of quality metrics for the LightGBM algorithm for the basic and improved models on the training and test sets.

Table 1. Comparison of quality metrics after adding features.

Sample	Model	R^2	Bias	MSE	MAE	WAPE
Train	Basic	0.841	0.000	63.199	2.033	0.708
Train	Improved	0.888	10.068	44.256	0.967	0.337
Test	Basic	0.729	−0.757	109.898	2.167	0.754
Test	Improved	0.758	9.699	98.208	1.495	0.520

The learning model stores in its structure information about the patterns between the features and the target variable, which allows us to determine to what extent each parameter affects the target variable. To evaluate the "importance" of the features, SHAP estimates were used. The most important feature was the Visibility of the product (the number of requests that will allow customers to see the product on the first page). This feature has a positive effect on demand, which means that the greater the number of requests that allow you to find a product, the more sales the product will have. The next most important feature is the brand of the product. Then there is the position of the product on the page, which has an inverse effect on the demand of the product.

Based on the information about the importance, managers can make decisions aimed at changing the values of indicators that will have the greatest impact on the product's demand. The resulting model allows you to analyze the change in demand for a product depending on price changes and other features. Thanks to this analysis, sellers can choose the optimal price for products depending on the current conditions and business requirements.

Maximizing Regularized DR-Submodular Functions on a Convex Set

Zhiyuan Dong, Yihan Wang, and Yang Zhou[(✉)]

School of Mathematics and Statistics, Shandong Normal University, Jinan, China
zhouyang@sdnu.edu.cn

The regularized Diminishing-Return (DR)-submodular maximization problem, which combines the objective of maximizing a DR-submodular function plus a linear regularization function, allows for a more flexible and controlled optimization process and has significant applications in areas such as feature selection, data summarization, and active learning. In this paper, we concentrate on approximation algorithms for solving the following problem

$$\begin{aligned} \max \quad & F(x) = G(x) + L(x) \\ \text{s.t.} \quad & x \in \mathcal{P} \subseteq [0,1]^n \end{aligned} \tag{1}$$

where $G : [0,1]^n \to \mathbb{R}^+$ is a DR-submodular function, $L(x) = \langle \ell, x \rangle$ is a linear function and $\mathcal{P}$ is the general convex set.

In the case where G is monotone under general solvable polytope constraints, Feldman [3] provides a bi-factor $(1 - 1/e, 1)$ approximation algorithm which means that the algorithm can return a solution x satisfying $G(x) + L(x) \geq (1 - 1/e)G(x^*) + L(x^*)$, where x^* denotes an optimal solution of the problem. For the non-monotone case, Lu et al. [4] propose a $(\frac{1}{e} - \varepsilon, 1)$ approximation guarantee for maximizing the multilinear relaxation $G - L$ subject to a matroid constraint, where L is non-negative. Moreover, Qi provides a more general result when ℓ is unrestricted in [6]. However, extending these results to general convex constraints, such as those encountered in many real-world applications, including negative parameter linear constraints, upper-bounded constraints, and lattice constraints, remains an open challenge.

The main contribution of this paper is the algorithm design for maximizing a regularized DR-submodular function on a general convex set, along with an approximation ratio analysis in its bi-factor form, which includes different cases of monotonicity for functions G and L. Our assumptions are as follows.

Assumption 1. For problem (1), we make the following assumptions:

1. $\mathcal{P} \subseteq [0,1]^n$ is a convex set, $\mathbf{0} = (0, \cdots, 0) \in \mathcal{P}$ and $G(\mathbf{0}) = 0$.
2. Function G is DR-submodular and continuously differentiable.
3. Three oracles are available: (i) computing the function value $G(x) + L(x)$ at any given point $x \in \mathcal{P}$, (ii) computing the gradient $\nabla G(x)$ at any given point $x \in \mathcal{P}$, and (iii) maximizing a linear function over $\mathcal{P}$.

This paper is supported by National Science Foundation of China (Nos. 12371099).

M. H. Hà et al. (Eds.): CSoNet 2023, LNCS 14479, pp. 421–422, 2024.
https://doi.org/10.1007/978-981-97-0669-3

For the case that G is monotone, we have the following result.

Theorem 1. *When G is monotone, there exists a polynomial-time algorithm that outputs a solution $x \in \mathcal{P}$ obeying*

$$G(x) + L(x) \geq (1 - \frac{1}{e})G(x^*) + L(x^*) - \varepsilon,$$

with $O(\frac{nD}{\varepsilon})$ iterations, where D is the gradient Lipschitz constant of G.

When function G is non-monotone, the design and analysis of algorithms will be influenced by the sign of ℓ. Therefore, we divide the discussion into three cases: $\ell \geq 0$, $\ell \leq 0$ and ℓ with no sign restrictions. For the first case $\ell \geq 0$, it can be observed that function $G + L$ remains a non-negative DR-submodular function. Thus by results in [1, 2, 5], the Frank-Wolfe algorithm can outputs a solution x satisfying $G(x) + L(x) \geq (\frac{1}{4} - \varepsilon)[G(x^*) + L(x^*)] - \varepsilon$. How to utilize the linearity of L to enhance this result will be the focus of our future work. For the case that $\ell \leq 0$, a novel result is presented in this paper as the following theorem.

Theorem 2. *For maximizing regularized non-monotonic DR-submodular functions, where $\ell \leq 0$, there exists an algorithm with $K = O(\frac{nD}{\varepsilon})$ iterations, that outputs a solution $x \in \mathcal{P}$ obeying*

$$G(x) + L(x) \geq \left(\frac{1}{4} - \varepsilon\right) G(x^*) + \log 2 \cdot L(x^*) - \varepsilon.$$

For the case that the sign of L is unlimited, we present an algorithm with a bi-factor approximation ratio as $(\frac{1}{4}, \frac{1}{2})$.

Theorem 3. *For maximizing regularized DR-submodular functions $G + L$, there exists a polynomial-time algorithm that outputs a solution $x \in \mathcal{P}$ obeying*

$$G(x) + L(x) \geq (\frac{1}{4} - \varepsilon)G(x^*) + (\frac{1}{2} - \varepsilon)L(x^*) - \varepsilon.$$

The iteration complexity is $O(\frac{n(D+M)}{\varepsilon})$, where $M = \max\{0, -\ell_1, \ldots, -\ell_n\}$.

References

1. Du, D.: Lyapunov function approach for approximation algorithm design and analysis: with applications in submodular maximization. ArXiv abs/2205.12442 (2022)
2. Du, D., Liu, Z., Wu, C., Xu, D., Zhou, Y.: An improved approximation algorithm for maximizing a DR-submodular function over a convex set. ArXiv abs/2203.14740 (2022)
3. Feldman, M.: Guess free maximization of submodular and linear sums. Algorithmica **83**, 853–878 (2018)
4. Lu, C., Yang, W., Gao, S.: Regularized non-monotone submodular maximization. ArXiv abs/2103.10008 (2021)
5. Mualem, L., Feldman, M.: Resolving the approximability of offline and online non-monotone DR-submodular maximization over general convex sets. In: International Conference on Artificial Intelligence and Statistics, pp. 2542–2564. PMLR (2023)
6. Qi, B.: On maximizing sums of non-monotone submodular and linear functions. arXiv preprint arXiv:2205.15874 (2022)

Activation and Deactivation Phenomena in Online Social Media Network Cascade Propagation with Geographic Considerations

Alexander Semenov[1], Alexander Nikolaev[2], Eduardo L. Pasiliao[3], and Vladimir Boginski[4(✉)]

[1] University of Florida, Gainesville, FL, USA
asemenov@ufl.edu
[2] University at Buffalo, Buffalo, NY, USA
anikolae@buffalo.edu
[3] Air Force Research Laboratory, Eglin AFB, FL, USA
eduardo.pasiliao@us.af.mil
[4] University of Central Florida, Orlando, FL, USA
vladimir.boginski@ucf.edu

Activation and influence propagation cascades are pervasive in the modern planetary scale online social media networks, where users influence each other's opinions, beliefs, etc. The most commonly used influence propagation models are based on activation thresholds, including linear threshold models, where a node in a network would "activate" if a certain minimum fraction of its neighbors are active. As an extension of such models, we consider the model of activation/influence propagation in networks based on the concept of "bandpass" thresholds: a node will "activate" if at least a certain minimum fraction of its neighbors are active and no more than a certain maximum fraction of neighbors are active. The respective hypothesis was originally mentioned in the seminal work on threshold models by Granovetter (1978); however, to our knowledge there have not been any rigorous mathematical/computational studies of double threshold models prior to our current and recent work. In addition, the considered activation/deactivation processes can be affected by geographic proximity factors (i.e., social media users being physically closely located). We present the results of real-world cascade traces of single- and bandpass-threshold cascades in city-wide and country-wide online social media networks based on anonymized user friendships data collected from VK.com in December 2016 [1].

Work Summary. In the first set of experiments, we examined the performance of seven seed selection heuristics across different seed set sizes, ranging from 1% to 10% of the network size. We assessed the percentage of network nodes active at the conclusion of the cascading process, also known as the "outbreak size." As an illustrative example for the network of VK.com users located in Kazakhstan, Figs. 1a and 1b show that all heuristics, except for the random selection, perform similarly well when the seed nodes reach 7% of the total size. However, both degree and PageRank perform effectively even with a small percentage of seed nodes when the bandpass model lower and upper thresholds are set at (0.5, 0.9). Somewhat surprisingly, for (0.2, 0.6) thresholds, *random* choice of seed nodes is

M. H. Hà et al. (Eds.): CSoNet 2023, LNCS 14479, pp. 423–425, 2024.
https://doi.org/10.1007/978-981-97-0669-3

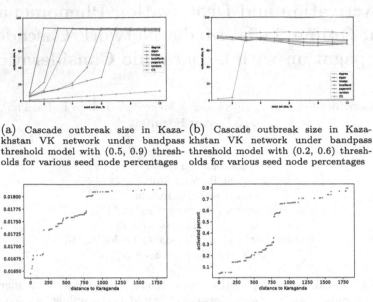

(a) Cascade outbreak size in Kazakhstan VK network under bandpass
threshold model with (0.5, 0.9) thresholds for various seed node percentages

(b) Cascade outbreak size in Kazakhstan VK network under bandpass
threshold model with (0.2, 0.6) thresholds for various seed node percentages

(c) Cumulative percentage of activated
nodes vs. distance to Karaganda: bandpass model with (0.5, 0.9) thresholds

(d) Cumulative percentage of activated
nodes vs. distance to Karaganda: bandpass model with (0.2, 0.6) thresholds

Fig. 1. (a), (b): Cascade outbreak size for the country-wide network corresponding
to VK.com users in Kazakhstan: bandpass model lower/upper thresholds: left-(0.5,
0.9); right-(0.2, 0.6). Horizontal axis shows seed set size (percentage of total number of
nodes), and vertical axis shows size of the outbreak (percentage activated nodes) at the
last stage of the cascade. Different color lines represent different strategies (heuristics)
for choosing seed nodes. (c), (d): Dependency of cumulative percentage of activated
nodes on the distance to Karaganda (seed nodes are selected from the top 10% of nodes
with the highest h-index, and they are filtered based on their location in Karaganda):
bandpass model lower/upper thresholds: left-(0.5, 0.9); right-(0.2, 0.6).

the most effective, compared to all the considered non-random "smart" heuristics for choosing the seed nodes. To illustrate the geographic aspect of cascade
propagation in a country-wide network, Figs. 1c and 1d show the dependency of
the cumulative percentage of activated nodes on their distance from the arbitrarily chosen city of Karaganda (under the assumption that all the initial seeds
are geographically clustered in this city). In the case of the bandpass model with
(0.5, 0.9) thresholds, only a small portion of the graph is activated, whereas in
the case of (0.2, 0.6) thresholds, a significant percentage of nodes is activated,
including those located geographically far away from the initial seed nodes cluster. In the presented work, we will discuss detailed results on the penetration of
the considered cascading processes under various initial conditions on threshold
values and seed node choice strategies.

Reference

1. Semenov, A., et al.: Exploring social media network landscape of post-soviet space. IEEE Access **7**, 411–426 (2019). https://doi.org/10.1109/ACCESS.2018.2885479

The Impact of News, Expert and Public Opinion on Painting Prices

Taisia Pimenova[1]($\boxtimes$), Valeria Kolycheva[1], Alexander Semenov[2], Dmitry Grigoriev[1], and Arsenii Pimenov[1]

[1] Center of Econometrics and Business Analytics, St. Petersburg State University, St Petersburg, Russia
tasia2001@yandex.ru
[2] Herbert Wertheim College of Engineering, University of Florida, Gainesville, USA

Abstract. Online reviews play a crucial role in determining the price of goods, and the art market is no exception. However, due to the varying levels of expertise and influence among participants, it is essential to analyze each group separately. In this work, we explore the influence of experts and public sentiment on painting prices. To investigate this, we employ a hedonic regression model with fixed effects for artists. Our dataset comprises 18,100 sold paintings at Sotheby's, Christie's and Phillips auction houses. Additionally, we examine the relationship between review sentiment and buyers' investment intentions, as purchasing paintings as an investment is a widespread practice in the secondary art market. Our results indicate that negative opinion from various sources and positive public opinion significantly influence the price of paintings in line with their respective valence. Furthermore, we observe that negative opinion from experts and news publications has a more pronounced effect on pricing. Our findings contribute to empirical research on the price determinants of artworks and examining online reviews from different sources.

Keywords: Art auctions · Hedonic model · Experts · Online reviews

1 Introduction

Development of the Internet and social networks brings the interaction between artists and art lovers to a whole new level. Large volumes of information posted on social media have opened up unprecedented opportunities to familiarize masses with art and turn art into an element of the everyday life of masses. Mentions of artists and their works on the Internet have become an integral part of their careers, alongside their exhibition portfolio, representation in collections, and auction statistics. Additionally, art is frequently viewed as an investment, attracting a distinct group of buyers known as investors. Their sensitivity to the market opinion may distinguish them from art lovers who are guided by other motives.

© The Author(s), under exclusive license to Springer Nature Singapore Pte Ltd. 2024
M. H. Hà et al. (Eds.): CSoNet 2023, LNCS 14479, pp. 426–430, 2024.
https://doi.org/10.1007/978-981-97-0669-3

The connection between the opinion of market participants and painting prices can be formally viewed through the conceptual model based on the theory of cultural and economic values of a cultural good [2, 11]. This approach recognizes that changes in cultural value are often mirrored by changes in economic value, thus with the economic value encompassing the cultural value [7].

The question of defining cultural value and its methods of assessment remains open. D. Throsby in [11] proposes attitudinal analysis as a way to assess the social and spiritual aspects. Analyzing public and expert online reviews is suitable for this purpose, as social media provides a large volume of publications related to the art market. The opinions of experts and the public can be linked to the economic value through the fame of artists, which can impact the prices of paintings.

Due to the diversity of the art world, experts can come from critics, dealers, collectors, artists, and other enthusiasts; however, a more specific set of characteristics is needed to identify social media specialists. Experts are gatekeepers and other intermediaries who have a significant influence in determining the value and worth of creative works, according to Victor Ginsburg [5]. Additionally, experts' assessments of cultural worth have a major impact on artists' financial success. A certain amount of cultural and educational capital is necessary for the estimation of intrinsic and acquired values [2, 9], identifying important aspects of market knowledge. The first question is how does the sentiment expressed by the public, art journalists and experts on social media influence the price of artworks and leads to first set of hypotheses.

H1a: Negative (positive) opinion of professionals expressed in online reviews leads to lower (higher) price of a painting.

H1b: Negative (positive) public opinion expressed in online reviews leads to lower (higher) price of a painting.

The role of an expert may also include influencing an artist's aesthetic quality and acting as an external reference for collectors and investors [6]. However, the internal relationship between the components may lead to a different impact value of reviews on price due to elements of economic value such as different investment intentions. Considering the cultural good as an investment may change the sensitivity to certain factors, for instance, increasing the relevance of market sentiment. This motivates the second set of hypotheses:

H2a: If a painting is considered as an investment, the opinion of professionals expressed in online reviews will affect the price more.

H2b: If a painting is considered as an investment, public opinion expressed in online reviews will affect the price more.

The following sections describe method for hypotheses testing, details of the data collection process and findings of this research.

2   Method

To investigate the effect of experts' and public opinion on the price of a painting, we analyzed 18106 paintings sold between the beginning of 2012 to the second half of 2021. The dataset includes 32 different painting styles with pop-art and cubism as the prevailing movements and 97 artists with 20 as the minimum number of paintings by a single author. 75% of all paintings were sold more than once, 89% were signed and 72% were framed. 8419 of all artworks were obtained from Sotheby's, 5983 from Christie's and remaining 3704 from Phillips auction house. In order to assess market sentiment, namely public opinion, we collected 512 thousand tweets with Twitter API and computed sentiment using the "Twitter-roBERTa-base-sentiment" model [3]. Following works on the tweets sentiment effect on the price of goods and financial asset, the event window is set to 60 days [8].

The list of expert accounts was created based on the description of an art expert in the preceding section in order to get professional opinions. First, a collection of accounts was created using the "ArtReview Power 100" [1], a yearly list of the most important figures in the field of art during the previous ten years. Subsequently, the accounts from the first group's subscriptions were examined to extract the Twitter users with the most followers among selected experts. Only art world-related accounts were chosen. The list was expanded by adding accounts of famous galleries, exhibitions and popular professional media about art since those accounts fit the definition of experts by influential power and confirmed expertise. To capture the influence power of experts more precisely, sentiment values were weighed by the number of retweets. 10161 tweets were collected from 53 experts with Andy Warhol as the most mentioned artist. Sentiment values were obtained with the same model as for public tweets.

A hedonic pricing model with artist fixed effects was estimated using the ordinary least squares method to test the first two hypotheses. This approach is used by the majority of studies and allows to find and assess the impact of price determinants [4, 10]. To capture distinct differences between segments, we analyze the moderating effects of features that cluster different behaviors. This approach enables us to assess the relative strength of influence. In this study, we use repeat sales as an indicator of investment intentions and examine how this feature interacts with three types of sentiment: news sentiment, expert sentiment, and public sentiment.

3   Results

Among the regression coefficients of two hedonic models for negative and positive experts' reviews, only negative opinion decreases painting prices significantly $(-0.158, t = -1.7, p < 0.1)$. These results provide support for the hypothesis $H1a$ for negative professional opinion, but for positive tweets the hypothesis is rejected. Secondly, for moderation effect estimation, the interaction term is calculated as the multiplication of the repeat sale feature and selected sentiment values. We find evidence that negative opinion of experts decreases painting prices more if the painting is considered as an investment. For positive reviews the interaction term states is insignificant.

We construct separate model for art journalists since news is regarded as a source of expert opinion but has a distinct format and tone. The significance of both the negative $(-0.211, t = -2.03, p < 0.1)$ and positive $(0.133, t = 1.87, p < 0.1)$ news impact on price is demonstrated by the hedonic model for the news emotion influence on price. When painting is considered as an investment, the moderation effect confirms the strengthened influence of news sentiment. Repeat sales boost sensitivity for negative news $(-0.2793$ vs. $-2.0169)$, but this is not supported experimentally for positive news.

As for public opinion, negative opinion lead to significantly lower prices $(-0.282, t = -2.27, p < 0.1)$. And in contrast to the opinion of experts, positive reviews significantly increase the price of reviewed paintings $(0.221, t = 1.77, p < 0.1)$, so the observed data allows not to reject hypothesis $H1b$ for both types of sentiment. Insignificance of interaction terms for both positive and negative public opinion lead to rejection of hypothesis $H2b$.

The findings are mostly in line with the existing literature. We find that positive public and negative opinion from all sources significantly affects the price of artworks in the direction of the valence. The imbalance between positive and negative sources can be motivated by the quantitative superiority of positive posts and comments in social media which leads consumers to extract and focus on the negative pieces of information. Further, the moderation analysis confirms an increased sensitivity to negative opinion from experts and art journalists if the art is considered as an investment. Considering the "cultural value determining" role and influence power of experts, signals of negative reviews are noted more carefully.

The secondary art market has demonstrated its sensitivity to reviews and opinions from individuals with varying levels of professionalism and influence. The emergence of social media and other platforms has made it simpler for art enthusiasts to express their opinions, elevating the interaction between the producer and the consumer of cultural commodities beyond what it was in previous centuries. Additionally, because of the speed at which information is shared, prospective buyers can examine a vast amount of pertinent data that may have an impact on their choices.

Acknowledgements. Dmitry Grigoriev and Arsenii Pimenov research for this paper was supported by a grant from the Russian Science Foundation (Project No. 22-18-00588). The authors are grateful to participants at the Center for Econometrics and Business Analytics (ceba-lab.org, CEBA) seminar series for helpful comments and suggestions.

References

1. Art review power 100 (2022). https://artreview.com/power-100/. Accessed 01 Oct 2022 https://artreview.com/power-100/, 2022. Accessed: 2022-10-01
2. Angelini, F., Castellani, M.: Cultural and economic value: a critical review. J. Cult. Econ. **43**(2), 173–188 (2019)
3. Barbieri, F., Camacho-Collados, J., Anke, L.E., Neves, L.: TweetEval: unified benchmark and comparative evaluation for tweet classification. In Findings of the Association for Computational Linguistics: EMNLP 2020, pp. 1644–1650, (2020). Association for Computational Linguistics

4. Cinefra, J., Garay, U., Mibelli, C., Pérez, E.: The determinants of art prices: an analysis of Joan Miró. Acad. Rev. Latinoam. Administración **32**(3), 373–391 (2019)
5. Ginsburgh, V.: Awards, success and aesthetic quality in the arts. J. Econ. Perspect. **17**, 99–111 (2003)
6. Hernando, E., Campo, S.: An artist's perceived value: development of a measurement scale. Int. J. Arts Manage. **19**, 33–47 (2017)
7. Hutter, M., Frey, B.S.: On the influence of cultural value on economic value. Rev. d'économie politique **120**(1), 35–46 (2010)
8. Oliveira, N., Cortez, P., Areal, N.: The impact of microblogging data for stock market prediction: Using twitter to predict returns, volatility, trading volume and survey sentiment indices. Expert Syst. Appl. **73**, 125–144 (2017)
9. Seaman, B.A.: Chapter 14 empirical studies of demand for the performing arts. In: Handbook of the Economics of Art and Culture, vol. 1. pp. 415–472. Elsevier (2006)
10. Stepanova, E.: The impact of color palettes on the prices of paintings. Empirical Econ. **56**(2), 755–773 (2019)
11. Throsby, D.: Economics and Culture. Cambridge University Press, Cambridge (2000)

Author Index

M. H. Hà et al. (Eds.): CSoNet 2023, LNCS 14479, pp. 431–433, 2024.
https://doi.org/10.1007/978-981-97-0669-3

Printed in the United States
by Baker & Taylor Publisher Services